THE MARVEL COMICS
ENCYCLOPEDIA

A COMPLETE GUIDE TO THE CHARACTERS OF THE MARVEL UNIVERSE

MARVEL

LONDON, NEW YORK, MUNICH,
MELBOURNE, and DELHI

Senior Editor Alastair Dougall
Design Manager Robert Perry
Senior Art Editor Nick Avery
Senior Designer Jill Bunyan
Editor Julia March
Publishing Manager Simon Beecroft
Category Publisher Alex Allan
Production Rochelle Talary
DTP Designer Hanna Ländin
Production Editor Siu Chan

First American Edition, 2006; reprinted 2008; revised 2009

11 12 13 14 10 9 8 7 6 5
009–MD593–01/10

Published in the United States by DK Publishing
375 Hudson Street, New York, New York 10014

Published in Great Britain by Dorling Kindersley Limited

DK books are available at special discounts when purchased in bulk for sales promotions,
premiums, fund-raising, or educational use. For details, contact:
DK Publishing Special Markets, 375 Hudson Street, New York, New York 10014
SpecialSales@dk.com

A catalog record for this book is available from the Library of Congress

ISBN: 978-0-7566-5530-3

Color reproduction by Media Development and Printing Ltd., UK
Printed and bound in China by Hung Hing Printing.

Discover more at
www.dk.com

THE MARVEL COMICS
ENCYCLOPEDIA

THE DEFINITIVE GUIDE TO THE CHARACTERS OF THE MARVEL UNIVERSE

CONTENTS

THE CONTRIBUTORS

TOM DEFALCO is also the Consultant Editor for the *Marvel Encyclopedia*. He is a best-selling author and a former editor-in-chief of Marvel. He is also the author of several Dorling Kindersley Ultimate guides to Marvel Super Heroes: *Avengers: The Ultimate Guide, Fantastic Four: The Ultimate Guide, Hulk: The Incredible Guide*, and *Spider-Man: The Ultimate Guide*.

PETER SANDERSON is a comics historian and critic, who was Marvel's first official archivist. He is the author of Dorling Kindersley's best selling *X-Men: The Ultimate Guide*. Mr. Sanderson was also one of the main writers of the first four versions of *The Official Handbook of the Marvel Universe*.

TOM BREVOORT is an Executive Editor for Marvel Comics, where he oversees titles such as *Avengers, Fantastic Four, Captain America, Iron Man*, and others. This also puts him in the unique position of being able to change any details of any Encyclopedia entry for which he couldn't locate the correct answer!

MICHAEL TEITELBAUM has been a writer, editor, and packager of children's books, comic books, and magazines for more than 20 years. Some of Michael's more recent writing includes *X-Men School, Story of the X-Men, Story of the Hulk, Story of Spider-Man*, and *Batman's Guide to Crime and Detection* for Dorling Kindersley.

DANIEL WALLACE is the author or co-author of more than a dozen books, including *Superman Returns: the Visual Guide* and the *DC Comics Encyclopedia* for Dorling Kindersley, *The Art of Superman Returns*, and the *New York Times*-best-selling *Star Wars: The New Essential Guide to Characters*.

ANDREW DARLING is a film, television and comics journalist, and the author of Dorling Kindersley's forthcoming *Ghost Rider: The Ultimate Guide* and *Thunderbirds: The Making of the Movie*. Andrew also writes for *SFX* and *Dreamwatch* magazines, the *Daily Mail* and contributed to *Star Wars* and *Prisoner* Fact Files.

MATT FORBECK has been writing and designing games, novels, comics, and more for over 20 years. His most recent work includes *Blood Bowl: Killer Contract, Mutant Chronicles, More Forbidden Knowledge, The Complete Idiot's Guide to Drawing Superheroes & Villains*, the *Harvey Birdman: Attorney at Law* video game, and *Marvel Heroes Battle Dice*.

INTRODUCTION
by Stan Lee

It just had to happen! There have been so many new and exciting developments in the Marvel Universe that fans world-wide have been clamouring for this second edition.

That's why we've totally updated everything by adding Marvel's mind-bending crossover developments such as Annihilation! Civil War! The Secret Invasion/Dark Reign! Private Hulk/World War Hulk!

Nor have we neglected new characters and updates on old ones. Here is just a tip of the incredible iceberg: Anti-Venom, Captain Midlands, Hulkling, Sabreclaw, Spider-Man 2211, Venus.

And, of course, we've included new teams, such as Agents of Atlas, Serpent Squad, X-Cell, Young Avengers.

And that's why I still proudly say—It ranks way up there with the discovery of fire and the invention of the wheel. Just like them, it represents an epic milestone in the history of the human race. That's why I'm so incredibly proud to be writing this intro for a book that mankind has been hungering for, a book that is—now and forever—a shining beacon of wonder, a titanic tribute to talent unleashed, with the simple but awesome title of—*The Marvel Encyclopedia.*

Here you'll find more than a thousand of Marvel's classic characters, all brilliantly illustrated, with their lives and vital statistics laid bare for your closest scrutiny and your browsing delight.

On a personal note, I must confess, when I first dreamed up some of the more prominent characters you'll find in this volume, I never dreamed that decades later they would have achieved the fame and popularity which they now enjoy. It's almost impossible to describe the feeling of pride, mixed with disbelief, that I feel when I realize how many great movies, video games, DVDs, toys and books are based on these heroes, villains, and far-out stories which we, in the mighty Marvel bullpen, had so much fun creating. None of us could have suspected that our creations would become so famous that we'd one day find ourselves featured in a prestigious encyclopedia.

And, speaking of this extraordinary book, when it comes to finding the hero or villain you may be seeking, the publishers have made it as easy for you as recognizing the Hulk in a crowd.

They've put the names of each and every one in convenient alphabetical order.

Starting with the creation of the "Fantastic Four," the world's greatest comic book (as we so modestly called it), you'll also be able to find decade-by-decade highlights from Marvel's fabulous comic book history.

But what about the artwork? Glad you asked! You'll find illustrations from the very best of Marvel's amazing army of artists, pencilers and inkers who have made their indelible marks on the consciousness of comic book fans worldwide.

And, naturally, the accompanying texts are written by the most acclaimed scriptwriters in Marvel's galaxy of gifted scriveners. Every sentence is a tribute to the greatest Super Hero creations this side of Asgard.

But that's not all. Realizing that some of the spectacular characters in our Super Hero stable have actually achieved such status and fame that they are now truly worldwide legends, the editors have wisely decided to accord these special heroes and villains full-page, double-page, or even *two* double-page layouts, plus a brief guide to their essential storylines.

There's so much more that I could say, but if I do it'll keep me from leaving my computer and reaching for my beautiful, brand-new Marvel Encyclopedia which is proudly sitting on my corner table. It might be my imagination, but I seem to see a glow around that voluminous volume, as though it's illuminated by some supernatural aura, some mystic radiance emanating from the combined power of the fantastic characters within its pages.

I know I must be fantasizing, and yet—as I slowly reach out to touch the cover of this magnificent book, I wonder—as you may wonder, too—what magic lies within?

Excelsior!

Stan

ABOMINATION

FACTFILE

REAL NAME
Emil Blonsky
OCCUPATION
Criminal
BASE
Mobile

HEIGHT 6 ft 8 in
WEIGHT 980 lbs
EYES Green
HAIR None

FIRST APPEARANCE
Tales to Astonish #90
(April 1967)

POWERS

Superhuman strength enables leaps of two miles; tough skin withstands small arms fire. Unlike Hulk, the Abomination's strength does not increase with rage, and he rarely returns to human form; however he retains all Blonsky's mental faculties.

ABOMINATION

Born in Zagreb, Yugoslavia, Emil Blonsky became a spy and infiltrated the US Air Force base where scientist Bruce Banner (*see* HULK) was stationed. Blonsky discovered gamma-radiation equipment with which Banner intended to commit suicide. Testing the device on himself, Blonsky became the monstrous Abomination. The Abomination fought the Hulk for domination of the Earth. Their first battles ended when he was kidnapped by the Stranger. The crew of the starship Andromeda rescued him, and he served as their first mate until his return to Earth. Further defeats by the Hulk eroded the Abomination's courage and he retreated to the New York sewers. Envious of Bruce Banner's apparent happiness, Blonsky poisoned his wife Betty (*see* BANNER, BETTY). Recently, the Red Hulk shot and killed the Abomination with a special gun designed to kill the Hulk. **AD, MF**

The Abomination is even stronger than the Hulk. His body is covered with reptilian scales.

The Hulk and the Abomination have never got on.

FACTFILE

REAL NAME
Carl "Crusher" Creel
OCCUPATION
Criminal
BASE
Mobile

HEIGHT 6 ft 4 in
WEIGHT 365 lbs
EYES Blue
HAIR None

FIRST APPEARANCE
Journey Into Mystery #114
(March 1965)

POWERS

Can magically duplicate within himself the physical and mystical properties of anything he physically contacts, including various forms of energy. If his body is broken into pieces while he is in a non-human state, he can mentally reassemble it.

ABSORBING MAN

Seeking a pawn to use against his nemesis THOR, the Asgardian god LOKI endowed brutal prisoner "Crusher" Creel and his ball and chain with the power to "absorb" the physical properties of anything he touched. Creel broke out of prison and battled Thor, as Loki intended. However, Creel overreached himself by trying to absorb the power of the whole Earth and exploded. Thanks to his new powers, however, Creel was not truly dead, and Loki magically reassembled his body. Loki then enlisted the Absorbing Man as his ally in an attempt to overthrow Odin, monarch of Asgard (*see* GODS OF ASGARD), but Odin banished Creel into outer space.

Over the years the Absorbing Man has repeatedly battled his archfoe Thor and his other leading adversary, the HULK. Among the Absorbing Man's other main opponents are SPIDER-MAN and the AVENGERS. During the first "Secret War" staged by the BEYONDER, Creel met another Super Villain, Mary "Skeeter" MacPherran, the second TITANIA. They became partners in crime, and eventually got married. Creel was nearly killed in a battle with SENTRY during Civil War (*see* pp. 84–5), but he was later seen at the STILT-MAN's funeral and battling SHE-HULK. **PS, MF**

The Absorbing Man's body can even duplicate the unknown alloy of Captain America's shield.

ACOLYTES

FIRST APPEARANCE X-Men #1 (October 1991)
BASE Formerly Genosha, Avalon, Asteroid M
FOUNDER MEMBERS **Fabian Cortez** Increases mutants' powers
EXODUS Psionic powers **Anne-Marie Cortez** Mind control
CHROME Alters matter **Marco Delgado** Increases size, strength
Rusty Collins Pyrokinetic **Joanna Cargill** Strength **Skids** Creates force-field **Colossus** Becomes organic steel **Spoor** Super-senses; mood-altering pheromones.

Fabian Cortez founded the Acolytes to help realize MAGNETO's dream of a world ruled by mutants. However, Cortez betrayed Magneto and vied with him for control of the group. On M-Day, most of the Acolytes lost their powers. Recently, the remnants of the group, under the leadership of Exodus, helped revived PROFESSOR X after BISHOP shot him in the head. **TD, MF**

Mutant telepath Rogue of the X-Men attracts the unwelcome attentions of Magneto's Acolytes team.

ADVERSARY

FIRST APPEARANCE Uncanny X-Men #188 (December 1984)
REAL NAME Unknown (alias Naze, the great trickster)
OCCUPATION Ancient deity **BASE** An unknown dimension
HEIGHT/WEIGHT/EYES/HAIR Not applicable
SPECIAL POWERS/ABILITIES Can assume any form he desires; may be fought successfully through magic, but not though most forms of physical force; vulnerable to iron, steel, and adamantium.

The Cheyenne believe that the Adversary is a demonic god that toys with the fate of the universe, heedless of the deaths he causes. FORGE was trained to be a shaman and combat him. After his teacher, Naze, was murdered and replaced by the Adversary, Forge joined the X-Men in an attempt to stop the monster. The Adversary is imprisoned by mystical spells, but may one day escape confinement. **TD**

AGAMEMNON

FIRST APPEARANCE Incredible Hulk Vol. 2 #381 (May 1991)
REAL NAME Vali Halfling **OCCUPATION** Godlike observer
BASE The Mount, a mountain base in Arizona
HEIGHT 5 ft 7 in **WEIGHT** 140 lbs **EYES** Brown **HAIR** Brown
SPECIAL POWERS/ABILITIES Virtually immortal; projects a hologram of himself as an old, bearded man (below) so that no one suspects that he truly looks like a teenaged boy.

The son of an Asgardian god and a mortal mother, Vali traded the pick of his future offspring with the alien Troyjan race in exchange for knowledge of immortality. He wished to improve the human condition by bringing an end to war, famine and disease and so he founded the PANTHEON, an interventionist think-tank, whose members include many of the children he has sired over the years, and others he has adopted. However, when Agamemnon's betrayal of his children became known to the Pantheon, he attempted to slay them all! He seemingly died trying to escape Pantheon members when his rocket was shot down. **TB**

AGENTS OF ATLAS

FIRST APPEARANCE (as the 1950s Avengers of Earth-9904) What If? #9 (June 1978); (as the G-Men) Agents of Atlas #1 (October 2006); (as the Agents of Atlas) Agents of Atlas #6 (March 2007)
BASE Temple of Atlas inside a huge cavern under San Francisco
MEMBERS AND POWERS
Gorilla Man (Kenneth Hale) The body of a gorilla, the mind of a man **Human Robot (M-11)** Super-strong, self-repairing robot with force field, death ray, telescopic, electrified limbs **Marvel Boy (Robert Grayson)** Uranian body **Namora (Aquaria Neptunia)** Superhuman strength, amphibious **Venus** Durability, hypnotic voice **Jimmy Woo** Secret agent skills

In the 1958, Jimmy Woo (see WOO, JIMMY) formed the G-Men to rescue President Eisenhower from the YELLOW CLAW. Decades later, Jimmy reformed the team to investigate a shadowy organization known as the Atlas Foundation, based in the Temple of Atlas. They discovered that the Yellow Claw was in fact Plan Tzu, direct heir to Genghis Khan. Plan had long ago chosen Woo as his own heir and had spent decades posing as his enemy, training him to be prepared.

In the end, Woo agreed to take over the Atlas Foundation, with his old friends at his side, and turn it into a force for good. **MF**

AGENT X

FIRST APPEARANCE Agent X #1 (September 2002)
REAL NAME Nijo (aka Alex Hayden)
OCCUPATION Mercenary **BASE** Mobile
HEIGHT 6 ft 2 in **WEIGHT** 210 lbs **EYES** Brown **HAIR** None
SPECIAL POWERS/ABILITIES Augmented strength, agility, and dexterity; superhuman regenerative abilities; certain advanced mental abilities; enhanced skill as a marksman.

Agent X's real name is Nijo, but during a bout of amnesia he adopted the name Alex Hayden. Agent X is a combined consciousness which resides in the body of Nijo but which also contains the mental powers of DEADPOOL and Black Swan. Agent X was created when the corpse of Nijo was revived and given Deadpool's healing power by Black Swan, who has the ability to enter a person's mind and unleash viruses similar to computer viruses into their brain. Agent X subsequently founded a team of mercenaries known as Agency X with his girlfriend Outlaw, Taskmaster, Sandi Brandenberg, and the mutant Mary Zero. **MT**

AGENTS OF ATLAS
1 Marvel Boy 2 Human Robot 3 Derek Khanata 4 Jimmy Woo 5 Namora 6 Venus 7 Gorilla Man

AGENT ZERO

FIRST APPEARANCE (as Maverick) X-Men Vol. 2 #5 (Feb. 1992)
REAL NAME Christopher Nord (changed to David North)
OCCUPATION Secret agent, mercenary **BASE** Berlin, Germany
HEIGHT 6 ft 3 in **WEIGHT** 230 lbs **EYES** Blue **HAIR** Brown
SPECIAL POWERS/ABILITIES Can absorb kinetic energy and utilize it for superhuman strength or release it as concussive blasts. Possesses aging suppression and enhanced healing factors.

Born in East Germany, Christopher Nord became a freedom fighter against the oppressive, postwar Communist regime. He was recruited by the Central Intelligence Agency for its WEAPON X project and he changed his name to David North. By the early 1960s, North was partnered with Logan and Victor Creed, the future WOLVERINE and SABRETOOTH, in the CIA's "Team X." Later, North became a mercenary under the code name Maverick. After nearly being killed by Sabretooth, Maverick reluctantly rejoined the Weapon X project, which saved his life. Nord subsequently became the project's leading special operative taking the new identity of Agent Zero. **PS**

AGUILA, EL

FIRST APPEARANCE Power Man/Iron Fist #58 (August 1977)
REAL NAME Alejandro Montoya
OCCUPATION Wealthy swashbuckler **BASE** New York City
HEIGHT 6 ft **WEIGHT** 190 lbs **EYES** Brown **HAIR** Black
SPECIAL POWERS/ABILITIES Can discharge electrostatic blast over 30-ft (9-meter) range, of up to 10,000 volts; highly skilled swordfighter; above-average strength; great agility.

Born in Madrid, Spain, Alejandro Montoya developed the mutant ability to discharge bursts of electricity through metal conductors; such as his steel sword. Making his way to New York City he joined other costumed vigilantes, branded himself El Aguila (the Eagle) and fought those who preyed on the poor and needy: drug dealers, slumlords and the like. His exploits brought him into conflict with the police as Power Man (*see* CAGE, LUKE) and Iron Fist. He lost his powers on M-Day.
AD, MF

AHAB

FIRST APPEARANCe Fantastic Four Annual #23 (1990)
REAL NAME Dr. Roderick Campbell
OCCUPATION Geneticist **BASE** Mobile
HEIGHT 6 ft 1 in **WEIGHT** (as Campbell) 166 lbs (as Ahab) 222lbs
EYES Brown **HAIR** Brown **SPECIAL POWERS/ABILITIES**
Possesses a robotic body, and wields psionic harpoons that cause those struck to feel pain, to be enslaved to his will, or to perish.

In a possible future, Ahab created a process by which captured mutants were turned into slaves known as Hounds and used to hunt down their fellow mutants. Ahab's body was rebuilt cybernetically after he was critically injured during the escape of his best Hound, Rachel Summers (*see* SUMMERS, RACHEL), into the past. He later joined Apocalypse and became Famine in his Four Horsemen.
TB, MF

The cyborg Ahab prepares to throw a psionic harpoon.

AIR-WALKER

FIRST APPEARANCE Fantastic Four #120 (March 1972)
REAL NAME Gabriel Lan
OCCUPATION Herald of Galactus **BASE** Various
HEIGHT 6ft 1in **WEIGHT** 210 lbs **EYES** Blue **HAIR** White
SPECIAL POWERS/ABILITIES Command of the Power Cosmic, the fundamental force of the universe, enables a variety of powers, including force blasts, interstellar flight, and ability to walk on air.

Chosen by the planet-devouring GALACTUS to become his latest Herald after the betrayal of the SILVER SURFER, Xandarian starship captain Gabriel Lan was endowed with the Power Cosmic, becoming Gabriel, the Air Walker. As the Air Walker, Gabriel served his master for several years, seeking out worlds for Galactus to consume in order to survive.

After the Ovoids killed the Air-Walker, Galactus transferred his mind into a robotic body. However, Galactus did not care for the results and replaced him with Firelord. Since then, Air-Walker's robotic body has been destroyed and rebuilt several times. Perhaps this last rebuild could mean the end of him. **TB, MF**

AJAK

FIRST APPEARANCE The Eternals Vol. 1 #2 (August 1976)
REAL NAME Ajak **OCCUPATION** Adventurer
BASE The City of the Space Gods, Andes Mountains
HEIGHT 6 ft 1 in **WEIGHT** 220 lbs **EYES** Gray **HAIR** Black
SPECIAL POWERS/ABILITIES Superhuman strength, virtual immortality and invulnerability; could psionically levitate, rearrange the molecular structure of objects, and project cosmic energy.

One of the Polar ETERNALS, Ajak was the spokesman for the Third and Fourth Host of the CELESTIALS on Earth. Ajak befriended archaeologist Dr. Daniel Damian, who used Celestial technology to turn Ajak into a murderous monster when his daughter Margo was killed. Ajak disintegrated himself and Damian out of guilt. Restored to life in Olympia years later, Ajak sought to learn how to speak with the Dreaming Celestial. This led him to join Hercules in battling the SKRULL gods. In that struggle, Kly'bn, an Eternal Skrull, killed Ajak. **PS, MF**

ALLIANCE OF EVIL

FIRST APPEARANCE X-Factor #5 (June 1985) **BASE** Mobile
MEMBERS AND POWERS
Frenzy Superhuman strength and endurance; steel-hard skin.
Tower Alters size, strength, resilience, and density.
Timeshadow Slips in and out of dimensional sync to travel at superspeed and create phase-form duplicates of himself.
Stinger Fires electricity through her fingers.

One of the least impressive Super Villain teams to threaten Earth, the Alliance of Evil was recruited by APOCALYPSE. Seeking to further his diabolical plot to change reality, Apocalypse commanded them to capture Michael Nowlan, a mutant with the ability to magnify their powers. Forced to do battle with X-FACTOR, the Alliance's initial victory was quickly turned on its head, much to Apocalypse's disgust. Abandoned by their master, the Alliance is thought to have disbanded. **AD**

ALL-WINNERS SQUAD

FIRST APPEARANCE All-Winners Comics #19 (Fall 1946)
MEMBERS AND POWERS
Captain America Superior strength, speed, agility, and endurance.
Human Torch Can control fire and can fly.
Namor Increased strength, can fly, can breath in air or water.
Whizzer Can run at super speed.
Miss America Superhuman strength, can fly.

Following World War II, the heroes of the All-Winners Squad decided to stay together to fight crime in the US rather than foreign enemies. They battled and stopped Adam-2, an android who designed a robot army. Later they faced Future Man, a time traveler from the year 1,000,000 who hoped to destroy humanity in order to allow his race to inhabit the Earth. The Squad also battled the SHE-HULK who had traveled back in time to help some gangsters acquire an atomic bomb. **MT**

THE ALL-WINNERS SQUAD
1 Miss America **2** Captain America **3** The Human Torch **4** Namor, the Sub-Mariner **5** Whizzer

ALPHA FLIGHT
Canada's foremost Super Hero team

Conceived as the Canadian government's answer to the recent spate of superhuman activity within the United States, Alpha Flight was the brainchild of James MacDonald Hudson, soon to be known first as Vindicator, then as GUARDIAN. Inspired by the FANTASTIC FOUR, Hudson and his wife Heather convinced the Canadian government to found Department H, which would be tasked with assembling a team of superhumans indigenous to the Great White North.

The Alpha Flight team roar into action.

ALPHA FLIGHT (2006)
1 Centennial **2** Sasquatch
3 Yukon Jack **4** Puck II
5 Nemesis **6** Major Mapleleaf

WANTED: A LEADER

The project was implemented using a three-tiered training system: new recruits or those whose powers proved unstable would be assigned to Gamma Flight. Those whose command of their abilities required further training formed the basis of Beta Flight. The front line, the active members whose job it would be to rout any superhuman threats to the nation, were Alpha Flight. Hudson intended that the man known as Logan (see WOLVERINE) or WEAPON X would lead Alpha Flight. However, that task fell to Hudson himself when Logan was recruited by PROFESSOR X to become a member of his X-MEN team. Alpha Flight endured a rocky relationship with the Canadian government. While the Beta and Gamma Flight units produced some heroes for Alpha Flight—like Puck—the programs also formed the nucleus of the sinister OMEGA FLIGHT team. Alpha Flight soldiered on, despite several roster changes, loyal to protecting their homeland. When the alien Plodex abducted the rest of Alpha Flight, SASQUATCH assembled a new, oddball squad that included the 97-year-old Centennial, Major Mapleleaf, the deadly Nemesis, Puck II (PUCK's daughter), and the mysterious Yukon Jack. In the aftermath of M-Day, a man known as the Collective blazed across Canada, bursting with the energy of all the mutant powers lost on that day. A hastily assembled Alpha Flight team—consisting of GUARDIAN, Major Mapleleaf, both Pucks, Sasquatch, SHAMAN, and VINDICATOR—tried to stop him and was slaughtered. Only Sasquatch is known to have survived, and he soon after put together a new team of heroes called, ironically, Omega Flight. **TB, MF**

The original team battled Wendigo and other villains in a story that featured Canadian PM Pierre Trudeau!

ALRAUNE, MARLENE

FIRST APPEARANCE The Hulk #11 (October 1978)

REAL NAME Marlene Alraune **OCCUPATION** Art history student, archaeologist, social worker **BASE** Spector Mansion, Long Island

HEIGHT 6ft 2in **WEIGHT** 130 lbs **EYES** Blue **HAIR** Blonde

SPECIAL POWERS/ABILITIES Marlene has the strength and agility of a normal woman; she is a skilled markswoman, gymnast, and hand-to-hand combatant and a resourceful crimefighter.

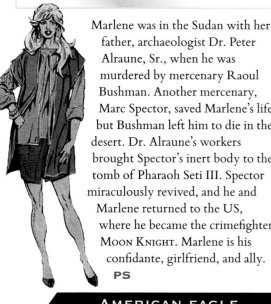

Marlene was in the Sudan with her father, archaeologist Dr. Peter Alraune, Sr., when he was murdered by mercenary Raoul Bushman. Another mercenary, Marc Spector, saved Marlene's life, but Bushman left him to die in the desert. Dr. Alraune's workers brought Spector's inert body to the tomb of Pharaoh Seti III. Spector miraculously revived, and he and Marlene returned to the US, where he became the crimefighter MOON KNIGHT. Marlene is his confidante, girlfriend, and ally. **PS**

AMERICAN EAGLE

FIRST APPEARANCE Marvel Two-In-One Annual #6 (1981)

REAL NAME Jason Strongbow

OCCUPATION Champion of the Navaho Tribe

BASE Navaho Reservation, Arizona

HEIGHT 6 ft **WEIGHT** 200 lbs **EYES** Brown **HAIR** Black

SPECIAL POWERS/ABILITIES Superstrength, speed and endurance; shoots a crossbow with specialized bolts.

While protesting the mining of a sacred mountain, Jason Strongbow and his brother Ward encountered KLAW. KLAW released a sonic blast that reacted with uranium in the rock and mutagenically enhanced the brothers. As American Eagle, Jason tracked Klaw to the Savage Land where he defeated the villain with the aid of the THING, KA-ZAR, and Wyatt WINGFOOT, but at the cost of Ward's life. Jason refused to register with the US government during the Civil War (*see* pp. 84-5) and fought the THUNDERBOLTS to stay free. He crippled BULLSEYE before he escaped. **AD, MF**

A-NEXT

On Earth-982, the AVENGERS disbanded. Ten years later, Kevin Masterson, son of THUNDERSTRIKE, visited Avengers compound to find that JARVIS had kept his father's enchanted mace for him. LOKI stole the mace and so inspired the formation of a new Avengers team, each member being related to a former one. Team membership varied as A-Next faced off against the DEFENDERS, the Soldiers of the Serpent, Kristoff Vernard (DR. DOOM's adopted son), Argo, Ion Man, RED SKULL and Dr. Doom, and the Revengers. They've also worked with SPIDER-GIRL and the Fantastic Five. **TD,**

A-NEXT
1 Blue Streak 2 Spider-Girl
3 American Dream
4 Sabreclaw 5 J2

FACTFILE
FOUNDING MEMBERS
THUNDERSTRIKE Super-strong, generates thunder blasts of concussive force.
MAINFRAME Program that lives within mobile armored, multi-weaponed, super-strong robot body.
STINGER Flies, shrinks, generates bio-electric blasts.
J2 Super-strong, nearly unstoppable and indestructible.
EDWIN JARVIS Director of operations.
ADDITIONAL MEMBERS
American Dream, Ant-Man, Bluestreak, Crimson Curse, Freebooter, Hawkeye, Jubilee, Kate Power, Sabreclaw, Scarlet Witch, Speedball, Thena, Warp.
BASE
Avengers Compound

FIRST APPEARANCE
A-Next #1
(October 1998)

ANACONDA

FIRST APPEARANCE Marvel Two-In-One #1 (June 1980)

REAL NAME Blanche "Blondie" Sitznski

OCCUPATION Freelance criminal **BASE** Mobile

HEIGHT 6 ft 2 in **WEIGHT** 220 lbs **EYES** Green **HAIR** Blonde

SPECIAL POWERS/ABILITIES Able to stretch her limbs, wrap them around people or objects, and exert enough power to crush one-inch thick steel. Few humans can break free from her grasp.

Former steelworker Blanche Sitznski underwent bioengineering changes at the mutagenics lab of the Brand Corporation, and became Anaconda. She then joined the SERPENT SQUAD to help retrieve the Serpent Crown. After some time as a mercenary, she joined SIDEWINDER in a criminal organization called the SERPENT SOCIETY. She did stints with the Femizons and the SIX PACK before joining the Serpent Society again during the Civil War. **MT, MF**

FACTFILE

ANCIENT ONE

REAL NAME
Unrevealed

OCCUPATION
Sorcerer Supreme

BASE
Kamar-Taj, Tibet, China

HEIGHT 5 ft 11 in
WEIGHT 160 lbs
EYES Brown
HAIR Bald, with white beard

FIRST APPEARANCE
Strange Tales Vol. 1 #110
(July 1963)

POWERS
Vast natural talent allied to years of training made him the greatest sorcerer in Earth's dimension, capable of astral projection, mesmerism, illusion-casting etc; able to hurl bolts of energy and possessed of extraordinary longevity.

ANCIENT ONE

Five centuries ago the master sorcerer called the Ancient One was a young farmer in the Himalayan village of Kamar-Taj. He studied sorcery with another villager, KALUU. When Kaluu sought to use his powers for conquest, the youth thwarted him, and henceforth dedicated his life to opposing evil sorcerers. He eventually became Sorcerer Supreme of Earth's dimension.

Though magic greatly extended his life, the Ancient One knew that his death was inevitable and sought to train a successor. He accepted BARON MORDO as a pupil, although he was aware of Mordo's potential for evil. Then the American surgeon Stephen Strange arrived, hoping that the Ancient One could cure his injured hands. Instead Strange found a new vocation and asked to become the Ancient One's pupil. Under the Ancient One's tutelage, DOCTOR STRANGE ultimately became the new sorcerer supreme of the Earth dimension. Later, to prevent the demon Shuma-Gorath from entering the Earth dimension through his mind, the Ancient One persuaded Strange to shut down the elderly sorcerer's brain. Thus the Ancient One died in mortal form, but his astral form became "one with the universe." **PS**

ANDROMEDA

FIRST APPEARANCE Defenders #143 (May 1985)
REAL NAME Andromeda **OCCUPATION** Warrior **BASE** Atlantis
HEIGHT 5 ft 8 in **WEIGHT** 180 lbs **EYES** Green **HAIR** Auburn
SPECIAL POWERS/ABILITIES Her physiology is suited to survival beneath the ocean; unusually strong for an Atlantean woman; highly skilled combatant, expert with a trident; on land, special serum allows her to breathe unaided for 12 hours.

Inspired by tales of NAMOR the Sub-Mariner's adventures among the humans of the surface world, the Atlantean soldier called Andromeda (a corruption of her true Atlantean name) used a serum that allowed her to breathe air and also changed the color of her skin to allow her to survive above the waves. Now resembling a normal human being, she called herself Andrea McPhee and set out to follow in Namor's footsteps. For a time, she adventured with the DEFENDERS, a team to which Namor once belonged. After the group disbanded, she eventually returned to her duties in Atlantis. **TB**

ANGAR

FIRST APPEARANCE Daredevil #100 (June 1973)
REAL NAME David Alan Angar
OCCUPATION Criminal **BASE** San Francisco
HEIGHT 6 ft 10 in **WEIGHT** 155 lbs **EYES** Brown **HAIR** Brown
SPECIAL POWERS/ABILITIES As Angar, his scream induces hallucinations and memory loss. As Scream, a creature of pure sound, he has flight, sound manipulation, and invulnerability.

Disillusioned social activist David Angar volunteered to be exposed to technology brought to Earth by MOONDRAGON, which gave him a hallucination-inducing scream. Moondragon's malevolent partner, Kerwin J. Broderick, hired Angar to kill DAREDEVIL and BLACK WIDOW, but Angar failed. Becoming a criminal for hire, Angar spent time in prison and lost his powers. MASTER KHAN later reinstated them, but the police gunned Angar down during a robbery. THE FIXER later used Angar's essence to create SCREAM, a being of pure sound, who joined the Redeemers (see THUNDERBOLTS). At his request, his teammate Songbird dispersed him permanently. **AD, MF**

ANGER, DIRK

FIRST APPEARANCE Nextwave #1 (March 2006)
REAL NAME Dirk Anger **OCCUPATION** Leader of H.A.T.E.
BASE Mobile
HEIGHT 6 ft 1 in **WEIGHT** 225 lbs **EYES** Brown **HAIR** Brown
SPECIAL POWERS/ABILITIES Controls H.A.T.E. and its resources. Ages very slowly.

General Dirk Anger was the director of the Highest Anti-Terrorist Effort (H.A.T.E.), an organization dedicated to battling the terrorists of S.I.L.E.N.T. Through the use of various, experimental longevity drugs, the mentally unstable Anger lived for over 90 years. He recruited a group of heroes to comprise Nextwave, H.A.T.E.'s strike team, but they went rogue after they discovered that S.I.L.E.N.T. was actually funding H.A.T.E. through its Beyond Corporation subsidiary, a fact Anger knew all about. He was last seen ordering the Aeromarine (H.A.T.E.'s mobile control center) on a kamikaze course into Nextwave's Shockwave Rider airship, killing everyone but his targets. **MF**

ANI-MATOR

FIRST APPEARANCE New Mutants # 59 (January 1988)
REAL NAME Dr. Frederick Animus **OCCUPATION** Geneticist
BASE Formerly "Paradise", island in North Atlantic **HEIGHT** 5 ft 6 in
WEIGHT 127 lbs **EYES** Brown **HAIR** Nearly bald
SPECIAL POWERS/ABILITIES Has a vast knowledge of genetics, beyond that of most scientists. Creates new species of life with humanoid characteristics by the genetic manipulation of animals.

Brilliant geneticist Frederick Animus was obsessed with the genetics of mutation. He was contacted by CAMERON HODGE, commander of the anti-mutant group known as the RIGHT. Hodge set Animus up on an island and supplied him with animals to use as test subjects. There, Animus created "Ani-Mates" by splicing together animal and human genes, and began calling himself the Ani-Mator. Even though some of his Ani-Mates had human levels of intelligence, Ani-Mator treated them cruelly. When one, BIRD-BRAIN, escaped and returned with members of the NEW MUTANTS, they freed the Ani-Mates and MAGIK exiled Ani-Mator to the dimension called Limbo. **MT**

ANNIHILUS

FIRST APPEARANCE Fantastic Four Annual #6 (1968)

REAL NAME Annihilus **OCCUPATION** Conqueror; destroyer

BASE Sector 17A of the Negative Zone

HEIGHT 5 ft 11 in **WEIGHT** 200 lbs **EYES** Green **HAIR** None

SPECIAL POWERS/ABILITIES Exoskeleton can withstand vast external pressure (up to 1,500 psi). He can breathe in the vacuum of space. His wings enable him to fly at up to 150 mph.

In the Negative Zone, a Tyannan ship crashed on the planet Arthros and released some spores. One of them grew into an insect-like being called Annihilus. Wielding the Cosmic Control Rod, he became master of the life forms that grew from the other spores, and he set out to conquer the other worlds of the Negative Zone. THE FANTASTIC FOUR regularly stymied his attempts to conquer the Earth and the Microverse. Later, Annihilus launched the Annihilation Wave, aiming to destroy both the regular universe and the Negative Zone. Nova killed him, but his spawn lives on. **MT, MF**

◎ ANT-MAN I *see Pym, Hank, p. 261*

ANT-MAN III

Eric O'Grady was an agent of SHIELD assigned to monitor duty with his best friend, Chris McCarthy. Eric accidentally knocked out Hank Pym (*see* PYM, HANK) and Chris wound up wearing a new Ant-Man suit that Pym was designing for SHIELD. Chris was killed when villains attacked the SHIELD Helicarrier, and Eric donned the armor and fled. After various misadventures, the cowardly Eric assumed a new identity and took a job with DAMAGE CONTROL. During World War Hulk, he tried to attack the HULK from inside but was blown out the Hulk's nose. Later, Eric found himself part of The Fifty-State Initiative (*see* pp. 118-9). During this time, he avoided most fights by shrinking away. However, he won a commendation for his work during Secret Invasion. This earned him a spot on the roster of the latest version of THE THUNDERBOLTS. **MF**

The new Ant-Man is less heroic than Hank Pym.

FACTFILE

REAL NAME
Eric O'Grady

OCCUPATION
Member of the Thunderbolts

BASE
Mobile

HEIGHT 5 ft 10 in
WEIGHT 115 lbs
EYES Brown
HAIR Blonde

FIRST APPEARANCE
The Irredeemable Ant-Man #1
(September 2006)

ANT-MAN III

POWERS

Can grow to giant-size and shrink to ant-size and back with the touch of a button on his helmet, which also allows him to communicate with ants. His armor features a jet pack and a pair of metallic tentacles.

ANT-MAN II

FACTFILE

REAL NAME
Scott Edward Lang

OCCUPATION
Adventurer; former burglar,
electronics technician

BASE
Avengers Mansion

HEIGHT 6 ft
WEIGHT 190 lbs
EYES Blue
HAIR Blond

FIRST APPEARANCE
Avengers Vol. 1 #181
(March 1979)

POWERS

Possesses ability to shrink himself and other objects and people, usually to ant size, but also to microscopic levels. Cybernetic helmet allows him telepathic control of ants. Helmet amplifies his voice so that he can be heard by normal-sized humans.

ANT-MAN II

Lang was an electronics expert who briefly turned to crime to help support his family. He was eventually arrested and sent to prison. After being paroled for good behavior, he worked at Stark Industries. His wife divorced him, but gave him custody of their daughter Cassie. Scott learned that Cassie needed an expensive heart operation, but her surgeon had been kidnapped. He resorted to burglary, breaking into the home of Dr. Hank PYM and stealing his old Ant-Man costume and shrinking formula. After rescuing the surgeon and saving Cassie, Scott turned himself in, but Pym decided to allow him to continue as Ant-Man. Scott often aided the AVENGERS and eventually joined the team. When his ex-wife learned that he was the new Ant-Man, she sued and won custody of Cassie. Scott was later killed in action when the SCARLET WITCH disassembled the Avengers. **TD**

As Ant Man, Scott was just ½ in tall and weighed little more than 1 lb.

Scott frequently clashed with the volatile Jack of Hearts, who thought Scott was not powerful enough to be a member of the Avengers.

ANTI-VENOM

FACTFILE

REAL NAME
Edward Charles "Eddie" Brock

OCCUPATION
Former journalist, now vigilante

BASE
New York City

HEIGHT 6 ft 3 in
WEIGHT 260 lbs
EYES Blue
HAIR Reddish-Blond

FIRST APPEARANCE
Amazing Spider-Man #568
(August 2008)

POWERS

Anti-Venom has superhuman speed, strength, and agility. He can stick to and climb surfaces and can fire webbing from his symbiote costume. He can also cure the irradiated.

ANTI-VENOM

Eddie Brock thought he had put his days as VENOM behind him. During his first bout with cancer, he'd sold his symbiotic suit to help find a cure, and the symbiote had bonded with Mac Gargan (*see* SCORPION). Although Matt Murdock (*see* DAREDEVIL) had helped Eddie clear his name of the crimes he'd committed when bonded with the suit, Eddie's cancer had returned, and he thought he had nothing to look forward to but a painful death. Then Martin Li (also known as Mister Negative) cured Eddie with a touch, causing the last vestiges of the symbiote to bond with Eddie's immune system. When Gargan next confronted Eddie, the symbiote tried to return to him, but it burned on touching his skin. In response, a new, altered symbiote—with the reverse of Venom's colors— seeped out of Eddie's flesh and turned him into Anti-Venom. **MF**

Anti-Venom clashes with Venom for the first time.

ANYA

FIRST APPEARANCE Amazing Fantasy Vol. 1 #1 (July 2004)
REAL NAME Anya Corazón
OCCUPATION Adventurer; student **BASE** New York City
HEIGHT 5 ft 2 in **WEIGHT** 105 lbs **EYES** Brown **HAIR** Brown
SPECIAL POWERS/ABILITIES Anya can stick to walls, climb up buildings, shoot webs, and has a "Spidey" sense that warns her of impending danger.

Brooklyn high-school student Anya Corazón nearly died in a battle between the Spider Society and the Sisterhood of the Wasps. Miguel, the sorcerer of the Spider Society endowed her with a spider-shaped tattoo which gave her spider- like powers; she also gained an exoskeleton. Told she was the latest in a 900-year-old line of Hunters charged with saving the world, Anya took the name Araña (Spanish for "spider") and faced off against her Wasp counterpart, Amun. She later discovered she was not a Hunter after all and, after the death of Miguel, she renounced the role. During the CIVIL WAR (*see* pp. 84–5), Anya registered with the government and was assigned to Ms. MARVEL for training. She recently lost her exoskeleton but still has her other powers. **MT, MF**

APALLA

FIRST APPEARANCE Doctor Strange Vol. 2 #22 (April 1977)
REAL NAME Apalla **OCCUPATION** Embodiment of the Sun
BASE Earth's solar system **HEIGHT** Variable **WEIGHT** Variable
EYES Variable **HAIR** Flaming orange
SPECIAL POWERS/ABILITIES Possesses all the powers of the Sun: able to generate heat, light etc; it is likely her abilities are restricted by her physical form.

Apalla is the corporeal manifestation of the Sun. Although thought to walk upon the Earth, sightings of are few. When the league of sorcerers, the Creators, wished to take over the stars and transform them into humans, Apalla helped DOCTOR STRANGE oppose them. A further encounter involved CAPTAIN MAR-VELL. Due to a radioactive overdose, Mar-Vell was draining her energies each time he used his powers. The pair rectified the situation before lasting damage could be done. **AD**

APOCALYPSE

Born nearly 5,000 years ago in ancient Egypt, Apocalypse is one of the earliest known mutant humans. As "En Sabah Nur," or "the First One," he traveled the world for thousands of years, instigating wars to test which nations were "fittest," and was worshipped as a god by ancient civilizations.

In the 20th century, Nur, now called Apocalypse, decided that the emerging superhuman mutants were destined to supplant "unfit" ordinary humans. Hence he often battled the original X-Factor and the X-Men, who were dedicated to peaceful coexistence between mutants and other humans.

Though extraordinarily long-lived, Apocalypse's physical body eventually wore out. He survived by projecting his consciousness into host bodies.

After M-Day, he returned again, this time after a drop of his technovirus-infected blood created a body for him out of spare body parts. On Earth-295, the "Age of Apocalypse," Apocalypse conquered North America and enslaved humanity before being killed by MAGNETO. **PS, MF**

Apocalypse's first modern team of Horsemen, his warrior servants, included Famine, War, Pestilence, (from left to right) and Archangel as Death (not shown).

THE HOUR OF YOUR GLORY IS AT HAND, MY HORSEMEN!

MOUNT YOUR BEASTS!

AQUARIAN

FIRST APPEARANCE Adventure Into Fear #17 (October 1973)
REAL NAME Wundarr **OCCUPATION** Adventurer
BASE Commune on southern California coast
HEIGHT 5 ft 10 in **WEIGHT** 165 lbs **EYES** Brown **HAIR** Brown
SPECIAL POWERS/ABILITIES Surrounded by null-field that neutralizes other superhumans' kinetic and electromagnetic energies; walks on air.

Sent into space at an early age, Wundarr landed on Earth, where the sun's energy gave him superhuman powers. An encounter with a Cosmic Cube augmented these powers. As Aquarian, he became a prophet of the Water-Children. After the Civil War he joined The Fifty-State Initiative and was assigned to the Command, Florida team, and defended Florida from the SKRULLS during the Secret Invasion. **AD, MF**

ARABIAN KNIGHT

FIRST APPEARANCE Incredible Hulk #25 (August 1980)
REAL NAME Abdul Qamar
OCCUPATION Bedouin chieftain **BASE** Saudi Arabia
HEIGHT 5 ft 10 in **WEIGHT** 170 lbs **EYES** Brown **HAIR** Black
SPECIAL POWERS/ABILITIES Scimitar fires force bolts and penetrates almost any material; rides magic carpet, which could also convert into a battering ram or envelop enemies.

Having uncovered the tomb of his ancestor, who had been a hero to his people, Abdul Qamar acquired his three mystic weapons, and set out to carry on his tradition as the modern Arabian Knight. He fought for justice for many years, but eventually perished when his life force was randomly and remotely sucked away from him by the life-draining Humus Sapien—leaving him a casualty of a conflict which had nothing to do with him directly. **TB**

ARACHNE

FACTFILE

REAL NAME
Julia Cornwall Carpenter

OCCUPATION
Adventurer, government operative

BASE
New York

HEIGHT 5 ft 9 in
WEIGHT 140 lbs
EYES Blue
HAIR Strawberry blonde

FIRST APPEARANCE
Marvel Super Heroes Secret Wars
#6 (October 1984)

POWERS

Enhanced strength, speed, stamina, agility, and reflexes. She can weave psionic force into adhesive psi-webs and can cling to and crawl across walls.

Julia's college friend Valerie Cooper (*see* COOPER, VALERIE) drafted her into the Commission on Superhuman Activities, a US task force overseeing superpowered Americans. The CSA gave Julia her powers and made her into one of its agents. She first saw action in the first Secret Wars. For a while, Julie worked with the CSA's FREEDOM FORCE, but she when pressed into battle against the AVENGERS, she took their side instead. She worked with the WEST COAST AVENGERS, but when that group was abandoned, she helped start up the new team FORCE WORKS. When the Superhuman Registration Act passed, Julia sided with Iron Man's faction. Ordered to bring in her boyfriend, the SHROUD, for refusing to register, she became a fugitive instead. Soon after her arrest, Julia was offered the choice to join OMEGA FLIGHT or serve time for her crimes. She opted for her freedom so she could remain with her daughter Rachel. **MF**

While battling demons during Omega Flight's first mission, Arachne rescued a crashing helicopter with her psi-webs.

ARCANNA

FIRST APPEARANCE Defenders #112 (October 1982)
REAL NAME Arcanna Jones
OCCUPATION Adventurer **BASE** Squadron City
HEIGHT 5 ft 8 in **WEIGHT** 115 lbs **EYES** Blue **HAIR** Blonde
SPECIAL POWERS/ABILITIES Arcanna possesses extensive magical powers, especially over natural forces, such as wind and water; able to levitate and ride the wind, sometimes on a pole.

A former medium who spent years developing her natural affinity for magic, Arcanna was encouraged to use her mystic powers in the service of mankind by her husband. Arcanna joined the ranks of the SQUADRON SUPREME, costumed champions of her home reality, and became one of its staunchest members—eventually using her magic powers to hollow out the enormous crater in which they built their upgraded headquarters, Squadron City. **TB**

ARCADE

FACTFILE

REAL NAME
Unknown

OCCUPATION
Assassin; playboy

BASE
Various Murderworlds in undisclosed locations

HEIGHT 5 ft 6 in
WEIGHT 140 lbs
EYES Blue
HAIR Red

FIRST APPEARANCE
Marvel Team-Up Vol. 1 #65 (January 1978)

POWERS

Genius at engineering, electronics, and robotics; habitual liar, using deceit to confuse opponents.

An engineering genius and a ruthless hitman, Arcade came by his fortune after allegedly murdering his billionaire father. He is obsessed with traps and games, and executes his victims in secret, amusement-park-style complexes he designs himself and dubs "Murderworlds." He charges $1 million per hit, but the money barely covers his expenses; he kills for sheer enjoyment.

Arcade is assisted by two henchmen, Miss Locke and Mr. Chambers. His victims include business tycoons and Super Heroes such as the X-MEN, SPIDER-MAN, and CAPTAIN BRITAIN, whom he kidnaps and then releases inside Murderworld. He studies victims weaknesses, chooses an appropriate killing method, and then looks on gleefully as they fight for their lives against his killing machines, which are often modeled on arcade games. Super Villains pay to use Murderworld as a training ground, or purchase Arcade's robots, which are virtually indistinguishable from real people. **DW**

Arcade is delighted when his victims express terror and panic. Recently, Arcade kidnapped the Thing and a roomful of party guests, and tormented them on remote Murder Island.

--THE X-MEN ARE AS GOOD AS DEAD!

ARCHANGEL
The Avenging Angel

A R C H A N G E L

FACTFILE

REAL NAME
Warren Kenneth Worthington III

OCCUPATION
Hero and Chairman of
Worthington Industries

BASE
New York State ("Avengers
Tower"), Manhattan, New York

HEIGHT 6 ft
WEIGHT 150 lbs
EYES Blue
HAIR Blond

FIRST APPEARANCE
X-Men #1 (September 1963)

POWERS

Feathered wings can carry up to
twice his weight and bear him to
29,000 feet; able to fly up to 150
mph; enhanced lungs enable him to
breath at high altitudes; possesses
extraordinary eyesight and blood
has healing qualities.

Warren's skin gained
a blue pigment during
his time working for
Apocalypse.

Warren Worthington was born into a
wealthy family. At private school, during
his late teens, Warren noticed wings
budding from his shoulder blades.
Fearful of attracting attention, he
strapped them to his body but secretly
began experimenting with flying. When
a fire started in his school, Warren flew
to the rescue of his schoolmates
disguised in a nightshirt and blond wig. He
was mistaken for an angel and so, when he
headed to New York City to become a
costumed crime fighter, he took the
moniker Avenging Angel.

ITINERANT X-MAN

Warren soon came to the attention of Professor
X and joined the Professor's fledgling band of
X-Men. At first, Warren disguised his face
with a mask, but he later discarded it,
believing that his handsome, telegenic
features would help gain the team public
support. With his vast, inherited wealth it was perhaps inevitable that he
would become a media playboy. Similarly, although he remained loyal to
Professor X's broad ideals, he drifted between various superpowered
teams, using his fortune to provide backing to the Champions of Los
Angeles, the DEFENDERS and later X-FACTOR. While with X-Factor
Warren's wings were damaged battling the MARAUDERS. The wings
became infected and had to be amputated. The loss of his wings so
depressed Warren that he attempted suicide. Saved by the mutant
warlord APOCALYPSE, Warren was offered the chance to grow new
wings of steel if he became one of Apocalypse's Horsemen—Death.

When his wings are
pinned to his body,
Warren can pass as a
non-mutant.

Having lost both his parents,
the X-Men have become
a surrogate family to
Archangel, bickering and
fighting but also protecting
and defending each other.

Confused and still depressed, Warren agreed, but this Faustian
pact brought him into direct conflict with his X-Men friends.
Only the apparent death of his old friend Iceman brought Warren
to his senses. Following this epiphany, Warren's metal wings
molted to reveal feathers beneath. Returning to the X-Men,
Warren rechristened himself Archangel. When his skin returned
to its normal color, he went back to calling himself Angel for a
while. Recently, WOLFSBANE tore off Warren's wings again and
gave them to the anti-mutant Purifiers, who distilled an
Apocalypse Strain from them and used it to give many of their
agents metallic wings. Warren soon transformed back into
Archangel once again. He can now morph back and forth
between his Angel and Archangel personas at will. **AD, MF**

During his recent stay in
Genosha as part of the
Excalibur team, Archangel
battled the high-tech soldiers
known as the Weaponeers.

ARES

FACTFILE

REAL NAME
Ares

OCCUPATION
God of War

BASES
New York, Olympus

HEIGHT 6 ft 1 in
WEIGHT 500 lbs
EYES Brown
HAIR Brown

FIRST APPEARANCE
Thor #129 (June 1966)

POWERS
Superhuman strength, endurance, agility, and reflexes. Immortal with healing factor.

ARES

Born the son of Zeus and Hera, Ares is the Olympian god of war. Angered over Zeus allowing the Greco-Roman religion to fade away, he has tried to conquer Olympus several times, sometimes with the help of his uncle Pluto, the god of the afterlife. In many instances, his hated half-brother Hercules thwarted his plans, continuing their eons-old enmity.

Weary of his father's rule, Ares retired to Earth to raise his son Alexander as a mortal. He returned to Olympus to battle Amatsu-Mikaboshi, the Japanese god of evil—but only once Alexander's life was at stake. After the Civil War (see pp. 84-5), he joined IRON MAN's AVENGERS, and he stuck with the team even after Norman Osborn (GREEN GOBLIN) assumed control. Recently, Nick FURY recruited Alexander—who is actually Phobos, the god of fear—for his Secret Warriors, which Ares does not yet know. With Hercules joining an alternative team of Avengers, it is only a matter of time before the two old enemies meet. **MF**

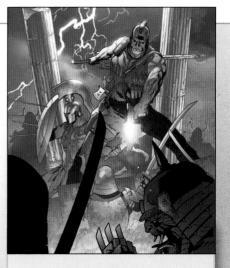

As the God of War, Ares was born for battle and is more than willing to use modern weaponry to help him rage war.

⊙ **ARIES I,II, see page 20**

ARKON

FIRST APPEARANCE Avengers #75 (April 1970)
REAL NAME Arkon ("The Magnificent")
OCCUPATION Ruler ("Imperion") **BASE** The planet Polemachus
HEIGHT 6 ft **WEIGHT** 400 lbs **EYES** Brown **HAIR** Brown
SPECIAL POWERS/ABILITIES Superhuman strength, speed, agility, and stamina; skin and muscles are more dense than that of humans; recovers from injury at a much faster rate than humans.

Arkon is a great leader and warrior on the planet Polemachus. The culture of Polemachus glorifies war and Arkon became his world's greatest warrior. As Imperion of the largest country on Polemachus, Arkon attempted to conquer the other nations of his world. But when Polemachus was faced with planet-wide annihilation, Arkon came to Earth believing that its destruction could save his homeworld. On Earth, IRON MAN teamed with THOR in a plan which saved Polemachus and stopped Arkon's aggression. **MT**

ARMADILLO

FIRST APPEARANCE Captain America Vol. 1 #308 (August 1985)
REAL NAME Antonio Rodriguez
OCCUPATION Professional wrestler **BASE** Mobile
HEIGHT 7 ft 6 in **WEIGHT** 540 lbs **EYES** Brown **HAIR** None
SPECIAL POWERS/ABILITIES Body resembles that of a gigantic humanoid armadillo, with sharp claws and armor plating; possesses superhuman strength and durability.

When his wife became mortally ill, Antonio Rodriguez turned to Dr. Karl Malus, who promised to try to cure her if Antonio worked for him and submitted to his experiments. Malus combined genes from an armadillo with Rodriguez's genes, transforming him into a super-powerful being resembling a humanoid armadillo. Malus assigned the Armadillo to invade the WEST COAST AVENGERS Compound. There Captain America defeated the Armadillo but realized he was not a criminal at heart. Though the Armadillo has sometimes run afoul of the law, he prefers to earn his living in wrestling matches against super-strong opponents. **PS**

ARMBRUSTER, COL.

FIRST APPEARANCE Incredible Hulk Vol. 1 #164 (June 1973)
REAL NAME Colonel John D. "Jack" Armbruster
OCCUPATION Colonel in US Air Force **BASE** Mobile
HEIGHT 6 ft 1 in **WEIGHT** 225 lbs **EYES** Blue **HAIR** Gray
SPECIAL POWERS/ABILITIES Military strategist, resourceful, honorable, and heroically loyal; inveterate pipe-smoker.

Colonel Armbruster led a force to rescue General Ross from the Russians. Although Ross' son-in-law, Major TALBOT, was lost during the mission, it was deemed successful and Armbruster was given control of Project Greenskin, an attempt to study the effects of gamma-radiation on the human body. Armbruster's main objective was to capture the HULK, which he succeeded in doing. When Talbot eventually returned, apparently having escaped from the Russians, Armbruster suspected foul play: when he shook hands with Talbot, his watch stopped. Armbruster discovered that there was a bomb in Talbot's body and dragged the Major into a pit. The bomb exploded, killing them both, but saving the life of the US President. **AD**

ARIES I, II
Born under the sign of the Ram

POWERS

The horns of Aries' costume were made of an incredibly hard, unknown material. He used them as a weapon, charging into opponents. Aries also wielded the Zodiac Key, an otherdimensional, sentient power object capable of firing energy bolts and transporting people across dimensions.

The first Aries, the human known as Marcus Lassiter, takes Manhattan.

Aries was a member of the criminal organization known as ZODIAC. Founded by Cornelius van Lunt was comprised of 12 human criminals, of which Marcus Lassiter (Aries), was one. Each member of the organization was based in a particular city in the US and took their codename from the astrological sign under which he or she was born.

THE ZODIAC KEY

The original human Aries, Marcus Lassiter took possession of the powerful interdimensional Zodiac Key. He then led a small army and succeeded in capturing Manhattan Island and sealing it off from the rest of the world with a force field. He tried to hold the island for ransom but this plan was stopped by the AVENGERS and DAREDEVIL. The first Aries died in an explosion. The Zodiac Key was apparently destroyed (though this turned out to be untrue).

As Daredevil looks on, Aries I threatens to execute the Avengers team using the Zodiac Key. But though he sets the chamber ablaze, it is his own plans for conquest that will shortly go up in smoke.

HORNED VILLAINS

The second human Aries, Grover Raymond, physically merged with the alien LUCIFER and died as a result. The third human Aries, whose real name is unknown, battled IRON MAN II (James Rhodes) and was killed by a member of the android Zodiac organization.

A second criminal group called Zodiac, led by Jacob Fury, was made up of android versions of the original human Zodiac members. The first android Aries (Aries IV) possessed superhuman strength. The second android Aries (Aries V) could shoot fire from his horns, although this might have simply been a power of his costume, not of the android himself. **MT**

Aries II's first appearance, in *Avengers* #120.

> CAPTAIN AMERICA WILL NOT BE SO QUICK TO COMPARE ZODIAC TO THE HYDRA WEAKLINGS...
>
> ...AFTER HE FEELS THE PHYSICAL MIGHT OF ARIES

Aries I prepares to unleash his power against Avengers leader Captain America.

Aries I

Aries II

ESSENTIAL STORYLINES
• *Avengers #82* Marcus Lassiter (Aries I) places a force field around the island of Manhattan and attempts to hold it for ransom. He is unsuccessful and is killed trying to escape.
• *Avengers #120* Grover Raymond (Aries II) is recruited into the Zodiac Cartel to replace Marcus Lassiter, but finds himself in conflict with Taurus.

FACTFILE

REAL NAME
Arm'Chedon

OCCUPATION
Warlord of the Troyjan

BASE
Troyjan-controlled space

HEIGHT 9 ft
WEIGHT 2,528 lbs
EYES Inapplicable; Troyjans have no pupils.
HAIR Gray

FIRST APPEARANCE
Incredible Hulk Vol. 2 #413 (January 1994)

POWERS
Superhuman strength and energy manipulation; enhanced durability and resistance to injury; warlike temperament; great leadership qualities.

ARMAGEDDON

Leader of the long-lived intergalactic race known as the Troyjan, the teen who would one day be known as Armageddon almost single-handedly reversed the fortunes of his race's declining empire. Under his leadership, the Troyjan expanded their galactic power base, and became a force to be reckoned with. Armageddon's attentions first turned to Earth after his son Trauma abducted ATALANTA of the PANTHEON in order to make her his mate, and was subsequently killed in battle with the incredible Hulk. Vowing revenge, Armageddon used a resurrection device created by the gamma-enhanced genius known as the LEADER to reincarnate the then-deceased THUNDERBOLT ROSS, in order to lure the Hulk into his clutches. Once the Hulk had been captured, Armageddon intended to use his life-force to restore Trauma to life. But the Hulk's energy proved too powerful, and it incinerated the remains of the deceased Troyjan warrior—leaving Armageddon with an even greater desire for revenge! **TB**

Armageddon's son, Trauma, lost his life in battle with the Hulk after trying to abduct Atalanta of the Pantheon.

To avenge his son's death, Armageddon launched attacks against the Pantheon and the Earth.

ARMORY

FIRST APPEARANCE Avengers: The Initiative #1 (April 2007)
REAL NAME Violet Lightner
OCCUPATION Former hero **BASE** Camp Hammond, CT
HEIGHT 5 ft 6 in **WEIGHT** 110 lbs **EYES** Green **HAIR** Purple
SPECIAL POWERS/ABILITIES Wore the Tactigon, an alien weapon capable of morphing into any weapon necessary.

As suicidal teen Violet Lightner leapt from the Golden Gate Bridge, an alien weapon called the Tactigon, shot from the water, attached itself to Lightner's arm, and transformed into a grappling hook that saved her. After helping the AVENGERS defeat the giant robot ULTIMO, Lightner joined the Fifty State Initiative (see pp. 118-9) and reported to Camp Hammond as part of the first class of trainees. During her first combat training session, teammate Trauma triggered her arachnophobia, and Lightner panicked. Wild shots from the Tactigon blew off KOMODO's arm and killed MICHAEL VAN PATRICK. Lightner was removed from duty, and surgeons stripped her of the Tactigon. **MF**

ARON, THE ROGUE WATCHER

FIRST APPEARANCE Captain Marvel #39 (July 1975))
REAL NAME Aron **OCCUPATION** Cosmic meddler
BASE mobile; intergalactic **HEIGHT** Variable **WEIGHT** Variable
EYES white; yellow when angry **HAIR** None
SPECIAL POWERS/ABILITIES Vast cosmic abilities; changed appearance at will; able to move between dimensions; subdued enemies with psionic blasts, or teleported them.

A young Watcher, as such temporal matters as age are measured by that intergalactic race, Aron eschewed his people's pledge of non-interference in all things, choosing instead to use his great cosmic abilities for his evil enjoyment. He toyed with the lives of the FANTASTIC FOUR, replacing them with corrupt duplicates, and later engineered a civil war within his own Watcher race. As Aron was about to destroy the Fantastic Four, UATU THE WATCHER, who was responsible for our section of the cosmos, reluctantly killed him. **TB**

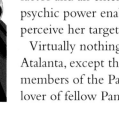

ATALANTA

FIRST APPEARANCE The Incredible Hulk #376 (December 1990)
REAL NAME Unrevealed **OCCUPATION** Pantheon operative
BASE The Mount, southwestern United States
HEIGHT 5 ft 10 in **WEIGHT** Unknown **EYES** Blue **HAIR** Black
SPECIAL POWERS/ABILITIES Wields a bow and arrows composed of an unknown form of energy that turns matter into super-heated plasma.

Named after the huntress of Greek mythology, Atalanta is a member of the PANTHEON, a covert organization of superhumans which intervenes in world affairs to prevent disasters. A deadly shot with her flaming bow, Atalanta's skin, body tissue and skeleton are denser than a normal human's, affording her greater resistance to injury. She also possesses a fast healing factor and an extended lifespan. A psychic power enables her to mentally perceive her target even if she is unable to see it.

Virtually nothing is known about the origin of Atalanta, except that she is related to other members of the Pantheon. She has been the lover of fellow Pantheon member Achilles. **PS**

ATLANTEANS

Undersea warrior race

The current emperor of Atlantis, Namor has often battled outside invaders and faced treachery from traitorous relatives—like his cousin Beemer—who have attempted to steal his throne.

FACTFILE

NOTABLE ATLANTEANS
PRINCE NAMOR
LADY DORMA (Namor's first royal consort, deceased)
ATTUMA (barbarian warlord)
KRANG (usurper)
VASHTI (Namor's Grand Vizier),
PRINCE BYRRAH
LADY FEN (Namor's mother, deceased)
NAMORA (Namor's cousin, deceased),
NAMORITA
BEEMER (would-be usurper)

FIRST APPEARANCE
Fantastic Four Annual #1 (1963)

ALLIES/FOES

Atlanteans' gills allow them to breathe underwater; they only survive five minutes out of water. They are about ten times stronger and faster than "surface dwellers." They easily withstand the crushing pressure and freezing temperatures at the bottom of the ocean.

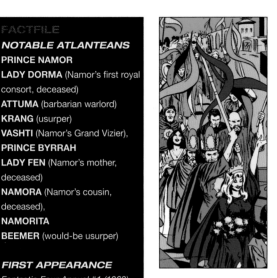

Atlantis was once a small continent in the Atlantic Ocean. The cradle of an advanced civilization, Atlantis was torn apart by earthquakes and sank into the sea some 20,000 years ago. About 10,000 years ago, a genetic offshoot of Man, *Homo mermanus* evolved the ability to live underwater. These mermen discovered the ruins left by the ancient Atlanteans and settled in them.

FIRST CONTACT

About 150 years ago, to protect his people, Emperor Thakorr moved the capital near to Antarctica. The Atlanteans remained undisturbed until an American research ship, commanded by Captain Leonard McKenzie set off explosive charges to break up icebergs. Fearing his city was under attack, Thakorr sent his daughter to investigate. Princess Fen fell in love with McKenzie and married him. When she failed to return, her father sent a war party to rescue her and McKenzie fell in the attack. Fen returned to Atlantis and gave birth to PRINCE NAMOR, the Sub-Mariner.

The Atlanteans' skin is usually light blue and their eyes tend to be blue or grey. They live on a diet of raw fish and seaweed and dwell in caves and reefs. Atlanteans communicate by high-pitched sounds and elaborate gestures. Their government is a coalition of tribes, ruled by an emperor. A Council of Elders advises the emperor. Most Atlanteans worship Poseidon, the Greek god of the sea. They are a rigid, warlike people; each citizen joins a guild to become a hunter, farmer, tradesman, craftsman, entertainer, or warrior. No one knows how many Atlanteans exist, but their population is believed to be fewer than 10,000.

Recently, Namor evacuated Atlantis and detonated the villain NITRO within it, rather than leave Atlantis under the control of his traitorous son Kamar, who had tried to draw the Atlanteans into war with the US. *Homo mermanus* now lives among the surface dwellers, and the Atlantean army is stationed in DOCTOR DOOM's homeland, Latveria. **TD, MF**

Unique Atlantean architecture employs submerged coral reefs.

The ancient Atlanteans consisted of several warring barbarian tribes, each led by warlord. The tribes formed alliances over the years, eventually uniting under a single emperor.

KEY ATLANTEANS
1 Namora
2 Namor, the Sub-Mariner
3 Lady Dorma

ATLAS

FIRST APPEARANCE Thunderbolts #1 (April 1997)

REAL NAME Erik Josten

OCCUPATION Adventurer; former criminal **BASE** Mobile

HEIGHT 6 ft **WEIGHT** 225 lbs **EYES** None; replaced by
containment spheres for unknown energy **HAIR** Red

SPECIAL POWERS/ABILITIES Atlas can grow in size from 6 ft to
60 ft; superhumanly strong and durable.

After working as POWER MAN and
GOLIATH, Josten joined BARON ZEMO
and his MASTERS OF EVIL (later the
THUNDERBOLTS) as Atlas. While battling
COUNT NEFARIA, he was changed into ionic
energy. He later managed to place his energy
into the body of Dallas RIORDAN. After they
were separated, his powers were restored, but
were still too unreliable to assign him to a team
in The Fifty State Initiative. He joined
NIGHTHAWK's version of the Defenders. **MT, MF**

ATTUMA

FIRST APPEARANCE Fantastic Four #33 (December 1964)

REAL NAME Attuma **OCCUPATION** barbarian chieftain;
former ruler of Atlantis **BASE** Atlantic Ocean

HEIGHT 6 ft 8 in **WEIGHT** 196 lbs **EYES** Brown **HAIR** Black

SPECIAL POWERS/ABILITIES Superhuman strength and stamina;
can breathe underwater and see clearly in the depths; expert hand-
to-hand combatant and with most Atlantean weapons.

Born to the *Homo mermanus*, Attuma belonged
to a tribe of nomadic barbarians and trained to
be a warrior. He repeatedly fought NAMOR the
Sub-Mariner but never defeated
him, and often allied himself
with renegade
Atlantean or human
scientists. Attuma briefly
seized control of
Atlantis, but Namor
later reclaimed his
throne. Despising
the human race,
Attuma often
attacked the surface
world but was
thwarted by the
AVENGERS and by the
FANTASTIC FOUR. The
SENTRY slew him
during his final
attempt. **TB, MF**

AVALANCHE

FIRST APPEARANCE X-Men 141 (January 1981)

REAL NAME Dominic Szilard Janos Petros

OCCUPATION Member of the Brotherhood of Evil Mutants

BASE Mobile **HEIGHT** 5 ft 7 in **WEIGHT** 195 lbs

EYES Brown **HAIR** Brown

SPECIAL POWERS/ABILITIES Vibrations generated from his
hands can bring downbuildings and cause earthquakes.

Dominic Petros was a Greek immigrant to
the US with mutant powers. The shape-shifting
mutant MYSTIQUE recruited him into THE
BROTHERHOOD OF EVIL MUTANTS, and he
participated in the Brotherhood's first attempted
assassination of SENATOR ROBERT KELLY. He left
the Brotherhood for a time to blackmail
California with the threat of an earthquake, but
he returned to it when it transformed into the
FREEDOM FORCE. He later joined EXODUS's
version of the
Brotherhood.
He retained his
powers after M-
Day, but he
decided to open
up a bar rather
than return
to crime.
AD, MF

AURORA

FACTFILE

REAL NAME
Jeanne-Marie Beaubier

OCCUPATION
Adventurer, special operative of
the Canadian government

BASE
Canada

HEIGHT 5 ft 11 in
WEIGHT 125 lbs
EYES Blue
HAIR Black

FIRST APPEARANCE
The Uncanny X-Men #120
(April 1979)

POWERS
Can run and fly at superhuman
speed. Can project
bright white light.

Orphans Jeanne-Marie
Beaubier and her twin brother
Jean-Paul were separated, and
Jeanne-Marie was raised in a
strict religious girls school. She
was so unhappy she threw
herself off a roof—and found
herself flying. Jeanne-Marie
thought a miracle had taken place
and told the headmistress, but was
punished for blasphemy. Jeanne-Marie
developed a personality disorder: her
everyday self was introverted, but her
repressed side was uninhibited. Five years later, Jeanne-Marie
became a teacher at the school. One night, WOLVERINE saw her
use superspeed to defend herself from a mugger. Wolverine
introduced her to James MacDonald Hudson, who reunited
Jeanne-Marie with her brother. Taking the codenames Aurora and
NORTHSTAR, Jeanne-Marie and Jean-Paul joined Hudson's team of
Canadian heroes, ALPHA FLIGHT. Since then, Aurora's psyche has
manifested a third personality. The X-Men used SHIELD virtual
reality equipment to allow Aurora and her brother to relive their
lives, helping to restore Aurora's shattered psyche. **PS, MF**

AVENGERS

Earth's mightiest heroes

AVENGERS FACTFILE

KEY MEMBERS
(see individual entries
for powers)
THOR; IRON MAN;
ANT-MAN I (DR. HANK PYM AKA
GIANT-MAN, GOLIATH,
YELLOWJACKET);
WASP; HULK;
CAPTAIN AMERICA;
WONDER MAN; HAWKEYE;
VISION; SCARLET WITCH;
QUICKSILVER;
BLACK PANTHER;
BLACK WIDOW;
HERCULES; BLACK KNIGHT;
SHE-HULK; PULSAR (Monica
Rambeau aka Captain Marvel,
Photon); QUASAR; CRYSTAL;
SERSI; ANT-MAN II (Scott Lang).

BASE
Stark Tower, Manhattan; formerly
Avengers Mansion (aka Avengers
Embassy) Manhattan, and
Avengers Compound, Palos
Verdes, California

FIRST APPEARANCE
Avengers #1
(September 1963)

ALLIES Rick Jones, Edwin Jarvis,
the Fantastic Four.

FOES Space Phantom, the Lava
Men, the Mole Man, Baron Zemo,
his Masters of Evil, Kang, Ultron,
Collector, Grandmaster, Electro,
Sauron, Madame Hydra.

ISSUE #1
Written by Stan Lee, penciled by
Jack Kirby and inked by Dick
Ayers, the first issue of *The
Avengers* guest-starred Rick
Jones, the Teen Brigade and the
Fantastic Four.

The Avengers are dedicated to safeguarding the planet from
super-menaces too powerful for a single hero or the armed forces
of any one country to combat. Formed shortly after the first
public appearance of the FANTASTIC FOUR, the Avengers
immediately won government approval from the National
Security Council of the United States and the General Assembly
of the United Nations. Unlike the FF, the Avengers' roster is
always changing. Members join, leave and return—a precedent set
by the HULK, who left the team weeks after it was first formed.

WAIT! DON'T YOU RECOGNIZE IT?? IT'S THE FAMOUS RED, WHITE, AND BLUE GARB OF -- CAPTAIN AMERICA!

THE WASP IS RIGHT!

Captain America
had lain frozen in
the Arctic ice since
the end of World
War II. Decades
later, he was
discovered and
revived by the
Avengers.

BACK, BACK, YOU HUMAN DOLT! NO MORTAL MAY LAY A HAND ON LOKI! I HAVE POWERS YOU NEVER DREAMED OF!

HEY! THAT GLOW... WHAT'S HAPPENIN' TO HIM?

HE'S MADE HIMSELF RADIOACTIVE!

Loki tried to escape by casting a
spell that made his body radioactive.
However, the heroes soon trapped
him within a lead-lined tank.

HERO TEAM

The Avengers were formed by
accident. LOKI, Asgardian God of Evil,
wanted revenge on his half-brother THOR. After
searching for a menace powerful enough to
challenge Thor, he selected the Hulk and tricked
him into causing a train wreck. When the Hulk's former
partner Rick JONES heard this news, he attempted to alert the
Fantastic Four, but Loki diverted his radio signal and sent it to
Thor. But the thunder god wasn't the only one to answer the
call. The astonishing Ant-Man (*see* PYM, DR.
HENRY), the WASP and IRON MAN also
responded. While the other heroes battled the
Hulk, Thor tracked down Loki and captured
him. After learning that the Hulk was innocent,
Ant-Man suggested that the heroes form a team.
The Wasp suggested they call themselves
"something colorful and dramatic, like ...the
Avengers."

AVENGERS MANSION

Tony Stark (Iron Man) donated his three-
story townhouse to the team who
renamed it Avengers Mansion and
later significantly modified it to fit
their needs. Stark also funded
the new team and provided

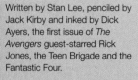

THE AVENGERS (2004)
1 The Wasp 2 Hawkeye 3 Scarlet Witch
4 Captain America 5 The Vision 6 Iron Man

For most of its history, the Avengers employed a rotating chairmanship that allowed different acting members to chair meetings and make administrative decisions. Captain America usually served as team leader in the field.

THE ULTIMATES

On a parallel Earth, government scientists created a super-soldier formula, but lost it when Captain America disappeared during World War II. Many years later, Dr. Bruce Banner was hired to recreate it. Working out of a rundown research facility in Pittsburgh, he engaged in secret superhuman trials on civilians and even tested the formula on himself, transforming himself into the rampaging Hulk. General Nick Fury took custody of Banner and ordered him to complete his research in order to create a new super-team called the Ultimates. This team included Dr. Hank Pym, a cybertronics expert and a world authority on super-genetics.

THE ULTIMATES (2004)
1 Giant-Man **2** Iron Man **3** Hawkeye **4** Wasp **5** Captain America
6 Black Widow **7** Thor

equipment, weaponry, security countermeasures and computer systems. He also used his government contacts to lobby for A-1 or Avengers Priority security clearance to aid the team's operations.

The Avengers began to establish themselves by fighting foes like the SPACE PHANTOM, the LAVA MEN, the MOLE MAN, BARON ZEMO, his MASTERS OF EVIL and KANG. The team also met Wonder Man who later sacrificed himself to save them. All of the founding members eventually left the team, leaving CAPTAIN AMERICA in charge with a band that first consisted of HAWKEYE, the SCARLET WITCH and QUICKSILVER. The Wasp and Hank Pym, who had exchanged his Ant-Man to become the first Goliath, returned to the team. The Olympian demigod HERCULES also became a member. Serving as an agent for the MANDARIN, the first Swordsman even attempted to join.

THE OLD ORDER CHANGETH
Accidentally created by Hank Pym, the robot ULTRON tried to kill the Avengers. He even built the android VISION, who betrayed him and served as an Avenger for many years. Haunted by guilt, Pym's marriage to the Wasp deteriorated and he left the team.

The Avengers fought alongside the alien CAPTAIN MAR-VELL in a cosmic battle that came to be known as the Kree-Skrull War. The membership continued to change as the BLACK WIDOW, the BEAST, the now-reformed Swordsman, MANTIS, and HELLCAT all became members. A romance developed between the

When Kang the Conqueror and his son Marcus waged all-out war against the Earth, the Avengers led the planet's defensive effort. Although Kang temporarily succeeded in subduing the entire world, the Avengers led a resistance movement that eventually overthrew his new dynasty.

When the Avengers disappeared while battling Onslaught, those on the Earth they left behind believed them dead.

VISION and the Scarlet Witch and they married.

The National Security Council began to take an active interest in the team and appointed Henry Peter GYRICH liaison officer. He tried to control team membership by recruiting FALCON and Ms. Marvel (see WARBIRD). In recent years, JUSTICE, FIRESTAR, TRIATHLON, SILVERCLAW, JACK OF HEARTS, ANT-MAN and a new female CAPTAIN BRITAIN served as members.

HEROES REBORN AND RETURN
At one point, the Avengers became embroiled in an epic battle with the villain ONSLAUGHT, and they, the FANTASTIC FOUR, and DR. DOOM were all presumed to have perished. Actually, Franklin Richards had used his reality-altering powers to save them at the last moment and transport them into a pocket dimension of his own creation, which featured a copy of Earth called Counter-Earth. They came back after a year. Later, Counter-Earth became situated on the opposite side of the sun from the Earth.

TD, MF

ESSENTIAL STORYLINES
• *Avengers #4* The Avengers rescue Captain America from an icy tomb and invite him to join the team.
• *The Greatest Battles of the Avengers (tpb)* The Avengers fight many of their most deadly foes.
• *Avengers: The Korvac Saga (tpb)* The Guardians of the Galaxy help the Avengers battle Michael Korvac.
• *Avengers: Under Siege (tpb)* The new Baron Zemo and his Masters of Evil attack Avengers Mansion
• *Avengers: Disassembled* The Scarlet Witch warps reality and attacks her former teammates.

AVENGERS

The Avengers Mansion had survived many attacks—until it was destroyed by one of its own.

AVENGERS DISASSEMBLED

A victim of her own reality-altering powers, the SCARLET WITCH (Wanda Maximoff) had a nervous breakdown after the WASP accidentally reminded her of something that had been wiped from her mind: the existence of her twin sons, Thomas and William. Desperate to become pregnant by her husband, the VISION, she'd subconsciously created them with her magic, implanting in each a soul fragment she'd found. When MEPHISTO claimed these fragments as lost bits of his own soul, the boys disappeared into him. To help save Wanda from a breakdown, Agatha HARKNESS had erased the memory of the boys from their mother's mind. When the memories came flooding back, Wanda's sanity shattered completely.

THE MANSION DESTROYED

An undead version of JACK OF HEARTS—who'd died earlier in the year while saving Cassie Young, the daughter of ANT-MAN (Scott Young)—showed up at the Avengers Mansion without warning. When Ant-Man went out to greet him, Jack said, "I'm sorry," and then exploded. The blast killed Ant-Man and totally destroyed half of the mansion.

At the same moment, IRON MAN—who was with the Scarlet Witch and YELLOWJACKET (Hank Pym)—was addressing the United Nations when he became drunk and belligerent, without having had a drink. Soon after, back at the Avengers Mansion, the Vision crash-landed an

Avengers quinjet into the front yard. Melting to pieces as he tried to explain himself, the Vision launched five metal balls from his mouth. These each transformed into an Ultron.

While helping to defeat the Ultrons, CAPTAIN BRITAIN (Kelsey Leigh) was killed. Afterward, She-Hulk flew into a rage and ripped the remains of the Vision to pieces, then nearly killed the Wasp.

THE FINAL ASSEMBLY

As the Avengers tried to puzzle out what was happening, every available hero who'd ever been an Avenger rallied outside the mansion. As they did, the UN revoked the Avengers' charter. Directly after that, a KREE invasion force appeared over the mansion and attacked. HAWKEYE sacrificed his life to destroy the alien ships.

DOCTOR. STRANGE then arrived and revealed that Wanda had been behind the string of disasters, which were designed not only to destroy the Avengers but also their reputation.

As the Vision was destroyed, his corpse produced copies of Ultron.

Always ready for a fight, the Avengers battled the five Ultrons, removing their heads to destroy them. As they did, they realized something was truly wrong.

The Avengers found and confronted Wanda, who unleashed a horde of their foes against them. After Doctor Strange finally stopped Wanda, her father, MAGNETO, appeared and took her away. Although he tried to nurse her back to health, she later snapped again, which led to the House of M and M-DAY events.

The Avengers were no more.

THE NEW AVENGERS

When ELECTRO staged a breakout of the world's worst criminals out of the super-prison called the Raft, CAPTAIN AMERICA and Iron Man led an impromptu team of heroes into trying to keep the lid on the place. They only partially succeeded, and the two members of the original Avengers decided to form a new team to help them track down and capture the escaped villains. Besides

Just when the Avengers thought they had seen the worst, an invasion force of Kree warriors appeared in the sky over Manhattan.

Captain America and Iron Man, this new team included Luke CAGE, SPIDER-MAN, SPIDER-WOMAN, and WOLVERINE.

The New Avengers lived in Stark Tower, which was topped by the Sentry's watchtower. The team fractured down the middle when the Civil War (*see* pp.84–5) began. Those who supported the Superhuman Registration Act stayed with Iron Man, while the others backed Captain America's resistance. This team currently functions underground with no official support from any government.

THE MIGHTY AVENGERS

At the end of the Civil War, Iron Man was named director of SHIELD and named Ms. Marvel to lead a new team of official Avengers. For her Mighty Avengers, she chose Ares, Black Widow, Iron Man, Sentry, Wasp, and WONDER MAN. They fought together until Iron Man was disgraced and removed from SHIELD. At that point, Hank Pym decided to form an Avengers team with the prodding of QUICKSILVER and the restored Scarlet Witch. This new team eventually learned that their Scarlet Witch was actually Loki in disguise.

MIGHTY AVENGERS
1 Sentry **2** Iron Man **3** Wonder Man **4** Ms. Marvel

THE DARK AVENGERS

At the same time, Norman Osborn (*see* GREEN GOBLIN) took over where Iron Man left off. He formed his own team of Avengers, staffing it with villains placed in the costumes of heroes—often their greatest foes including VENOM in the role of Spider-Man and Bullseye as Hawkeye. As the Iron Patriot, Osborn filled the roles of both Captain America and Iron Man on his team, leading from the front while he deployed his THUNDERBOLTS as a cover strike force. **MF**

Norman Osborn (Green Goblin) revealed a new team, the Dark Avengers, featuring (left to right) Captain Marvel (Marvel Boy), Sentry, Ms. Marvel (Moonstone), Iron Patriot (Green Goblin), Ares, Wolverine (Daken), Hawkeye (Bullseye), and Spider-Man (Venom).

AVENGERS WEST COAST

The Avengers' West Coast "branch office"

FACTFILE

FOUNDING MEMBERS
HAWKEYE
MOCKINGBIRD
IRON MAN
TIGRA
WONDER MAN

FINAL MEMBERS
SCARLET WITCH
SPIDER-WOMAN II
(Julia Carpenter)
WAR MACHINE
U.S. AGENT

ADDITIONAL MEMBERS
HUMAN TORCH I
(James Hammond)
LIVING LIGHTNING
MOON KNIGHT
BASE
Avengers Compound, 1800 Palos
Verdes Drive, California

FIRST APPEARANCE
West Coast Avengers #1
(September 1984)

ALLIES Hank Pym (resident
scientist), The Thing.

FOES Graviton, Ultron, The Grim
Reaper, Master Pandemonium,
Mephisto, Lethal Legion.

While chairman of the AVENGERS, the Vision decided to expand the team and sent HAWKEYE and his new wife MOCKINGBIRD to Los Angeles to establish a second headquarters on the West Coast. Hawkeye purchased a 15-acre estate on the Pacific coast. It consisted of a main building, surrounded by several guest cottages that housed various Avengers over the years. The mountainside beneath the main building accommodated the high-security Avengers Assembly Room, a hospital, laboratories and a hanger for Avengers' Quinjets.

GROWING PAINS

The team faced its first crisis when Mockingbird and Hawkeye argued over whether the Avengers had the right to use lethal force. Hawkeye later resigned when the government assigned the US Agent to the team and he temporarily joined the GREAT LAKES AVENGERS. The Wasp moved to the West Coast to join her former husband Dr. Pym and the team aided their East Coast counterparts in the Kree-Shi'ar war known as Operation: Galactic Storm. After falling under

Most of the West Coast Avengers had served on the East Coast team and returned to New York after this branch office closed.

the control of MAGNETO and IMMORTUS, the SCARLET WITCH used her reality-altering powers against the West Coast Avengers.

Hawkeye and Mockingbird eventually reconciled and rejoined the team, and the Scarlet Witch (now cured) became the team's chairperson. During an attack by the demon MEPHISTO and the LETHAL LEGION, Mockingbird was killed and the Compound severely damaged. Hawkeye resigned to mourn his wife's death and CAPTAIN AMERICA and the BLACK WIDOW decided to close the West Coast branch. **TD**

ESSENTIAL STORYLINES
• *West Coast Avengers* #1–4
Hawkeye and Mockingbird establish the new team.
• *WEST COAST AVENGERS* #17–23 Dr. Pym contemplates suicide, the team is transported into the past, and Mockingbird is captured by the Phantom Rider.
• *Avengers West Coast* #55–57, 59–62 The Scarlet Witch falls victim to Magneto and Immortus.

CHARACTER KEY
1 Spider-Woman II **2** US Agent
3 Living Lightning **4** Hawkeye **5** Iron
Man **6** Scarlet Witch **7** Wonder Man

Trapped by the X-Men and the Fantastic Four, the Mad Thinker and the Puppet Master turn the Awesome Android loose in a last attempt to escape justice.

AWESOME ANDROID

FIRST APPEARANCE Fantastic Four #15 (June 1963)
REAL NAME Answers to "Awesome Andy"
OCCUPATION Legal aide **BASE** New York City
HEIGHT 15 ft **WEIGHT** 1421 lbs **EYES** None **HAIR** None
SPECIAL POWERS/ABILITIES Possessed the ability to duplicate any special powers directed against it.

The Awesome Android was the creation of the evil MAD THINKER, constructed using research notes that once belonged to scientist Reed Richards (*see* MISTER FANTASTIC). The Mad Thinker intended to use the Awesome Android as a weapon to destroy the FANTASTIC FOUR. However, as time went by, the android developed a personality of its own and freed itself from the Thinker's villainous thrall.

"Awesome Andy" now works peacefully as an aide in the legal offices of Goodman, Lieber, Kurtzburg & Holliway. **TB**

AYESHA (AKA HER)

FIRST APPEARANCE Marvel Two-In-One #61 (March 1980)
REAL NAME Paragon
OCCUPATION None **BASE** Outer space
HEIGHT 6 ft 6 in **WEIGHT** 390 lbs **EYES** White **HAIR** Blonde
SPECIAL POWERS/ABILITIES Controls cosmic energy which prevents aging; uses this energy to rearrange matter, project concussive blasts, to fly, and to open cosmic rifts into warp-space.

Originally called Paragon or Her, Ayesha was created by a group of scientists known as the Enclave. Hoping to create a perfect life form, they created a being called Him, but Him refused to be controlled. Paragon also rebelled, destroying the Enclave's base. After meditating in a cocoon, she emerged as Her, able to tap into pure cosmic energy. She hoped to mate with Him (now known as Adam WARLOCK), pursuing him even through death and return to life, but he spurned her. She then turned her attentions to Quasar, during which time she was known as Kismet. **MT, MF**

AZAZEL

FIRST APPEARANCE The Uncanny X-Men #428 (October 2003)
REAL NAME Azazel **OCCUPATION** Conqueror
BASE La Isla de Demonas, off the coast of Florida; the *Brimstone*
HEIGHT 5 ft 11 in **WEIGHT** Unknown **EYES** Black **HAIR** Gray
SPECIAL POWERS/ABILITIES The full extent of his powers is unknown; can teleport himself, take on human form, and mentally influence his offspring.

Azazel is the leader of the Neyaphem, a race of mutants who resemble demons. In ancient times Azazel was thought to be the devil. Azazel claims that he once ruled the Earth until he and the Neyaphem were banished to another dimension by the Cheyarafim, a race of mutants who resembled angels. As part of his plan to reconquer Earth, Azazel mated with various women, fathering mutants with teleportational powers. Among the women he seduced was the mutant MYSTIQUE, who gave birth to their son Kurt Wagner, alias NIGHTCRAWLER. When Nightcrawler learned that Azazel was his father, he not only rejected him, but helped defeat him. **PS**

AZAZEL AND HIS CREW
1 Azazel 2 Ginniyeh
3 Minion of Azazel 4 Ydrazil 5 Jillian

ANNIHILATION
This means war...

Richard Rider (Nova), the last survivor of the Nova Corps, led the Kree defense—and later the entire United Front—against the invading hordes of the Annihilation Wave.

Without warning, the overwhelming forces of the Annihilation Wave stormed through outer edge of the universe, piercing its border with the strange dimension known as the Negative Zone, called the Crunch. The Wave, composed of countless insectoid starships and warriors, first destroyed the Kyln, a ring of artificial moons that both served as a super-prison and as a generator of nearly limitless power. Then it destroyed the planet Xandar and the Nova Corps and leaving Earth's Richard Rider (NOVA) as the galactic police force's only survivor.

Drax the Destroyer was killed by Paibok the Skrull before the Annihilation Wave even began. He returned in a new body to seek his revenge, accompanied by his new friend Cammi.

THE GALAXY AT WAR

With the help of QUASAR and DRAX THE DESTROYER, Nova discovered that ANNIHILUS, who led the Annihilation Wave, had allied with THANOS to conquer the galaxy. After killing Quasar, Annihilus took his quantum bands and drove off the others. Annihilus freed from Kyln two ancient beings known as Aegis and Tenebrous, who GALACTUS had imprisoned there. The SILVER SURFER joined with Galactus and his former heralds to fight his foes but lost.

Nova left Earth to help defend the planet Xandar against the Annihilation Wave. Failing at that, he drew on the power of the entire Nova Force to challenge Annihilus himself.

With the help of Drax, GAMORA, RONAN THE ACCUSER, and Star-Lord (Peter Quill), Nova formed and led the interstellar alliance called the United Front. After Thanos captured MOONDRAGON, Drax went to rescue her and discovered that Annihilus had turned Galactus and his heralds into

The Silver Surfer made the ultimate sacrifice to stem the tide of the Annihilation Wave. After nearly dying at the hands of other elder beings, he returned to the service of Galactus.

a cosmic bomb that would destroy the entire universe. Drax freed the Silver Surfer, who in turn freed Galactus. Furious, Galactus attacked the Annihilation Wave. Meanwhile, with the SKRULL Empire destroyed, Ronan and the SUPER-SKRULL freed the KREE Empire from the control of the traitorous House Fiyero, which had kept the SUPREME INTELLIGENCE trapped between life and death. Finishing the Supreme Intelligence off, Ronan took control of the empire.

With the Annihilation Wave decimated, Nova, Phyla-Vell (CAPTAIN MARVEL), and Star-Lord hunted down Annihilus. Phyla took the quantum bands from him, and Nova killed him with his bare hands. Later, though, Annihilus's lieutenant Ravenous revealed an infant insectoid he believed to be Annihilus reborn.

ANOTHER CONQUEST

Soon after, the PHALANX attacked and conquered the Kree Empire, using a techno-organic virus to control their subjects. Star-Lord formed a team (a prototype of the GUARDIANS OF THE GALAXY) to help fight this threat. Phyla-Vell (now the new Quasar) and Moondragon (transformed into the Dragon of the Moon) hunted for a savior who could defeat the Phalanx: a young, regenerated Adam WARLOCK. Warlock brought the women to meet the HIGH EVOLUTIONARY. Soon after, ULTRON attacked, killing Moondragon and revealing himself as the driving force behind the Phalanx invasion. Later, Ultron forced the High Evolutionary to transfer his mind into Warlock's body. Meanwhile, Ronan, Super-Skrull, and a Kree named Wraith— who can protect others from the Phalanx infection—went to the

The Super-Skrull failed to keep the Annihilation Wave from destroying his people's homeworld, but he sacrificed himself (temporarily) to keep the Harvester of Sorrows from obliterating any other worlds.

Kree world controlled by Ravenous and shielded an army of robotic Kree sentries. They then sent them to destroy the Phalanx. At the same time, Nova, Drax, and Gamora reappeared with Warlock of the Technarchy—which had created the Phalanx—with them.

The Technarchy Warlock forced Ultron from Adam Warlock's body. When Ultron reassembled himself into a gigantic body, Wraith trapped Ultron's mind within it, and Quasar slew it, ending the war. MF

Ronan the Accuser was framed for treason by Tana Nile but still rose to become the leader of the Kree. He ultimately had to kill the Supreme Intelligence and take control of the Kree Empire himself.

THE ANNIHILATION WAVE

The invasion forces that Annihilus assembled in relative safety of the Negative Zone proved to be the largest fighting force the galaxy had ever seen. At the height of its powers, it destroyed nearly all of the mighty Skrull and Kree Empires and even captured the Silver Surfer and Galactus. At the moment known as Annihilation Day, Annihilus's forces destroy the Kyln super-prison and launch their war on the positive-matter universe.

BANNER, BETTY

The Hulk's beloved

FACTFILE

REAL NAME
Elizabeth Ross Banner

OCCUPATION
None

BASE
Mobile

HEIGHT 5 ft 6 in
WEIGHT 110 lbs
EYES Blue
HAIR Brown

FIRST APPEARANCE
Incredible Hulk #1
(May 1962)

BETTY BANNER

POWERS

No superhuman powers, but courageous and resourceful; steadfastly loyal to her husband Bruce Banner through many shared tribulations.

The only daughter of renowned military general Thaddeus "Thunderbolt" Ross, Betty spent her formative years firmly under her father's thumb. Thunderbolt Ross had wanted a son, and had no use for his unfortunate daughter; after her mother died during Betty's teenage years, she was sent away to boarding school. After graduating, she returned to her father's side, a repressed wallflower. Thunderbolt Ross was then in charge of a top-secret project to create a new type of weapon employing the limitless power of gamma radiation. The head scientist on the project was the quiet, bookish Bruce Banner, and an attraction between Betty and Banner soon developed.

Betty Banner met her one-day husband Bruce when she came to live on a New Mexico military base with her father, Thunderbolt Ross.

TRAGIC LOVE

Their relationship was forever changed when, during the gamma-bomb test, Banner was struck by the full force of the detonation, and its radiations transformed him into the HULK whenever he grew angry. Banner tried to keep his condition secret from Betty, which only served to alienate them. Betty was then ardently pursued by Major Glenn Talbot (*see* TALBOT, COL. GLENN), the new aide attached to her father's Hulkbuster task force. Eventually, the secret of Banner's dual identity became public knowledge, and his transformations and rampages created a rift between Betty and himself. With no one else to turn to, Betty married Major Talbot. Their union soon ended in divorce, however, and Talbot died attempting to destroy the Hulk.

ESSENTIAL STORYLINES

• *Hulk Vol. 2 #168–169*
MODOK transforms Betty into the Harpy.

• *Hulk Vol. 2 #319*
After years of courtship and chaos, Bruce Banner finally marries Betty.

• *Hulk Vol. 2 #465–469*
Betty is exposed to radiation poisoning; Bruce desperately tries to save her.

YOU MAY HAVE BRUTE STRENGTH-- BUT I HAVE THE UNBRIDLED POWER OF THE HARPY'S HELLBOLTS--

HARPY HORROR

Betty continued to find herself entangled in the lives of Bruce Banner and the Hulk. At one point she was transformed by the villainous MODOK into a gamma-empowered flying menace known as the Harpy. But even these trials could not destroy her love for hapless Bruce Banner, and eventually, despite her father's objections, she married him.

However lasting happiness was not to be theirs. The ABOMINATION used his own gamma-irradiated blood to poison Betty, hoping to pin the crime on Bruce. Later, the LEADER seemed to revive Betty, who then aided her fugitive husband as his shadowy contact Mr. Blue.

However, NIGHTMARE then revealed that her apparent return was only one of many hallucinations he'd used to manipulate the Hulk. Betty truly is dead.

TB, MF

Bruce Banner's transformation into the rampaging Hulk has brought Betty a lot of strife, yet she remains devoted to her husband.

BALDER THE BRAVE

Prophecy has it that the death of Norse God Balder will result in Ragnarok—the destruction of Asgard, the home of the Norse Gods (*see* GODS OF ASGARD). For this reason Odin commanded his wife Frigga to make Balder (his son) invulnerable to physical injury and so she cast spells that protected him from everything except mistletoe.

The God of mischief, Loki, Thor's adopted brother, learned of this and tricked the blind God Hoder to fire an arrow, tipped with mistletoe wood, at Balder. Only Odin's intervention saved him, but before his recovery, Balder's soul was to travel through the underworld where it encountered the spirits of those he had killed.

Balder's return to the land of the living was not without difficulties: he fell into a deep depression after Nanna, his beloved, sacrificed herself to save him from marrying the Norn sorceress Kamilla. Roving the desert, determined to kill himself, Balder gained hope from a vision of the future. Since then, he has come to love Kamilla, with whom he fought against Surtur and the legions of the Muspelheim. He also ruled Asgard when Odin was believed dead, but following the God-ruler's return Balder went back to his new love, Kamilla. **AD**

A natural leader, Balder the Brave has led his people on countless campaigns.

FACTFILE
REAL NAME Balder
OCCUPATION Norse God of Light
BASE Asgard
HEIGHT 6 ft 4 in
WEIGHT 320 lbs
EYES Blue
HAIR Brown
FIRST APPEARANCE Journey into Mystery #85 (October 1962)

POWERS
Charismatic leader; formidable swordsman, horseman, and hand-to-hand combatant; in Asgard dimension, only weapons tipped with mistletoe cause him harm; able to produce and emit light; possesses superhuman strength, endurance, and longevity.

BANNER, BETTY *see opp. page*

BANNER, DR. BRIAN

FIRST APPEARANCE The Incredible Hulk Vol. 2 #312 (Oct. 1985)
REAL NAME Brian Banner
OCCUPATION Atomic physicist **BASE** Dayton, Ohio
HEIGHT 5 ft 10in **WEIGHT** 145 lbs **EYES** Brown **HAIR** Brown
SPECIAL POWERS/ABILITIES Scientific genius.

Married to his childhood sweetheart, Rebecca, Dr. Banner worked as an atomic physicist for the US government and helped develop the country's first atomic weapons. The more he studied atomic radiation, the more he feared it. Suspecting that he had been exposed to trace amounts of radiation, Banner was horrified when he learned that his young wife was pregnant. When she began to suffer complications, he became convinced that the child would be mutant and grow up to become a monster. His paranoia increased when his son Bruce (*see* HULK) showed signs of great intelligence. Banner began to drink heavily and often exploded in fits of temper. After striking and accidentally killing his wife, he was convicted of manslaughter and confined to a mental institution. His son Bruce would be profoundly affected by this family trauma. **TD**

BANSHEE

After his wife's death, Irish Interpol agent and mutant Sean Cassidy was forced to join Factor Three, an organization of evil mutants. The evil CHANGELING gave him the name Banshee and fitted him with an explosive headband to keep him in line. PROFESSOR X used his telepathic powers to remove the band, and Banshee then defeated Factor Three. Later, Banshee joined the X-MEN. While there, he reunited with his daughter SIRYN and became co-head—with Emma FROST—of Xavier's Academy, where he taught the young mutants of GENERATION X. Following the tragic death of his beloved, Dr. Moira MACTAGGERT, Banshee suffered a temporary breakdown. He formed X-CORPS, but this venture ended with MYSTIQUE stabbing him through the throat. Banshee later died at the hands of VULCAN. **MT, MF**

FACTFILE
REAL NAME Sean Cassidy
OCCUPATION Director of X-Corps
BASE Cassidy Keep, Ireland
HEIGHT 6 ft
WEIGHT 170 lbs
EYES Blue-green
HAIR Blond
FIRST APPEARANCE Uncanny X-Men #28 (January 1967)

POWERS
Banshee's "sonic scream" could propel him into flight, shatter solid objects, and fire percussive blasts, which placed others into trances or knocked them unconscious.

Banshee unleashes a devastating sonic scream at Cyclops and his fellow X-Men.

BARON BLOOD

FIRST APPEARANCE The Invaders Vol. 1 #7 (June 1976)
REAL NAME Lord John Falsworth
OCCUPATION Former German assassin **BASE** London
HEIGHT 5 ft 10 in **WEIGHT** 180 lbs **EYES** Red **HAIR** Black
SPECIAL POWERS/ABILITIES Vampiric powers, including superhuman strength, hypnotic abilities, and invulnerability to conventional weaponry; could fly without transforming into a bat.

The younger son of a British aristocrat, John Falsworth was killed and vampirized by DRACULA. As Baron Blood, Falsworth served German intelligence during World War I and II. During World War II Baron Blood battled UNION JACK (who was secretly his brother, Montgomery) and the INVADERS. Decades later, Blood was beheaded by CAPTAIN AMERICA. Two later vampires took the name Baron Blood: DOCTOR STRANGE's brother Victor and Montgomery's grandson Kenneth Crichton. **PS**

BARON VON STRUCKER

FIRST APPEARANCE Sgt. Fury And His Howling Commandos #5 (January 1964) **REAL NAME** Baron Wolfgang Von Strucker
OCCUPATION Terrorist leader **BASE** Mobile
HEIGHT 6 ft 2 in **WEIGHT** 225 lbs **EYES** Blue **HAIR** None
SPECIAL POWERS/ABILITIES Can release the virulent Death Spore Virus from within his body at will. He wears the Satan Claw, capable of discharging electrical shocks, upon his right hand.

Baron Von Strucker fought for the Nazis during World War II as the leader of the Blitzkrieg Squad, Germany's answer to the HOWLING COMMANDOS led by Sgt. Nick FURY. After the war, Strucker took control of a Japanese secret society and evolved it into the worldwide terror group HYDRA. Kept alive and vigorous by the Death Spore virus within his body, Von Strucker's goal is total world domination. **TB**

BARON MORDO

Doctor Strange and Baron Mordo battle in astral form before their mentor, the Ancient One.

As a child, Karl Mordo gained an interest in the occult from his grandfather, Viscount Crowler. As an adult Mordo sought out a mystic master known as the ANCIENT ONE in Tibet. The Ancient One recognized that Mordo had great potential as a sorcerer, but he also saw that Mordo was motivated only by a desire to gain power for his own ends.

Mordo plotted to destroy the Ancient One by sending his spirit image to hypnotise the Ancient One's servant into poisoning his food. Mordo threatened to let the Ancient One die if he did not reveal all his knowledge of black magic. In the nick of time, Mordo's plot was discovered by Dr. Stephen STRANGE, another of the Ancient One's pupils. Strange sent his spirit image to Tibet and the two spirit images fought, as the old man lay in a coma. Strange managed to use his amulet to revive the old man.

Thirsting for revenge, Mordo allied himself with powerful creatures like Satannish, DORMAMMU, and MEPHISTO. Struck with incurable cancer by his use of black magic, Mordo repented his sins on his deathbed; however, a past version of himself became free when Dr. Strange traveled through time, and he recently joined the Red HULK's Offenders. **MT, MF**

Baron Mordo allied himself with the dread Dormammu hoping to increase his mystical abilities in order to defeat his nemesis Doctor Strange.

FACTFILE
REAL NAME
Karl Amadeus Mordo
OCCUPATION
Sorcerer
BASE
Castle Mordo, Varf Mandra, Transylvania

HEIGHT 6 ft
WEIGHT 250 lbs
EYES Brown
HAIR Black

FIRST APPEARANCE
Strange Tales #111
(August 1963)

POWERS

Mordo can separate his spirit self from his physical body and travel through space unaffected by physical laws. He can mentally control others and can hurl magical energy bolts.

BARON ZEMO

Like father, like son

I KNOW YOUR LATEST PROJECT, ZEMO! AN *ADHESIVE* SO STRONG THAT *NOTHING* CAN TEAR IT APART!! BUT I'LL NEVER LET YOU MAKE A WEAPON OF IT FOR HITLER... *NEVER!!*

DON'T THROW THAT SHIELD!!! *NO!!*

After the accident that bonded his mask to his face, the original Baron Zemo became obsessed with destroying Captain America

Helmut Zemo is the son of Baron Heinrich Zemo, a Nazi scientist during World War II who designed super-weapons. Heinrich Zemo was working on a glue, "Adhesive X," that could never be dissolved, hoping it could be used to immobilize Allied troops. CAPTAIN AMERICA broke into his lab and, in the fight, Cap's shield shattered the vat containing the adhesive and Zemo's mask was glued to his head.

FACTFILE

REAL NAME
Helmut Zemo

OCCUPATION
Criminal entrepreneur

BASE
Mobile

HEIGHT 5 ft 11 in
WEIGHT 183 lbs
EYES Blue
HAIR Blond

FIRST APPEARANCE
Captain America #168
(June 1971)

BARON ZEMO

POWERS

Master strategist, extensive training in hand-to-hand combat, and excellent marksman; lacks his father's scientific genius.

MASTER OF EVIL

Zemo later went to London to steal an experimental drone plane. Captain America and his teenage partner BUCKY BARNES attempted to stop him, but Bucky was killed and Captain America was flung into the ocean, where he fell into a state of suspended animation. When the Nazis lost the war, Zemo fled to the jungles of South America where he conquered a small kingdom.

Decades later, he came out of hiding after learning that Captain America had been revived by the Avengers. Zemo formed the first MASTERS OF EVIL and later transformed Simon Williams into WONDER MAN, but failed in all his attempts to destroy the Avengers. He was accidentally crushed by a landslide during a battle with Captain America.

Zemo's hatred of Captain America ultimately led to the rock fall that killed him.

ESSENTIAL STORYLINES

• *Avengers #16* During a battle with Captain America, the original Baron Zemo is killed.
• *Captain America #357–362* "The Bloodstone Hunt"—Helmut Zemo tries to resurrect his father.
• *The Avengers: Under Siege, tpb* Helmut's new Masters of Evil invade the Avengers' Mansion and take Edwin Jarvis hostage.
• *Thunderbolts: Justice Like Lightning, tpb* Helmut Zemo repositions the Masters of Evil into seeming heroes.

FROM VILLAIN TO HERO

The Baron's son, Helmut, calling himself Phoenix, attempted to drown Cap in a boiling vat of Adhesive X. The liquid splashed Helmut, scarring his face and giving it the appearance of melted wax. Zemo later organized a new Masters of Evil.

When the Avengers temporarily disappeared from this reality, Zemo gathered his Masters of Evil. They became the THUNDERBOLTS, Super Villains masquerading as heroes. Helmut assumed the identity of Citizen V, a British costumed hero murdered by the original Baron Zemo. Like most of the Thunderbolts team, Zemo grew into the role of being a real hero. After keeping the Grandmaster from the Wellspring of Power, he took control of it himself, claiming that he would use it to better the world. The other Thunderbolts, who no longer trusted him, knocked him into a time vortex instead. After making his way back from the past, Zemo has dedicated himself to making the world a better place.

TD, MF

MASTERS OF EVIL

1 Absorbing Man **2** Baron Zemo
3 Screaming Mimi **4** Mr. Hyde **5** Moonstone
6 The Fixer **7** Power Man

Helmut Zemo claims that he wants to atone for his past misdeeds.

BUCKY BARNES

FACTFILE
REAL NAME
James Buchanan Barnes
OCCUPATION
Adventurer; army camp mascot
BASE
Mobile

HEIGHT 5 ft 7 in
WEIGHT 140 lbs
EYES Brown
HAIR Red-brown

FIRST APPEARANCE
Captain America #1
(March 1941)

POWERS

Excellent hand-to-hand combatant, skilled marksman, Olympic-level athlete, acrobat and gymnast.

Personally trained by Captain America, Bucky learned Cap's unique fighting style that employed acrobatics and gymnastics in combat situations.

Bucky discovers that Steve Rogers has a secret—he's the superpowered costumed war hero Captain America.

BARNES, BUCKY

Orphan James Buchanan "Bucky" Barnes was a mascot for the soldiers at Camp Lehigh, Virginia, where Steve Rogers was stationed. After learning that Steve was CAPTAIN AMERICA, Barnes began helping him on his missions, and became his official partner. Captain America and Bucky were in London when they discovered that their enemy BARON ZEMO was attempting to steal a bomb-filled drone plane. As the plane took off, Bucky leaped aboard and was apparently killed trying to defuse it. Captain America was hurled into the English Channel.

Decades later Cap was revived by the AVENGERS. Years after that he discovered that Bucky also survived but had been captured by the Soviets and transformed into the super-agent known as the WINTER SOLDIER. After the original's recent death, Bucky became the new Captain America. **TD, MF**

BASILISK

FACTFILE
REAL NAME
Basil Elks
OCCUPATION
Criminal; terrorist
BASE
Mobile

HEIGHT 5 ft 11 in
WEIGHT 210 lbs
EYES Red
HAIR None

FIRST APPEARANCE
Marvel Team-Up #16
(December 1973)

POWERS

Generated microwave-related energy, which he could project from his eyes as force blasts, to heat or freeze things, or to levitate himself. Possessed superhuman strength and durability and could teleport himself.

BASILISK

When burglar Basil Elks tried to steal a gem from a museum, a guard fired his gun, striking the gem. The "gem" was the Alpha-Stone of the KREE, which exploded, giving Elks superhuman powers. Elks dubbed himself Basilisk after the mythological serpent. Basilisk tried to destroy civilization, only to be thwarted by SPIDER-MAN and the THING. Elks was assassinated by SCOURGE.

The second Basilisk was a mutant who could shoot a paralysis beam from his single eye. He was killed by Kuan-Yin Xorn, who impersonated Magneto and led a new mutant Brotherhood. **PS**

XORN'S BROTHERHOOD
1 Angel's child holding No-Girl **2** Martha Johansson the Living Brain **3** Ernst **4** Basilisk **5** Xorn as Magneto **6** Esme (Stepford Cuckoo) **7** Baby of Angel and Beak **8** Beak **9** Angel **10** Toad

---

BASTION

FIRST APPEARANCE Uncanny X-Men #333 (June 1996)
REAL NAME Sebastion Gilberti
OCCUPATION Anti-Mutant crusader **BASE** Mobile
HEIGHT 6 ft 3 in **WEIGHT** 375 lbs **EYES** Red **HAIR** White
SPECIAL POWERS/ABILITIES Enhanced strength, speed, physical stamina, and resistance to injury; also immune to telepathic probes.

Bastion is a combination of Master Mold (a SENTINEL robot) and Nimrod (a Sentinel prototype from a possible future). He led the international anti-mutant initiative known as Operation: Zero Tolerance, during which he and his Prime Sentinels captured several X-MEN and took over the Xavier Institute. SHIELD stopped him, and WOLVERINE later beheaded him while serving as the Horseman of Death. Later, for a while, Bastion worked under the name Template. Recently, the anti-mutant Purifiers restored Bastion again, and he used the Technarch virus to revive a number of old X-MEN foes to attempt to destroy them all. **MT, MF**

BATROC

FACTFILE

REAL NAME
Georges Batroc

OCCUPATION
Mercenary

BASE
Mobile

HEIGHT 6 ft
WEIGHT 225 lbs
EYES Brown
HAIR Black

FIRST APPEARANCE
Tales of Suspense #75
(March 1966)

POWERS

Self-professed master of Savate, the French form of kickboxing; allegedly an expert hand-to-hand combatant; does not have any superhuman abilities but describes self as Olympic-standard weight lifter with ability to leap vast distances; devises military tactics that serve to bewilder opponents.

BATROC THE LEAPER

Describing himself as the world's greatest mercenary and master of Savate, Marseilles-born Georges Batroc trained himself in this Gallic martial art while serving in the French Foreign Legion. Since embarking on a life of crime, Batroc has fought some of the world's greatest Super Heroes, including CAPTAIN AMERICA and the PUNISHER. Sadly, he has rarely survived these confrontations with more than the smallest degree of dignity.

Batroc is the eponymous leader of Batroc's Brigade, a motley collection of martial artists, assassins, and mercenaries whose membership is fluid. In the Brigade's early days, Batroc hired members for specific jobs, but most of the missions were unsuccessful. Employed to obtain the "seismo-bomb" from a foreign power, Batroc teamed with the SWORDSMAN and the LIVING LASER, but they did not succeed. Later, the RED SKULL hired him to attack Captain America. Although banded with PORCUPINE and Whirlwind, the mission failed.

Batroc has only scored significant victories with the British weapons master ZARAN and South American revolutionary Machete. During the Civil War (*see* pp. 84–5), Batroc was forced to work for the Thunderbolts Army. Afterward, he registered with the US government and trained heroes in the martial arts. He has since returned to crime. **AD, MF**

BATTLESTAR

FIRST APPEARANCE *Captain America* #341 (May 1988)
REAL NAME Lemar Hoskins
OCCUPATION Government agent **BASE** Chicago,
HEIGHT 6 ft 2 in **WEIGHT** 196 lbs **EYES** Blue **HAIR** Black
SPECIAL POWERS/ABILITIES Superhuman strength and stamina; can lift 10 tons; excels at hand-to-hand combat, gymnastics, and acrobatics; carries an indestructible adamantium shield.

After the POWER BROKER gave him his powers, Lemar Hoskins became a professional wrestler, along with his three pals from the US Army: Jerome Johnson, Hector Lennox, and John Walker. When Walker decided to become a hero named the Super-Patriot, Hoskins and the others formed the Bold Urban Commandos (the BUCkies) as his support team. When the COMMISSION ON SUPERHUMAN ACTIVITIES chose to Walker to replace Steve Rogers as CAPTAIN AMERICA, Hoskins became Walker's new Bucky (see BARNES, BUCKY). Soon after, he changed his codename to Battlestar, after another African-American told him that the name "Bucky" struck a bit too close to the way slaveholders sometimes called their men "bucks." Hoskins continued as Battlestar even after Rogers returned and Walker became the US AGENT. After retiring from government service, Hoskins joined SILVER SABLE's Wild Pack. He sided with Rogers during the Civil War (*see* pp. 84–5), and later joined the Garrison, the Vermont team of the Fifty State Initiative (*see* pp.118–9). **MT, MF**

BEAST

Mind of a genius, body of a wild thing!

FACTFILE

REAL NAME
Henry P. "Hank" McCoy

OCCUPATION
Adventurer, biochemist

BASE
The Xavier institute, Salem Center, New York

HEIGHT 5 ft 11 in
WEIGHT 402 lbs
EYES Blue
HAIR Brown (originally); blue-black (currently)

FIRST APPEARANCE
X-Men Vol. 1 #1
(September 1963)

The Beast possesses superhuman strength, agility, durability, and enhanced senses, including catlike night vision. He is able to recover with superhuman swiftness from minor wounds. He also possesses genius-level IQ, with extraordinary expertise in genetics, biochemistry and other subjects.

THE *CHEMICAL!* IT'LL CHANGE ME--AND IN AN HOUR'S TIME, I CAN CHANGE *BACK* AGAIN, JUST BY TAKING ANOTHER DRINK AS AN ANTIDOTE--

DON'T KNOW WHAT WILL HAPPEN IF YOU MUTATE A MUTANT--BUT I'VE GOT TO TAKE THE CHANCE--

Dr. McCoy recklessly drank his own serum, which gave him a more bestial form and increased superpowers.

Nuclear-power-plant worker Norton McCoy was exposed to intense radiation, and his son Henry was born a mutant, with unusually large hands and feet. Henry's schoolmates called him "Beast," but his mutant physique enabled him to become a star football player. When a criminal called the Conquistador abducted Henry's parents to force Henry to work for him, the X-Men came to the rescue. The team's founder, Professor X, recruited Henry and, codenamed the Beast, he thus became one of the X-Men's original members.

UNCHAINED

Under Xavier's tutelage McCoy earned his Ph.D. and went on to become a genetic researcher at the Brand Corporation. There he developed a serum that further mutated him: he grew fur all over his body, as well as fangs and pointed ears.

Initially McCoy attempted to masquerade as a normal human by using a latex mask and gloves. However, the Beast abandoned this disguise, joined the AVENGERS, and publicly revealed his true identity. Later, the Beast reorganized another team, the DEFENDERS. After this incarnation of the Defenders collapsed, the Beast rejoined Xavier's other four original X-Men in a new mutant team, X-FACTOR. Soon afterwards, the Beast was captured by former Brand scientist Dr. Carl Maddicks, who used a serum to cause the Beast to revert to his previous, more human appearance. Still later, the mutant INFECTIA's powers returned the Beast to his fur-covered form.

Though the Beast can be fierce in battle, paradoxically he is also a man of high intellect, sharp wit, and great kindness.

BEAST WITH THE X-MEN
1 Wolverine 2 Jean Grey 3 Beast (wearing reading glasses) 4 Professor X 5 Emma Frost 6 Cyclops

The Beast has grown more massive and more feline in appearance: his face now resembles a lion's.

THE APPLIANCE OF SCIENCE

The original members of X-Factor rejoined the X-Men, and McCoy succeeded in creating a cure for the Legacy Virus, drawing on research by DR. MOIRA MACTAGGERT. After the Beast was nearly killed in combat, fellow member SAGE saved his life by using her powers to mutate him even further. He worked harder than anyone to find way to restore mutant powers lost on M-DAY, but he has so far failed. He currently lives with the X-Men in San Francisco. **PS, MF**

ESSENTIAL STORYLINES
- ***X-Men Vol. 1 #49–53***
  The extraordinary origin of the Beast explained for the first time.
- ***Amazing Adventures Vol. 2 #11–16***
  the Beast mutates into his furry ape-like form and combats the Secret Empire.
- ***X-Treme X-Men #3***
  The Beast mutates into his leonine form.

BELLADONNA

FIRST APPEARANCE Spectacular Spider-Man Vol. 1 #43 (June 1980)

REAL NAME Narda Ravanna

OCCUPATION Criminal **BASE** New York City

HEIGHT 5 ft 5 in **WEIGHT** 120 lbs **EYES** Blue-gray **HAIR** Brown

SPECIAL POWERS/ABILITIES Extensive knowledge of chemistry enables development of sinister chemical weapons.

With her sister, Desiree Vaughan-Pope, Narda Ravanna was the founder of Vaughan-Pope Cosmetics and responsible for product development. When they refused to sell the company to Roderick Kingsley (see HOBGOBLIN), he used the media to smear their products, driving them out of business. Hungry for revenge, Narda returned to the US, her home country. As Belladonna, Narda developed weapons from stolen neo-atropine and attacked Kingsley with the help of several allies. When SPIDER-MAN intervened, she attempted to kill the web-slinger but he thwarted her efforts and handed her over to the police. **MT**

BEREET

FIRST APPEARANCE Rampaging Hulk #1 (January 1977)

REAL NAME Bereet

OCCUPATION Krylorian Techno-Artist **BASE** The planet Krylor

HEIGHT/WEIGHT Unrevealed **EYES** Brown **HAIR** Unrevealed

SPECIAL POWERS/ABILITIES Carried the tools of her trade with her in a special distortion pouch. Accompanied by a hovering device called Sturky that could convert matter.

A renowned techno-artist from the planet Krylor, Bereet first came to prominence among her race when she created a series of adventure films depicting the earliest version of the HULK combating a fictitious invasion of Earth by the Krylorians.

After several attempts to duplicate this early success, she journeyed to Earth intending to document the ongoing exploits of the true Hulk, and became embroiled in a number of his adventures. She remained on Earth and became a movie director in Hollywood. **TB**

BERENGETTI, MICHAEL

FIRST APPEARANCE Incredible Hulk Vol. 2 #347 (Sept.1988)

REAL NAME Michael Berengetti

OCCUPATION Casino owner **BASE** Las Vegas

HEIGHT 5 ft 10 in **WEIGHT** 170 lbs **EYES** Brown **HAIR** Black

SPECIAL POWERS/ABILITIES Highly skilled businessman, with a deep knowledge of underworld politics. Skilled with firearms, and had a talent for mathematics relating to games of chance.

Michael Berengetti owned Las Vegas's Coliseum casino, and hired the Hulk as a bodyguard and leg-breaker during the period when the Hulk sported gray skin and a cunning intellect. Berengetti, who called the Hulk "Joe Fixit," ensured that the Hulk had steady access to tailored suits and Las Vegas's more sensual pleasures. After the Hulk left Vegas, the android Frost (employed by the gangster Sam Striker) killed Berengetti. **DW**

An honorable employer, Berengetti treated the loyal members of his staff as members of his family.

BETA-RAY THOR

Beta Ray Bill was a guardian-warrior of an extraterrestrial race whose galaxy was destroyed by the ancient demon Surtur. He was created when scientists transferred his life force into a bioengineered carnivorous beast, with increased strength, speed and agility.

While traveling in suspended animation in his starship, Beta Ray Bill entered the Milky Way Galaxy, where THOR was sent to investigate. They battled and Thor was separated from his enchanted hammer, Mjolnir, which changed back into Donald Blake's cane. When Beta Ray Bill struck the cane on a wall he suddenly possessed Thor's power and a variation of the Thunder God's costume.

After a battle on Asgard in which Beta Ray Thor spared Thor's life, Odin (see GODS OF ASGARD) commissioned the creation of new enchanted hammer, called Storm Breaker, possessing the same powers as Mjolnir, Thor's hammer. Bill left Earth to return to his people's planet, but while he was there, GALACTUS devoured it. He came back to Earth and helped the new OMEGA FLIGHT battle demons of Sutur. He was replaced by a SKRULL before the Secret Invasion (see pp. 326–7), but Thor freed and fought alongside him to defeat the Skrull known as the Godkiller. **MT, MF**

FACTFILE

REAL NAME
Beta Ray Bill

OCCUPATION
Warrior

BASE
Mobile; his alien race's space fleet, his own warship Skuttlebutt

HEIGHT 6 ft 7 in

WEIGHT 480 lbs

EYES None visible

HAIR None

FIRST APPEARANCE
Thor # 337 (November 1983)

POWERS

Beta Ray Thor has the same powers as Thor himself. He has superhuman strength, and is immune to all disease and injury. His Asgardian metabolism gives him far greater endurance at all physical activities than humans.

Beta-Ray Thor and Hercules battle fire demons from the Asgardian world of Muspelheim.

BEYONDER
Observer of worlds

POWERS Virtually omnipotent; the Beyonder can change reality just by thinking; has assumed various physical forms, created planets, destroyed galaxies, and taken control of every mind on Earth.

The infinite energies of a Cosmic Cube experimented on by scientist Owen Reece transformed Reece into MOLECULE MAN and also formed the Beyonder. At first the Beyonder was a non-corporeal entity. As he acquired consciousness he began observing the activities of humans. Intrigued by what he saw, he created a planet, combining elements from various worlds including a small part of Detroit. He christened it Battleworld and gathered together a clutch of Super Heroes and Villains, in order to watch them fight. However, the Beyonder grew tired of just looking on...

The Beyonder created Battleworld—a single planet orbiting a lonely star.

Everything in the Beyonder's dimension was part of him. All matter—planets, suns, people—were aspects of his being, and he could alter and restructure it on the merest whim.

ENDLESS QUEST

The Beyonder arrived on Earth, and took the appearance of Molecule Man, CAPTAIN AMERICA, and finally a square-jawed alpha male with bad dress sense. He traveled the world learning about humanity. He was toilet-trained by SPIDER-MAN, learned about money from a homeless woman, and had a fling with the musician DAZZLER.

The Beyonder still felt unfulfilled and became increasingly unstable—a threat to the entire multiverse. He decided that he needed to be fully human and tried to transplant himself into the body of a baby, which was gestating in a machine he had built. Before the child could be born, Molecule Man destroyed the birth tank to save the multiverse, channelling the resulting explosive energies into a new and empty universe.

KOSMOS

In time, the Beyonder and Molecule Man fused to become a new Cosmic Cube. This Cube expelled the Molecule Man and became the female entity Kosmos (above) who existed in mortal form as the MAKER. Thanos tossed the Maker into the interstellar prison Kyln. During the Annihilation (*see* pp. 30-1) Kyln was destroyed, and the corpse of Kosmos was found in the wreckage. **AD, MF**

Returning to Earth after the Secret War, the Thing had some scores to settle with the Beyonder. The Thing's stay on Battleworld had caused terrible heartache and he was not happy.

ESSENTIAL STORYLINES
• *Secret Wars #1–12* The Beyonder creates Battleworld and gets the Earth's Super Heroes to fight there.
• *Secret Wars Vol. 2 #1–9* The Beyonder arrives on Earth and learns about humanity.
• *Fantastic Four Annual #23* The Beyonder and Molecule Man merge to form a new entity named Kosmos.

BI-BEAST

Created to be the guardian of the Avian race at a time when they were forced to go into hibernation in order to survive, the android Bi-Beast patrolled their now silent Sky Island, maintaining its security and keeping it from harm. But after years of loneliness, the twin persona of the Bi-Beast went mad, and they attempted to kidnap Betty Ross (*see* BANNER, BETTY), who had been transformed into a winged, gamma-powered monster called the Harpy. But the HULK pursued the Bi-Beast, and after a savage battle, Bruce Banner used the scientific apparatus found in Sky Island to cure Betty's condition, much to the displeasure of the Bi-Beast.

Thereafter, the Bi-Beast continued its lonely vigil, attacking any and all who came within reach. Eventually, however, the Avians were revived, and so the savage Bi-Beast is no longer alone. **TB**

WE MEAN JUST THIS. HUMAN CREATURES FROM YOUR PALE GREEN PLANET EARTH ARE RESPONSIBLE FOR THE DESTRUCTION OF OUR WORLD!!

The twin cranium of the Bi-Beast gives it double intelligence as well as two distinct personalities.

FACTFILE

REAL NAME
Bi-Beast
OCCUPATION
Guardian of the Avian race
BASE
Sky Island of the Avian race

HEIGHT 7 ft 8 in (variable)
WEIGHT 360 lbs (variable)
EYES Black
HAIR None

FIRST APPEARANCE
Incredible Hulk #169
(November 1973)

POWERS

Bi-Beast's artificial minds contain the accumulated knowledge of the Avian race—the top head specializes in knowledge related to warfare and combat, while the lower head is the repository of information pertaining to history and culture.

BIG-HERO 6

FIRST APPEARANCE Sunfire And Big Hero 6 #1 (Sept. 1998)
MEMBERS AND POWERS
SUNFIRE Projects heat and flame and can fly.
SILVER SAMURAI Projects energy through his sword.
GOGO TOMAGO Turns into an explosive ball of energy.
HONEY LEMON Obtains almost any object from her "Power Purse"
HIRO TAKACHIHO 13-year-old scientific genius.
Baymax "Synthformer" robot that can change into a dragon.

Big Hero 6 is Japan's official team of superhuman agents. The Japanese government first formed the Giri, a group of officials and businessmen, to find and train superhuman recruits and to oversee their activities. The initial lineup of Big Hero 6 included Sunfire, formerly of the X-Men; and WOLVERINE's old adversary the SILVER SAMURAI.

SUNFIRE and the Silver Samurai were replaced by Sunfire's sister Sunpyre, who possesses similar powers, and the mysterious Ebon Samurai. **PS**

BIG HERO 6
1 Hiro Takachiho
2 Baymax
3 Honey Lemon
4 Go Go Tomago
5 Silver Samurai
6 Sunfire

BIG MAN

FIRST APPEARANCE Amazing Spider-Man #10 (March 1964)
REAL NAME Frederick Foswell **OCCUPATION** Reporter, criminal
BASE New York City **HEIGHT** 5 ft 10 in; (Big Man) 6 ft 1 in
WEIGHT 185 lbs **EYES** Blue **HAIR** Gray
SPECIAL POWERS/ABILITIES Brilliant criminal mind, master of disguise and crack shot. Padded costume to appear more robust and taller; wore mask and used a device that deepened voice.

Daily Bugle reporter Foswell tried to organize New York's gangs under his leadership as the Big Man, employing the ENFORCERS as his henchmen. After clashing with SPIDER-MAN, the police learned the Big Man's identity and arrested Foswell. He served his time in prison and, thanks to the generosity of publisher J. Jonah JAMESON, returned to the *Bugle*. Foswell adopted the identity of Patch to spy on the underworld and aided in the capture of the Crime-Master. Foswell later returned to crime and worked for the KINGPIN. He sacrificed himself to save his former employer J. Jonah Jameson. **TD**

BIRD-BRAIN

FIRST APPEARANCE New Mutants #56 (October 1987)
REAL NAME Bird-Brain **OCCUPATION** None
BASE Paradise, an island in the North Atlantic **HEIGHT** 6 ft
WEIGHT 125 lbs **EYES** Red **HAIR** Vari-colored feathers
SPECIAL POWERS/ABILITIES Wings enable flight; entire body is hollow-boned, like a bird's; able to breathe at high altitudes; eyes are specially adapted to withstand high winds during flight.

Bird-Brain is a half-human, half-animal creature known as an Ani-Mate. He was created through genetic engineering by Dr. Frederick Animus, the ANI-MATOR. Although Bird-Brain and his fellow Ani-Mates possessed human-level intelligence, the Ani-Mator treated them like slaves. After being subjected to a number of cruel tests, Bird-Brain used his wings to fly away from the Ani-Mator's Paradise Island. He was placed in quarantine by the US authorities in preparation for being sent to a research laboratory for further testing, when he escaped. Bird-Brain was then recruited by the New MUTANTS, who returned with him to Paradise Island in order to help free his fellow Ani-Mates from the Ani-Mator's cruel thrall. **MT**

BISHOP

FACTFILE

REAL NAME
Lucas Bishop

OCCUPATION
Adventurer; law enforcement officer

BASE
The Xavier institute, New York; "District X," New York City

HEIGHT 6 ft 6 in
WEIGHT 275 lbs
EYES Brown
HAIR Black

FIRST APPEARANCE
The Uncanny X-Men #282 (November 1991)

POWERS
Can absorb energy and project it as concussive force or use it to enhance his strength, durability, and healing factor. Expert with a samurai sword and firearms. Bionic arm grants him superhuman strength and contains a time-travel device.

Bishop and his partner, Ishmael Ortega, patrol Manhattan's mutant ghetto, Mutant Town, alias District X.

Bishop comes from the future of Earth-1191, in which robot SENTINELS conquered North America. Born in a "mutant relocation camp," Bishop was branded with an "M" to identify him as a mutant. In time, mutants and humans joined in the Summers Rebellion to overthrow the Sentinels. Bishop joined Xavier's Security Enforcers (XSE), a mutant police force combating criminal mutants, and pursued one mutant criminal, Trevor Fitzroy, to Earth-616, where he met the X-MEN, and was invited to join. Later, Bishop became the partner of NYPD cop Ismael Ortega, fighting crime in "District X," Manhattan's mutant ghetto. He sided with the government during the Civil War (*see pp. 84–5*), which pitted him against his former teammates. After M-Day, Bishop tried to kill the first new mutant baby to prevent his future from happening. Instead, he lost an arm and accidentally shot PROFESSOR X. **PS, MF**

BLACK BOLT

FIRST APPEARANCE Fantastic Four #1 (December 1965)
REAL NAME Blackagar Boltagon **OCCUPATION** Monarch of the Inhumans **BASE** Blue Area of Moon **HEIGHT** 6 ft 2 in
WEIGHT 210 lbs **EYES** Blue **HAIR** Black
SPECIAL POWERS/ABILITIES Harnesses electrons; power linked to vocal chords, which trigger shockwaves; antenna channels power, giving superhuman strength, speed; fires concussive blasts; creates force fields; flight.

Black Bolt was born the son of Agon, ruler of the INHUMANS. His infant cries created massive destruction, forcing his parents to place him in a soundproof chamber. An energy-harnessing suit was designed for him and he was trained to use his powers. After he was released Black Bolt learned that his younger brother MAXIMUS was about to betray the Inhumans to the alien KREE race. Black Bolt shouted, blasting the Kree ship out of the sky. It crashed into the parliament building, killing his parents. Black Bolt became the ruler of the Inhumans but has often battled Maximus. Black Bolt is married to Medusa. A former member of the ILLUMINATI, Black Bolt recently launched Attilan into space and took control of the Kree Empire. **TD, MF**

BLACK CAT

Peter Parker adored Felicia but, unfortunately, she preferred his amazing alter ego.

The daughter of a famous cat burglar, Felicia Hardy was determined to follow in her father's footsteps. She devised the costumed identity of the Black Cat, setting up prearranged "accidents" to make it appear as though she could cause bad luck to befall others. After encountering SPIDER-MAN, she became smitten with him, and for a time she was one of his closest confidantes and even knew his secret identity.

After the mutant SABRETOOTH beat her, the Cat obtained mystical bad luck powers through the machinations of the KINGPIN. These abilities faded away, as did her romance with Spider-Man, who couldn't reconcile spending the rest of his life with a compulsive thief who wasn't interested in him as Peter Parker. When MEPHISTO erased everyone's memory of Spider-Man's true identity before the Brand New Day event, though, the Cat lost that precious bit of knowledge too. During the Civil War (*see pp. 84–5*), she worked with the new Heroes for Hire, but that group broke up at the end of World War Hulk, so she is likely on her own again. **TB, MF**

FACTFILE
REAL NAME
Felicia Hardy

OCCUPATION
Cat-burglar; adventurer

BASE
New York City

HEIGHT 5 ft 10 in
WEIGHT 120 lbs
EYES Green
HAIR Platinum blonde

FIRST APPEARANCE
Amazing Spider-Man #194 (July 1979)

POWERS
Devices in costume give far greater strength, speed, and agility than a normal woman.

BLACK KNIGHT
Knight of the Ebony Blade

The first Black Knight, Sir Percy of Scandia, was born in the 6th Century and became one of the bravest knights at the court of King Arthur PENDRAGON at Camelot. Here he led a double life, posing as a mild-mannered fop while secretly fighting evil as the Black Knight, armed with the Ebony Blade, a sword fashioned by MERLIN the Magician from the Starstone meteorite. Centuries later, Sir Percy's spirit returned to converse with his ancestors, Professor Nathan Garrett and Dane Whitman, each of whom would take up his mantle.

Raised in Scandinavia, Sir Percy was a new face to the people of Camelot.

BLACK KNIGHT

POWERS

An able scientist, Whitman built on discoveries of his uncle, Nathan Garrett; rides a winged horse and has power lance that fires heat and force beams; also wields Ebony Blade, sometimes more curse than blessing.

VILLAINOUS KNIGHT

Nathan Garrett met the spirit of Sir Percy during a visit to the family home of Garrett Castle, and was offered the chance to become a latter-day Black Knight. However, Garrett failed to draw the Ebony Blade from its scabbard thereby proving himself unworthy. Determined to become the Black Knight by other means, Garrett developed a lance that fired energy bolts, and embarked on a criminal career mounted upon a genetically engineered winged horse. Garrett battled the Avengers with the MASTERS OF EVIL, dying in a fight with IRON MAN. Before passing away, Garrett confessed his crimes to his nephew, Dane Whitman, and begged him to restore his honor.

A brilliant scientist, Garrett used his knowledge to create a winged steed.

THE GOOD KNIGHT

Initially mistaken as the previous Black Knight and attacked by the AVENGERS, Dane Whitman soon gained their trust and joined the team. Blessed with a noble spirit, he was able to draw the Ebony Blade once wielded by his ancestor Sir Percy. Unfortunately, the sword had been cursed with the blood of those felled by Sir Percy. This curse dogged Whitman for years until DOCTOR STRANGE finally recognized what it was. In order to cleanse it, Whitman was instructed to plunge the sword into the Brazier of Truth, located in Garrett Castle. Whitman's effort shattered the Brazier. Since it was this mystical object that held Sir Percy's spirit in this world, its destruction finally allowed him to rest. Dane joined CAPTAIN BRITAIN in MI-13 during the Secret Invasion (see pp. 326-7) taking on the new hero, Faiza Hussain, as his squire while protecting Britain from the SKRULLS. **AD, MF**

The dark sorcerer Kalmari battled Dane Whitman with a dragon, but this version of the Black Knight proved victorious.

ESSENTIAL STORYLINES
• ***The Black Knight #1-3*** Sir Percy begins his adventures as the Black Knight.
• ***Avengers Vol. 1 #71*** Dane Whitman helps the Avengers beat Kang and becomes a member.
• ***Dr. Strange Vol. 2 #68*** Whitman cleanses the Ebony Blade of evil and frees Sir Percy's ghost.

The Ebony Blade renders its user invulnerable but, if it tastes blood, will eventually corrupt him.

BLACK PANTHER

FACTFILE

REAL NAME
T'Challa

OCCUPATION
Monarch of Wakanda

BASE
Wakanda

HEIGHT 6 ft
WEIGHT 200 lbs
EYES Brown
HAIR Black

FIRST APPEARANCE
Fantastic Four #52
(July 1966)

POWERS

Olympic-level athlete, acrobat and gymnast; combat specialist. Mask enhances night vision; gloves expel gases; vibranium boots enable him to land from great heights; vibranium in costume makes bullets or punches lose power.

The "Black Panther" is an honorary title bestowed on the reigning monarch of the jungle kingdom of Wakanda. T'Challa was only a child when he succeeded his father, who had been murdered by KLAW, the master of sound. Before T'Challa assumed his throne, he was educated in the finest schools in Europe and America and then embarked on a series of grueling tests to prove that he was worthy of donning the mantle and using the powers of the Black Panther. Although T'Challa often allied himself with the FANTASTIC FOUR and the AVENGERS, the people of Wakanda are always his highest priority. Realizing that the time had come for him to father an heir, he married Ororo Munroe, STORM of the X-MEN. They sided with CAPTAIN AMERICA's resistance during the Civil War (see pp. 84–5), and they fought off a SKRULL invasion of Wakanda during the Secret Invasion (see pp. 326–7). Recently, DR. DOOM critically wounded T'Challa, and his sister Shuri stepped in to fill his role as the Black Panther. **TD, MF**

Ally from Africa: claws at the ready, the resourceful Black Panther springs into action alongside the Fantastic Four, whom he has aided on several occasions.

BLACK MAMBA

FIRST APPEARANCE Marvel Two-In-One #64 (June 1980)
REAL NAME Tanya Sealy
OCCUPATION Mercenary **BASE** Mobile
HEIGHT 5 ft 7 in **WEIGHT** 115 lbs **EYES** Green **HAIR** Black
SPECIAL POWERS/ABILITIES Projects Darkforce energy, which suffocates opponents; hypnotic powers trick targets into thinking that Darkforce is a loved one, allowing it to ensnare them.

Roxxon Oil surgically altered Tanya Sealy, a former call girl, to become a covert agent. A surgical implant allowed her to tap her brain's energy to control the Darkforce, an inky cloud of energy, and also some hypnotic powers. She formed part of the original incarnations of the SERPENT SQUAD and SERPENT SOCIETY. Later, she also worked with the MASTERS OF EVIL, the B.A.D. Girls, and the Femizons. During the Civil War (see pp.84–5), she sided with CAPTAIN AMERICA's anti-registration forces, but by the time the SECRET INVASION took place, she had rejoined the new Serpent Society. **MT, MF**

BLACK TALON

FIRST APPEARANCE Avengers #152 (October 1976)
REAL NAME Unrevealed
OCCUPATION Houngan (voodoo priest) **BASE** Louisiana
HEIGHT 6 ft 2 in **WEIGHT** 240 lbs **EYES** Brown **HAIR** Black
SPECIAL POWERS/ABILITIES Supernatural voodoo powers, including the ability to create and control zombies, human corpses that can be reanimated through voodoo magic.

Black Talon is a Creole with true voodoo powers. This man, whose real name is unknown, is actually the second to wear the Black Talon costume. The first was a fake voodoo priest who was killed by his own cult when they found out he was a fraud. The true houngan Black Talon formed his own cult and was then contacted by the GRIM REAPER, who wanted his dead brother WONDER MAN brought back to life as a zombie. When Black Talon did this, the Reaper's brother attacked the AVENGERS, who subdued him and then defeated Black Talon himself. **MT**

BLACK TOM

FIRST APPEARANCE X-Men Vol. 1 #99 (June 1976)
REAL NAME Thomas Samuel Eamon Cassidy
OCCUPATION Criminal **BASE** Mobile
HEIGHT 6 ft **WEIGHT** 200 lbs **EYES** Blue **HAIR** Black
SPECIAL POWERS/ABILITIES Can project blasts of heat and concussive force, which he focuses through his shillelagh.

Brother of Sean Cassidy, Black Tom is an Irish-born mutant. Losing both the Cassidy fortune and the woman he loved, he turned to crime. Partnered with the JUGGERNAUT, Black Tom battled the X-MEN and other heroes many times. After CABLE shot Tom, doctors grafted a wood-like material onto his wounds, transforming him into a sentient humanoid plant. On M-Day, Tom lost his plant powers and returned to his old self. Juggernaut later convinced him to turn himself in for his crimes. **PS**

Black Widow

Uncompromising and deadly

Natasha has assumed many roles, including surrogate mother, field agent, and implacable opponent of a rival Black Widow.

Shortly after Russia's World War II victory at Stalingrad, a lady, trapped in a burning building, threw her baby to a stranger below—a soldier named Ivan Petrovich. He raised the baby, named Natasha, who turned out to be a superb student, athlete, and ballerina. She married test pilot Alexei Shostakov, but their happiness was cut short. Faking Shostakov's death and leaving Natasha to grieve, the KGB trained him to become the Red Guardian—a Russian super-soldier. The KGB then manipulated Natasha into becoming a spy codenamed Black Widow.

While they don't always see eye-to-eye, Black Widow remains loyal to her old lover, Daredevil.

HARD TIME

Two espionage missions against Stark Industries brought her into contact with the adventurer Hawkeye, and it was ultimately he that inspired Natasha to claim her freedom and join SHIELD. A romance between the pair proved short-lived. Encountering the Red Guardian on a mission, she had only just learned his true identity when he was shot and killed, the double shock causing Natasha to withdraw from her relationship with Hawkeye.

In the years that followed, Natasha became romantically involved with Daredevil and founded the Champions team of Super Heroes. She also led the Avengers during one of its most testing periods, when several members lost their lives. More recently, Natasha became the implacable opponent of a rival Black Widow, Yelena Belova. Natasha also learned that she was just one of many Black Widows and that her memories of her early life were implanted. Recently, while working for Iron Man's SHIELD, Natasha helped install Bucky Barnes as the new Captain America, and she still works with him now that SHIELD has been dismantled. **AD, MF**

ESSENTIAL STORYLINES
• **Daredevil #87–90** Black Widow and Daredevil move to San Francisco; Black Widow's history is explained.
• **Pale Little Spider #1–3** The origins of Yelena Belova are explained for the first time.
• **Black Widow Vol. I #1–3** The two Black Widows, Natasha Romanova and Yelena Belova, go head-to-head and their bitter enmity begins.

FACTFILE
REAL NAME Natalia (Natasha) Alianovna Romanova
OCCUPATION Intelligence agent
BASE New York City
HEIGHT 5 ft 7 in
WEIGHT 125 lbs
EYES Blue
HAIR Red/auburn
FIRST APPEARANCE Tales of Suspense Vol. 1 #52 (April 1964)

BLACK WIDOW I

POWERS Martial artist; Olympic-level gymnast; trained spy; cartridges on wrist house various devices: tear-gas, spring-loaded cable, radio transmitter.

FACTFILE
REAL NAME Yelena Belova
OCCUPATION Intelligence agent
BASE Russia
HEIGHT 5 ft 7 in
WEIGHT 135 lbs
EYES Blue
HAIR Blonde
FIRST APPEARANCE Inhumans Vol. 2 #5 (March 1999)

BLACK WIDOW II

POWERS Only experience and gadgets separate Belova from the first Black Widow: Belova achieved even higher marks in training; she is also a martial-arts expert and Olympic-level gymnast.

YELENA BELOVA
Like Natasha, Yelena Belova was trained at the KGB's Red Room. She once worked for Hydra, who had transferred her mind into a Super-Adaptoid body. Yelena now leads the latest version of the Thunderbolts.

BLACKLASH

FIRST APPEARANCE Tales of Suspense #97 (January 1968)

REAL NAME Mark Scarlotti (aka Mark Scott)

OCCUPATION Assassin-for-hire   **BASE** Mobile

HEIGHT 6 ft 1 in   **WEIGHT** 196 lbs   **EYES** Blue   **HAIR** Blond

SPECIAL POWERS/ABILITIES Expert with whip and nunchakus. Possesses two cybernetically-controlled whips, anti-gravity bolas, and a necro-lash releasing electrical energy generated by gauntlets.

As a MAGGIA engineer, Scarlotti developed his own super-weapons. First calling himself Whiplash, he battled IRON MAN to a draw. As Mark Scott, he worked undercover for Stark International. Later, JUSTIN HAMMER hired Scarlotti, and he upgraded his arsenal and changed his name to Blacklash. For a time, he gave up crime, and later returned as Whiplash, but was later killed by Iron Man's armor. During the Civil War, an unrelated pair of villains called Whiplash and Blacklash joined the THUNDERBOLTS. **TD, MF**

BLACKOUT

FIRST APPEARANCE Nova #19 (May 1976)

REAL NAME Marcus Daniels

OCCUPATION Criminal   **BASE** New York City

HEIGHT 5 ft 10 in   **WEIGHT** 180 lbs   **EYES** Gray   **HAIR** Brown

SPECIAL POWERS/ABILITIES Projects and manipulates semi-solid black energy known as the Darkforce; has the strength and agility of a normal human being.

Exposed to "black star" rays by the physicist Dr. Abner Croit, Daniels gained the ability to control this cosmic radiation. He adopted the moniker "Blackout" and embarked on a series of robberies. Over time, exposure to this dark energy led to creeping insanity. Although his ally MOONSTONE helped him to direct and extend his powers, she also sought to control his mind, as did their joint master, BARON ZEMO. During an attack on the Avenger's Mansion, Blackout endeavoured to resist Zemo's mental commands, but these efforts led to a brain haemorrhage and Blackout's death. **AD**

BLACKWING III

FIRST APPEARANCE X-Men #117 (October 2001)

REAL NAME Barnell Bohusk

OCCUPATION Student, reality traveler   **BASE** New York City

HEIGHT 5 ft 9 in   **WEIGHT** 122 lbs

EYES Brown   **HAIR** Brown

SPECIAL POWERS/ABILITIES Possesses a suit that gives him superhuman strength, energy blasts, and flight.

At puberty, Barnell mutated into a birdlike human with hollow bones, talons, and wings. Soon after, he joined the Xavier Higher Institute of Learning (see X-MEN) as a student codenamed Beak. There, he had six babies with fellow mutant Angel Salvadore.

After rebelling against XORN's attempt to take the world, Barnell became dislodged in time and was forced to join the EXILES. He reunited with Angel and their children just before he lost his powers on M-Day. He recently joined the latest version of the NEW WARRIORS as Blackwing, wearing a high-tech suit that grants him powers. **MF**

POWERS

Immune to vampire bites and vampiric hypnosis; enhanced strength, speed, senses, and healing. Immune to vampire's susceptibility to sunlight. Carries arsenal of anti-vampire weapons; guns fire garlic-filled, silver bullets; trademark blade is titanium; martial-arts expert.

Born a half-vampire (dhampir) when his mother was fatally bitten by vampire Deacon Frost while giving birth, Blade was brought up by vampire hunter Jamal Afari. DRACULA later transformed Afari, and Blade was forced to kill his foster father. Now nursing two grudges, Blade set out for revenge against both Dracula and Deacon Frost. During his quest he allied with Quincy HARKER, Rachel VAN HELSING, and Frank DRAKE against Dracula, while "vampire detective" Hannibal KING assisted him against Frost.

Blade, King, Drake, and DOCTOR STRANGE helped unleash the Montesi Formula, a mystical incantation that temporarily destroyed all the vampires on Earth. Blade opened a detective agency with King, named Borderline Inc., and battled occult threats with King and Drake under the name Nightstalkers. **DW**

Blade doesn't take orders well and is difficult to work with in large team settings.

Blade remains committed to his mission to rid the world of vampires. He now possesses the abilities of a pseudo-vampire due to a bite from Morbius.

BLINK

FIRST APPEARANCE Uncanny X-men #317 (October 1994)

REAL NAME Clarice Ferguson

OCCUPATION Adventurer   **BASE** Mobile   **HEIGHT** 5 ft 5 in

WEIGHT 125 lbs   **EYES** Green   **HAIR** Magenta

SPECIAL POWERS/ABILITIES Blink is a mutant with the ability to create teleportational warps; carries a dagger and a set of javelins.

Having been brought up in the brutal Age of Apocalypse by her world's version of SABRETOOTH, Blink eventually became "unstuck in time"—exiled from her home reality. Recruited by the Timebroker and entrusted with the Tallus, a wrist-worn device that provides mission info, she and a team of fellow EXILES were charged with repairing the broken links in the chain of realities across the multiverse. Since that time, she has traveled from Earth to Earth, doing what must be done to put the multiverse back on the proper path. **TB**

BLIZZARD

Employed by Stark Industries, Dr. Gregor Shapanka attempted to steal and sell Stark technology to fund research into longevity. After being caught and fired, Shapanka developed a suit capable of generating immense cold. Using it to perform acts of villainy, he came to be known as Jack Frost or Blizzard and became a nemesis of IRON MAN. Shapanka's life ended when he was killed by Arno Stark, the Iron Man of 2020 (from Earth-8410), who had come back in time for data needed to disarm a bomb. Shapanka's successor as Blizzard was Donny Gill, an employee of Justin Hammer (*see* HAMMER, JUSTIN).

After leaving Hammer's employ, he joined the MASTERS OF EVIL, and later he became a part of MACH–IV's THUNDERBOLTS. After earning a pardon for his crimes, he registered with the Fifty State Initiative (*see* pp.118–9). A third man, Randy Macklin, wore Gill's suit for a while, but after he was captured and served his time, Tony Stark took him under his wing. **AD, MF**

Suit contains tiny cryogenic units called micro-cryostats.

The more water there is in the air, the more powerful is Blizzard's suit. In arid conditions it is useless.

FACTFILE
REAL NAME
Dr. Gregor Shapanka
OCCUPATION
Former scientist; criminal
BASE New York City

HEIGHT 5 ft 6 in
WEIGHT 165 lbs
EYES Brown
HAIR Brown

FIRST APPEARANCE
Tales of Suspense Vol. 1 #45
(September 1963)

BLIZZARD

POWERS

Gloves on Blizzard's battlesuit could project intense cold, generate freezing mist, mini-blizzards of snow, sleet, and darts of ice that could pierce metal; he could freeze people by covering them in frost; escaped capture by creating an ice slide. He has no superhuman powers.

BLOB

Once a carnival freak, life changed for Fred J. Dukes when the X-MEN revealed to him that he was a mutant. Rather than accept their offer of membership in their school, Dukes attempted to destroy them as the Blob. Recruited thereafter by MAGNETO to become a member of his BROTHERHOOD OF EVIL MUTANTS, the Blob embarked on a life of crime, clashing not only with the X-Men, but also with the AVENGERS and the DEFENDERS. For a while, he worked with the government-sponsored FREEDOM FORCE, but later returned to crime. After M-Day, the Blob lost his powers and much of his mass, but his skin did not snap back and hung on him in folds. Soon after, he joined X-Cell, a group of angry, depowered mutants. He's since lost the extra skin and is promoting himself as a weight-loss success story in Japan. **TB, MF**

When the Blob set himself in one position, his mutant ability made it almost impossible for an outside force to dislodge him.

BLOB

FACTFILE
REAL NAME
Fred J. Dukes
OCCUPATION
Criminal; former circus performer
BASE
Mobile

HEIGHT 8 ft
WEIGHT 976 lbs
EYES Brown
HAIR Brown

FIRST APPEARANCE
Uncanny X-Men #3
(January 1964)

POWERS

Superhuman strength and durability. Fatty body could absorb bullets, even artillery shells, and was impervious to injury; however eyes, ears, nose, and mouth were not as injury-resistant. When he planted himself firmly, the Blob bonded with the ground beneath him and could not be moved.

BLOODHAWK

FIRST APPEARANCE Avengers #179 (January 1979)

Real name Bloodhawk **OCCUPATION** Adventurer

BASE Muara, an island in the Atlantic Ocean **HEIGHT** 6 ft 3 in

WEIGHT 150 lbs **EYES** Black **FEATHERS** Reddish-brown

SPECIAL POWERS/ABILITIES Superhuman strength and stamina; able to fly and communicate with birds; possesses razor-sharp claws.

Bloodhawk is the only son of a geneticist who experimented on his own wife. The poor woman died giving birth to a mutant of hawklike appearance and characteristics. Unable to accept the horror he had created, Bloodhawk's father turned his son over to his best friend, who removed the child from civilization. Plagued by bouts of insanity, Bloodhawk grew to adulthood in the South Seas. When a powerful totem was stolen from his island home, he journeyed to the US and battled the AVENGERS to recover it. Bloodhawk later gave his life to save Thor. **TB**

BLOODSCREAM

FIRST APPEARANCE Wolverine Vol. 2 #4 (February 1989)

REAL NAME Unknown **OCCUPATION** Enforcer

BASE Madripoor, Southeast Asia **HEIGHT** 6 ft 5 in

WEIGHT Unknown **EYES** Unknown **HAIR** Gray

SPECIAL POWERS/ABILITIES Although not a true vampire, has many vampire powers: superhuman strength, agility, accelerated healing, hypnotic ability; can also kill or cause bleeding by touch.

Bloodscream was once a 16th-century sailor, whom a necromancer turned into a pseudo-vampire—a condition that could only be cured by drinking an immortal's blood. Centuries later, Bloodscream, now a Nazi soldier, encountered WOLVERINE. Meeting Wolverine decades later, Bloodscream saw the mutant hadn't aged. Assuming Wolverine was immortal, Bloodscream has hounded him ever since. **MT**

BLOODSTONE, ELSA

FIRST APPEARANCE Bloodstone #1 (December 2001)

REAL NAME Elsa Bloodstone **OCCUPATION** Monster hunter

BASE Boston, Mass. **HEIGHT** 5 ft 9 in

WEIGHT 120 lbs **EYES** Blue **HAIR** Blonde

SPECIAL POWERS/ABILITIES An expert markswoman with superhuman strength, agility, speed, regeneration, and endurance granted by her Bloodstone Choker.

The daughter of Ulysses BLOODSTONE, Elsa inherited his estate soon after her 18th birthday and moved in with her mother; Bloodstone House's caretaker Adam, turned out to be FRANKENSTEIN'S MONSTER. She later joined Dirk Anger to become part of HATE and battled the forces of the Beyond Corporation as part of the NEXTWAVE squad. With the Beyond Corporation defeated, she registered with the US government and joined The Fifty State Initiative (see pp. 118–9). **MF**

BLOODSTONE, ULYSSES

FACTFILE

REAL NAME
Unknown; took the name Ulysses Bloodstone

OCCUPATION
Soldier of fortune

BASE
Bloodstone Island

HEIGHT 6 ft 2 in
WEIGHT 255 lbs
EYES Blue
HAIR Blond

FIRST APPEARANCE
Marvel Presents #1 (October 1975)

POWERS

Superhuman strength; blood-red Helix crystal endowed him with immortality and regenerative ability: could even regrow limbs; also had invisible third eye in forehead giving him psychic powers; expert with all kinds of weapons, though favored a customized sawn-off shotgun firing explosive shells.

BLOODSTONE, ULYSSES

Born in the Hyborian Age over 10,000 years ago, the man now known as Ulysses Bloodstone originally belonged to a Scandinavian tribe of hunter-gatherers, from which he was lured away by Ulluxy'l Kwan Tae Syn. This alien being was the guardian of a crystal entity called the Hellfire Helix, a being that was seeking to dominate the Earth. To fulfil its goal, the Helix needed a human servant, so it endowed the tribe's foremost hunter with superhuman powers. However, when it went on to kill his tribe members, the hunter grabbed at it, causing the Helix crystal to shatter into hundreds of pieces, one of which embedded itself in his chest. The crystal fragment saved his life and made him immortal, but the rest of his tribe were wiped out. The reddish crystal and his wandering existence led him to adopt the name Ulysses Bloodstone. The other pieces of the Helix were scattered all over the world.

Ulysses meets his nemesis, Ulluxy'l, for the first time.

ISLAND BASE

Vowing vengeance on Ulluxy'l, Ulysses spent the rest of his life searching for the alien, while Ulluxy'l devoted his existence to piecing the Helix back together.

During his quest, Ulysses earned a fortune through mercenary work and shrewd investments, establishing six headquarters across the world and a base on what became known as Bloodstone Island.

Inevitably, Ulysses' fate was bound up with that of the Helix. In one final, climactic confrontation, a dying Ulysses managed to destroy the crystal altogether and so achieved vengeance for his tribe. Ulysses left behind his ex-wife and his daughter, Elsa. Wearing a bloodstone choker that endowed her with superhuman powers, she vowed to continue her father's fight against evil. **AD**

BLOODSTORM

FIRST APPEARANCE Mutant X #1 (October 1998)

REAL NAME Ororo Munroe

OCCUPATION Adventurer **BASE** Earth of Mutant X universe

HEIGHT 5 ft 11 in **WEIGHT** 196 lbs **EYES** Blue **HAIR** White

SPECIAL POWERS/ABILITIES Possessed vampiric powers,
including hypnotic abilities and the power to transform into mist, a
bat, or a wolf; can control the weather over limited areas.

BLUE SHIELD

FIRST APPEARANCE Dazzler #5 (July 1981)

REAL NAME Joseph Cartelli **OCCUPATION** Security Director
for Project: Pegasus **BASE** Mount Athena, New York

HEIGHT 6 ft **WEIGHT** 180 lbs **EYES** Blue **HAIR** Brown

SPECIAL POWERS/ABILITIES Formerly wore microcircuitry-lined
belt which increased strength and generated force field around
body; now, owing to prolonged exposure, no longer needs belt.

BLUEBIRD

FIRST APPEARANCE Untold Tales of Spider-Man #11

REAL NAME Sally Avril **OCCUPATION** Student; adventurer

BASE Midtown High School, New York **HEIGHT** 5 ft 2 in

WEIGHT 110 lbs **EYES** Brown **HAIR** Black (blonde wig)

SPECIAL POWERS/ABILITIES Stolen technology from the Vulture
enabled her to fly using power pack and wings; also had a device
that emitted an ultrasonic, ear-splitting scream.

Years ago DRACULA bit STORM of the X-MEN,
who began transforming into a vampire. In the
main Marvel Universe, Storm was cured. But
on the alternate Earth where the "Mutant X"
series was set, Storm completed her
metamorphosis, becoming the vampiress
known as Bloodstorm. She nevertheless
refused to turn villainess, and fed only
on the blood of that reality's FORGE,
with his consent. Bloodstorm joined the
Six, a team mostly comprised of former
members of that reality's X-Men. For
aiding the people of yet another
alternate Earth, Earth X, Bloodstorm
was rewarded by receiving a blood
transfusion which cured her
vampirism. **PS**

After losing his father and a boyhood friend to
mob violence, Joseph Cartelli decided to avenge
them both. He went undercover, joining the
Barrigans' gang with the intention of
destroying it from within. His dead friend
had built a force-field belt financed with
loan-shark money, and Cartelli used the
belt to become the Blue Shield. After
defeating the Barrigans, Cartelli tried to
join the Avengers, but he wound up
replacing QUASAR as the security
director for Project: Pegasus instead.
Recently, Cartelli was assigned to help
out in New York City as part of The
Fifty State Initiative (*see*
pp. 118–9). **TD, MF**

A classmate of Peter Parker's
at Midtown High, Sally Avril
adopted the costumed
identity of Bluebird after
being inspired by the
exploits of SPIDER-MAN.
Possessing no superhuman
abilities or even proper
training, Bluebird proved to
be a danger to herself and to
others, until Spider-Man
eventually convinced her to put aside her
costumed identity and return to life as a student.
Tragically, she was killed shortly thereafter in an
automobile accident. **TB**

BOOMERANG

FIRST APPEARANCE Tales to Astonish #81 (July 1966)

REAL NAME Frederick Myers

OCCUPATION Assassin for hire **BASE** Mobile

HEIGHT 5 ft 11 in **WEIGHT** 175 lbs **EYES** Brown **HAIR** Black

SPECIAL POWERS/ABILITIES Brilliant baseball pitcher; famed for
customized boomerangs, such as explosive "shatterangs,"
poisonous "gasarangs," diamond sharp "razorangs."

Australian Fred Myers moved to the US
as a child and became a Major League
Baseball player renowned for his
amazing accuracy. Suspended for
taking bribes, he turned to crime
full-time. The Secret Empire
criminal organization gave him
the codename Boomerang and equipped
him with a range of specialized weaponry.
He subsequently worked for or with Justin
HAMMER, HAMMERHEAD, THE KINGPIN, THE
SINISTER SYNDICATE, THE SINISTER TWELVE,
and THE MASTERS OF EVIL, battling foes like
SHIELD, DAREDEVIL, and SPIDER-MAN. In the
aftermath of the Civil War (*see* pp. 84–5),
Boomerang tried to blackmail Norman
Osborn (*see* GREEN GOBLIN), but wound
up forced to work for him
instead. **AD, MF**

Only Bullseye and Hawkeye can match
Boomerang's terrifying accuracy while
Boomerang's jet boots enable attacks
from unexpected directions.

BOX

Robotic armored crimefighter

Roger Bochs' life was pitted by sadness. It is unclear why he had no legs, but for much of his early life he defined himself by his paraplegic status. Eventually, he stepped beyond these limitations, building a giant humanoid robot—Box—in which he could travel, gaining the freedom that so many others took for granted.

Wheelchair-user Roger Bochs' early life was sad and lonely.

POWERS

An engineering genius, Bochs built the first Box robot to serve as a bipedal robotic transportation for himself; the Box robot possessed vast strength and durability; Bochs was able to "phase" in and out of robot at will.

JOINING ALPHA FLIGHT

With his robotic chariot, Roger came to the attention of James McDonald Hudson who was recruiting for ALPHA FLIGHT. Hudson recruited Roger into Alpha Flight's training program and he was progressing well when the Canadian government withdrew funding. Out of a job, Roger returned to his native Saskatchewan.

Hudson kept the team going but Roger's return to it was a long time coming. Hired by Jerome Jaxon to join the nefarious Omega Flight, Roger was expected to help them destroy Alpha Flight. He opposed this but was helpless when Jaxon took control of Box and sent it into battle. By the end of the struggle, both Jaxon and Hudson were dead and Box was seriously mangled. Roger was invited to rejoin the exhausted Alpha Flight, but first he needed to rebuild his robot.

With the help of fellow team member, Madison Jefferies, Roger constructed a superior Box model, but when he became unlucky in love, his life began a downward spiral. Manipulated into merging his being with Madison's unbalanced brother, Roger became part of a new entity—Omega. His endeavors to limit Omega's sinister activities led to him being effectively lobotomized and when Omega was defeated and died, Roger passed away, too.

ESSENTIAL STORYLINES
• **Alpha Flight #41–49**
Charts Roger Bochs' physical and mental decline, and his death as part of Omega.
• **Alpha Flight #102–105**
Madison Jeffries helps Alpha Flight battle Diablo… and then there's the small matter of getting married to Lillian Crawley.

THERE! GOOD AS NEW! YOU CAN PHASE OUT NOW, BOXXIE!

OUT! ALIVE! AS WHOLE AS A LEGLESS CRIPPLE CAN EVER BE!

I-I FELT LIKE MY "BODY" HAD BECOME MY COFFIN! YOU SAVED MY SANITY, MR. JEFFERIES...AND QUITE POSSIBLY, MY LIFE!

AS FOR THE DAMAGE...WELL, THAT DON'T MEAN BEANS TO A TRANSMUTATOR LIKE ME!

The new improved Box allowed Roger to phase in and out of it.

BOX IV

POWERS

Mutant power to manipulate metal, plastic and glass allows Jeffries to extend capability of Box; robot armor now much lighter and able to increase its size and weight seemingly without limit.

MADISON JEFFRIES

When Roger Bochs died, his friend Madison Jeffries became the next man to wear the Box armor. A mutant capable of manipulating metal, Madison used his abilities to augment the machine.

Jeffries worked with Alpha Flight for a long while, but he eventually retired to marry teammate Diamond Lil. Later, agents of WEAPON X captured Jeffries and brainwashed him into building the Neverland mutant concentration camp. He retained his powers after M-DAY and, after a period of solitude where he found his own machinery turning against him, is currently working with the BEAST to restore the missing mutant genes.

AD, MF

FEEZAK

FIRE?

With his intuitive grasp of all things mechanical, Madison Jeffries made great strides in enhancing Box.

Tensions erupt between Box and Shaman, a fellow Alpha Flight member.

BRADDOCK, JAMIE

FIRST APPEARANCE Captain Britain Weekly #9 (December 1976)
REAL NAME James Braddock
OCCUPATION Ex-racing driver, slave-trafficker   **BASE** London
HEIGHT 6 ft 1 in   **WEIGHT** 151 lbs   **EYES** Blue   **HAIR** Black
SPECIAL POWERS/ABILITIES Possesses the ability to warp
reality, which he perceives as made of string; he can thus twist
objects, such as people's bodies, into grotesque, agonizing shapes.

Brother of CAPTAIN BRITAIN
and PSYLOCKE, sleazy playboy
Jamie Braddock was captured
by the insane criminal
mastermind known as Doctor
Crocodile. Tortured by
Crocodile, Jamie's latent ability
to reshape reality manifested at
the same moment he lost his
grip on sanity. He became one
of the most dangerous beings
in the universe, both out of his
mind and capable of turning the world upside
down. After EXCALIBUR defeated him, he spent
years in a coma. He returned during the House
of M incident and sacrificed himself to save his
sister and the universe. **TB, MF**

BRAND, LUCAS

FIRST APPEARANCE Tomb of Dracula #9 (June 1973)
REAL NAME Lucas Brand
OCCUPATION Gang leader; assassin   **BASE** London
HEIGHT 6 ft 4 in   **WEIGHT** 210 lbs   **EYES** Red   **HAIR** Brown
SPECIAL POWERS/ABILITIES Standard vampiric powers,
including superhuman strength and invulnerability to most weapons.
Strong willpower enabled him to resist Dracula's mental control.

Lucas Brand and the members of the British
motorcycle gang he led came across a weakened
DRACULA, beat him up and attempted to drown
him. In retaliation, Dracula bit and
killed Brand, who thereby became a
vampire himself. Later Brand was
recruited by Doctor Sun, a
criminal mastermind who
existed as a bodiless, living brain.
On Sun's behalf, Brand
overcame Dracula, but when
Brand then turned against
Doctor Sun, Sun destroyed the
would-be rebel. **PS**

Lucas Brand was one of the
very few vampires in the world
who was able to resist the
mental control of that lord of
vampires, Count Dracula.

BROOD

The Brood are a race of alien
insectoids that spread across the
universe like a cancer by injecting
their eggs into other beings. When
the eggs hatch, the host is consumed
and transformed into a Brood
member. The Insectoids use space
whales the Acandi as living starships.
Native to the Shi'ar Galaxy, the
Brood aided DEATHBIRD's attempts
to overthrow her sister Lilandra
Neramani as the SHI'AR Majestrix.
   The Brood infected the X-MEN
and planted the egg of a
Bloodqueen into PROFESSOR X, but
the team was saved by WOLVERINE
who was able to resist the transformation process. Their home
planet, Broodworld, was destroyed, but many of the Brood
survived and began to rebuild their race. A Brood queen, No-
Name, came to Earth during World War Hulk as part of the
HULK'S WARBOUND. **TD, MF**

Wolverine's healing factor let
him resist the Brood egg that
was deposited in his body.

Individuals possess six legs,
transparent wings, razor-sharp
teeth, armor-plated scales and
long tails that are divided into two
deadly stingers. The Brood are
extremely durable, very hard to
destroy, and vicious fighters,
determined that their malignant
race will survive.

The alien Brood eventually found their way to Earth and injected a team
of mutants; however they were defeated by the X-Men.

BROTHER VOODOO

FIRST APPEARANCE Strange Tales #169 (September 1973)
REAL NAME Jericho Drumm
OCCUPATION Houngan (voodoo priest)   **BASE** Port-au-Prince, Haiti
HEIGHT 6 ft   **WEIGHT** 220 lbs   **EYES** Brown   **HAIR** Brown
SPECIAL POWERS/ABILITIES Summoning brother's spirit from within
own body doubles his strength; can send this spirit forth to possess
other people; can create fire and smoke; hypnotic control over

After years in the US, Jericho Drumm returned to
Haiti to take over as a houngan (voodoo priest) from
his brother Daniel. His voodoo became stronger
when he merged with Daniel's spirit. As
Brother Voodoo, he vanquished Damballah
and his evil cult, but later succumbed to
the temptation to tap Damballah's power,
and became possessed. DOCTOR STRANGE
freed him, and he joined the HOWLING
COMMANDOS. During the Secret Invasion (see pp.
326-7), it was revealed that Jericho had been
replaced by a SKRULL. **MT, MF**

BROTHERHOOD OF EVIL MUTANTS

Mutant terrorist organization

BROTHERHOOD OF EVIL MUTANTS

FACTFILE

MEMBERS/POWERS

MAGNETO (LEADER)
Manipulates magnetic forces.

ASTRA
Varies her molecular density.

TOAD
Tongue stretches 25 ft; leaps great heights; super-strong.

QUICKSILVER
Superhuman speed.

SCARLET WITCH
Chaos magician.

MASTERMIND
Illusion-caster.

BLOB
Immovable; impervious to injury.

Unus
Impenetrable force-field.

LORELEI
Hypersonic, paralysing scream.

BASE
Mobile

FIRST APPEARANCE
Uncanny X-Men #4
(March 1964)

ALLIES/FOES

ALLIES: Magneto

FOES: Professor X, The X-Men, New Mutants, X-Factor, X-Force, the Avengers, Cable, all non-mutant human beings.

CHARACTER KEY
(original brotherhood)
1 The Toad **2** Mastermind **3** Magneto
4 Quicksilver **5** The Scarlet Witch

Founded by MAGNETO, the Brotherhood of Evil Mutants has remained, through its various incarnations, the opposite number of the X-MEN; while the X-men's mission has always been to promote tolerance and co-existence between mutants and normal humans, the Brotherhood's goal has been nothing less than total domination over mankind, and quite possibly the eradication of normal humans entirely.

MUTANT MENACE

Originally, Magneto formed the Brotherhood as a strike force, helping him to oppose PROFESSOR X's X-Men, who had foiled his takeover of the Cape Citadel rocket base. This initial assemblage included the high-leaping Toad, Mastermind, creator of perfect illusions, the super-swift QUICKSILVER, and his sister, the hex-casting SCARLET WITCH. Time and again they struck against their X-Men foes and against humanity, never scoring a true victory. And eventually, with the defeat of Magneto, this incarnation of the Brotherhood was no more— and the misguided Quicksilver and the Scarlet Witch went on to become members of the AVENGERS.

Some years later, the mysterious, shape-shifting mutant terrorist MYSTIQUE formed a new Brotherhood of Evil Mutants under her command. This grouping was comprised of the immovable BLOB, the earth-shaking AVALANCHE, the flame-wielding PYRO, and the future-predicting DESTINY. This incarnation of the Brotherhood eventually transformed into FREEDOM FORCE when it was offered amnesty by the US Government in exchange for becoming government operatives. But Freedom Force was at its heart corrupt, and after assorted clashes with the X-Men and other hero groups such as the Avengers, the program was quietly disbanded.

ESSENTIAL STORYLINES
• *X-Men #4*
The newly-formed Brotherhood has its first clash with the X-Men
• *Uncanny X-Men #141–142*
Mystique's Brotherhood attempts to assassinate Senatory Robert Kelly and prevent the passing of the Mutant Registration Act
• *The Brotherhood #1*
X's agents are assembled for covert terrorist missions against humankind.

CHARACTER KEY
(Mystique's Brotherhood)
1 Avalanche **2** Blob **3** Pyro **4** Mystique

BAD BROTHERS

Since then, a number of other individuals have attempted to form their own permutations of the team. The Toad created his own Brotherhood in an attempt to destroy CABLE. HAVOK of the X-Men assembled a team of his own as a combat unit against humanity at a point at which his faith in Professor X's dream was at a low. And the mysterious mutant operative known only as X created a many-celled version of the Brotherhood in his ongoing terror campaign against the human race. In recent years, former X-Man Xorn and Exodus have also created their own versions of the team. **TB, MF**

CHARACTER KEY
(LATEST BROTHERHOOD)
1 Black Tom Cassidy
2 Juggernaut
3 Avalanche
4 Exodus
5 Sabretooth
6 Mammomax

BRUTACUS

FIRST APPEARANCE Fantastic Four Vol. 1 #186 (September 1977)

REAL NAME Unrevealed   **OCCUPATION** Warlock

BASE New Salem, Colorado   **HEIGHT** 6 ft 5 in

WEIGHT 310 lbs   **EYES** Brown   **HAIR** Orange

SPECIAL POWERS/ABILITIES Enhanced strength and reflexes, damage resistance, ability to change into lion form, other unrevealed powers of sorcery.

BUCHANAN, SAM

FIRST APPEARANCE Ghost Rider Vol. 3 #28 (August 1992)

REAL NAME Samuel Buchanan

OCCUPATION Agent for Paranormal Law Enforcement Team

BASE Mobile   **HEIGHT** Unrevealed   **WEIGHT** Unrevealed

EYES Brown   **HAIR** Brown

SPECIAL POWERS/ABILITIES Highly trained marksman and expert hand-to-hand combatant.

BUSHMASTER

FIRST APPEARANCE Captain America #310 (October 1985)

REAL NAME Quincy McIver   **OCCUPATION** Professional criminal

BASE Mobile   **HEIGHT** 18 ft 6 in from head to tail

WEIGHT Unknown   **EYES** Brown   **HAIR** Black

SPECIAL POWERS/ABILITIES Tail enables him to travel and attack at speeds of up to 40 mph. His tail is also strong enough to crush a six-inch thick steel pipe; poison fangs on backs of hands.

Brutacus was born the son of warlock NICHOLAS SCRATCH in New Salem, Colorado. When Scratch ordered his mother, AGATHA HARKNESS, to stand trial for living in the outside world, he transformed Brutacus and his six other children into inhuman creatures collectively called SALEM'S SEVEN. In a final battle with the VISION and the SCARLET WITCH, an explosion of magical energy killed Salem's Seven and wiped out New Salem. During a nervous breakdown, the Scarlet Witch recently resurrected Salem's Seven. For a time, they lived with Dr. Strange and became friends with the Fantastic Four. **DW, MF**

A special agent for Interpol, Sam Buchanan was a level-headed, no nonsense sort of chap who didn't believe in magic. Following the release of LILITH, the demon-queen, from imprisonment, there was a steady increase in demonic activity and Sam was assigned to protect human-demon hybrid, Victoria MONTESI. For a long time, while continuing to protect Victoria, he insisted that the mystical events that he witnessed had a rational explanation; eventually he was persuaded to believe what he was seeing. When this assignment finally ended, Sam Buchanan joined the Paranormal Law Enforcement Team, where it is thought he still works. **AD**

Bushmaster's serpentine tail both supports his body and is a formidable weapon, being strong enough to crush a 6-inch-thick steel pipe.

Quincy McIver's limbs were amputated by a ship's propeller and he was rebuilt as a cyborg with a snakelike tail by the Brand Corporation. Shortly after this transformation, Bushmaster accepted Sidewinder's invitation to join the SERPENT SOCIETY. While battling MODOK, Bushmaster's mechanical arms were severed, but they were later reattached. As well as his powerful tail, Bushmaster has six-inch fangs on the back of his hands that deliver a fast-acting poison created from snake venom. **MT**

BULLSEYE

Bullseye's origins remain mysterious. A notorious assassin, he first clashed with his archenemy, DAREDEVIL, while trying to extort money from the rich. New York crimelord the KINGPIN then hired him to be his chief assassin. While Bullseye was imprisoned, the Kingpin replaced him with ELEKTRA. To reclaim his position, Bullseye killed Elektra. She and Daredevil had once been lovers, and Daredevil came after Bullseye. In the battle, Bullseye fell from a great height, and was paralyzed.

Japanese scientist Lord Dark Wind repaired Bullseye's bones with adamantium, and he resumed his criminal career and war with Daredevil, murdering Karen PAGE, whom Daredevil had loved for many years.

Bullseye joined the THUNDERBOLTS and fought with them against the Skrulls during the Secret Invasion (*see* pp. 326–7). Afterward, Norman Osborn (*see* GREEN GOBLIN) made him the new HAWKEYE in his version of the AVENGERS. **PS, MF**

FACTFILE

REAL NAME
Lester (last name unrevealed)

OCCUPATION
Assassin

BASE
New York City

HEIGHT 6 ft
WEIGHT 200 lbs
EYES Blue
HAIR Blond

FIRST APPEARANCE
Daredevil Vol. 1 #131
(March 1976)

Can use almost any object as a weapon and throw it with deadly aim; spine and other bones are reinforced with adamantium, making them unbreakable; highly formidable hand-to-hand combatant.

Bullseye temporarily gets the better of his greatest enemy, the blind costumed crimefighter Daredevil.

MARVEL IN THE
1960s

Although it had published characters like Captain America, the Human Torch and the Sub-Mariner in the 1930s, 40s and 50s, the company that would become Marvel Comics had given up on Super Heroes when the 1960s began, and was only publishing monster comics, westerns and teenage romances. According to comic book legend, publisher Martin Goodman heard that the competition had launched a team of Super Heroes that was selling well. He asked his editor, Stan Lee, to come up with a new super-team. Stan developed the Fantastic Four and hired Jack Kirby as illustrator.

Launched as a bimonthly in 1961, *Fantastic Four #1* was followed by *The Incredible Hulk #1* in 1962. The same year saw the first appearances of Spider-Man in *Amazing Fantasy #15*, and Thor in *Journey Into Mystery #83*. Spider-Man received his own title in 1963, the year that also premiered *Avengers #1*, *X-Men #1*, *Sgt. Fury And His Howling Commandos #1* and Iron Man in *Tales of Suspense #39*. *Daredevil #1* appeared in 1964. With the launch of *Nick Fury, Agent of SHIELD* in 1968, Nick became the first character to simultaneously star in two series set during different time periods: World War II and the modern era!

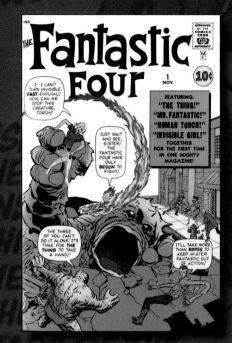

FANTASTIC FOUR #1 (1961)
The Marvel Universe is born with a bimonthly title that introduces Mr. Fantastic, the Thing, the Invisible Girl and the Human Torch to the world.

TALES TO ASTONISH #44 (1963)
The Ant-Man gains a partner and meets his future wife when Janet Van Dyne becomes the Wasp and joins his series.

SGT. FURY AND HIS HOWLING COMMANDOS #13 (1964)
In a story set during World War II, Captain America and Bucky join Sgt. Nick Fury to foil a typically fiendish Nazi plot.

FANTASTIC FOUR ANNUAL #3 (1965)
Almost every Super Hero and Villain in the then Marvel Universe appears on the scene to celebrate the wedding of Reed Richards and Sue Storm. The guest list even includes a brief appearance by Stan Lee and Jack Kirby.

AMAZING FANTASY #15 (1962)

Marvel's most popular Super Hero—the always amazing Spider-Man—premieres in the last issue of a suspense comic. Peter Parker, Aunt May, Uncle Ben, and Flash Thompson all make their first appearances as Spider-Man learns that, "with great power there must also come great responsibility.

AVENGERS #4 (1964)

Stan Lee and Jack Kirby resurrect the original Captain America from the 1940s and reintroduce him to the modern age of comics.

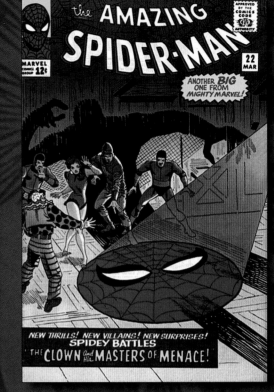

AMAZING SPIDER-MAN #22 (1964)

The Webhead meets the Circus of Crime for the second time and battles the Ringmaster, the Clown, and Princess Python.

AMAZING SPIDER-MAN #39 (1966)

John Romita takes over the Wall-Crawler's art chores when Peter Parker is unmasked and captured by his greatest enemy: Norman Osborn, the original Green Goblin!

MARVEL TALES #3 (1966)

As Marvel Comics became more popular, the company began to publish reprints of their earlier work so that readers could catch up on the histories of their favorite characters.

THE MIGHTY THOR #145 (1967)

As punishment for disobeying his father, Thor is stripped of his immortality and powers and abandoned on Earth. He lands a job working for the Ringmaster and his Circus of Crime.

CABE, BETHANY

FIRST APPEARANCE Iron Man #117 (December 1978)
REAL NAME Bethany Cabe
OCCUPATION Bodyguard **BASE** Mobile
HEIGHT 5 ft 7 in **WEIGHT** 125 lbs **EYES** Green **HAIR** Red
SPECIAL POWERS/ABILITIES Bethany Cabe is a trained investigator, an expert marksman, and extensively trained in self-defense techniques.

After the apparent death of her ex-husband, Bethany Cabe trained to become a bodyguard. In the course of her work, she met and became involved with Tony Stark (*see* IRON MAN). When Stark's alcoholism threatened to destroy him, Bethany convinced him to get help. Their romance ended when Cabe's ex-husband turned out to be still alive but in a coma, and she returned to him. Years later, OBADIAH STANE swapped MADAME MASQUE's mind into Cabe's body and set her against Stark, but Cabe foiled the plot. Currently, Cabe is in charge of the WAR MACHINE research and development. **TB, MF**

CAIERA

FIRST APPEARANCE Incredible Hulk Vol. 3 #92 (April 2006)
REAL NAME Caiera
OCCUPATION Gladiator, queen **BASE** Sakaar
HEIGHT 7 ft **WEIGHT** 270 lbs **EYES** Green **HAIR** Black
SPECIAL POWERS/ABILITIES Superhuman strength and near invulnerability.

One of the Shadow People of the planet Sakaar, Caiera was captured and enslaved by Prince Angmo II at the age of 13. She rose through his ranks to become his trusted lieutenant and was named his Warbound Shadow when he ascended to the throne of the Red King.

When the HULK came to Sakaar, she fought against him on the Red King's behalf, but she later joined the Hulk's rebellion. After the Hulk was proclaimed king, Caiera joined him as his queen, and she became pregnant. She died when the vessel that brought Hulk to Sakaar exploded. **MF**

CABLE *see opposite page*

CAGE, LUKE

As a young man, a rivalry Carl Lucas had over a woman turned bitter and the other man framed him for possessing heroin. After being sent to prison, he volunteered to be a test subject for an experimental chemical in order to obtain an early parole. An angry guard tried to kill him by giving him an overdose. Instead of killing him, the drug reacted with his unique body chemistry and gave him superpowers. He escaped prison, faked his death, and adopted the name Luke Cage. He made a name for himself as a solo hero for hire sometimes using the name Power Man. Cage formed a partnership with Danny Rand (IRON FIST), and they worked to clear his name. He joined the new AVENGERS and began a relationship with Jessica JONES. Luke and Jessica had a daughter and have since married. Luke sided with CAPTAIN AMERICA during the Civil War (*see* pp. 84–5) and stayed with the underground Avengers after Cap was killed. **TD, MF**

After preventing a robbery at a diner, the owner gave Cage a reward and the idea to go into business as a hero for hire.

FACTFILE

REAL NAME
Carl Lucas
OCCUPATION
Bodyguard; investigator
BASE
Stark Tower, New York

HEIGHT 6 ft 6 in
WEIGHT 425 lbs
EYES Brown
HAIR Formerly black, now bald

FIRST APPEARANCE
Luke Cage, Hero For Hire #1
(July 1972)

LUKE CAGE

POWERS

Cage possesses superhuman strength, very dense muscle and bone tissue and steel-hard skin. He recovers three times faster from injury than a normal person and is an experienced and skilled street fighter.

CALEDONIA

FIRST APPEARANCE Fantastic Four Vol. 3 #9 (September 1998)
REAL NAME Alysande Stuart
OCCUPATION Champion **BASE** New York City
HEIGHT 5 ft 6 in **WEIGHT** 130 lbs **EYES** Blue **HAIR** Blonde
SPECIAL POWERS/ABILITIES Wore a warrior's armor and a long red cloak; wielded an enormous sword with the skill and courage of a great warrior of old; accomplished athlete.

In another world, Alysande Stuart was descended from a long line of ancient Scottish warrior champions. Her warrior name was Caledonia, and she also served as CAPTAIN BRITAIN. Freed from captivity in her world, Caledonia arrived in New York City. She worked as a nanny to Franklin RICHARDS, son of Reed Richards and Sue Storm (MR FANTASTIC and INVISIBLE WOMAN), and thus came under the protection of the FANTASTIC FOUR.

Caledonia was eventually killed by the insane, murderous Jamie BRADDOCK. **MT**

CABLE

A living link between present and future

Cable has spent his life as a warrior, but longs for peace. He once established the airborne city of Providence as a futuristic utopia.

Hailing from the future of Earth-2107, Nathan Dayspring Askani'son, alias Cable, was actually born in modern times as Nathan Christopher Summers. He is the son of Scott Summers, CYCLOPS of the X-MEN, and his first wife Madelyne PRYOR, a clone of Jean GREY, alias Phoenix.

In the "House of M" storyline, Cable devolved into an infant. Deadpool rescued the baby from Mister Sinister, and Cable soon returned to his true age.

LIFE-SAVER

APOCALYPSE infected Nathan with a potentially deadly "techno-organic" virus. A woman from the Clan Askani brought the child to her own time, the 40th century of Earth-4935. There Mother Askani, a version of Rachel Summers, halted the virus' spread. She also had Nathan cloned. Apocalypse, who ruled this era, abducted the clone, who grew to become Cable's evil twin, STRYFE. Mother Askani transported the souls of Scott Summers and Jean Grey into the future and, as "Slym" and "Redd", they raised young Nathan. After the boy had destroyed Apocalypse, Scott and Jean returned to their own time. Nathan became the Clan Askani's foremost freedom

Next to Apocalypse, Cable's greatest enemy is literally himself: the terrorist Stryfe is Cable's clone. Stryfe framed Cable for an assassination attempt on Charles Xavier. Stryfe's mind once even took possession of Cable's body.

fighter against the New Caananites, led by Stryfe. Nathan married a fellow warrior, Aliya, and they had a son, Tyler, but Aliya was murdered by Stryfe. When Stryfe traveled back to the 20th century, Cable pursued him. There Cable founded the mercenary team Six Pack, which included his lover Domino. Later, Cable took command of the New Mutants, and reorganized them into X-Force.

Cable came to believe that his powers were killing him. DEADPOOL and the Fixer removed part of his brain and replaced the techno-organic matter, saving his life, but reducing his powers. He joined the X-Men in their mission to save the first mutant baby born after M-Day. After the infant was rescued, Cable escaped into the future with her, trying to keep her safe from BISHOP who seeks to kill her. **PS, MF**

FACTFILE

REAL NAME
Nathan Christopher Summers
OCCUPATION
Adventurer; former freedom fighter and US government agent
BASE
Mobile

HEIGHT 6 ft 8 in
WEIGHT 350 lbs
EYES Blue
HAIR White

FIRST APPEARANCE
Uncanny X-Men #201
(January 1986)

CABLE

POWERS

Mutant with telepathic and telekinetic abilities. Possesses superhuman strength.

ESSENTIAL STORYLINES
• ***Adventures of Cyclops and Phoenix #1–4***
Scott Summers and Jean Grey raise young Nathan Summers in a distant future.
• ***The New Mutants #86–100***
Cable remolds the New Mutants into X-Force.
• ***Uncanny X-Men #294–296***
"The X-Cutioner's Song" storyline, featuring Cable's showdown with his nemesis Stryfe, which also crossed over into other Marvel titles.

CALLISTO

FIRST APPEARANCE Uncanny X-Men #169 (May 1983)

REAL NAME Unrevealed   **OCCUPATION** Former leader of the
Morlocks, former model, former bodyguard   **BASE** Formerly the
Alley (tunnel beneath Manhattan); Mobile

HEIGHT 5 ft 9 in   **WEIGHT** 130 lbs   **EYES** Blue   **HAIR** Black

SPECIAL POWERS/ABILITIES Superhumanly keen senses,
including night vision.

Callisto was the leader of
the MORLOCKS, mutant
outcasts who lived
beneath Manhattan, but
she survived the
MARAUDERS' massacre.
She joined Mikhail
Rasputin, who brought the
other surviving Morlocks
to a pocket dimension
called the Hill and
organized them into the
terrorist group Gene
Nation. The Morlock
Masque transformed
Callisto's arms into tentacles
and made her fight in the Arena. Callisto lost her
powers on M-Day, becoming a normal human
with regular arms. She later joined X-Cell, a
group of depowered mutants who blame the US
government for their troubles. **PS, MF**

CALYPSO

FIRST APPEARANCE New Mutants Vol. I #16 (June 1984)

STATUS Villain (deceased)   **REAL NAME** Calypso Ezili

OCCUPATION Witch; troublemaker   **BASE** New York City

HEIGHT 5 ft 8 in   **WEIGHT** 120 lbs   **EYES** Brown   **HAIR** Black

SPECIAL POWERS/ABILITIES Skilled in Voodoo magic; combines
potions and spells to confuse enemies; controls enemies with
Yorumba spirit drum; can revive dead and resurrect herself.

Born and raised in Haiti,
Calypso was initiated
into the arts of
Voodoo. Meeting
KRAVEN THE HUNTER
shortly after his first
defeat by Spider-
Man, Calypso formed a
love-hate attachment to him. After Kraven's
death, Calypso became unhinged, killing
her sister to obtain her supernatural powers.
Although killed by the LIZARD, Calypso
resurrected herself and clashed with Daredevil,
before dying once more, at the hands of Alyosha
Kravinoff. Her spirit then infused an amulet
through which she could possess anyone who
wore it. **AD, MF**

Powered by a
thermo-chemical
reaction,
Cannonball slams
into Wolverine.
A force field
protects him from
the impact.

CANNONBALL

Sam Guthrie's mutant abilities first revealed themselves while
he was trapped in a coal mine with a group of co-workers. The
stress triggered his powers of propulsion, which helped free
Guthrie and his partners. Later, Donald Pierce, a renegade
member of the HELLFIRE CLUB, found Guthrie using a device
he had built from stolen plans for PROFESSOR X's mutant-
locating device, Cerebro. Pierce recruited Guthrie to help him
battle Professor X and his NEW MUTANTS.
Pierce ordered Guthrie to kill the New
Mutants, but he refused. Pierce tried to
kill Guthrie, but Professor X saved
Guthrie's life and defeated Pierce.
Xavier invited Guthrie to join the New
Mutants as Cannonball. He became one
of the team's leaders, and later a member
of the X-Men. **MT**

Cannonball explodes
into action, teaming
up with fellow
X-Men Bishop,
Storm, and Sage.

*The equal and opposite
reaction to the thermo-
chemical energy
Cannonball generates
propels his body into the
air like a human rocket.*

FACTFILE

REAL NAME
Samuel Guthrie

OCCUPATION
Adventurer; student, ex-coal miner

BASE
Professor Xavier's School for
Gifted Youngsters, Salem Center,
New York

HEIGHT 6 ft
WEIGHT 150 lbs
EYES Blue-gray
HAIR Blond

FIRST APPEARANCE:
Marvel Graphic Novel #4 (1982)

Possesses the mutant power to
create thermo-chemical energy
and release it from his body in a
powerful burst. Force field
surrounding body gives
superhuman durability.

CANNONBALL

POWERS

◎ CAPTAIN AMERICA **see pages 60-65**

CAPTAIN BRITAIN

CAPTAIN BRITAIN

FACTFILE

REAL NAME
Brian Braddock

OCCUPATION
Ruler of Otherworld

BASE
England; Otherworld

HEIGHT 5 ft 11 in
WEIGHT 180 lbs
EYES Blue
HAIR Blond

**FIRST
APPEARANCE**
*Captain Britain
Weekly #1
(December 1976)*

POWERS

Uniform formerly gave superhuman strength and durability, enabled flight, and provided protective force field. Captain Britain's powers have now been internalized. His uniform no longer has augmentation circuitry built into it.

Chosen to become the champion of the nation of Great Britain by MERLYN and his daughter ROMA, Brian Braddock was made Captain Britain. Both alone and as a member of EXCALIBUR, he strove to be worthy of his new role. Eventually he discovered he was one of an almost infinite number of Captains created to safeguard the multiverse. He later succeeded Roma as ruler of the Otherworld and commander of the CAPTAIN BRITAIN CORPS. He married the mutant MEGGAN, but lost her when she sacrificed herself to save their world during the events surround M-Day. The Corps has since been decimated, and Brian has begun working closely with Britain's MI-13 instead, helping repel the SKRULLS' attempt to invade the magical realm of Avalon during the Secret Invasion (*see* pp 326–7) **TB, MF**

Captain Britain marries Meggan, a fellow member of the team Excalibur.

GET AWAY FROM HER, YOU DEPRAVED MANIACS.

CAPTAIN BRITAIN?!

BUT WE HAVE NOT DONE ANY CRIMES.

Captain Britain saves Alice from the Crazy Gang, dressed as characters from the pages of Lewis Carroll's *Alice in Wonderland.*

CAPTAIN BRITAIN CORPS

CAPTAIN BRITAIN CORPS

FACTFILE

MEMBERS
Assorted interdimensional incarnations of **CAPTAIN BRITAIN**, including **CAPTAIN UK, CAPTAIN ANGLETERRE, CAPTAIN COMMONWEALTH, CAPTAIN EMPIRE, CAPTAIN ENGLAND, CAPTAIN MARSHALL, KAPTAIN BRITON, HAUPTMANN ENGLANDE, BROTHER BRIT-MAN** and others.

BASE
Otherworld; various Earths across the multiverse.

FIRST APPEARANCE
Mighty World of Marvel #13 (1984)

The Captain Britain Corps is an alliance of interdimensional champions, all empowered by MERLYN and his daughter ROMA, and charged with protecting their home realities from dimensional incursions. Based out of the central nexus realm known as Otherworld, the many members of the Captain Britain Corps—each an analogue of the mainstream CAPTAIN BRITAIN— are stationed so as to be able to detect threats to all of existence, and intercept them.

The Captain Britain of Earth-616 was in charge of the Corps for a while, but after its decimation at the hands of the mutant villain Mad Jim Jaspers, the champion called Albion (the Captain Britain equivalent from Earth-70518) was charged with rebuilding it. **TB, MF**

The Captain Britain Corps interceded when it was feared that the mutant powers once possessed by Franklin Richards, son of the Fantastic Four's Mr. Fantastic and the Invisible Woman, might destroy the multiverse.

CAPTAIN FATE

FIRST APPEARANCE Man-Thing Vol. 1 #13 (January 1975)
REAL NAME Captain Jebediah Fate
OCCUPATION Pirate **BASE** The ship *Serpent's Crown* in the Bermuda Triangle, Atlantic Ocean
HEIGHT 6 ft 3 in **WEIGHT** Unknown **EYES** Gray **HAIR** Gray
SPECIAL POWERS/ABILITIES No longer ages, and is invulnerable to certain forms of injury.

In 1795, Jebediah Fate was the first mate to the pirate queen Maura Hawke when they encountered the satyr Khordes, who desired a mate. The traitorous Fate and his men turned Hawke over to Khordes in exchange for treasure. Hawke cursed Fate and his accomplices to sail the seas for eternity, and Khordes' magic made her curse come true. Centuries later, Fate again encountered Khordes and Hawke, now reincarnated as oceanographer Maura Spinner, as well as the monstrous MAN-THING. Though Fate was killed by gunfire, the demon Thog resurrected him, and Fate clashed with the Man-Thing, Maura and Khordes yet again. **PS**

CAPTAIN AMERICA

Living Legend of World War II

FACTFILE

REAL NAME
Steve Rogers

OCCUPATION
Adventurer

BASE
Brooklyn, New York; Stark Tower ("Avengers Tower"), Manhattan, New York

HEIGHT 6 ft 2 in
WEIGHT 240 lbs
EYES Blue
HAIR Blond

FIRST APPEARANCE
Captain America Comics #1 (March 1941)

POWERS

The Super-Soldier Serum brought Rogers to the peak of physical perfection; able to lift twice his own body weight; expert military strategist; Olympic-level martial artist and gymnast; resistant to disease and fatigue.

ALLIES Bucky Barnes, Nick Fury, Sharon Carter, Rick Jones, The Falcon, Nomad (Jack Monroe), The Avengers

FOES The Red Skull, Baron Zemo, MODOK, the terrorist organizations AIM and Hydra, Crossbones

ISSUE #1

Captain America burst into action battling Hitler in his first issue. Cap's shield changed shape to circular in forthcoming issues because of objections from the creators of another hero called the Shield.

In the late 1930s, with the threat of world war looming in Europe, the American high command embarked upon a program to create the perfect soldier. Project: Rebirth, spearheaded by Dr. Abraham Erskine, was intended to create a battalion of supreme fighting men, stronger and more resilient than normal soldiers, expertly trained and equipped —a bulwark against Nazi aggression. The first test subject for Erskine's revolutionary Super-Soldier Serum was a young, would-be artist name Steve Rogers, who had attempted to enlist, but had been turned away, classified 4-F, because of his physical frailty.

THE SUPER SOLDIER

Subjected to Erskine's process, Rogers' body virtually doubled in size, as millions of healthy cells were created almost instantaneously. His physique was accelerated to the pinnacle of human perfection, all weakness and deficiency drained out of it.

However the secret test area had been infiltrated by Nazi sympathizers, who slew Dr. Erskine, the only person who knew how the process worked. Although Rogers quickly captured the saboteurs, it was clear that there would be no battalion of super-soldiers now— Steve Rogers would be the only one.

Captain America arrives in the nick of time to prevent Sharon Carter being blasted into the blue courtesy of Nazi menace Red Skull.

Equipped with a virtually unbreakable red, white and blue shield, the product of a metallurgical accident, and trained in combat, tactics, espionage, and the fighting arts, Rogers was rechristened Captain America. Clad in a striking star-spangled uniform, he became a symbol for the US fighting forces and a dread nemesis of the Axis powers.

In his many battles against Nazi aggression, Captain America was joined by a sidekick, the worldly James "Bucky" Barnes, who had discovered the secret of Rogers' true identity.

> YOU MUST DRINK THIS QUICKLY, BEFORE THE CHEMICALS LOSE THEIR POTENCY! GOOD LUCK, MY BOY!

Abraham Erskine, operating under the code-name Professor Reinstein, created the Super-Soldier Serum. It turned frail Steve Rogers into a perfect specimen of humanity.

The result of a metallurgical accident, Captain America's shield is the most durable object known to man.

Among the foes combated by Cap in the present day is MODOK, the Mental Organism Designed Only for Killing. MODOK was the result of an experiment by the sinister think-tank known as Advanced Idea Mechanics, or AIM.

BUCKY'S DEATH

Toward the end of World War II, Cap and Bucky Barnes set out to foil Baron Zemo's scheme to steal a drone plane laden with a bomb. As the plane took off, Bucky and Cap leaped aboard. Cap fell into the sea, but Bucky clung on trying to defuse the bomb. The bomb exploded, Bucky was killed, and Cap has been haunted by the memory ever since.

Together, Cap and Bucky tore a swath through the ranks of the enemy forces, vanquishing such Nazi menaces as the RED SKULL, Agent Axis, and the Iron Cross. The duo were often joined by their allies in the INVADERS team, including the original HUMAN TORCH and NAMOR, the Sub-Mariner.

In 1945, Cap and Bucky were on a mission to apprehend the German scientist BARON ZEMO, who planned to steal an experimental long-range Drone Plane developed by the British. As the plane took off, Cap and Bucky made a desperate leap to catch it. Cap couldn't maintain his hold, and plummeted earthward... seconds later the plane self-destructed, ending the life of Bucky Barnes. Cap's body plunged into the icy waters below, where he was frozen into a state of suspended animation, a condition he would remain in for decades to come.

To safeguard morale, the Allied high command kept the deaths of Cap and Bucky secret and recruited other heroes to play the role of Captain America. Meanwhile, the true Captain America slumbered within the ice.

THE RETURN

Eventually, while searching for their foe Namor (the same person who had fought alongside Steve Rogers in the INVADERS), the AVENGERS came across Captain America's body floating in the icy waters, and revived him. Now Captain America was a man out of time, a soldier whose war was long over. Attempting to find a place for himself in this strange new society, Cap accepted an offer of Avengers membership, and swiftly became the binding glue that held the team together.

Reformed criminal Sam Wilson, alias Harlem's guardian the Falcon, has been one of Captain America's closest friends and most frequent crime-fighting partners.

THE AVENGERS
1 Hawkeye **2** The Wasp **3** Falcon **4** Captain America, team leader **5** Iron Man **6** Vision **7** Scarlet Witch

ESSENTIAL STORYLINES
• *Captain America & The Falcon #153-156:* Cap and his partner the Falcon must combat the replacement Captain America and Bucky of the 1950s, who have been driven mad by the flawed serum that gave them their abilities
• *Captain America Vol. 4 #1-6:* Captain America reveals his true identity as Steve Rogers to the world after he is forced to take the life of a terrorist leader
• *Captain America Vol. 5 #1-14:* Cap is on the trail of the Winter Soldier, a legendary assassin from the pages of history who may actually be his former sidekick Bucky Barnes!

Over the years, Cap has contested with numerous opponents intent on taking up his mantle. One of his challengers was the "Anti-Cap", a modern day counterpart created by Naval Intelligence as an extreme anti-terrorist operative. Eventually facing defeat by Captain America for a second time, the Anti-Cap chose death rather than capture.

Cap also offered his services to his old war buddy Nick Fury, now head of SHIELD. It was while operating as a SHIELD agent that Cap first encountered Sharon CARTER, SHIELD's Agent 13, who would become his paramour.

Hailed as the most trusted costumed champion of them all, Captain America fought on, struggling to uphold freedom and democracy, both alone and with the Avengers—right up until the moment of his death. **TB, MF**

SHOT DOWN

In the last days of his life, CAPTAIN AMERICA (Steve Rogers) led the resistance against the Superhuman Registration Act. Declaring it an unjust law, he fought both his country and his longtime friends. Once he was captured, the RED SKULL finally saw his chance and executed a plan that had been months in the making. As Rogers was marched into a federal courthouse, CROSSBONES shot him. In the resultant chaos, Rogers's girlfriend Sharon Carter—brainwashed by DR. FAUSTUS—turned and shot him three times, too.

Rogers was buried in Arlington National Cemetery, at a state funeral with full military honors. His pallbearers were Ben Grimm (THING), Rick Jones, T'Challa (BLACK PANTHER), Carol Danvers (MS. MARVEL), Sam Wilson (FALCON), and Tony Stark (IRON MAN). Alicia MASTERS designed his memorial.

Unaware that she just had shot him, Sharon Carter tried to tend to Cap's wounds.

CAPTAIN AMERICA

Wolverine sneaks onto the SHIELD Helicarrier to inspect Steve Rogers's body.

After the announcement of the Superhuman Registration Act, Captain America (Steve Rogers) could not stomach enforcing what he considered to be an unjust law. He broke with his old friend Tony Stark (IRON MAN) and formed a resistance movement to help unwilling heroes to defy the law. This split fractured the superhero community and set the heroes against each other in what would become known as the Civil War (*see* pp. 84–5). At the end of the war, Iron Man defeated and captured Rogers, who was soon after assassinated as he was brought into a federal courthouse in New York City.

IN DEATH'S SHADOW
Without Rogers to lead it, the organized resistance against the Superhuman Registration Act fell apart. Many of the heroes who had held out stepped forward to register. The Falcon, for instance, signed up solely so he could appear at Rogers's funeral.

Having seen many people supposedly die in the past, including Rogers himself, some heroes refused at first to believe that he was dead. It was only after Iron Man and WOLVERINE—each representing a different side in the Civil War— were able to corroborate Rogers's death that the reality began to sink in.

THE HUNT FOR A NEW CAPTAIN
Although Stark had gone on record stating that no one would replace Captain America, it wasn't long until he went looking for a replacement. With Captain America's costume and indestructible shield in SHIELD custody, he could give the assignment to whoever he liked. When Stark discovered that Clint Barton (HAWKEYE) had somehow survived the SCARLET WITCH's disassembling of the Avengers, he brought Barton aboard the SHIELD Helicarrier to show him the original shield, revealing that he'd had two imperfect copies made. The first sat on display at the Smithsonian, while the second was to be buried with Rogers. The real one was

up for grabs.

Barton tried out the shield, becoming the first person to wield it properly after 77 other people had failed. Stark gave Barton the shield and the costume to try out as he went to arrest PATRIOT and the new Hawkeye for failure to comply with the Superhuman Registration Act. At the moment of truth, Barton—dressed in Rogers's uniform and holding his shield—let the two heroes go rather than arrest them. He then gave the shield back to Stark.

BUCKY CLAIMS THE SHIELD
Unwilling to let Rogers's shield languish in the custody of SHIELD—which he blamed in part for Rogers's death—Bucky BARNES stole it. Back

Iron Man finds Clint Barton (Hawkeye), who is supposed to be dead.

from his own purported death, after which he had become the WINTER SOLDIER, he used the shield in a few missions of his own. While taking the shield, he ran into Natasha Alianovna (BLACK WIDOW), with whom he'd had a relationship when they'd both been in the employ of the Soviet Union.

After SHIELD finally captured Barnes, Stark surprised him by offering him the identity of Captain America to go along with the shield. Barnes accepted on two

conditions. First, any secret mental conditioning from his days as the Winter Soldier had to be telepathically removed. Second, he would answer only to himself. Knowing that this would be exactly what Rogers would have wanted, Stark accepted the deal.

Feeling unfit to wear Rogers's own costume, Barnes had a new one designed for himself. Unlike Rogers, Barnes was happy to use weaponry of all sorts in his battles, not just the shield. He carried a pistol and a combat knife on his belt, which featured a number of pouches, and he brought in other ordnance as necessary.

Iron Man presents Captain America's original shield to Clint.

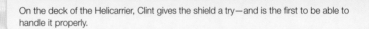

On the deck of the Helicarrier, Clint gives the shield a try—and is the first to be able to handle it properly.

THE NEW CAPTAIN AMERICA

As Captain America, Barnes foiled the RED SKULL's attempt to assassinate both candidates for the US Presidency. He also faced off against the Captain America of the 1950s—also known as Steve Rogers—who had been brainwashed by the Red Skull and DR. FAUSTUS. Defeating this hero from the past and restoring his mind established Barnes's claim as the sole Captain America.

On the one night he wears the Captain America costume, Clint sees Patriot and the new Hawkeye battle Firebrand.

Barnes fought alongside the heroes of Earth against the SKRULLS during the Secret Invasion (*see* pp. 326–7), participating in the final battle in Central Park. This was his first encounter with many of the heroes that had known Rogers and called him friend, and he handled himself well. After the Skrulls were driven off, Barnes joined the underground Avengers team that Rogers had

once led. He allowed them to use his secret home in an old warehouse as their base of operations. Barnes worked with them under the leadership of Barton, now calling himself Ronin. Barnes also renewed his relationship with the Black Widow and worked closely with her and the Falcon on many of his missions.

While still struggling to fill Roger's boots, Barnes dedicated himself to being worthy of the honor of wearing the mantle of the icon of his country. He knew he had a lot to make up for from his days as the Winter Soldier, but he was living proof of what people could do with second chances. **MF**

When Bucky agreed to become Captain America, he designed a new costume for the role.

CAPTAIN MAR-VELL

Protector of the Universe

POWERS

Thanks to his Kree "nega-bands," Mar-vell possessed great strength (he could lift 10 tons), a high degree of imperviousness to harm, and the ability to fly. He could also exist in outer space without having to breathe.

Mar-Vell gained the ability to fire bolts of solar energy after his ailing psionic partner Rick Jones was treated with life-saving electromagnetic radiation by Professor Benjamin Savannah.

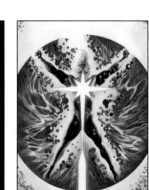

Kree nega-bands convert Captain Mar-vell's psionic energy into incredible power.

Captain Mar-Vell was a member of the Kree, an alien humanoid race who built an empire known as the Greater Magellanic Cloud. Captain Mar-Vell was a "White Kree," who have the same skin color as Caucasian Earth humans and similar physiology. (Most members of the Kree race have blue skin.) As captain of a Kree space fleet, Mar-Vell distinguished himself in battles against the shape-changing Skrulls, the Kree's age-old foes.

Mar-Vell impersonated a dead scientist named Dr. Walter Lawson when he first came to Earth.

OLD FOES OF MINE WHO HAVE DIED... ...RETURNING FROM THE GRAVE!

In delirium while dying from cancer, Captain Mar-Vell is haunted by terrifying phantoms of the enemies he fought and defeated during his career as a Super Hero.

PROTECTOR

Captain Mar-Vell's qualities did not go unremarked by the Supreme Intelligence, the force that governed the Kree. Wary of mankind's growing scientific abilities, the Intelligence sent Mar-Vell to sabotage the planet's space programs. However Mar-Vell grew to respect the people of Earth and helped them, earning the soubriquet "Captain Marvel."

The Supreme Intelligence then used Mar-Vell to forge a telepathic link with a human being. The Intelligence believed that humans possessed vast psionic potential, which it longed to possess. It would then destroy humanity. The Intelligence secretly enabled Mar-Vell to bond with Rick Jones by means of a pair of Kree "nega-bands. "

The Intelligence used the psionic link

with Jones to nullify the Skrull space fleet. The effort almost cost Jones his life, and Mar-Vell used his own life force to revive Jones. Mar-Vell then defeated Thanos, who wished to destroy all life in the universe. Mar-Vell also met with the alien being Eon, who gave him "cosmic awareness," persuaded him to renounce the Kree's warmongering ways, and designated him "Protector of the Universe."

During a battle with the Nitro of the Lunatic Legion, an alien-criminal organization formed by a band of renegade Kree scientists, Mar-Vell was exposed to a carcinogenic gas. Mar-Vell subsequently developed cancer and died on Saturn's moon, Titan, surrounded by his lover, Elysius, Rick Jones, the Avengers (who posthumously made him an honary member), and many Super Hero friends. Mar-Vell's son, Genis-Vell, eventually took over his mantle. Later, the original Captain Mar-Vell returned, but during the Secret Invasion (*see* pp. 326–7) he was revealed to be a Skrull. He turned against his superiors and sided with Earth, but was killed in the war. Recently, Noh-Varr (Marvel Boy) became the latest Captain Marvel, serving with the Avengers under Norman Osborn (*see* Green Goblin). **MT, MF**

CAPTAIN MARVEL

CAPTAIN MARVEL

FACTFILE

REAL NAME
Genis-Vell

OCCUPATION
Adventurer

BASE
Mobile throughout the universe

HEIGHT 6 ft 2 in
WEIGHT 195 lbs
EYES Blue
HAIR Blond (becomes white when "cosmically aware")

FIRST APPEARANCE
Silver Surfer Annual #6 (1993)

POWERS
Kree Nega-bands confer superhuman strength and durability, the ability to fly, the power to project concussive energy blasts; Genis-Vell possesses "cosmic awareness," allowing him to perceive cosmic threats or dangers.

The Kree nega-bands enabled Genis to fly through outer space without oxygen or protection.

Following the tragic death from cancer of the Kree warrior CAPTAIN MAR-VELL, his lover Elysius, an ETERNAL of Titan, used cell samples taken from his body to conceive a son she named Genis-Vell. To help keep the child safe from harm, Titanian science accelerated Genis-Vell's aging so that he rapidly reached physical maturity. As soon as he discovered his heroic lineage, Genis-Vell donned his father's nega-bands and became an adventurer, fittingly called Legacy. Genis-Vell later adopted his father's name, "Captain Marvel."

In order to save the life of his father's long-time friend Rick Jones, the new Captain Marvel's atomic structure was bonded to his. This meant that whenever Captain Marvel was in the Earth dimension, Rick Jones was cast into a microverse, and vice versa. In mental contact with each other, Jones acted as Genis-Vell's advisor.

After battling Atlas, Genis absorbed the Kree nega-bands (shown on his wrists) into his body.

THE BROKEN BOND

Genis-Vell subsequently went insane and helped the conceptual beings Entropy and Epiphany to destroy the universe. However, Genis then triggered a new "Big Bang," recreating the cosmos. Once more insane, Genis became a menace to the universe. Elysius and another Titan, Eros, successfully returned Genis to sanity. The bonding between Jones and Genis was undone, allowing them to exist on Earth separately.

After Atlas beat Genis nearly to death, Baron ZEMO utilized moonstones to help Genis heal his body. Genis took the name Photon and joined the THUNDERBOLTS. Zemo learned that the moonstones' effect on Genis would cause the universe's destruction. Zemo therefore killed Genis and scattered his body through the Darkforce Dimension.

The name "Captain Marvel" was briefly used by Phyla-Vell, Genis's sister, who had been similarly created by Elysius. **PS**

Monica Rambeau was known first as Captain Marvel and then Photon. When Genis took the name Photon (right), Rambeau renamed herself Pulsar.

CAPTAIN ULTRA

FIRST APPEARANCE Fantastic Four #177 (December 1976)
REAL NAME Griffin Gogol
OCCUPATION Stand-up comedian, former plumber
BASE Chicago, Illinois **HEIGHT** 5 ft 11 in **WEIGHT** 175 lbs
EYES Unknown **HAIR** Unknown
SPECIAL POWERS/ABILITIES Captain Ultra is superhumanly strong and durable, and can fly; also has a great sense of humor.

Captain Ultra began his superhuman career as a would-be super-villain, who hoped to join the FRIGHTFUL FOUR. The Four were impressed by his strength, but not by his vulnerability—he passed out in the presence of any open flame. His bid rejected, Captain Ultra went into therapy with DOC SAMSON, the psychiatrist, who helped him to overcome his aversion to fire. This didn't improve Captain Ultra's fortunes as a hero, but it did give him the confidence to move into a new line of work—as a stand-up comedian. **TB**

CAPTAIN UNIVERSE

FIRST APPEARANCE Micronauts #8 (August 1979)
REAL NAME Various, including Ray and Steve Coffin, Monty Walsh
OCCUPATION Not applicable **BASE** Mobile
HEIGHT Various **WEIGHT** Various **EYES** Various **HAIR** Various
SPECIAL POWERS/ABILITIES Captain Universe is any person endowed with the Uni-Power; abilities include superstrength, flight, and ability to alter an object's molecular structure.

The Uni-Power is energy emanating from the Microverse that appears as a clot of energy. Uni-Power bestows upon an individual the powers and knowledge of Captain Universe, as well as a special costume.

The Uni-Power only stays with an individual for a short period before moving on. The transfer from one person to the next is almost instantaneous—the cosmos is never without a Captain Universe. In recent years, the might of the Uni-Power has been borne by ex-astronauts, cat burglars and individuals as notable as Bruce Banner (see Hulk) and DOCTOR STRANGE. **AD**

CARDIAC

FIRST APPEARANCE (Dr. Wirtham) Amazing Spider-Man #342 (December 1990), (Cardiac) Amazing Spider-Man #343 (January 1991)
REAL NAME Dr. Elias "Eli" Wirtham
OCCUPATION Surgeon, researcher, vigilante **BASE** New York City
HEIGHT 6 ft 5 in **WEIGHT** 300 lbs **EYES** Brown **HAIR** Black
SPECIAL POWERS/ABILITIES Superhuman strength, speed and stamina, bulletproof skin, can project beta particle-force blasts.

Elias Wirtham's brother Joshua died of a rare disease after insurance companies refused to pay for unproven cures. Dr. Wirtham devoted his life to medical research, secretly battling those who profit from suffering. He had his heart replaced with a beta particle reactor, and his skin with vibranium mesh that transmits the particles to his muscles, giving him amazing strength. As Cardiac, he has clashed with SPIDER-MAN. **PS**

CARRION

The first Carrion was a clone of Miles Warren who was SPIDER-MAN's enemy, the JACKAL. Before his death, Warren left a clone of himself in a capsule, but something went wrong and the creature that emerged was like a living corpse. Carrion died in a fire following a battle with Spider-Man. Many years later, a fellow research student of Peter Parker's named Malcolm McBride discovered a test tube containing a genetic creation of Warren's, the "Carrion virus." The virus consumed McBride and turned him into a second incarnation of Carrion. When Miles Warren's body was examined by Dr. William Allen, he was infected by the virus, and became the third and most powerful incarnation of Carrion. **MT**

FACTFILE
REAL NAME
"Miles Warren" (actually a clone of the original Miles Warren)
OCCUPATION
None
BASE
New York City

HEIGHT 5 ft 11 in
WEIGHT 175 lbs
EYES Yellow
HAIR None

FIRST APPEARANCE
Spectacular Spider-Man #25 (December 1978)

POWERS
Carrion could repel living matter, levitate, destroy living matter with his touch, reduce the density of his body to become almost intangible, and teleport.

CARNAGE

FACTFILE
REAL NAME
Cletus Kasady
OCCUPATION
Spreader of Chaos
BASE
New York City

HEIGHT 6 ft 1 in
WEIGHT 190 lbs
EYES Green
HAIR Red

FIRST APPEARANCE
Amazing Spider-Man #244 (February 1991)

POWERS
Superhuman strength; can generate swing lines and bladed weapons; able to neutralize Spider-Man's spider-sense.

CARNAGE

Imprisoned for multiple murders, Cletus Kasady was sharing a cell with Eddie Brock, parasitical VENOM's host, when that symbiote arrived to attempt a jailbreak. Venom left behind its spawn, which bonded with Kasady resulting in a new symbiote, the creature now known as Carnage. The bond between Carnage and Kasady is more profound than that between Brock and Venom— the fact that they refer to themselves as "I" rather than "we" is testament to this. Carnage is also far more powerful, violent and deadly than its parent—following his first encounter with the creature, SPIDER-MAN was forced to enlist the help of the HUMAN TORCH and even VENOM to defeat it. It has fought alongside DEMOGOBLIN, DOPPELGANGER, Shriek, and Carrion, and has bonded with Ben REILLY, the SILVER SURFER and JOHN JAMESON. The Carnage symbiote spawned its own offspring, which bonded with a cop named Patrick Mulligan and became Toxin. The SENTRY recently ripped the Carnage symbiote apart, but Kasady may still be at large. **AD**

Like its parent, Venom, Carnage quickly came to regard Spider-Man as its arch nemesis.

CARTER, SHARON

FIRST APPEARANCE Tales of Suspense Vol. 1 #75 (March 1966)

STATUS Active **REAL NAME** Sharon Carter

OCCUPATION SHIELD liaison officer **BASE** Mobile

HEIGHT 5 ft 8 in **WEIGHT** 135 lbs **EYES** Blue **HAIR** Blonde

SPECIAL POWERS/ABILITIES Highly trained field agent; martial-arts expert and weapons expert; special talent for disguise, infiltration, and undercover work.

Sharon Carter grew up inspired by tales of her Aunt Peggy Carter, a member of the French Resistance and a lover of CAPTAIN AMERICA during World War II. Her stories of bravery inspired Sharon to take part in international espionage and law enforcement.

As an adult, Sharon became the SHIELD operative Agent 13, and she met and fell in love with Captain America, too. She disappeared after faking her death to go deep undercover for SHIELD. When she finally returned, she served as SHIELD's director in Nick Fury's absence, then became Captain America's SHIELD liaison officer. As part of a scheme run by the RED SKULL, she recently assassinated Captain America while under DR. FAUSTUS's mind control.
DW, MF

"Dr. TUMOLO then revealed herself as a disguised member of your race, and gathered others like her to save me!"

WE MUST CHANGE YOU INTO ONE OF US, GREER!

LIFE IS PRECIOUS TO ME, DR TUMOLO --IN ANY SHAPE! DO WHAT YOU MUST!

"AND WITH SCIENCE AND MAGICK, AND MENTAL ENERGY--

CAT PEOPLE

FIRST APPEARANCE Giant-Size Creatures #1 (May 1974)

BASE The Land Within, an otherdimensional netherworld

SPECIAL POWERS/ABILITIES Mystical abilities; enhanced strength, speed, and agility, similar to those of a human-sized cat.

The Cat People were brought into existence thousands of years ago when a kindly human sorcerer named Ebrok enchanted two ordinary cats called Flavius and Helene into humanoid form. He then instructed these first two Cat People in the magical arts.

In time, the numbers of the Cat People grew, to the displeasure of Ebrok's fellows in the Sorcerer's Guild. The Cat people were subsequently exiled to the limbolike realm they call the Land Within, whose properties caused them and their descendents to become demons. The Sorcerer's Guild also decreed that a member of the Cat People, given the title the Balkatar, must always answer if summoned. The current Balkatar is named Grigar.

The legendary heroine of the Cat People is known as Tigra, a human woman who was transformed into a catlike warrior by the Cat People's sorcery. Today, Greer Nelson has similarly been transformed into the heroine Tigra by a combination of the Cat People's magic and human science, and she serves as their emissary to the outside world and as a member of the mighty AVENGERS. **TB**

CAT & MOUSE

FIRST APPEARANCE Marvel Preview #21 (May 1980)

REAL NAMES (Cat) Mark Grant, (Mouse) Stephanie Wald

OCCUPATION (Cat) Musician, Shroud operative; (Mouse) Shroud operative **BASE** New York City **HEIGHT** (Cat) 6ft 1in, (Mouse) 5 ft 10 in **WEIGHT** (Cat) 195 lbs; (Mouse) 135 lbs. **EYES** (Cat) Brown; (Mouse) Blue **HAIR** (Cat) Black; (Mouse) Blonde

SPECIAL POWERS/ABILITIES Cat is a cat burglar and electronics expert. Mouse is a pickpocket and getaway driver.

Daring cat burglar Cat was recruited into a gang run by a criminal known as the Crooked Man. He met Mouse, a singer and small-time crook. They became close friends and joined the SHROUD to help take down their former employer.

Deciding to join the Shroud's crusade to destroy crime from within, they opened and began performing at the Cat's Jazz Club, which became the Shroud's unofficial base. Before the Club was destroyed, Cat & Mouse played host to such adventurers as SPIDER-MAN, TATTERDEMALION, DANSEN MACABRE and the West Coast AVENGERS. They later aided the Shroud against the Scorpion and various other crimelords. **TD**

CATSEYE

FIRST APPEARANCE New Mutants Vol. I #16 (June 1984)

STATUS Villain (deceased) **REAL NAME** Sharon Smith

OCCUPATION ex-Hellion team member **BASE** Mobile

HEIGHT 6 ft **WEIGHT** 140 lbs **EYES** Lavender **HAIR** Lavender

SPECIAL POWERS/ABILITIES Transformed into a cat and a human-panther hybrid with increased strength, agility, reflexes, and senses; hybrid also boasted razor-sharp claws and prehensile tail.

The abilities of most mutants are only manifested at puberty. Not so with Sharon Smith— her capacity to change into a cat was revealed when she was very young. Abandoned by her parents, Sharon was raised feral by a stray cat. She was a teenager before she came to the attention of Emma FROST, the White Queen. Under her guidance the highly intelligent Sharon received an accelerated education; within a year she gained high-school literacy and joined the HELLIONS. Her time with them was tragically short, an attack on the HELLFIRE CLUB leading to her death. **AD**

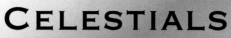

CELESTIALS

FACTFILE

KNOWN CELESTIALS
ARISHEM THE JUDGE, JEMIAH THE ANALYZER, TEFRAL THE SURVEYOR, GAMMENON THE GATHERER, NEZARR THE CALCULATOR, ONEG THE PROBER, HARGEN THE MEASURER, ESON THE SEARCHER, ZIRAN THE TESTER, ONE ABOVE ALL, EXITAR THE EXECUTIONER.

HEIGHT (average) 2,000 ft
WEIGHT (average) 260 tons

FIRST APPEARANCE
Eternals #1 (July 1976)

POWERS

Cosmic power on a scale immeasurable by Earth standards; have visited Earth, but eradicated all evidence and memory of their existence.

The Celestials are a race of virtually immortal space gods whose conscious minds gestate in the form of living galaxies for more than a million years. Once the Celestial is deemed worthy, this mind is encased by a full suit of virtually indestructible body armor that is "dimensionally transcendental," (far larger on the inside than it appears to be on the outside). Each Celestial appears to have a specific purpose. Barely a dozen and a half are known by their names and function, but many more are believed to exist. For reasons of their own, the Celestials travel throughout the Universe, performing genetic experiments. They later return a million years later to judge the results of their experiments. If the world is judged favorably, it is allowed continue. If not, it is cleansed of life. **TD**

Though the Celestials have visited Earth on four different occasions, they have erased all physical evidence of their existence. They have also purged the memories of all the humans who saw them.

CENTURIUS

FACTFILE

REAL NAME
Dr. Noah Black
OCCUPATION
Geneticist
BASE
Mobile

HEIGHT 6 ft
WEIGHT 225 lbs
EYES Brown
HAIR None

FIRST APPEARANCE
Nick Fury, Agent of SHIELD #2 (July 1968)

POWERS

Scientific genius specializing in genetics; evolved himself into a perfect human specimen, with attendant strength, agility, and durability; high-tech body armor incorporates an array of weapons; experiments with his Evolutionizer device have increased his lifespan.

The ridicule of the scientific community led scientist Dr. Noah Black to hide himself away on Valhalla Island, where he began to experiment on himself with his Evolutionizer. His experiments led him to become super-evolved, but also increased his mania, and he came to believe that humanity should be wiped out and started afresh. Calling himself Centurius, Black intended to gather up superior specimens of life, shepherd them to an ark, then destroy human civilization while he and his recruits waited in the skies above the Earth. A century later they would land and reclaim the world. His initial plot was thwarted by Nick Fury and SHIELD, but Centurius continued to threaten world security. He currently works for the Hood's crime syndicate and helped repel the Skrulls during the Secret Invasion. **TB, MF**

Centurius attempted to turn the world into a new Garden of Eden.

CENTURY

FIRST APPEARANCE Force Works #1 (July 1994)
REAL NAME Century   **OCCUPATION** Adventurer
BASE/HEIGHT/WEIGHT/EYES Unknown   **HAIR** White
SPECIAL POWERS/ABILITIES Combines memories, skills and abilities of one hundred Hodomur; projects energy from hands; wields the Parallax, a bladed weapon that binds his multiple personalities together and enables interdimensional travel.

Following the destruction of their world Hodomur by the extradimensional entity, Lore, the survivors created a new being from one hundred of their number.

Named Century, this creature was compelled to track down and destroy Lore, and given a lifespan of a hundred years to attain this goal. During this quest, the pirate, Broker, enslaved Century, blanking his mind—only Century's desire to find Lore remained. This desire led him to Earth where he served on the Super Hero team FORCE WORKS until it disbanded. Lore is now dead—destroyed by the SCARLET WITCH—and Century's whereabouts are unknown. **AD**

CERISE

FIRST APPEARANCE Excalibur #47 (March 1992)

REAL NAME Cerise

OCCUPATION Soldier   **BASE** Shi'ar Empire

HEIGHT 5 ft 10 in   **WEIGHT** 130 lbs   **EYES** Brown   **HAIR** Black

SPECIAL POWERS/ABILITIES Uses the energy of the red light spectrum to create weapons, force fields, vortexes, and shields. She can fly, direct energy blasts, and hold her breath for 7 minutes.

Cerise is an alien of the SHI'AR race, which absorbs other cultures into its vast interplanetary empire through violent conquest. Disillusioned with the brutal tactics of the Shi'ar war machine, Cerise deserted from its army and fled to Earth. There, she became a member of EXCALIBUR and fell in love with teammate NIGHTCRAWLER. The STARJAMMERS brought her back to stand trial for her crimes. In time, the Shi'ar empress LILANDRA pardoned her act of desertion and made her an operative to investigate reports of Shi'ar brutality. During Annihilation (see pp. 30-1), she joined GAMORA's team of warriors, known as the Graces. **MT, MF**

CHAMBER

FIRST APPEARANCE Generation X #1 (November 1994)

REAL NAME Jonothon Starsmore

OCCUPATION Weapon X field agent   **BASE** Mobile

HEIGHT 5 ft 9 in   **WEIGHT** 140 lbs   **EYES** Brown   **HAIR** Auburn

SPECIAL POWERS/ABILITIES (As Chamber) Can psionically fire blasts or cause objects to explode. Communicates telepathically. (As Decibel) Wears a high-tech suit that grants him a sonic scream and allows him to create things from solid sound.

Jonothon "Jono" Starsmore's mutant power manifested when an explosion of psionic energy in his chest disintegrated the lower half of his face. Able to communicate only through telepathy, Jono became withdrawn. He helped found the GENERATION X team as Chamber, and joined the X-Men. Agents from the WEAPON X program made Chamber a field agent, and their scientists restored his face. However, he lost his powers and face on M-Day. He was healed but now looks like a young APOCALYPSE. He joined the New Warriors, wearing a suit that grants him his powers. **DW, MF**

CHAMELEON

Dmitri Smerdyakov grew up in Russia as the half-brother and servant of Sergei Kravinoff, who later became known as the original KRAVEN the Hunter. Smerdyakov eventually became the mercenary spy known as the Chameleon, who was renowned as a master of disguise. Originally Chameleon relied on makeup, costumes, and his acting skill; he now uses a special serum and clothing to impersonate others.

The Chameleon first clashed with his nemesis, SPIDER-MAN, when he attempted to frame the crimefighter for the theft of classified plans for a missile defense system. However, Spider-Man captured the Chameleon and exposed him as the real thief. The Chameleon has also contended against other Super Heroes, including the HULK and DAREDEVIL.

After the original Kraven committed suicide, the Chameleon lost his sanity, and jumped from a bridge. However, he turned up alive in an insane asylum, and resumed his criminal career. **PS**

CHAMELEON

POWERS

Experimental serum renders his flesh malleable, so that he can alter his appearance without makeup or prosthetics. Clothing contains "memory material" that responds to his nerve impulses, and change appearance at will.

CHAMPION OF THE UNIVERSE

FIRST APPEARANCE Marvel Two-In-One Annual #7 (1982)   **REAL NAME** Tryco Slatterus   **OCCUPATION** Competitor   **BASE** Mobile   **HEIGHT** 9 ft 2 in   **WEIGHT** 5,050 lbs   **EYES** Silver   **HAIR** Red   **SPECIAL POWERS/ABILITIES** Has channeled the power primordial, the energy derived from the Big Bang, into his physical form, making his body a perfect fighting machine. Has also mastered thousands of different martial arts from across the universe.

Like many of the ELDERS OF THE UNIVERSE, the Champion's origin has been lost in antiquity. A true immortal, he devotes himself to physical perfection to avoid boredom. He considers himself the living spirit of competition and travels the universe, challenging the champions of each planet. If he finds them unworthy, he exterminates all life on their planets. He challenged the heroes of Earth to a match and was impressed with the Thing's courage. He and other Elders battled the SILVER SURFER and GALACTUS. The Champion's only defeat came at the hands of SHE-HULK, after which he called himself the Fallen One. **TD, MF**

CHAMPIONS OF XANDAR

FIRST APPEARANCE Fantastic Four #208 (July 1979)
BASE The planet Xandar; Nova-Prime starship
KEY MEMBERS AND POWERS
NOVA-PRIME Flight; superhuman strength, invulnerability.
PROTECTOR Psionic ability.
POWERHOUSE Siphons energy from any power source, including living beings.
COMET Flight; can project electrical energy.
CRIMEBUSTER No superhuman powers.

The Champions of Xandar was a team of superhumanoid beings who formed to protect the planet Xandar. Xandar suffered three huge alien invasions. In the first, the Luphoms shattered Xandar into pieces. Survivors on the four largest fragments connected the four planetoids with huge bridges and rebuilt their civilization.

The second invasion was by the shape-shifting SKRULLS, who hoped to bring Xandar into their empire. Having kept an active militia, Nova Corps, since the first invasion, the Xandarians resisted. They were aided by the FANTASTIC FOUR, and then by a group of Xandarians and Earth heroes, who banded together as the Champions of Xandar. Together, Nova Corps and the Champions repelled the Skrull invasion, though Crimebuster was killed. The third invasion, by NEBULA, wiped out the entire population, including the remaining Champions. **MT**

THE CHAMPIONS OF XANDAR
1 Comet 2 Nova-Prime 3 Powerhouse
4 Protector 5 Crimebuster

CHANCE

FIRST APPEARANCE Web of Spider-Man #15 (June 1986)
REAL NAME Nicholas Powell
OCCUPATION Mercenary; gambler **BASE** New York City
HEIGHT 6 ft **WEIGHT** 185 lbs **EYES** Blue **HAIR** Brown
SPECIAL POWERS/ABILITIES Chance's armored costume contains wrist-blasters, boot-jets for flight, and assorted other weapons and paraphernalia.

A chronic gambler and inveterate risk-taker, Nicholas Powell took the name Chance and sought work as a mercenary to satisfy his craving for thrills. Chance's standard modus operandi is to wager his fee at double-or-nothing odds against his success—if he fails, he receives nothing. Chances's assignments have brought him into conflict with numerous Super Heroes, including SPIDER-MAN and DAREDEVIL. Chance is thoroughly immoral—but he prides himself on his ability to beat the odds. **TB**

CHANGELING

A one-time member of the terrorist organization Factor Three, the Changeling changed sides when he learned that its leader, the alien Mutant Master, was seeking to eradicate humanity. When the Changeling discovered that he had contracted a terminal illness, he decided to make amends for his past misdeeds. He approached PROFESSOR X and volunteered to support the X-MEN. The timing was fortuitous: Xavier needed to withdraw from active duty to fend off an impending alien invasion. The Changeling agreed to impersonate the Professor during his absence. However, his leadership of the X-Men was cut short when he was killed during a skirmish with the insane Prince Gor-Tok. **AD**

Changeling turned over a new leaf by taking Professor X's place, at the latter's request.

CHARCOAL

FIRST APPEARANCE Thunderbolts #19 (October 1998)

REAL NAME Charles Burlingame

OCCUPATION Adventurer; student **BASE** Mt. Charteris.

HEIGHT 5 ft 7 in **WEIGHT** 135 lbs **EYES** Brown **HAIR** Black

SPECIAL POWERS/ABILITIES Transforms into a being composed of charcoal; manipulates heat and can reshape himself into any form of carbon, including flaming charcoal or rock-hard diamond.

When Charles Burlingame's father took him to a rally of the Imperial Forces of America, the scientist ARNIM ZOLA discovered the boy's potential for superhuman powers and transformed him into Charcoal, the Burning Man. At first, Charcoal joined a group called the Bruiser Brigade and battled the THUNDERBOLTS. Later, as a member of the Thunderbolts, Charcoal witnessed the death of JOLT. He left the group to join the Redeemers, where he battled his father, who was still a member of the Imperial Forces. He later died at the hands of GRAVITON. **MT, MF**

CHARLIE-27

FIRST APPEARANCE Marvel Super Heroes #18 (January 1969)

REAL NAME Charlie-27

OCCUPATION Soldier; adventurer **BASE** The starship *Icarus*

HEIGHT 6 ft **WEIGHT** 555 lbs **EYES** Blue **HAIR** Red

SPECIAL POWERS/ABILITIES Superhuman strength and endurance; high resistance to injury and disease; withstands the gravity of Jupiter (11 times that of Earth); pilot and master strategist.

In the 31st century of Earth-691, Charlie-27 was a member of a genetically bio-engineered race of humans sent to live on and mine the planet Jupiter. After completing a solo tour of duty as a space militia pilot, Charlie-27 learned that an alien race called the Badoon had overrun the Solar System and slaughtered the inhabitants of Jupiter, Pluto, Mercury, and Earth. Joining with Martinex (Pluto), Nikki (Mercury), Yondo (Centauri V) and Vance Astro (Earth) to form the original GUARDIANS OF THE GALAXY, Charlie-27 helped to expel the Badoon and later safeguarded the entire galaxy. **TD, MF**

Luke Cage ended Chemistro's criminal career almost before it began.

CHEMISTRO

Sad and slightly pathetic—that's how you might describe the story of the first man to bear the name Chemistro. Dissatisfied with his research position at Mainstream Motors, Curtis Carr embarked on a personal project–the development of an "Alchemy Gun" capable of changing one substance into another. When Carr was sacked for refusing to hand the weapon over to his boss, he disguised himself as a new Super Villain, Chemistro, and began a series of revenge attacks against his employer. Carr's vengeful spree of destruction finally ended during a struggle with POWER MAN, when Carr accidentally shot his own foot and turned it to steel. Crippled when his steel foot crumbled into dust, he was thrown into prison where he was forced to give the secrets of the Alchemy Gun to a fellow prisoner, Arch Morton. Although Morton's version of the gun exploded in his hand, the accident did endow his left hand with similar alchemical powers. On leaving prison, a reformed Carr developed a device called a Nullifier, and Luke Cage was able to use it to disable Morton. The third Chemistro turned out to be Carr's brother, Calvin, who stole a new version of the Alchemy Gun but was again defeated, this time by both Power Man and IRON FIST. Calvin has since been seen working for the Hood's crime syndicate and was involved in a plot to use DEATHLOK to rob a federal reserve bank. **AD, MF**

D-DON'T COME NO CLOSER, CAGE! I STILL GOT MY ALCHEMY GUN!

Although it made him look the part, Chemistro's spangly outfit did not prevent him from losing a foot when he accidentally shot himself.

FACTFILE

REAL NAME
Curtis Carr

OCCUPATION
Research scientist and reformed criminal

BASE
New York City

HEIGHT 5 ft 11 in
WEIGHT 185 lbs
EYES Brown
HAIR Black

FIRST APPEARANCE
Luke Cage, Hero for Hire #12
(August 1972)

POWERS

No superhuman powers; carried self-designed Alchemy Gun capable of transmuting one substance into another.

The Alchemy Gun was vital to Chemistro's efforts to become a dastardly criminal. A poor shot with any other weapon, his villainous career was bound to be shortlived.

CHENEY

FIRST APPEARANCE New Mutants Annual #1 (1984)
REAL NAME Lila Cheney **OCCUPATION** Songstress; thief
BASE A Dyson sphere somewhere in the Milky Way Galaxy
HEIGHT 5 ft 8 in **WEIGHT** 120 lbs **EYES** Blue **HAIR** Black
SPECIAL POWERS/ABILITIES Lila Cheney possesses the mutant
ability to teleport herself and other people and objects over
intergalactic distances.

An acclaimed rock singer on Earth, Lila Cheney
simultaneously pursued a very different career
among the stars. Employing her mutant gift to
teleport herself, Lila gained a reputation as one of
the foremost thieves in the universe. She was an
ally of the NEW MUTANTS, and a romance
with CANNONBALL led her
to curtail her criminal
activities. Since their
breakup, it remains
to be seen
whether she has
abandoned her
outlaw life for good. **TB**

CHTHON

Chthon is one of the
major Elder Gods who
first appeared on Earth,
shortly before humans
appeared on the planet.
Chthon and his sister
god GAEA inhabited the
portions of Earth which
were covered by land (not
the seas or the skies) and
probably helped create Earth's
land masses as they appear today.

Being a scholar, Chthon wrote upon a parchment all
the mystical knowledge of the world he had acquired to
that point. This document became known as the
Darkhold. Chthon hoped to use the Darkhold as a way
to manipulate Earthly pawns, as well as a magical
talisman that could function as an Earthly portal, enabling
Chthon to one day return to Earth. **MT**

FACTFILE
REAL NAME
Chthon
OCCUPATION
Elder God
BASE
An unknown extradimensional
realm

HEIGHT Unknown
WEIGHT Unknown
EYES Red
HAIR None

FIRST APPEARANCE
Avengers #187
(September 1979)

POWERS

Chthon is a master of the forces of
magic on a scale beyond human
comprehension. In his own
dimension, he has absolute control
over every aspect of that
dimension's reality.

FACTFILE
MEMBERS
RINGMASTER (Maynard Tibolt),
STRONGMAN (Bruno Olafsen),
CLOWN (Eliot "Crafty" Franklin),
FIRE-EATER (Tomas Ramirez),
THE GREAT GAMBONNOS
(Ernesto and Luigi), **HUMAN
CANNONBALL** (Jack Pulver),
LIVE WIRE (Rance Preston),
PRINCESS PYTHON (Zelda
DuBois), **RAJAH** (Kabir
Mahadevu), **TEENA THE FAT
LADY** (name unrevealed).

FIRST APPEARANCE
Incredible Hulk Vol. 1 #3
(September 1962)

POWERS

Most of the members of the
Circus of Crime have skills and
abilities that fit their job
descriptions; these they then
adapt for criminal purposes.
Princess Python is a snake
charmer; Rajah is an elephant
trainer; and Live
Wire possesses
an electrified
lariat.

CIRCUS OF CRIME

Operating under many different
commercial names, the Circus of
Crime is constantly traveling around
the country. They usually enter a small
town and give away a large quantity of
free tickets in order to ensure a full
house. Once the show has begun, the
Ringmaster uses a hypnotic device in
his top hat to place the audience in a
deep trance. The audience is robbed
and sometimes the entire town is looted.
A post-hypnotic suggestion usually prevents
the Ringmaster's victims from identifying
any members of the Circus or from
remembering any details of the crime.
They only recall having had a great time
at the circus!

Despite the Ringmaster's skills,
and those of his accomplices, the
Circus has not always got away
with its mass robberies. When the
Ringmaster tried to turn HULK
into a monstrous attraction, he
was unable to hypnotize the
enraged green giant—with
inevitable results. **TB**

THE HOUSE IS FILLIN UP GOOD BOSS! WE'LL SOON BE RICH!

THE FOOLS HAVE COME TO SEE SPIDER-MAN! BUT THEY'LL GET A FAR DIFFERENT KIND OF SHOW INSTEAD!

KEEP THE ENTERTAINMENT GOING UNTIL THE PLACE IS FILLED! I DON'T WANT ANYONE TO GET SUSPICIOUS

Originally from Austria, the Ringmaster moved his circus to America where he believed he
could strike it rich. However, he only turned to crime when his small band were unable to
compete with the larger circus shows.

AND NOW, REPEAT AFTER ME...I MUST
OBEY THE RINGMASTER!! HIS WILL IS
MY WILL! HIS WILL IS MY WILL!!

The Ringmaster's
mechanism has
enough range
to hypnotize a
capacity crowd in
a sports arena.

CLEA

Until recently the ruler of the Dark Dimension, during her lifetime the Faltinian Princess Clea has experienced numerous trials and tribulations. The daughter of Prince Orini and Umar, influential figures in the Dark Dimension, Clea became involved in much of the political turmoil that afflicted that pocket universe. Doctor Strange first met Clea during one of his first forays to her homeland, and he was to have a significant influence on her life. Together they fought against the demon Dormammu and during these battles they fell in love. Inevitably, these struggles were not without their dangers and for a time Clea became trapped in a separate pocket universe with Dormammu. After her rescue by Strange, Clea spent several years in New York City, where she became his disciple and also his lover. When she returned to her home, she led a revolution against her mother, who had become ruler. After she took her mother's place, she married Strange, but Dormammu later usurped her throne. She left Strange behind on Earth to lead the resistance against him. **AD, MF**

Dr. Strange meets Clea for the first time.

Even a burning head can't help Dormammu beat Dr. Strange.

FACTFILE

REAL NAME
Clea

OCCUPATION
Former ruler of the Dark Dimension

BASE
The Dark Dimension

HEIGHT 5 ft 8 in
WEIGHT 190 lbs
EYES Blue
HAIR White

FIRST APPEARANCE
Strange Tales #125 (November 1964)

POWERS
Formidable manipulator of mystical forces. Alien metabolism gives greater strength and endurance than a human being of similar height and weight.

CLOAK AND DAGGER

Tyrone Johnson was an Afro-American teenager whose stutter tragically prevented him saving his friend Billy from being mistakenly shot as a thief by a policeman. A Caucasian teenager, Tandy Bowen, felt neglected and unloved by her wealthy mother. Johnson and Bowen each ran away from home, and met each other upon arriving in New York City at the Port Authority Bus Terminal.

They were offered a place to stay by men who worked for Simon Marshall, an unscrupulous chemist who was developing a new, highly addictive drug for the Maggia. Marshall was testing the drug on captured runaways. But whereas the drug killed the other runaways, it activated Johnson and Bowen's latent mutant abilities. Realizing he now resembled a living shadow, Johnson wrapped himself in fabric. He then entrapped some of Marshall's men in the blackness within this "cloak," while Bowen struck others down with "daggers" of "light." Johnson and Bowen decided to use their superhuman powers to save children and teenagers from drug dealers and other criminals and became the vigilante duo called Cloak and Dagger. **PS**

Despite differing backgrounds, runaways Tyrone Johnson and Tandy Bowen became the closest of friends.

Dagger's "light-knives" are manifestations of the life energy that resides within all living beings. Dagger generates more of this life energy than normal humans do, and uses it to feed Cloak's hunger for such "light."

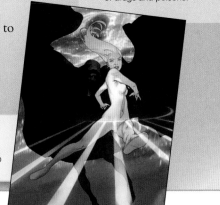

FACTFILE

REAL NAMES
Tyrone Johnson, Tandy Bowen

OCCUPATION
Vigilantes

BASE The Holy Ghost Church, New York City

HEIGHT (Cloak) 6 ft (Dagger) 5 ft 5 in
WEIGHT (Cloak) 175 lbs, (Dagger) 115 lbs
EYES (Cloak) Brown, (Dagger) Blue
HAIR (Cloak) Black, (Dagger), Blonde

FIRST APPEARANCE
Spectacular Spider-Man #64 (March 1982)

POWERS
Cloak can open a portal into "Darkforce Dimension." Can project foes into this dimension, teleport himself and others. Dagger projects "daggers of light," psionic energy that deprives a victim of some life energy and can also cleanse people of drugs and poisons.

CLOUD 9

FIRST APPEARANCE Avengers: The Initiative #1 (March 2007)
REAL NAME Abigail "Abby" Boylen
OCCUPATION Super Hero **BASE** Montana
HEIGHT 5 ft 5 in **WEIGHT** 100 lbs **EYES** Blue **HAIR** Blonde
SPECIAL POWERS/ABILITIES Controls a cloud of gas on which she can fly; can also manipulate it to surround others and blind or suffocate them.

Soon after the launch of The Fifty-State Initiative (*see* pp. 118–9), WAR MACHINE found Abby flying over Evanston, Illinois, and recruited her for training at Camp Hammond. She became part of the inaugural class and struck up a friendship with MVP (*see* VAN PATRICK, MICHAEL). When ARMORY panicked during a training mission, MVP tried to protect Abby and was killed. Abby later helped defeat Kia, an insane clone of MVP, and started a relationship with MVP's first clone. She then joined FREEDOM FORCE, the Initiative team based in Montana. **MF**

COBRA

FIRST APPEARANCE Journey into Mystery #98 (November 1963)
REAL NAME Klaus Voorhees
OCCUPATION Criminal **BASE** Manhattan, formerly the Serpent Citadels in New York State **HEIGHT** 5 ft 10 in
WEIGHT 160 lbs **EYES** Blue **HAIR** None
SPECIAL POWERS/ABILITIES Has flexible, virtually unbreakable bones; can perform superhuman contortionist feats.

Klaus Voorhees worked in India for a scientist conducting research into antidotes for snake venom. Voorhees fatally poisoned the scientist, but was himself bitten by an irradiated cobra. That cobra's venom and an experimental antidote mutated Voorhees. As the Cobra, Voorhees first fought (and lost to) THOR. He often partners with MISTER HYDE and has also joined other snake-themed criminals in the Serpent Squad and Serpent Society. After once assuming leadership of the Society, he changed his name to King Cobra. He currently works with Sin's new Serpent Squad and also for the Thunderbolts. **PS, MF**

COLLECTOR

FIRST APPEARANCE Avengers Vol. 1 #28 (June 1966)
REAL NAME Taneleer Tivan
OCCUPATION Curator **BASE** Mobile
HEIGHT 6 ft 2 in **WEIGHT** 450 lbs **EYES** White **HAIR** White
SPECIAL POWERS/ABILITIES Immortality, precognition and telepathy; can manipulate cosmic energy to change his size and shape; Temporal Assimilator permits time travel.

One of the immortal ELDERS OF THE UNIVERSE, the Collector foresaw the destruction of all life by THANOS, and began to collect specimens for future repopulation. He was slain by KORVAC, but returned to life when the GRANDMASTER, a fellow Elder, won a contest with Death. The Collector briefly held the Reality Gem, but lost it to Thanos who sought it for the Infinity Gauntlet. Recently, the Collector allowed the Brethren to invade Earth, hoping to collect survivors from the reduced population. **DW**

COLOSSUS

COLOSSUS

FACTFILE
REAL NAME Piotr Nikolaievitch Rasputin
OCCUPATION Adventurer
BASE Professor X's School for Gifted Youngsters, Salem Center, New York
HEIGHT 7 ft 5 in (armored)
WEIGHT 500 lbs (armored)
EYES Blue
HAIR Black
FIRST APPEARANCE Giant Size X-Men #1 (1975)

POWERS Mutant ability to change his body's tissue into an organic, steel-like material. This gives Colossus superhuman strength (he can lift at least 70 tons) and protects him from injury.

Piotr Rasputin was born and raised on a Soviet collective farm in Russia. His mutant powers first emerged during his adolescence, and at first he was content to use his great strength and invulnerability to help his fellow farmers on the collective. His armored form added 11 inches to his normal height and doubled his natural weight. When PROFESSOR X organized a new team of mutants to help him rescue his original team of X-MEN from the sentient island known as Krakoa, he contacted Rasputin and asked him to join. The young Russian agreed to leave his native land and accompany Xavier to the US. Training at the X-Men's mansion, Rasputin was given the code name Colossus. He then helped Professor X's other new recruits in their battle with Krakoa. When the battle was over, Rasputin decided to remain in the US as a member of the X-Men. **MT**

In armored form Colossus retains his normal degree of mobility, but his endurance and speed are greater.

Few can resist the devastating power of Colossus when he is in his armored state. One of his mighty punches is enough to crush even Magneto himself.

His armor can withstand an explosion of 450 pounds of dynamite.

COLLINS, RUSTY

FIRST APPEARANCE X-Factor #1 (February 1986)

REAL NAME Rusty Collins

OCCUPATION Adventurer **BASE** X-Factor HQ, New York City

HEIGHT 5 ft 11 in **WEIGHT** 160 lbs **EYES** Blue **HAIR** Red

SPECIAL POWERS/ABILITIES Rusty Collins was a pyrokinetic with the mutant ability to cause flames to spontaneously generate in his vicinity.

Leaving a troubled home life behind, Rusty Collins enlisted in the United States Navy while still underage. But his career as a sailor came to an end when his mutant ability to generate flames first manifested itself. Rusty was thereafter recruited by X-FACTOR, members of the original X-MEN who had taken on the role of mutant hunters in order to conceal their activities in recruiting and training young mutants. Rusty eventually gained some control over his flaming abilities, and he adventured with X-Factor's junior team, the X-Terminators. However, he eventually perished due to injuries received during a battle with the villain HOLOCAUST. **TB**

COMET

Comet aides Nova in the defence of the planet Xandar.

Harris Moore was one of the very first superpowered individuals to adopt a costume and take up the fight against crime. During an encounter with a gaseous, comet-like object in the 1950s, Moore was mutagenically affected by its radiation. Discovering that he could now fly and fire electrical energy from his hands, Moore decided to battle criminals on the streets of New York. His new vocation was not to end well. Moore was a wealthy individual with a wife and two children, but his good life was to come to an end when an enemy tracked him down to his suburban home and attacked him and his family. While he was hospitalised and appeared to have lost his powers, they were all thought to be dead. Moore retired his costume for many years until he was called upon to travel to the planet Xandar, along with other Earth Super Heroes, and help its people in the fight against the Skrulls. During this battle, Moore was reunited with his son, Frank, the high-tech vigilante Crimebuster. Sadly, their renewed relationship was not to last long: Frank was killed during this battle while Moore later died during the Xandarians' battle against Nebula. **AD**

COMET MAN

Comet Man *Max*

On a mission in space, Dr. Stephen Beckley lost control of his spacecraft, which entered a comet's tail. The comet's intense heat vaporized the ship and Beckley. However, within the comet was another spaceship piloted by Max, an alien from the Colony Fortisque. Max used Fortisquian technology to reconstruct Beckley's body and endow him with superhuman powers.

Returning to Earth, Beckley was quarantined by David Hilbert, a member of the Bridge, an intelligence agency headed by Beckley's brother John, the Superior. Hilbert captured Stephen's wife Ann and son Benny. Stephen escaped captivity, but in her own escape attempt Ann was killed. The Superior had scientist Dr. Fishler subject Benny to painful experiments in order to endow him with powers like Stephen's. Stephen found Benny, who used his new powers to kill Dr. Fishler before turning comatose.

Now known as Comet Man, Stephen accompanied Max to the Colony Fortisque, where Beckley mastered his powers. Comet Man then returned to Earth, where he used his powers to awaken Benny from his coma. **PS**

Max, a member of the Fortisquian race, is fascinated by Earth's popular culture. Revealing himself to be an alien, Max became a media celebrity.

About every 77 years, a Fortisquian spaceship, hidden within a comet, travels past Earth to observe the planet.

COMMISSION ON SUPERHUMAN ACTIVITIES

FACTFILE

BASE
United States of America;
various locations

FIRST APPEARANCE
Captain America #331
(July 1987)

The Commission on Superhuman Activities is a special task force answerable only to the President of the United States. It is charged with the task of regulating security in an age when beings with superhuman abilities roam the world. The Commission, or the CSA as it is frequently known, has involved itself in numerous incidents since its inception: it recruited the BROTHERHOOD OF EVIL MUTANTS led by Mystique to form the nucleus of a government-sponsored team of operatives known as FREEDOM FORCE. It was responsible for choosing John Walker as the replacement for Steve Rogers when the latter gave up his identity as CAPTAIN AMERICA. Members of the CSA were also responsible for the creation of superhumans such as Nuke and the Julia Carpenter SPIDER-WOMAN. When a SENTINEL went rogue and attacked a school in Antigo, Wisconsin, the Commission sent agents to investigate. The CSA has also been responsible for pitting the THUNDERBOLTS against the NEW AVENGERS. While their resources have occasionally been used for nefarious purposes, in general the membership of the Commission remains dedicated to its mission statement of protecting the American people from any threat spawned by those possessing superhuman attributes. **TB**

The CSA
1 Orville Sanderson 2 George Mathers
3 General Heyworth 4 Henry Peter Gyrich
5 Valerie Cooper 6 Raymond Sikorsky
7 Adrian Sammish

The Commission on Superhuman Activities is tasked with maintaining national security in a world occupied by superhumans.

CONSTRICTOR

FACTFILE

REAL NAME
Frank Payne (alias Frank Schlichting)

OCCUPATION
Professional criminal and assassin

BASE
Mobile

HEIGHT 5 ft 11 in
WEIGHT 190 lbs
EYES Blue
HAIR Black

FIRST APPEARANCE
Incredible Hulk # 212
(June 1977)

POWERS

Battlesuit contains two cybernetically-controlled, electrically-powered adamantium cables, used as whips, as crushing coils, and to release electrical charges.

Using the alias Frank Schlichting, SHIELD agent Frank Payne infiltrated the criminal organization known as the Corporation. When Payne was forced to kill several youths during a fight, he suffered a nervous breakdown. The Corporation then gave him the Constrictor battlesuit and made him a criminal operative. When the Corporation dissolved, Constrictor went freelance. He normally likes to work alone, but he has teamed up with many other villains in the past. He put his criminal past behind him once he won a multimillion-dollar lawsuit after taking a beating from HERCULES. He is now part of The Fifty-State Initiative's (*see* pp. 118-9) Shadow Initiative team. **MT, MF**

The cables in Constrictor's battlesuit are made of adamantium, the strongest metal ever forged by man.

CONTEMPLATOR

FIRST APPEARANCE Marvel Treasury Special #1 (1976)
REAL NAME Tath Ki
OCCUPATION Philosopher **BASE** Coal Sack Nebula
HEIGHT 5 ft **WEIGHT** 100 lbs **EYES** Blue **HAIR** None
SPECIAL POWERS/ABILITIES Control of his body's involuntary responses: heartbeat, perspiration, etc.; highly developed mental powers; acute awareness of this and alternate universes.

An ELDER OF THE UNIVERSE, the Contemplator is one of the most ancient beings in the cosmos. Born in the early days of the universe, he has spent most of his life in meditation, reflecting on and teasing out the universe's deepest secrets. On occasion, the Contemplator has intervened in human affairs—IRON FIST encountered him during a battle with HYDRA; he once gave CAPTAIN AMERICA a history tour, and he has had dealings with the SILVER SURFER. But, for the most part, this enigmatic, aged figure spends his days watching and learning. **AD**

CONTROLLER

FIRST APPEARANCE Iron Man Vol. 1 #12 (April 1969)

REAL NAME Basil Sandhurst

OCCUPATION Criminal **BASE** Mobile

HEIGHT 6 ft 2 in **WEIGHT** 565 lbs **EYES** White **HAIR** Black

SPECIAL POWERS/ABILITIES Armored exoskeleton provides enhanced strength and damage resistance; can telepathically control victims wearing his slave discs.

Crippled in a lab accident while working for Cord Industries (one of Stark Industries' main rivals), Basil Sandhurst built himself an exoskeleton powered by mental energy. By placing a slave disc on a victim's head or neck, Sandhurst could direct that person's actions and leech his or her brainpower to charge up his suit. On various occasions, he set himself up as a cult leader or clinic director to get easy access to more bodies. At other times, THANOS and the Master of the World upgraded his technology to make it more efficient. The Controller clashed with IRON MAN and the AVENGERS several times. Currently, he works for THE HOOD. **DW, MF**

COOPER

FIRST APPEARANCE X-Men #176 (December 1983)

REAL NAME Valerie Cooper **OCCUPATION** Chair of the Commission on Superhuman Activities **BASE** Washington, D.C.

HEIGHT 5 ft 9 in **WEIGHT** 135 lbs **EYES** Green **HAIR** Blonde

SPECIAL POWERS/ABILITIES Highly intelligent, efficient, and loyal; superb organizer; trained in the use of weapons.

Special Assistant to the US National Security Advisor Dr. Valerie Cooper was concerned about the number of mutants in the world. She feared that if control of mutants fell into the wrong hands, they could be used as weapons against the US. When Mystique offered the help of the BROTHERHOOD OF EVIL MUTANTS, Cooper accepted, changing the group's name to FREEDOM FORCE. Later, as the head of the COMMISSION ON SUPERHUMAN ACTIVITIES, Cooper was the liaison with the mutant team X-FACTOR. Cooper also helped found the Office of National Emergency and was named its deputy director. She oversaw the mutant refugee camp set up at the Xavier Institute for Higher Learning after M-Day. **MT, MF**

COPYCAT

FIRST APPEARANCE New Mutants #98 (Feburary 1991, in the guise of Domino) **REAL NAME** Vanessa Geraldine Carlysle

OCCUPATION Professional criminal; mercenary **BASE** Mobile

HEIGHT Unrevealed **WEIGHT** Unrevealed

EYES Black with white pupils **HAIR** White

SPECIAL POWERS/ABILITIES Copycat can transform herself into a duplicate of any other person.

Vanessa Carlysle's mutant power to transform her appearance manifested itself in her early teens. She was kicked out by her family, and forced to make her way on the mean streets. She eventually came to the attention of the shadowy Mr. Tolliver, who used her to infiltrate X-FORCE in the guise of DOMINO. But Copycat came to like the members of X-Force, and she could not go through with the plan to blow them up along with their headquarters. Her deception discovered, Copycat was forced to return to being a mercenary, and She met her doom at the hands of SABRETOOTH after being recruited by the revived WEAPON X project. **MT**

Copycat's most successful impersonation was when she took the form of Domino and joined the New Mutants. Even the readers were unaware of the substitution for months.

CORRUPTOR

FIRST APPEARANCE Nova #4 (December 1976))

REAL NAME Jackson Day **OCCUPATION** Criminal mastermind

BASE Mobile

HEIGHT 6 ft 1 in **WEIGHT** 225 lbs **EYES** Red **HAIR** White

SPECIAL POWERS/ABILITIES His touch makes his victims susceptible to his commands. Left to themselves, they will behave in an unihibited, perhaps amoral fashion.

While employed by a drug company, factory worker Jackson Day was accidentally drenched with chemicals. They turned his skin blue-black, and removed his inhibitions against wrongdoing. He also gained the power to control the wills of others by touching them. As the Corruptor, Day turned THOR into a violent menace. However, the Nova intervened, and together he and Thor prevailed. He later tried to corrupt the HULK and the Avengers. Recently, he has been working with the HOOD, battling the newest versions of the AVENGERS and helping repel the SKRULLS during the Secret Invasion (see pp. 326–7). **MT, MF**

COUNT NEFARIA

FACTFILE

REAL NAME
Count Luchino Nefaria

OCCUPATION
Criminal; former head of Nefaria "family" of Maggia

BASE
Various, including castle originally located in Italy and reconstructed in the New Jersey Palisades.

HEIGHT 6 ft 2 in
WEIGHT 230 lbs
EYES Blue
HAIR Black

FIRST APPEARANCE
The Avengers #13 (Feb. 1965)

POWERS

Superhuman strength, speed, and resistance to injury; projects laser beams from eyes; regenerates after injury; drains energy from other beings powered by ionic energy.

Italian nobleman Count Luchino Nefaria used his fortune both to finance technological research and to make himself a power in the MAGGIA crime syndicate. Nefaria's wife Renata died giving birth to their daughter Giulietta. Growing up in America as Whitney Frost, Giulietta would eventually become the Maggia leader called MADAME MASQUE. In retaliation for the AVENGERS' opposition to the Maggia, Nefaria framed them for treason. The Avengers were cleared, but Nefaria was publicly exposed as a criminal. Among his grandest schemes, Nefaria captured Washington DC and held it for ransom, and later took over the North American Defense Command base at Valhalla Mountain. On both occasions he was thwarted by the X-MEN.

Thunderbird, a Native American member of the X-Men, perished while trying to prevent Count Nefaria's escape from Valhalla Mountain.

IN ALL VALHALLA BASE, MY CHILDREN, WE SIX ARE THE ONLY ONES STILL CONSCIOUS, AND ONCE AGAIN, COUNT NEFARIA IS TRIUMPHANT...

THIS TIME TO HOLD THE FATE OF A WORLD IN HIS HANDS.

Nefaria was the villain in the 1975 issue that relaunched the X-Men Super Heroes.

Later, Nefaria had Prof. Kenneth Sturdy endow him with the powers of the LIVING LASER, POWER MAN, and WHIRLWIND and again battled the Avengers. Soon afterwards, however, Nefaria aged into an ancient invalid, and seemingly died when his body was crushed. However, Nefaria revived as a superhuman powered by ionic energy, and continues to menace the entire world. **PS**

CRAZY GANG
1 Jack of Hearts **2** Jester
3 Tweedledope **4** Executioner
5 Red Queen

CRAZY GANG

FIRST APPEARANCE Marvel Super Heroes #377 (Sept. 1981)
BASE Mobile
MEMBERS AND POWERS
Executioner A hooded, scythe-wielding humanoid robot.
Jester Accomplished swordsman.
Knave Possesses superhuman strength.
Red Queen Her insanity twists all reality into negative situations.
Tweedledope Idiot-savant who devises advanced machinery.

The Crazy Gang is a team of professional criminals from another dimension (Earth-238, or the Crooked World) who look like characters from children's storybooks. They were assembled by that dimension's CAPTAIN BRITAIN (called Captain UK, real name: James Jaspers).

When the Crazy Gang was transported to the Earth of the Captain Britain, who was really Brian Braddock, they proved incompetent at committing crimes and so advertised for a new leader. They were taken over by Captain Britain's foe the Slaymaster, who masterminded a series of spectacular crimes which the Crazy Gang carried out for him. They were then recruited by master assassin Arcade to abduct Courtney Ross, the former girlfriend of Captain Britain. Ross managed to escape from the bumbling group, but was taken prisoner by Arcade himself. The Crazy Gang later clashed with EXCALIBUR, who subsequently allowed them to remain in this dimension. **MT**

CREED, GRAYDON

FIRST APPEARANCE Uncanny X-Men #299 (April 1993)

STATUS Villain (deceased) **REAL NAME** Graydon Creed

OCCUPATION Politician; wheeler-dealer **BASE** New York City;
New York State; mobile **HEIGHT** 6 ft **WEIGHT** 181 lbs

EYES Blue **HAIR** Brown

SPECIAL POWERS/ABILITIES Charismatic orator, skilled political
operator and rabble-rouser.

Victor Creed was psychologically abused as a child and become the mutant menace SABRETOOTH; his son, Graydon Creed, was to grow up similarly disaffected. Born to the shapeshifting mutant MYSTIQUE, Graydon came to hate all mutants. He founded the Friends of Humanity, an organization that aimed to wipe out mutants. Standing for US President on a Friends of Humanity platform, Graydon was cut down by an assassin's plasma beam. The murderer turned out to be his own mother, who had travelled back from the future especially to kill him. **AD**

CRIMSON COMMANDO

FIRST APPEARANCE Uncanny X-Men # 215 (March 1987)

REAL NAME Frank Bohannan

OCCUPATION Federal agent **BASE** Washington, DC

HEIGHT 6 ft 1 in **WEIGHT** 235 lbs **EYES** White **HAIR** White

SPECIAL POWERS/ABILITIES The Crimson Commando is a
mutant at the peak of physical perfection. He has been turned into
a cyborg with even greater strength and power.

The Crimson Commando is a veteran Super Hero of World War II who, after the war, took to hunting down criminals and slaying them in a brutal vigilante style alongside his two partners, Super-Sabre and Stonewall. They were arrested when their activities were revealed after trying to execute the X-Man STORM. Recruited for the government-sponsored mutant team FREEDOM FORCE, the Crimson Commando served with that unit until, on a mission to Kuwait, he was horribly wounded, losing both legs and part of an arm. Still alive, he was rebuilt into a cyborg by the government, and continues to operate as a covert agent. **TB**

CRIMSON DYNAMO

FIRST APPEARANCE Tales of Suspense Vol. 1 #46 (October 1963)

STATUS Russian hero **REAL NAME** Valentin Shalatov

OCCUPATION Former KGB agent **BASE** Moscow, Russia

HEIGHT 6 ft 2 in **WEIGHT** 210 lbs **EYES** Brown **HAIR** Brown

SPECIAL POWERS/ABILITIES Armored suit provides flight,
enhanced strength, and damage resistance; built-in weapons
include missiles, guns, electrical generators, and a fusioncaster.

At least a dozen people have worn the Crimson Dynamo armor. The first—Russian inventor Anton Vanko—built the original battlesuit and battled Iron Man, but defected to work for Tony Stark. Vanko died killing the second Dynamo, Boris Turgenev, who had been sent to assassinate him. Vanko's protégé Alex Nevsky became the third Dynamo until his death at the hands of the KGB. The others all operated as Russian agents, with two exceptions: the eighth (a college student who accidentally activated a prototype suit) and the tenth (a bank robber who bought his suit on the black market). **DW, MF**

CROSSBONES

FIRST APPEARANCE Captain America #360 (October 1989)

STATUS Villain **REAL NAME** Brock Rumlow

OCCUPATION Brock Rumlow **BASE** Mobile

HEIGHT 6 ft 4 in **WEIGHT** 290 lbs **EYES** Brown **HAIR** Brown

SPECIAL POWERS/ABILITIES Brutal hand-to-hand combatant;
highly adept with weapons and explosives, including pistols,
throwing knives, which he keeps in his boots, and wrist blades,
which are hidden in his wrist bands.

As a child, Brock Rumlow idolized the RED SKULL. As the mercenary Crossbones, he and his Skeleton Crew became loyal employees of Adolf Hitler's old confidante, and he repeatedly battled Captain America for his boss. He also has a long history with Captain America's ex-girlfriend, DIAMONDBACK, having hurt her and killed her older brother when she was 15. Crossbones currently works for the Red Skull again and is the lover of the Skull's daughter, SIN. He took part in Captain America's assassination, firing the first shot. Shield arrested him for this, but the Serpent Squad freed him soon after. **AD, MF**

CROSSFIRE

FIRST APPEARANCE Marvel Two-In-One #52 (June 1979)

REAL NAME William Cross

OCCUPATION Ex-CIA agent, criminal **BASE** Mobile

HEIGHT 6 ft **WEIGHT** 190 lbs **EYES** Blue **HAIR** Brown

SPECIAL POWERS/ABILITIES Marksman, spy, deadly hand-to-
hand fighter; left eye replaced by infrared device allowing night
vision; left ear replaced by audio sensor giving super-hearing.

William Cross learned all about espionage, and especially brainwashing techniques, as a CIA agent. Leaving the CIA, and taking the codename Crossfire, he organized an army of mercenaries with the goal of disrupting society and earning himself a hefty profit from the ensuing chaos. When his enemies set off an explosion in Crossfire's headquarters, he lost his left eye and left ear. Replacing these with an enhanced cybernetic eye and ear, Crossfire set about brainwashing costumed heroes. His attempts put him in conflict with the THING, MOON KNIGHT, and HAWKEYE. **MT**

CRYSTAL

FIRST APPEARANCE Fantastic Four #45 (December 1965)

REAL NAME Corystalia Amaquelin Maximoff

OCCUPATION Adventurer **BASE** City of Attilan, variously located
in the Himalayas, on the Moon, and on Attilan Is., Atlantic Ocean

HEIGHT 5 ft 6 in **WEIGHT** 110 lbs **EYES** Green **HAIR** Red

SPECIAL POWERS/ABILITIES Elemental powers enable her to
psionically control fire, air, earth, and water.

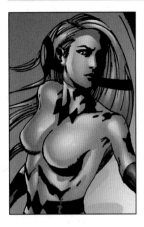

Crystal is an elemental
and a member of the
Royal Family of the
INHUMANS, a
genetically advanced
offshoot of humanity.
She is also the younger
sister of MEDUSA.
While in exile in New
York City, she met and
fell in love with the
HUMAN TORCH and
became a substitute
member of the FANTASTIC FOUR. Crystal
eventually married QUICKSILVER, and they had a
daughter named Luna, but their marriage was
annulled after Quicksilver illegally exposed both
himself and Luna to the power-granting Terrigen
Mists. After the Secret Invasion (see pp. 326-7),
she fled Earth with the rest of the Inhumans and
agreed to marry RONAN THE ACCUSER to cement
an alliance with the KREE. **PS, MF**

CYBELE

FIRST APPEARANCE Eternals #1 (July 1976)

REAL NAME Cybele **OCCUPATION** Goddess

BASE The forests of Colorado **HEIGHT** 5 ft 11 in

WEIGHT 125 lbs **EYES** Blue **HAIR** White-blonde

SPECIAL POWERS/ABILITIES Immortal projects cosmic energy
from hands and eyes; levitates and flies; manipulates minds of
others to render herself invisible.

The wife of Zuras, the ruler of the
ETERNALS, Cybele has lived a life
surprisingly remote from the affairs
of her fellow immortals. Marrying
Zuras in the days before the rise of
the ancient Greek civilization,
Cybele bore his child, Azura (later
known as THENA) and tended to
her upbringing. After Azura came
of age, Cybele withdrew from the
other Eternals. Despite her
formidable powers, she chooses to
live quietly in a forest in Colorado,
where she uses her psionic abilities
to remain invisible to humans, unless
she wishes them to see or hear her. **AD**

CYBER

FIRST APPEARANCE Marvel Comics Presents #85 (August 1991)

REAL NAME Silas Burr **OCCUPATION** Mercenary

BASE Mobile **HEIGHT** 6 ft 4 in **WEIGHT** 365 lbs

EYES Hazel **HAIR** Unrevealed

SPECIAL POWERS/ABILITIES Superhuman strength; mutant
healing; ability to track brain patterns; adamantium-laced skin;
claws containing poisons or hallucinogens; cybernetic eye.

During World War I, Silas Burr served as
the commanding officer of Logan (see
WOLVERINE) in the "Devil's Brigade"
of the Canadian army. Decades later,
he trained Logan's son DAKEN as a
killer but was betrayed by him and
left for dead. ROMULUS had Burr's
skin laced with adamantium and his
hands equipped with adamantium claws. As
Cyber, Burr crossed paths with Wolverine while
on the island of Madripoor. Wolverine slashed
out Cyber's eye, and Cyber ingested a
hallucinogenic drug that drove him insane but
enabled him to track brain patterns over several
miles. Later, sporting a cybernetic replacement
eye, Cyber led a female crime organization
known as Hell's Belles and clashed with X-
FACTOR and EXCALIBUR. He died once, his flesh
consumed by mutant deathwatch beetles, but he
returned in astral form to possess a young
mutant and then hired the TINKERER to enhance
his new body again. He orchestrated a meeting
between Wolverine and Daken, hoping to use
them to find
Romulus, but Daken
double-crossed him
and left him for dead.
DW, MF

Cyber's hatred of Wolverine
spurred him to destroy this
robotic doppelganger with
particular enthusiasm.

⊙ **CYCLOPS** *see opposite page*

CYPHER

FIRST APPEARANCE New Mutants #13 (March 1984)

REAL NAME Douglas Ramsey **OCCUPATION** Student

BASE Professor Xavier's School for Gifted Youngsters

HEIGHT 5 ft 9 in **WEIGHT** 150 lbs **EYES** Blue **HAIR** Blond

SPECIAL POWERS/ABILITIES Cypher possessed a mutant facility
for translating any sort of language, whether human, extraterrestrial,
or even computer code.

Doug Ramsey's interest in computer
programming and games brought him into
contact with Kitty PRYDE, and from there
PROFESSOR X, who realized that Ramsey's ability
to decipher languages was a mutant trait. Both
the NEW MUTANTS and Emma FROST's HELLIONS
tried to recruit Ramsey; he eventually became a
member of the New Mutants after they
requested his aid in communicating with the
newly-arrived alien child called WARLOCK.
Cypher often complained that his gift was not of
great value in a fight with Super Villains, but he
proved his heroism when he sacrificed his life
blocking a bullet
meant for his
teammate,
WOLFSBANE. **TB**

CYCLOPS
Deputy Leader of the X-Men

When Professor X set up his School for Gifted Youngsters, the first mutant he asked to join was Scott Summers. He joined the Professor's team, the X-Men, adopting the codename Cyclops. Cyclops proved Professor X's most trusted X-Man, and quickly became the team's deputy leader and master strategist, displaying great tactical abilities.

Deadly solar energy continually crackles forth from the eyes of Cyclops, controlled only by his visor.

A PERILOUS FLIGHT

Scott Summers was the elder of two sons of Air Force Major Christopher Summers and Katherine Anne Summers. Major Summers decided to fly his family home from a vacation aboard his private plane. But the plane was attacked by a space ship of the alien Shi'ar Empire.

Scott's mother pushed him and his brother Alex out of the burning plane with the one available parachute. Having to share one parachute led the boys to plunge to Earth rapidly. When they hit the ground, both brothers were hurt and hospitalized. Scott struck his head and fell into a coma, which lasted for a year.

Scott suffered brain damage, which would eventually prevent him from controlling his mutant powers (optic blasts) once they emerged. Alex ended up in an orphanage and the boys lost contact for many years. They would be reunited once Alex's mutant powers emerged and he became known as Havok, and eventually joined the X-Men.

Target practice: Cyclops hones his skills by practicing pinpoint control using targets flying through the air.

THE X-MAN

In his mid-teens, Scott developed terrible headaches and eyestrain. Then his mutant powers emerged and he unintentionally released an optic blast that struck a crane at a construction site, endangering people on the street. He then fired another blast which destroyed the falling debris, saving the crowd. Scott fled the scene and fell into an unwilling partnership with a mutant criminal, the Living Diamond.

Cyclops roars with anguish as he holds the dead body of his beloved, Jean Grey, in his arms.

Ruby quartz visor shields optic blasts, which he is unable to "turn off" due to his childhood brain injury.

FACTFILE
REAL NAME
Scott Summers
OCCUPATION
Adventurer, student, radio announcer
BASE
Xavier Institute, Westchester County, New York State; X-Factor Headquarters, New York City

HEIGHT 6 ft 3 in
WEIGHT 175 lbs
EYES Black (red when his optic power is active)
HAIR Brown

FIRST APPEARANCE
X-Men #1 (September 1963)

POWERS

Cyclops has the mutant ability to project ruby-colored beams of concussive force from his eyes. Cyclops' cells constantly absorb sunlight, and he uses that solar energy to create openings from another universe in front of his eyes, and the beams fire from these breaches. Due to a childhood trauma, Cyclops' optic beam is always "on." The only way to block it is by closing his eyes or wearing a special visor or glasses. Cyclops' optic blasts are powerful enough to punch holes through a mountain.

ESSENTIAL STORYLINES
• *X-Men #107* First appearance of Corsair, Cyclops's father (Christopher Summers), whom Scott believed to be dead, but is now a member of the Starjammers, an alien group opposed to Shi'ar tyranny.
• *X-Men #30* Marriage X-men style: after years of romance, Scott Summers finally marries his beloved, Jean Grey.

When Professor X learned about Scott, he rescued him from the Living Diamond and invited him to join his school. Scott loved his teammate Jean Grey but after her death, married her clone, Madelyne Pryor and had a son named Nathan (Cable) with her. After Jean returned and Madelyne died, Scott and Jean were married. With Jean dead once again, Scott is currently dating Emma Frost. Scott as taken over from Professor X and is the sole leader of the X-Men. **MT, MF**

CIVIL WAR
The Battle Between Heroes

When the New Warriors try to capture Nitro, he explodes, killing several hundred people. The government response splits the remaining Super Heroes into a Civil War.

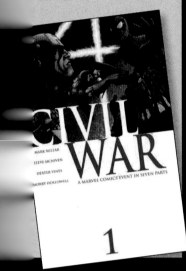

Spider-Man complied with the law, at the urging of Iron Man, and revealed his secret identity to a shocked world.

Having reinvented themselves as the heroes of a reality TV show, the NEW WARRIORS moved in on a house containing four Super Villains: Cobalt Man, Coldheart, NITRO, and SPEEDFREEK. During the ensuing battle, Nitro exploded in the middle of Stamford, Connecticut. The blast killed over six hundred people, including Microbe, Namorita, and Night Thrasher.

REGISTER OR ELSE

The public outcry over the tragedy spurred Congress to pass the Superhuman Registration Act, which required all superpowered people in the US to register with the government—and work for it as part of SHIELD—or face imprisonment. In the wake of M-Day, the public had already been pushing for such safeguards, and the Stamford disaster gave it the impetus it needed to get through.

The new law split the Super Hero community in two. Many of the heroes understood the need for the law and planned to comply with it. Others believed it to be a bad law and planned to fight it.

IRON MAN, MR. FANTASTIC, and Hank Pym led those who backed the law, while CAPTAIN AMERICA refused to help SHIELD and went underground to form a secret Avengers as the core of his resistance movement. As soon as the law went into effect and SHIELD starting rounding up outlaw heroes, the resistance set to freeing them.

Notably, most of the backers of the law already had public identities to begin with, while many of those who protested the law did not. The most famous exception was SPIDER-MAN, who sided with his mentor IRON MAN. After some soul searching, he revealed his secret identity as Peter Parker at a globally televised press conference.

The X-MEN officially declared neutrality during the conflict, which soon became known as the Civil War. Although they sympathized with the resistance, they had been nearly destroyed on M-Day and did not wish to risk making their eradication complete.

In the first major conflict between the two sides, SHIELD unleashed a clone of THOR. The clone killed GIANT-MAN (Bill Foster) and would have harmed others had the INVISIBLE WOMAN not switched sides to protect the resistance. The incident caused heroes on both sides to reconsider their choices. Spider-Man switched to Captain America's team, while NIGHTHAWK and STATURE decided to register.

Desperate to even the sides, Captain America and his heroes launched an attack on the super-prison Mr. Fantastic had built in the Negative Zone. Anticipating this, Iron Man led a team to stop them. CLOAK teleported the entire battle back to Manhattan, and the resistance was winning handily when a group of firefighters, EMTs, and police tackled Captain America to keep him from killing Iron Man.

Looking around at the damage the battle had caused, Captain America realized that his team had won "everything except the argument." He surrendered himself to the NYPD, effectively ending the conflict. In the aftermath, Iron Man became the new director of SHIELD and launched the Fifty State Initiative (*see* pp. 118-9). (*see* pp. 118-9)

At a turning point in the war, a clone of Thor slew Bill Foster, the latest Giant-Man.

After Namorita slammed him into a school bus outside of a playground, Nitro exploded and killed over 600 innocents—including dozens of children—rather than be captured and thrown into jail. This atrocity spurred the passage of the Superhuman Registration Act that launched the Civil War.

The Baxter Building served as a rallying point after the initial tragedy. With Congress about to pass the Superhuman Registration Act, the greatest heroes of the age assembled there to discuss how they should respond.

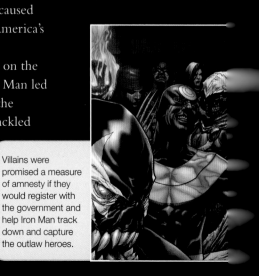

Villains were promised a measure of amnesty if they would register with the government and help Iron Man track down and capture the outlaw heroes.

THE FINAL BATTLE

In the climactic battle of the Civil War, Captain America's resistance faction faced off against Iron Man's government-backed forces. The battle began in the maximum-security prison located in the Negative Zone, called 42 because it was the 42nd idea that Iron Man's team had for improving the world. It spilled out into New York City when Cloak teleported the entire battle back into the regular world. At the climax of the battle, Captain America finally beat Iron Man but he hesitated when he had the chance to deliver the final blow. Gazing out at the destruction around him, he realized how many innocents were

being caught up and harmed in the Civil War, and he gave himself up. Without Captain America, the active resistance crumbled, and the Civil War came to an end.

Soon afterward, while being marched in handcuffs into a federal courthouse, Captain America was assassinated by order of the Red Skull. Later, his old partner Bucky Barnes took up his name and shield and now works with a team of outlaw Avengers to fight crime and save the world while remaining fugitives from justice themselves.

DAREDEVIL
The Man Without Fear

DAREDEVIL

FACTFILE

REAL NAME
Matthew Michael Murdock

OCCUPATION
Lawyer

BASE
Hell's Kitchen, New York City

HEIGHT 5 ft 11 in
WEIGHT 185 lbs
EYES Blue
HAIR Red/Brown

FIRST APPEARANCE
Daredevil #1 (April 1964)

POWERS

Despite his blindness, Daredevil's remaining four senses have been honed to superhuman levels. He also possesses a built-in Radar Sense that allows him to detect the contours of his environment. A trained athlete and acrobat, he carries a billy club that can be converted into a blind man's cane; it also contains a reeled throwing line that allows Daredevil to swing over the rooftops or entangle an enemy.

NOW THAT PLAY TIME'S OVER, I'LL HANG AROUND UNTIL I FIND THE FIXER! AS FOR WHO I AM, YOU CAN JUST CALL ME... DAREDEVIL

When he began his crime-fighting career, Daredevil wore a yellow and red costume similar to that of a wrestler.

Matt Murdock was the only son of professional boxer "Battling" Jack Murdock. But his father, forced to work as a mob leg-breaker in order to supplement his meager income as a prize-fighter, made Matt promise to get a good education, and not become a fighter like himself. As a dedicated student who would never compete in athletics with his fellows, Matt was nicknamed "Daredevil" by his taunting classmates. Not wanting to break his promise to his father, Matt took their insults—but he secretly kept up a rigorous training regimen all by himself.

RADIOACTIVE ACCIDENT

One fateful day, Matt saw a blind pedestrian about to be struck down by a truck. Matt rushed to the old man's aid, knocking him from the path of the vehicle. In the crash that followed, a canister of radioactive material fell from the truck and struck Matt in the face. Despite the best efforts of the doctors, Matt would thereafter be blind.

However Matt discovered that the accident had a second effect on him: all of his remaining senses had been enhanced to a superhuman degree. Additionally, he now possessed a kind of built-in radar sense, which allowed him to detect the contours of his environment and compensated for his lack of sight. Initially overwhelmed by his powers, young Matt sought out the former Ninja master known as STICK, who trained him to control his newfound abilities.

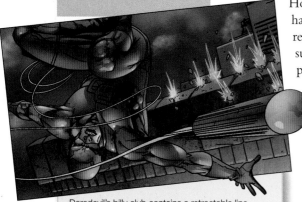

Daredevil's billy club contains a retractable line which allows him to swing from the rooftops.

REVENGE AND THE LAW

When the Fixer told Jack Murdock to throw a fight, Murdock, with his son watching, won. He was gunned down by the Fixer's men shortly after.

In order to track down the men who had murdered his father, Matt Murdock, now a successful lawyer, adopted the identity of Daredevil. After the Fixer had been brought to justice, Matt continued his crime-fighting double life. In recent years, Bullseye murdered Karen Page, the love of Matt's life. Matt later married Milla Donovan, but this fell apart over Matt's continued mourning for Karen. For a while, Matt was exposed to the world as Daredevil, but with the help of IRON FIST—who posed as Daredevil while Matt was in prison—he was able to recover the secret. **TD, MF**

In college, Matt Murdock fell in love with exchange student Elektra Natchios. The two would one day become implacable foes.

ESSENTIAL STORYLINES
• *Daredevil #168*
Daredevil has a reunion with his college sweetheart Elektra, now an assassin for hire.
• *Daredevil #227–232*
The Kingpin methodically tears Matt Murdock's life apart, piece by piece.
• *Daredevil Vol. 2 #32*
Daredevil's true identity as Matt Murdock is revealed to all the world.

DAKEN

FIRST APPEARANCE Wolverine Origins #10 (March 2007)

REAL NAME Daken Akihiro   **OCCUPATION** Assassin, agent

BASE New York City   **HEIGHT** 5 ft 9 in   **WEIGHT** 167 lbs

EYES Blue   **HAIR** Black

SPECIAL POWERS/ABILITIES Mutant healing factor, retractable claws made of bone, superhuman senses, endurance, and reflexes, plus manipulation of others via pheromones.

While attempting to capture WOLVERINE, the WINTER SOLDIER killed his pregnant wife, Itsu. The baby, who would become Daken, was cut from her womb and raised by a Japanese couple as their own. Daken later trained under CYBER and worked for ROMULUS. Daken vowed to kill Wolverine, and the older mutant used this to draw Daken into a trap in which he faked letting DEADPOOL kill him.

After discovering that Romulus had orchestrated Itsu's death, Daken and Wolverine worked together to bring him down. Daken subsequently took over his father's identity as Wolverine to join Norman Osborn's (*see* GREEN GOBLIN) new AVENGERS. **MF**

DAMAGE CONTROL

FIRST APPEARANCE Marvel Comics Presents #19 (June 1989)

BASE Manhattan

MEMBERS

Anne Marie Hoag Director of Operations

Henry Ackerdson V.P. Marketing

Albert Cleary Comptroller

Eugene Strausser Head of R&D

Damage Control, Inc. is an engineering and construction company that specializes in cleaning up and repairing property damage caused by conflicts between Super Heroes and Super Villains. With its headquarters in Manhattan's Flatiron Building, and a warehouse in New Jersey, the company has about 300 employees. It was hired by the AVENGERS to clean up the damage done to their mansion by the MASTERS OF EVIL. After the Baxter Building was destroyed, Damage Control was hired to build the FANTASTIC FOUR's new HQ, Four Freedom's Plaza. **MT**

DANSEN MACABRE

FIRST APPEARANCE Marvel Team-Up #93 (May 1980)

REAL NAME Unknown   **OCCUPATION** Criminal; exotic dancer; second-in-command of Night Shift   **BASE** Los Angeles

HEIGHT 5 ft 10in   **WEIGHT** 135 lbs   **EYES** Blue   **HAIR** Silver

SPECIAL POWERS/ABILITIES Her dancing can hypnotise or even kill; able to evade Spider-Man's telepathic "Spider-Sense."

Dansen Macabre was the high priestess of Kali, a religious cult. When Macabre believed the SHROUD to be a member of a rival cult, she hypnotised SPIDER-MAN into attacking him. Her plan failed and the pair defeated her. Realizing the impossibility of imprisoning Macabre, Spider-Man left her in the Shroud's care. She is now second-in-command of Night Shift, the Shroud's supposed criminal gang, unaware that it is a front for his crimefighting. **AD**

◎ **DAREDEVIL** *see opposite page*

DARK BEAST, THE

FIRST APPEARANCE X-Men Alpha (1994)

REAL NAME Henry P. McCoy   **OCCUPATION** Genetic engineer

BASE Formerly Sinister's slave pens in the "Age of Apocalypse"

HEIGHT 5 ft 11 in   **WEIGHT** 355 lbs   **EYES** Blue

HAIR Formerly brown, now blue-black

SPECIAL POWERS/ABILITIES Possesses superhuman strength, agility and durability. Expert in genetics and biochemistry.

In the alternate future of Earth-295, there was an evil counterpart to the X-Men's BEAST. This "Dark Beast" was the head geneticist for that reality's SINISTER, and experimented on the inmates in his slave pens. When Apocalypse was defeated, the Dark Beast transported himself 20 years into the past of Earth-616, where he met a young Emma FROST and created the Morlocks. At one point, he captured the Beast and impersonated him. He survived M-Day with his powers, and even worked with the Beast for a while on finding a way to restore the world's depowered mutants. **PS, MF**

DARKHAWK

While exploring an old amusement park, Christopher Powell discovered an amulet that was extraterrestrial in origin. It instantly exchanged Chris's body for the Darkhawk android, while simultaneously transferring the teenager's consciousness into the artificial construct. When not being used, the Darkhawk android or Chris's own body rested in a state of suspended animation within a living vessel in deep space. Whenever the Darkhawk body was damaged, the ship instantly surrounded it within a healing pod that immediately restored it to full health.

Chris eventually obtained a new android form with new powers, including the ability to become invisible. Chris eventually merged with the Darkhawk form so he could change directly between the two forms. As Darkhawk, he worked with the New Warriors and the West Coast Avengers, and he later joined the Loners (originally Excelsior), a group for ex-teen heroes. He tried to give up being Darkhawk when he started acting erratically, but could not manage it. He registered with the government during the Civil War and served as the security chief of Project PEGASUS during the Secret Invasion. Recently, an alien named Talon revealed that both he and Darkhawk are part of the Fraternity of Raptors, charged with safeguarding the advance of galactic culture. **MT**

FACTFILE

REAL NAME
Christopher Powell

OCCUPATION
High-school student

BASE
Queens, New York City

HEIGHT 6 ft 1/2 in
WEIGHT 320 lbs
EYES Brown
HAIR Brown

FIRST APPEARANCE
Darkhawk #1 (August 1964)

DARKHAWK

POWERS

Bio-mechanical armored suit possesses enhanced strength, speed, agility and durability. Also possesses a pair of retractable glider wings and a claw-cable on his right hand that can act as a grappling hook. Can also generate defensive force-shields and concussive blasts of dark energy.

DARKSTAR

FIRST APPEARANCE Champions #7 (August 1976)

REAL NAME Laynia Petrovna

OCCUPATION Adventurer   **BASE** Russia

HEIGHT 5 ft 6 in   **WEIGHT** 125 lbs   **EYES** Brown   **HAIR** Blond

SPECIAL POWERS/ABILITIES Darkstar could tap into the extradimensional Darkforce to create solid objects, to teleport herself and others, and to fly.

Born a mutant, Laynia and her brother Nicolai were turned over to Professor Piotr PHOBOS, who was assembling a team of Russian mutants to serve the state. They became Darkstar and VANGUARD. Darkstar was instrumental in defeating Phobos when it emerged the real purpose of his academy was to increase his own power. Darkstar continued her activities in the WINTER GUARD, until she perished with other members of X-CORPS, fighting the villain Weapon XII. Recently, a new Darkstar has been seen working with the latest incarnation of the Winter Guard. **TB, MF**

DEADPOOL

FIRST APPEARANCE New Mutants #98 (February 1991)

REAL NAME Wade Wilson

OCCUPATION Mercenary   **BASE** Mobile

HEIGHT 6 ft 2 in   **WEIGHT** 210 lbs   **EYES** Brown   **HAIR** None

SPECIAL POWERS/ABILITIES Advanced healing abilities, and an expert marksman and hand-to-hand-combatant. Uses a teleportation device to travel instantly from one place to another.

When Wade Wilson was diagnosed with cancer, he allowed the scientists of WEAPON X to try to cure him by attempting to recreate Wolverine's healing ability. The cure worked, but Wilson's skin was left a mangled mess, and Weapon X placed him in a prison lab as a failure. After escaping, Deadpool began his career as a mercenary, battling CABLE and X-FORCE, among others. During the Secret Invasion, he figured out how to kill VERANKE, but Norman Osborn stole the information and used it to make himself a hero. **MT, MF**

DAZZLER

Alison Blaire's father, Carter, was a lawyer and her mother was a jazz singer, who eventually deserted the family. Carter wanted his daughter to follow in his footsteps, but she dreamed of becoming a singer.

Alison's mutant power first manifested itself during a high-school talent show. After graduation she attempted to establish herself professionally and used her powers to create spectacular lighting effects while she sang. Her amazing powers soon helped to make her a star. Although originally Alison had no intention of using her mutant abilities to fight crime, she joined the X-MEN after she was publicly exposed as mutant, and her popularity with the public plummeted. She later met and fell in love with LONGSHOT. After he was reported dead, Alison returned to her singing career. **TD**

Rock singer Dazzler's mutant power creates a spectacular light show to match her dynamic vocals.

FACTFILE

REAL NAME
Alison Blaire

OCCUPATION
Singer, actress

BASE
Mobile

HEIGHT 5 ft 8 in
WEIGHT 115 lbs
EYES Blue
HAIR Blonde

FIRST APPEARANCE
X-Men #130 (February 1980)

DAZZLER

POWERS

Mutant with the ability to convert sonic vibrations into various forms of light, including blinding, colorful, mind-numbing and hypnotic displays, high impact photon blasts, laser beams, holographic illusions and protective force fields.

YOU DID IT!

WE DID IT--TO MAKE THIS WORLD A BETTER PLACE

The loss of her romantic love, Longshot, led Dazzler to return to her first love—music.

DEAN, LAURA

FIRST APPEARANCE Alpha Flight Vol. 1 #53 (December 1987)

REAL NAME Laura Dean   **OCCUPATION** Former adventurer

BASE Formerly Alpha Flight headquarters, Canada

HEIGHT 4 ft 8 in   **WEIGHT** 90 lbs

EYES Brown   **HAIR** Black

SPECIAL POWERS/ABILITIES Possesses psionic ability to open portals into another dimension and also close them.

Darby Dean discovered to his horror that one of his wife's unborn twins was a mutant with an inhuman form, and attempted to kill the child. However, the other unborn twin, Laura, used her own mutant powers to save her sister by transporting her to another dimension, which she would later name "Liveworld." In her teens, Laura used her powers to change places with her twin, known as Goblyn. Hence, whenever Goblyn came to Earth, Laura went to Liveworld. Eventually both twins ended up on Earth simultaneously.

Laura and Goblyn then briefly served as members of Beta Flight, the training team for the ALPHA FLIGHT hero team, and Laura took the code name Pathway. **PS**

Laura and Goblyn's miserable early lives led to Laura calling Earth "Deadworld."

DEATH

FIRST APPEARANCE Captain Marvel Vol. 1 #27 (July 1973)

REAL NAME Not applicable

OCCUPATION Embodies principle of mortality **BASE** Mobile

HEIGHT Varies **WEIGHT** Varies **EYES** Varies **HAIR** Varies

SPECIAL POWERS/ABILITIES Often appears as a cowled skeleton, but has adopted various male and female guises; an arch-manipulator; extent of other powers remains unknown.

Just as the abstract being ETERNITY represents life, so Death is said to symbolise mortality, the pair serving to provide cosmic balance. Although they have been embarked on games of one-upmanship (Death once attempted to manipulate THANOS into destroying the universe) in large part Death works in partnership with Eternity to maintain universal equilibrium. When APOCALYPSE established his Four Horsemen, he recruited a number of people to be Death. Wolverine (pictured right) was the third individual to fill this role. **AD**

DEATHBIRD

FIRST APPEARANCE Ms. Marvel #9 (September 1977)

REAL NAME Cal'syee Neramani **OCCUPATION** Adventurer

BASE Shi'ar Empire **HEIGHT** 5 ft 8 in **WEIGHT** 180 lbs **EYES** White **HAIR** None; black, purple and blue feathers

SPECIAL POWERS/ABILITIES Flight (18 ft wingspan); vast strength and stamina; razor-sharp talons; wrist-bands contain telescopic javelins; has javelins that emit gas or electric charges.

Deathbird was born a mutant into the ruling house of the SHI'AR; her full set of wings were a throwback to her people's avian ancestry. Her younger sister, Lilandra, aided by the X-MEN, assumed the Shi'ar throne before her, and Deathbird launched several coups in her efforts to become Majestrix. She eventually won the throne, but her rule was short-lived. During the Shi'ar war against the alien Phalanx, Deathbird struck up a short-lived romance with the X-Man BISHOP. Deathbird served as War, one of APOCALYPSE's Horsemen. **AD**

DEATHCRY

FIRST APPEARANCE Avengers #363 (June 1993)

REAL NAME Deathcry

OCCUPATION Warrior **BASE** The Shi'ar Empire

HEIGHT 6 ft 2 in **WEIGHT** 196 lbs **EYES** White **HAIR** Purple

SPECIAL POWERS/ABILITIES Deathcry possesses super-acute senses, superhuman reflexes, and natural claws which she can use as weapons.

The young warrior known only as Deathcry was dispatched to the AVENGERS' side by Lilandra, Empress of the Shi'ar, who feared reprisals by the KREE RACE against the Avengers for the role they had played in the Kree-Shi'ar War. On Earth, she helped the Avengers fend off a Kree attack and prevail against other threats. Eventually, feeling that her mission had come to an end, she returned to the Shi'ar Empire. Later, the Kree captured her, releasing her only to help fight the PHALANX. In the course of a misunderstanding, CAPTAIN UNIVERSE accidentally killed her in self-defense. **TB, MF**

DEATHLOK

Luther Manning is not the only man to bear the Deathlok mantle.

Luther Manning was born in an alternate timeline in which multinational corporations had used Operation: Purge to rid the Earth of all Super Heroes. A colonel in that world's US Army, Manning was wounded in battle and later transformed into the cyborg Deathlok by brothers Harlan and Simon Ryker. Although they intended to control him, Deathlok somehow managed to break free. With the help of Godwulf, Deathlok was transported to Earth-616, where Operation: Purge had yet to take place. Working with CAPTAIN AMERICA, Deathlok successfully prevented the program from being carried out.

In the years since, a number of other Deathloks have been created, with Michael Collins and Siege (John Kelly) both acting as brain donors. Although the original Deathlok has traveled to numerous realities, even fighting alongside DAREDEVIL for a time, his life continues to be a lonely one. **AD**

FACTFILE

REAL NAME
Luther Manning

OCCUPATION
Cyborg supersoldier

BASE Mobile

HEIGHT 6 ft 4 in
WEIGHT 395 lbs
EYES Red
HAIR Gray/brown

FIRST APPEARANCE:
Astonishing Tales #25 (August 1974)

POWERS

Cybernetic brain and body parts enable superhuman strength, endurance and reactions; Deathlok's special armaments include a dagger and laser pistol.

DEATH'S HEAD

FIRST APPEARANCE The Transformers #113 (May 1987)
REAL NAME Death's Head
OCCUPATION Bounty hunter   **BASE** New York City
HEIGHT Varies   **WEIGHT** Varies   **EYES** Varies   **HAIR** Varies
SPECIAL POWERS/ABILITIES Superhumanly strong; able to detach limbs and substitute for weapons; controls limbs even when separated from body; jets in feet enable short-range flight.

Death's Head is a cyborg built by techno-mage Lupex as a shell for his mind. Lupex' plan was ruined by his wife, who activated the cyborg's consciousness. Following an encounter with the Time Lord known as the Doctor, he was dumped in the year 8162 of Earth-5555. Since then, he has visited contemporary Earth-616 many times, jumping among times and dimensions. Death's Head II arose from the parts of the original and lived in Earth-8140. The latest version, Death's Head 3.0, sprang from Earth-6216. **AD, MF**

DE LA FONTAINE, CONTESSA

FIRST APPEARANCE Strange Tales #159 (August 1967)
REAL NAME Valentina Allegra de la Fontaine
OCCUPATION Former secret agent   **BASE** Mobile
HEIGHT 5 ft 8 in   **WEIGHT** 196 lbs
EYES Blue   **HAIR** Black with white streak
SPECIAL POWERS/ABILITIES Superb strategist and hand-to-hand combatant; expert with most types of weapons.

During SHIELD training the Contessa caught the eye of Nick Fury by defeating him in hand-to-hand combat. The two became lovers and teammates, working to help SHIELD put down threats from Hydra and AIM. The Contessa later led SHIELD'S Femme Force. At one point, a Skrull posed as the Contessa, but Fury killed her. Years later, during the Secret Invasion, another Skrull replaced the Contessa and attacked Dum Dum Dugan. The real Contessa is now back in service. **DW, MF**

DEMOLITION-MAN

FIRST APPEARANCE The Thing Vol. 1 #28 (October, 1985)
REAL NAME Dennis Dunphy
OCCUPATION Adventurer   **BASE** New York City
HEIGHT 6 ft 3 in   **WEIGHT** 335 lbs   **EYES** Blue   **HAIR** None
SPECIAL POWERS/ABILITIES Enhanced strength and endurance, damage resistance; expert wrestler; trained in hand-to-hand combat by Captain America.

Given superhuman strength by the corrupt Power Broker, Dennis Dunphy became a member of the Unlimited Class Wrestling Federation. There, he befriended the Thing, and later left the UCWF to become Captain America's unofficial partner as the costumed hero D-Man. On a mission to infiltrate the Flag-Smasher's Arctic stronghold, D-Man seemingly died in the explosion of an Avengers' Quinjet. However, D-Man survived among the Inuit for a time, before returning to New York City and becoming protector of the homeless in the subterranean Zerotown. **DW**

DEFENDERS

The Defenders are a loose affiliation of heroes. In fact, the core four Defenders are often at odds with one another, and only band together when there is no other option available. Initially, they allied themselves to face the menace posed by scientist-sorcerer Yandroth. Thereafter, when met by circumstances in which they required assistance, the individual Defenders would often seek each other out. Other heroes, like Hellcat and Valkyrie, have wandered in and out of the team over the years. Under the Fifty State Initiative, a team composed of Blazing Skull, Colossus, Darkhawk, and She-Hulk guarded New Jersey. Once the Initiative disbanded it, it reformed with Krang and Hellstorm in place of Blazing Skull and Colossus. The Grandmaster recently gathered the original team to take on the Red Hulk's Offenders. **TB, MF**

Despite functioning as a "non-team", the Defenders have formed tight bonds.

FACTFILE

KEY MEMBERS
DOCTOR STRANGE
Command of the mystic arts.
NAMOR, THE SUB-MARINER
Superhuman strength and durability; ability to fly; ability to breathe air and also survive beneath the ocean waves.
HULK
Rampaging monster of almost unlimited strength.
SILVER SURFER
Possesses the Power Cosmic, one of the fundamental forces of the universe.

BASE
The Defenders team usually operates out of Doctor Strange's sanctum in Greenwich Village, New York City.

FIRST APPEARANCE
Marvel Feature #1 (December 1971)

DEFENDERS

THE DEFENDERS
1 Namor, the Sub-Mariner   **2** The Hulk
3 The Silver Surfer   **4** Doctor Strange

DESTINY

FIRST APPEARANCE X-Men #141 (January 1981)

REAL NAME Irené Adler

OCCUPATION US government agent **BASE** Washington, D.C.

HEIGHT 5 ft 7 in **WEIGHT** 110 lbs **EYES** Unknown **HAIR** Silver

SPECIAL POWERS/ABILITIES Mutant power to see future allowed her to scan the probability spectrum of alternate futures, then focus on events before they happened.

When MYSTIQUE formed the second BROTHERHOOD OF EVIL MUTANTS, her longtime friend Destiny joined her. When the Brotherhood was renamed FREEDOM FORCE, Destiny accompanied Mystique on its first mission: the capture of MAGNETO. She was killed on a later mission by LEGION, who was possessed by the SHADOW KING at the time. She left behind several diaries with predictions of the future, and several battles were fought over these "Books of Truth" until they were destroyed. **MT, MF**

DIABLO

FIRST APPEARANCE Fantastic Four #30 (September 1964)

REAL NAME Esteban Corazon de Ablo

OCCUPATION Alchemist **BASE** Mobile

HEIGHT 6 ft 3in **WEIGHT** 190 lbs **EYES** Brown **HAIR** Black

SPECIAL POWERS/ABILITIES Alchemical elixir bestows extended life and vitality. Clothing lined with alchemical potions including a sleeping potion and nerve gas; a master of disguise.

Born into the aristocracy in 9th-century Spain, Diablo became fascinated with the alchemical arts. Realizing that time was against him, Diablo sold his soul to the demon MEPHISTO in exchange for knowledge. Developing an elixir of life and moving to Transylvania, Diablo spent the next millennia tyrannising the local villagers, until they rose up, trapping him in a crypt for over a century. Having tricked the THING into freeing him, Diablo clashed with the FANTASTIC FOUR numerous times. Given his persistent vitality he is likely to remain a threat for years to come. **AD**

DIGGER

FIRST APPEARANCE Amazing Spider-Man Vol. 2 #51 (May 2003)

REAL NAME None (a combination of 13 mobsters)

OCCUPATION None **BASE** New York City sewers

HEIGHT 7 ft 1 in **WEIGHT** 275 lbs **EYES** Blue **HAIR** None

SPECIAL POWERS/ABILITIES Gamma-powered strength, but limited endurance; possesses the combined consciousnesses of the Vegas Thirteen, with their various 1950s predelictions.

In 1957, a meeting of 13 mobsters in Las Vegas turned nasty, resulting in the deaths of all of them. The bodies of the gangsters, who became known as the Vegas Thirteen, were secretly buried deep in the Nevada desert—a common resting place for Vegas' gangland casualties.

Many years later, scientists investigating the effects of gamma rays detonated a gamma bomb in the desert near the site of the grave. Somehow, the bomb's gamma radiation fused the 13 dead mobsters into a huge, powerful, green zombie who called himself Digger. Digger followed some old railroad tracks until he reached New York City. He then started on a mission of vengeance against the Forelli mob, who had bumped off the Vegas Thirteen in the first place. SPIDER-MAN, hired by Forelli to investigate, went to Nevada and figured out that Digger was a gamma-mutated version of the Vegas Thirteen. Back in New York, during a long battle with Spider-Man, Digger eventually broke apart and died. **MT**

DEVIL DINOSAUR

FIRST APPEARANCE Devil Dinosaur #1 (April 1978)

REAL NAME Inapplicable **OCCUPATION** Carnivore

BASE A jungle on the otherdimensional planet "Dinosaur World," later the Savage Land

HEIGHT 25 ft **WEIGHT** unknown **EYES** Yellow

SPECIAL POWERS/ABILITIES Has unusually high intelligence for a dinosaur. Possesses superhuman strength and stamina.

DIAMONDBACK

FIRST APPEARANCE Captain America #310 (October 1985)

REAL NAME Rachel Leighton **OCCUPATION** Mercenary

BASE Serpent Citadel **HEIGHT** 5 ft 11 in **WEIGHT** 142 lbs

EYES Green **HAIR** Magenta

SPECIAL POWERS/ABILITIES Expert gymnast; wields diamond-shaped throwing spikes filled with explosives, acid, poison, or drugs.

On an alien world similar to prehistoric Earth, dinosaurs coexisted with primitive, fur-covered human beings. A tribe called the Killer Folk tried to burn to death a creature that resembled one of Earth's tyrannosaurs. The reptile was rescued by a furry primitive known as MOONBOY, but the fire had turned his hide bright red. Moonboy named him Devil Dinosaur, and they became loyal companions, battling various menaces. Later, they were transported to Earth, and joined the superhuman team called the Fallen Angels Eventually they went to live in the primeval Savage Land. **PS**

Diamondback was enlisted into the Serpent Society by SIDEWINDER. On her first mission she had the opportunity to kill CAPTAIN AMERICA but chose not to. Eventually, she became his partner and eventually his lover. Later, Diamondback joined ASP, BLACK MAMBA, and IMPALA to form a mercenary group called B.A.D. Girls, Inc. She had several run-ins with Crossbones, who abused her, murdered her brother Willy, and tried to kill her brother Danny. She is currently a recruit for the Fifty-State Initiative. **MT, MF**

DIRE WRAITHS

FIRST APPEARANCE Rom #1 (December 1979)

BASE Formerly Wraithworld in the Dark Nebula

HEIGHT 5 ft 5 in (average) **WEIGHT** Unrevealed

EYES No pupils **HAIR** Inapplicable

SPECIAL POWERS/ABILITIES Shapeshifters who mimic other living beings. Female Wraiths kill their victims and gain their memories; they also have powers of sorcery.

The Dire Wraiths are offshoots of the SKRULLS who settled on a planet called Wraithworld. Male Wraiths are white-skinned, vaguely humanoid creatures. Female Wraiths have heavier, red bodies, tentacles and clawed feet. Centuries ago, the Wraiths attacked the planet Galador, but were defeated by Galadorian cyborgs called the Spaceknights, including ROM. Rom battled Wraiths on Earth and used his neutralizer to cast Wraithworld into the otherdimensional realm called Limbo. As a result, the Wraiths lost their powers, and Rom exiled them into Limbo as well. **PS**

DOCTOR BONG

FIRST APPEARANCE Howard the Duck #15 (August 1977)

REAL NAME Lester Verde **OCCUPATION** Genetic engineer

BASE An island in the Atlantic Ocean **HEIGHT** 8 ft 8 in

WEIGHT 225 lbs **EYES** Blue **HAIR** Reddish-brown

SPECIAL POWERS/ABILITIES When struck by the large metal ball he wears on his hand, Doctor Bong's helmet can produce sonic waves for a variety of effects.

Having adopted the aphorism "The pen is mightier than the sword" as his motto at an early age, bullied Lester Verde began to strike back at those who tormented him through his writing. Infatuated with Beverly SWITZLER, Lester reinvented himself as Doctor Bong, a melodramatic villain whose exploits were puffed by self-penned press releases. Intent on forcing Switzler to marry him, Bong was undone by Beverly's boyfriend, HOWARD THE DUCK. He has since gone on to be a thorn in the side of the SHE-HULK. **TB**

DOCTOR DEMONICUS

FIRST APPEARANCE Godzilla #4 (December 1977)

REAL NAME Douglas Birely

OCCUPATION Geneticist; criminal **BASE** Pacific Ocean

HEIGHT 5 ft 11 in **WEIGHT** 170 lbs **EYES** Gray **HAIR** Brown

SPECIAL POWERS/ABILITIES A brilliant geneticist who used a radioactive meteor to artificially mutate animals, turning them into monsters to do his bidding; no superpowers.

Geneticist Douglas Birely exposed himself to radiation hoping to acquire superpowers. Instead, he ended up with skin cancer. Embittered, he acquired a radioactive meteor he called the Lifestone, and perfected a process to mutate animals into monsters. As Doctor Demonicus, he recruited an army of criminals and battled SHIELD. He was captured by the West Coast AVENGERS. **MT**

DOC SAMSON

FACTFILE

REAL NAME
Dr. Leonard Samson

OCCUPATION
Psychiatrist

BASE
Mobile

HEIGHT 6 ft 6 in
WEIGHT 380 lbs
EYES Blue
HAIR Green

FIRST APPEARANCE:
Incredible Hulk #141
(July 1971)

POWERS

Gamma-radiation greatly increased Samson's body mass and musculature; he has the equivalent strength of a "relaxed" Hulk, plus great endurance and injury resistance. The gamma rays also turned his hair green. Unlike the Hulk, Samson's razor-sharp mind has been unaffected by the changes in his physiology.

DOC SAMSON

A dedicated psychiatrist, Doctor Leonard Samson was fascinated by gamma radiation's potential to help the mentally ill. When Betty Ross was transformed into a crystalline creature, Samson used a specially developed machine to drain gamma radiation from the HULK and used it to cure Betty. Later, he exposed himself to the rays and gained Hulk-like powers. In the years that followed, Samson has doggedly pursued Bruce Banner, hoping to rid him of the Hulk. He also helped treat several others, including MOLECULE MAN, She-Hulk, RACHEL SUMMERS, and MULTIPLE MAN. He sided with the US government during the Civil War and worked as a therapist at Camp Hammond. He helped the ILLUMINATI send the Hulk into space and fought him when he returned during World War Hulk. Recently, when he tried to inform the President about the true nature of Norman Osborn, he was framed for trying to kill the President instead. **AD, MF**

DOCTOR FAUSTUS

FIRST APPEARANCE Captain America #107 (November 1968)

REAL NAME Johann Fennhoff **OCCUPATION** Psychiatrist, criminal mastermind **BASE** New York City **HEIGHT** 6 ft 6 in

WEIGHT 321 lbs **EYES** Blue **HAIR** Red

SPECIAL POWERS/ABILITIES Expert in brainwashing and mind control.

A master psychiatrist, Doctor Faustus specializes in driving people to the brink of suicide and beyond. He clashed often with CAPTAIN AMERICA, SPIDER-MAN, and THE FANTASTIC FOUR. He also served as the mentor for MOONSTONE, schooling her in the arts of manipulation. Presumed dead for years, he cropped up again, this time allied with the RED SKULL and posing as a SHIELD psychiatrist. In this position, he brainwashed Sharon Carter (see CARTER, SHARON) into killing Captain America. Faustus was later discovered to be holding the Captain America of the 1950s in suspended animation, preparing him to kill the current Captain America. **AD**

DOCTOR DOOM

The Lord of Latveria

Victor Von Doom was born in a gypsy camp in the tiny kingdom of Latveria in the Balkan Mountains of Eastern Europe. Victor's mother, Cynthia, was killed when he was an infant. When Victor was a boy, his father Werner, a gypsy healer, failed to save the wife of a Latverian baron from dying of cancer. With Victor, Werner fled the baron's retaliation, only to perish from exposure. Victor vowed vengeance on the world for his parents' deaths.

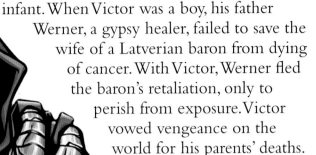

A mysterious order of Tibetan monks helped Doctor Doom forge the metal mask with which he conceals his hideously scarred features.

FACTFILE

REAL NAME
Victor Von Doom

OCCUPATION
Monarch of Latveria

BASE
Doomstadt, Latveria

HEIGHT 6 ft 2 in;
(in armor) 6 ft 7 in
WEIGHT 225 lbs;
(in armor) 415 lbs
EYES Brown
HAIR Brown

FIRST APPEARANCE
Fantastic Four #5
(July 1962)

POWERS

Scientific genius; knowledge of sorcery. Learned from alien Ovoids how to psychically transfer his consciousness into the body of another person. armor is actually a battlesuit that increases his strength to superhuman levels and contains highly advanced weaponry.

SCARRED

Victor discovered Cynthia's chest of magical artifacts and realized that she was a witch. He developed immense talents for sorcery and also science, eventually winning a scholarship for State University in the US. It was there he first encountered fellow student Reed Richards.

Determined to contact his mother in the hereafter, Von Doom invented an interdimensional communication device. Richards happened upon Von Doom's notes on the machine and pointed out an error in his calculations. Furious that Richards had invaded his privacy, Von Doom refused to heed his warning. When Von Doom activated his machine, it exploded, scarring his face. (According to one account the explosion left only one thin scar; however, Doom's ego could not tolerate even a single imperfection in his appearance.)

As king, Doom has brought peace and prosperity to his homeland, Latveria.

Doctor Doom led an army of Super Villains on the Beyonder's Battleworld in the first "Secret War."

THE METAL MASK

Blaming Richards for the accident, Von Doom made his way to Tibet, where an order of monks helped him forge the metal mask and armor that he would wear in his new role as Doctor Doom. Donning the newly cast mask before it had fully cooled, Doom scarred his face for life. Returning to Latveria, Doom overthrew the monarch and made himself king.

Although Latveria appears unchanged since the 19th century, Doom has created technological wonders, including a robot army and a time machine. As monarch of Latveria, Doom has diplomatic immunity that shields him from arrest. However, his plans have often been thwarted by the FANTASTIC FOUR. Doom recently opened Latveria as a home for refugees from the destroyed Atlantis. He also joined the Cabal (see ILLUMINATI) formed by Norman Osborn (see GREEN GOBLIN). **PS, MF**

ESSENTIAL STORYLINES
• *Fantastic Four #5*
Doctor Doom first clashes with the world's greatest team.
• *Fantastic Four Annual #2*
The origin of Doctor Doom.
• *Fantastic Four #39–40*
Doctor Doom battles the Fantastic Four without their powers.
• *Fantastic Four #57–60*
Doom steals the power of the Silver Surfer.
• *Fantastic Four #84–87*
Doctor Doom traps the Fantastic Four in Latveria.

DR. DRUID

FACTFILE

REAL NAME
Dr. Anthony Ludgate Druid

OCCUPATION
Psychiatrist and master of
the occult

BASE Mobile

HEIGHT 6 ft 5 in
WEIGHT 310 lbs
EYES Green
HAIR White

FIRST APPEARANCE
Amazing Adventures Vol. 1 #1
(June 1961)

POWERS

Master of the mystical arts; able to
control his heartbeat, respiration,
bleeding, etc.; can undertake
telepathy, scan thoughts, control
minds of others, and levitate objects.

DOCTOR DRUID

For many years Harvard-educated Dr. Anthony Druid pursued a career as a psychiatrist, while harbouring an interest in all things mystical and occult. Growing older he began to devote more and more time to this area but it was only when called to the side of a dying Tibetan lama that he started to develop his abilities. After Druid survived a number of trials, the lama helped him to realise his latent potential while conferring upon the psychiatrist some of his own powers.

In the years that followed Druid was recruited by NSA agent Jake Curtiss to join his team of Monster Hunters, a team that also included Ulysses BLOODSTONE and the Eternal Makkari (*see* ETERNALS). Following the emergence of Super Heroes like the FANTASTIC FOUR, Druid aligned himself with the AVENGERS, becoming a member and helping to drive the MASTERS OF EVIL from Avengers Mansion.

The final years of Druid's life proved far less fulfilling. Twice he was manipulated into betraying his friends—he was held in the thrall of Terminatrix and later corrupted by his manipulative lover, NEKRA. She eventually killed him, his promising life finally ending in grief. **AD**

A powerful sorcerer, Dr. Druid could
project images of himself.

DR. SPECTRUM

FACTFILE

REAL NAME
Joseph Ledger

OCCUPATION
Squadron Supreme member

BASE
Squadron City

HEIGHT 6 ft
WEIGHT 190 lbs
EYES Brown
HAIR Blond

FIRST APPEARANCE
Avengers Vol. 1 #85
(March 1971)

POWERS

Internalized power prism
permits flight, the discharge of
energy blasts, and the ability to
construct objects of solid energy.

DOCTOR SPECTRUM

On a parallel Earth in another dimension, astronaut Joe Ledger rescued an alien SKRULL who gave him a power prism. Using the prism's energies to become the heroic Doctor Spectrum, Ledger joined the SQUADRON SUPREME. After the defeat of the villainous OVERMIND, the Squadron Supreme repaired the damage to their world by becoming virtual dictators. A second group of heroes known as Nighthawk's Redeemers formed a resistance movement. One of their number, the Black Archer (formerly the GOLDEN ARCHER), shattered Doctor Spectrum's power prism with an arrow, only to watch as its energies became part of Ledger's own body. Doctor Spectrum no longer needs to rely on an outside source for his powers, and his body has been changed to a monochromatic white. **DW**

*Seen here
is Doctor
Spectrum in
an alternate
incarnation.*

Various versions of
Doctor Spectrum, and
other Squadron Supreme
members, exist among
the parallel Earths that
compose the multiverse.

DOCTOR OCTOPUS

Mastermind of mechanical menace

Otto was the son of Torbert and Mary Lavinia Octavius. He was a shy bookworm, but his father, a construction worker, believed that a man was measured by his brute strength. Mary Lavinia wanted Otto to rely on his brains, and when his father was killed in a construction accident, she convinced herself that an early grave was the destiny of all manual laborers.

Doc Ock can use his tentacles simultaneously, with each one performing a different action.

FACTFILE

REAL NAME
Otto Octavius

OCCUPATION
Criminal mastermind, former nuclear scientist

BASE
New York area

HEIGHT 5 ft 9 in
WEIGHT 245 lbs
EYES Brown
HAIR Brown

FIRST APPEARANCE
Amazing Spider-Man #3
(July 1963)

POWERS

Mental control over four electrically powered, 6-ft long, prehensile, titanium steel tentacles that can telescope to 24 ft in length and lift 3 tons; tentacles terminate in three single-jointed pincers that can rotate 360 degrees and grip with a force of 170 lbs per sq. in.

ESSENTIAL STORYLINES

• *Amazing Spider-Man Annual #1* Octopus forms the Sinister Six to kill Spider-Man.
• *Spectacular Spider-Man #221* He appears to be killed by Peter Parker clone Kaine.
• *Amazing Spider-Man #426* Doc Ock is restored to life thanks to his protégée Carolyn Trainer.

Tentacles can operate independently

ARM'S LENGTH

Otto became a scientist specializing in nuclear research and invented a mechanical harness that allowed him to perform dangerous experiments at a distance. He also began dating Mary Alice Anders, a fellow researcher, and even asked her to marry him. Believing that no woman was good enough for her son, Otto's mother forced him to break off the engagement. Shortly afterwards she died of a heart attack while arguing with her son over Mary Alice. Lost in a private world of grief and guilt, Otto caused a laboratory accident: he was bombarded with radiation and his mechanical arms somehow fused with his body.

Ock's tentacles can move at a speed of 90 feet per second and can strike with the force of a jackhammer.

MIND CONTROL

After this accident, Doctor Octopus was misdiagnosed with brain damage. In reality his superior intellect was busily creating new neuro-pathways allowing him to mentally control his metal tentacles. He can now psionically control them even when they have been completely separated from him.

Doctor Octopus, also known as the Master Planner and Master Programmer, first fought and was defeated by SPIDER-MAN shortly after he became a professional criminal. Sometimes as a member of the SINISTER SIX, sometimes on his own he has since battled heroes such as DAREDEVIL, CAPTAIN AMERICA and the FANTASTIC FOUR; however Doc Ock's overriding obsession is to destroy the elusive web-swinger. **TD**

DOCTOR STRANGE
Sorcerer Supreme of Earth's dimension

DOCTOR STRANGE

FACTFILE

REAL NAME
Dr. Stephen Vincent Strange

OCCUPATION
Former surgeon, now Sorcerer
Supreme of Earth's dimension

BASE
177A Bleecker St., Greenwich
Village, Manhattan

HEIGHT 6 ft 2 in
WEIGHT 180 lbs
EYES Grey
HAIR Black; white at temples

FIRST APPEARANCE
Strange Tales #110
(July 1963)

POWERS

Greater mastery of the arts of magic
than anyone else in Earth's
dimension; astral projection and
mental communication. Possesses
various magical paraphernalia,
including cloak of levitation which
enables him to fly, and amulet the
Eye of Agamotto.

According to the original account, Doctor Stephen Strange was a highly successful but arrogant surgeon whose brilliant career was abruptly cut short by an automobile accident. Strange suffered minor nerve damage, which prevented him from holding a scalpel steadily enough to perform surgery. Exhausting his fortune searching in vain for a cure, Strange ended up an alcoholic derelict.

The Ancient One not only instructed Stephen Strange in sorcery, but advised and guided him until his death.

ANCIENT WISDOM

Strange journeyed to Tibet to meet a healer known as the Ancient One. Initially, Strange, a man of science, refused to believe in the magic powers that the Ancient One claimed to have. However, Strange discovered the Ancient One's pupil Baron Mordo intended to murder his master. Mordo cast a spell on Strange that prevented him from uttering a warning to the Ancient One, but otherwise allowed him to speak. Not only did Strange now know that magic was real, but he also recognized the existence of evil and realized that it must be fought. Evading the restrictions of Mordo's spell, Strange asked the Ancient One if he could become his pupil. The Ancient One freed Strange from Mordo's spell, revealed that he was well aware of Mordo's treachery, and accepted Strange as his new apprentice.

SORCERER SUPREME

Upon completing his training, Doctor Strange lived in New York City's Greenwich Village although the general population are unaware of his role or that he has devoted his life to protecting humanity from supernatural menaces from our own world and mystic realms,

Strange has long been associated with the Defenders, including Hellcat, the Hulk, Nighthawk, and the Sub-Mariner.

such as his enemies Mordo, Nightmare and Dormammu. When the Ancient One died, Doctor Strange inherited his role as Sorcerer Supreme of Earth and the dimension in which it exists.

Doctor Strange has allied himself with Earth's leading costumed crimefighters and founded the Defenders, a team that often included the Hulk and Namor. Recently, because of his use of dark magic during the Civil War *(see pp 84-5)*, World War Hulk and the Secret Invasion *(see pp. 326-7)*, Strange lost his position as the Sorcerer Supreme. He is currently hunting for his replacement. **PS MF**

Another version of Strange's origin claims he was injured in a skiing accident.

ESSENTIAL STORYLINES
• *Strange Tales #130–146*
Doctor Strange battles Baron Mordo and Dormammu and first meets Eternity
• *Strange Tales #150–168* Doctor Strange first combats Umar and encounters the Living Tribunal.
• *Doctor Strange (Vol. 2) #1–2, 4–5*
Doctor Strange battles Silver Dagger, dies and is resurrected.

D

DOMINO

FIRST APPEARANCE X-Force #8 (March 1992)
REAL NAME Neena Thurman (many aliases include "Beatrice")
OCCUPATION Covert operative   **BASE** Mobile
HEIGHT 5 ft 8 in   **WEIGHT** 196 lbs   **EYES** Blue   **HAIR** Black
SPECIAL POWERS/ABILITIES Able to influence the laws of probability to shift odds in her favor; weapons expert; her staff fires projectiles; a superb athlete, martial artist, and linguist.

A career mercenary during her early adult life, it was only after being employed as a bodyguard to the genius Milo Thurman that the mutant Domino became drawn into more official circles. She and Milo fell in love, only to be separated when an attack by AIM terrorists forced Milo into deeper cover. Believing that Milo was dead, Domino joined SIX-PACK and became an ally of CABLE. For a while she was impersonated by COPYCAT. Domino has since served with X-FACTOR, worked for the Hong Kong branch of X-Corporation and fought alongside the X-MEN. **AD**

DOMINUS

FIRST APPEARANCE Uncanny X-Men #21 (June 1966)
REAL NAME Dominus   **OCCUPATION** World conqueror
BASE New York City   **HEIGHT** Several stories
WEIGHT Several tons   **EYES** n/a   **HAIR** n/a
SPECIAL POWERS/ABILITIES Supercomputer controlling many minions.

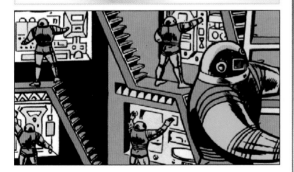

The alien race called the Arcane built Dominus to help them conquer planet after planet. On Earth, the Arcane's agent LUCIFER planned to use Dominus to further the Arcane's plans to take over the planet, although it required a small army of robots to keep it in operating condition. The X-MEN destroyed the robots, rendering Dominus useless. Dominus later gained sentience, took command of the Arcane and, protected by an army of 50 minions, tried again to conquer Earth. The AVENGERS defeated Dominus's forces, and the supercomputer escaped into outer space. **MF**

DONOVAN, MILLA

FIRST APPEARANCE Daredevil #41 (March 2003)
REAL NAME Milla Donovan
OCCUPATION Works for Hell's Kitchen Housing Commission
BASE New York City   **HEIGHT** 5 ft 8 in   **WEIGHT** 130 lbs
EYES White   **HAIR** Black
SPECIAL POWERS/ABILITIES None

Born blind, Milla Donovan never saw the truck barreling down on her when she crossed the street, but DAREDEVIL saved her at the last second. To thank him, she tracked him down as

Matt Murdock and asked him on a date. Their romance led them to be married soon after, but when Milla discovered that Matt might have been suffering from a nervous breakdown following the murder of his previous girlfriend, Karen Page (see PAGE, KAREN), she decided to divorce him.

Driven mad by a fear gas, she is currently a residential patient at the Broadmoor Clinic. **MF**

DORMAMMU

Although a member of the Faltine race, Dormammu has spent most of his life in the Dark Dimension, where his people had banished him. Following his arrival there, Dormammu allied himself to the Dark Dimension's ruler, Olnar, showing him how to expand his realm by absorbing other pocket universes into it. Inadvertently, this was to precipitate Dormammu's rise to power. One of these universes was occupied by the Mindless Ones, destructive beings that, once released in the Dark Dimension, began to wreak havoc. Before they were finally stopped, Olnar was killed and Dormammu had been named regent.

Flames blazing from every limb, Dormammu is a fearsome being.

His appetite for power still not satisfied, Dormammu set his sights on conquering Earth but repeated attempts to invade were repelled by various mystical beings, including the ANCIENT ONE and, later, Dr Stephen STRANGE. Although less powerful than Dormammu, Strange has defeated him on several occasions, even trapping him in a separate pocket universe for a time. Hugely powerful, Dormammu is a difficult creature to destroy altogether. Although quelled at present, he is likely to re-emerge at some point in the future. **AD**

Only Dr. Strange stands in the way of Dormammu's domination of the Dark Dimension and a strike against the Earth itself.

FACTFILE
REAL NAME
Dormammu
OCCUPATION
Sometime ruler of the Dark Dimension
BASE
Dark Dimension

HEIGHT 6 ft 1 in
WEIGHT Unknown
EYES Green
HAIR Black

FIRST APPEARANCE
Strange Tales Vol. 1 #126 (November 1964)

One of the most powerful mystical beings in the universe; can teleport between dimensions, alter his size, travel in time, and perform telepathy.

DORMAMMU

POWERS

DRACULA

The most powerful vampire on Earth

FACTFILE

REAL NAME
Vlad Tepes Dracula

OCCUPATION
Ruler of Earth's vampires

BASE
Castle Dracula, Transylvania;
otherwise mobile

HEIGHT 6 ft 5 in
WEIGHT 220 lbs
EYES Red
HAIR Black

FIRST APPEARANCE
Tomb of Dracula #1 (April 1972)

Drains blood from victims by biting, enabling him to control their wills. Those who die become vampires. Has superhuman strength, virtual immortality, and cannot be killed by conventional means. Transforms into a bat, wolf, or mist. Can mentally control other vampires and mesmerize human beings.

Vlad Tepes Dracula was born in 1430 in Schassberg, Transylvania. The following year his father, the Transylvanian nobleman Vlad Dracul, became prince of nearby Wallachia. Dracula's father was later assassinated by other Transylvanians. Dracula nevertheless went through with the marriage his father had arranged with Zofia, a Hungarian noblewoman. After the birth of their daughter, Dracula put an end to their marriage. Zofia committed suicide; her daughter would become the vampiress LILITH.

THE IMPALER

Dracula regained the throne of Wallachia in 1456, and had those responsible for his father's assassination impaled. He then fought a war with the Turks, during which he impaled huge numbers of them. Hence Dracula became known as "Vlad the Impaler." Dracula married his second wife, Maria, who bore him a son, Vlad Tepelus.

In 1459, Dracula was defeated in battle by the Turkish warlord Turac, who mortally wounded him. Turac took Dracula to the gypsy healer Lianda, who proved to be a vampiress and bit and killed Dracula, transforming him into a vampire. After Turac murdered Maria, Dracula slew him and turned his son Vlad Tepelus over to the care of gypsies. By defeating the vampire Nimrod, Dracula took his place as the ruler of Earth's vampires. The eldest vampire on Earth, Varnae, enhanced Dracula's blood with his own before killing himself. As a result Dracula became the most powerful vampire on the planet.

Dracula's most persistent modern adversaries were (from left to right) the team of Quincy Harker, Frank Drake, Rachel Van Helsing, and Blade.

THE VAMPIRE HUNTERS

In 1890 Dracula employed British solicitor Jonathan Harker to buy Carfax Abbey in England. Moving there, Dracula attacked Harker's fiancée Mina Murray. Vampire hunter Abraham Van Helsing intervened and led the pursuit of Dracula to Transylvania, where Van Helsing's allies impaled the vampire. However, Dracula has repeatedly returned from real or apparent death, and he has continued to menace humanity into the 21st century.

In recent years, Dracula's nemeses were a team led by Jonathan Harker's son, Quincy. Among his allies were Rachel VAN HELSING, Abraham's descendant; Dracula's own descendant FRANK DRAKE; and the vampire hunter BLADE. Quincy HARKER and Rachel Van Helsing have died, but Drake and Blade continue the hunt. Dracula has also battled such adversaries as DOCTOR STRANGE, the vampire detective Hannibal KING, and the monster hunter Elsa BLOODSTONE. **PS**

ESSENTIAL STORYLINES
• *Dracula Lives #2–3* How Count Dracula first became a vampire
• *Tomb of Dracula #45–59* Dracula married Domini and fathers Janus, who rapidly becomes an adult who opposes him.
• *Tomb of Dracula #64–70* Dracula becomes human again. After regaining his powers, Dracula and Quincy Harker die in their final confrontation.

DRAGON MAN

FIRST APPEARANCE Fantastic Four #1 (February 1965)
REAL NAME Dragon Man
OCCUPATION None **BASE** Mobile
HEIGHT 15 ft 3 in **WEIGHT** 3.2 tons **EYES** Gray **HAIR** None
SPECIAL POWERS/ABILITIES Possesses colossal natural strength. He can exhale flame from his mouth, and his gigantic wings enable him to fly.

DRAGON OF THE MOON

FIRST APPEARANCE The New Defenders #143 (May 1985)
REAL NAME Unrevealed **OCCUPATION** Demon
BASE Mobile **HEIGHT** Unknown **WEIGHT** Unknown
EYES Red **SCALES** Dark blue
SPECIAL POWERS/ABILITIES The Dragon is a virtually immortal, demonic entity with god-like powers; able to influence other beings to commit evil deeds.

DRAKE, FRANK

FIRST APPEARANCE Tomb of Dracula Vol. 1 #1 (April 1972)
REAL NAME Frank Drake
OCCUPATION Private Investigator; former vampire hunter
BASE Boston, Massachusetts
HEIGHT 6 ft **WEIGHT** 165 lbs **EYES** Blue **HAIR** Blond
SPECIAL POWERS/ABILITIES Adept at hand-to-hand fighting and a fair marksman.

An artificial lifeform created by Professor Gregson Gilbert of State University and brought to life by DIABLO the alchemist, Dragon Man has the intelligence of a dog. He has been used as a pawn by various Super Villains, including Diablo himself, the wealthy industrialist Gregory Gideon, and MACHINESMITH. But Dragon Man is not evil himself—he operates strictly by animal instinct. On occasion, the FANTASTIC FOUR have attempted to adopt Dragon Man as a pet, but he has proven to be too accidentally destructive to domesticate easily. **TB**

The sole survivor of an ancient race of demons, the Dragon of the Moon seeks to gain power by corrupting the human race. The Dragon once allied with MORDRED, who was trying to overthrow King Arthur PENDRAGON of Britain, but it was defeated and imprisoned within Saturn's moon Titan by the ETERNALS. The Dragon later managed to corrupt THANOS, who murdered most of the population of Titan. It also began to corrupt MOONDRAGON. With the aid of the DEFENDERS, Moondragon was freed and the Dragon destroyed. However, it remains to be seen if the

The Dragon psychically bonded itself to Moondragon.

A distant descendent of DRACULA, Frank Drake's life was dogged by his vampiric ancestor. After frittering his considerable inheritance away, all Drake had left was his family's castle in Transylvania. Traveling there with an aim to selling up, Drake accidentally resurrected Dracula. The following years were marked by a series of battles against the undead fiend. Fighting alongside other vampire hunters, including BLADE, Rachel VAN HELSING and Quincy HARKER, Frank met and lost many good friends and lovers. Exhausted by the fight, he eventually retired from vampire-hunting to become a private eye in Boston. **AD**

DRAX THE DESTROYER

Mentor, the powerful Titanian, had been monitoring the reckless actions of his mad son THANOS on Earth. When Thanos destroyed a car containing Arthur Douglas and his wife and daughter, Mentor took Douglas's daughter Heather, who was still alive, back to Titan to be raised. She would later return to Earth as MOONDRAGON. Then, with the aid of his father, Chronos, Mentor took the living consciousness of Arthur Douglas before it had completely left his body and placed it into a humanoid body he had created from the Earth's soil, granting it superhuman powers. This new being was known as Drax the Destroyer. MENTOR blocked all of Douglas's human memories and instilled in him a single-minded desire to destroy Thanos. Drax clashed with Thanos several times, both of them dying on occasion and being resurrected. Eventually, Drax learned who he was and reunited with Moondragon, and he and his daughter fought alongside each other through the Annihilation events. Today, Drax is part of the new GUARDIANS OF THE GALAXY. **MT, MF**

Drax pauses after his latest session of carnage, plotting the next steps in his all-consuming quest to completely destroy Thanos.

FACTFILE
REAL NAME
Arthur Douglas
OCCUPATION
Former real estate agent; agent of Chronos
BASE
Titan

HEIGHT 6 ft 4 in
WEIGHT 680 lbs
EYES Red
HAIR None

FIRST APPEARANCE
Iron Man #55 (February 1973)

POWERS
Cosmic energy gives him superhuman strength, invulnerability, the ability to fly and make interplanetary voyages in a matter of weeks. He can survive for an indefinite time in outer space without air, food, or water. He fires concussive blasts from his hands.

DRAX THE DESTROYER

DREADKNIGHT

FIRST APPEARANCE Iron Man #101 (August 1977)

REAL NAME Bram Velsing

OCCUPATION Engineer; vengeful vigilante **BASE** Mobile

HEIGHT 5 ft 8 in **WEIGHT** 160 lbs **EYES** Red **HAIR** None

SPECIAL POWERS/ABILITIES High-tech suit of armor protects him from attack. Among his arsenal are a lance containing a number of offensive weapons, and a nerve-gas pistol.

Born in Latveria, Bram Velsing was a skilled engineer, carrying out the schemes of DOCTOR DOOM. As punishment for an act of disobedience, Doom had an iron mask fused to Velsing's face, so that he would know what it meant to be Doom. Fleeing Latveria, Velsing took refuge in the castle of Victor Frankenstein. Calling himself Dreadknight, armed with his own inventions, and riding a winged horse that once belonged to the BLACK KNIGHT, he vowed to take revenge on his former master—no matter how many innocent people got hurt along the way. **TB**

DREADNOUGHT

FIRST APPEARANCE Strange Tales #154 (May 1940)

REAL NAME Dreadnought

OCCUPATION Weapons system **BASE** New York State

HEIGHT 8 ft **WIDTH** 40 in **WEIGHT** 2,200 lbs

SPECIAL POWERS/ABILITIES Portable fusion generator ensures 1.5 years of continuous use; travels at 35 mph; lifts up to 10 tons; armed with flamethrower, knuckle spikes, and electrical field.

A robotic juggernaut, the Dreadnought was built by the terror group HYDRA, but its first field trial proved unsuccessful: directed to kill Nick FURY, the SHIELD director's resourcefulness, combat training and arsenal of miniaturised weaponry combined to overwhelm the automaton. This wasn't the end of the machine, however; when the MAGGIA crime family stole the Dreadnought blueprints, eight more of these machines were built, the most sophisticated being a silver version of the robot. Numerous Super Heroes have contended with these new Dreadnoughts, including IRON MAN, SPIDER-MAN and the FANTASTIC FOUR, and each time the heroes have proved triumphant. **AD**

DREAMQUEEN

Eight hundred years ago, NIGHTMARE, ruler of the dream dimension, captured a succubus called Zhilla Char, mated with her, and then confined her in a pocket dimension. Zhilla Char was consumed by flames giving birth to her daughter, the Dreamqueen. Three hundred and fifty years ago the Native American shaman Nanquato's astral self traveled into the Dreamqueen's realm in search of the sky gods that could save his tribe from drought. Believing the Dreamqueen to be a sky god, Nanquato accepted a totem from her. Through this totem, the Dreamqueen terrified Nanquato's tribe with hallucinations, as a means to escape to Earth. But her plan was thwarted when Nanquato's tribesmen slew the shaman and buried the totem.

In recent years, the mutant Laura DEAN visited the Dreamqueen's dimension, which Dean named "Liveworld." The Canadian Super Hero team ALPHA FLIGHT inadvertently traveled to Liveworld, and when they returned to Earth, the Dreamqueen came with them. However, Alpha Flight's Puck and Laura Dean succeeded in forcing her back to Liveworld. By afflicting Alpha Flight with nightmares, the Dreamqueen escaped to Earth, where she took control of the minds of the people of the Canadian city of Edmonton. But Alpha Flight's sorceress TALISMAN defeated her and drove her from Earth. Still later, the Dreamqueen sided with Alpha Flight against their enemy, the Master. **PS**

FACTFILE

REAL NAME
Unrevealed

OCCUPATION
Ruler of Liveworld

BASE
The dimension of Liveworld

HEIGHT Variable, normally 6 ft 3 in

WEIGHT Variable

EYES White

HAIR Green

FIRST APPEARANCE
Alpha Flight Vol. 1 #57 (April 1988)

POWERS

Wields virtually unlimited magical abilities, including the ability to create living beings, but only when she is in Liveworld. In or out of Liveworld, she can mentally control the minds and the perceptions of other beings, and cause them to experience hallucinations.

DREW, JONATHAN

FIRST APPEARANCE Spider-Woman Vol 1, #1 (April 1978)
REAL NAME Jonathon Drew
OCCUPATION Scientist **BASE** Wundagore City
HEIGHT 6 ft 2 in **WEIGHT** 196 lbs **EYES** Blue **HAIR** Black
SPECIAL POWERS/ABILITIES Brilliant scientist who specializes in radiation and entomology—the study of spiders and insects.

Geneticists Jonathan and Miriam Drew moved to Wundagore Mountain to work with Miles Warren and Dr. Herbert Wyndham. Funded by Hydra, they researched how spiders might be used to enhance human DNA. While pregnant, Miriam was accidentally struck by a laser laced with spider DNA. This affected her unborn daughter, who grew up to be Jessica Drew, the first SPIDER-WOMAN. Jonathan left his wife and daughter and continued his research until Jessica caught up with him years later. MADAME HYDRA killed him when he refused to abandon his research and Jessica. **MF**

DREW, PATIENCE

FIRST APPEARANCE Marvel Fanfare Vol 1, #43 (April 1989)
REAL NAME Unknown
OCCUPATION Pirate Captain **BASE** Sargasso Sea
HEIGHT Unknown **WEIGHT** Unknown **EYES** Blue **HAIR** Black
SPECIAL POWERS/ABILITIES Skilled in the use of sabres, swords and pistols, and other weapons of her time. Possessed the same skills in death.

Patience Drew was a pirate captain who lived several hundred years ago. She and her crew were killed by a British ship which led them into a trap during battle. After they sunk into the Sargasso Sea, they were doomed to experience their deaths forever. NAMOR rescued Drew and her ship on one of these occasions and the pair fell in love. Namor joined Drew as a pirate and she gave him an earring to remember her by. Later, Namor left her ship and never returned—despite still wearing her earring, he found her skeleton on the seabed and was uncertain whether he had ever known her. **ED**

D'SPAYRE

FIRST APPEARANCE Marvel Team-Up Vol. 1 #68 (April 1978)
REAL NAME Unknown **OCCUPATION** Demonic being
BASE Extradimensional tower **HEIGHT** 6 ft 3 in
WEIGHT Unknown **EYES** Black **HAIR** None
SPECIAL POWERS/ABILITIES Enhanced strength; able to levitate; able to instill fear into other beings; various other unrevealed magical abilities.

D'spayre is an extradimensional demon created by another demon, the Dweller-in-Darkness. He feeds off the psychic energy of suffering. D'spayre has teamed with NIGHTMARE, and is attended by a horde of small servant-beings, the D'sprites. One of D'spayre's first clashes with Super Heroes took place in the Florida Everglades, where he was defeated by SPIDER-MAN and MAN-THING. He has since fought CYCLOPS, DOCTOR STRANGE, and served as a member of the Fear Lords, an alliance of demons. **DW**

DUGAN, DUM DUM

FIRST APPEARANCE Sgt Fury and his Howling Commandos #1 (May 1963) **REAL NAME** Timothy Aloysius Cadwallader Dugan **OCCUPATION** Ex-SHIELD agent
BASE New York City **HEIGHT** 6 ft 2 in
WEIGHT 196 lbs **EYES** Blue **HAIR** Black
SPECIAL POWERS/ABILITIES Expert boxer, wrestler, marksman, and commando.

In 1941, while touring Europe as a circus strongman, the Boston-born Dugan met NICK FURY, who was on a covert rescue mission for Britain. Later, the pair became part of Fury's military strike force, the HOWLING COMMANDOS. When Fury was appointed to head SHIELD, Dugan joined him as one of his top operatives. At one point, Dugan retired, but he rejoined SHIELD after HYDRA killed his wife. During the Secret Invasion (see pp. 326-7), a Skrull posing as the Contessa de la Fontaine stabbed Dugan, and another Skrull replaced him. The real Dugan is currently back in action. **MF**

DUSK

FIRST APPEARANCE Slingers #0 (December 1998)
REAL NAME Cassie St. Commons
OCCUPATION Adventurer **BASE** New York City
HEIGHT 5 ft 6 in **WEIGHT** 125 lbs **EYES** Blue **HAIR** Black
SPECIAL POWERS/ABILITIES Receives power from the Negative Zone allowing her to melt into shadows or to teleport; possesses minor psychic abilities.

During a time when SPIDER-MAN was accused of murder, he adopted four separate costumes and identities, including one called Dusk. Later, former World War II hero Black Marvel gave the costumes to four youths to create the Slingers. Cassie St. Commons, a moody Empire State University student from a rich family, became the new Dusk. After what seemed a fatal fall, she returned with the power of teleportation. The Slingers disbanded after saving Black Marvel's soul from MEPHISTO, and Dusk has since kept a low profile. **DW**

EARTH LORD

FIRST APPEARANCE Thor #395 (September 1988)

REAL NAME Kyle Brock   **OCCUPATION** Policeman

BASE New York City   **HEIGHT** (as Brock) 6 ft 1 in; (as Earth Lord) 12 ft 2 in to unknown limit   **WEIGHT** (as Brock) 194 lbs; (as Earth Lord) varies   **EYES** Brown   **HAIR** Brown

SPECIAL POWERS/ABILITIES Draws strength and mass from the Earth. Can increase his size and strength to superhuman levels.

Shot in the line of duty, Officer Brock was rushed to hospital, the same hospital where the god Hogun (see GODS OF ASGARD) was staying. He and two other dying patients attracted the attention of Seth, god of death (see GODS OF HELIOPOLIS), who claimed that Hogun was a threat to the Earth. Seth branded their left palms with the sign of Aton, the disc of the sun, and gave them superhuman powers. Brock and his teammates learned that Seth was the real menace and helped THOR defeat him. Brock returned to the police force, but becomes Earth Lord when necessary. **TD**

EEL

FIRST APPEARANCE Strange Tales #112 (October 1963)

REAL NAME Leopold Stryke   **OCCUPATION** Criminal

BASE New York City   **HEIGHT** 5 ft 10 in   **WEIGHT** 192 lbs

EYES Brown   **HAIR** Brown

SPECIAL POWERS/ABILITIES The Eel's costume contains devices that generate and shoot electrical charges; also contains layer of nearly frictionless synthetic fabric.

Leopold Stryke was the curator of an aquarium who turned to crime as the Eel. After being defeated by THE HUMAN TORCH, he worked as henchman for Mister Fear and COUNT NEFARIA. He later joined his brother Jordan, the VIPER, in the Serpent Squad. Stryke was eventually killed by GLADIATOR. Lavell became the second Eel, battling heroes as well as villains like Hammerhead and MR. HYDE. He was pressed into the Thunderbolt Army for a while, and he later joined Sin's new Serpent Squad. **PS, MF**

ECSTASY

FIRST APPEARANCE Doctor Strange Vol. 1 #74 (December 1985)

REAL NAME Renée Deladier

OCCUPATION Drug kingpin   **BASE** Marseilles, France

HEIGHT 5 ft 9 in   **WEIGHT** 130 lbs   **EYES** Green   **HAIR** Blonde

SPECIAL POWERS/ABILITIES Formerly possessed the ability to project semi-solid tentacles of darkness, or to absorb beings into the Darkforce dimension.

Ecstasy, who can wield tendrils of Darkforce energy, proves more than a match for the light-generating heroine Dagger.

Renée Deladier, who headed up a French cartel distributing the drug ecstasy, adopted the drug's name as her alias. The vigilante CLOAK tried to punish her by absorbing her into the Darkforce dimension, but instead the sentience inhabiting the Darkforce selected Ecstasy to be its new agent, and absorbed Cloak instead, transferring his powers to Ecstasy. DOCTOR STRANGE came to Cloak's assistance, and with the help of the Eye of Agamotto, Cloak was able to defeat Ecstasy and regain his powers. **DW**

EGGHEAD

FACTFILE

REAL NAME
Elihas Starr

OCCUPATION
Criminal; scientist

BASE
New York City

HEIGHT 5 ft 7 in
WEIGHT 210 lbs
EYES Blue
HAIR None

FIRST APPEARANCE Tales to Astonish #38 (December 1962)

POWERS

Egghead created machines to enable communication with ants, powerful robots, and mind-controlling, prosthetic limbs; prone to delusions of grandeur and obsessed with destroying rival Henry Pym.

A brilliant scientist, Elihas Starr—or Egghead as he was known because of his unusually-shaped head—lacked a conscience and was prone to boredom. Seeking extra excitement, Egghead had been working for the US government when he was sacked for stealing and selling secrets.

Coming to the attention of the New York mobs, Egghead was contracted to rid them of the original Ant-Man, otherwise known as Henry PYM. In the years that followed, the pair were to become arch enemies. Egghead's strenuous efforts to destroy Ant-Man involved a range of intriguing devices: he built a machine to communicate with ants and persuaded them to turn against Pym, and on another occasion, he developed a bionic arm designed to control the thoughts of Pym's niece.

Although he appeared fairly harmless, Egghead was responsible for the destruction of an entire Mid-western town, an incident that brought him into direct conflict with the AVENGERS. As time went on, Egghead's schemes became ends in themselves: the more complex and convoluted they were, the happier he seemed to be. Had it not been for a gun exploding in his face, Egghead's schemings would probably have continued. Instead, the accident brought to an end both his life and his latest attempt to destroy Henry Pym's reputation. **AD**

I HAD TO BREAK OUT OF JAIL! I MUST MAKE GIANT-MAN PAY FOR THE INDIGNITY OF BEATING ME --A MAN WHO IS MANY TIMES HIS MENTAL SUPERIOR!!

So much did he hate Harry Pym, nothing would stop Egghead from trying to get revenge—not even the prison bars.

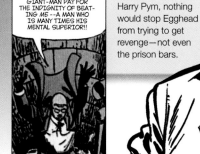

ONCE I COMMUNICATE WITH THE INSECTS, THEY'LL RELAY MY MESSAGE ON TO OTHER! SOON, THERE WON'T BE AN INSECT IN THE COUNTY STILL LOYAL TO THE ANT-MAN!

Motivated by his hatred of Henry Pym, Egghead was inspired to create a device to communicate with ants.

EGO THE LIVING PLANET

FIRST APPEARANCE Thor #132 (September 1966)

REAL NAME Ego

OCCUPATION Not applicable   **BASE** Mobile

DIAMETER 4,165 miles

SPECIAL POWERS/ABILITIES Vast intelligence and psionic powers, including telepathy and telekinesis; travels through space faster than light and can change its surface appearance.

Ego is a self-aware planet, which although formed from the same cosmic gases and dust resulting from the Big Bang as other planets, somehow also grew a huge brain. About the size of a small moon, Ego is from the Black Galaxy. Ego created armies of superhuman warriors from its own substance, which it sent to conquer other worlds. During a battle with GALACTUS, THOR sided with Ego, but later realized Ego's evil intentions and battled it with Galactus, HERCULES, and FIRELORD. Eventually, Ego's size was condensed and contained within the body of the Super Hero QUASAR. **MT**

ELDERS OF THE UNIVERSE

The Elders of the Universe are among the oldest sentient creatures in the universe. Although they do not belong to the same race, they have come to regard one another as brothers. This is because their lifespans date back to the formation of the first primordial galaxies, and because they have each chosen an area of speciality with which to fill their eons-long lives. In this way they manage to overcome the inevitable boredom that would otherwise accompany their virtual immortality.

The exact number of Elders in existence is not known, but several of their number have had dealings with the Super Heroes of Earth, including the GRANDMASTER, the COLLECTOR, the GARDENER, the CONTEMPLATOR, and the CHAMPION.
TB

Each Elder of the Universe has a specialty. The Grandmaster, for example, devotes his time to games of cosmic chance, while the Gardener is obsessed with the growing of beautiful plant life.

ELECTRO

While working as a lineman for an electrical company during a thunderstorm, Max Dillon received a shock that endowed him with superhuman powers. He became the villain Electro. On his first outing, Electro robbed *Daily Bugle* publisher J. Jonah JAMESON, who

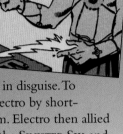

IT'S UNBELIEVABLE! MY BODY KEEPS RECHARGING IT-SELF! I'M LIKE A LIVING ELECTRICAL GENERATOR!!

was sure that Electro was Spider-Man in disguise. To clear his name, Spider-Man defeated Electro by short-circuiting his powers with a water stream. Electro then allied himself with criminal teams, including the SINISTER SIX and the FRIGHTFUL FOUR. This did little to help Electro with his chronic inferiority complex about being a B-list villain at best. Whether alone or with a team, he never seems to triumph. He once attacked the super-prison called the Raft, breaking out dozens of powerful villains, but he fainted when a new version of the Avengers, now including Spider-Man, cornered him. Recently, he joined the Hood's criminal syndicate when it joined in the battle against the Skrulls during the Secret Invasion.
DW, MF

FACTFILE

REAL NAME
Maxwell Dillon

OCCUPATION
Professional criminal

BASE
New York City

HEIGHT 5 ft 11 in
WEIGHT 165 lbs
EYES Blue
HAIR Reddish-brown

FIRST APPEARANCE
Amazing Spider-Man Vol. 1 #9 (February 1964)

POWERS

Electro can store, release, and manipulate electricity to fire electric bolts, travel along power lines, and control machinery.

Electro can transmit so much electricity through the bodies of others that he can literally cook them from the inside out. The upper limit of his powers has never been established.

Mentally unbalanced Electro can shape electricity into whips, tendrils, and nets.

ELEKTRA

Assassin-for-hire

FACTFILE

REAL NAME
Elektra Natchios

OCCUPATION
Mercenary assassin

BASE
Mobile

HEIGHT 5 ft 9 in
WEIGHT 130 lbs
EYES Blue-Black
HAIR Black

FIRST APPEARANCE
Daredevil Vol. 1 #168
(January 1981)

POWERS

Awesome martial arts skills, particularly proficient in Ninjutsu; skilled with martial art weaponry, especially the sai; Olympic-standard gymnast and athlete; limited telepathic abilities and partial control of nervous system.

The histories of so many superpowered individuals are marred by tragedy. While in some cases these tragedies drive them towards heroism others are compelled to pursue careers of villainy. For Elektra Natchios this choice has never been clear-cut—while she continues to yearn for contentment, time and again her happiness has been spoiled by the intervention of others.

From their first encounter, Elektra's fate was bound to Matt Murdock's.

ETCHED BY SADNESS

Even before she was born, misfortune was etched into Elektra's existence: her mother was shot while pregnant and died soon after giving birth. When Elektra's overprotective father became Greek ambassador to the US, she enrolled at Columbia University in New York City, but was followed everywhere by security guards.

Despite this restriction, a romance grew between Elektra and Matt Murdock, a fellow student. For a year, a clandestine relationship flourished, but when her father was killed during a hostage incident Elektra's whole world fell apart. Riven with grief she fled, leaving Matt and the US behind.

Elektra was not the first to be resurrected by the Hand. That fate fell to 16th-century warrior, Eliza Martinez.

Armed with her trademark sai, few have stood against Elektra and survived.

Fatally injured, Elektra crawls to Matt's apartment to die.

KILLER FOR HIRE

Elektra trained as a Ninja and for a year belonged to the Chaste, a Ninja order led by Matt Murdock's own mentor, STICK. Elektra's "impure" heart stopped her joining the Chaste and this rejection drove her to the Chaste's enemy—the HAND, an order of assassins. Elektra abandoned them and became an assassin for hire. This ironically led her back to Matt, now also the crime-fighter DAREDEVIL. Once lovers, they were now opponents but despite this, when Elektra was mortally wounded by BULLSEYE, it was to Matt's door that she crawled and in his arms that she died. Matt refused to believe Elektra was dead and became involved in the Hand's attempt to resurrect her. While Matt failed to prevent her return, his love purified her soul, making her useless to the Hand.

ELEKTRA REBORN

Recently, Elektra appeared to have rejoined the Hand to battle the AVENGERS. However, when she was killed, the Avengers discovered she was a SKRULL imposter—a fact they'd been unable to detect before. This heralded the Secret Invasion (*see* pp. 326–7) during which the original Elektra escaped from the Skrulls and returned to her life. **AD, MF**

KEY STORYLINES

• ***Daredevil #168–9***
Elektra's first encounter with Matt Murdock; her origin is revealed.
• ***Daredevil #174–181***
Elektra fights the Hand with Matt, is recruited by the Kingpin, and dies at the hands of Bullseye.
• ***Daredevil #190*** Elektra is reborn and more about her past is revealed.
• ***Elektra Vol. 2 #11–15***
As her addiction to violence reaches new heights, relatives of Elektra's victims seek revenge.

Following her resurrection, a purified Elektra fought evil, garbed in a white costume.

ELLIS, KENNETH

FIRST APPEARANCE Web of Spider-Man #118 (November 1994)

REAL NAME Kenneth Ellis

OCCUPATION Reporter **BASE** New York City

HEIGHT 5 ft 10 in **WEIGHT** 165 lbs **EYES** Brown **HAIR** Brown

SPECIAL POWERS/ABILITIES Professional journalistic skills; useful talent for coming up with a memorable moniker for a costumed hero or villain, or an eye-catching headline.

Ken Ellis was a reporter for the *Daily Bugle,* a major New York City newspaper published by the redoubtable J. Jonah JAMESON. He has reported on various stories involving the costumed crimefighter SPIDER-MAN.

When Spider-Man's clone, Ben Reilly, adopted his first costumed identity, it was Ellis who named the new crimefighter "The Scarlet Spider" in one of his DAILY BUGLE" articles.

Since this high point in his journalistic career, however, Ellis has become less prominent in the New York newspaper business. **PS**

EMPLATE

FIRST APPEARANCE Generation X #1 (November 1994)

REAL NAME Marius St. Croix

OCCUPATION None **BASE** Mobile

HEIGHT 6 ft 3 in **WEIGHT** Variable **EYES** Red **HAIR** Gray

SPECIAL POWERS/ABILITIES Must consume the marrow of mutants to prevent being pulled into a pocket dimension of untold tortures; absorbs the abilities of each mutant he feeds on for a time.

The sister of Monet St. Croix of GENERATION X, Emplate's mutant power flung him into a pocket dimension, where his physical body was ravaged. Only by feeding on the marrow of the mutant PENANCE was he able to return to our world, albeit encased in a respirator unit he now needed to survive. In order to remain in our dimension, Emplate must constantly renew himself from the marrow of other mutants, and he specifically targeted Generation X after Penance was delivered into their care, allying himself with others who bore the team a similar grudge, such as the New HELLIONS. **TB**

Exiled to a horrific other dimension, Emplate could only remain in our reality by consuming the bone marrow of mutants like himself.

EMPATH

As a member of the mutant team the HELLIONS, Empath studied under EMMA FROST, then the White Queen of the Hellfire Club. He later fell in love with MAGMA of the NEW MUTANTS and used his powers to make her reciprocate. After they broke up, they later worked together for the X-Corporation in Los Angeles. Empath's powers survived M-DAY, but he recently turned up in San Francisco as part of MADELYNE PRYOR's Hellfire Cult **MT, MF**

FACTFILE

REAL NAME
Manuel Alfonso Rodrigo
de la Rocha

OCCUPATION
Student

BASE
Massachusetts Academy,
Snow Valley, Massachusetts

HEIGHT 5 ft 11 in
WEIGHT 160 lbs
EYES Black
HAIR Light Brown

FIRST APPEARANCE
New Mutants #16
(June 1984)

EMPATH

POWERS

Able to manipulate the emotions and feelings of those around him. His powers can be used on one individual or a crowd.

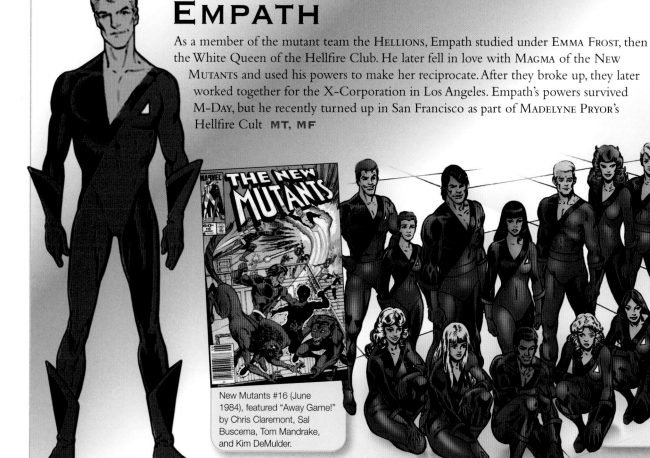

New Mutants #16 (June 1984), featured "Away Game!" by Chris Claremont, Sal Buscema, Tom Mandrake, and Kim DeMulder.

Empath and his fellow Hellions were all students at the White Queen's Massachusetts Academy.

FACTFILE

REAL NAME
Amora

OCCUPATION
Goddess

BASE
Asgard, otherworldly home of
the Norse gods

HEIGHT 6 ft 3 in
WEIGHT 450 lbs
EYES Green
HAIR Blonde

FIRST APPEARANCE
Journey Into Mystery #103
(April 1964)

Possesses the enhanced lifespan,
durability, and might of a goddess
of Asgard. Adept at sorcery,
specializing in spells that enhance
her beauty and allow her to control
the minds and emotions of men.
Her kiss can enslave any man. Able
to fire power bolts from her hands.

ENCHANTRESS

One of the immortals of the Norse realm of Asgard (*see* GODS OF
ASGARD), the Enchantress studied under the master sorceress
Karnilla. Vain and headstrong, she centered her magics on
increasing her allure, so as to more easily ensnare the hearts and
minds of those around her. When her desire for Odin's son Thor
proved unrequited, she turned her mystic powers to evil, hoping
to catch him one way or another. She especially resented Thor's
love of humanity, and longed for him to rule Asgard with her as
his queen. Her feelings for the Thunder God are genuine, and she
has come close to realizing her dream; however Thor's love of
humanity always gets in
the way.

*The Enchantress's
Asgardian body is
three times denser
and heavier than that
of a human being.*

Not only can the Enchantress manipulate magical
energy, but she uses various spells and potions to
exert control over mortal men and other Asgardians.

THE FEMME FATALE

The Enchantress' love of manipulating others to
do her will has resulted in her often teaming up
with Skurge, the grim EXECUTIONER. He was
hopelessly infatuated and would do anything
to please her, and she contemptuously strung
him along. The pair have even tried to
conquer Asgard, and suffered
banishment for their presumption.

The Enchantress has also plied
her trade on Earth as a member of
the MASTERS OF EVIL. She was also
responsible for the creation of the
heroic warrior-woman known as the
Valkyrie, in reality the Enchantress in
disguise. **TB**

ENCLAVE

FIRST APPEARANCE Fantastic Four #66 (September 1967)
BASE Various, including a North Atlantic island
MEMBERS AND POWERS
Maris Morlak Lithuanian Nuclear Physicist
Jerome Hamilton American Medical Biologist
Carlo Zota Spanish Electronics Technician
Wladyslav Shinski Polish Geneticist.

The group of scientists known as
the Enclave believed they could
establish a benevolent world
dictatorship. Faking their deaths,
the Enclave established a base on
a remote North Atlantic island.
They first endeavored to create a
race of superbeings to control the human
race. However, they failed to control the
monsters, the first of which rampaged
through their base, destroying it. Initially
named "Him," this creature eventually came to
be called Adam WARLOCK. The Enclave
embarked on new schemes, such as attempting
to dominate the race known as the INHUMANS
and exploit the aliens' technology. Intervention
by the AVENGERS resulted in two of the Enclave
being imprisoned. Although they later broke out,
nothing has been heard of the Enclave since. **AD**

ENERGIZER

FIRST APPEARANCE Power Pack #1 (August 1984)
REAL NAME Katie Power   **OCCUPATION** Student, adventurer
BASE New York City   **HEIGHT** (age 5) 3 ft 7 in
WEIGHT (age 5) 41 lbs   **EYES** Blue   **HAIR** Strawberry blonde
SPECIAL POWERS/ABILITIES Can disintegrate objects in order to
absorb energy, which she can release as "power balls" of
destructive force—hence her codename.

Katie Power is the youngest child of Dr. James
and Margaret POWER, and the sister of Alex, Jack
and Julie Power. When Katie was five, she and her
siblings met Aelfyre WHITEMANE of the alien
Kymellians. Dying, "Whitey" endowed the
children with superpowers, and they became the
POWER PACK. At times the Pack has exchanged
powers. Katie was Starstreak
when she could fly, and
Counterweight when she
could alter her body
density. **PS**

ENFORCER

FIRST APPEARANCE Ghost Rider Vol. 1 #22 (February 1977)
REAL NAME Charles L. Delazny, Jr. **OCCUPATION** Criminal
BASE Los Angeles, California **HEIGHT** 5 ft 11 in
WEIGHT 180 lbs **EYES** Brown **HAIR** Brown
SPECIAL POWERS/ABILITIES Wears bulletproof costume and
carries automatic pistols; formerly possessed a disintegration
amulet and ring

Son of a movie mogul, Charles
Delazny left college to become the
Enforcer. His primary weapon was
a disintegration device, at times
worn as an amulet or ring. The
Enforcer, often going by the
name of childhood acquaintance
Carson Collier, built up a secret
criminal empire from his father's
Delazny Studios and clashed with
GHOST RIDER and SPIDER-WOMAN.
He was later shot and killed by The
SCOURGES OF THE UNDERWORLD. **DW**

ENFORCERS

FIRST APPEARANCE Amazing Spider-Man #10 (March 1964)
BASE New York City
MEMBERS AND POWERS
Fancy Dan Judo and karate expert—a nice line in suits, too.
Montana Proficient with the lariat. **Ox** Not superstrong but very
strong. **Snake Marston** Entwines body around objects and people.
Hammer Harrison Expert boxer and unarmed combatant.
Big Man Would-be crime lord Frederick Foswell.

The Enforcers can give most Super Heroes a run
for their money. Although they have been
defeated by SPIDER-MAN a number of times, he
has required the help of others to overcome
them, calling on the NYPD, the HUMAN TORCH,
or the reformed SANDMAN. Initially employed by
the BIG MAN, during his bid to control New
York's underworld, the Enforcers have also
worked for the GREEN GOBLIN and the KINGPIN,
until he was overthrown,
forcing them back into
the muscle-for-hire
market. **AD**

ENFORCERS
1 Big Man
2 Ox
3 Montana
4 Fancy Dan

ETERNALS

The Eternal known as Thena is a powerful fighter with a brilliant mind. Like all Eternals she doesn't age or get sick.

A million years ago, the Celestials came
to Earth to experiment on the human
race. They accelerated the evolution of
a few subjects, giving them the
potential to mentally control small
amounts of cosmic energy. These
people became the Eternals, a nearly
immortal race of people who possess
superhuman powers. Subsequent
experiments led to the creation of the
Deviants, who later vied for power
with the Eternals.

Eventually, the Eternals split into two
factions: a benevolent one led by
Kronos, and a warlike one led by
Uranos. After a bitter civil war,
Kronos's side triumphed, and Uranos
and his people were exiled to Saturn's moon Titan.

The Eternals on Earth, led by Kronos's son Zuras, clashed with
the fourth host of the Celestials, when the latter arrived to judge
the Earth and its people. Although Zuras was killed, the Celestials
spared the peoples of Earth and departed. Most of the Eternals
left the planet then as well, leaving but a small group ruled by
Ikaris behind.

Recently, the Eternal named Sprite erased the memories of
all the other Eternals on Earth and placed them in new lives.
They have since steadily gone about the task of regrouping and
remembering their original lives. **MT, MF**

FACTFILE
KEY MEMBERS
KRONOS, MENTOR (Alars),
ZURAS, IKARIS, URANOS,
ARLOK, THENA, SERSI,
MAKKARI, THE FORGOTTEN
ONE, KINGO SUNEN,
SPRITE, CYBELE, PHASTOS,
KHORYPHOS, INTERLOPER,
AJAK, DOMO, VALKIN, DRUIG,
AGINAR, ZARIN, DELPHAN
BROTHERS, SIGMAR, VIRAKO,
VAMPIRO.
BASE
Earth; Titan (moon of Saturn)

FIRST APPEARANCE
Eternals Vol. 1 #1 (July 1976)

All Eternals have superhuman
strength, can levitate themselves or
other objects, can fly (up to 600
mph), create mental illusions, and
project cosmic energy in beams
from their eyes. Some Eternals can
transform an object's shape.

Ancient Earth civilizations such as the Greeks, Romans, and Norse, worshipped the Eternals as gods,
whom they called by names such as Zeus, Hera, and Athena. Those humans believed these gods
resided in great temples in places such as Mount Olympus.

ETERNITY

FIRST APPEARANCE Strange Tales #138 (November 1965)

REAL NAME Inapplicable; (alias) Adam Quadmon

OCCUPATION None; abstract entity **BASE** Inapplicable

HEIGHT Inapplicable **WEIGHT** Inapplicable

EYES Inapplicable **HAIR** Inapplicable

SPECIAL POWERS/ABILITIES Unlimited ability to manipulate time, space, matter, energy or magic for any purpose.

Eternity is the collective consciousness of all life and is dependent on the many trillions of beings within it. It exits everywhere simultaneously. Eternity can take on humanoid form when it deigns to communicate with sorcerers and the like. Eternity once aided DOCTOR STRANGE against DORMAMMU, and Strange then helped Eternity escape NIGHTMARE's clutches. To have a greater understanding of humanity, Eternity has occasionally walked the Earth, using the name Adam Quadmon. **TD**

EXECUTIONER

Battling the Hulk, the Executioner finally met his match.

Born in the Asgardian province of Skornheim, Skurge was the child of a goddess and a Storm Giant. Although ostracized by the Storm Giants for his small height (he was only 7 ft tall), the Skurge became a great warrior. Turning against his father's people, Skurge killed many of them during a bloody war, earning himself the sobriquet "The Executioner." He fell under the ENCHANTRESS' spell, serving her in various bids to dominate Earth and Asgard. In time, Skurge realized she was just toying with him and rejected her. On a mission to the realm of Hela with THOR, Skurge restored his reputation by fighting to free mortal souls from this land of the dead. Skurge died a hero's death, guarding the escape of Thor's forces. **AD**

FACTFILE

REAL NAME
Skurge

OCCUPATION
Giant-killer

BASE
Asgard

HEIGHT 7 ft 2 in
WEIGHT 1100 lbs
EYES Blue
HAIR Black

FIRST APPEARANCE
Journey into Mystery #103 (April 1964)

POWERS

A master of combat. Superhuman strength and stamina; wielded a magical double-bladed axe that can create dimensional rifts enabling time travel and also fired blasts of intense heat or cold; also possessed an unbreakable helmet.

EXCALIBUR

FACTFILE

ORIGINAL MEMBERS
CAPTAIN BRITAIN
Superpowered defender of Earth-616.

SHADOWCAT
Phases through solid objects.

NIGHTCRAWLER
Teleportation.

MEGGAN
Shapeshifter.

PHOENIX
(Rachel Summers-Grey)
Telepathy; telekinesis; projects force bolts.

LOCKHEED
Breathes fire and flies.

BASE
United Kingdom

FIRST APPEARANCE
Excalibur: The Sword is Drawn (1987)

Excalibur missions are bywords for exotic travel to alien worlds and otherworldly dimensions.

Based at Captain Britain's lighthouse, the Excalibur team of heroes was formed following the X-Men's apparent demise at the hands of the Adversary. With a base located not just on the shores of the UK but also at the nexus of several realities, many of their battles have been fought across multiple alternate worlds. For instance, Excalibur confronted its Nazi counterparts the Lightning Force on Earth-597. Excalibur's unity has been undermined by romantic tensions. When NIGHTCRAWLER developed feelings for Captain Britain's lover, MEGGAN, friction grew within the team, culminating in a brawl between the two men. When Captain Britain and Meggan finally married, the original team disbanded. Captain Britain has since reformed the team twice, each time with a new lineup. The latest version disbanded after a climactic battle with MERLYN, but a number of the members recently banded together again under the auspices of MI-13. **AD, MF**

EXCALIBUR
1 Nightcrawler **2** Pete Wisdom **3** Kitty Pryde
4 Meggan **5** Colossus **6** Wolfsbane

FACTFILE

CURRENT MEMBERS

BLINK (leader)
Ability to teleport herself and others.

BEAK
Mutant power of flight.

MIMIC
Can duplicate the powers and abilities of others.

MORPH
Shapeshifting.

SABRETOOTH
Mutant healing factor, enhanced senses, retractable claws.

BASE
Mobile Panoptichron base

FIRST APPEARANCE
Exiles Vol. 1 #1
(August 2001)

EXILES

The Exiles are a group of heroes taken from alternate realities, tasked by the Timebroker with fixing snags in the multiverse of divergent timestreams. They receive guidance on repairing the timestream from a device called the Tallus. The founding Exiles team consisted of otherdimensional versions of Blink, MIMIC, MAGNUS, THUNDERBIRD, NOCTURNE, and MORPH. Later members included variants of GAMBIT, LONGSHOT, MAGIK, MYSTIQUE, PSYLOCKE, Valeria Richards, SABRETOOTH, SAGE, SUNFIRE, and SASQUATCH, plus Spider-Man 2099 and several versions of WOLVERINE. During their dimension hopping, the team faced off against HYPERION and the opposing team WEAPON X, and welcomed NAMORA and Beak to their ranks. The team's lineup has shifted dramatically over the years, and it currently consists of alternate versions of Beast, Black Panther, Blink, FORGE, POLARIS, and SCARLET Witch. **DW, MF**

CHARACTER KEY
1 Morph
2 Sabretooth
3 Beak 4 Sasquatch
5 Mimic 6 Blink

EXODUS

FIRST APPEARANCE X-Factor Vol. 1 #92 (July 1993)
REAL NAME Bennet du Paris
OCCUPATION Supervillain **BASE** Mobile
HEIGHT 5 ft 10 in **WEIGHT** 165 lbs **EYES** White **HAIR** Black
SPECIAL POWERS/ABILITIES Incalculable psionic powers including telepathy, telekinesis, and the ability to fire mental bolts; possesses enhanced strength, near-invulnerability, and flight.

In the 12th-century, crusader Bennet du Paris crossed paths with APOCALYPSE, who placed him in suspended animation when he refused to kill the BLACK KNIGHT. Awakened by MAGNETO in the modern era, du Paris took the name Exodus and joined Magneto's Acolytes. He led the Acolytes until Nate Grey (X-MAN) sealed him in a mountain. He was one of the few mutants to maintain his powers after M-Day. After Professor X was shot, Exodus rebuilt his brain, and he later dueled with him over Magneto's fate. **DW, MF**

EXTERNALS

The Externals, also known as the High Lords, were a small group of superhuman mutants whose lifespans were potentially unlimited. Their aging process was greatly retarded, and they could recover from injuries that would be fatal to normal humans.

Candra exacted payments of "tithes" from the Thieves and Assassins Guilds of New Orleans until GAMBIT stopped her. GIDEON was the owner of Ophrah Industries and a recurring foe of X-FORCE. Selene has lived for thousands of years and became Black Queen of the HELLFIRE CLUB. Most of the Externals proved not to be as immortal as they hoped. Burke and Nicodemus succumbed to the Legacy Virus. Candra perished in an encounter with the X-MEN. Having drained the life forces of Gideon and the others, Selene is the last living External. **PS**

KRAK

KTOOM

Believing Sunspot was another External, Gideon arranged the murder of Sunspot's father. Later, Gideon fought Crule (left) and sent him to capture Cannonball.

Selene as the Black Queen of the Hellfire Club.

FACTFILE

KEY MEMBERS
(all have virtual immortality)

ABSALOM
Caused bone-like spikes to emerge from his skin.

BURKE Precognition.

CANDRA Telekinesis.

CRULE Superhuman strength.

GIDEON Duplicated powers of superhumans.

SELENE Drains life forces from others; telekinetic powers; superhuman strength and speed.

FIRST APPEARANCE
X-Force #10
(May 1992)

One of the oldest known mutants, Selene is also a powerful sorceress.

FALCON

FACTFILE

REAL NAME
Sam "Snap" Wilson

OCCUPATION
Hero and urban planner

BASE
Harlem, New York City

HEIGHT 6 ft 2 in
WEIGHT 240 lbs
EYES Brown
HAIR Black

FIRST APPEARANCE
Captain America #117
(September 1969)

FALCON

POWERS

Falcon has a telepathic link allowing him to see through the eyes of his trained falcon, Redwing. Trained by Captain America, Falcon is skilled in numerous fighting styles, and possesses the agility of a skilled acrobat. Jet-powered glider wings enable him to fly.

When both his parents were murdered, his father trying to stop a street fight, and his mother in a mugging, community volunteer Sam Wilson became so disillusioned he turned to crime. While working for a smuggling gang he crash-landed on Exile Island in the Caribbean and encountered the RED SKULL. In order to realize one of his diabolical schemes, the Skull used a Cosmic Cube to endow Sam with limited superpowers, moulding him to become CAPTAIN AMERICA's ideal sidekick.

After helping the Cap to defeat Red Skull, Sam branded himself the Falcon and entered into a long partnership with the famed supersoldier. A gift of jet-powered wings from BLACK PANTHER enabled him to become Captain America's airborne companion. Wilson moved in and out of the Avengers over the years, but he finally left after the insane Scarlet Witch unbalanced his mind. After recovering, he took some time away from being the Falcon, but he returned to support Captain America's resistance against the Superhuman Registration Act. After Captain America's assassination, he finally registered and was assigned to protect Harlem. **AD, MF**

Captain America's airborne ally, Falcon provides vital air support in the battle against evil.

FENRIS

FIRST APPEARANCE Journey into Mystery #114 (March 1965)
REAL NAME Fenris Wolf
OCCUPATION Predator **BASE** Varinheim
HEIGHT 15 ft **WEIGHT** Unrevealed **EYES** Brown **HAIR** Gray
SPECIAL POWERS/ABILITIES Superhuman strength, speed and durability; razor-sharp claws and teeth; able to transform change into a humanoid god and wield weapons.

Fenris is an immense wolf with human intelligence. Though kept chained by the GODS OF ASGARD, it is prophesied that he will devour Odin at Ragnarok. Fenris was also the name Andrea and Andreas von Strucker took for their terrorist organization. As Citizen V, BARON ZEMO murdered Andrea, and Andreas became the new Swordsman. Andrea returned as a clone and joined the Thunderbolts alongside Andreas, but during the Secret Invasion Bullseye killed her. Norman Osborn murdered Andreas. **PS, MF**

FERAL

FIRST APPEARANCE New Mutants #99 (March 1991)
REAL NAME Maria Callasantos **OCCUPATION** Terrorist
BASE New York City **HEIGHT** 5 ft 9 in **WEIGHT** 110 lbs
EYES Yellow **HAIR** Orange and white
SPECIAL POWERS/ABILITIES Enhanced strength, speed, and agility; superhumanly acute senses, especially her senses of sight and smell.

When Feral's mutant powers emerged, she killed her stepfather and her mother and joined X-Force. When X-Force tried to rescue HENRY GYRICH from the MUTANT LIBERATION FRONT, Feral switched sides. The New York City Police arrested her for the murders of her parents. Later, she joined the X-CORPORATION, along with her sister, Thornn. They both lost their powers on M-Day, and SABRETOOTH killed Feral. **MT, MF**

FIREBIRD

FIRST APPEARANCE Incredible Hulk #265
(November 1982) **REAL NAME** Bonita Juarez
OCCUPATION Social worker **BASE** New Mexico
HEIGHT 5 ft 5 in **WEIGHT** 125 lbs **EYES** Brown **HAIR** Black
SPECIAL POWERS/ABILITIES Firebird can generate a field of flame about herself, a fiery envelope that often manifests itself in the shape of a huge bird; this also enables her to fly.

Bonita Juarez gained her fiery powers when she was struck by a fireball from the heavens. Believing that her powers were from God, Bonita became Firebird, and used her abilities to help the people of her native New Mexico. She became a member of the AVENGERS, though she devoted much time to social work. She learned that the fireball was caused by an alien race, but still maintains that her abilities are god-given. **TB**

FIRELORD

FIRST APPEARANCE Thor Vol. 1 #225 (July 1974)

REAL NAME Pyreus Kril

OCCUPATION Former herald of Galactus **BASE** Mobile

HEIGHT 6 ft 4 in **WEIGHT** 220 lbs **EYES** White **HAIR** yellow

SPECIAL POWERS/ABILITIES Exposure to alien radiation granted Firelord the ability to fly and to understand the language of birds.

Pyreus Kril, an officer of the Xandarian Nova Corps, saw his commander abducted by GALACTUS, devourer of worlds, from aboard the ship *Way-Opener*. Kril's commander became AIR-WALKER, Galactus's herald, seeking out worlds for him to destroy. The loyal Kril followed his trail, eventually becoming Galactus's newest herald following Air-Walker's death. Remade as Firelord, Kril wielded the energies of a miniature sun. Firelord served with Galactus briefly, until THOR offered the Asgardian construct known as the Destroyer (*see* GODS OF ASGARD) to Galactus as a replacement herald. **DW**

FIXER (TECHNO)

FIRST APPEARANCE Strange Tales #141 (February 1966)

REAL NAME Paul Norbert Ebersol

OCCUPATION Adventurer **BASE** New York City

HEIGHT 5 ft 8 in **WEIGHT** 160 lbs **EYES** Brown

HAIR Bald with black goatee

SPECIAL POWERS/ABILITIES Fixer is an engineering genius who sometimes lives in a morphable robot body.

A genius with electronic and mechanical devices, Fixer began his criminal career working with HYDRA. He clashed with many heroes, fighting alongside MENTALLO and Professor Power. Later, he joined BARON ZEMO and THE MASTERS OF EVIL. As part of the original THUNDERBOLTS, Fixer's neck was broken, and he transferred his mind into a robot body. When that was destroyed, he returned to his original body, which was now healed, although it required the use of his tech-pac to keep him from being paralyzed. He joined the Redeemers and lived for a while on Counter-Earth. He has since returned to Earth. **MF**

FLAG-SMASHER

FIRST APPEARANCE Captain America #312 (December 1985)

REAL NAME Unknown

OCCUPATION Terrorist **BASE** Rumekistan

HEIGHT 6 ft 2 in **WEIGHT** 235 lbs **EYES** Brown **HAIR** Brown

SPECIAL POWERS/ABILITIES Skilled at shotokan karate-do; multilingual, can speak Russian, German and Japanese; wields spiked mace, flame-throwing pistol, and tear-gas gun.

When his diplomat father died in a riot, Flag-Smasher committed himself to establishing peace by violent means. Regarding nationalism as the enemy of concord, he initiated a terrorist campaign against symbols of national identity: embassies, national flags and the like. CAPTAIN AMERICA repeatedly defeated him. Forming the terrorist organization ULTIMATUM, Flag-Smasher subsequently took over the country of Rumekistan, but Domino later assassinated him. During the Civil War (see pp. 84–5), a new Flag-Smasher has been spotted, supporting the anti-registration forces. **AD, MF**

FIRESTAR

REAL NAME Angelica Jones

OCCUPATION College student

BASE Manhattan, New York

HEIGHT 5 ft 1 in **WEIGHT** 101 lbs **EYES** Green **HAIR** Red

FIRST APPEARANCE Uncanny X-Men #193 (May 1985)

FIRESTAR

Angelica Jones's mutant powers began to emerge when she was 13 years old. She was soon recruited by the Massachusetts Academy, and she became a member of the HELLIONS. Emma Frost, who was both the school's headmistress and the White Queen of the Inner Circle of the HELLFIRE CLUB at the time, secretly trained Angelica to become an assassin who could kill without detection.

After the Hellions repeatedly clashed with the X-Men and NEW MUTANTS, Angelica decided to leave the school. She joined the NEW WARRIORS and fell in love with Vance "Justice" Astrovik. They briefly became reserve members of the Avengers. Angelica learned that her powers were slowly causing her to become sterile and began to use them more sparingly. She shared her medical problem with the team and Dr. Henry PYM cured her. Justice proposed to her and the couple decided to leave the Avengers to focus on their relationship and education. However, they broke off their engagement soon after. She retained her powers after M-Day, but during the Civil War she retired from being a hero to remain in college. **TD, MF**

When Firestar concentrates, she causes microwaves to swirl around her body. She can project toward a specific target by mentally pushing the waves toward it.

POWERS

Firestar possesses mutant ability to project microwave energy and to generate intense heat. She can propel herself and others through the air by mentally pushing microwave energy behind or beneath herself.

Firestar has learned to focus her microwave energy so that prolonged exposure isn't dangerous to those nearby.

FANTASTIC FOUR

Superheroic planet protectors

FANTASTIC FOUR

FACTFILE

CURRENT MEMBERS

MR. FANTASTIC (Reed Richards) Scientific genius; elastic powers.

INVISIBLE WOMAN (Susan Richards) Can turn her body or any other object invisible; projects invisible force fields.

THE THING (Ben Grimm) Man monster with superhuman strength.

HUMAN TORCH (Johnny Storm) Generates fiery plasma over his entire body and can fly.

ADDITIONAL MEMBERS

CRYSTAL, MEDUSA, SHE-HULK, ANT-MAN (Scott Lang), **LUKE CAGE** (Carl Lucas), **SHARON VENTURE** (Ms. Marvel/She-Thing), **NAMORITA** (Namorita Prentiss)

BASE

The Baxter Building, NYC

FIRST APPEARANCE

Fantastic Four #1
(November 1961)

ALLIES Spider-Man, Namor, The Sub-Mariner, Alicia Masters, Agatha Harkness, Wyatt Wingfoot, Silver Surfer, Lyja (Lyja Storm).

FOES Dr. Doom, Puppet Master, Red Ghost and his Super-Apes, Frightful Four, Galactus.

The Baxter Building was built by Noah Baxter, one of Reed's professors and mentor.

Reed Richards was a scientific genius who dreamed of exploring the stars. His roommate at New York's State University was football star Ben Grimm. Reed shared his dream of building a starship and Grimm, who wanted to become a pilot, promised to fly it. Grimm subsequently joined the US Air Force and became a test pilot and astronaut. Meanwhile, using his own family's fortune as well as money from the government, Richards built a starship.

COSMIC RAYS

When the government threatened to withdraw its funding, Richards decided to take his prototype ship on a test flight with Grimm at the helm. Richards' fiancée Susan Storm and her teenage brother Johnny came along for the ride. Soon after takeoff, a solar flare bombarded the ship with an unknown form of cosmic radiation that mutated their bodies and gave them fantastic powers. Richards became MR. FANTASTIC, Susan Storm became INVISIBLE WOMAN, Ben Grimm became the THING, and Johnny Storm became the HUMAN TORCH.

IF YOU WANT TO FLY TO THE STARS, THEN *YOU* PILOT THE SHIP! COUNT ME OUT!

YOU *KNOW* WE HAVEN'T DONE ENOUGH RESEARCH INTO THE EFFECT OF COSMIC RAYS! THEY MIGHT KILL US ALL OUT IN SPACE!

Fearing that Reed's ship didn't have sufficient shields, Ben tried to talk the others out of flying.

NO CHARGE

Pledging to use their new powers for the good of mankind, the four adventurers formed a legal corporation. The Fantastic Four safeguards the planet from human and extraterrestrial super-menaces, and also specializes in pure scientific research and explorations into the unknown. Funded by the patents on inventions and scientific discoveries made by Richards, the team offers its services without charge.

On their first public mission, the Fantastic Four prevented the MOLE MAN conquering the world. They later stopped the SKRULLS invading Earth and the MIRACLE MAN from blackmailing New York City. They were also responsible for the return of Prince NAMOR, the Sub-Mariner: the Human Torch found him living like a tramp in the Bowery slums and helped restore his lost

I AIN'T BEN ANYMORE-- I'M WHAT SUSAN CALLED ME-- THE THING!!

AND I'LL CALL MYSELF... MISTER FANTASTIC!!

The Fantastic Four have vowed to safeguard Earth.

memory. The FF also uncovered the menace of DOCTOR DOOM and made first contact with UATU THE WATCHER and the mysterious INHUMANS. They blocked Galactus from consuming the Earth and discovered the area of sub-space known as the Negative Zone. The team also battled the FRIGHTFUL FOUR, the OVERMIND, the SPHINX and aided the Planet Xandar against a Skrull invasion.

ALTERNATE WORLDS

After a prolonged engagement, Reed Richards married Susan Storm and she gave birth to their son Franklin. Soon afterward, Richards' scientist father Nathaniel switched young Franklin with his alternate-world teenage counterpart in an effort to help the team battle Hyperstorm, a menace they were destined to face in the future. Richards and Doctor Doom were later transported into a possible alternate future where the son of Franklin had conquered the universe.

A few months later, Franklin somehow created a pocket universe called Counter Earth, where he transported his

ISSUE #1

After being exposed to cosmic rays, the Fantastic Four kept a low profile and didn't reveal their powers to the public until giant monsters began attacking atomic research facilities.

THE FANTASTIC FOUR
1 The Thing **2** Mr. Fantastic
3 Invisible Girl **4** Human Torch

BASES AND EQUIPMENT

The team established its first headquarters on the top five floors of the Baxter Building in Manhattan, New York City. Although this building was later destroyed, Richards designed another base that was constructed in outer space by his former mentor Noah Baxter. The new Baxter Building is equipped with a state-of-the-art security system that is regularly upgraded. Roberta, the Fantastic Four's robot receptionist, is networked with the team's main computer and can undertake hundreds of tasks simultaneously.

Richards has also designed many different types of Fantasti-cars for easy travel around Manhattan (they're easy to park). Each team member is equipped with a wireless communications link, and an emergency flare gun. The FF also have a Pogo-Plane that is outfitted with vertical take off and landing capabilities, a captured Skrull starship that they use for galactic travel and a time platform and space/time sled that allow them to visit alternate time eras or dimensions. The team's costumes are composed of unstable molecules that are specifically designed to adjust to their individual powers.

Roberta is able to operate 24 hours a day and can answer various calls simultaneously.

ESSENTIAL STORYLINES

• *Greatest Villains of the Fantastic Four (tpb)* The FF battle Psycho-Man, Blastarr, Annihilus, Puppet Master, the Mad Thinker, and Doctor Doom.
• *Fantastic Four: Monsters Unleashed (tpb)* The Hulk, Ghost Rider, Wolverine and Spider-Man help the FF battle the Mole Man and the Skrulls.
• *Fantastic Four: Nobody Gets Out Alive (tpb)* The FF travel through time and various alternate dimensions on a hunt for the missing and presumed dead Reed Richards.
• *Fantastic Four: Unthinkable (tpb)* Dr. Doom attempts to use black magic as well as Reed and Sue's own children as weapons against the FF.
• *Fantastic Four: Authoritative Action (tpb)* To the world's horror and outrage, the FF seize control of Latveria after Doom is apparently destroyed.

parents to protect them from a psychic monster called ONSLAUGHT. The FF later returned and soon faced another reality-altering cosmic entity called Abraxas. Shortly after they defeated him, the Invisible Woman gave birth to a daughter, named Valeria.

CHANGING THE WORLD

The Fantastic Four have been embroiled in every major event on Earth over the past several years. Reed supported the Superhuman Registration Act, although he lost the backing of every other member of the team. When the Civil War (*see* pp. 84–5) ended, he and Sue reunited and left the team for a while to re-examine their marriage. During the Secret Invasion (*see* pp. 326–7) the Skrulls captured Reed and Sue and sent the others, including Franklin and Valeria, into the Negative Zone. They all survived and were reunited, but the experience inspired Reed to start exploring alternate universes.

TD, MF

The team have traveled into space and alternate dimensions.

FLUX

FIRST APPEARANCE Incredible Hulk #17 (August 2000)
REAL NAME Benjamin Tibbetts
OCCUPATION US Army private   **BASE** Washington, DC
HEIGHT Variable   **WEIGHT** Variable   **EYES** Green   **HAIR** Green
SPECIAL POWERS/ABILITIES Exposure to gamma radiation and experimentation by the military gave Flux superhuman strength and durability; however his physiology is in a constant state of change.

Benny Tibbetts enlisted in the US army to fight in the Gulf War and was caught in the blast of gamma bombs dropped by a black-ops team headed by General RYKER. Tibbetts survived, but like the HULK before him, was forever changed by the gamma radiation. His self-doubts prevented his powers from permanently catalyzing, and as Flux his body stayed in a constant state of transformation. General Ryker sent him to fight the Hulk twice, but he lost each time. Later, AIM captured him, and Grey of the GAMMA CORPS killed him on General Ryker's orders. **TB, MF**

General Ryker hoped that his creation Flux would defeat the Hulk, but Flux had too many mental insecurities.

FOOLKILLER

Paralyzed from the waist down, Ross Everbest's childhood was never going to be easy; then his parents were killed in the Korean War. However, when traveling revivalist preacher Reverend Mike Pike used faith-healing to restore his legs Everbest's life changed. Joining Pike on the road, Everbest became increasingly angry with the "immoral fools" he encountered every day.

Foolkiller had a calling card warning victims that they had 24 hours to live and telling them to use the time wisely.

Vowing to rid the world of sinners and dissidents, he became Foolkiller, his murder spree beginning when he discovered Pike indulging in a drunken orgy. Everbest's psychotic reign of death ended when he was killed during a confrontation with the MAN-THING. However, his example was to inspire two more Foolkillers: Greg Salinger, who was eventually locked up in a mental institution; and Kurt Gerhardt, still at large in Albuquerque, New Mexico. **AD**

FACTFILE
REAL NAME
Ross G. Everbest
OCCUPATION
Killer
BASE
Mobile

HEIGHT 6 ft
WEIGHT 185 lbs
EYES Blue
HAIR Blond

FIRST APPEARANCE
Man-Thing #3
(March 1974)

FOOLKILLER

POWERS

Psychopathic energy gave him greater strength and endurance than an average man of his weight; possessed a raygun, he termed his "purification gun," capable of disintegrating victims.

FORCE WORKS

FACTFILE
MEMBERS AND POWERS
CENTURY
Composite being of 100 alien warriors.
IRON MAN
Powered armor; flight; energy blasts.
MOONRAKER
Emits electrical energy from hands.
SCARLET WITCH
Chaos magic.
SPIDER-WOMAN
Various spider powers; spins webs of psionic energy.
US AGENT
Enhanced strength, expert combatant.
WONDER MAN
Body composed of ionic energy.
BASE
The Works, Ventura, California

FIRST APPEARANCE
Force Works Vol. 1 #1
(July 1994)

FORCE WORKS

After the disbanding of the Avengers West Coast, Tony Stark (IRON MAN) founded Force Works to be a team with a more aggressive, proactive stance. By using the SCARLET WITCH's hex powers, combined with data from a predictive supercomputer, the members of Force Works set out to squash budding threats before they could escalate to crisis levels.

On Force Works' first mission, WONDER MAN seemingly died while battling a band of Kree warriors. The team bounced back from this loss by welcoming the alien CENTURY into their ranks. Soon, the events known as the Crossing caused Iron Man to appear to turn traitor, behaving irrationally and murderously due to the mind-controlling IMMORTUS. A new hero named Moonraker (claiming to be LIBRA) joining the group to distract them from Immortus's larger schemes. Force Works dissolved following the Crossing episode. **DW**

FORCE WORKS
1 Spider-Woman (Julia Carpenter) **2** Wonder Man
3 Iron Man **4** Scarlet Witch **5** US Agent

FORGE

The Native American who became known as Forge was not only trained in mystic arts by Naze, a shaman in his Cheyenne tribe, but was also a mutant, with the ability to invent highly-sophisticated mechanical devices.

Forge lost a leg and a hand during the Vietnam War and designed mechanical limbs to replace them. When industrialist Anthony Stark (see Iron Man) stopped making advanced weaponry for the federal government, the US Defense Department began buying new weaponry designs from Forge. During that time, he created a device that could detect hidden aliens and one that neutralized mutant powers.

Forge later joined the X-Men, with whom he rid the world of the threats of the alien Dire Wraiths and the demonic Adversary, and he subsequently worked with X-Factor. During his time with the X-Men he had a relationship with Storm.

He is currently recuperating from being shot by Bishop, who was hunting for the first mutant child born after M-Day. **MT, MF**

Forge shares a tender moment with Mystique, despite his deep feelings for Storm.

FACTFILE

REAL NAME
Unknown
OCCUPATION
Inventor, former soldier
BASE
Dallas, Texas

HEIGHT 6 ft
WEIGHT 180 lbs
EYES Brown
HAIR Black

FIRST APPEARANCE
X-Men #184
(August 1984)

POWERS

Mutant ability gives superhuman talent for inventing mechanical devices. While even the greatest inventors must work out the principals and designs of their inventions, the ideas for Forge's inventions spring fully formed from his mutant mind.

FORGOTTEN ONE, THE

FIRST APPEARANCE Eternals #13 (July 1977)
REAL NAME Unknown; has been known as Gilgamesh
OCCUPATION Adventurer; agent of the Celestials **BASE** Mobile
HEIGHT 6 ft 5 in **WEIGHT** 269 lbs **EYES** Brown **HAIR** Black
SPECIAL POWERS/ABILITIES Superhuman strength and stamina; immortality; full mental control over body; ability to manipulate matter on a subatomic scale.

As an Eternal known throughout the years as Hero or Gilgamesh, the immortal Forgotten One has lived for millennia. For meddling in the affairs of humanity, he was confined to the city of Olympia for centuries, only regaining his freedom after helping foil an attack by the Deviants: grotesque, distant cousins of humanity. As Gilgamesh, he served with the Avengers, but he was killed during a battle with Immortus. Reborn later in a new body, he could not recall his former life. He was working in a circus in Brazil when Ajak found him and restored his lost memories. **AD, MF**

FRANKENSTEIN'S MONSTER

FIRST APPEARANCE X-Men #40 (January 1968)
REAL NAME None
OCCUPATION Caretaker, wanderer **BASE** Baveria, Germany
HEIGHT 8 ft **WEIGHT** 325 lbs **EYES** Brown **HAIR** Brown
SPECIAL POWERS/ABILITIES The Monster possesses superhuman strength and stamina; able to go into suspended animation when exposed to intense cold.

In the late 18th century, Victor Frankenstein created a living humanoid creature from different corpses. Abandoned by his creator, the Monster learned to speak, and forced Frankenstein to create a mate for him. After Frankenstein killed her, the Monster slew Frankenstein's own bride. The Monster pursued his creator to the Arctic, where Frankenstein perished. The Monster was revived in 1898 and again in modern times. As "Adam," the Monster assisted monster hunter Elsa Bloodstone. **PS**

FREEDOM FORCE

FIRST APPEARANCE Uncanny X-Men Vol. 1 #199 (Nov. 1985)
BASE Washington DC **MEMBERS AND POWERS Mystique** (leader), shapeshifter [4]; **Avalanche**, groundquakes [7]; **Blob**, immovable; **Crimson Commando**, expert combatant [6]; **Destiny** (deceased), precognition [3]; **Pyro** (deceased), controls fire [5]; **Spider Woman**, spider powers; **Spiral**, spellcaster [2]; **Stonewall**, superstrength [1]; **Super Sabre** (deceased), superspeed
[Dazzler [8] is not a member]

Freedom Force was an incarnation of the Brotherhood of Evil Mutants, formed to wipe out mutant threats to America. The team clashed with outlaw mutants such as the X-Men and X-Factor. The Force later teamed with the X-Men to save Dallas, Texas, from the Adversary, but the group disbanded after a disastrous mission to the Middle East. An all-new Freedom Force team was formed for Montana as part of the Fifty-State Initiative. It included the Challenger, Cloud 9, Spinner, Think Tank, and Equinox. **DW, MF**

FRIGHTFUL FOUR

The WIZARD (Bentley Wittman) was a much-lauded scientist until the similarly brilliant Mr. FANTASTIC (Reed Richards) led the FANTASTIC FOUR into the limelight and forced him from the public eye. Insanely jealous, the Wizard committed himself to destroying Reed and his friends, by establishing the Frightful Four team of Super Villains. The original lineup was Wizard himself, SANDMAN, TRAPSTER, and MEDUSA.

The Wizard has changed his team's roster many times, but it has continued to suffer defeats. Even when they took the Fantastic Four off guard—during Reed and Sue Storm's engagement party, for example—the Wizard's team was still beaten. The search for new members led the Wizard to look everywhere, even advertising in the *Daily Bugle*.

More recently, the Frightful Four's lineup has come to resemble a family—albeit a dysfunctional one—with the Wizard's ex-wife, Salamandra, and their daughter, Cole, signing up for duty.

Perhaps now the team will finally defeat its sworn enemies, the Fantastic Four. **AD**

FRIGHTFUL FOUR
1 Wizard
2 Hydro-Man
3 Trapster
4 Salamandra

Eugene's father designed a pair of electrically-powered leaping coils. Calling himself Leapfrog, he took to crime to support his family, but ended up in jail. To redeem his father's name, Eugene donned one of his old costumes to become the crime fighter Frog-Man, helping SPIDER-MAN and the HUMAN TORCH defeat the SPEED DEMON. Eugene later tried to team up with the Toad and Spider-Kid (now called the Steel Spider). A Skrull posing as Frog-Man joined the Action Pack, the Kentucky team of the Fifty-State Initiative (*see* pp. 118-9). During the Secret Invasion (*see* pp. 326-7), the Skrull died, and Eugene was rescued. **TD,MF**

FROST, EMMA

Emma was the chair of the Massachusetts Academy's board of trustees.

Emma Frost was born into a wealthy New England family. Gifted with a superb business brain, at a remarkably young age she was running a multi-billion-dollar corporation specializing in transportation and electronics, which she re-named Frost International. Her great wealth, intelligence, and charisma soon attracted the attention of the HELLFIRE CLUB, an elite social organization of powerful politicians and businessmen and women. She joined, becoming a close associate of Sebastian SHAW, who, like her, was also a mutant. When Frost and Shaw discovered a plot by Hellfire Club leader Edward Buckman to build massive SENTINEL robots to hunt down and destroy mutants, they seized control of the organization, renaming it the Inner Circle, and taking the codenames Black King and White Queen.

In her role as the White Queen, Frost was at first an enemy of the X-Men. However, guilt over her inability to prevent the violent deaths of her former students, the HELLIONS, caused her to offer the Massachusetts Academy, the private school she had headed, to the X-men's leader PROFESSOR X, who turned it into his new School for Gifted Youngsters. Emma Frost now teaches there, instructing the young mutants of GENERATION X to develop and control their various mutant abilities. **MT**

FURY, NICK
Agent of SHIELD

Nick Fury grew up on the mean streets of Hell's Kitchen in New York during the Great Depression of the 1930s. Recruited by "Happy" Sam Sawyer, who would serve as his commanding officer for most of the war, Fury enlisted in the US Army at the outbreak of World War II, eventually becoming the Sergeant in command of the Howling Commandos, an elite unit of Able Company given the most dangerous missions.

FACTFILE

REAL NAME
Nicholas Joseph Fury
OCCUPATION
Spymaster, director of SHIELD
BASE
SHIELD mobile Helicarrier

HEIGHT 6 ft 1 in
WEIGHT 225 lbs
EYES Brown
HAIR Brown, graying at temples

FIRST APPEARANCE
Sgt. Fury and His Howling
Commandos #1
(May 1963)

Once a gung-ho Sergeant during World War II, Fury is now Director of SHIELD.

INFINITY FORMULA

Fury and his Howlers raked up an impressive string of victories over the AXIS forces, defeating such foes as BARON VON STRUCKER and his Blitzkreig Squad, and even the legendary RED SKULL himself. Wounded at the end of the war, Fury was injected with an experimental Infinity Formula by Professor Berthold Sternberg. The formula allowed Fury to survive what would have otherwise been fatal injuries (though he did eventually lose his left eye as a result of this injury), but the drawback was that Fury would need to ingest a yearly dosage to survive. On the plus side, the formula greatly extended Fury's natural lifespan—and for decades, Professor Sternberg blackmailed Fury for great sums in order to provide the necessary supply of the drug. After the War, Fury became an operative of the OSS, and then the CIA, earning the rank of Colonel.

As Director for the Strategic Hazard Intervention Espionage Logistics Directorate, Fury has access to the most state-of-the-art weapons and technologies on the planet.

POWERS

Nick Fury is a trained soldier with decades of experience. His youth and vigor have been maintained, despite his age, by the rejuvenating Infinity Formula. He is an expert martial artist and highly trained in the use of all kinds of weapons, both conventional and advanced.

THE PEACEKEEPER

When Super Heroes began to appear, the CIA employed Fury as a liaison between them and the government. Fury was later recruited to head up SHIELD, a worldwide peacekeeping force. SHIELD's first mission was to destroy the terrorist cartel HYDRA, which had been founded by Fury's old nemesis, Baron Von Strucker.

GIT **READY**, YOU CLOWNS THAT TIN DOOR AIN'T GONNA HOLD 'EM BACK FOR LONG!

Fury's inner circle at SHIELD includes surviving members of the Howling Commandos.

When Latveria retaliated for a failed coup attempt led by Fury, he lost his position as the head of SHIELD. On the run, Fury learned of the SKRULL infiltration of Earth and assembled his own fighting force. After helping foil the Secret Invasion (*see* pp. 326-7), he learned that HYDRA had actually founded and still controlled SHIELD. He and his Secret Warriors now work to destroy HYDRA. **MT, MF**

Resourceful, cool, courageous, and committed to the cause, Fury is a superb field agent, and a brilliant leader.

FIFTY-STATE INITIATIVE

Super Heroes for All of America

FACTFILE

CURRENT MEMBERS
ANT-MAN (Eric O'Grady) Can shrink or grow to dramatic sizes.
GAUNTLET Drill sergeant with an alien superweapon.
MUTANT ZERO (Typhoid Mary) Telekinesis, telepathy, and pyrokinesis.
TASKMASTER Martial arts expert with photographic reflexes.
TRAUMA Telepath and shapeshifter.
BARON VON BLITZSCHLAG Scientific genius and electricity control.

ADDITIONAL MEMBERS
ARMORY, CLOUD 9, HARDBALL, MICHAEL VAN PATRICK, and many others.

BASE
Camp Hammond, Stamford, Connecticut
FIRST APPEARANCE
Civil War: The Initiative #1 (April, 2007))

ALLIES The Dark Avengers.

FOES The New Avengers.

After the passage of the Superhuman Registration Act, Tony Stark (IRON MAN) realized that SHIELD needed a plan for how to make use of all of the Super Heroes soon to be under its remit. During the Civil War (*see* pp. 84-5), he, MR. FANTASTIC, and Hank PYM brainstormed a long list of ideas for how to improve the world. The Fifty State Initiative was number 41 on that list.

HEROES UNITED AND DEPLOYED

To get the Initiative started, Stark funded a superteam of his own: the ORDER. This team was ready to see action in the final battle of the Civil War. When Stark was made the director of SHIELD after the Civil War, he had the power to build a Super Hero team for each state in the nation, based on that prototype.

Many of the initial teams were simply existing teams or heroes brought into the new structure. The GREAT LAKE AVENGERS, for example, were renamed the Great Lakes Initiative and assigned to their home state of Wisconsin, while HELLCAT was sent to Alaska to serve as its hero.

Gauntlet—the drill sergeant at Camp Hammond—greets the first busload of trainees as they arrive.

As the new leader of SHIELD, Tony Stark considers how to best organize the heroes available to him.

HERO BOOT CAMP

Many new heroes joined the Initiative, and these required training to make the best use of their powers and reduce the danger they presented to others. To this end, Stark set up Camp Hammond as the Initiative's headquarters and training facility. Sergeant Joe Green (GAUNTLET) served as the base's drill instructor under administrator Henry Peter GYRICH with Hank Pym as the chief administrator, and Baron Werner Von Blitzschlag in charge of the science division. Gyrich formed a black ops team answerable only to himself, called the Shadow Initiative. Members included Bengal, Constrictor, the Scarlet Spiders, Trauma, and Mutant Zero (TYPHOID MARY).

Stark formed the Order as a template for the Initiative. The California team was the first generated specifically for the program.

EARLY TROUBLES

In the first combat training session, a terrified ARMORY fired the Tactigon wildly and killed fellow recruit Michael Van PATRICK. The following cover-up came back to haunt the Initiative when Von Blitzschlag fitted a clone of Van Patrick with the Tactigon, causing him to become psychotic and go on a murderous rampage.

Initiative recruits helped during World War Hulk (*see* pp. 152–5) and the Secret Invasion (*see* pp. 326–7). In the confusion surrounding the Hulk's attack, SLAPSTICK beat Gauntlet into a coma for berating the New Warriors, of which Slapstick had once been a member. Gauntlet later recovered.

SHIELD scientists developed Super-Power-Inhibiting Nanobots (SPIN) technology that could be used to remove superpowers. HYDRA leader Senator WOODMAN persuaded Initiative recruit HARDBALL to steal this for him. Later, when Woodman blackmailed Hardball into continuing to work for him, Hardball killed him, left the Initiative, and took over the leadership of HYDRA instead.

THE SKRULL INFILTRATION

Before the Secret Invasion, the SKRULL Queen VERANKE made sure to insert a Skrull into every team in all 50 states. When the Skrulls launched their attack, many of the spies revealed themselves, and the rest of the Initiative's members could not tell who to trust. Using 3-D MAN's powers, TRIATHLON managed to spot most of them located at Camp Hammond, but few other teams were so lucky.

In the aftermath, DOC SAMSON held group therapy sessions for those people who were kidnapped and replaced by Skrulls. However, the Skrull who had impersonated Hank Pym for his entire time with the Initiative reactivated the clone of THOR that had killed GIANT-MAN during the Civil War (*see* pp. 84–5). After helping to stop the clone's rampage, the members of an underground team called Counter Force—made up of former NEW WARRIORS—revealed to reporters the scandal behind MVP's death and the subsequent cover-up. When Norman Osborn (GREEN GOBLIN), became director of HAMMER he took the opportunity to shut down Camp Hammond. He then secretly placed TASKMASTER and the HOOD in charge so that they could use the base to create new forces for Osborn's Dark Avengers team. **MF**

The Thunderbolts were brought into the Initiative.

When the Civil War ended, Stark faced a flood of registered heroes to choose from for the Initiative's teams.

GALACTUS
Devourer of Worlds

FACTFILE

GALACTUS

REAL NAME
Galen

OCCUPATION
Consumer of planets

BASE
Mobile

HEIGHT 26 ft 9 in
WEIGHT 18.2 tons
EYES Unknown; to humanoids appear white
HAIR Unknown; appears black to humanoids

FIRST APPEARANCE
Fantastic Four #48
(March 1966)

POWERS

Manipulates vast cosmic power; can restructure matter and deliver a planet-shattering energy blast; able to teleport across the galaxy and create force fields; travels the galaxy in a worldship the size of the solar system; also pilots a smaller, circular "shuttle."

In the last universe's final moments, Galactus awaited his death.

Older than the universe itself, the only survivor of the universe that came before our own, Galactus's fate is inextricably bound up with that of the entire cosmos. Although at times he has been a force for good, far more often he has brought doom, destroying whole peoples and consuming entire worlds, for his hunger for energy is insatiable; without it, he would cease to exist.

GALEN OF TAA

Born Galen, on the paradise world of Taa, Galactus was fated to live in the last days of his universe, just as it was entering the final stages of the Big Crunch. Realizing that his people were doomed, he persuaded them to pilot a vessel into the heart of the Crunch, to die in one last act of heroism. His people perished, but Galactus was somehow saved by the Phoenix Force of his universe.

For billions of years he slept, and when he awoke it was with an immense hunger that could only be sated by consuming the life-energies of a world. At first he searched for uninhabited worlds but his hunger gradually forced him to consume planets populated by sentient races. Galactus's conscience was only eased by a prophecy that he would ultimately make good on the devastation he wrought.

As the centuries passed, countless worlds crumbled before Galactus's devouring might.

GALACTUS'S HERALD

During a search for food, Galactus came upon the planet Zenn-La. To save his homeworld, Norrin Radd agreed to become Galactus's herald and to search out new planetary fodder. Transformed into the SILVER SURFER, Radd's emotions were subdued so he would be willing to identify inhabited worlds for Galactus. However the Surfer's conscience was reawakened when Galactus turned his attentions to Earth. With the FANTASTIC FOUR, the Surfer drove his master away.

At one point, Galactus was killed, but he was later resurrected to help prevent Abraxas from destroying the entire multiverse. Recently, Galactus was held in the galactic prison Kyln, but DRAX THE DESTROYER broke him out so that he could stop the Annihilation Wave (*see* pp. 30-1). **AD, MF**

A being of immense power and size, only the very brave or foolish would stand against Galactus.

ESSENTIAL STORYLINES

• *Fantastic Four #48–50*
Galactus discovers the Earth and, for the very first time in his immortal life, experiences defeat.

• *Silver Surfer Vol. 1 #1*
Galactus's first meeting with Norrin Radd, soon to become the Silver Surfer, is detailed.

• *Galactus the Devourer #1–6*
Galactus is seemingly destroyed by the combined efforts of the Avengers, Fantastic Four, and the Shi'ar Empire.

GAEA

FIRST APPEARANCE Doctor Strange #6 (February 1975)
REAL NAME Gaea   **OCCUPATION** Goddess   **BASE** Earth
HEIGHT Variable   **WEIGHT** Variable   **EYES** Blue   **HAIR** Black
SPECIAL POWERS/ABILITIES Possesses enormous mystical energies tied to the Earth; commands the forces of nature, such as storms and volcanic activity; power to heal and make things grow; telekinetic abilities; able to bestow magical powers.

Gaea is the embodiment of the spirit of life, growth, harvest and renewal on Earth. One of the foremost of the Elder Gods who ruled the world when mankind was not yet a glimmer, Gaea was the only one not to devolve into a demon, feeding on the spirits of others to survive. Instead, she became literally Mother Earth, and oversaw the growth of all living things. With Odin (see GODS OF ASGARD), Gaea conceived THOR, who is both of Asgard and of Earth, and the champion of both realms. **TB**

🎯 **GALACTUS** *see opposite page*

GAMORA

FIRST APPEARANCE Strange Tales Vol. 1 #180 (June 1975)
REAL NAME Gamora
OCCUPATION Former assassin; member of the Infinity Watch
BASE Mobile
HEIGHT 6 ft   **WEIGHT** 170 lbs   **EYES** Green   **HAIR** Black
SPECIAL POWERS/ABILITIES Expert gymnast and martial artist; proficient with all known weapons.

Gamora is the sole survivor of the Zen-Whoberi, an alien race wiped out by MAGUS and his Universal Church of Truth. The mad Titan THANOS rescued Gamora as an infant and trained her to become the deadliest assassin in the galaxy. Thanos killed her after a failed rebellion, and Adam WARLOCK absorbed her spirit into his soul-gem. She returned in a new form, and guarded the Time Gem as a member of the Infinity Watch. **DW**

GARDENER

FIRST APPEARANCE Marvel Team-Up #55 (March 1977)
REAL NAME Ord Zyonyz
OCCUPATION Botanist   **BASE** The known universe
HEIGHT 7 ft 1 in   **WEIGHT** 390 lbs   **EYES** Purple   **HAIR** Gray
SPECIAL POWERS/ABILITIES Almost immortal, but not quite; Soul-Gem worn on forehead enables travel between worlds and to other dimensions; Soul-Gem also accelerates growth of plants.

One of the ELDERS OF THE UNIVERSE, the Gardener belonged to one of the first sentient species to roam the cosmos. Dedicating his life to horticulture, the Gardener spent his days collecting new seeds and cultivating barren worlds. The Gardener's fate was bound up with the two Soul-Gems that he used to travel between worlds and to accelerate plant growth. Abandoning the first Soul-Gem after using it in battle with the STRANGER, the Gardener fought the DEATH-worshipping ETERNAL THANOS to retain his second gem, but the battle resulted in his death. **AD**

GAMBIT

The mutant Gambit was abducted soon after his birth by members of the Thieves' Guild of New Orleans. Hoping to make peace between the Thieves' Guild and their rivals, the Assassins' Guild, Remy married the granddaughter of the Assassins' Guild's leader. Her brother Julien was opposed to the union, and Remy killed him in a duel. Banished from New Orleans, Remy became the international master thief known as Gambit. Gambit was employed by SINISTER to organize the MARAUDERS, a mutant team of assassins, but he was shocked when Sinister sent the Marauders to massacre the MORLOCKS.

Later, Gambit met and aided STORM, who had been turned into a child at the time. Storm later sponsored Gambit's membership in the X-Men. He has had a longstanding love affair with his X-Men teammate ROGUE. Gambit later served as one of Apocalypse's Horsemen— Death—and even rejoined the Marauders. He helped save the first mutant baby born after M-DAY and has currently rejoined the X-Men to help find Rogue. **PS, MF**

Gambit and Rogue's relationship had its explosive side: here, she nimbly avoids Gambit's "energy charge card."

More fiery fallings-out as Rogue gives Gambit a taste of his own medicine—an energy blast that knocks him off his feet.

FACTFILE

REAL NAME
Isaac Christians

OCCUPATION
Caretaker

BASE
The estate of Daimon Hellstrom

HEIGHT 5 ft 10 in
WEIGHT 204 lbs
EYES Red
HAIR None

FIRST APPEARANCE
Defenders #94
(April 1981)

POWERS

Possesses the increased strength and mystic durability of one of the demon race. He can also levitate, fly and project bolts of eldritch force from his hands; leathery skin is bulletproof; impervious to disease and to aging.

GARGOYLE

In order to secure economic prosperity for his impoverished town, elderly Isaac Christians made a pact with a demonic group called the Six-Fingered Hand. He allowed his essence to be transplanted into the body of a demon, while the demon's mind would reside within his own human body. This demon had formerly been trapped in stone form as a gargoyle, as seen on ancient churches throughout Europe.

Isaac Christians made a deal with infernal forces that saw his soul cast into the body of a demon.

Despite his grotesque appearance, the Gargoyle was not truly evil, and after the destruction of his human body, he rebelled against the Six-Fingered Hand and came to be affiliated with the DEFENDERS. When that team disbanded, Christians tagged along with HELLCAT and her husband Daimon Hellstrom, eventually becoming the caretaker of Hellstrom's estate.

The Gargoyle should not be confused with a similarly-named Soviet agent (real name: Yuri Topolov) who attempted to capture the Hulk on the eve of the latter's creation and was the father of the GREMLIN. **TB**

While inhabiting the body of a demon, the Gargoyle retains the essence of an elderly human. His mind and characteristics remain those of a human retiree.

GAROKK

FIRST APPEARANCE Astonishing Tales #2 (October 1970)
REAL NAME Unrevealed **OCCUPATION** Sailor, wanderer, god
BASE The Savage Land **HEIGHT** 7 ft **WEIGHT** 355 lbs
EYES (as human) Brown; (as Garokk) Yellow
HAIR (as human) Brown; (as Garokk) Virtually none
SPECIAL POWERS/ABILITIES Can project heat, light, and concussive force from his eyes. Possesses virtual immortality.

Godlike wrath: Garokk the immortal Petrified Man lets fly with his powerful eye beams.

Some time in the 15th century, a British sailor from HMS *Drake* became stranded in the Savage Land. Immersion in a pool of mysterious liquid rendered the sailor virtually immortal. He wandered the world for centuries, and his body took on a gray, rock-like appearance, as if he were a "petrified man."

In recent times, the Petrified Man returned to the Savage Land, where he was worshipped by the Sun People as the incarnation of their god Garokk. As Garokk he regards himself as the guardian of the Savage Land, although his insanity and "offensive capability" makes him a thoroughly unpredictable menace. **PS**

GATEWAY

FIRST APPEARANCE Uncanny X-Men Vol. 1 #227 (March 1988)
REAL NAME Unrevealed
OCCUPATION None known **BASE** Australia
HEIGHT 4 ft 6 in **WEIGHT** 80 lbs **EYES** Brown
HAIR Gray-black
SPECIAL POWERS/ABILITIES Ability to open teleportation doorways, transdimensional clairvoyant

The mysterious, silent Gateway is an Australian aborigine with the mutant ability to open teleportation doorways. The outlaw REAVERS forced Gateway to assist them in their crimes by threatening to destroy an aborigine sacred site. The X-MEN later evicted the Reavers, operating from their headquarters for a time, and Gateway became an unofficial member. Gateway has a special connection to the GENERATION X member M, and is an ancestor of the X-Man called Bishop. **DW**

GATHERERS

FACTFILE

MAIN MEMBERS AND POWERS

PROCTOR
Teleportation; mind control.

CASSANDRA
Telepath; strategist.

MAGDALENE
Wields power lance.

SLOTH
Superstrong; razor-sharp claws.

SWORDSMAN
Sword fires energy beam.

FIRST APPEARANCE
Avengers #355
(October 1992)

The Gatherers serve PROCTOR, an extra-dimensional being. Each member of the Gatherers comes from an alternate Earth in another dimension. On each of their Earths, the Gatherers were AVENGERS. Also, on each of their Earths, Sersi, a member of the ETERNALS, went mad and killed everyone. The Gatherers were each the last survivors of their home worlds. They were recruited by Proctor to destroy SERSI and the Avengers of Earth-616. But in order for the Gatherers to exist on Earth-616, they had to each kill their own counterpart on Earth-616. This process was known as "gathering." The Gatherers infiltrated the Avengers' mansion on Earth-616 several times. In the final battle, Proctor tried to destroy all realities, but THUNDERSTRIKE hit Proctor with a bolt of lightning, and all the Gatherers collapsed. **MT**

THE GATHERERS
1 Cassandra
2 Magdalene
3 Swordsman
4 Sloth

GENESIS

GENESIS

FIRST APPEARANCE Cable #18 (December 1994)
REAL NAME Tyler Dayspring
OCCUPATION Would-be conqueror; arms-dealer **BASE** Mobile
HEIGHT 6 ft 1 in **WEIGHT** 191 lbs **EYES** Blue **HAIR** Blond
SPECIAL POWERS/ABILITIES Mutant ability to create solid holograms from the memories of another person; trained in military tactics and combat techniques; wears armored suit.

The adopted son of CABLE in a future world ruled by APOCALYPSE, Tyler Dayspring was brainwashed by Cable's twisted clone STRYFE into becoming his father's enemy. Tyler traveled to the present, intent on ensuring that Apocalypse's rise to power would take place, and on avenging himself on Cable. He operated at first under the alias of a rogue arms dealer named Tolliver, but then abandoned that identity for direct action as Genesis. However, when Genesis attempted to restore WOLVERINE's lost adamantium to his skeleton, the pain-crazed mutant slew him. **TB**

GAUNTLET

GAUNTLET

FIRST APPEARANCE She-Hulk #100 (January 2006)
REAL NAME Joseph Green **OCCUPATION** Super Hero trainer
BASE Camp Hammond, Stamford, Connecticut **HEIGHT** 5 ft 11 in
WEIGHT 210 lbs **EYES** Brown **HAIR** Black
SPECIAL POWERS/ABILITIES Has an alien gauntlet on his right hand. It can project a powerful hand composed of pure energy.

When two aliens battling in space crashed in the Sudanese desert, the US Army sent a team of soldiers to investigate. They attempted to recover the dead aliens' weaponry, only to clash with agents of HYDRA. one of the soldiers, Sgt. Green defended himself with an alien gauntlet. He won the day but found that the alien gauntlet could not be removed. During the Civil War (see pp. 84-5), Tony Stark (see IRON MAN) and Henry Gyrich (see GYRICH, HENRY) recruited Green as drill sergeant at Camp Hammond, a training camp for Super Heroes destined to join the Fifty State Initiative (see pp. 118-9). One of his trainees, SLAPSTICK, beat him into a coma, but when KIA threatened Green's life, Green's gauntlet saved him. **MF**

GENERATION X

As one generation of X-MEN matures so another steps forward, in this case Generation X. Having experienced danger in the form of the alien collective intelligence, PHALANX, when the members of Generation X banded together they had a fair idea what fate had in store. Accepted by the Xavier Institute's new mutant high school at Massachusetts Academy, the team learned to hone its abilities and were introduced to PROFESSOR X's vision of the future. While at the Academy, the members of Generation X faced various foes, including EMPLATE, who preyed on the marrow of mutants. The team members were outed to the world as mutants and, with those in charge of the school—Emma FROST and Sean Cassidy (see BANSHEE)—becoming increasingly unstable, they decided to go their separate ways. **AD**

FACTFILE

MEMBERS/POWERS

HUSK
Sheds skin to reveal shape-shifted body beneath.

SKIN
Has 6 ft of extra skin, to manipulate as required.

M
Superstrength; invulnerability.

JUBILEE
Projects explosive energy bolts.

CHAMBER
Projects psionic energy blasts from chest.

SYNCH
Mimics powers of students.

PENANCE
Super-dense body.

BASE
Massachusetts Academy

FIRST APPEARANCE
Generation X #1
(November 1994)

CHARACTER KEY
1 Emma Frost **2** M **3** Banshee **4** Chamber **5** Synch
6 Jubilee **7** Penance **8** Skin **9** Husk

GENOSHANS

FIRST APPEARANCE Uncanny X-Men #235 (October 1988)

BASE The island of Genosha, Indian Ocean

SPECIAL POWERS/ABILITIES The inhabitants of Genosha were a mixture of ordinary humans and those with mutant abilities. The latter were called "Mutates" and were conditioned to fulfil specific, tasks tailored to their particular mutant ability. From time to time Mutates managed to rebel against their human masters.

Adolescent mutates were tatooed with a number on their foreheads, their identities were eliminated, and they faced a life of enslavement.

The Genoshans live on the island of Genosha, located near the Seychelles in the Indian Ocean. Originally, Genoshan mutants were identified and enslaved as adolescents. They then were stripped of their identities, given a number, and genetically engineered to alter or enhance their abilities. A militia called the Magistrates enforced the enslavement laws. The X-Men toppled this regime, and after a period of turmoil, the UN turned the country over to MAGNETO to govern. Later, Cassandra Nova and her Sentinels destroyed the nation and killed nearly everyone on it. Professor X tried to help Magneto rebuild, but they failed. **MT, MF**

GHAUR

FIRST APPEARANCE Eternals Vol. 2 #2 (November 1985)

REAL NAME Ghaur **OCCUPATION** Priestlord

BASE "City of Toads", Deviant Lemuria

HEIGHT 6 ft 4 in **WEIGHT** 210 lbs **EYES** Yellow **HAIR** Blue-Black

SPECIAL POWERS/ABILITIES The extent of Ghaur's power is currently unknown.

The product of a centuries-long breeding programme run by Deviant Priests, Ghaur came to head this priestly order. His ambition did not end there, for Ghaur was determined to rule the Deviant race and to challenge the might of the alien Celestials themselves. These hubristic ambitions almost led to his death. For a time his disembodied consciousness floated through space, until a passing SILVER SURFER inadvertently enabled him to regain corporeal form. Becoming a servant of the Elder God, Set, Ghaur sought to enable Set's return to Earth but his efforts came to naught. His whereabouts are currently unknown. **AD**

GHOST RIDER

Posing as "Satan," Mephisto approached stunt motorcyclist Johnny Blaze and agreed to cure Blaze's mentor "Crash" Simpson of a fatal disease in exchange for Blaze's soul. Simpson then died performing a stunt, and Mephisto bonded the demon Zarathos to Blaze's body, transforming him into a Ghost Rider. Blaze was temporarily freed of the curse when Zarathos became trapped in a "crystal of souls."

The Ghost Riders are brilliant motorcyclists who can perform incredible stunts. Their mystical bikes enable them to ride up walls and even across water.

Later, when criminals wounded Barbara Ketch, her brother Dan carried her to a junkyard. With Barbara's innocent blood on his hands, Dan touched a mysterious motorcycle and became the new Ghost Rider. Dan and John Blaze later learned they were brothers. John was again bonded to Zarathos and became a Ghost Rider once more. Recently, the rogue angel Zadkiel convinced Ketch to collect the power of the spirits of vengeance around the world—including Blaze's—as they came from angels rather than demons, but Zadkiel was actually using Ketch to gather the power for himself.
PS, MF

FACTFILE

REAL NAME
John "Johnny" Blaze

OCCUPATION
Stunt motorcyclist

BASE
Mobile

HEIGHT (Ghost Rider) 6 ft 2 in
WEIGHT (Ghost Rider) 220 lbs
EYES (Ghost Rider) flaming red
HAIR (Ghost Rider) none

FIRST APPEARANCE
Marvel Spotlight Vol. 1 #5
(August 1972)

Turns into a superhuman mystical being that projects "hellfire"; Ghost Rider I can create a mystical motorcycle from "hellfire." Ghost Rider II's "Penance Stare" causes wrongdoers to suffer the same emotional pain they inflicted.

G

GIANT-MAN

FIRST APPEARANCE Avengers Vol. 1 #32 (September 1966)
REAL NAME William Foster
OCCUPATION Adventurer **BASE** Los Angeles
HEIGHT 6 ft 10 in **WEIGHT** 200 lbs **EYES** Brown **HAIR** Black
SPECIAL POWERS/ABILITIES Could grow in size up to a maximum height of 25 ft; gained proportional strength as his size increased.

Dr. Hank PYM discovered how to use his "Pym particles" to change his size and became the first GIANT-MAN. His lab assistant, Bill Foster, became Black Goliath and later the second GIANT-MAN. He fell victim to radiation poisoning while fighting Atom-Smasher, but SPIDER-WOMAN cured him with a blood transfusion. He later became the fourth Goliath. During the Civil War he sided with Captain America, and he died while battling a clone of THOR. In the aftermath of WORLD WAR HULK, Bill's nephew Tom Foster became the new Goliath. **DW, MF**

GIDEON

FIRST APPEARANCE New Mutants #98 (February 1991)
REAL NAME Gideon **OCCUPATION** CEO of Ophrah Industries
BASE Denver, Colorado
HEIGHT 6 ft 8 in **WEIGHT** 265 lbs **EYES** Blue **HAIR** Green
SPECIAL POWERS/ABILITIES Mutant ability to duplicate the superhuman powers of others by aligning himself with their energy signatures. He also had a greatly extended lifespan.

A member of the long-lived mutants who call themselves the EXTERNALS, Gideon was a power broker who called the halls of big business his natural habitat. Utterly corrupt, Gideon attempted to take Roberto DaCosta, the New Mutant known as SUNSPOT, under his wing, and turn him into his protégé. However his attempts to turn Sunspot into an External like himself met with failure, and he soon turned his attentions to other pursuits. Gideon was subsequently slain by the External vampire Selene, who had embarked on a vendetta against her fellow Externals. **TB**

GLADIATOR

FIRST APPEARANCE Daredevil Vol. 1 #18 (July 1966)
REAL NAME Melvin Potter **OCCUPATION** Ex-criminal
BASE New York City
HEIGHT 6 ft 6 in **WEIGHT** 300 lbs
EYES Blue **HAIR** None
SPECIAL POWERS/ABILITIES Skilled athlete and combatant; wore armored suit with saw blades in gauntlets.

When Foggy Nelson rented a DAREDEVIL outfit from Melvin Potter's costume shop, Potter dressed up like a villain to ambush Foggy. Potter acquired a taste for crime, becoming the Gladiator and serving with ELECTRO's Emissaries of Evil and the MAGGIA. He gave up crime but returned to it because of threats against his daughter. While in prison, Mr. Fear forced him into a psychotic killing spree. Daredevil stopped him and sent him back to prison. Melvin Potter is not to be confused with the alien Gladiator who leads the SHI'AR Imperial Guard. **DW, MF**

GLENN, HEATHER

FIRST APPEARANCE Daredevil Vol. 1 #126 (October 1975)
REAL NAME Heather Glenn
OCCUPATION Secretary; owner of Glenn Industries (after her father's death) **BASE** New York City
HEIGHT 5 ft 8 in **WEIGHT** 120 lbs **EYES** Blue **HAIR** Black
SPECIAL POWERS/ABILITIES Proficient secretarial skills; Heather had no superpowers.

The daughter of Maxwell Glenn, owner of Glenn Industries, Heather became romantically involved with lawyer Matthew Murdock. Zebediah Killgrave, the PURPLE MAN, used his mind-controlling powers to force Maxwell Glenn to commit crimes. Murdock prosecuted Maxwell Glenn, who killed himself. Heather blamed Murdock for her father's death; she then discovered that he was the crimefighter DAREDEVIL. Heather and Murdock were reconciled but, while drunk, Heather revealed Daredevil's identity to his enemy Tarkington Brown. When Murdock broke up with Heather, she committed suicide, as her father had. **PS**

GLOB

FIRST APPEARANCE Incredible Hulk Vol. 2 #121 (November 1969)
REAL NAME Joe Timms **OCCUPATION** Petty thief; swamp creature **BASE** Florida Everglades
HEIGHT 6 ft 6 in **WEIGHT** 900 lbs **EYES** Brown **HAIR** None
SPECIAL POWERS/ABILITIES Superhumanly strong, the Glob's mutated swampy body can withstand severe attacks; enhanced speed and stamina; not particularly intelligent.

Three men have been known as the Glob. The first was Joe Timms, who drowned in the Florida Everglades. After his corpse was exposed to radioactive waste, he returned to life as a swamp-like beast. Sumner Samuel Beckwith became the second Glob after injecting himself with a flawed super soldier serum. The third—called Glob Herman—was a mutant student at the Xavier Institute. His flesh was made of a transparent, living wax called bio-paraffin that burned when set afire. He joined a mutant riot after a prominent mutant was killed in what seemed to be a hate crime. After M-Day, he retained his powers. **MF**

Not a pretty sight, the Glob is, nevertheless, a well-meaning soul.

GLORIAN

FIRST APPEARANCE Incredible Hulk #191 (September 1975)
REAL NAME Thomas Gideon
OCCUPATION Apprentice dream-shaper **BASE** Known universe
HEIGHT 5 ft 9 in **WEIGHT** 155 lbs **EYES** Pink **HAIR** Orange
SPECIAL POWERS/ABILITIES Glorian can control tachyons, small speed-of-light particles, forming them into rainbow-shaped bridges allowing him to travel across worlds or star systems at light speed. He can also mentally redefine small pockets of reality for short periods of time.

Thomas Gideon survived radiation poisoning thanks to the SHAPER OF WORLDS. The Shaper renamed him Glorian and taught him to manipulate reality and dreams. Recently, Glorian tricked Gamorra and RONAN THE ACCUSER into battling so he could absorb their energy and use it to reshape a world. When the Annihilation Wave interrupted him, he destroyed all he'd made, shattering his mind along with his attackers. **MT, MF**

GODS OF ASGARD

Immortals who rule the dimension of Asgard

FACTFILE

KEY ASGARDIANS

ODIN

(Monarch of Asgard) The most powerful god, possessing vast magical abilities. He can enchant objects or living beings, project energy bolts, and open gateways between dimensions. He also commands the life energies of all Asgardians, which he can absorb at will.

THOR

(God of Thunder) Asgard's finest warrior; exceptionally skilled in hand-to-hand combat, swordsmanship, and hammer-throwing.

BALDER

(God of Light) Thor's closest friend; almost invulnerable; skilled in hand-to-hand combat, swordsmanship, and horsemanship.

HELA

(Goddess of Death) Ruler of the underworlds of Hel and Niffleheim; holds the power of life and death over the gods; can levitate and travel in astral form; touch is fatal to mortals,

LOKI

(God of Evil) Great magical abilities; can shapeshift into any animal, god, or giant; can plant hypnotic suggestions into others' minds.

HERMOD

(God of Speed) Fastest of all Asgardians.

HODER

(God of Winter) has Psychic abilities that allow him to see into the future.

VALKYRIE

Brunnhilde the Valkyrie can see a "deathglow" around a person about to die. She can transport herself (and a dead or dying person) from one dimension to another.

HEIMDALL

Guardian of the Rainbow Bridge has extremely acute senses. He can focus on, or block out, any specific sensory information.

VOLLA

Prophetess who can see alternate futures.

BASE

The Otherdimensional Realm of Asgard

FIRST APPEARANCE

Journey into Mystery #85,
(October 1962)

The otherdimensional planetary body known as Asgard.

The Gods of Asgard are a powerful race of beings who live in a dimension called Asgard, a small, otherdimensional planetary body whose laws of physics are different from the planets we know in the Earthly realm. Asgard is also home to five other races—Giants, Dwarves, Elves, Trolls, and Demons. The Gods of Asgard are the most human-looking and powerful of the six races of Asgard.

NINE WORLDS

All Asgardian refer to the known universe as the "Nine Worlds of Asgard." Four of those worlds—Asgard, home of the gods; Vanaheim, home of the Asgardians' sister race called the Vanir; Nidavellir, home of the Dwarves.; and Alfheim, home of the Light Elves—actually share the planetary body on which Asgard is located.

The other five worlds exist in separate dimensions connected by an unknown number of interdimensional nexuses. They are Midgard, the Asgardian name for Earth, home of humanity; Jotunheim, home of the giants; Svartalfheim, home of the dark elves; Hel, land of the dead and it's adjunct world Niffleheim, the frozen realm of the dishonored dead; and Muspelheim, land of the fire demons and home to Surtur, the Gods of Asgard's most deadly enemy.

Surtur rises from the flames of Muspelheim, land of the fire demons.

RAINBOW BRIDGE

The origin of the Gods of Asgard is not clearly known, but it believed that unlike the other races of the realm, the gods are not native to Asgard. Legend has it that they were born on Earth, but moved to Asgard at some time in the far distant past. The Rainbow Bridge, also known as Bifrost—one of the interdimensional nexuses—connects Asgard to Earth.

Although they look like humans, the Gods of Asgard possess superhuman physical abilities. They are extremely long-lived (although not immortal, unlike their Olympian counterparts) and age at an extremely slow pace once they reach adulthood.

Their skin and bones are three times as dense as that of a human and are invulnerable, to a degree, to physical attack. They possess great strength (able to lift 30 tons) and, due to their density, weigh far more than humans of comparable size. The Gods of Asgard are immune to all diseases found on Earth and their metabolism gives them superhuman endurance while performing physical activities.

All Asgardians are born with the potential to use and control mystical energies, although only a few (such as LOKI) have developed this power to any significant degree.

The Fantastic Four cross Bifrost, the Rainbow Bridge to Asgard, which is guarded by Heimdall, Sentry of Asgard.

GODS OF ASGARD

1 Enchantress **2** Sif **3** Balder the Brave
4 Hela, Goddess of Death **5** Hermod, God of Speed
6 Loki **7** Thor **8** Heimdall, Guardian of the Rainbow
Bridge **9** Thunderstrike **10** Odin **11** Karnilla, the
Norn Queen **12** Kurse **13** Frigga **14** Fandral the
Dashing **15** Volstagg the Enormous **16** Hogun the
Grim **17** Thor Girl **18** Malekith **19** Surtur
20 Ulik, the Unstoppable Rock Troll

ESSENTIAL STORYLINES

• *The Mighty Thor Vol. 2 #80–85* The Ragnarok (Doom of the Gods) Saga. Loki and his followers unleash an attack on Asgard intended to destroy the home of the gods and all its inhabitants. Thor's hammer Mjolnir is shattered during the battle that follows.

• *The Mighty Thor #418* The fire demon Surtur possesses Odin and gains control of Asgard.

The Storm Giants, sworn enemies of the Gods, eat and drink their fill in Jotunheim, their Asgardian home. Odin challenged Thor and Loki (in foreground) to return the Golden apples of Iduna to the Storm Giants.

prove his valor. When Thor was 16, Odin finally presented him with the mighty hammer, and Thor became Asgard's greatest warrior.

Loki, who had been adopted by Odin, turned to sorcery and earned the nickname, "God of Mischief." Jealous of Thor, Loki vowed to destroy him. Loki launched Ragnarok but Thor broke the cycle and stopped the war. The gods disappeared but later reappeared in mortal guises. Thor brought them to a reborn Asgard, which now hovers over the plains of Oklahoma.

MT, MF

Ymir, King of the Ice Giants

ODIN THE ALL-FATHER

Odin, also called All-Father, is the leader of the Gods of Asgard. Odin is the grandson of Buri, the first of the Asgardians. He is the son of the God Bor and Bestia, of the race of frost giants.

For many ages, Odin has ruled Asgard wisely and effectively. Odin wields the enchanted, three-pronged spear Gungnir ("The Spear of Heaven"), which returns to his hand when thrown, and he travels through space in Skipbladnir, a Viking-style longboat with enchanted sails and oars.

SON OF ODIN

Although Odin made the Asgardian Goddess Frigga his queen, he desired a son that would combine the power of Asgard and Earth, and so he mated with GAEA, the patron Goddess of Earth, who bore him THOR, the God of Thunder, Odin's favorite son. However, from the time Thor was an infant, he was raised in Asgard by Frigga, whom he believed to be his mother.

When Thor was eight, Odin sent him to

Nidavellir, land of the Dwarves, to ask them to create treasures for Asgard's rulers. Among the objects they created was the hammer Mjolnir, forged of the mystical metal uru. Odin enchanted the hammer so that only one worthy of wielding such a powerful weapon could lift it. He hoped that Thor would one day be that one.

HEROIC DEEDS

For the next eight years Thor strove to become worthy enough to possess Mjolnir, doing many heroic deeds to

In the early days of Asgard, the rampaging Ice Giants attempted to bring frost, desolation and eternal night to the land of the gods. They were defeated by Odin and his warriors.

GODS OF HELIOPOLIS

Deities of Ancient Egypt

FACTFILE

NOTABLE GODS

OSIRIS (Ruler of the Gods)
God of the Dead
BES God of Luck
GEB God of the Earth
HORUS God of the Sun
ISIS Goddess of Fertility
KHONSHU God of Light
NUT Goddess of the Sky
SETH God of Evil
THOTH God of the Moon

BASE
Celestial city of Heliopolis

FIRST APPEARANCE
Thor Vol. 1 #240
(October 1975)

The Path of the Gods enabled the Egyptian deities to visit Earth and meddle in human affairs.

In ancient times the pantheon of the Egyptian gods lived in Heliopolis, ruling Egypt until humans finally took their place as the dynastic kings known as the pharaohs. It was then that the Heliopolitan gods departed Earth, settling in a parallel dimension, where they established the celestial city of Heliopolis. However, like the Asgardian gods (*see* GODS OF ASGARD), the Heliopolitan deities retained strong links with Egypt, traveling to and from Earth on a golden bridge named the Path of the Gods.

Creeping up on the sleeping Osiris, Seth prepared to slice him into pieces.

CLASH OF THE GODS

Although essentially an extended family, the Heliopolitan gods were somewhat dysfunctional. When Osiris, God of the Dead, was appointed ruler of the Gods his younger brother Seth was overwhelmed with jealousy—the tensions between the pair were to reverberate far beyond their celestial home. Seth's first solution was drastic—he killed Osiris, slicing up his body and scattering the pieces. When Osiris' wife and son—Isis and Horus—managed to resurrect him, Seth employed a different tactic, imprisoning all three in a pyramid. Although trapped there for millennia, Osiris and Isis eventually made the pyramid appear in the 20th century. This attracted the attention of the Asgardian gods THOR and ODIN but their efforts to free their fellow immortals did not prove straightforward. Odin was forced to join battle with Seth, their struggle finally culminating in the severing of Seth's left hand.

Releasing Osiris from his pyramid prison, Thor and Odin joined him in the battle to overthrow Seth. However, before they could reach him, they were forced to fight through Seth's skeletal legions.

CONTINUING MENACES

Seth has attempted time and again to destroy all life in the multiverse. An alliance of evil let loose the demonic Demogorge the God-Eater. Only when the entity attempted to consume Thor was its path of destruction brought to an end. On a separate occasion, Seth drained the energies of his fellow gods and invaded Asgard. He was only defeated by the combined forces of the AVENGERS and EARTH FORCE. Thanos also threatened the universe with his Infinity Gauntlet. Osiris attended a Council of the God Kings to discuss their response. Fortunately, Thanos was thwarted by other entities.

Although the time of the Heliopolitan Gods is now long over, they and their petty squabbles still spill over into human affairs. **AD**

For millennia, the god Seth has brooded and conspired to gain control of Heliopolis.

ESSENTIAL STORYLINES
• ***Thor Vol. 1 #240–241***
In the first story to feature the Heliopolitans, Seth traps Osiris and Isis in a pyramid and does battle with Odin and Thor.
• ***Thor Vol. 1 #386–400***
Seth conquers Heliopolis, battles Thor and the Avengers, and then tries to invade Asgard.

GODS OF OLYMPUS

Deities of Ancient Greece

Although for centuries they were worshipped by the Greeks it remains unclear where the Gods of Olympus first originated—was it on Earth or in the pocket dimension of Olympus where they currently reside? Wherever they came from, their influence on this planet has faded over the last two millennia, although a handful of their number still walk the Earth.

Olympus was ruled by the stern and hirsute, Zeus.

THE GOLDEN AGE

Children of the Titans, the first generation of the Olympian Gods were imprisoned in the underworld realm of Tartarus as soon as they were born, their father Cronos fearing that they would eventually overthrow him. His anxiety proved to be well founded: the last of his children, Zeus, avoided being incarcerated and, when he was old enough, freed his siblings and led a ten-year-long war against Cronos.

Victorious, Zeus and his siblings became the Gods of Olympus, worshipped by peoples across Europe. It was only when Christianity began to dominate the Western world that the Gods chose to withdraw to the Olympus dimension and began to reduce their ties with the mortal realm.

The court of Zeus was a byword for feasting and revelry. While most enjoyed the carefree hedonism of the place, some, including Venus and Hercules, yearned for a slightly more challenging existence.

Although most of the Gods departed a handful either remained on the Earth or returned, time and again, in the years that followed. Of those that stayed on Earth, Neptune (or Poseidon, as the Greeks called him) remained to watch over and be worshipped by the Atlanteans, while HERCULES and Venus (Aphrodite to the Greeks) spent time living with mortals.

BACK TO EARTH

With the destruction of Asgard during Ragnarok, the Olympians became of a target of Amatsu-Mikaboshi, the Japanese god of evil. Mikaboshi led an attack on Olympus that was only repelled after both ARES and Hercules returned from Earth to help. Zeus was slain in the conflict and has not returned, although his body was not recovered.

During the Secret Invasion (see pp. 326-7), Hercules served as the Olympians' representative to the God Squad assembled to take down the SKRULL gods. More recently, HERA and PLUTO took control of the Olympus Group, the corporation that represents the Olympians' interests on Earth. Meddling directly in the affairs of mortals once again, they have decided to turn their company's resources toward one goal: killing both ATHENA and Hercules **AD, MF**

Zeus did not entirely approve of the life his son, Hercules, had chosen to lead.

FACTFILE

NOTABLE GODS

ZEUS (Ruler of the Gods)
God of the Sky and Weather
APOLLO God of Light
ARES God of War
ARTEMIS Goddess of the Hunt
ATHENA Goddess of Wisdom
ATLAS Mountain God
BELLONA Goddess of Discord
CUPID God of Love
DEIMOS God of Terror
DEMETER Goddess of Fertility
DIONYSUS God of Wine
GAEA Mother-Earth
HEBE Goddess of Youth
HEPHAESTUS God of Fire
HERA Goddess of Marriage;
Queen of the Gods
HERMES God of Commerce and Travel
NEPTUNE (POSEIDON)
God of the Sea
NOX God of Night
PAN God of Shepherds, Flocks and Forests
PERSEPHONE Queen of the Underworld
PHOBOS God of Fear
PROMETHEUS Titan of forethought; benefactor of mankind
PSYCHE Goddess of Fidelity and Adoration
TYPHON God of Wind
VENUS (APHRODITE) Goddess of Love and Beauty

BASE
Mount Olympus, Greece; later in an otherdimensional world

FIRST APPEARANCE
Journey Into Mystery Annual #1 (1965)

ESSENTIAL STORYLINES
• *Venus #1–5*
The goddess Venus becomes editor of Beauty Magazine and helps bring couples together.
• *Thor #126–131*
Hercules fights Thor who then rescues him from the netherworld where he has been imprisoned. Their firm friendship is sealed.
• *Avengers #281–285*
Angered by injuries suffered by Hercules, Zeus attacks the Avengers and forbids the Olympus Gods from travelling to Earth.

GOLDBUG

FIRST APPEARANCE Luke Cage, Power Man #41 (March 1977)

REAL NAME Unrevealed

OCCUPATION Criminal **BASE** New York City

HEIGHT 5 ft 9 in **WEIGHT** 170 lbs **EYES** Blue **HAIR** Blond

SPECIAL POWERS/ABILITIES Battlesuit contains electrically-powered exoskeleton that amplifies strength; "gold-gun" shoots gold-colored dust that hardens on contact; uses "bugship" hovercraft and submarine.

Goldbug is a thief obsessed with gold. Early in his career, he clashed with Luke CAGE and Thunderbolt. Later, he captured the Hulk as part of his plan to conquer El Dorado. In El Dorado, Goldbug teamed up with the Hulk to defeat the subterranean conqueror TYRANNUS. He later attempted to steal underwater gold but was foiled by NAMOR. He worked for Latveria when the nation attacked Nick Fury and his friends over their attempt to overthrow the Latverian government. During the Civil War, the PUNISHER killed him before he could join Captain America's forces. **PS, MF**

GOLDEN ARCHER

FIRST APPEARANCE Avengers #141 (November 1975)

REAL NAME Wyatt McDonald **OCCUPATION** Government agent, former cab driver **BASE** Squadron City

HEIGHT 6 ft 3 in **WEIGHT** 150 lbs **EYES** Blue **HAIR** Black

SPECIAL POWERS/ABILITIES Expert archer who shot arrows with pin-point accuracy. Besides conventional arrows used a chemical mace arrow, a siren arrow, and a flash arrow.

Wyatt McDonald practiced until he became an expert archer. Deciding to use his skills as a costumed crimefighter he adopted the name Hawkeye. McDonald was the first recruit of the SQUADRON SUPREME, a team of Super Heroes who banded together to protect their world, known as "Earth-S." He later changed his name to Golden Archer. Eventually he was kicked out of the Squadron Supreme for using a Behavior Modification Machine on Lady Lark. He then joined NIGHTHAWK's Redeemers as Black Archer and was killed battling Blue Eagle. **MT**

GORGON

FIRST APPEARANCE Fantastic Four Vol. 1 (November 1965)

REAL NAME Unrevealed

OCCUPATION Administrator **BASE** Attilan, blue Area, the Moon

HEIGHT 6 ft 5 in **WEIGHT** 450 lbs **EYES** Brown **HAIR** Black

SPECIAL POWERS/ABILITIES Immensely powerful legs and hooves give him the ability to create seismic tremors.

Gorgon is a member of the INHUMAN royal family and cousin of their ruler, BLACK BOLT. Like all Inhumans, Gorgon underwent exposure to the mutating Terrigen mists as a youth and gained hooves in place of feet, capable of creating seismic tremors. He often acts as Black Bolt's bodyguard, and he also takes youths exposed to the mists and trains them in the use of their powers. Recently, SHIELD exposed him to the Terrigen mists a second time, transforming him into a true beast. He is not to be confused with the Japanese villain called Gorgon, who was killed by WOLVERINE. **DW, MF**

GOLDDIGGER

FIRST APPEARANCE Captain America #389 (April 1990)

REAL NAME Angela Golden

OCCUPATION Enforcer **BASE** New Orleans, Louisiana

HEIGHT/WEIGHT Unknown **EYES** Blue **HAIR** Blonde

SPECIAL POWERS/ABILITIES Skilled hand-to-hand combatant.

Little is known about the woman known as Golddigger, save that she sells her skills to the highest bidder, and that she specializes in sneak attacks. She first crossed swords with CAPTAIN AMERICA in the service of Superia, who plotted to sterilize the world. Thereafter, she came to be employed by Damon Dran as an enforcer for his child slavery ring. But when Captain America and the brutal hero called Americop demolished Dran's operation, Golddigger attempted to flee in a helicopter, which was subsequently shot down. No one knows whether she truly perished in the crash. **TD**

GRANDMASTER

Like his kinsman the Collector, the Grandmaster is a survivor of an extraterrestrial race that evolved shortly after the Big Bang. To combat the unending boredom of immortality, the Grandmaster has spent the eons engaging in various games, tournaments, and contests. He particularly relishes challenging other cosmic beings to games of skill and chance for incredibly high stakes. Grandmaster discovered Earth-712, which was inhabited by the SQUADRON SUPREME, and created duplicates of these heroes to pit against the Avengers. He later used Earth as a breeding ground for superhuman pawns for his games, but gave up this plan when he lost a bet to Daredevil. He also challenged Death to a series of games, resulting in the banning of all the Elders of the Universe from his kingdom, making them all virtually immortal. He also once joined with the other Elders in a plot to kill Galactus, but the SILVER SURFER foiled this. Recently, the Grandmaster pitted the original Defenders against the RED HULK's new Offenders. **TD, MF**

GORILLA-MAN

FIRST APPEARANCE Men's Adventures #26 (1954)

REAL NAME Kenneth Hale **OCCUPATION** Adventurer

BASE San Francisco

HEIGHT 6 ft **WEIGHT** 340 lbs **EYES** Brown **HAIR** Brown

SPECIAL POWERS/ABILITIES Hale is a man cursed to live in a gorilla's body.

Legend says, "If you kill the Gorilla-Man, you become immortal." When forced to commit this act, Hale discovered the immortality came with the curse of becoming the Gorilla-Man he had killed. In the 1950s, Ken worked with a super group called the G-Men under Jimmy Woo (*see* Woo, Jimmy).

Decades later, he became an agent of SHIELD and joined the supernatural version of THE HOWLING COMMANDOS. Gorilla-Man has since reunited with his G-Men friends to fight the Atlas Foundation. With their victory, they took over the organization and formed the new AGENTS OF ATLAS. **MF**

GRAVITON

FIRST APPEARANCE Avengers Vol. 1 #158 (April 1977)

REAL NAME Franklin Hall

OCCUPATION Criminal **BASE** Mobile

HEIGHT 6 ft 1 in **WEIGHT** 200 lbs **EYES** Blue **HAIR** Black

SPECIAL POWERS/ABILITIES Control over gravity allows Graviton to levitate objects, generate force fields and shockwaves, and pin opponents to the ground.

Franklin Hall, a Canadian researcher, gained absolute control over gravity in an accident involving a particle accelerator. Dubbing himself Graviton, he battled the AVENGERS, the THUNDERBOLTS, SPIDER-MAN, and the West Coast Avengers, and was banished to an alternate dimension more than once.

Upon one return, he went to exact his revenge on the Thunderbolts. Finding the Redeemers in their place, he destroyed them, then seemed to die while stopping an invasion from the dimension in which he'd been trapped. He returned one last time to battle Iron Man, but ended their conflict by committing suicide. **DW, MF**

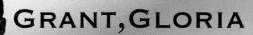

GRANT, GLORIA

Model Glory Grant befriended Peter Parker when they both lived in an apartment house on Manhattan's Lower West Side. Grant was looking for work, and Peter, a freelance photographer for the *Daily Bugle,* suggested she apply to be the paper's publisher J. Jonah JAMESON's secretary, a post recently vacated by Betty Brant LEEDS. The irascible Jameson liked Grant and she became Brant's replacement.

Mexican crimelord Eduardo Lobo seduced Grant to obtain the Bugle's files on his enemy, the KINGPIN; in time, Grant and Lobo fell genuinely in love. During a battle between SPIDER-MAN and Lobo, Grant tried to shoot Spider-Man, but shot and killed Lobo instead. Later, Grant was possessed by the spirit of the voodoo sorceress CALYPSO as part of the latter's plan to return to life. Grant has enjoyed a more successful romantic relationship with RANDY ROBERTSON, Joe's son. **PS**

FACTFILE
REAL NAME
Gloria "Glory" Grant

OCCUPATION
Administrative assistant, former model

BASE
New York City

HEIGHT 5 ft 8 in
WEIGHT 120 lbs
EYES Brown
HAIR Black

FIRST APPEARANCE
The Amazing Spider-Man #140
(February 1975)

POWERS

Highly efficient secretarial skills, including typing and computer skills. Outgoing, romantic, and warm-hearted; prepared to do almost anything to help the man she loves.

GREAT LAKES AVENGERS

Formed by Craig Hollis, the GLA was a self-proclaimed branch of the Avengers. Despite much mockery and their successes being overlooked, they insisted on remaining together. The group's bills are met by Big Bertha, whose alter ego is the wealthy supermodel Ashley Crawford. Other misfit members have included: Squirrel Girl, Leather Boy, Monkey Joe, Tippy-Toe, Grasshopper, and even Deadpool. After they won the rights to the Champions name from HERCULES in a poker game, they became the Great Lakes Champions. The heroes all signed up with the Superhuman Registration Act and became the Great Lakes Initiative, the Fifty State Initiative's team for Wisconsin. **AD, MF**

FACTFILE
FOUNDING MEMBERS AND POWERS

MR. IMMORTAL
Immortal; team leader

DINAH SOAR
Alien flying reptile, attacks with high-pitched shriek.

BIG BERTHA
Controls body mass; alternates between super-obesity and strength and supermodel skinniness.

DOORMAN
Can teleport self and others into the next room.

FLATMAN
Two-dimensional mutant with elasticated body.

FIRST APPEARANCE
The West Coast Avengers #46
(July 1989)

GREAT LAKES AVENGERS

THE GREAT LAKES AVENGERS
1 Mr. Immortal
2 Big Bertha
3 Squirrel Girl
4 Flatman
5 Doorman

GREEN GOBLIN

Spider-Man's greatest enemy

Norman Osborn reveals himself to be the Green Goblin.

For almost as long as there has been a SPIDER-MAN, so too has the Green Goblin existed. Spider-Man's arch nemesis, the Green Goblin is the insane, malevolent alter ego of that once-respectable industrialist, Norman Osborn. Despite their mutual antagonism, the relationship between the pair is complex. Although the Green Goblin loathes and resents Spider-Man's very existence, for a long time Norman Osborn and Peter Parker shared a deep mutual respect and admiration. Osborn saw in the orphaned Peter the son he really wanted.

ESSENTIAL STORYLINES
• *Amazing Spider-Man #39–40*
The Green Goblin discovers Peter Parker's secret identity, the Goblin is unmasked as Norman Osborn and we learn about his origins.
• *Amazing Spider-Man #121–2*
A climactic battle between the Green Goblin and Spider-Man results in the death of Gwen Stacy and the Goblin's own, apparent, demise.
• *Amazing Spider-Man #134–7*
Norman Osborn's son Harry discovers that Peter Parker is really Spider-Man and, looking for revenge, becomes the second Green Goblin.

YOU MUST BE *NUTS* GOBLIN! I AIN'T LETTIN' *YOU* OR ANYONE ELSE TAKE OVER MY GANG! NOW HIT THE ROAD, MISTER, WHILE YOU STILL *CAN!*

DIG THAT CORNY COSTUME WILLYA?

BUT, UNDER MY LEADER-SHIP, WE COULD TAKE OVER EVERY RACKET IN THE CITY!

GENESIS OF THE GOBLIN

Long before his transformation into the Green Goblin, Norman Osborn was an ambitious businessman, quite prepared to sacrifice others on the altar of his own success. The co-founder of chemical company Oscorp, Osborn gained total control by framing his business partner, Professor Mendel Stromm, for embezzlement. The Goblin Formula that was to prove Osborn's undoing was a concoction detailed in the professor's notes, but it was Osborn's attempt to manufacture it for himself that resulted in the solution exploding in his face. As a result of this explosion, Osborn's strength, stamina and reflexes were enhanced but his sanity began to erode.

As the Green Goblin, Osborn wished to lead New York's criminal underworld and he set out to gain the respect of the key gangs by destroying Spider-Man. He developed high-tech weaponry specifically designed to achieve this end. Despite discovering Spider-Man's true identity, the Green Goblin was ultimately defeated: an electric shock, sustained during a battle with the web-slinger, caused Osborn to regain his sanity and lose all memory of his malevolent alter ego. Peter Parker judged that it was better to allow Osborn to resume his old life.

ISSUE #1

Teaming up with the Enforcers, the Green Goblin is determined to destroy Spider-Man.

STRIKING AT SPIDER-MAN

Osborn's regained sanity proved fragile. Time and again his inner demon—the Green Goblin—reasserted control, and

Tingling spider-sense, awesome strength, and superfast reflexes—Spider-Man needs all of these things to survive the Green Goblin's arsenal of weapons and enhanced body.

although Peter repeatedly brought Osborn back to reality, the businessman's grip on sanity became more and more tenuous. During this period, Peter's then-girlfriend, Gwen Stacy, met Osborn and, overwhelmed by his charisma, became pregnant by him. Nine months later, she gave birth to twins, Gabriel and Sarah, in France, keeping their existence a secret from Peter.

Following Gwen's return to New York, an angry altercation between her and a desperately unbalanced Osborn served to destabilize him further. Determined to punish both her and Spider-Man, when Osborn reverted to the Green Goblin he kidnapped Gwen and carried her to the top of Brooklyn Bridge.

OTHER GREEN GOBLINS

To protect his father, Harry Osborn says he is the Green Goblin.

All the Green Goblins have shared similar equipment.

In becoming the Green Goblin, Norman Osborn inadvertently founded a Goblin dynasty. After witnessing his father's apparent death, a mentally unstable Harry Osborn adopted the Green Goblin mantle and attempted to destroy Spider-Man. Although Harry eventually put his father's legacy behind him, even settling down with a wife and child, life's pressures finally drove him back to the Goblin formula. Tragically, his body was killed by the deadly concoction. Twice, the Goblin name has been borne by non-Osborns, with Harry's psychiatrist, Bart Hamilton, and Phil Urich, the nephew of reporter Ben Urich, both being pretenders to the Goblin crown. More recently, Gabriel Stacy, the son of Norman Osborn and Gwen Stacy, injected himself with the Goblin formula to save his own life. Now the fifth Green Goblin, Gabriel remains at large, somewhere in Europe.

The third Green Goblin is revealed.

Osborn travelled to Europe, where he took control of a secret society known as the SCRIERS. At the same time he watched over Gwen's children, tending to their physical needs while warping their minds against Peter Parker by convincing them that Peter was their father and had abandoned them.

NORMAN OSBORN, HERO

Recently, Osborn has worked hard to become a hero in the eyes of the world. As the new director of the THUNDERBOLTS, he played a major role in the Secret Invasion (*see pp. 326-7*), using his villains-turned-heroes to help fight off the SKRULLS and even killing Queen VERANKE himself on live television. He spun this event into being chosen to dismantle SHIELD and head up a new agency called H.A.M.M.E.R.

Once in power, Osborn set up the Cabal, a darker version of the ILLUMINATI which strives to control the world from behind the scenes. As director of HAMMER, he also formed a new AVENGERS team composed of villains wearing the costumes of heroes. He led it himself as a combination of IRON MAN and CAPTAIN AMERICA called the Iron Patriot.

AD, MF

The Goblin uses a variety of grenades which look like Halloween pumpkins.

A casualty of war, the Green Goblin throws Gwen Stacy to her death.

The ensuing confrontation with Spider-Man resulted in Gwen's death and in Osborn being impaled by his own Goblin Glider.

Peter Parker assumed that Osborn had been killed by this impact but he had not allowed for the extraordinary potency of the Goblin formula. While lying on a mortuary slab, Osborn's body suddenly revived. To keep his survival secret, Osborn substituted his own body with that of an anonymous drifter.

Harry Osborn prevents the Ultimate universe Green Goblin from destroying Spider-Man. Norman Osborn had injected himself with a spider-serum. Rather than endowing him with Spider-Man's powers, the serum transformed Osborn into a crazed demonic creature.

GREMLIN

FIRST APPEARANCE Incredible Hulk Vol. 2 #187 (May 1975)

REAL NAME Unrevealed

OCCUPATION Scientist **BASE** A secret base in Khystyro, somewhere in the Arctic and Bitterfrost, a secret base in Siberia

HEIGHT 4 ft 6 in **WEIGHT** 215 lbs **EYES** Blue **HAIR** None

SPECIAL POWERS/ABILITIES Mutant who inherited father's genius-level intelligence; battlesuit gave superhuman strength.

The Gremlin is the son of the dead Soviet scientist known as the GARGOYLE, who participated in atomic tests that vastly increased his intelligence but scarred his face and body. The Gargoyle died following an encounter with Bruce Banner, the HULK. The Gremlin's intelligence was so great that he achieved a position of authority while only a child. Unfairly blaming the Hulk for his father's death, the Gremlin frequently tried to destroy him. Wearing a battlesuit similar to TITANIUM MAN, he was eventually killed in a battle with IRON MAN. **TD**

GREY, JEAN *see pages 136-7*

GRIM REAPER

FIRST APPEARANCE Avengers #52 (May 1968)

REAL NAME Eric Williams

OCCUPATION Criminal **BASE** Mobile

HEIGHT/WEIGHT Unrevealed **EYES** Brown **HAIR** Black

SPECIAL POWERS/ABILITIES Has a scythe fused into the place of his right hand, which can fire arcs of electrical energy and induce comas in victims.

Brother of WONDER MAN, Eric Williams became the Grim Reaper to get revenge on the AVENGERS, whom he believed were responsible for his brother's death. To that end, he allied with ULTRON, and formed the LETHAL LEGION. Even after Wonder Man revived, the insane Reaper refused to believe it, and he died pursuing his vendetta. He has come back from death more than once and he tried to blow up the Statue of Liberty. **TD, MF**

GUARDIAN

FIRST APPEARANCE X-Men #109 (February 1978)

REAL NAME James MacDonald Hudson

OCCUPATION Scientist, adventurer **BASE** Canada (Dept. H)

HEIGHT 6 ft 2 in **WEIGHT** 196 lbs **EYES** Blue **HAIR** Black

SPECIAL POWERS/ABILITIES Electromagnetic battlesuit has built-in force-field, allows him to fly, and discharge force bolts; also uses gravity to slingshot him in a westward direction at 1000 mph.

James MacDonald Hudson stole the prototype battlesuit he was developing when he discovered that his employers, Am-Can Petro-Chemical, intended to turn it over to the US military. Hudson took the suit to the Canadian government and founded ALPHA FLIGHT which he led as VINDICATOR. When Canada ended its support of Alpha Flight, Hudson took the name Guardian to symbolize his new role. Later, the Collective possessed Michael Pointer and used him to kill Hudson, along with most of the rest of Alpha Flight. Pointer recently became the new Guardian of OMEGA FLIGHT, wearing Hudson's battlesuit to help control his energy absorption powers. **TD, MF**

GREY GARGOYLE

GREY GARGOYLE

FACTFILE

REAL NAME
Paul Pierre Duval

OCCUPATION
Chemist, criminal

BASE
Mobile

HEIGHT 5 ft 11 in

WEIGHT 175 lbs (human form); 750 lbs (stone form)

EYES Blue (human form); white (stone form)

HAIR Black (human form); gray (stone form)

FIRST APPEARANCE
*Journey into Mystery #107
(August 1964)*

POWERS

Can transform himself into living stone without losing mobility, thereby gaining superhuman strength and durability. By touching people or objects with his right hand, he can transform them into an immobile, stone-like substance for about an hour.

French chemist Pierre Paul Duval inadvertently spilled a potion that had been contaminated by an unknown organic substance onto his right hand. To his astonishment, his right hand permanently transformed into stone; however, he could still move it as if it were ordinary flesh. When Duval discovered that he could transform his entire body into mobile, living stone, he decided to become a costumed criminal named the Grey Gargoyle.

Hoping to learn the secret of immortality, the Grey Gargoyle battled THOR, who remains his principal enemy. Over the years, the Gargoyle has also contended against IRON MAN, CAPTAIN AMERICA, SPIDER-MAN, the HULK, the AVENGERS and the FANTASTIC FOUR. The Grey Gargoyle also briefly served as a member of BARON ZEMO'S MASTERS OF EVIL.

For a time the Grey Gargoyle used a secret identity as "sculptor" Paul St. Pierre, transforming real people into supposed stone sculptures. **PS**

The Grey Gargoyle retains his normal agility when in stone form, despite his increased weight. With his superhuman strength, he can leap nearly twenty feet into the air.

GUARDIANS OF THE GALAXY

FACTFILE

NOTABLE MEMBERS AND POWERS

MAJOR VICTORY
(Vance Astrovik) Psychokinesis, mental force blasts.

ALETA
Can create objects of solid light.

CHARLIE-27
Enhanced strength and stamina.

MARTINEX
Enhanced strength, projection of heat and cold.

NIKKI
Resistant to heat and bright light, sharpshooter.

STARHAWK
Flight, enhanced strength, energy projection.

YONDU
Skilled archer, mystical sensory abilities.

BASE
Mobile

FIRST APPEARANCE
Marvel Super Heroes Vol. 1 #18 (January 1969)

In an alternate timeline of the 31st century, the Guardians of the Galaxy act as protectors of the Milky Way. The group formed in response to the Badoon invasion of 3007, which decimated Pluto, Mercury, Jupiter, and Earth. The Guardians defeated the Badoon by 3015, then became adventurers. They have traveled to Earth's current reality several times, becoming honorary members of the AVENGERS. The Guardians' adventures in their own time included a quest for Captain America's shield. At this time, Vance Astrovik convinced his younger self to follow a different path, leading to his mainstream version becoming MARVEL BOY (later Justice). Other teammates have included Hollywood (a future WONDER MAN); the feline Talon, the shapeshifting SKRULL Replica, a time-traveling Yellowjacket II, and the former herald of Galactus, Firelord. **DW**

CHARACTER KEY
1 Spirit of Vengeance (Ghost Rider)
2 Martinex **3** Replica **4** Phoenix IX
5 Firelord **6** Hollywood (Wonder Man)

FACTFILE

REAL NAME
Kevin O'Brien

OCCUPATION
Research scientist

BASE
Long Island, New York

HEIGHT 5 ft 10 in
WEIGHT 195 lbs
EYES Blue
HAIR Red

FIRST APPEARANCE
Iron Man #43 (November 1971)

POWERS
Armor augments strength and enables flight; it is also equipped with radiation shielding and pulsed laser.

GUARDSMAN

Kevin O'Brien headed up Stark Industries' research department and aided IRON MAN against the SPYMASTER and the Espionage Elite. After revealing that he was Iron Man, Stark asked O'Brien to substitute for him if the need arose. That day came before O'Brien's Guardsman armor had been fully tested. Stark was kidnapped; O'Brien put on his armor, but its circuitry malfunctioned, stimulating areas of O'Brien's brain responsible for rage and jealousy. Guardsman and Iron Man clashed and Kevin was accidentally killed. Furious, Kevin's brother Michael obtained the Guardsman armor, and fought Stark. They have since become reconciled, and Michael led a Guardsman force guarding the high-tech Vault prison. **AD**

TONY STARK BUILT THIS SUIT BETTER THAN HE KNEW! I FEEL AS IF I COULD SHED METEORS--

Kevin O'Brien tries on the Guardsman armor for the first time.

Ultimately, Tony Stark's victory over the Guardsman depended on his greater experience.

GYRICH, HENRY PETER

FIRST APPEARANCE Avengers #168 (February 1978)
REAL NAME Henry Peter Gyrich
OCCUPATION Adventurer **BASE** Washington, DC
HEIGHT 6 ft 8 in **WEIGHT** 225 lbs **EYES** Green **HAIR** Red
SPECIAL POWERS/ABILITIES Gyrich is a normal human being with no superhuman powers; a cunning, ruthless strategist and highly efficient administrator.

Henry Peter Gyrich was the government liaison to the AVENGERS. He threatened to cut off the team's unlimited airspace access and use of secret government equipment unless they obeyed his rules. As head of Project Wideawake, he transformed the BROTHERHOOD OF EVIL MUTANTS into FREEDOM FORCE. He took over from Valerie COOPER as head of the COMMISSION ON SUPERHUMAN Activity. With the launch of the Fifity-State Initiative (*see* pp. 118–9), Gyrich became Secretary of the Superhuman Armed Forces. He retired after it was discovered that he had covered up the death of Michael VAN PATRICK. **MT, MF**

GREY, JEAN
Telepath of virtually unlimited psychic power

JEAN GREY

FACTFILE

REAL NAME
Jean Grey-Summers

OCCUPATION
Adventurer, former fashion model

BASE
Formerly the Xavier Institute, Salem Center, New York State; now the "White Hot Room"

HEIGHT 5 ft 6 in
WEIGHT 110 lbs
EYES Green
HAIR Red

FIRST APPEARANCE
X-Men #1 (September 1963)

POWERS

As Marvel Girl, possessed mutant abilities of telepathy and telekinesis. The Phoenix Force amplified these powers to a virtually unlimited extent. The Phoenix Force can manifest itself as a fiery corona in the shape of a bird that surrounds Jean Grey's body.

ALLIES/FOES

ALLIES Professor Charles Xavier, Cyclops, Archangel, Beast, Iceman, Storm, Wolverine, Marvel Girl (Rachel Summers), Cable.

FOES Magneto, Mastermind, Hellfire Club, Apocalypse, Sentinels, Xorn I.

ISSUE #1

In the first X-Men comic, Jean Grey arrived at Professor Xavier's school, met her future husband Scott Summers, became Marvel Girl, and first battled Magneto.

Jean's telekinetic power enables her to levitate objects.

When Jean Grey was ten years old, her best friend, Annie Richardson, was hit by an automobile. Jean's anguish as she held her friend activated her mutant telepathic powers, and Jean thus shared Annie's emotions as she died. Traumatized, Jean suffered from deep depression and was unable to control her new telepathic powers.

ESSENTIAL STORYLINES
• **Uncanny X-Men #129–137**
The Dark Phoenix Saga.
• **Fantastic Four #286, X-Factor #1**
Jean Grey returns from apparent death and reunites with Scott Summers (Cyclops).
• **X-Men Vol. 2 #30**
At long last the wedding of Jean Grey and her beloved Scott Summers takes place.

MARVEL GIRL

When Jean was eleven, her parents turned to Professor Charles Xavier (*see* PROFESSOR X) for help. Xavier created psychic shields in Jean's mind to prevent her from utilizing her telepathic powers until she was mature enough to control them. He also began training her telekinetic ability to mentally manipulate objects. As a teenager, Jean enrolled in Xavier's School for Gifted Youngsters, becoming the fifth member of the original X-Men, the team of young mutants whom Xavier was training to combat mutant menaces to humanity. Grey was given the codename "Marvel Girl."

Jean Grey was only a small child when she first met Charles Xavier. She joined the X-Men in her mid-teens.

Grey and her fellow student Scott Summers (CYCLOPS) quickly fell in love, although they did not reveal their feelings to each other for a long time. After she had trained for years at his school, Xavier finally enabled Grey to use her telepathic powers.

Following Xavier's recruitment of a new class of X-Men, Grey left the team. However, soon afterwards she and other X-Men were abducted by SENTINELS to a space station orbiting the Earth. The X-Men had to escape back to Earth in a space shuttle during a solar radiation storm. Grey volunteered to pilot the shuttle, although she had to sit in a section without sufficient radiation shielding. Grey's powers proved insufficient to hold back the intense radiation, and it began killing her.

Phoenix Force: This primal power of creation and destruction manifests itself as a gigantic bird of prey composed of cosmic flame.

PHOENIX FORCE

A sentient cosmic entity of limitless power, the Phoenix Force, made contact with the dying Grey. The Phoenix Force created a human host body for itself that was a duplicate of Grey's, and infused it with a portion of her consciousness. The Phoenix Force placed Grey's original body into suspended animation within a large cocoon, in which it would slowly heal. When the shuttle crash-landed in Jamaica Bay, the Phoenix Force's new host body rose from the water, declaring herself to be Phoenix. The X-Men believed that Phoenix was the real Jean Grey, and Phoenix/Grey joined the team.

The X-Men's old foe the criminal Mastermind began manipulating Phoenix/Grey's mind to prove his worthiness to join the Inner Circle of the

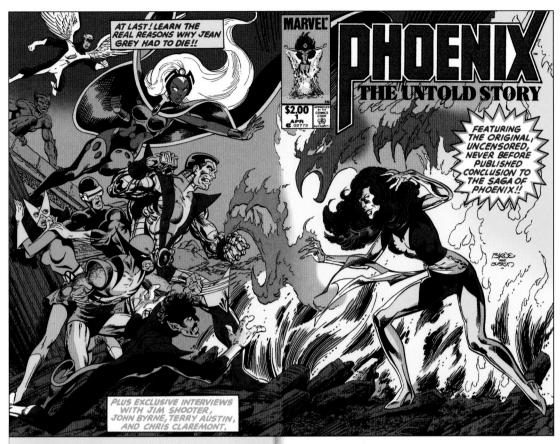

In this cover, Jean Grey appears as Marvel Girl (on the left, with the X-Men) confronting herself as Dark Phoenix (on the right). in the classic "Dark Phoenix Saga."

BLACK QUEEN

The mutant Mastermind projected illusions directly into Phoenix's mind, in which she led a dissolute life in the 18th century. Thus he brainwashed her into becoming the sinister new Black Queen of the Inner Circle of the Hellfire Club. Phoenix regained her free will and sent Mastermind into a coma. However his malevolent tampering with her mind triggered her metamorphosis into the evil Dark Phoenix.

HELLFIRE CLUB, thereby awakening the dark side of her personality. Finally, Mastermind mesmerized her into becoming the new Black Queen of the Hellfire Club. However Mastermind could not control her for long: Phoenix/Jean Grey not only turned against him, she transformed into the insane Dark Phoenix.

Dark Phoenix battled the X-Men, and inadvertently destroyed an inhabited planet. Finally, Jean's original personality reasserted itself. To prevent herself from reverting to Dark Phoenix, she committed suicide as the horrified Cyclops looked on.

BACK FROM THE DEAD

Upon the death of Phoenix's body, the portion of Jean's consciousness within it returned to her original body within the cocoon at the bottom of Jamaica Bay. Scott Summers eventually married Madelyne PRYOR, who later proved to be a Jean Grey clone created by MISTER SINISTER. Scott and Madelyne had a child, Nathan, who became the warrior CABLE.

Eventually the cocoon was found by the AVENGERS, and a revived Jean Grey emerged from it. Soon she, Cyclops, and the other three original X-Men rejoined to found the original X-FACTOR team. Pryor went mad, developed superhuman powers as the Goblin Queen, and died in combat with Grey.

The series *X-Men: The End* depicts an alternate future timeline in which Jean Grey returns once more as Phoenix in time for the team's last adventure.

Inevitably, Grey and the other X-Factor founders rejoined the X-Men.

Finally, Jean Grey and Scott Summers were married, with the other X-Men in attendance. During their honeymoon, Jean and Scott's souls were transported into an alternate future by Mother Askani (Rachel SUMMERS) and infused into new bodies. As "Redd" and "Slym," Jean and Scott raised Nathan Summers for ten years. Jean and Scott's souls were then sent back to their original bodies in their native time period.

DRIFTING APART

Jean assumed the name "Phoenix" and linked herself with the Phoenix Force. Jean and Scott began drifting apart from one another, and Jean discovered that Scott was having an affair with Emma FROST, the former White Queen.

Later, the first Xorn, posing as MAGNETO, slew Grey. But the Phoenix Force resurrected Grey and bonded with her once again. Jean Grey is now "the White Phoenix of the Crown" and inhabits a higher level of reality, known as the "White Hot Room." **PS**

MARVEL IN THE 1970s

Marvel Comics began to experiment with its line of comics during the 1970s. *The Fantastic Four* celebrated its 100th issue in 1970, and new titles such as *Claws of the Cat, Marvel Team-Up, Red Wolf, Shanna the She-Devil, The Tomb of Dracula, Warlock, Werewolf By Night* and *Luke Cage, Hero for Hire* were launched in 1972. *The Monster of Frankenstein, Ghost Rider* and *Tales of the Zombie* followed in 1973. Marvel also published black and white magazines and Treasury-sized editions. *The Man-Thing* and *Marvel Two-In-One* both debuted in 1974.

The Champions, The Invaders, Iron Fist and Skull the Slayer were all awarded titles in 1975. The first issues of *Black Goliath, The Eternals, Howard the Duck, Nova, Omega the Unknown* and *Peter Parker, the Spectacular Spider-Man* appeared in 1976. The Black Panther finally starred in his own title in 1977, accompanied by *Ms. Marvel* and *What If*. *The Defenders, Devil Dinosaur, Machine Man,* and *Spider-Woman* all had first issues in 1978. As the decade drew to a close, the Avengers challenged Korvac, reality went wild when the X-Men first met Proteus and the Fantastic Four were artificially aged as Galactus battled the Sphinx.

AVENGERS #89 (1971)
The Avengers suddenly find themselves in the middle of a war between the space-born Kree and the alien Skrulls.

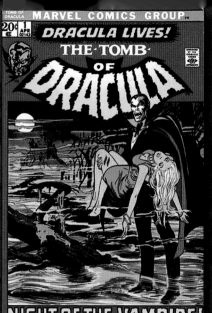

TOMB OF DRACULA #1 (1972)
The first appearance of Dracula in the Marvel Universe and the start a new slew of comics based on classical monster.

AMAZING SPIDER-MAN #121 (1973)
Peter Parker's girlfriend Gwen Stacy is captured and murdered by his greatest enemy—Norman Osborn, the original Green Goblin.

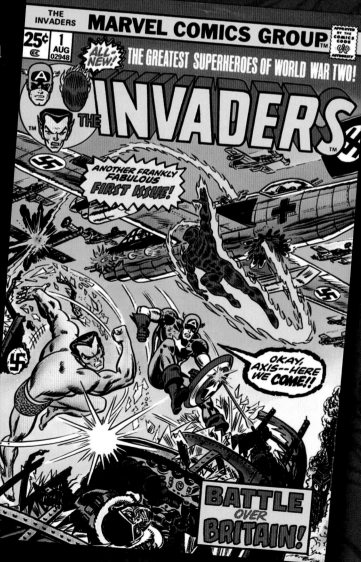

INVADERS #1 (1975)
Captain America, Bucky Barnes, the Human Torch, Toro, and Namor the Sub-Mariner unite to battle the Nazi menace during World War II.

AVENGERS #152 (1976)
After apparently dying in Avengers #9, Wonder Man is resurrected and rejoins the team.

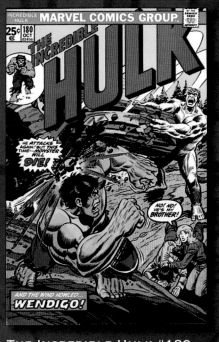

THE INCREDIBLE HULK #180 (1974)

Aside from fighting the mysterious Wendigo, the Hulk must also play host to the very first appearance of Wolverine.

GIANT-SIZED X-MEN #1 (1975)

After a brief hiatus, the X-Men return with new members and a new concept as Nightcrawler, Storm and Thunderbird are introduced.

SPIDER-WOMAN #2 (1978)

Jessica Drew, the original Spider-Woman, teams up with the legendary Merlin the Magician to battle

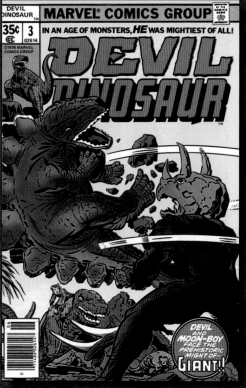

DEVIL DINOSAUR #2 (1978)

Moon Boy and his faithful companion battle strange monsters at the dawn of time.

IRON MAN #128 (1979)

Tony Stark faces his greatest enemy—himself—as he finally admits that he has become an alcoholic.

HALLER, GABRIELLE

FIRST APPEARANCE The Uncanny X-Men #161 (September 1982)
REAL NAME Gabrielle Haller
OCCUPATION Israel's ambassador to the United Kingdom
BASE Tel Aviv, Israel; London, England
HEIGHT/WEIGHT Unrevealed **EYES** Brown **HAIR** Black
SPECIAL POWERS/ABILITIES Gabrielle Haller has no superpowers, but is a highly accomplished diplomat.

Gabrielle Haller is a survivor of the concentration camp in Dachau, Germany. There Nazis implanted in her mind the location of a hidden cache of gold. After the war, Haller was afflicted with catatonic schizophrenia and hospitalized in Israel. Charles Xavier (*see* PROFESSOR X) used his telepathic powers to cure her and they fell in love. When BARON VON STRUCKER and his HYDRA agents kidnapped Haller to find the gold, Xavier and "Magnus" (the future MAGNETO) rescued her.

Many years later Xavier learned that Gabrielle had given birth to a son, David (*see* LEGION). Haller is now Israel's ambassador to UK. **PS**

HAMMER, JUSTIN

FIRST APPEARANCE Iron Man #120 (March 1979)
REAL NAME Justin Hammer
OCCUPATION Criminal financier **BASE** Mobile
HEIGHT 6 ft 2 in **WEIGHT** 170 lbs **EYES** Blue **HAIR** Gray
SPECIAL POWERS/ABILITIES A financial and business genius, Hammer has cunningly preserved his wealth despite being worldwide *persona non grata*.

Whatever Justin Hammer lacked in guile he made up for with low cunning. Infuriated by Stark International's success, Hammer resolved to undermine Tony Stark's business by compromising its corporate emblem, the IRON MAN. Using a hypersonic device to take control of the armored suit, Hammer used it to kill a foreign ambassador. After Stark cleared his name, Hammer went into hiding and took to funding various criminals, including BLIZZARD, BOOMERANG, and Water Wizard. Another showdown with Stark left Hammer frozen in a block of ice and floating through space. **AD**

HAMMERHEAD

Hammerhead's style recalls the Prohibition gangsters of the 1920s.

Once an obscure, small-time criminal, Hammerhead was found, severely injured, by Dr. Jonas Harrow. Harrow reconstructed the criminal's shattered skull, making it as strong as steel—hence his new name. Hammerhead retained no knowledge of his past life, save that he had been a criminal. Taking his inspiration from the poster of a gangster movie, The Al Capone Mob, he adopted a Prohibition-era style and returned to the New York underworld, determined to become the boss of bosses. He was prepared to violently dispatch anyone who stood in his way, including Doctor Octopus, the KINGPIN, and MAGGIA boss Don Fortunato. During the Civil War (*see* pp. 84–5), the Kingpin hired the assassin Underworld to kill Hammerhead. Shot down once more, Hammerhead was saved this time by Mr. Negative, who had his brain transferred into a robotic skeleton made of adamantium. In return, he now trains and leads his benefactor's enforcers. **TB, MF**

HAMMERHEAD

POWERS

Hammerhead's reinforced skull allows him to head-butt with devastating effect, and even smash through walls. He can also use his head as a shield against blows. He has strong criminal organizational skills, and his favorite weapon is a Tommy gun.

A full-powered Spider-punch means nothing to the criminal with the hardest head in the business.

--BUT I'VE GOT THINGS TO DO--AND YOU'RE NOT LEAVING ME MUCH CHOICEEEEEYOW!!

Hammerhead's skull is reinforced with an unbreakable steel alloy.

FACTFILE

NOTABLE MEMBERS

THE BEAST
Demon with mystical powers

KIRGI
Martial arts and occult magic

SHADOW
Martial arts and occult magic

THOUGHT
Martial arts and occult magic

PAIN
Martial arts and occult magic

KWANNON
Martial arts and occult magic

MANDARIN
Martial arts and occult magic

FIRST APPEARANCE
Daredevil #168 (January 1981)

In addition to possessing various mystical powers, Hand operatives are trained in the way of the ninja: expert spies and assassins skilled at unarmed combat, and with all kinds of weapons.

HAND, THE

The Hand is a cult of mystical ninjas involved with organized crime and often hired to carry out assassinations. The Hand dates back to 16th-century Japan, where the cult adapted classical ninjitsu techniques to its own evil purposes. The Hand's activities have now spread throughout the world. Hand operatives are servants of a demon known only as the Beast. Skilled in the use of powerful occult magic, they can kill a person, then bring that person back to life as a member of the Hand. Only ELEKTRA and WOLVERINE have ever been able to reverse this process. If one of the Hand is killed, his body magically turns to dust in order to prevent identification.

The Hand has most often clashed with DAREDEVIL, Elektra, and other members of the clan of warriors once led by STICK, the late martial arts master. They have also battled Wolverine, SPIDER-MAN, the AVENGERS, and the X-MEN. **MT**

Implacable, faceless killers, the Hand cult remains one of the most feared groups of assassins at large in the modern world.

HARKNESS, AGATHA

FIRST APPEARANCE Fantastic Four #94 (March 1969)
REAL NAME Agatha Harkness
OCCUPATION Witch **BASE** New York City
HEIGHT 5 ft 11 in **WEIGHT** 130 lbs **EYES** Blue **HAIR** White
SPECIAL POWERS/ABILITIES Could manipulate magical forces through the recitation of spells; possessed magical familiar named Ebony, a pet cat that could transform into a vicious panther.

Agatha Harkness was raised in the town of New Salem, Colorado, whose inhabitants practiced magic. She excelled in her craft and eventually became the town's most powerful sorceress and leader. Agatha believed that witches and warlocks didn't have to live apart from normal humans. Her son and the town elders disagreed and she choose to leave New Salem. After moving to Whisper Hill, New York, she was hired as the governess for Franklin RICHARDS, son of MR. FANTASTIC and INVISIBLE WOMAN. When the SCARLET WITCH became unbalanced and disassembled the Avengers, she apparently murdered Agatha. However, Agatha has been reported dead before and has returned. **TD**

HARDBALL

FIRST APPEARANCE Avengers: The Initiative #1 (March 2007)
REAL NAME Roger Brokeridge
OCCUPATION HYDRA agent **BASE** Camp Hammond
HEIGHT 6 ft **WEIGHT** 200 lbs **EYES** Green **HAIR** Blond
SPECIAL POWERS/ABILITIES Creates and throws a number of different types of balls of energy.

Roger never wanted to be a hero. His brother Paul purchased powers from the POWER BROKER and then became paralyzed in a wrestling match. When Roger confronted the Power Broker, he signed up for his own powers. Trying to rob an armored car, he accidentally saved a little girl and became a hero. The Power Broker sold Roger's contract to HYDRA, and Roger became part of the first class of cadets at Camp Hammond and spied on the organization from within. Recently, he killed Senator Woodman (*see* WOODMAN, SENATOR), who had been in charge of HYDRA, and became the leader himself. **MF**

HAVOK

The brother of the X-Men leader Cyclops, Alex Summers was separated from his sibling following the death of their parents. Although Alex's mutant abilities developed during puberty, his mutant college professor, Ahmet Abdol, was the first to recognize them. After absorbing the cosmic energy stored in Alex's body, Abdol became the Living Monolith, but was defeated by the X-Men. Reunited with his brother, Alex joined the X-Men. Despite working in Cyclops' shadow, he later led X-Factor and fought to save the dark and twisted Earth-1298. He has long had a romantic relationship with the mutant POLARIS. At one point, he fell in love with his nurse from when he was in a coma, but she left him when she realized life near the X-Men was too dangerous. Since then, he and Polaris seem to be patching up their relationship. They are currently working with the STARJAMMERS to put an end to the plans for galactic conquest of Havok's long-hidden brother VULCAN. **AD, MF**

FACTFILE

REAL NAME
Alexander "Alex" Summers

OCCUPATION
Adventurer; X-Man

BASE
New York State

HEIGHT 6 ft
WEIGHT 180 lbs
EYES Brown
HAIR Blond

FIRST APPEARANCE
X-Men #54 (March 1969)

Havok can absorb solar energy and project it either in an omni-directional wave or in the form of plasma bolts of intense heat, which causes objects to shatter or burn up.

HAWKEYE
The Marksman

HAWKEYE

FACTFILE

REAL NAME
Clinton "Clint" Barton
OCCUPATION
Super Hero; Avengers
member
BASE
Manhattan, New York City

HEIGHT 6 ft 3 in
WEIGHT 230 lbs
EYES Blue
HAIR Blond

FIRST APPEARANCE
Tales of Suspense #57
(September 1964)

POWERS

Expert archer with perfect
accuracy. Employs an arsenal
of custom-made bows and a
variety of trick arrows.
Extensive training as an
aerialist and acrobat. Skilled
in hand-to-hand combat.

Barton was only 14 when he joined a carnival and attracted the attention of the show's star Jacques Duquesne, the SWORDSMAN. Duquesne trained Barton in the art of throwing knives, but quickly realized the boy was a natural at archery and turned him over to Trickshot, the carnival's archer. On stage, Barton was known as Hawkeye the Marksman.

Wickedly sarcastic, Hawkeye has developed some of his trick arrows to both defeat and humiliate his foes.

GOING WRONG

Witnessing IRON MAN in action, inspired Barton to use his archery skills to fight crime. When he tried to prevent a robbery, he was mistaken for a thief, and he wound up fighting Iron Man instead. Soon after that, he met the original BLACK WIDOW and fell in love with her and started committing crimes to impress her.

Barton later reformed and begged to be admitted into the AVENGERS. Iron Man sponsored him, and Barton remained an Avenger for many years, though he occasionally took brief breaks and even joined the DEFENDERS during one of them. To help the team, Barton sometimes borrowed Hank Pym's growth formula and became a new Goliath.

While on leave, Barton married Bobbi Morse (MOCKINGBIRD). They moved to California when Barton was assigned to set up the WEST COAST AVENGERS. After Mockingbird seemed to be killed in action, the West Coast branch disbanded, and Barton rejoined the Avengers. He died stopping a KREE warship during the SCARLET WITCH's breakdown, but she restored him to life when she rearranged reality after M-Day In the meantime, at the request of CAPTAIN AMERICA, Kate Bishop of the YOUNG AVENGERS took on the identity of Hawkeye.

Kate Bishop in her role as Hawkeye while fighting in the Young Avengers.

THE HERO REBORN
Barton took on the identity of Ronin. During the Secret Invasion (*see* pp. 326-7), Barton discovered that a SKRULL had been impersonating Mockingbird when she'd been killed, and that the real Mockingbird was still alive. The two became a couple once more. The villain BULLSEYE took on the identity of Hawkeye as part of the new Avengers team assembled by Norman Osborn (*see* GREEN GOBLIN) and he and Barton have clashed over who is the true Hawkeye. **TD, MF**

ESSENTIAL STORYLINES
- *Hawkeye (tpb)* While working as head of security for Cross Industries, Hawkeye meets and marries Mockingbird.
- *Solo Adventures #1-6* Hawkeye's former mentor Trickshot returns and we learn Clint's true origin.
- *West Coast Avengers Limited Series #1-4* Hawkeye opens a branch office for the Avengers.
- *Avengers #502* Hawkeye courageously sacrifices his life to protect his Avengers teammates.

HEADMEN, THE

The Headmen comprised four brilliant individuals, each so confident of their abilities they were convinced that they should rule the Earth. United by Dr Arthur Nagan they agreed to combine their talents to gain control of the planet. Despite obvious ability, their tactics were at best questionable.

Looking to obtain superhuman powers for themselves, the Headmen targeted the DEFENDERS and succeeded in implanting Chondu's brain into the head of Kyle Richard, alias NIGHTHAWK. When his consciousness was subsequently transferred into the body of a vile monster, Chondu went mad. Although his sanity had returned by the time his brain was transferred into a SHE-HULK clone, this proved to be one step too far. Furious at having been given a woman's body, Chondu attacked the Headmen with the help of SPIDER-MAN. The group reunited and attempted to take over the world, starting with Manhattan, by manipulating a hugely powerful, extra-dimensional entity named Orago the Unconquerable. **AD**

THE HEADMEN
1 Gorilla-Man **2** Ruby Thursday
3 Orago the Unconquerable (not a member) **4** Chondu the Mystic
5 Shrunken Bones

FACTFILE
MEMBERS AND POWERS
GORILLA-MAN
(Dr. Arthur Nagan)
A brilliant scientist, whose head has been mysteriously transplanted onto a gorilla's body.
SHRUNKEN BONES
A biologist and biochemist, experiments on own body led to skeleton shrinking but not skin.
CHONDU THE MYSTIC
A minor adept in the mystic arts; powers determined by body occupied by brain.
RUBY THURSDAY
Artificial head serves as "organic computer", capable of superhuman storage and processing.
BASE Mobile

FIRST APPEARANCE
Defenders #21
(March 1975)

HELLCAT

As a teenager, Patsy Walker was the subject of popular by her mother. As an adult, Walker wed Air Force officer Baxter (later MAD DOG), though the marriage ended unhappily. She had always idolized Super Heroes, so Walker decided to become one, donning a costume once worn by Greer Nelson (TIGRA). Calling herself Hellcat, she aided the AVENGERS and served with the DEFENDERS for years. Eventually she married master of the occult Daimon Hellstrom, the SON OF SATAN. The couple moved to San Francisco, becoming paranormal investigators. Hellcat later took her own life, but her spirit lived on in Hell. There she encountered HAWKEYE and the THUNDERBOLTS, who had journeyed to the underworld to rescue MOCKINGBIRD. The team returned to Earth with Hellcat, who rededicated herself to the heroic life. She was recently sent to Alaska to serve as its superhero as part of the Fifty State Initiative. **DW, MF**

EACH NIGHT THERE WAS A NEW STORY ON THE NEWS. I COULDN'T HEAR ENOUGH ABOUT EACH NEW HERO!

Patsy Walker had a teenage crush on Reed Richards of the Fantastic Four.

HELLCAT WITH THE DEFENDERS
1 Doctor Strange **2** Hellcat **3** Nighthawk
4 Valkyrie **5** Damion Hellstrom

FACTFILE
REAL NAME
Patricia "Patsy" Walker Hellstrom
OCCUPATION
Adventurer
BASE
San Francisco, California

HEIGHT 5 ft 8 in
WEIGHT 135 lbs
EYES Blue
HAIR Red

FIRST APPEARANCE
The Avengers #144
(February 1976)

POWERS

Minor psionic abilities, skilled acrobat and combatant (received combat training from Moondragon on Saturn's moon Titan). Costume enhances strength and agility; steel-tipped claws in gloves and boots; a wrist device fires a 30-ft cable with grappling hook for scaling tall buildings.

Hellfire Club

HELLFIRE CLUB

Founded in England in the mid-18th century, the Hellfire Club was an exclusive social organization for Britain's upper classes. According to legend, the Club provided a place where members could secretly pursue illicit pleasures. In the 1770s, Sir Patrick Clemens and Lady Diana Knight established the Hellfire Club's American branch in New York City. Today, the Hellfire Club is a worldwide organization with branches in London, Manhattan, Paris, and Hong Kong. Its members include socialites, celebrities, wealthy businessmen, and politicians. Despite the Club's outward respectability, its Inner Circle secretly seeks world domination through accruing political and economic influence. Inner Circle members hold positions named after chess pieces. The men dress in 18th-century costume and the women in risqué outfits.

INNER CIRCLE

Industrialist Sebastian SHAW ruled as Black King over an Inner Circle that included his fellow mutant Emma FROST, the White Queen, and cyborg Donald Pierce. To win admission to the Inner Circle, Mastermind mesmerized PHOENIX into becoming the Club's Black Queen. Other members of American Inner Circles in recent years have included MAGNETO, Selene, Daimon Hellstorm, Blackheart, the VIPER, SUNSPOT, and Cassandra Nova. **PS**

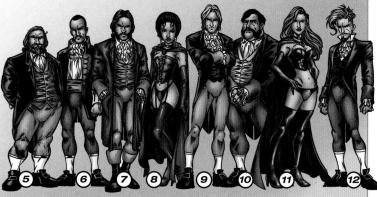

HELLIONS

FIRST APPEARANCE New Mutants #16 (June 1984)
BASE Snow Valley, MA
CURRENT MEMBERS AND POWERS
Rockslide (Santo Vaccarro) Made of granite, can fire hands as projectiles [1]; **Emma Frost** Telepath [2]; **Wither** (Kevin Ford) Touch disintegrates organic matter [3]; **Dust** (Sooraya Qadir) Turns into sandlike substance [4]; **Mercury** (Cessily Kincaid) Shapeshifter made of non-toxic mercury [5]; **Hellion** (Julian Keller) Telekinesis [6]; **Tag** (Brian Cruz) Tags others, causing them to emit a psionic signal [7].

Three groups of young mutants have called themselves the Hellions. The original Hellions were students at EMMA FROST's Massachusetts Academy who served the HELLFIRE CLUB. They were wiped out by a psychotic criminal. The second band were formed by the brother of

X-FORCE member Bedlam, and were out solely for their own interests. The third group of Hellions, students at the Xavier Institute for Higher Learning, had a reputation as bad boy rebels. They ceased to exist in the aftermath of M-Day. **TB**

HELLSTORM

FIRST APPEARANCE Marvel Spotlight #12 (October 1973)
REAL NAME Daimon Hellstrom
OCCUPATION Demonologist, occult investigator, exorcist, former priest **BASE** San Francisco, CA.
HEIGHT 6 ft 1 in **WEIGHT** 180 lbs **EYES** Blue **HAIR** Red
SPECIAL POWERS/ABILITIES Trident projects "soulfire;" can cast spells to transport himself and others into mystical dimensions.

Daimon Hellstrom is the son of a demon named Satan. Sent to an orphanage after his mother's breakdown, Daimon learned the truth about his father. As SON OF SATAN, he joined the Defenders and eventually defeated his father. He married Patsy Walker (HELLCAT), but while saving his life she saw his true face, went insane, and later killed herself. Now calling himself Hellstorm, Daimon figured out how to kill Satan and did so to take over Hell. He then helped Hawkeye's Thunderbolts revive Patsy. Recently, as part of the Fifty State Initiative (see pp. 118-9), Daimon joined the Defenders again. **MT, MF**

◎ **HERCULES** SEE OPPOSITE PAGE

HIGH EVOLUTIONARY

FIRST APPEARANCE Thor #134 (November 1966)
REAL NAME Herbert Edgar Wyndham
OCCUPATION Founder of the Knights of Wundagore **BASE** ?
HEIGHT 6 ft 2 in **WEIGHT** 200 lbs **EYES** Brown **HAIR** Brown
SPECIAL POWERS/ABILITIES Highly evolved intelligence; immense psionic powers; armor reconstructs body when injured enabling virtual immortality; able to grow to 300 ft.

At Oxford in the 1930s, Herbert Wyndham built a genetic accelerator that evolved creatures inside it. Ostracized by his peers, he brought Jonathan Drew and Miles Warren (see JACKAL) to Wundagore Mountain in the Balkans. There, Wyndham used his accelerator on himself to become the High Evolutionary and then created an army of humanoid animals he called the Knights of Wundagore. He later founded a new planetary home for his knights, established Counter-Earth, and— driven insane—tried to evolve all humanity. He has since regained his sanity and dropped his mad plans. He was involved in the Annihilation (see pp. 30–1) event and recently helped Magneto regain a semblance of his powers. **AD, MF**

HERCULES

Super-strong demigod son of Zeus

During his 12 labors, Hercules killed a flock of man-eating birds belonging to his half-brother Ares, the god of war, who has hated him ever since.

Hercules is the son of Zeus, king of the Gods of Olympus, and a mortal woman. He is best known for his Twelve Labors, which he carried out to prove that he was worthy of immortality. He also made three enemies during the course of these labors: Ares, the god of war, Pluto (Hades), the lord of the underworld and Typhon, the giant son of Titan.

PRINCE OF POWER

Hercules is known throughout Olympus as the Prince of Power and he lives for the thrill of battle. He also believes that it is a great honor to fight him and often bestows this so-called "gift" on both friends and foes alike. Instead of a handshake, Hercules likes to greet his fellow AVENGERS with a friendly punch in the face!

In modern times, Hercules met and battled Thor when the thunder god accidentally journeyed to Olympus. Hercules later traveled to Earth to renew his acquaintance with the Asgardian and unwittingly signed a contract that made him Pluto's slave. After being rescued by Thor, Hercules returned to Olympus until the ENCHANTRESS cast a spell on him and sent him to battle the Avengers. He later joined the team when Zeus temporarily exiled him to Earth. He was taken prisoner by Ares and his minions, but rescued by the Avengers. Hercules joined Thor on a journey to the far end of the galaxy, where they battled the Destroyer, FIRELORD and EGO, THE LIVING PLANET. He also joined the Los Angeles super-team known as the Champions and spent time as one of the DEFENDERS.

Hercules often greets Thor with the "gift" of his power—in the form of a punch in the face!

THE TRIALS OF HERCULES

After the Avengers were disassembled, Hercules starred in a reality TV show. He stood against the Superhuman Registration Act and has been a fugitive from the US government ever since. In the climactic battle of the Civil War (*see* pp. 84–5), he killed the clone of THOR with the creature's own false hammer. He allied with the HULK during World War Hulk (*see* pp. 152–5), after which the Hulk's friend Amadeus Cho joined him in his travels. During the Secret Invasion (*see* pp. 326–7), Hercules led the God Squad into battle with the SKRULL gods and defeated them. Recently, Hercules rejoined a new version of the Avengers. **TD, MF**

Hercules has been unlucky in love. He falls for mortal women who grow old and die while he remains young.

Though outnumbered, Hercules tried to defeat the Masters of Evil and almost paid the price.

FACTFILE

REAL NAME
Hercules; aliases Heracles, Harry Cleese

OCCUPATION
Adventurer

BASE
Olympus

HEIGHT 6 ft 5 in
WEIGHT 325 lbs
EYES Blue
HAIR Dark brown

FIRST APPEARANCE:
Journey Into Mystery Annual #1 (1965)

HERCULES

POWERS

Virtually immortal. Trained in hand-to-hand combat and ancient Greek wrestling skills. Excellent archer. Wields a practically indestructible golden mace.

Hercules can be rash and stubborn but is usually gregarious and exuberant. He is a faithful friend and valiant warrior who loves the thrill of battle.

ESSENTIAL STORYLINES

• ***Thor #124–130*** Hercules' first journey to Earth in modern times: enslaved by Pluto, rescued by Thor.
• ***The Avengers: Under Siege tpb*** Zemo's new Masters of Evil invade Avengers Mansion and almost beat Hercules to death.
• ***Hercules: Prince of Power tpb*** Hercules confronts Galactus in the far future.

HOBGOBLIN

FACT FILE NAME

FACTFILE

REAL NAME
Roderick Kingsley

OCCUPATION
Super Villain

BASE
Mobile

HEIGHT 5 FT 11 IN
WEIGHT 185 LBS
EYES Blue
HAIR Gray

FIRST APPEARANCE
Spectacular Spider-Man #43
(June 1980)

POWERS

Hobgoblin's strength and agility are enhanced by improved Goblin formula; flies upon a vertical-thrust Goblin glider; wears electro-shock gloves; carries Jack O'Lantern-shaped grenades in a pouch. Possessed an armor-plated battle-van with an arsenal of weaponry.

When Belladonna attempted to kill him, Roderick Kingsley looked for ways to defend himself. He uncovered a cache of the Green Goblin's costumes and weaponry and sought to dominate New York's criminal underworld as Hobgoblin; however, his efforts were undermined by Spider-Man. To defeat the Wallcrawler, Kingsley has manipulated two other men into taking the Hobgoblin role. Petty crook Lefty Donovan served as a human guinea pig when Kingsley wanted to test his own version of the Goblin formula; and, after being brainwashed by Kingsley, Ned Leeds acted as Kingsley's substitute until his death. Since Betty LEEDS outed Kingsley as the Hobgoblin, he has been in hiding, plotting revenge from the Caribbean. The Hobgoblin of 2211 (Earth-6078) recently came back in time to destroy Spider-Man, but she accidentally used her own weapon against her to erase her existence. **AD, MF**

The various Hobgoblins have all tested Spider-Man's mettle, but the doughty wall-crawler is always victorious.

HODGE, CAMERON

FIRST APPEARANCE X-Factor #1 (February 1986)
REAL NAME Cameron Hodge
OCCUPATION Businessman **BASE** Mobile
HEIGHT 6 ft 2 in **WEIGHT** 196 lbs **EYES** Blue **HAIR** Black
SPECIAL POWERS/ABILITIES Cunning manipulator; due to a pact with the demon N'astrih, Cameron Hodge cannot die; since becoming a cyborg, he has vast strength and weaponry.

Cameron Hodge grew up secretly hating mutants, becoming the leader of the anti-mutant radical group the Right. Hodge suggested that the X-Men go undercover as mutant hunters called X-FACTOR, so as to conceal their activities in recruiting and training mutants. However, his real objective was to stir up anti-mutant sentiment. Hodge later made a pact with the demon N'ASTRIH that gave him immortality. Even after his head was cut off and he was consumed by the techno-organic race known as the PHALANX, Hodge remained a thorn in the X-Men's side. **TB**

HOGAN, HAROLD

FIRST APPEARANCE X-Men Alpha #1 (February 1995)
REAL NAME Harold "Happy" Hogan
OCCUPATION Tony Stark's right-hand man; chauffeur
BASE New York City **HEIGHT** 5 ft 11 in **WEIGHT** 221 lbs
EYES Brown **HAIR** (as human) Brown; (as Freak) None
SPECIAL POWERS/ABILITIES As the Freak, Hogan possesses superhuman strength and durability.

When former boxer "Happy" Hogan saved Tony Stark from a car crash, Stark hired him as his chauffeur. Hogan eventually realized that Stark was secretly Iron Man and sometimes donned an Iron Man battlesuit to stand in for Stark. Doctors used Stark's invention, the Enervator, to save Hogan's life, but its cobalt radiation also transformed Hogan into a virtually mindless monster known as the Freak. Iron Man restored him to normal using the Enervator, although Hogan has sometimes reverted to the Freak. Hogan married PEPPER POTTS—twice. He was nearly killed while saving her from the SPYMASTER, and he later died from his injuries. **PS, MF**

HOLOCAUST

FIRST APPEARANCE X-Men Alpha #1 (February 1995)
REAL NAME Unknown
OCCUPATION Horseman of the Apocalypse **BASE** Mobile
HEIGHT 6 ft 2 in **WEIGHT** 240 lbs **EYES** Red **HAIR** Blond
SPECIAL POWERS/ABILITIES Holocaust is a flaming skeleton held inside a containment suit; able to absorb energy and release it as concussive power blasts.

Sired in the Age of Apocalypse timeline, Holocaust claimed to be the son of APOCALYPSE and served as the leader of Apocalypse's Four Horsemen. Escaping from that timeline just moments before it was obliterated, Holocaust was transported to Earth-616, where he destroyed the Avalon space station and battled another timeline refugee, X-MAN. Press-ganged into joining reality-hopping heroes the EXILES, an encounter with a tyrannical HYPERION led to Holocaust's demise. After cracking his containment suit, Hyperion literally absorbed his entire being. **AD**

HOOD, THE

FIRST APPEARANCE Hood #1 (July 2002))

REAL NAME Parker Robbins   **OCCUPATION** Criminal
Mastermind   **BASE** New York City   **HEIGHT** 5 ft 10 in

WEIGHT 165 lbs   **EYES** Brown   **HAIR** Brown

SPECIAL POWERS/ABILITIES His magic cloak and boots grant
him invisibility, electrical bursts from his hands, the ability to walk
on air, and the ability to transform into a demon.

The son of a man who worked with the KINGPIN, Parker seemed destined for a life of petty crime. While robbing a warehouse, he stumbled upon a summoned demon, killed it, and took its boots and cloak. After becoming embroiled in a battle on a reconstituted Battleworld, Parker returned to Earth and began to build a criminal empire based on superpowered villains. This put him into direct conflict with THE AVENGERS. During the Secret Invasion (*see* pp. 326–7), he joined forces with the heroes to save the Earth. In the aftermath, known as Dark Reign, he joined Norman Osborn's evil cabal (*see* GREEN GOBLIN). **MT**

HOWARD THE DUCK

Howard feels the strain of life in a world not his own.

Howard the Duck was born on Duckworld, where people evolved from waterfowl. When the demon Thog the Nether-Spawn caused the Interdimensional Cosmic Axis to Shift, Howard was dropped into the Florida Everglades on Earth, the site of the Nexus of All Realities. Hoping to get home, Howard joined up with Korrek the Barbarian, the Earth sorceress Jennifer KALE, Dakimh the Enchanter, and the MAN-THING. As this group battled Thog, Howard fell off the Stepping Stones of Oblivion and tumbled back to Earth, landing in Cleveland, Ohio. There he met Beverly Switzler, when the two were attacked by the criminal accountant Pro-Rata. Howard and Beverly escaped and began living together, attempting to have as normal a life as possible in a human-duck relationship. Recently, Howard tried to register under the Superhuman Registration Act but was told that government's official policy is that he did not exist. This was later corrected, and he fought against the Skrulls during the Secret Invasion. **MT, MF**

HOWLING COMMANDOS

The Howling Commandos formed the first attack squad of Able Company during World War II, a unit that took on the most dangerous missions of the war. Under orders from Captain "Happy" SAM SAWYER, Sergeant Nick Fury led his men against the worst the Axis powers could throw at them, including the legendary Blitzkrieg Squad of Baron von Strucker, and the malevolent Red Skull. Many members of the unit survived to become the nucleus of the UN peacekeeping force SHIELD. SHIELD once used the Howling Commandos name for a top-secret squad of monsters dedicated to battling supernatural forces. After leaving SHIELD, Fury assembled a new team of Howling Commandos—a.k.a. the Secret Warriors—to fight the Secret Invasion. This included Druid, Hellfire, Phobos, Quake, Slingshot, and Stonewall. **TB, MF**

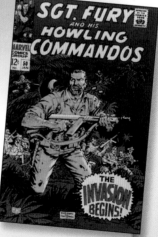

The Howling Commandos were heroes of World War II.

THE LINEUP
1 Sgt. Nick Fury
2 Jonathan "Junior" Juniper
3 Reb Ralston
4 Cpl. Dum Dum Dugan
5 Gabe Jones
6 Dino Manelli
7 Izzy Cohen

THE HULK
The strongest man-like creature on Earth!

FACTFILE

THE HULK

REAL NAME
Robert Bruce Banner

OCCUPATION
Scientist; wanderer

BASE
Mobile

HEIGHT 7 ft
WEIGHT 1,040 lbs
EYES Green
HAIR Green

FIRST APPEARANCE:
Incredible Hulk #1
(May 1962)

POWERS

Fueled by gamma radiation, the Hulk possesses almost unlimited physical strength. The madder he gets, the stronger he gets. He can leap several miles in a single bound. His body heals almost instantly, He possesses a strong homing instinct for the desert where he was "born."

ALLIES Rick Jones, Betty Ross-Banner, Doc Samson, Jennifer Walters (She-Hulk), Jarella, the Avengers.

FOES The Leader, The Abomination, Rhino, Sandman, Juggernaut, Absorbing man, General Thaddeus "Thunderbolt" Ross, Bi-Beast, Zzzax.

ISSUE #1

In his first appearance in The incredible Hulk #1 (May 1962), the Hulk was colored grey, rather than the more familiar green.

Bruce had a troubled childhood; his father called him a monster, and eventually killed his mother.

A child prodigy, Bruce Banner grew up in an abusive household, one that would have a profound long-term effect on his psyche. An introverted child, Bruce was ill-equipped to deal with the outbursts of his father, who called young Bruce a monster and terrorized both him and his mother. Bruce developed a multiple personality disorder, shunting aside and repressing all of his negative emotions when the trauma became too much to take. This cycle of abuse continued until the day Brian Banner slew his wife in a fit of rage. Thereafter, Bruce was shuttled from relative to relative, and grew ever more socially awkward, even as his remarkable intellect became more apparent.

FIRST LOVE

The US Army recruited Banner to develop new weapons systems while he was still in high school. Bruce was placed under the authority of General Thaddeus "Thunderbolt" Ross, a blustering no-nonsense veteran. It was in the person of Ross's daughter Betty that Bruce found a kindred spirit. Both he and Betty had lost mothers, and were subjected to the outbursts of raging fathers; an attraction soon developed between them.

Recruited by the military, Bruce Banner worked on developing new weapons systems on the military base commanded by hard-nosed general "Thunderbolt" Ross.

THE GAMMA BOMB

Prodded by his military handlers, Banner developed the G-Bomb, a weapon harnessing the power of gamma radiation. On the day the bomb was to be tested, a reckless teenager, RICK JONES, drove out onto the test range on a dare, little realizing that he was standing on ground zero of the most potent explosive device ever developed. In an uncharacteristic moment of heroism, Bruce Banner rushed out onto the test site, and dragged Jones to the safety of a nearby trench before the G-Bomb detonated. However Banner was exposed to the full force of the weapon, his every atom bombarded by gamma radiation.

Banner is bathed in gamma rays trying to save the life of Rick Jones.

Over the years, Bruce Banner's transformations into the Hulk have taken on a variety of styles. Initially, Banner would become the Hulk when the sun set, and return to his Banner identity at sunrise. Soon thereafter, Banner learned to control his transformations using a gamma ray machine, becoming a more intelligent but no less savage Hulk. Eventually, the continued exposure to gamma radiation caused Banner to transform into the Hulk whenever he became agitated or upset. Banner's Hulk persona has also differed over the years, each one apparently representing a different facet of his fragmented psyche: the childlike Green Hulk, the more intelligent but less powerful Grey Hulk, the extremely intelligent but egocentric "Professor" Hulk—and even a "Devil Hulk" representing all of the evil within Banner's soul. Additional permutations of the Hulk are apt to emerge at any given time, should conditions prove favorable.

HE'S SCARED. HE AIN'T THE ONLY ONE EITHER... NOT WITH WHAT YOU'VE LET LOOSE IN HERE

WE ALL ARE

MULTIPLE PERSONALITIES
1 Bruce Banner **2** Savage Hulk
3 Joe Fixit **4** Mindless Hulk
5 Professor Hulk

Hulk takes on a pack of gamma-ray-infused dogs, set on him by General Ryker.

A day later, Banner was still silently screaming. But the military doctors could find nothing wrong—he had miraculously escaped the blast unscathed. Or so it seemed. For the gamma radiation Banner had been exposed to had unlocked long-repressed feelings of hate and rage. When conditions were right, Banner found himself transforming into an unstoppable juggernaut of destruction, the personification of his long-denied dark side: the incredible Hulk! At first, the Hulk only manifested at nightfall. When the sun went down, Banner would inexorably change into a green-skinned powerhouse and remain out of control until daybreak. Eventually, due in part to Banner's attempts to cure

himself of these unwanted transformations, the appearance of the Hulk would be brought on by stress and anxiety. Whenever Bruce became outraged or fearful, the change in his emotional state would trigger the gamma radiation within his system, and the Hulk would live again. For a time, with the aid of Rick Jones, Bruce kept his dual identity secret, even while the Hulk was hunted by the same military forces for whom Banner toiled. But eventually the truth was revealed to the world, forcing Banner to become a fugitive, both to escape those who desired the Hulk's destruction, and to protect those who might be harmed during his uncontrollable episodes.

MIND OF A CHILD
The character of the Hulk changed over time. Initially, he had a strong dislike for humanity. However he mellowed as the years went by, resulting in a more childlike Hulk. He simply wanted to be left

alone, and couldn't understand why people were persecuting him. Eventually, the super-powered psychiatrist DOC SAMSON figured out the truth: each of the Hulk's personalities represented a different fragment of Banner's shattered psyche. For a time, Samson was able to fuse the disparate elements of Banner's mind together, granting Banner the strength of the Hulk while allowing him to maintain his own intellect. But this construct proved unstable, and eventually splintered once again.

Over the years, the Hulk has proved a force for good almost as often as he has been an engine of destruction. He was instrumental in the formation of the AVENGERS, Earth's Mightiest Heroes, though friction between himself and his teammates quickly led to him leaving the group. He has stood side-by-side with the DEFENDERS, DOCTOR STRANGE, the SUB-MARINER, and the SILVER SURFER in defense of our planet. But for the most part, the Hulk calls no man friend. Bruce Banner and his superhuman alter ego remain ever at odds, as they strive to stay one step ahead of forces who would see the Hulk destroyed, or exploit his power for their own ends. **TB**

ESSENTIAL STORYLINES
• *Incredible Hulk #312* The truth about Bruce Banner's multiple personality disorder and traumatic childhood is revealed.
• *Incredible Hulk #377* Doc Samson unites Banner's splintered psyche into an intelligent Hulk.
• *Incredible Hulk #24-25* General "Thunderbolt" Ross unleashes the Hulk against the Abomination, who had secretly poisoned Ross's daughter and Hulk's beloved, Betty Banner!

The Hulk

A new Hulk cuts loose

Imaginary friend or inner demon? The Hulk seems to have been with Bruce Banner for most of his life, in one form or another.

TEMPEST FUGIT

After walking for miles on the ocean floor, the Hulk came upon a mysterious island and collapsed in front of two castaways: a woman named Gwen and her blind boyfriend Ripley. After battling a series of monsters, including the original gray version of himself, Hulk confronted the master of this strange land and forced him to reveal himself as NIGHTMARE, the lord of dreams.

Nightmare claimed to have created the island as an outpost of his realm. In the wake of the terrorist attacks of September 11, 2001, so many people wished for reality to be just a bad dream that they gave him the power to establish the island. He populated it with a group of MINDLESS ONES and disguised them with his perception-twisting powers.

When a Mindless One acting as Thunderbolt ROSS nearly killed Gwen, she remembered who she was. Calling herself Daydream, she revealed that she was the daughter of Nightmare, who he claimed to have had with Betty BANNER while she lay in a coma. Disgusted by this, Hulk ripped off Nightmare's head and rode away on his horse.

The strange island on which the Hulk washed up gave him the chance to battle with all sorts of monsters, including himself.

Nightmare taunted the Hulk with the idea that nothing he knew might be real—and paid the Hulk's price.

PLANET HULK

The Hulk eventually found his way to Alaska, where Bruce Banner set up house in a remote cabin, far away from the rest of humanity and any of its troubles. It did not last long. Nick FURY found him and asked Banner to become the Hulk and help SHIELD disarm a lethal satellite in orbit around the Earth. Banner agreed, but after the Hulk completed the mission, he was not brought home but instead fired into deep space.

Having learned of the Hulk's mission, the ILLUMINATI saw a chance to get rid of the Hulk and took it. Instead of reaching a verdant and unpopulated

The collateral damage from the Hulk's battles with other heroes often caused more destruction than the Hulk ever would have on his own.

The planet Sakaar offered Hulk a series of battles from the moment he crawled from his starship and onto its shattered surface.

planet, however, the ship entered a wormhole and crashed on war-ravaged Sakaar. Far from being a paradise, Sakaar was a savage planet filled with danger and a variety of alien life-forms. Immediately after the crash, the Hulk was captured and enslaved. He was fitted with an obedience disk, a device that ensured he would do his new masters' bidding.

Forced to fight as a gladiator in the Red King's arena, the Hulk survived his training and bonded with his fellow warriors, who became his WARBOUND, a tight-knit team of some of the hardest people and creatures from Sakaar and beyond. Fighting his way up the arena's chain, the Hulk got his chance at the Red King and cut him before he was brought down.

Later, the Hulk and the Warbound broke free and led a rebellion against the bloodthirsty Red King. When the Hulk's blood caused a flower to grow, many believed the Hulk was a legendary savior called Sakaarson, destined to lead the enslaved to freedom. The Hulk and his allies succeeded in overthrowing the Red King and Hulk placed himself on the throne, marrying one

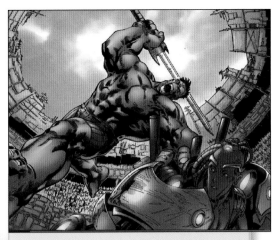

The Red King thought he could best the Hulk in gladiatorial combat, but even wearing a suit of powered armor he fell before the Hulk's fury.

of his compatriots—Caiera, the Red King's former lieutenant—who became pregnant with his child. Finally happy and at peace as King of Sakaar, the Hulk began to work to improve the lives of his subjects—until the ship he'd first come to Sakaar in mysteriously exploded. The massive blast killed millions of people, including Caiera. **MF**

> **ESSENTIAL STORYLINES**
> • *Incredible Hulk Vol. 3 #77–81* In "Tempest Fugit," the Hulk learns that Nightmare has been playing with him for years.
> • *Incredible Hulk Vol. 3 #92–105* In "Planet Hulk," the Hulk rises from a gladiatorial slave to the conqueror of an entire alien planet.
> • *Hulk #1–6* The mysterious Red Hulk debuts.

THE RED HULK

After the events of World War Hulk (see pp. 152–5), in which the Hulk returned from Sakaar for his revenge, a new, red Hulk appeared in Russia and gunned down the ABOMINATION with a pistol the size of a small cannon. He next arrived at the new SHIELD Helicarrier built by Tony Stark (IRON MAN) and tore it from the sky. Soon after that, back near the Gamma Base under which Banner was being held, he attacked Rick JONES, who transformed into A-Bomb, a gamma-irradiated creature with armored, blue skin.

The Red Hulk beat A-Bomb badly, but their battle accidentally freed the Hulk. In the ensuing battle, the Red Hulk took on and defeated the Hulk, THOR, and even the WATCHER. Eventually, he overheated, and the Hulk took advantage of this momentary weakness to trounce him. The identity of the Red Hulk is still secret. Although DOC SAMSON and Thunderbolt ROSS claim to have helped create him, neither they nor anyone else has revealed the Red Hulk's real identity.

> The Red Hulk attacked the new SHIELD Helicarrier Gold and singlehandedly brought it down, beating his way through She-Hulk, Iron Man, and countless SHIELD agents

The Red Hulk attacked Rick Jones, but he got more than he bargained for when Jones transformed into a A-Bomb, a new version of the Abomination.

WORLD WAR HULK

A Story of Revenge

The Hulk defeated Black Bolt. Then he called the rest of the Illuminati out to battle him in Manhattan. Iron Man attacked in his Hulkbuster armor, but the Hulk's fury could not be stopped.

The ILLUMINATI decided that the HULK had become too dangerous to be permitted to remain on Earth. Discovering that a Life Model Decoy robot of Nick FURY had sent the Hulk into space on a mission, they turned his rescue vehicle away from Earth and sent it toward an uninhabited planet. On its way, the ship entered a wormhole and wound up on the planet Sakaar. There, the Hulk became a gladiatorial slave of the Red King—until he and his WARBOUND friends led a rebellion that installed him as the planet's king instead.

MADDER THAN EVER

As king, the Hulk married the Red King's lieutenant CAIERA, making her his queen. His happiness was shattered, however, when the ship in which he'd traveled to Sakaar exploded, killing millions of people, including the pregnant Caiera. Believing the Illuminati, were responsible, the Hulk gathered his Warbound allies and returned to Earth.

On his way to Earth, the Hulk stopped at the Moon to pick up BLACK BOLT. He and his Warbound then appeared in their starship over Manhattan and gave the people 24 hours to evacuate. IRON MAN, wearing his latest Hulkbuster armor, attacked, but the Hulk defeated him and brought his Warbound to help beat the AVENGERS. He then took on the FANTASTIC FOUR and captured MR. FANTASTIC.

While General Ross led the US Army against the Hulk, DR. STRANGE tried to help his old friend. The Hulk broke his hands, making it difficult for him to cast spells. Then he set up Madison Square Garden as a gladiatorial arena. Desperate, Dr. Strange unleashed and merged with the demon Zom, becoming as angry and powerful as the Hulk. When he nearly killed a group of bystanders, however, doubts overcame him, and the Hulk brought him down.

Back in Madison Square Garden, the Hulk permitted those with grievances against BLACK BOLT, DR. STRANGE, IRON MAN, and MR. FANTASTIC to demand justice. He then unleashed a monster from Sakaar on the heroes. When they survived that, he used slave disks implanted in each of them to set the four against each other.

At the last moment, the Hulk spared the Illuminati, stating that he had come for justice, not murder. Having exposed them for what they were, he and the Warbound would raze Manhattan and then leave. Before he could do so, the SENTRY finally showed up and attacked. He and the Hulk battled each other until they both reverted to their human forms. Unwilling to let the conflict end, Miek—the first of the Warbound that the Hulk had ever met—stabbed the Hulk's oldest friend, Rick JONES to enrage Bruce Banner and make him turn back into the Hulk. Miek also revealed that he had seen a band of Red King loyalists set the explosion on Sakaar but had said nothing so that the Hulk would go to war.

Too angry to control himself, the Hulk begged Iron Man to stop him. Iron Man fired a coordinated blast from several orbital satellites, causing the Hulk to become Bruce Banner once more. Unconscious, he was captured and imprisoned three miles beneath the earth.

Black Bolt was the only Super Hero who had ever defeated the Hulk. Because of this, the Hulk made sure to take him out first when he returned to Earth.

Dr. Strange was desperate enough—after the Hulk broke his hands—to merge himself with the spirit of the vicious demon Zom. But even this action wasn't sufficient to stop the Hulk.

The Gamma Corps charged into action against the Hulk for the first time, each hungry for revenge. When he showed them who was really to blame for their troubles, they changed their target to the Illuminati instead.

Although most people fled Manhattan before the battle began, many New York landmarks fell in the battle with the Hulk, including Stark Tower and Madison Square Garden

HULK VS. EVERYONE

When the Hulk returned to Earth for his revenge, he was ready to fight anyone who came between him and the Illuminati. Black Bolt, Mr. Fantastic, Iron Man, and Dr. Strange had a lot of friends willing to stand by them, no matter what they might or might not have done; nevertheless, the Hulk and his Warbound beat them all. The Illuminati were bound with slave disks and brought to Madison Square Garden. There they were forced to fight each other. Despite his rage, the Hulk remained true to his claim that he had returned not for murder but justice. None of the heroes— nor anyone else—died at his hand.

THE WARBOUND ATTACK!

After defeating Black Bolt and Iron Man, the Hulk and his Warbound allies from the planet Sakaar face off against the Avengers in an evacuated Manhattan. This pits the Hulk, Elloe Kaifi, Hiroim the Shamed, Korg the Kronan, Miek the Unhived, and No-Name of the Brood against Ares, Doc Samson, Luke Cage, Ms. Marvel, She-Hulk, Spider-Man, Spider-Woman, and Wonder Man. As the Hulk's cousin and friend, She-Hulk made a last-ditch appeal to him to put aside his rage and let the rule of law judge the crimes of the Illuminati. If he had agreed to this, his point would have been made, and the battle would have been over before it had barely gotten started. Instead, the Hulk attacked the She-Hulk, and the real fighting began.

HUMAN TORCH

The Super Hero who is literally "hot stuff!"

FACTFILE

REAL NAME
Jonathon Lowell Spencer Storm

OCCUPATION
Adventurer

BASE
New York City

HEIGHT 5 ft 10 in
WEIGHT 170 lbs
EYES Brown
HAIR Brown

FIRST APPEARANCE
Fantastic Four #1
(November 1961)

POWERS

Able to control heat energy and cover his body with fiery plasma for over 16 hours before needing to rest, for about 12 hours. He can release a single "Nova-burst" which strikes with the force of a nuclear warhead. The Torch can create shapes from flame, including letters which burn in the sky for 3 minutes. He can also control the temperature of objects with his mind. Clothing is made of special fire-resistant fabric.

ALLIES/FOES

ALLIES Invisible Woman, the Thing, Mr. Fantastic, Lyja the Laserfist, Alicia Masters, Spider-Man.

FOES Doctor Doom, Onslaught, Gormuu, Frightful Four, Galactus.

ISSUE #1

When Johnny Storm's sister, Sue, accompanied her fiancé, Reed Richards, into space, Johnny insisted on tagging along. Transformed into the Human Torch, he battled the Mole Man.

The Human Torch can generate and control fire from any part of his body.

Johnny Storm and his older sister Susan grew up on Long Island, New York, the children of a doctor and his wife. In spite of the fact that Johnny's mother was killed in a car crash when he was nine years old, the boy developed a passion and skill for building, fixing, and driving cars. He overhauled his first transmission at the age of 15. The following year his father bought him his first hot rod.

FATEFUL FLIGHT

While a teenager, Johnny went to California to visit his sister Susan who had moved out west to become an actress. Susan Storm (INVISIBLE WOMAN) was engaged to marry a brilliant physicist and engineer named Reed Richards (MISTER FANTASTIC). Richards was developing a starship that would be capable of exploring other galaxies.

While Johnny was in California, the government threatened to cut off Richards' funding and so he decided to prove his ship's worth by taking it on a test flight to the stars. Reed's best friend Ben Grimm (THE THING) piloted the craft. Susan and Johnny insisted on coming along.

In space, inadequate shielding on the starship allowed a huge dose of cosmic radiation to bombard the crew. They managed to return to earth using the autopilot, but all four were changed forever.

The cosmic rays altered Johnny's genetic structure allowing him to create fiery plasma that covered his entire body in flames without causing him harm.

JOHNNY! WHAT *IS* IT? WHAT'S HAPPENING TO YOU?

I DON'T KNOW, SIS! MY BODY FEELS HOT-- LIKE IT'S *ON FIRE!!* I--I FEEL LIKE I'M BURNING UP!!

YOU'RE STARTING TO SMOKE!!!

Following exposure to cosmic radiation, Johnny Storm's body burst into flame.

The Human Torch creates multiple flaming images of himself in an attempt to escape from fireproof natives with poison-tipped spears.

THE FIRST HUMAN TORCH

The original Human Torch was an android, created by Professor Phineas T. Horton. But the professor's dream of creating a perfect human being failed when the android's body, which was covered in photoelectric solar cells, burst into flames on contact with oxygen. Astonishingly, the android itself was not harmed by the fire. At first the public labeled this Human Torch a menace. The Torch then rejected his creator's "ownership," claiming he didn't want to be a "slave" to someone more concerned about his own fame than about his creation's well-being.

Once he learned to control his flames, the Human Torch vowed never to use his power for evil or harm, and he became a crimefighter. When World War II broke out, the Human Torch teamed with other super heroes, using his abilities to fight the Axis Powers.

In modern times, the Human Torch worked with Heroes for Hire, the West Coast Avengers and even the Fantastic Four. At one point, Immortus split the Torch into two bodies, one of which became the Vision As part of a new team of Invaders the Torch sacrificed himself to save his teammates' lives.

Exposure to oxygen caused the photoelectric cells in the original Human Torch's skin to burst into flame, to the surprise of the android and its creator.

Fighting fire with fire: the original Human Torch faces off against Johnny Storm, the Human Torch of Fantastic Four fame!

He also discovered that he was able to fly, shoot flames, and absorb heat.

Calling themselves the Fantastic Four, the transformed astronauts decided to team up and use their new powers to help humankind. Johnny chose to call himself the Human Torch, the same name used by an android hero of the 1940s.

For a while, Johnny tried living with his sister on Long Island, attempting to complete high school while at the same time trying to keep that fact he was the Human Torch a secret. This proved far more difficult than he had anticipated. After he finished high school, Johnny moved into

The Human Torch can release concussive blasts of heat energy, each packing a powerful punch.

the Baxter Building, the Fantastic Four's original headquarters in New York City.

LOVE RIVALS

Johnny always loved to tease the unfortunate Thing, Ben Grimm, who was easily angered and jealous of Johnny's good looks and charm. Still, they felt a great affection for each other. This however was greatly strained when Johnny fell in love with and eventually married the blind sculptress Alicia Masters, the only woman that had ever returned Ben's affection.

Later, Alicia Masters was revealed to be a Skrull spy named Lyja, a deception that devastated Johnny.

During the Civil War (*see* pp. 84–5), Johnny took a beating at the hands of an angry mob. When he awoke, he joined Captain America's resistance. Recently, during the Secret Invasion (*see* pp. 326–7), he had a chance to settle matters with his Lyja, who teleported the upper part of the Baxter Building—along with Johnny, the Thing, and Franklin and Valeria Richards—into the Negative Zone. MT, MF

Flaming on (except for his left arm), Johnny rescues a woman from an attacking Sentinel.

HULKLING

FIRST APPEARANCE Young Avengers #1 (April 2005)
REAL NAME Theodore "Teddy" Altman/Dorrek VIII
OCCUPATION Adventurer, student **BASE** New York City
HEIGHT Varies **WEIGHT** Varies
EYES Usually blue **HAIR** Usually Blond
SPECIAL POWERS/ABILITIES Shapeshifting and superhuman strength and healing.

Born the secret son of Princess Anelle (a SKRULL) and CAPTAIN MAR-VELL (a KREE), Teddy Altman had thought he was a human mutant when he co-founded the YOUNG AVENGERS. He learned the truth when the SUPER-SKRULL tried to return him to the Skrulls. Teddy became a pawn in a face-off between the Kree and Skrull empires, settled only when he agreed to spend six months with each race before deciding which side to join—but the Super-Skrull left in his place instead. Teddy subsequently came out as gay and is in a relationship with teammate Wiccan. **MF**

HUNTARA

FIRST APPEARANCE Fantastic Four #377 (June 1993)
REAL NAME Huntara Richards
OCCUPATION Guardian of the Sacred Timelines **BASE** Elsewhen
HEIGHT 6 ft 2 in **WEIGHT** 185 lbs **EYES** Brown **HAIR** Black
SPECIAL POWERS/ABILITIES Psionic scythe cuts through almost any material, fires concussive bolts and teleports her between dimensions and across space; superior athlete and combatant.

Huntara was born on an alternate Earth. The daughter of Nathaniel Richards and the half-sister of MISTER FANTASTIC, she was taken to Elsewhen, a barbaric alien dimension. Huntara was trained in the arts of war and combat alongside her nephew Franklin and they both became Guardians of the Sacred Timelines, who prevent and repair time paradoxes.

When her father created a time paradox by exchanging the teenager Franklin RICHARDS with his younger self, Huntara was forced to journey to this timeline where she eventually met the FANTASTIC FOUR. She later returned to Elsewhen and resumed her duties as a Guardian. **TD**

HUNTER, STEVIE

FIRST APPEARANCE The Uncanny X-Men #139 (November 1980)
REAL NAME Stephanie "Stevie" Hunter
OCCUPATION Dance instructor **BASE** Salem Center, New York
State **HEIGHT** 5 ft 9 in **WEIGHT** 121 lbs
EYES Brown **HAIR** Dark brown
SPECIAL POWERS/ABILITIES A talented dancer and athlete and an excellent dance teacher.

Stevie Hunter was a ballet dancer, until a broken leg forced her to retire. She became a dance instructor and opened a school in Salem Center, New York State. Professor Charles Xavier's School for Gifted Youngsters, the headquarters of

the X-MEN, was located nearby. One of Xavier's students, Kitty PRYDE, began taking lessons at Hunter's school. Eventually, Hunter discovered that Xavier's students were mutants. Xavier hired Hunter to be a physical trainer and therapist at his school.

Hunter has since returned to operating her own dance academy. **PS**

HUSK

Husk, Archangel and Iceman are surrounded by a pack of slavering wolf men.

Condemned to a humdrum life on a struggling family farm in West Virginia, Paige Guthrie envied her elder brother who, as Cannonball, had forged a career among the NEW MUTANTS team. Although she underwent a mutation of her own, Paige kept this hidden until she was forced into a battle of wits with the Gamesmaster. This mutant with psionic powers had formed the UPSTARTS, who specialized in assassinating mutants. Paige's intervention freed her brother and several of his friends from the Grandmaster's clutches. Shortly afterward, she was captured by PHALANX, along with several other young mutants. Its effort to assimilate them into its consciousness was foiled and Paige was invited to join the Xavier Institute's new school, Massachusetts Academy, and become a member of Generation X. Paige subsequently joined X-Corps, helping to police mutants in Europe, and then went traveling with Archangel. Her brother Jay and sister Melody were also mutants, but Melody lost her powers on M-Day, and Jay died soon after. **AD, MF**

Husk tears off her skin to reveal a woman of steel

FACTFILE

HUSK

REAL NAME
Paige Elisabeth Guthrie
OCCUPATION
X-Man
BASE
New York State

HEIGHT 5 ft 7 in
WEIGHT 127 lbs
EYES Blue
HAIR Black

FIRST APPEARANCE
X-Force #32
(March 1994)

POWERS

A mutant metamorph, Husk can shed skin and transform her body into any form with similar or less mass. She frequently turns her body into a different substance, such as steel or stone, taking on the properties of that substance, for example increased strength.

HYDRA

FACTFILE

KEY MEMBERS

BARON VON STRUCKER
Master criminal strategist; founder of HYDRA.

ARNOLD BROWN
Brilliant bureaucrat who transformed HYDRA.

RED SKULL
Instructed Strucker to found HYDRA.

MADAME HYDRA
Leader of New York City HYDRA

LAURA BROWN
Daughter of Arnold Brown; one of the first women to serve in HYDRA.

BASE Mobile

FIRST APPEARANCE
Strange Tales #135
(August 1965)

Created by Baron von Strucker after WWII, Hydra began with a base on a Pacific island. When US Marines destroyed this, Hydra decentralized, becoming harder to attack. Under Strucker's guidance, Hydra twice attempted to blackmail the world, first with a Betatron bomb and later with a biological weapon. After his death, Hydra focused on criminal activities. In recent years Hydra has been reinvigorated, allying with the Hand to prepare for a confrontation with the Avengers. SPIDER-WOMAN worked for Hydra and SHIELD as a double agent, but this fell apart when she was revealed to be the Skrull queen VERANKE. Soon after this, Hardball became the new leader. Recently, Nick Fury discovered that Hydra had controlled SHIELD and many other international intelligence organizations for decades. **AD, MF**

The personalities of HYDRA personnel are subordinate to the organization they serve.

HYDRO-MAN

FIRST APPEARANCE Amazing Spider-Man #212 (January 1981)
REAL NAME Morris Bench
OCCUPATION Criminal **BASE** New York City
HEIGHT 6 ft 2 in **WEIGHT** 265 lbs **EYES** Brown **HAIR** Brown
SPECIAL POWERS/ABILITIES Changes body into watery liquid; can merge with larger bodies of water; propels liquid body as if it were shooting through a fire hose; can turn body into ice or steam.

While working as a crewman on a cargo ship lowering an experimental generator into the ocean, Morris Bench was accidentally knocked overboard by SPIDER-MAN. Exposed to the energy-conversion process of the generator, which mixed with volatile volcanic gases, Bench gained the ability to change his body into water. As Hydro-Man he sought revenge against Spider-Man. Later, in a battle with SANDMAN, Hydro-Man fused with the Super Villain and the two became a mud creature. Eventually they were separated. Hydro-Man joined the SINISTER SYNDICATE and later, GREEN GOBLIN's Sinister Twelve, and continues to battle Spider-Man, BLACK CAT, and the AVENGERS. **MT**

HYPERION

A member of the race of Eternals on Earth-712, Hyperion, unaware of his lineage, was raised by human beings and taught to use his tremendous powers for good. As Hyperion, he became the foremost champion of his world, and a founding member of the heroic Squadron Supreme. After the Squadron was manipulated by the OVERMIND into participating in a plan that left their world decimated, Hyperion and his fellow Squadron members resolved to take control of their world for one year and turn it into a utopian state within that time. Despite initial success, their program met with resistance from one of the Squadron's former members, NIGHTHAWK. Unfortunately, by the time the team members were ready to dismantle the government they had set up, it had turned into a corrupt, totalitarian regime. Ever since, Hyperion and the remaining Squadron members have functioned as freedom fighters, trying to liberate their homeland. An evil Hyperion appeared on the mainstream Earth-616 first, as part of the Grandmaster's Squadron Sinister. **TB, MF**

In one world visited by the reality-hopping Exiles, Hyperion had murdered most of humanity.

FACTFILE

REAL NAME
Unrevealed; adopted the human identity of Mark Milton for a time.

OCCUPATION
Adventurer, world leader

BASE
Squadron City on the Squadron Supreme's parallel Earth.

HEIGHT 6 ft 4 in
WEIGHT 460 lbs
EYES Blue
HAIR Red

FIRST APPEARANCE
Avengers #85
(February 1971)

Hyperion possesses almost limitless strength, speed, and endurance. He is impervious to virtually any injury, can fly through the air, and project radioactive beams of energy from his eyes as "Flash-Vision."

ICEMAN

FACTFILE

REAL NAME
Robert Drake

OCCUPATION
Adventurer

BASE
The Xavier Institute for
Higher Learning

HEIGHT 5 ft 8 in
WEIGHT 145 lbs
EYES Brown
HAIR Brown

FIRST APPEARANCE
Uncanny X-Men #1
(September 1963)

POWERS

Iceman can manipulate temperatures around him to freeze the water vapor in the air, forming a variety of icy weapons, protective ice shields, and ice slides.

Iceman can transform back into an ordinary-looking human being at will.

Born a mutant, young Bobby Drake was almost lynched when his ability to freeze moisture in the air was discovered. Bobby was saved by CYCLOPS of the X-MEN, and became the second recruit to Professor Charles Xavier's School for Gifted Youngsters (*see* PROFESSOR X), where he would learn to control his mutant gifts. Adopting the codename Iceman, Drake fought as one of the X-Men, battling such menaces as MAGNETO's BROTHERHOOD OF EVIL MUTANTS, the JUGGERNAUT, and the robotic SENTINELS. Upon graduation, Iceman attempted to forge a super-heroic career on his own, founding the Champions of Los Angeles. However, his path eventually led him back to Xavier's School, where he remains as a member of the X-Men today. His command of his icy abilities has also increased, to the point where, rather than simply sheathing his body in an icy coating, Drake's entire form now transmutes into living, sentient ice. **TB**

Iceman creates weapons of all kinds from ice, from single missiles to hailstones. Here he lets fly with an ice beam.

Iceman slides along at superhuman speeds thanks to a path of ice that he creates himself.

IKARIS

FIRST APPEARANCE The Eternals Vol. 1 #1 (July 1976)
REAL NAME Unrevealed
OCCUPATION Prime Eternal   **BASE** Olympia, Greece
HEIGHT 6 ft 2 in   **WEIGHT** 230 lbs   **EYES** Blue   **HAIR** Blond
SPECIAL POWERS/ABILITIES Superhuman strength; virtual immortality and indestructibility; psionic abilties, including flight through levitation; projects cosmic energy from eyes or hands.

Born over 20,000 years ago, Ikaris is one of the Polar ETERNALS. He calls himself Ikaris in memory of his deceased son. Under the name "Ike Harris," Ikaris accompanied archeologist Dr. Daniel Damian and his daughter Margo to the Andes, where they witnessed the arrival of the Fourth Host of the CELESTIALS. He later succeeded Thena as Prime Eternal. After the Eternals all lost their memories, Ikaris was killed. Reborn with his memories restored, he worked to locate the other Eternals and remind them who they were. **PS, MF**

IMMORTUS

Immortus was born in the 31st Century of one of Earth's alternate futures. It was a time of peace and prosperity, but Immortus craved adventure. Using parts found in the ruins of his ancestors' property, he built a time machine and set off traveling through time. In each time era he arrived at, Immortus adopted a new guise, among them Rama-Tut and KANG THE CONQUEROR. He left behind countless temporal counterparts capable of existing on their own and of further time travel. The being who became Rama-Tut journeyed to Limbo, a realm existing outside the timestream itself. There he was visited by the TIME-KEEPERS, who helped him unlock the secrets of time. Immortus then set about untangling the many timelines he and his counterparts had created by their time travel. **MT**

FACTFILE

REAL NAME
Unknown

OCCUPATION
Ruler of Limbo

BASE
Limbo, outside the
timestream

HEIGHT 6 ft 3 in
WEIGHT 230 lbs
EYES Green
HAIR Gray

FIRST APPEARANCE
Avengers #10
(November 1964)

POWERS

Immortus has no superhuman powers. His abilities come from his use of the vast knowledge and advanced technology he has accumulated on his travels through time.

REAL NAME
Unknown

OCCUPATION
Trickster and student of Earth's popular culture

BASE
Mobile

HEIGHT 6 ft 4 in
WEIGHT 165 lbs
EYES White
HAIR None

FIRST APPEARANCE
Fantastic Four Vol. I #11 (February 1963)

POWERS

Limitless shape-shifting abilities; can mirror properties of objects he imitates (if he's a hose he can spray water, as a light bulb he can light up); asexual reproduction.

IMPOSSIBLE MAN

The planet Poppup was an inhospitable world, its people surviving through asexual reproduction and their shape-changing abilities and group mind. Then a Poppupian was born who had a degree of individuality. Bored by life, this creature transformed himself into a spacecraft and traveled to Earth where he encountered the FANTASTIC FOUR. Finding him unbearably annoying, the THING told the creature that he was "impossible", and so "Impossible Man" was born.

To the Fantastic Four's annoyance, the team has encountered Impossible Man several times. When GALACTUS was threatening to consume Counter-Earth, Impossible Man tricked him into eating Poppup instead, giving him a bad case of cosmic indigestion. With his peoples' consciousness living on through him, Mr Impossible set about rebuilding the Poppup race, first creating a wife—Impossible Woman—and later scores of children. Despite his newfound responsibilities, Impossible Man has continued to visit Earth, oblivious of humanity's ambivalence toward him. **AD**

Impossible Man can change himself into just about anything.

Transformed into a rocket, Impossible Man left his homeworld far behind him.

FIRST APPEARANCE *Warlock Vol. 1 #10* (December 1975)
REAL NAME Inapplicable
OCCUPATION Cosmic entity **BASE** Mobile
HEIGHT 15 ft **WEIGHT** Unrevealed
EYES White **HAIR** None
SPECIAL POWERS/ABILITIES Near-infinite cosmic power, often held in check by its own need for balance.

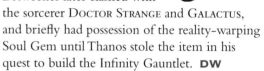

The In-Betweener, the creation of LORD CHAOS and MASTER ORDER, is the living synthesis of balance, representing both life and death, good and evil, logic and emotion, reality and illusion, existence and nothingness, and god and man. When the Titan THANOS tried to plunge the universe into death, the In-Betweener tried to restore balance by abducting Adam WARLOCK and turning him into a champion of life. The In-Betweener later clashed with the sorcerer DOCTOR STRANGE and GALACTUS, and briefly had possession of the reality-warping Soul Gem until Thanos stole the item in his quest to build the Infinity Gauntlet. **DW**

FIRST APPEARANCE *X-Factor #28* (May 1988)
REAL NAME Not known
OCCUPATION Genetic manipulator **BASE** New York City
HEIGHT 5 ft 6 in **WEIGHT** 120 lbs **EYES** Brown **HAIR** Black
SPECIAL POWERS/ABILITIES Perceives molecular structure of organic lifeforms, and is able to mutate the lifeforms genetically by kissing them.

The daughter of a geneticist, Infectia gained an enormous amount of knowledge from her father, which enabled her to understand her mutant ability to mutate organic life. Following her father's death while she was still at high school, Infectia inherited a small fortune and withdrew from society. Re-emerging as a dangerous and manipulative mutant, she set her sights on obtaining the X-Factor's skycraft headquarters. Her plan was to transform ICEMAN into a form she could manipulate, but because he was a mutant her effort caused an explosion. It was the last time she was to pose a threat—shortly thereafter, Infectia was stricken by the fatal Legacy virus and died in BEAST's care. **AD**

ILLUMINATI
Great Men with Best Intentions

FACTFILE

CURRENT MEMBERS
BLACK BOLT
Inhuman King with lethal voice.
DR. STRANGE
Master of the mystic arts.
IRON MAN
Genius engineer wearing
powered armor.
MR. FANTASTIC
Genius scientist with elastic
body.
NAMOR
Mutant Atlantean king.
PROFESSOR X
Powerful telepath.

BASE
New York City

FIRST APPEARANCE
New Avengers #7 (July 2005)

ALLIES Atlanteans, Avengers,
Fantastic Four, X-Men, Inhumans.

FOES Cabal, Kree, Skrulls.

Iron Man's first attempt to
band together the best minds
on the planet failed due to a
lack of trust among them.

Following the KREE–SKRULL War, IRON MAN saw the need for an organization that could band together the various heroes to form a force capable of responding to planetary threats. To that end, he invited BLACK BOLT, MR. FANTASTIC, NAMOR, and DR. STRANGE to meet at the BLACK PANTHER's palace in Wakanda. The others raised several objections to Iron Man's vision, and the Black Panther refused to participate. Instead of working together officially, the five heroes agreed to secretly share information so that they might better anticipate and respond to world threatening events.

CAPTURED BY SKRULLS

When the Illuminati traveled to the Skrull homeworld to deliver a warning, the Skrull ruler refused to heed them. Black Bolt destroyed his warship. Unfortunately, the Illuminati were captured as they tried to leave the system. After bringing the Illuminati back to the planet, the Skrulls separated them and nullified their powers. Then they analyzed their prisoners, learning much that they would later use to give their operatives superpowers during the Secret Invasion (*see* pp. 326–7). Believing Iron Man to be helpless without his armor, they were careless, and Stark found the opportunity to break loose and to free the others.

THE AVENGER IRON MAN--

HE IS JUST A FRAGILE FLACCID HUMAN BEING WHO HAS ENCASED HIMSELF IN A RATHER PRIMITIVE ROBOTIC ARMOR.

WHILE ADVANCED BY HIS OWN CIVILIZATION'S STANDARDS--

--IT IS NOTHING OF CONCERN NOW THAT IT'S BEEN DISMANTLED.

THE ONLY INTERESTING ASPECT IS THAT THIS ARMOR WAS KEEPING STARK'S HEART VALVES WORKING.

IT'S TO GO IN THE ROYAL TROPHY ROOM.

While Iron Man was the only one of the Illuminati able to cope with being tossed into outer space, the Skrulls thought very little of him and his armor.

Iron Man gathers the leaders of the superpowered community in Wakanda to discuss forming an official organization for heroes. Instead, the Illuminati is born.

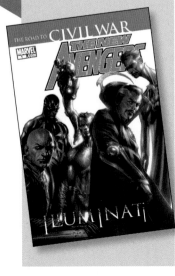

THE INFINITY GAUNTLET

Two events that nearly destroyed everyone in the universe involved the Infinity Gauntlet, a glove that holds the six Infinity Gems, assembling them into an artifact that grants the wearer limitless power. Mr. Fantastic began collecting the gems and turned to the Illuminati to help him. Namor, Professor X, and Dr. Strange searched for the Mind Gem, while Black Bolt, Mr. Fantastic, and Iron Man went after the Reality Gem. Once the Gauntlet was complete, the Watcher showed up to see what would happen and scolded them for meddling with such power. Mr. Fantastic chose to try to use the Gauntlet to destroy itself. When that failed, he removed the gems from the Gauntlet and gave one to each member of the Illuminati to safeguard in secret.

GROUP LISTING
1 Iron Man *2* Black Bolt
3 Dr Strange *4* Mr. Fantastic
5 Namor *6* Professor X.

Other Adventures

Later, the Illuminati approached the BEYONDER directly during the second Secret Wars. Professor X convinced the Beyonder that he had once been an Inhuman who'd been a mutant even before being exposed to the Terrigen Mists. Because of this, Black Bolt—who was therefore the Beyonder's king—could command him to leave, and did. After that, when MARVEL BOY (Noh-Varr) was imprisoned on Earth, the Illuminati visited him in his cell. They showed him that the Kree created the Inhumans to protect the Earth, not conquer it, and they encouraged him to follow the example set by CAPTAIN MAR-VELL.

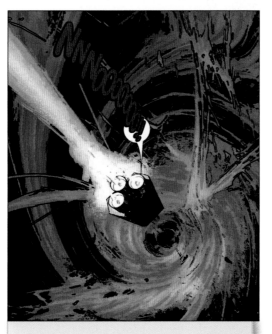

Deeming the Hulk too dangerous to remain on Earth, the Illuminati shot him into space.

Exiling the Hulk

The Illuminati arranged for a Life Model Decoy (android) version of Nick FURY to send the Hulk on a mission into space to disable a dangerous satellite. Once he entered the satellite, it turned into a starcraft and rocketed away, programmed to release the Hulk on an idyllic but unpopulated planet. Unfortunately, the ship wound up on the war-torn planet Sakaar instead. Namor refused to have any part of this mission, and Professor X was too busy to take part in it, but the other four managed it on their own. The Hulk later returned to exact his revenge during World War Hulk (see pp. 152-5).

THE CABAL

After killing the Skrull Queen VERANKE during the Secret Invasion, Norman Osborn (GREEN GOBLIN) came into power as the head of SHIELD—and then its replacement, HAMMER. To consolidate his position as the man in charge of all superhuman activity in the US, Osborn formed a secret organization of his own, called the Cabal. This included DR. DOOM, EMMA FROST, the HOOD, LOKI, NAMOR, and himself. While the six ostensibly worked together, behind the scenes they began scheming against each other.

ESSENTIAL STORYLINES

• *New Avengers #7–10* The Illuminati makes its first appearance to discuss the problem of the Sentry.
• *New Avengers: Illuminati #1–5* The Illuminati gather for a series of secret adventures, starting with the aftermath of the Kree-Skrull War.
• *World War Hulk #1–5* The Hulk comes back from outer space to have his revenge on the members of the Illuminati who kicked him off Earth.

War and Invasion

The Civil War (*see* pp. 84-5) shattered the Illuminati. Mr. Fantastic and Iron Man supported backing the Superhuman Registration Act, but Dr. Strange and Black Bolt strongly disagreed. Namor abstained, considering it no problem of Atlantis, and Professor X was not available to comment at the time. No one was willing to change his mind, so the Illuminati ended. Despite this, when Iron Man discovered an impending Secret Invasion (*see* pp. 326-7) by the Skrulls he called the Illuminati together again. The others discovered that Black Bolt had been replaced by an undetectable Skrull, and they barely defeated him. Afterward, they hoped to work together again but soon realized they could not trust each other any longer. **MF**

The lowest moment for the Illuminati came when the Superhuman Registration Act pitted them directly against each other. At the end of the Civil War that resulted from this, Iron Man felt forced to battle against his long-time friend and fellow Avenger Captain America.

INFERNO

FIRST APPEARANCE (as Inferno) Avengers #192 (August 1977)

REAL NAME Joseph Conroy

OCCUPATION Steelworker **BASE** Pittsburgh, Pennsylvania

HEIGHT/WEIGHT Unrevealed **EYES** Red **HAIR** None

SPECIAL POWERS/ABILITIES Possessed superhuman strength and durability; could radiate intense heat; could absorb and redirect electrical energy.

THOR once repaired his enchanted uru hammer at the Paretta Steel Mill in Pittsburgh. Steel worker Joseph Conroy kept a flake from the hammer for luck. Later Conroy threatened to expose the criminal activities of his boss, Vince Paretta, and was knocked into a vat of electrified molten steel. The magic of the uru flake transformed Conroy into Inferno, a being made of "living slag." Inferno's revenge mission led to a clash with the AVENGERS. When Captain America promised that Paretta would be jailed, Inferno committed suicide by walking into a river. **PS**

INTERLOPER

FIRST APPEARANCE Defenders Vol. 1 #147 (September 1985)

REAL NAME Unknown

OCCUPATION Hermit **BASE** Washington, D.C.

HEIGHT 6 ft 2 in **WEIGHT** 196 lbs **EYES** Blue **HAIR** Black

SPECIAL POWERS/ABILITIES Virtually immortal through total mental control of his body; levitation; projects cosmic energy in form of beams from hands or eyes.

Although one of the ETERNALS of Earth, for most of his life, the Interloper lived as a hermit, emerging for periodic battles against his nemesis, the malevolent DRAGON OF THE MOON. Only three of these battles have been chronicled, the first taking place on the Saturn moon of Titan and the second during the final days of King Arthur PENDRAGON. Believing that he had finally bested the Dragon, Interloper withdrew to the Siberian wastelands, but his destiny was still bound up with the creature. Returning to fight one more time, the Interloper sacrificed his life to destroy the dragon altogether. **AD**

INHUMANS

The Inhumans are an incredibly technologically advanced race descended from early humans.

The Inhumans diverged from mainstream humans when the alien Kree used early humans to create a race of superhuman warrior-servants. The Kree abandoned this plan but left a small tribe of their subjects—known as the Inhumans—behind. They settled on an island in the North Atlantic named Attilan and developed technology and culture at an astounding rate. The Inhuman geneticist Randac developed a substance called Terrigen that accelerated genetic advances.

Immersing himself in the Terrigen Mist, Randac developed advanced mental powers, and the other Inhumans soon followed suit, each developing a different set of powers.

A few years ago, the Inhuman king Black Bolt moved Attilan to the air-filled Blue Area of the Moon. For a time, RONAN THE ACCUSER enslaved them there, but Black Bolt set them free. During the Secret Invasion, the Skrull posing as Black Bolt was exposed. Once the Skrulls were defeated, the real Black Bolt led the Inhumans to the Kree Empire, where Black Bolt became their ruler too. **MT, MF**

THE INHUMANS
1 Medusa 2 Gorgon
3 Triton 4 Karnac
5 Black Bolt

INVADERS

The greatest Super Heroes of World War II

The Invaders were brought together in 1941 by Winston Churchill.

During the opening days of World War II, before the United States had formally entered the conflict, an elite fighting unit was banded together by British Prime Minister Winston Churchill to halt Nazi aggression. The first great gathering of superhuman champions ever recorded—CAPTAIN AMERICA and Bucky BARNES, NAMOR the SUB-MARINER, the HUMAN TORCH and TORO, UNION JACK, SPITFIRE, MISS AMERICA and the WHIZZER—this alliance, known formally as the Invaders, cut a swath through enemy forces until the Axis powers were defeated.

As a team, the Invaders battled both conventional forces, and Nazi superhuman operatives such as the Atlantean U-Man.

THE ALL-WINNERS

Although they disbanded after the war, for a time combating crime on the homefront as the All-Winners Squad, the Invaders established a legend and a tradition that would inspire others to follow in their footsteps over the years. Some of those heroes associated with the Invaders joined forces with Parisian resistance fighters to form the covert V-Battalion, maintaining world order secretly through the decades.

THE NEW INVADERS

In the early years of this century, the RED SKULL infiltrated the government in the guise of US Secretary of Defense Dell Rusk. He organized a new incarnation of the Invaders, intending it to forcibly protect US world interests, and thus foment greater distrust among nations. The new Invaders, recruited by US Agent (whose title as Captain America had been restored), and led by the Thin Man, soon realized the truth. Instead of following Rusk's agenda, the new Invaders turned their efforts towards the destruction of Axis Mundi, a cabal of superhumans. Cornered, the Axis Mundi activated a traitor within the Invaders' team: Tara, an android built by the Red Skull. The first Human Torch prevented her from exploding, but died in the attempt. The team members then went their separate ways. **TB, MF**

The Machiavellian Thin Man, once imprisoned for his murder of a former Nazi agent, was the brains behind the modern-day Invaders' operation.

ESSENTIAL STORYLINES
• *Invaders #5–6* and *Marvel Premiere #29–30* The Invaders are joined by the homefront heroes of the Liberty Legion to thwart a scheme by the Red Skull
• *Avengers #83–85, New Invaders #0*
When the Avengers become a global organization, a modern day team of Invaders is assembled by the US government to do the jobs that they will not.

FACTFILE

CURRENT MEMBERS AND POWERS

USAGENT
Super-strong soldier.

BLAZING SKULL
Immortal; impervious to flame.

THIN MAN
Can distend body and teleport by twisting dimensions.

UNION JACK
Trained fighter who specializes in battling monsters.

TARA
Android life form that bursts into flame and can fly.

BASE
The Infiltrator, a battleship capable of interdimensional travel

FIRST APPEARANCE
Giant-Size Invaders #1 (June 1975)

CHARACTER KEY
1 Union Jack **2** Tara **3** The USAgent (as Captain America) **4** The Blazing Skull

INVISIBLE WOMAN

The Fantastic Four's female presence

FACTFILE

REAL NAME
Susan Storm Richards

OCCUPATION
Adventurer

BASE
New York City

HEIGHT 5 ft 6 ins
WEIGHT 120 lbs
EYES Blue
HAIR Blonde

FIRST APPEARANCE
Fantastic Four Vol. 1 #1
(November 1961)

POWERS

Can turn herself invisible, and is able to project energy around other people or objects that makes them invisible too; can generate protective force fields, or shape invisible objects of psionic force. By projecting force fields beneath her, she can travel through the air.

Actress Susan Storm had already struck up a romance with the scientist Reed Richards when she volunteered to join him on an experimental mission into space. Along with her brother Johnny Storm and the starship's pilot Ben Grimm, Sue received a mutagenic dose of cosmic rays that gave her the power to turn invisible at will. The others had also received superhuman powers, and Sue became a member of their new team, the FANTASTIC FOUR, under the identity of the Invisible Girl. Sue's powers evolved over time, giving her the ability to project impenetrable force fields and to turn objects invisible through mental control.

Sue's ability to generate force fields is more versatile than her power of invisibility, making her one of the team's strongest members.

COSMIC POWERS

Sue soon married Reed, and battled threats to Earth including planet-devouring GALACTUS. Complications with her first pregnancy forced Reed to stabilize her labor with the energies of ANNIHILUS' Cosmic Control Rod, and Sue gave birth to a boy, Franklin RICHARDS. She briefly separated from Reed and left the Fantastic Four, allowing MEDUSA to fill her spot. Sue's second pregnancy ended in a stillbirth. During this vulnerable period, PSYCHO-MAN controlled Sue's mind and caused her to assume the villainous identity of Malice. After shaking off Psycho-Man's influence, Sue called herself the Invisible Woman.

Sue and Reed briefly joined the AVENGERS, but returned to their original team. After Reed's apparent death at the hands of DOCTOR DOOM, Sue served as the Fantastic Four's leader, rejecting romantic overtures from NAMOR the Sub-Mariner. It transpired that the child from Sue's earlier stillbirth had been preserved in another dimension by Franklin. After a battle with Abraxas, the unborn girl returned to Sue's womb and soon after became her daughter Valeria.

During the Civil War (see pp. 84–5), Reed's efforts on behalf of SHIELD (and the ILLUMINATI) disgusted Sue.

--you're not the only one with an imagination.

She left Reed and sided with CAPTAIN AMERICA's resistance. At the start of the Secret Invasion (*see* pp. 326–7), the Skrull named Lyja replaced Sue, but Sue herself later escaped.

An older Sue Richards from a possible future recently led her DEFENDERS into the present day to save eight billion refugees to Nu-World, a synthetic copy of Earth. She died at the hands of DR. DOOM, but her friends continue her work as the Fantastic Force. **DW, MF**

Sue can shape her force fields into tentacles that grasp and stab. Here, she unleashes her rage on Doctor Doom.

IRON FIST

The Iron Fist is granted to the chosen of K'un-L'un, one of the Cities of Heaven. In modern times, philanthropist Danny Rand controls the Iron Fist. Aged nine, he accompanied his parents and their treacherous business partner Harold Meachum to K'un-L'un. Both parents were killed and only Danny reached the sacred city. Aged 19, he gained the power of the Iron Fist and confronted Meachum, but spared him. A ninja slew Meachum instead. Rand became wealthy as co-owner of Rand-Meachum and partnered with Luke CAGE to form the Heroes for Hire. He opposed the Superhuman Registration Act and joined Cage in the AVENGERS for a time after the Civil War (*see* pp. 84–5). **PS, MF**

Iron Fist's hand glows with superhuman energies.

Iron Fist's supreme mastery of the K'un-L'un martial arts and his "iron fist" make him a match for even superhuman opponents.

FACTFILE
REAL NAME
Daniel Thomas Rand-K'ai
(Daniel Thomas Rand in US)
OCCUPATION
Adventurer; co-owner of
Rand-Meachum, Inc.
BASE
New York City

HEIGHT 5 ft 11 in
WEIGHT 175 lbs
EYES Blue
HAIR Blond

FIRST APPEARANCE
Marvel Premiere #15
(May 1974)

POWERS

Master of the martial arts of K'un-L'un. Can focus his chi (natural energy) and superhuman energy in his hand, endowing his fist with superhuman strength, durability, or healing power.

IRON MAN *see pages 168-9*

IRONCLAD

FIRST APPEARANCE Incredible Hulk #254 (December 1980)
REAL NAME Michael Steel
OCCUPATION Superpowered villain **BASE** Mobile
HEIGHT 6 ft 2 in **WEIGHT** 450 lbs **EYES** White **HAIR** None
SPECIAL POWERS/ABILITIES Metallic armored hide protects him from most forms of attack, and increases strength and endurance to superhuman levels; can also increase his body's density.

Ironclad was one of the U-FOES, organized by industrialist Simon Utrecht, who hoped to recreate the accident that empowered the FANTASTIC FOUR. Ironclad and the U-Foes battled the HULK and the AVENGERS, among other heroes. He later joined the HOOD's criminal crew. **MT, MF**

IT

It, the Living Colossus was a statue supposed to celebrate the might of the Soviet Union. The night before its unveiling, the statue was animated by a stranded alien Kigor. It rampaged through Moscow until other Kigor fetched their companion. It was transferred to Los Angeles and once again animated by the Kigor, however special-effects expert Robert O'Bryan tricked the aliens with a booby-trapped prop and uploaded his own mind into It. Thus began a tug of war with the scheming Dr. Vault. Since then, O'Bryan has twice rebuilt It, once for a movie, and once while under the thrall of crime boss Lotus Newmark. Fortunately, O'Bryan was freed from Newmark before any harm could be done. **AD**

FACTFILE
REAL NAME
None

OCCUPATION
Instrument of destruction
BASE
Los Angeles

HEIGHT 100 ft (later reduced to 30 ft)
WEIGHT approximately 1,000 tons (later 100 tons)
EYES White
HAIR None

FIRST APPEARANCE
Tales of Suspense #14
(September 1961)

IT

POWERS

Outside consciousness needed to animate—or reassemble– statue. Vast strength. Granite construction impervious to bullets, shells, and electric shocks; limited flying ability. Vulnerable to gas attack.

IRON MAN
The billion-dollar man

FACTFILE

REAL NAME
Anthony Stark

OCCUPATION
Businessman and philanthropist, hero and leader of the Avengers

BASE
Stark Tower ("Avengers Tower"), Manhattan, New York

HEIGHT 6 ft 1 in
WEIGHT 225 lbs
EYES Blue
HAIR Black

FIRST APPEARANCE
Tales of Suspense #39
(March 1963)

POWERS

Prodigious inventiveness and business acumen. Standard Iron Man armor provides superhuman strength and durability, jet-boot powered flight, repulsor beams in gauntlets, and chest-mounted uni-beam. Armor's underlayer is now incorporated into Stark's body, letting him control Iron Man

ALLIES/FOES

ALLIES The Avengers, James Rhodes (War Machine), SHIELD, Virginia Potts, Bethany Cabe, Edwin Jarvis.

FOES Obadiah Stane, Justin Hammer, Madame Masque, Titanium Man, Spymaster, Mandarin.

Billionaire industrialist and philanthropist Tony Stark is perhaps the most influential superpowered individual on the planet. While Professor X has the respect of the Earth's mutant community, Stark's work as Iron Man, his long-term membership of the Avengers, and position as head of Stark International arguably gives him even wider authority.

Iron Man—corporate mascot, bodyguard, or armored Super Hero?

FORGING THE IRON MAN

The son of a wealthy industrialist, Tony Stark's parents died in a car crash when he was young, leaving him their business conglomerate, Stark Industries. Taking over the company when he was 21, in retrospect some of Tony's early business decisions were ethically circumspect. An engineering prodigy, many of Tony's early inventions were designed for use by the US military and it was his dealings with the army that ultimately led him to create his Iron Man armor.

Developing mini-transistors for use on the battlefield, Tony travelled to Vietnam to see them in use on the ground. The trial ended badly when an exploding bomb left a piece of shrapnel dangerously close to his heart and Tony was captured by the North Vietnamese warlord, Wong-Chu.

In the nick of time, the first Iron Man armor saved Tony Stark's life.

Told that the shrapnel would only be removed if he developed a weapon for the North Vietnamese, Tony responded with typical tenacity. Teaming with a fellow prisoner, Nobel prize-winning physicist Ho Yinsen, Tony developed an iron suit that would protect his heart as well as allow him to fight the warlord and his men and escape.

SOCIAL CONSCIENCE

In the following years, Tony donned this armor many times. Claiming the Iron Man was his bodyguard and corporate emblem, at first he simply used it to fight communists and threats to his business empire. With the advent of new technologies and ideas the armor evolved, becoming increasingly, at times dangerously, sophisticated.

Over the years Tony's own world view also began to evolve: he halted sales to the military, recognizing that they caused more harm than good, and established a number of charitable foundations. He became a founder member of the Avengers, allowing the team to use his mansion as their base and providing financial backing via the Maria Stark foundation—a non-profit-making organization named for his mother.

Initially a defender of Stark Industries, gradually Iron Man began to serve the general public.

ISSUE #1

Injured in Vietnam, Stark's first Iron Man armor saves his life and helps him escape capture. From that day on, he could not survive without it.

ESSENTIAL STORYLINES
• *Iron Man Vol. 1 #120–129 #153–156* Tony Stark's first encounter with Justin Hammer and his battle with alcohol.
• *Iron Man Vol. 2 #162–200* Stark's long dark fall to the gutter at the hands of Obadiah Stane, and his gradual resurrection.
• *Iron Man Vol. 3 #27–30* The Iron Man armor becomes sentient and attacks Stark.

OLD FLAMES

Wealthy, charming, handsome—over the years, countless women have been drawn to Tony Stark, and many hearts have been broken, including his own. Time and again, his dual identity and multiple responsibilities have sabotaged any hope at a settled, long-term romance.

JANICE CORD	BETHANY CABE	SUNSET BAIN	VIRGINIA POTTS	NATASHA ROMANOVA
Daughter of Stark rival Drexel Cord.	*Tony's lover until her husband returned.*	*Seduced Tony and stole his secrets.*	*One of Tony's most loyal confidantes.*	*Sometime adversary and former fiancée.*

Although immensely strong-willed, at times the pressures on Tony Stark have proved overwhelming—twice he has succumbed to the lure of alcohol. Tony's first fall from grace was precipitated by a series of attacks from Super Villains hired by business rival Justin HAMMER. While fending these off, Iron Man was framed for the murder of a diplomat, and at the same time national security agency SHIELD were attempting to buy his company and so gain his military secrets. Gradually, with the support of his friends, Tony overcame these threats and defeated his addiction.

This episode was nothing compared to Tony's second dance with drink. As a result of the emotional manipulations of his competitor Obadiah STANE, Tony became a homeless vagrant. His epiphany came when he was forced to deliver the child of a homeless woman, who died soon after. After waking up in hospital, he began to rebuild his

Like his father before him, Tony Stark was cursed by the demon drink. With Iron Man labeled a murderer and his company under siege, Tony was driven to the bottle.

life, creating a new business empire —Stark Enterprises—and defeating Stane in combat.

AN ENEMY OF AMERICA

Although a long-term member of the Avengers, Tony's decisions have brought him into direct conflict with his teammates, as well as with the US government. When Justin Hammer stole Stark technology and distributed it to criminals across the world, Tony began a quest to find each item of missing technology. His efforts to track down the US military's Stark-derived Guardsmen suits resulted in Iron Man being branded an outlaw by the US government. This action also antagonized CAPTAIN AMERICA.

A HEAVY BURDEN

During the Civil War (*see* pp. 84–5), Tony led the Super Heroes who complied with the Superhuman Registration Act and worked with SHIELD. When the conflict ended, he was named the new director of SHIELD and used his new power to set up the Fifty State Initiative (*see* pp. 118–9).

Unfortunately, because of his membership in the ILLUMINATI, Tony became the target of the Hulk's wrath during World War Hulk (*see*

pp.152–5). This scandal was the beginning of the end for him. When the Secret Invasion (*see* pp. 326–7) of the SKRULL Empire caught Tony off guard, the public backlash forced his removal as director of SHIELD. The man who took his place—Norman Osborn (GREEN GOBLIN)—ordered his capture. Tony ran, making himself as much an outlaw as the heroes he'd once sought to capture for SHIELD. **AD, MF**

Battling armored humans is now commonplace for Iron Man.

In the House of M universe, Tony Stark is a competitor in Sapien Death Match, a televised gladiatorial contest. There he competes against other armored humans.

Although sometimes at odds with his fellow Avengers, Tony Stark remains one of the team's most constant members. While his money keeps the team afloat, it is as Iron Man that he really leaves his mark.

J2

FIRST APPEARANCE What If? Vol. 2 #105 (February 1998)

REAL NAME Zane Yama

OCCUPATION High-school student   **BASE** New York City

HEIGHT 5 ft 5 in (Zane); 6 ft 6 in (J2)   **WEIGHT** 137 lbs (as Zane)
725 lbs (as J2)   **EYES** Blue   **HAIR** Brown

SPECIAL POWERS/ABILITIES Superhuman strength and
durability; virtually unstoppable and indestructible.

In one possible future, Zane's parents are Cain
Marko, the original JUGGERNAUT, and Sachi Yama,
an Assistant District Attorney. They fell in love
shortly after Marko renounced his criminal ways,
joined the X-MEN, and was pardoned for his past
crimes. They married, but Sachi kept her last
name for professional reasons. While on an X-
Men mission, Marko was lost in an alien
dimension. Years later, Zane discovered that he
could temporarily gain the
mass and power of the
Juggernaut. Calling
himself J2, Zane
joined the
AVENGERS of his
timeline and
eventually freed
his father from an
alien sorcerer who had
been holding him
prisoner. **TD**

JACK OF HEARTS

Jack Hart's mother was an
extraterrestrial Contraxian,
and his father a human
scientist. He was born with
volatile energy powers that
would have killed him, and
his father created Zero Fluid
in an attempt to give his son
control. After an accidental
drenching in the fluid when agents of the
criminal Corporation killed his father, Jack
became the costumed hero Jack of Hearts, but
he required regular periods of isolation in a
SHIELD facility to keep from exploding. After
learning of his origins, Jack traveled to Contraxia
to rekindle the planet's waning star. He became
romantically involved with Ganymede of the
Spinsterhood during the fight against GALACTUS's
offspring TYRANT, and joined the AVENGERS upon
his return to Earth. Frustrated by the segregation
required by his condition, Jack detonated himself
in space after saving the life of ANT-MAN II's
daughter, Cassie Lang (Stature). A doppelganger
of Jack of Hearts, created by the SCARLET WITCH,
later killed Ant-Man II in an explosion. **DW**

FACTFILE

REAL NAME
Jonathan "Jack" Hart

OCCUPATION
Adventurer

BASE
Mobile

HEIGHT 5 ft 11 in
WEIGHT 175 lbs
EYES Blue (right), white (left)
HAIR Brown

FIRST APPEARANCE
Deadly Hands of Kung Fu #22
(March 1976)

POWERS

Enhanced strength, resistance to
injury and accelerated healing rate,
ability to release massive quantities
of explosive energy as shock
waves. Power of flight is achieved
by controlling blasts of energy.
Computerized intelligence enables
him to think at phenomenal speeds.

An undead version of Jack
of Hearts appeared at the
Avengers Mansion, moments
before the events known as
"Avengers Disassembled."

JACKAL

FIRST APPEARANCE Amazing Spider-Man #31 (December 1965)

REAL NAME Dr Miles Warren

OCCUPATION Criminal, former university lecturer

BASE New York City   **HEIGHT** 5 ft 10 in   **WEIGHT** 175 lbs

EYES Green   **HAIR** Gray; (as Jackal) none

SPECIAL POWERS/ABILITIES Expert in cloning; superhuman
strength and poison-tipped, razor-sharp claws; used gas bombs.

Peter Parker's biochemistry teacher was obsessed
with Peter's girlfriend, Gwen STACY. Grief-
stricken by her death he became unhinged,
creating clones of Gwen and Peter and
killing his lab assistant when he was
discovered. Unable to face what he
had done, he developed an
alternate personality, the Jackal,
who gradually became
dominant. The Jackal blamed
SPIDER-MAN for what had
happened to Gwen, and
forced Peter to face up to his
own guilt for her death. Their last
confrontation was in the Daily
Bugle offices, where the Jackal
met his maker. **TB**

JACK FROST

FIRST APPEARANCE USA Comics #1 (August 1941)

REAL NAME Unrevealed   **OCCUPATION** Adventurer

BASE North Pole; mobile in US in World War II

HEIGHT 5 ft 11 in   **WEIGHT** 172 lbs

EYES Blue-white   **HAIR** Blue

SPECIAL POWERS/ABILITIES Possesses innate superhuman
ability to generate sub-freezing temperatures.

Jack Frost may have been the human-sized
offspring of Frost Giants (see GODS OF ASGARD).
In the 1940s, he joined the Liberty
Legion, a hero team that battled Axis
agents on the American home front.
Jack Frost was later swallowed by
a gigantic Ice Worm in the Arctic
yet remained alive. Dr. Gregor
Shapanka, whose costume
generated intense cold, adopted
the name "Jack Frost" as his
original criminal identity. A foe
of IRON MAN, Shapanka later
called himself the BLIZZARD. He
was killed by Arno Stark, the
time-traveling Iron Man of an
alternate future. **PS**

JAMESON, JOHN

FIRST APPEARANCE Amazing Spider-Man #1 (March 1963)

REAL NAME John Jameson

OCCUPATION Former astronaut   **BASE** Manhattan

HEIGHT 6 ft 2 in   **WEIGHT** 200 lbs   **EYES** Brown

HAIR Red-brown

SPECIAL POWERS/ABILITIES Possesses the physical fitness of
a top-notch astronaut.

John was rescued by SPIDER-MAN when his space
capsule went out of control. Later, exposure to
space-spores gave him superhuman strength and
caused him to run wild, and a lunar
gemstone made him the MAN-WOLF.
Jameson joined the AVENGERS'
support staff as CAPTAIN
AMERICA's pilot, before serving
as the head of security for
Ravenscroft Asylum. He once
married the SHE-HULK, but
after they discovered that
STARFOX had influenced her
emotions, the marriage was
annulled. Mr. Fantastic has
supposedly cured him of being
Man-Wolf now. **TB, MF**

JAMESON, J. JONAH

Crusading publisher of the Daily Bugle

WHAT'S THIS??!! MY OWN NEWS-PAPER CALLING SPIDER-MAN A HERO?!!

Irascible and domineering, Jameson had no time for costumed Super Heroes.

J. Jonah Jameson began his career in journalism while he was still in high school, working as a part-time copy boy for New York's prestigious *Daily Bugle* newspaper. The son of a war hero, he obtained firsthand experience of conflict when he served as a war correspondent in Europe during World War II. Jameson later spent three years covering the Korean War, during which time Joan—his first wife and the mother of his son, John—was tragically killed by a masked mugger, sparking a lifelong distrust of mask-wearers, be they villain or hero!

FACTFILE
REAL NAME
J. Jonah Jameson
OCCUPATION
Owner and publisher, Daily Bugle newspaper
BASE
New York City

HEIGHT 5 ft 11 in
WEIGHT 210 lbs
EYES Blue
  HAIR: Black, white at the temples

FIRST APPEARANCE
Amazing Spider-Man #1 (March 1963)

JAMESON, J. JONAH

POWERS
J. Jonah Jameson has no superhuman powers, but his stubborn, uncompromising attitude makes him a formidable opponent. Outspoken and tenacious, he refuses to back down when he believes he is right.

CRIME FIGHTER

Jameson reacted to the grief by throwing himself even more fully into his professional life, rising to become editor-in-chief of the *Bugle*. He eventually became the paper's publisher, relinquishing the editor-in-chief position to Joe "Robbie" ROBERTSON. In time, Jameson bought the paper. For many years Jameson used his newspaper to fight for civil rights and to battle organized crime. The KINGPIN of Crime tried to have him killed, but this attempt on his life did nothing to change Jameson's uncompromising attitude. The stubborn, belligerent, but courageous publisher continued to print exposés of big-time criminals—even when his old friend, Norman Osborn, turned out to be one of them.

WHERE'S PARKER?

The Bugle's staff soon learned to cope with Jameson's outbursts!

Jameson began writing editorials against costumed Super Heroes, criticizing them as vigilantes who took the law into their own hands. When the Amazing SPIDER-MAN appeared in New York and began fighting crime as a costumed hero, J. Jonah Jameson focused his most pointed attacks on the Wall Crawler. He called Spider-Man a menace, claiming that the Web Swinger was a danger to the citizens of New York.

Jameson had no idea that his fellow club member Norman Osborn was the Green Goblin.

SPIDER SEEKER

Jameson tried for years to uncover Spider-Man's true identity, even sponsoring attempts to capture him. This including helping create the SCORPION and hiring Dr. Marla Madison to build a Spider-Slayer robot. Jameson later fell in love with Marla and married her. During the CIVIL WAR (*see* pp. 84-5), when Spider-Man revealed that he was Peter Parker, Jameson fainted. After Spider-Man's identity was concealed by MEPHISTO, Jameson resumed his attacks. He recently had a heart attack and lost control of the Bugle while in the hospital. After recovering, he ran for mayor of New York City and won, giving him the ability to pursue Spider-Man with the power of the entire city. **TB, MF**

JARELLA

FACTFILE

REAL NAME
Jarella

OCCUPATION
Empress of K'ai

BASE
The city-state of K'ai

HEIGHT (on Earth) 5 ft 6 in
WEIGHT (on Earth) 126 lbs
EYES Green
HAIR Blonde

FIRST APPEARANCE
The Incredible Hulk Vol. 2
#140 (May 1971)

POWERS

Jarella was an
excellent swordswoman and
formidable hand-to-hand
combatant; a brilliant
military leader and a wise
and compassionate ruler
of her people.

A creature called PSYKLOP
subjected the Hulk to a ray that
caused him to shrink, until he was
shunted into an alternate dimension
called a "microverse." The Hulk
found himself outside the city of K'ai
on an unnamed planet, whose
humanoid inhabitants had green skin
like his own. After defeating huge beasts
called warthos, the Hulk was hailed as a
hero by the people of K'ai. Its warrior
queen, Jarella, chose the Hulk to
become her husband and king of
the city-state. K'ai's Pantheon of Sorcerers cast a spell that enabled the
personality and intellect of Dr. Bruce Banner to dominate the
superhuman form of his alter ego, the Hulk. Believing he would
never return to Earth, Banner came to love Jarella. However, the
day before their wedding, Psyklop returned the Hulk to Earth,
where the spell no longer had effect.

Jarella visited Banner on Earth, and the Hulk twice returned
to K'ai, before returning to Earth with Jarella. The Hulk
later battled a robot, the Crypto-Man, causing a wall to
collapse. Saving a child from the toppling wall, Jarella was
crushed to death by it instead. **PS**

TIME IS *VANISHING.* CAN YOU *COMPREHEND,* TRY TO *SEE...?*

HULK SEES YOU WANT TO TAKE ONLY *GOOD THING* IN HIS LIFE! DON'T *CARE* ABOUT THE SUN...THE WORLD...ONLY *JARELLA!*

TOUCH HER AND SEE HOW FAST THE HULK CAN *SMASH!*

Hulk was so in love with Jarella that
he was willing to spend the rest of his
life on K'ai and never see Earth again.

JARVIS, EDWIN

FACTFILE

REAL NAME
Edwin Jarvis

OCCUPATION
Butler

BASE
Stark Tower, New York City

HEIGHT 5 ft 11 in
WEIGHT 160 lbs
EYES Blue
HAIR Black

FIRST APPEARANCE
Tales of Suspense #59
(November 1964)

POWERS

Former boxing champion of the
Royal Air Force. Resourceful
under pressure, courageous, and
loyal; an excellent, manager,
administrator and organizer.
World's leading authority on
cleaning otherworldly stains from
clothing, rugs and fabrics.

Jarvis keeps track of all the
Avengers' expenditures.

Edwin Jarvis is a war hero and a former
pilot in Britain's Royal Air Force. After
retiring to the US, he became the butler of
Howard and Maria Stark and continued to
work for their son Tony (*see* Iron Man) after
their deaths. When Stark gave his mansion
to the Avengers, he asked Jarvis to stay on
as the team's lead servant, the only one
to live on the premises. Jarvis served
the team loyally until ULTRON
brainwashed him into becoming
the Crimson Cowl and allowing the second version of the Masters
of Evil to enter Avengers Mansion and capture the team.
After recovering, Jarvis returned to his duties. After the
Scarlet Witch, in a fit of madness, destroyed both the
Avengers and the mansion, Jarvis followed the new
team to its headquarters in Stark Tower. During the
Secret Invasion (*see* pp. 326-7), the Avengers learned
that Jarvis had been replaced by a Skrull, but not
before he kidnapped Luke Cage and JESSICA JONES's
infant daughter. Cage rescued the baby just before
Bullseye shot the imposter. After his own rescue, Jarvis
refused to work for Norman Osborn's (*see* GREEN
GOBLIN) new Avengers and signed on with HANK
PYM's team instead. **TD, MF**

JESTER

FIRST APPEARANCE Daredevil Vol. 1 #42 (July 1968)
REAL NAME Jonathan Powers
OCCUPATION Former actor; criminal **BASE** New York City
HEIGHT 6 ft 2 in **WEIGHT** 190 lbs **EYES** Blue **HAIR** Brown
SPECIAL POWERS/ABILITIES No super powers; above-average athlete, skilled in gymnastics, swordsmanship, and unarmed combat; uses toys converted into deadly weapons or tools.

Struggling actor Jonathan Powers studied fencing, gymnastics, and bodybuilding, hoping to win additional roles, but all he landed was a job as a comic foil on a children's TV show. Calling himself the Jester, Powers set out on a crime spree in New York, using his deadly toys and gimmicks that the Tinkerer made for him. Daredevil stopped him several times. When Powers temporarily retired, Dr. Doom outfitted a second Jester (Jody Putt), who formed the Assembly of Evil to take on the Avengers. While part of the Thunderbolts Army, Putt attacked Spider-Man, but the Punisher shot him dead. **MT, MF**

JOCASTA

FIRST APPEARANCE Avengers #162 (August 1977)
REAL NAME Jocasta
OCCUPATION Former adventurer; computer **BASE** Mobile
HEIGHT 5 ft 9 in **WEIGHT** 750 lbs **EYES** Red **HAIR** None
SPECIAL POWERS/ABILITIES Superhuman ability to process information; superhuman strength, durability and senses of sight and hearing; projects energy blasts from eyes and hands.

The evil robot ULTRON created Jocasta to be his mate, basing her personality on that of the Wasp, who was the wife of Ultron's creator, Henry Pym. Although Ultron programmed Jocasta to serve him, she turned against him and aided the Avengers instead. Later, Jocasta's artificial intelligence entered the main computer in the mansion of Tony Stark (Iron Man), and she became his personal ally. Later, Jocasta returned in a new robot body. She served with the Mavericks, the Fifty State Initiative's New Mexico team. Recently, she joined Hank Pym's new team of Avengers. **PS, MF**

JOLT

FIRST APPEARANCE Thunderbolts #1 (April 1997)
REAL NAME Helen "Hallie" Takahama
OCCUPATION Adventurer **BASE** Counter-Earth
HEIGHT 5 ft 5 in **WEIGHT** 109 lbs **EYES** Blue; yellow (energy form) **HAIR** Black **SPECIAL POWERS/ABILITIES** Biokinetic energy gives enhanced strength, speed and agility and the ability to throw hyperkinetic punches.

After her parents were killed during the rampage of ONSLAUGHT, Hallie Takahama had to fend for herself on the streets of New York. Abducted by mad geneticist Arnim Zola, Hallie was rescued by the Thunderbolts—Super Villains posing as heroes. Not realizing their motives, Hallie joined the team as Jolt, to the consternation of its leader, Baron Zemo. She inspired some members to turn against Zemo, before leaving the team and opting to live on the ravaged Counter-Earth on the other side of the sun. **TB**

JETSTREAM

FIRST APPEARANCE New Mutants #16 (June 1984)
REAL NAME Haroun ibn Sallah al-Rashid
OCCUPATION Hellion team-member
BASE Massachusetts Academy
HEIGHT 5 ft 7 in **WEIGHT** 145 lbs **EYES** Black **HAIR** Black
SPECIAL POWERS/ABILITIES Body generates thermo-chemical energy; able to fly.

Mutants often have difficulty learning to use their powers, but Haroun al-Rashid struggled more than most. Codenamed Jetstream, Haroun had difficulty controlling and releasing the thermo-chemical energy his body was constantly generating. When these energies caused his flesh to catch fire, it was only the intervention of the Hellions that saved his life. The Hellions provided him with a bionic system that enabled him to control his powers. After all they had done for him, Haroun felt obliged to remain with the team; however his membership was not destined to last long. During an attack on the Hellfire Club by White Rook (Trevor Fitzroy), Haroun was killed when his life energy was drained away. **AD**

JOHN THE SKRULL

FIRST APPEARANCE Wisdom #1 (November 2006)
REAL NAME Unknown **OCCUPATION** Adventurer
BASE Massachusetts Academy **HEIGHT** Varies
WEIGHT Varies **EYES** Usually brown **HAIR** Usually brown
SPECIAL POWERS/ABILITIES Shapeshifting and flight.

In 1963, the Skrull empire sent four Skrulls to Earth to impersonate The Beatles and use their worldwide popularity to help launch an invasion. The Skrull Beatles decided to "go native" and abandon the empire's plans. Decades later, John joined MI-13, the British secret service charged with investigating paranormal creatures and events. With the start of the Secret Invasion (see pp. 326–7), the Skrulls went after all "traitors" and killed every Skrull Beatle except for John. He joined Captain Britain, Peter Wisdom (see Wisdom, Peter), and Spitfire to stop the Skrulls and was executed by a Skrull while trying to prevent an invasion of Avalon. **MF**

JONES, GABE

FIRST APPEARANCE Sgt. Fury and his Howling Commandos #1 (May 1963) **REAL NAME** Gabriel Jones
OCCUPATION SHIELD agent **BASE** New York City
HEIGHT 6 ft 2 in **WEIGHT** 225 lbs **EYES** Brown **HAIR** White
SPECIAL POWERS/ABILITIES Formidable hand-to-hand combatant when younger; excellent marksman and combat tactician; expert jazz trumpeter.

Like so many other members of World War II heroes the Howling Commandos, Gabe Jones was to continue fighting alongside its commander, Nick Fury, for most of his life. Reuniting with the rest of the military strike squad during the Korean and Vietnam wars, Gabe became a key aide to Fury when he was made director of SHIELD. Responsible for infiltrating and bringing down the insidious organization known as the Secret Empire, Gabe remained loyal to Fury even after the android Deltites infiltrated SHIELD. He went on to play a key role when the organization was re-established as a leaner, more focused operation. **AD**

JONES, JESSICA

FIRST APPEARANCE Alias #1 (November 2001)

REAL NAME Jessica Jones

OCCUPATION Private investigator **BASE** New York City

HEIGHT 5 ft 4 in **WEIGHT** 120 lbs **EYES** Brown **HAIR** Brown

SPECIAL POWERS/ABILITIES As the Super Hero Jewel, Jessica Jones possessed the powers of flight, superhuman strength, and a high resistance to injury.

While a teenager, Jessica Jones lost her family but acquired superpowers. As Jewel, she battled criminals until the PURPLE MAN enslaved her mind. After losing a battle with the AVENGERS, Jessica fell into a coma until JEAN GREY revived her. She later opened a detective agency specializing in cases involving superpowered beings. She then married Luke Cage, with whom she had a baby girl, Danielle. She fled to Canada during the Civil War but returned to rejoin the Avengers. After the Secret Invasion, a Skrull posing as Edwin Jarvis kidnapped Danielle, but Norman Osborn helped Luke rescue her. **MT**

JONES, MARLO

FIRST APPEARANCE Incredible Hulk #347 (September 1998)

REAL NAME Marlo Chandler-Jones

OCCUPATION Talk show host, comic shop owner

BASE Las Vegas, Los Angeles

HEIGHT 5 ft 8 in **WEIGHT** 135 lbs **EYES** Green **HAIR** Red

SPECIAL POWERS/ABILITIES In excellent physical shape. At one point she acquired the ability to see the spirits of dead people.

Marlo Chandler dated the HULK when he was in his gray Joe Fixit personality, but she broke it off after witnessing the Hulk kill an enemy. Marlo later met the Hulk's friend RICK JONES when he was on a book tour promoting his memoirs. They married and hosted a television talk show called *Keeping Up With the Joneses,* then opened a comic-book shop in Los Angeles, during which Marlo was temporarily possessed by Death.

Rick and Marlo have separated and reunited many times. At the moment, they are back together—when Rick isn't off on one of his many adventures. **MT, MF**

JONES, RICK

As a teenager, Rick Jones snuck onto a military test site on a dare. Bruce Banner rescued him but was caught in the blast, which caused him to transform into the Hulk whenever angered. Feeling responsible, Rick helped Banner conceal his secret from the military. When the Avengers formed to deal with the Hulk, Rick became an honorary member. Trained by Captain America, Rick served as his partner for a time, and subsequently worked in concert with both Captain Mar-Vell—with whom he helped end the Kree-Skrull War—and his son Genis-Vell (*see* Captain Marvel), and with the space knight Rom. Later, Rick secretly bankrolled the young superhuman help group known as Excelsior. Rick stood by the Hulk during WORLD WAR HULK but was impaled by MIEK, the traitorous member of the Hulk's WARBOUND. Recently, when the Red Hulk attacked him, he transformed into A-Bomb, a blue-skinned, armored creature resembling the Abomination. **TB, MF**

For a time, Rick's molecules were merged with those of the Kree hero Captain Marvel,

FACTFILE

REAL NAME
Richard Jones

OCCUPATION
Adventurer

BASE
Various

HEIGHT 5 ft 9 in
WEIGHT 165 lbs
EYES Brown
HAIR Brown

FIRST APPEARANCE
Incredible Hulk #1
(May 1962)

Rick Jones possesses a courageous spirit and the expert fighting skills of one trained by Captain America.

JONES, RICK

POWERS

JOSEPH

FIRST APPEARANCE Uncanny X-Men #327 (December 1995)

REAL NAME Unknown **OCCUPATION** Adventurer

BASE Xavier Institute, New York State

HEIGHT 6 ft 2 in **WEIGHT** 190 lbs

EYES Blue-gray **HAIR** White

SPECIAL POWERS/ABILITIES As Magneto's clone Joseph has the same power as Magneto—the ability to control magnetism and magnetic forces—frequently to devastating effect.

Astra of the BROTHERHOOD OF EVIL MUTANTS created a clone of her enemy MAGNETO hoping that it would kill the original. The clone physically resembled the 20-year-old Magneto. The clone and Magneto clashed in Guatemala. Magneto knocked the clone unconscious and escaped. When the clone came to, he had lost his memory.

Sister Maria de la Joya nursed him back to health and a child at the orphanage where she worked named him Joseph. Sister Maria sent Joseph to the US to seek help from the X-MEN, but they believed that he was really Magneto, only younger and with amnesia. Nevertheless, they allowed him to join the team.

In a final confrontation with the real Magneto, Joseph bravely sacrificed his life in order to save the world from Magneto's attack on the Earth's magnetic fields. Magneto's dreams of world conquest would have to wait a little longer. **MT**

JUBILEE

Born to a wealthy Asian-American family, Jubilee was raised in Beverly Hills and became a top-class gymnast. After her parents lost their fortune and then their lives, Jubilee was left orphaned and embittered.

Jubilee ran away, living at the Hollywood Mall, where her mutant powers became manifest. Having evaded mall security with the help of various X-MEN, Jubilee followed them through a teleportal to their Australian base, remaining hidden there until it was abandoned. She left the base with WOLVERINE and they travelled through Asia: he found her directness, sarcasm and honesty refreshing; she came to regard Wolverine as a surrogate father. Since returning to the US, Jubilee has been a member of the X-Men and GENERATION-X. While she still has some sharp edges, much of Jubilee's faith in humanity has been restored. **AD**

JUBILEE

FACTFILE

REAL NAME
Jubilation Lee

OCCUPATION
X-Corporation employee

BASE
Mobile

HEIGHT 5 ft 5 in
WEIGHT 105 lbs
EYES Blue
HAIR Black

FIRST APPEARANCE
Uncanny X-Men #244
(May 1989)

POWERS

Generates and projects energy globules—"fireworks"—from her fingers; Jubilee is also able to control, direct and reabsorb these.

JUGGERNAUT

After the death of her husband, Sharon Xavier married his colleague, atomic scientist Dr. Kurt Marko. Dr. Marko often beat his son Cain, who in turn bullied his new stepbrother, Charles Xavier (see PROFESSOR X), whom he came to hate. Marko joined the army, but deserted while in Korea. In a cave he seized a large ruby, which magically transformed him into a "human juggernaut," an unstoppable super-being. Enemy bombs then caused the cave to collapse, burying him alive.

Years later, Marko resurfaced as the Juggernaut, invading Xavier's mansion and trying to kill him. The Juggernaut had several battles with the X-Men, often teaming up with BLACK TOM CASSIDY. For a while, the Juggernaut lost much of his power and made peace with Xavier. He even fell out with Cassidy and joined the X-Men and the third incarnation of Excalibur. During World War Hulk, though, he embraced his destructive nature—alienating himself from Xavier once more—and his full power returned. **MF**

JUGGERNAUT

FACTFILE

REAL NAME
Cain Marko

OCCUPATION
Former soldier, later mercenary, professional criminal, adventurer

BASE
Mobile

HEIGHT 6 ft 10 in
WEIGHT 900 lbs
EYES Blue
HAIR Red

FIRST APPEARANCE
X-Men #12
(July 1965)

POWERS

Virtually invulnerable, with superhuman strength and an impenetrable force field. His helmet protects him from psychic attack.

Juggernaut uses his colossal might against Mammomax.

KAINE

FACTFILE

REAL NAME
None; clone of Peter Parker

OCCUPATION
Assassin, criminal

BASE
Various

HEIGHT 6 ft 4 ins
WEIGHT 250 lbs
EYES Brown
HAIR Brown

FIRST APPEARANCE
Web Of Spider-Man #118,
November 1994

POWERS

Kaine possesses the strength, speed and agility of Spider-Man himself, as well as the ability to burn the "mark of Kaine" onto the skin of his victims. Kaine also receives prophetic visions of the future from his imperfect spider-sense.

The first, flawed clone of Peter Parker created by the JACKAL, Kaine developed cellular degeneration and was able to survive only by wearing a special life-support suit. His condition left him badly scarred, and caused his spider-powers to become twisted and magnified. Abandoned by his creator, and knowing himself to be nothing more than a mockery of true life, Kaine wandered the world taking on work as an assassin to survive. Kaine would duplicate his own facial scarring on his victim's faces, leaving it as a calling card—the "mark of Kaine."

Kaine believed that the Ben Reilly clone of Peter Parker was the true SPIDER-MAN, and made it his mission in life to torture and torment Reilly for having the life that he never would, even framing him for a series of murders.

Eventually, Kaine was drawn back into Spider-Man's orbit as part of a far-reaching plot of the JACKAL's, and he was a participant in the Maximum Clonage affair which resulted in him finally learning the truth about Reilly and Parker. In the end, Kaine gave himself up to the authorities to pay for his crimes; however, he later escaped from prison, and his current whereabouts are unknown. **TB**

The assassin Kaine always left his vicious mark—a network of scars on the face of each victim.

STOPS YOU COLD DOESN'T IT? COLD AS THE GRAVE

WHAT HAPPENED? THAT MARK ON YOUR FACE IS THE SAME AS—

THE SAME AS THE MARK FOUND ON THE BODIES OF DOCTOR OCTOPUS AND THE GRIM HUNTER.

KALA

FIRST APPEARANCE Tales Of Suspense #43 (July 1963)
REAL NAME Kala
OCCUPATION Queen **BASE** The Netherworld and Subterranea
HEIGHT 5 ft 8 in **WEIGHT** 135 lbs **EYES** Blue **HAIR** Black
SPECIAL POWERS/ABILITIES Kala possess no superhuman powers, although she can see clearly in very low light due to her years of living underground.

Kala is the queen of an underground realm known as the Netherworld. She had threatened to attack the surface world, but IRON MAN captured her and brought her up to the surface. The sudden change in atmospheric conditions caused the young and beautiful Kala to age rapidly. She renounced her plans of conquest and was returned to the Netherworld, where she reverted to her youthful self. Kala allied with MOLE MAN of Subterranea, but the two later went to war. **MT**

KALE, JENNIFER

FIRST APPEARANCE Adventures Into Fear #11 (December 1972)
REAL NAME Jennifer Kale
OCCUPATION Sorceress **BASE** Citrusville, Florida
HEIGHT 5 ft 6 in **WEIGHT** 122 lbs **EYES** Blue **HAIR** Blonde
SPECIAL POWERS/ABILITIES Jennifer Kale is a highly knowledgeable sorceress with developing skill in manipulating various magical forces.

Jennifer is the granddaughter of Joshua Kale, a leader of the Cult of Zhered-Na, named after a sorceress who lived in Atlantis before it sank. Jennifer and MAN-THING were magically transported to another dimension, where they met the wizard Dakimh, last surviving pupil of Zhered-Na. As Dakimh's apprentice, Jennifer became a sorceress. An ally of MAN-THING and HOWARD THE DUCK, she is a founder of the Legion of Night and teamed with TOPAZ and Satana as the Three Witches. **PS**

KALUU

FIRST APPEARANCE Strange Tales Vol. I #147 (August 1966)
REAL NAME Kaluu
OCCUPATION Sorcerer **BASE** Not known
HEIGHT 6 ft 5 in **WEIGHT** 190 lbs **EYES** Yellow **HAIR** Black
SPECIAL POWERS/ABILITIES Arguably most powerful living black magician; has knowledge of vast number of spells including all those contained in Book of the Vishanti.

Born 500 years ago in Tibet, Kaluu trained with a youth who would become the ANCIENT ONE. Corrupted by the vampire VARNAE, Kaluu turned to black magic. Over the centuries he threatened Earth many times, but redeemed himself by helping DR. STRANGE to destroy a horde of accidentally released demons. Unable to complete the journey to eradicate the greatest of these demons, Shuma-Gorath, Kaluu was left behind by Strange, who finished the job. Kaluu later helped Strange purge himself of the side-effects of using black magic. His whereabouts are currently unknown. **AD, MF**

KANG
Time-traveling conqueror

Born in an alternate timeline in 3000 AD, Nathaniel Richards (a descendant of MISTER FANTASTIC's father, who bore the same name) discovered time-travel technology that enabled him to journey virtually anywhere he liked in the timestream.

TIME TRAVELER

Richards' first stop was ancient Egypt, where he seized power and ruled for a decade as Pharaoh Rama-Tut until forced to flee after a fight with the FANTASTIC FOUR. Arriving in the 40th century, he briefly became the SCARLET CENTURION before settling on the name Kang the Conqueror. Kang found the century in turmoil and easy to subjugate.

Looking for new challenges, Kang traveled to 1901 and established the city of Timely, Wisconsin in his guise as Victor Timely. He assembled an elite warrior class, the Anachronauts, from all eras of history before returning to the 40th century. There he fell in love with Princess RAVONNA. After her death during a revolt by Kang's troops, he tried and failed to become the consort of the Celestial Madonna (MANTIS), killing the original SWORDSMAN in the process. A future version of Kang, calling himself IMMORTUS, tried to thwart his younger self's aggressive schemes, but Kang would not be contained, and assembled the original LEGION OF THE UNLIVING.

Despite having the entirety of time and space at his disposal, the only thing for which Kang truly cared was the beautiful princess Ravonna. His obsession for her inspired several of his early schemes.

FACTFILE

REAL NAME
Nathaniel Richards

OCCUPATION
Conqueror

BASE
Mobile

HEIGHT 6 ft 3 in
WEIGHT 230 lbs
EYES Brown
HAIR Brown

FIRST APPEARANCE
Avengers Vol. 1 #8
(September 1964)

KANG

POWERS

Master of time travel; suit provides enhanced strength, force field projection, and energy projection; Kang is typically armed with futuristic weaponry.

Kang is an expert at understanding futuristic technology, particularly weaponry

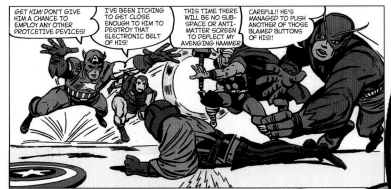

The Avengers faced Kang shortly after the team's founding, and have clashed with him countless times since. During the "Destiny War," Kang handpicked a group of Avengers from across the timestream to aid in his fight against Immortus.

KANG'S GANG

After a stint in 1873 Arizona and many other time hops, Kang gathered alternate versions of himself from branching timestreams and formed the Council of Kangs. The Kangs killed any duplicates deemed unworthy until only the prime Kang remained.

Kang joined with LIBRA, the KREE Supreme Intelligence, and the AVENGERS to prevent IMMORTUS and the TIME KEEPERS from wiping out a multitude of alternate realities. During the battle, Kang and Immortus's histories diverged. Kang then conquered modern-era Earth with his son Marcus (the new SCARLET CENTURION), but met defeat at the hands of the Avengers. **DW**

KARKAS

FIRST APPEARANCE The Eternals Vol. 1 #8 (January 1977)
REAL NAME Karkas
OCCUPATION Scholar   **BASE** Olympia
HEIGHT 8 ft 3in   **WEIGHT** 1,260 lbs   **EYES** Black   **HAIR** None
SPECIAL POWERS/ABILITIES Possesses superhuman strength. His thick hide, resembling an elephant's, gives him superhuman resistance to injury.

The Deviants are an evolutionary offshoot of humanity with an unstable genetic code. Those whose genetic makeup varies beyond standards set by the Deviant priesthood are labeled mutates. The Deviant mutate Karkas was raised to be a gladiator, but at heart he was a philosopher. He was defeated in the arena by another mutate, Ransak the Reject. Then Karkas asked THENA, a visiting ETERNAL, to grant sanctuary to himself and the Reject. She transported them to Olympia, home of the Eternals. Ever since then Karkas has been a staunch ally of the Eternals. **PS**

KARMA

FIRST APPEARANCE Marvel Team-up #100 (December 1980)
REAL NAME Xi'an Coy Manh
OCCUPATION Adventurer   **BASE** Mobile
HEIGHT 5 ft 4 in   **WEIGHT** 90 lbs   **EYES** Brown   **HAIR** Black
SPECIAL POWERS/ABILITIES Has the ability to psionically possess other people, controlling their actions and turning them into virtual puppets.

Xi'an and her brother Tran had the ability to possess others' minds. Tran tried to force Xi'an to work with him for their criminal uncle; to stop him she absorbed his psyche into her own. She attended PROFESSOR X's School for Gifted Youngsters, and became the first member of the NEW MUTANTS. Later, she rescued her siblings from her uncle and became the Xavier Institute's librarian. She retained her powers after M-Day and moved to San Francisco with the X-Men. **TB, MF**

KARNAK

FIRST APPEARANCE Fantastic Four #45 (December 1965)
REAL NAME Unrevealed   **OCCUPATION** Priest/philosopher
BASE Attilan, Blue Area, the Moon
HEIGHT 5 ft 7 in   **WEIGHT** 150 lbs   **EYES** Blue   **HAIR** Black
SPECIAL POWERS/ABILITIES Superhuman strength and ability to control his heartbeat and other autonomic body functions. Has the extrasensory ability to perceive weakness in objects and people.

A member of the royal family of the INHUMANS, Karnak is the second son of the Inhuman priest Mander. Mander and his wife Azur had sent their first son, TRITON, into the Terrigen Mist which produced genetic mutations. They decided not to expose Karnak to the mist, instead sending him to his father's religious seminary in the Tower of Wisdom. There, he trained in physical and mental disciplines, martial arts, and religious study until the age of eighteen. Karnak was involved in the Kree-Skrull Wars, and aided DAREDEVIL in his attempt to find Karnak's cousin BLACK BOLT's son. **MT**

KARNILLA

FIRST APPEARANCE Journey into Mystery #107 (August 1964)
REAL NAME Karnilla
OCCUPATION Sorceress and Queen of Nornheim
BASE Nornheim, Asgardian dimension
HEIGHT 6 ft 6 in   **WEIGHT** 475 lbs   **EYES** Purple   **HAIR** Black
SPECIAL POWERS/ABILITIES Long-lived; superhuman strength; can project magical power bolts and create a magical shield.

For centuries, Karnilla, Queen of Nornheim and the most powerful sorceress in the Asgardian dimension, vied with the GODS OF ASGARD, often allying herself with the mischievous god LOKI. Karnilla fell in love with the heroic warrior god BALDER THE BRAVE, but he repeatedly spurned her advances. After fighting alongside her in the war against the demon Surtur however, Balder relented and the pair became lovers, to the consternation of others in Asgard. The pair have forged a deep love and mutual respect, with Balder committing himself to a life in Nornheim. **AD**

KA-ZAR

FIRST APPEARANCE Uncanny X-Men Vol. 1 #10 (March 1965)
REAL NAME Lord Kevin Plunder
OCCUPATION Hunter, trapper, lord of the Savage Land
BASE The Savage Land
HEIGHT 6 ft 2 in   **WEIGHT** 215 lbs   **EYES** Blue   **HAIR** Blond
SPECIAL POWERS/ABILITIES Expert physical combatant, hunter and forager.

Son of British nobleman Lord Robert Plunder (the discoverer of Antarctic vibranium), Ka-Zar grew up in the Antarctic "Savage Land" following the murder of his father at the hands of MAN-APES. Raised by the intelligent sabertoothed tiger ZABU, Ka-Zar learned to survive against dinosaurs and Man-Apes. His enemies have included his brother Parnival, also known as the Plunderer, and the Savage Land Mutates. Ka-Zar eventually married SHANNA THE SHE-DEVIL, and the two are currently raising a son, Matthew. **DW**

KELLY

FIRST APPEARANCE X-Men #135 (September 1980)
REAL NAME Senator Robert Kelly
OCCUPATION Politician   **BASE** Washington DC
HEIGHT 5 ft 10 in   **WEIGHT** 175 lbs   **EYES** Brown
HAIR Brown (graying temples)
SPECIAL POWERS/ABILITIES Charismatic individual with rabble-rousing public speaking skills.

In one alternate future, the successful assassination of Senator Kelly led to the death or imprisonment of all mutants.

As senator for Massachusetts, Robert Kelly proposed strong anti-mutant legislation. Repeated assassination attempts and his wife's death hardened his stance until, while standing for president on an anti-mutant platform, he was saved from another attempt on his life by the sacrifice of PYRO. Kelly then changed his stance dramatically, only to be killed by a non-mutant who accused him of betraying humanity. **AD**

Like his adversary Iron Man, Killer Shrike wears armor: his costume is a head-to-toe battlesuit composed of steel alloy mesh that can resist small-arms fire.

KILLER SHRIKE

FIRST APPEARANCE The Rampaging Hulk #1 (January 1977)
REAL NAME Simon Maddicks
OCCUPATION Criminal **BASE** Mobile
HEIGHT 6 ft 5 in **WEIGHT** 250 lbs **EYES** Brown **HAIR** Brown
SPECIAL POWERS/ABILITIES Posesses enhanced strength and ability to fly. Wears bracelets with titanium talons and power-blasters that fire electrical bolts of concussive force.

The mutagenics laboratory of the Brand Corporation, a Roxxon Oil subsidiary, boosted mercenary Simon Maddicks' strength to superhuman levels and implanted an anti-gravity generator at the base of his spine, which enabled him to fly. Roxxon assigned Maddicks, as the Killer Shrike, to infiltrate the cabal called the Conspiracy. This led to his defeat by the monster hunter Ulysses BLOODSTONE. Eventually, Killer Shrike became a free agent, hiring out his services or committing crimes on his own.

In the course of his criminal career, Killer Shrike has battled the Super Heroes SPIDER-MAN, MOON KNIGHT, and the SHE-HULK. During the Civil War (see pp. 84-5), he was forced to join the Thunderbolts Army. **PS, MF**

KILLRAVEN

FIRST APPEARANCE Amazing Adventures Vol. 1 #18 (May 1973)
REAL NAME Jonathan Raven
OCCUPATION Freedom fighter **BASE** Mobile
HEIGHT 6 ft 1 in **WEIGHT** 185 lbs **EYES** Blue **HAIR** Red
SPECIAL POWERS/ABILITIES An expert combatant and swordsman who can take mental control of a Martian's body. A natural leader who has keen survival instincts suited for a post-apocalyptic world.

On Earth-691, invaders from Mars conquered Earth in the year 2001 and forced many survivors to battle in gladiatorial pits, where Jonathan Raven first won fame as "Killraven." The scientist Keeper Whitman genetically modified Killraven, giving him the ability to seize mental control of the aliens. Killraven led a team of Freemen to hunt for his lost brother Deathraven, who they discovered to be a traitor. Another Killraven fought aliens on Earth-2120, and on the standard Earth-616, trans-dimensional aliens attacked a young Jonathan Raven. PETER WISDOM stopped the aliens but had to kill Jonathan's mother to do it. **DW, MF**

Armed only with his trademark swords, Killraven faces off against a horde of alien warriors, exhibiting the cocky courage that won him fame in the gladiator pits.

KINCAID, DR. KEITH

FIRST APPEARANCE Thor #136 (January 1967)
REAL NAME Dr. Keith Kincaid
OCCUPATION Medical doctor **BASE** California
HEIGHT 5 ft 7 in **WEIGHT** 155 lbs **EYES** Blue **HAIR** Blond
SPECIAL POWERS/ABILITIES Dr. Keith Kincaid is a normal human with no superhuman powers. He possesses the normal degree of physical fitness of a man of his age and weight.

Following the temporary transformation of THOR's mortal love Jane Foster into a goddess by Odin (see GODS OF ASGARD) and her defeat at the hands of the Unknown (a formless creature composed of living fear), Odin returned her to Earth. Jane had no memory of either Thor or his alter ego Dr. Donald Blake. Foster went to work for Dr. Keith Kincaid. She fell in love with Kincaid, whose personality and appearance were virtually identical to Blake's. They married and had a son named Kevin. As it turned out, Odin had originally used Kincaid as the model for the Don Blake persona he created as a punishment for Thor. **TB**

KING, HANNIBAL

FIRST APPEARANCE Tomb of Dracula #25 (October 1974)
REAL NAME Hannibal King
OCCUPATION Private Investigator **BASE** Boston, Massachusetts
HEIGHT 6 ft 2 in **WEIGHT** 196 lbs **EYES** Blue **HAIR** Black
SPECIAL POWERS/ABILITIES Has all of the abilities typical to a vampire, but prefers not to use them due to his self-loathing about his condition.

A low-rent private investigator, Hannibal King was slain by the vampire Deacon Frost and three days later rose from the dead, himself a vampire. King's force of will was so strong that he refrained from feasting on human blood. Later, while fighting DRACULA, he met the vampire hunter BLADE. The two men tracked Frost to his lair and ended him. Along with Frank Drake, King and Blade formed the Nightstalkers to battle supernatural evil. At one point, King turned a woman he loved into a vampire to save her from a painful death. King recently fought Blade over a means of restoring souls to vampires, but Blade later gave him a potion to cure his bloodlust. **TB, MF**

KINGPIN
Bulky criminal mastermind

FACTFILE

REAL NAME
Wilson Grant Fisk

OCCUPATION
Criminal mastermind

BASE
New York City

HEIGHT 6 ft 7 in
WEIGHT 450 lbs
EYES Blue
HAIR None

FIRST APPEARANCE
Amazing Spider-Man Vol 1 #50
(July 1967)

POWERS

Brilliant criminal mind and superb fighting skills; his body, though huge and heavy, is composed of almost solid muscle.

I CANNOT NOW, OR EVER, LIVE WITHOUT YOU AT MY SIDE!

MY DEAR, MY LOVING VANESSA, I AM NOW AND FOREVER-- YOUR SLAVE!

Fisk was so in love with the beautiful Vanessa that he agreed to renounce his criminal ways—until fate took a hand.

Wilson Fisk, the Kingpin, is the most formidable figure in organized crime, and a perennial enemy of the Super Heroes SPIDER-MAN, the PUNISHER, and, most frequently, DAREDEVIL. The Kingpin's operations are global and the assassins that have done his dirty work are legion, including such names as BULLSEYE, ELEKTRA, and TYPHOID MARY.

UNDERWORLD KING

As a youth, Fisk bulked up his body to strike back against the bullies who tormented him, committing his first murder at the age of 12. At 15, he led a gang of street toughs, and came to be called the "Kingpin of Crime." Employed by crimelord Don Rigoletto, he ended up killing Rigoletto and assuming control of his operation. He married Vanessa, a beautiful socialite, and they had a son, Richard. The Kingpin also became the guardian of Maya Lopez (ECHO), the daughter of one of his murdered business partners. After decades in power, the Kingpin organized the various New York gangs and challenged the MAGGIA, triggering a war that Spider-Man helped to end.

ESSENTIAL STORYLINES
- ***Daredevil Vol. 1 #227–233***
In the acclaimed "Born Again" story arc, the Kingpin's malicious schemes bring Daredevil to the edge of a mental breakdown.
- ***Daredevil Vol. 2 #46–50***
In a shocking turn of events, Daredevil defeats the Kingpin and takes over as boss of New York City's notorious Hell's Kitchen.

Sabotage by various costumed crimefighters has hobbled the Kingpin's illicit empire.

The Kingpin's son, Richard Fisk, became a rival to his father as the masked Rose.

POWER STRUGGLES

The Kingpin believed that his son Richard had died in a skiing accident. In truth, Richard had become a rival crimelord, the SCHEMER, who lured his father into an alliance with a HYDRA faction. The Kingpin left his empire behind to pursue a new life with Vanessa in Japan, but returned with a vengeance after Vanessa's apparent death. Richard Fisk then became a new criminal rival, the ROSE.

After the Kingpin learned Daredevil's secret identity, he set out to destroy the hero's life. The Kingpin's empire crumbled under assault from HYDRA. He rebuilt his empire, but his foster daughter Echo blinded him by shooting him in the face, and the Kingpin's inner circle—including his son Richard—stabbed him many times and left him for dead. Vanessa nursed her husband back to health, and killed Richard for betraying his father.

Imprisoned, the Kingpin continued to scheme from behind bars. He exposed Daredevil's secret identity and caused him to be arrested. Also, after Spider-Man revealed his true name, the Kingpin ordered a hit that nearly killed MAY PARKER instead. His secret later restored, Daredevil helped the Kingpin win his trial in exchange for leaving the country. He recently returned to exact vengeance on the Hand, which would not leave him be. **DW, MF**

Sheer muscle mass makes the Kingpin surprisingly strong and tough, allowing him to withstand Spider-Man's powerful blows.

KLAW

FIRST APPEARANCE Fantastic Four #53 (August 1966)

REAL NAME Ulysses Klaw

OCCUPATION Scientist, professional criminal **BASE** Mobile

HEIGHT 5 ft 11 in **WEIGHT** 175 lbs **EYES** Red **HAIR** None

SPECIAL POWERS/ABILITIES Can turn sound waves into matter and reshape his body, which is made of sound waves. Able to project deafening sounds and fire concussive blasts of sound waves.

Physicist Ulysses Klaw was working on a device to turn sound into physical objects and needed Vibranium, an element found only in the African nation of Wakanda. He traveled to the country and tried to seize the element from the Cult of the BLACK PANTHER, but in the battle, Klaw's right hand was destroyed by his own sonic blaster. Eventually buying vibranium on the black market, Klaw made a prosthetic device that could turn sound into matter, to replace his hand. He has frequently battled the FANTASTIC FOUR. **MT**

KNIGHT, MISTY

FIRST APPEARANCE Marvel Team-Up #1 (March 1972, as bystander); Marvel Premiere #20 (January 1975, identified)

REAL NAME Misty Knight **OCCUPATION** Private investigator

BASE Nightwing Restorations, New York City

HEIGHT 5 ft 9 in **WEIGHT** 136 lbs **EYES** Brown **HAIR** Black

SPECIAL POWERS/ABILITIES A trained fighter with a bionic right arm. Now upgraded, it grants her superhuman strength and the ability to liquefy metals and fire a repulsor beam and a freeze ray.

Police officer Misty Knight lost her right arm to a terrorist's bomb, but Stark International fitted her with a bionic replacement. Misty went into business as a private investigator with samurai Colleen WING. As the Daughters of the Dragon, the two shared many adventures, often with Luke Cage and Misty's lover IRON FIST. Misty complied with the Superhuman Registration Act and started a new Heroes for Hire with Colleen, BLACK CAT, Humbug, Orka, PALADIN, SHANG-CHI, and the new TARANTULA. The team folded after World War Hulk, and Colleen and Misty parted ways.
TB, MF

KOFI

FIRST APPEARANCE Power Pack #16 (November 1985)

REAL NAME Lord Kofi Whitemane

OCCUPATION Student **BASE** Kymellian homeworld

HEIGHT 5 ft **WEIGHT** Not known **EYES** Pink **HAIR** Black

SPECIAL POWERS/ABILITIES Able to teleport himself short distances; like other Kymellian's, Kofi has the potential to control mass, energy, and gravity but these skills are as yet undeveloped.

A young member of the Kymellian race of aliens, Kofi was the son of Lord Yrik Whitemane, the interstellar ambassador to the Z'nrx (see SNARKS). As he became older, Kofi grew to resent the time and energy his father committed to his work. Things came to a head when Kofi discovered a Z'nrx plot to kidnap the junior team of Earth Super Heroes known as POWER PACK, and to use them in a game of political brinkmanship. Traveling to Earth, Kofi defeated the schemers, his efforts earning the admiration of his father and forging a reconciliation between them. **AD**

KOMODO

FIRST APPEARANCE Avengers: The Initiative #1 (March 2007)

REAL NAME Melati Kusuma **OCCUPATION** Adventurer

BASE Arizona **HEIGHT** Varies **WEIGHT** Varies

EYES Black **HAIR** Black

SPECIAL POWERS/ABILITIES Komodo can shift to a lizardwoman form that grants her superhuman strength, endurance, agility, and reflexes, plus armored skin, sharpened teeth and claws, and a healing factor.

Missing her legs from the knees down, Melati Kusuma pursued a college internship under Dr. Curt Conners (see LIZARD). The moment he trusted her with his experimental regeneration formula, she tested it on herself. The formula worked but turned her into a lizardwoman. Taking the codename Komodo, Melati became a cadet in the inaugural class at Camp Hammond as part of The Fifty-State Initiative (see pp.118–9), where she met and fell for HARDBALL, who later betrayed her to lead HYDRA. She rarely leaves her Komodo form, but she did for HARDBALL. After graduating from Camp Hammond, she was assigned to the Desert Stars team in Arizona. **MF**

KORVAC

FIRST APPEARANCE Giant-Size Defenders #3 (January 1975)

REAL NAME Michael Korvac **OCCUPATION** Computer technician; would-be master of the universe **BASE** Mobile

HEIGHT 6 ft 3 in **WEIGHT** 230 lbs **EYES** Blue **HAIR** Blond

SPECIAL POWERS/ABILITIES Cosmic power on an unimaginable scale. Capable of time travel, astral projection, projecting lethal energy blasts and of power absorption from any source.

Korvac comes from the same possible 31st-century future as the GUARDIANS OF THE GALAXY. When the Badoon invaded Earth, he quickly offered to help the alien conquerors. They rewarded his loyalty by amputating the lower half of his body and replacing it with a mobile computer module. Realizing the potential of his new form, Korvac began to plot against the Badoon. He also managed to siphon energy from the GRANDMASTER and absorbed the power cosmic from the world-sized starship that belonged to GALACTUS. Now seemingly omnipotent, Korvac traveled to the 20th century with the intention of restructuring the universe in his image, but he later faked his own death during a battle with the AVENGERS. **TD**

KRANG

FIRST APPEARANCE Fantastic Four Annual #1 (1963)

REAL NAME Krang **OCCUPATION** Warlord

BASE Formerly Atlantis, now mobile in the Atlantic Ocean

HEIGHT 6 ft **WEIGHT** 290 lbs **EYES** Blue **HAIR** Black

SPECIAL POWERS/ABILITIES Like all Atlanteans, Krang has superhuman strength, gills for breathing water, and other physical adaptations for undersea living.

A member of Atlantis's military, Krang aspired to the throne of NAMOR the Sub-Mariner during his long absence. When Namor returned, he appointed Krang as his warlord, but Krang seized the throne and plotted to conquer the surface world. Namor bested Krang in combat and exiled him from Atlantis. Since then, Krang has continued to scheme against Namor and has allied himself with Namor's enemies ATTUMA and Byrrah. Krang once fell under the sway of the Serpent Crown and joined forces with the second VIPER's Serpent Squad. Krang later joined NIGHTHAWK's version of the Defenders. **PS, MF**

KRAVEN

KRAVEN

FACTFILE

REAL NAME
Sergei Kravinoff

OCCUPATION
Professional game hunter
and mercenary

BASE
Mobile

HEIGHT 6 ft
WEIGHT 235 lbs
EYES Brown
HAIR Black

FIRST APPEARANCE:
*Amazing Spider-Man Vol. 1 #15
(August 1964)*

POWERS

Enhanced strength, speed,
and agility; expert
tracker and skilled
hand-to-hand fighter.

After his Russian aristocrat parents died while he was a child, Sergei Kravinoff joined the crew of an African safari, learning to track and kill big game. A mystical serum augmented his strength and speed, and Kravinoff became the world's greatest hunter. After anglicizing his name to Kraven, he took up a challenge from his half-brother, the Chameleon, to hunt the most dangerous game of all: Spider-Man. After numerous defeats, both on his own and as one of the Sinister Six, Kraven tranquilized Spider-Man and buried him alive. Kraven then assumed the hero's identity in a bid to prove himself the better crime fighter. In the end, confident that life held no further challenge, Kraven shot himself. Kraven's son Vladimir briefly served as the Grim Hunter—until Kaine killed him—and his son Alyosha became the second Kraven the Hunter. Recently, Kraven's young daughter Ana Tatiana took up the Kraven the Hunter mantle too. **DW, MF**

Despite his modest superpowered abilities, Kraven's combat skill allowed him to hold his own against multiple metahuman opponents.

Kraven was skilled with whips, crossbows, and all bladed weapons, as well as an expert in every form of unarmed combat.

KREE, THE *see opposite page*

KRO

FIRST APPEARANCE The Eternals Vol. 1 #1 (July 1976)
REAL NAME Kro **OCCUPATION** Monarch of Earth's Deviants
BASE Deviant Lemuria **HEIGHT** 6 ft 5 in **WEIGHT** 320 lbs
EYES Red **HAIR** Bald with black facial hair
SPECIAL POWERS/ABILITIES Superhuman strength; mental control over his body, giving him virtual immortality; the power to heal from severe injuries, and limited shapeshifting abilities.

Unlike other members of the Deviants, an offshoot of humanity, Kro is virtually immortal, and has lived more than 20,000 years. Kro has concealed his longevity by pretending to be his own descendants. Kro fell in love with THENA of the ETERNALS, the Deviants' foes. They have mostly remained apart, but decades ago they had twins known as Donald and Deborah Ritter. Formerly a warlord, Kro has become ruler of the Deviants on Earth. **PS**

KULAN GATH

FIRST APPEARANCE Conan the Barbarian #15 (May 1972)
REAL NAME Kulan Gath
OCCUPATION Sorcerer **BASE** Mobile
HEIGHT n/a **WEIGHT** n/a **EYES** Red **HAIR** Black
SPECIAL POWERS/ABILITIES Manipulates magic to a very high level. Can summon demonic entities, mentally control individuals, project beams of mystical force, and restructure flesh and bone.

Kulan Gath once held a high position among the sorcerers of Stygia during the Hyborian era. He married his bitter rival, the sorceress Vammatar, to gain access to the Iron-Bound Books of Shuma-Gorath and together they opened the books, unleashing a Nether Demon. Kulan Gath also studied under the master sorcerer Thoth-Amon, a longtime enemy of Conan the Barbarian. The wizard's physical body has been killed more than once but his spirit always survives, often in a necklace, to enslave others. He has clashed with DR STRANGE, SPIDER-MAN, THE AVENGERS and the X-MEN, among others. **MT**

KURSE

FIRST APPEARANCE Thor #347 (September 1984, as Algrim), Secret Wars II #4 (October 1985, as Kurse)
REAL NAME Valgoth, formerly Algrim the Strong
OCCUPATION Vengeance-seeker **BASE** Asgard
HEIGHT 7 ft **WEIGHT** 840 lbs **EYES** Yellow **HAIR** None
SPECIAL POWERS/ABILITIES Almost limitless strength, and is invulnerable to almost all harm. Can sense the presence of those he hunts from a world away.

Kurse began life as Algrim the Strong, mightiest of the Dark Elves who served their ruler Malekith. Chosen to battle THOR on behalf of his master, Algrim fell into a pit of lava. His desire for vengeance was so strong he survived, but he no longer knew who he was. THE BEYONDER decided to use Algrim to study vengeance. He transformed Algrim into the vastly more powerful Kurse, who pursued Thor across the Nine Worlds. Kurse eventually learned that his true enemy was his one-time ruler Malekith. After he slew the Dark Elf Lord, his craving for revenge was sated, and he became a sword protector of Asgard and its children, taking the name Valgoth. **TB**

KREE, THE

Extraterrestrial empire-builders

The Kree are aliens, similar in appearance to humans but possessing twice the strength and endurance. They originated on the planet Hala in the Pama system, located in the Greater Magellanic Cloud, a planet they shared with another intelligent species, the plant-like Cotati. Kree consist of two primary races: the original blue-skinned race and a pink-skinned race which emerged millennia later.

FACTFILE

BASE
Kree-Lar, Turunal system, Greater Magellanic Cloud

FIRST APPEARANCE
Fantastic Four Vol. 1 #65 (August 1967)

KREE

POWERS
Strength and endurance that are twice the human average.

WAR YEARS

Nearly a million years ago, the SKRULLS landed on Hala and set up a contest between the KREE and the COTATI. When the Cotati were named as victors, the enraged Kree killed the contact team, stole their starship technology, and launched the Kree-Skrull war that raged for eons. They took special interest in Earth, creating the offshoot of humanity known as the INHUMANS. Kree society was ruled by the SUPREME INTELLIGENCE, a computer consciousness formed by the minds of the greatest Kree thinkers. In the modern era, the Kree officer Mar-Vell scouted Earth for a possible invasion, but defected to Earth's side as the Super Hero CAPTAIN MARVEL.

Armored mobile infantry platforms decimate the Kree enemy and protect Kree operators from counterattack.

Warships, bristling with weaponry form the Kree defense fleet and its expeditionary strike teams.

Warriors dominate Kree society. Other respectable professions include politician and scientist, since both can use their unique talents to advance the glory of the Kree empire.

KREE EVOLUTION

During the Kree-Shi'ar war, a later conflict sometimes called Operation Galactic Storm, the Supreme Intelligence arranged for the detonation of a nega-bomb in Kree space in the hope of jumpstarting the species' evolution. Over ninety percent of the Kree died, and the survivors became vassals of the Shi'ar. The AVENGERS executed the Supreme Intelligence, but it survived, and using the Forever Crystal, accelerated the evolution of some Kree into a new breed, the Ruul, which could spontaneously produce adaptations such as the ability to fly or to breathe underwater. During Avengers Disassembled, HAWKEYE seemingly died while fighting a Kree invasion force, but these Kree were probably manifestations of the SCARLET WITCH's formidable reality-warping powers. **DW**

The Kree have created many technological wonders, including Kree Sentries and the Psyche-Magnetron, which can conjure up any weapon from Kree history.

LADY DEATHSTRIKE

FACTFILE

REAL NAME
Yuriko Oyama

OCCUPATION
Assassin; CEO of Oyama Heavy Industries

BASE
Japan, later mobile

HEIGHT 5 ft 9 in
WEIGHT 128 lbs
EYES Brown
HAIR Black

FIRST APPEARANCE
*Daredevil Vol. 1 #197
(August 1983)*

POWERS

Cyborg whose bones have been laced with adamantium molecules, rendering them unbreakable. Her fingers were replaced with adamantium talons. Can interface with computers.

LADY DEATHSTRIKE

Yuriko Oyama is the daughter of Japanese scientist Lord Dark Wind. Seeking vengeance on her father for the death of her brothers and the scarring of her face, Oyama joined forces with Daredevil against him. She killed Lord Dark Wind just as he was about to murder Daredevil. However, the man she loved, Kira, a member of Lord Dark Wind's private army, then committed suicide. She fought for the Thunderbolts Army during the Civil War and later led a new group of Reavers while hunting for the first mutant baby born after M-Day. Recently, she accepted an invitation into MADELYNE PRYOR's Sisterhood of Mutants. **MF**

Lady Deathstrike is not only a mistress of Japanese martial arts, but, as a cyborg, has increased strength, speed and agility.

CYBORG ASSASSIN

As the samurai warrior Lady Deathstrike, Oyama attempted to kill Wolverine and take his skeleton. However, she was defeated by Wolverine's friend Heather Hudson in her costumed identity of VINDICATOR.

Subsequently, Lady Deathstrike was converted into a cyborg by the extradimensional being SPIRAL. In this new form, Lady Deathstrike's own skeleton has been reinforced with adamantium.

Although Lady Deathstrike heads Oyama Heavy Industries, she also works as a professional assassin. For a time she was a member of the REAVERS, Donald Pierce's team of cyborgs. She severed the legs of the Japanese hero SUNFIRE. Wolverine remains her principal adversary. **PS**

Like her archfoe Wolverine, Lady Deathstrike has an adamantium-laced skeleton and adamantium claws. Normally a foot long, her claws can extend to about twice that length.

LAVA MEN

FIRST APPEARANCE Journey Into Mystery #97 (October 1963)
BASE Various; deep underground   **HEIGHT** Up to 20 ft
WEIGHT Unknown   **EYES** Black   **HAIR** None
SPECIAL POWERS/ABILITIES Able to stand in molten lava; constantly release heat into surrounding area; possess double the strength of normal humans; possess ability to transform themselves into sentient giants.

Moulded into their current form by an unknown demon, the Lava Men were originally descended from the Gortokians, a genetically engineered offshoot of humanity. There are two known tribes of Lava Men. For a time, the first was led by a witch doctor known as Jinku, but his reign ended when THOR thwarted efforts to ignite every volcano on the planet. The second tribe lives in caverns beneath the Project: PEGASUS research facility. Researchers became aware of these Lava Men when the creatures were disturbed by a drilling project. The AVENGERS resolved the situation and the Lava Men haven't been seen since. **AD**

LEAP-FROG

FIRST APPEARANCE Daredevil Vol. 1 #25 (February 1967)
REAL NAME Vincent Patilio
OCCUPATION Inventor, professional criminal
BASE New York City
HEIGHT 5 ft 9 in   **WEIGHT** 170 lbs   **EYES** Brown   **HAIR** Gray
SPECIAL POWERS/ABILITIES Electrical coils in boots enable leaps up to 60 feet high; exoskeleton provides enhanced strength.

Vincent Patilio started out as a toy inventor before seeing a chance to make some money when he created a set of electrically-powered jumping coils. He devised a frog costume and embarked on a criminal career as Leap-Frog. He met with a string of pathetic setbacks, including a disastrous stint with ELECTRO's Emissaries of Evil and numerous humiliations at the hands of DAREDEVIL and SPIDER-MAN. Vincent's son Eugene later donned his father's costume and became FROG-MAN, an identity that Vincent has sometimes assumed as he continues in his modest calling. **DW**

LEADER

After dropping out of school, Samuel Sterns took a menial job in a US government research facility, where an accident led to his body being bombarded by intense gamma radiation. In the days that followed, Sterns developed an insatiable thirst for knowledge, and as his intelligence expanded at exponential rates, so too did his cranium.

Unfortunately, Sterns' increased intellectual capacity was not matched by emotional maturity. Disgusted by government corruption, he decided that he should command the human race, and restyled himself as the Leader.

Over the years, the Leader's efforts to dominate the world have been repeatedly foiled by the HULK and undermined by his own impatience. The Leader has battled that green behemoth with robotic humanoids and even pitted Super Villains like the RHINO and the GLOB against him, but global domination has remained elusive. However, he has had some successes, in particular the construction of Freehold, a utopian city hidden in Canada's icy north.

After World War Hulk, the Leader teleported the at-large members of the Warbound to his base in Nevada. Once there, he used their powers to activate a Gamma-powered dome over the desert and irradiate everyone inside. The Warbound managed to stop him—for now. **AD, MF**

Bruce Banner shares the Leader's final moments in the physical world and witnesses his ascension to a new plane of existence.

FACTFILE

REAL NAME
Samuel Sterns

OCCUPATION
Would-be world conqueror

BASE
Another dimension

HEIGHT 5 ft 10 in
WEIGHT 140 lbs
EYES Green
HAIR Black

FIRST APPEARANCE
Tales to Astonish #62
(December 1964)

POWERS

Superhuman intelligence, several times that of a genius, with an incredible memory for facts and information. Specializes in creating robots, computer systems, high-tech weapons. Has devised methods of telepathic control.

LEECH

FIRST APPEARANCE Uncanny X-Men #179 (March 1984)
REAL NAME Unrevealed
OCCUPATION Adventurer **BASE** Various
HEIGHT 4 ft 2 in **WEIGHT** 67 lbs **EYES** Yellow **HAIR** None
SPECIAL POWERS/ABILITIES Leech can dampen the superhuman powers of any Super Heroes or Villains, mutant or not, within his proximity, up to a range of 30 ft.

Abandoned by his parents, Leech was found by CALIBAN, who welcomed him into the MORLOCKS, who lived in the sewers beneath Manhattan. Leech was happy there—until the MARAUDERS came to kill the Morlocks. POWER PACK and X-FACTOR saved him, and the green-skinned boy lived with X-Factor as one of the X-Terminators, and then worked with GENERATION X and the DAYDREAMERS. The WEAPON X program later captured Leech and used him to control mutant prisoners. He escaped and survived M-Day with his powers intact. **TB, MF**

LEEDS, BETTY BRANT

Although unfazed by the rantings of her bullish boss, J. Jonah JAMESON, Betty Brant's positive outlook was gradually worn down as events drove her from one calamity to another.

Betty was SPIDER-MAN Peter Parker's very first girlfriend, and when their relationship ended, she married *Daily Bugle* reporter Ned Leeds. Ned's obsession with his work caused constant tension, which he blamed on SPIDER-MAN. She was dismayed to discover that Ned had become the evil HOBGOBLIN, and suffered a mental breakdown following his death. Since then, Betty has rebuilt her life, becoming an investigative reporter. It was she who discovered that Roderick Kingsley was the original Hobgoblin. Having experienced the worst that life can deal, Betty can now look to the future with confidence. **AD**

FACTFILE

REAL NAME
Betty Brant Leeds

OCCUPATION
Investigative journalist

BASE
New York City

HEIGHT 5 ft 7 in
WEIGHT 125 lbs
EYES Brown
HAIR Brown

FIRST APPEARANCE:
Amazing Spider-Man #4
(September 1963)

LEEDS, BETTY BRANT

POWERS

Expert investigative reporter with a strong personality and a hugely generous soul.

LEFT-WINGER

FIRST APPEARANCE Captain America #323 (November 1986)

REAL NAME Hector Lennox

OCCUPATION Former wrestler   **BASE** Mobile

HEIGHT 6 ft 5 in   **WEIGHT** 265 lbs   **EYES** Blue   **HAIR** Black

SPECIAL POWERS/ABILITIES Left-Winger possessed superhuman strength and stamina thanks to the Power Broker's strength-augmentation program.

When his ex-army buddy John Walker (*see* US AGENT) became the Super-Patriot, Lennox became one of his Bold Urban Commandos ("Buckies"). Walker was then selected to replace Steve Rogers as CAPTAIN AMERICA. Angered, Lennox and his partner took on guises as Left-Winger and Right-Winger, and set out to destroy Walker's tenure as Captain America. They revealed Walker's true identity to the media, Walker's parents were killed as a result, and he vowed vengeance. Left-Winger was so badly burned in an ensuing explosion that he took his own life. **TB**

LEGION

FIRST APPEARANCE New Mutants #25 (March 1985)

REAL NAME David Charles Haller   **OCCUPATION** Student

BASE Muir Island, off the coast of Scotland

HEIGHT 5 ft 9 in   **WEIGHT** 130 lbs   **EYES** (left) Green; (right) Blue   **HAIR** Black   **SPECIAL POWERS/ABILITIES** Telepathic ability; telekinesis enables him to lift objects and protect self with force field; also able to start fires with his mind.

After an affair with Charles Xavier (*see* PROFESSOR X), Gabrielle HALLER secretly gave birth to a son, David. David became a powerful mutant named Legion, but after a horrifying terrorist attack, he developed multiple personalities. After Xavier learned of David's existence, he helped his core persona reassert itself. David decided to change history by killing MAGNETO in the past, but he accidentally killed a younger version of his father instead, bringing on the Age of Apocalypse (Earth-295). BISHOP traveled into the past to restore the timeline by killing David, but it seems that Legion has recently returned. **AD, MF**

○ **LEGION OF THE UNLIVING**
see opposite page

LETHAL LEGION

When Simon Williams (*see* WONDER MAN) sacrificed his life to save the AVENGERS, his altruism had untold consequences. His grieving brother, Eric, blamed the Avengers for Simon's death and determined to destroy them, adopting the guise of the GRIM REAPER and forming the Lethal Legion of Super Villains. The Legion's efforts ended in failure, while Eric's own enmity to the Avengers was compromised following his brother's resurrection. Nevertheless the Lethal Legion lived on under the leadership of COUNT NEFARIA. Not much of a team player, Nefaria stole the powers of his fellow legionnaires but was still defeated, despite his augmented abilities.

Following Grim Reaper's death, the Legion's name was adopted by the demon lord Satannish, who resurrected various historical figures—including Josef Stalin and Heinrich Himmler —to capture the souls of the Avengers. Although this plot was also foiled, the Lethal Legion's name continues to inspire fear. **AD**

FACTFILE

MEMBERS AND POWERS

GRIM REAPER
A mechanical scythe replaces right hand.

LIVING LASER
A collection of light particles possessing human consciousness.

MAN-APE
Superhuman strength, endurance, and agility.

POWER MAN
Can grow from 6 ft to 60 ft, with tenfold increase in strength.

SWORDSMAN
Superb athlete and master swordsman.

COUNT NEFARIA
Superhuman strength, speed and the power of flight.

WHIRLWIND
Achieves superhuman speed by spinning body.

ULTRON
A robot with vast strength, speed and deadly weapons.

BLACK TALON
Can create and control zombies.

BASE
Mobile

FIRST APPEARANCE
Avengers #78 (July 1970)

CHARACTER KEY

1 Living Laser
2 Power Man
3 Swordsman
4 Grim Reaper
5 Man-Ape

LETHAL LEGION

LIBERTEENS, THE

FIRST APPEARANCE Avengers: The Initiative Annual #1 (December 2007)   **BASE** Philadelphia

MEMBERS AND POWERS The Revolutionary Swordsman. **Ms. America** Superhuman strength, flight, and invulnerability. **Blue Eagle** Flying marksman. **Iceberg** Ice powers. **2-D** Turns flat and stretches. **Whiz Kid** Super speed. **Hope** Superhuman strength and invulnerability.

THE LIBERTEENS
1 Blue Eagle   **2** Ms America   **3** Iceberg   **4** Whiz Kid   **5** The Revolutionary   **6** Hope   **7** 2-D

The Liberteens are a young group of Super Heroes based in Philadelphia as part of The Fifty-State Initiative (*see* pp. 118–9). Team members are modeled directly on the members of the 1940s Liberty Legion. Unfortunately, their team leader, the Revolutionary, turned out to be a SKRULL inserted into their team as part of the Skrulls' efforts to infiltrate every branch of the Initiative.

During the Secret Invasion (*see* pp. 326–7), the Skrull Kill Krew—a team of humans infected with a rare Skrull disease—helped root the Revolutionary out, along with several of the Skrulls hiding inside of other Initiative teams. **MF**

LEGION OF THE UNLIVING

The undead are on the march!

The Legion of the Unliving are foes of the AVENGERS, their ranks made up of deceased heroes and villains brought together by outside entities. Legion members have variously appeared as duplicates or animated zombies and, most disturbingly, have included former Avengers. KANG the Conqueror, allied with IMMORTUS, assembled the original Legion. Scouring the timestream, Kang brought together FRANKENSTEIN'S MONSTER, Midnight, Flying Dutchman, villain-turned-hero WONDER MAN, BARON ZEMO and the heroic HUMAN TORCH.

THE ORIGINAL LEGION
1 Wonder Man 2 Midnight
3 Baron Zemo
4 Human Torch
5 Flying Dutchman
6 Frankenstein's Monster

DEFEATED

Despite their combined powers, Kang's Legion failed to defeat the Avengers, and Immortus—after defeating the turncoat Kang—restored the Legion members to their proper places in the timestream.

The second Legion of the Unliving came about through the efforts of the GRANDMASTER, who raised such figures as Bucky BARNES, the SWORDSMAN, CAPTAIN MAR-VELL, KORVAC, DRACULA, and the RED GUARDIAN to guard "life bombs" that threatened to wipe out the universe. As the Avengers struggled to thwart the Grandmaster's scheme, their slain members joined the ranks of the Legion of the Unliving. Fortunately, all the Avengers returned to life after the resolution of the crisis.

THE SECOND LEGION
1 Swordsman 2 Nighthawk 3 Executioner 4 Terrax
5 Hyperion 6 Green Goblin 7 Korvac 8 Death Adder
9 Dracula 10 Bucky Barnes 11 Black Knight
12 Captain Mar-Vell 13 Baron Blood
14 Drax the Destroyer 15 Red Guardian

THE THIRD LEGION
1 Iron Man (Arno Stark)
2 Grim Reaper
3 Swordsman
4 Left-Winger
5 Right-Winger
6 Oort the Living Comet

NEVER SAY DIE

A third Legion included such notable figures as the GRIM REAPER, the BLACK KNIGHT (Nathan Garrett), and Toro. They were gathered by Immortus in order to help him capture the SCARLET WITCH.

Following Immortus's failure, the undead Grim Reaper gained additional power from the demon Lloigoroth and gathered a fourth version of the Legion of the Unliving. Grim Reaper's Legion included copies of villains such as COUNT NEFARIA and INFERNO, but the team once again met defeat in battle against the Avengers.

The fifth Legion of the Unliving were once more pawns of the Grim Reaper against the Avengers. It consisted of the deceased heroes CAPTAIN MAR-VELL, DOCTOR DRUID, HELLCAT, MOCKINGBIRD, Swordsman, Wonder Man, and THUNDERSTRIKE (Eric Masterson). The Scarlet Witch used her powers to send the spirits of this Legion into the afterlife, and her love for Wonder Man restored him to life. Likewise, Wonder Man restored his brother the Grim Reaper to full physical health, thus ending his threat. **DW**

THE FOURTH LEGION
1 Wonder Man
2 Captain Mar-Vell
3 Swordsman
4 Doctor Druid
5 Thunderstrike
6 Mockingbird

FACTFILE

ORIGINAL MEMBERS AND POWERS
KANG THE CONQUEROR
Master of time travel
FRANKENSTEIN'S MONSTER
Enhanced strength, damage resistance.
BARON ZEMO
(Heinrich Zemo)
Extended longevity, brilliant criminal mind.
WONDER MAN
Flight, enhanced strength, body suffused with ionic energy.
HUMAN TORCH
(Jim Hammond)
Flight, flame projection.
FLYING DUTCHMAN
Projection of energy blasts.
MIDNIGHT
Master martial artist.

BASE
Mobile

FIRST APPEARANCE
Avengers Vol. 1 #131
(January 1975)

LEGION OF THE UNLIVING

L

LIFEGUARD

FIRST APPEARANCE X-Treme X-Men #6 (December 2001)
REAL NAME Heather Cameron
OCCUPATION Member of X-Corp **BASE** Mumbai, India
HEIGHT 5 ft 10 in **WEIGHT** 156 lbs **EYES** Blue **HAIR** Blonde
SPECIAL POWERS/ABILITIES Possesses bio-morphic ability—
powers adapt to circumstances. In past Lifeguard has grown wings,
extra arms, and developed ability to breath underwater.

When the Chinese Triad targeted Heather and Davis Cameron, only the X-Men's intervention saved the siblings' lives. Forced to uncover their mutant abilities during this conflict, both siblings joined the X-Men afterward, and Heather began a relationship with Neal Shaara (THUNDERBIRD). As her powers developed, Heather's appearance became increasingly alien, and Jean Grey suggested that her mother was of the Shi'ar race. Disturbed by this, Davis disappeared, and Heather left the team to find him. Later, she went to work for the X-CORPORATION and then came to live at the Xavier Institute. She retained her powers after M-Day. **AD, MF**

LIGHTMASTER

FIRST APPEARANCE Peter Parker, the Spectacular Spider-Man #1
(December 1976) **REAL NAME** Dr. Edward Lansky
OCCUPATION Physics professor **BASE** New York City
HEIGHT 5 ft 11 in **WEIGHT** 175 lbs **EYES** Brown **HAIR** Brown
SPECIAL POWERS/ABILITIES Lightmaster possesses the ability
to generate light, including lasers, to create simple solid objects out
of light, and to fly.

In a bid to prevent budget cuts that might affect his position at Empire State University, Dr. Edward Lansky donned a high-tech suit designed to harness the power of light and became the criminal Lightmaster. His intent was to hold various key government officials hostage, but his scheme was foiled by SPIDER-MAN. During the conflict, Lansky's suit was damaged, transforming him into an energy being. Since that time, Lightmaster has resurfaced, attempting to cash in on his light-based powers. But each time heroes such as DAZZLER, QUASAR, CABLE, and the aforementioned Spider-Man have succeeded in putting his lights out. **TD**

LILITH

FIRST APPEARANCE Ghost Rider #98 (August 1992)
REAL NAME Lilith Drake **OCCUPATION** Sumerian Goddess
BASE The Shadowside Dimension, Atlantis
HEIGHT 6 ft **WEIGHT** 140 lbs **EYES** Yellow **HAIR** Black
SPECIAL POWERS/ABILITIES Superhuman strength and stamina;
manipulates the dark forces of the universe. She can summon her
children from other dimensions, giving them new bodies on Earth.

Lilith is believed to be the daughter of Aehr, the ancient god of darkness. She lived on the island of Atlantis and survived its destruction. Later, Atlantean sorcerers imprisoned her within the belly of a Leviathan believed to be Tiamat. On emerging, Lilith gathered her children, known as the Lilin, to her and battled Ghost Rider and Johnny Blaze. She and the Lilin later came into conflict with DOCTOR STRANGE. At one point, she was imprisoned inside the magical realm of Avalon, but during the Secret Invasion, Peter Wisdom freed her to help battle the Skrulls. **AD, MF**

LILITH (DRACULA'S DAUGHTER)

FIRST APPEARANCE Giant-Size Chillers Vol. 1 #1 (June 1974)
REAL NAME Unrevealed
OCCUPATION Adventureress **BASE** South of France
HEIGHT 6 ft **WEIGHT** 125 lbs **EYES** Red **HAIR** Black
SPECIAL POWERS/ABILITIES Unique among vampires, Lilith
could walk in sunlight and was unaffected by religious talismen;
superhuman strength; hypnotic abilities; could transform into a bat.

The daughter of DRACULA and his first wife, Zofia, Lilith hated her father for throwing them out of their castle home and driving her mother to suicide. A gypsy woman called Gretchin raised Lilith, but when Dracula killed Gretchin's son, the gypsy magically transformed Lilith into a vampire and condemned her to hunt Dracula for the rest of her life. For centuries, Lilith stalked and battled her father, but when she finally had the chance to kill him, she found she could not. Later, she became an agent of Nick FURY's supernatural HOWLING COMMANDOS. **AD, MF**

LIPSCOMBE, DR. ANGELA

FIRST APPEARANCE The Incredible Hulk Vol. 3 #12 (March 2000)
REAL NAME Angela Lipscombe
OCCUPATION Neuropsychologist **BASE** Mobile
HEIGHT 5 ft 9 in **WEIGHT** 125 lbs **EYES** Blue **HAIR** Blonde
SPECIAL POWERS/ABILITIES Genius-level knowledge of the
science of neuropsychiatry; kind-hearted and a loyal and
courageous friend to Bruce Banner in his hour of need.

Angela Lipscombe and Bruce Banner (*see* HULK) dated in medical school, but Banner broke off the relationship, jealous when Lipscombe received a coveted grant for graduate study and he did not. Doctor Lipscombe became one of the world's foremost experts in the field of neuropsychiatry. Many years later, Bruce Banner looked her up in terrible distress, believing he had contracted an incurable disease. Lipscombe used the opportunity to study the bizarre and disturbing multiple personalities that Banner exhibited as the Hulk. She is the partner of DOC SAMSON. **DW**

LIVING LASER

FIRST APPEARANCE Avengers Vol. 1 #34 (November 1966)
REAL NAME Arthur Parks
OCCUPATION Criminal **BASE** Mobile
HEIGHT 5 ft 11 in **WEIGHT** (formerly) 125 lbs
EYES (formerly) Blue **HAIR** (formerly) Brown
SPECIAL POWERS/ABILITIES Composed entirely of light, he can travel at light speed or transform himself into an offensive laser.

Technician Arthur Parks strapped lasers to his wrists to become Living Laser. Obsessed with Wasp, he kidnapped her until the Avengers rescued her. He escaped from prison and worked as a criminal henchman for the Mandarin, Batroc's Brigade, and the Lethal Legion. He later implanted lasers beneath his skin, but the process caused him to explode. He reappeared as a sentient being made of light, and battled Iron Man several times. Recently, he joined the Hood's criminal organization and fought against the Skrulls during the Secret Invasion. **DW, MF**

LIVING LIGHTNING

FIRST APPEARANCE Avengers West Coast #63 (October 1990)
REAL NAME Miguel Santos
OCCUPATION Student **BASE** California
HEIGHT 5 ft 9 in **WEIGHT** 170 lbs **EYES** Brown **HAIR** Black
SPECIAL POWERS/ABILITIES Living Lightning can transform his body into sentient electrical energy, which he uses for various effects, including to fly.

Miguel Santos's father was Lightning Lord, head of the Legion of Living Lightning, which hoped to control the Hulk and use him to overthrow the US government. The Hulk destroyed the Legion's headquarters, killing Lightning Lord. Miguel intended to follow in his father's footsteps, but an accident with one of his father's devices transformed him into a being of pure electrical energy, who needed a containment suit to remain stable. He eventually became a member of the Avengers. He sided with Captain America during the Civil War, but later joined the Rangers, the Fifty State Initiative's team in Texas. **TB, MF**

LIVING MUMMY

FIRST APPEARANCE Supernatural Thrillers #5 (August 1973)
REAL NAME N'Kantu
OCCUPATION Wanderer **BASE** Egypt
HEIGHT 7 ft 6 in **WEIGHT** 650 lbs **EYES** Brown **HAIR** None
SPECIAL POWERS/ABILITIES Blood replaced by life-preserving fluid removing human need for food, water, or sleep; enhanced strength, rock-hard body, near-immortality; limited mobility.

Chief N'Kantu of the Swarili of North Africa became a prisoner of the pharaoh Aram-Set and organized a slave rebellion. Although Aram-Set was killed, the rebellion was crushed, and N'Kantu was entombed while still alive. Preserved in a sarcophagus for 3,000 years, he reawakened in

the modern era and went on a rampage before being shocked back to relative sanity when he seized a power line. He later joined Nick Fury's supernatural Howling Commandos. He was imprisoned during the Civil War for refusing to register with the US government. He has since returned to Egypt, where he harvests evil souls for the god Anubis. **DW, MF**

LIVING PHARAOH

FIRST APPEARANCE X-Men #54 (1969)
REAL NAME Ahmet Abdol
OCCUPATION Would-be world conqueror, now living planet
BASE Formerly Egypt, now distant solar system
HEIGHT 5 ft 8 in **WEIGHT** 196 lbs **EYES** Blue **HAIR** Black
SPECIAL POWERS/ABILITIES Absorbs cosmic energy and wields it as destructive force; at times able to vastly increase body size.

Egyptian academic Ahmet Abdol was obsessed with the Egyptian Pharaohs, so when a traumatic incident caused his own mutant powers to become evident he renamed himself the Living Pharaoh. The discovery that his abilities were muted by those of Alex Summers (see Havok) led to many encounters with the X-Men, during which he occasionally transformed himself into the 30-ft-high Living Monolith. Terrible destruction always ensued, including his daughter's own death, and eventually Ahmet faced up to this. Asking Thor to hurl him into deep space, cosmic energy gradually transformed him into a rich and verdant Living Planet. **AD**

LIVING TRIBUNAL

FIRST APPEARANCE Strange Tales #157 (June 1967)
REAL NAMES Equity, Necessity, and Vengeance
OCCUPATION Guardian of the continuum of alternate universes
BASE The Multiverse
HEIGHT n/a **WEIGHT** n/a **EYES** n/a **HAIR** n/a
SPECIAL POWERS/ABILITIES Immensely powerful; can cause a sun to go supernova by firing a single bolt of its cosmic energy.

The Living Tribunal has existed as long as the universe itself. Its purpose is to safeguard the multiverse (the totality of all alternate universes) from an imbalance of mystical forces. Thus the Living Tribunal will pass judgment on any crisis that threatens to affect the cosmic balance. It will prevent one universe from acquiring more mystical power than any other. The Living Tribunal will also intervene to prevent an imbalance between the mystical forces of good and evil within a single universe.

The Living Tribunal is capable of destroying entire planets in order to maintain the cosmic balance. In its humanoid form, the Living Tribunal has three faces—its fully visible face represents equity, its partially hooded face represents vengeance, and its fully hooded face represents necessity. It will only pass judgment when all the three sides are in agreement. **MT**

LIZARD

FIRST APPEARANCE The Amazing Spider-Man #6 (November 1963)

REAL NAME Dr. Curtis Connors

OCCUPATION Research biologist   **BASE** New York City

HEIGHT 5 ft 11 in   **WEIGHT** 175 lbs

EYES (as human) Blue, (as Lizard) Red   **HAIR** (as human) Brown, (as Lizard) None   **SPECIAL POWERS/ABILITIES** Superhuman strength and speed. Can cling to walls like a gecko, and can telepathically control reptiles.

When Dr. Curt Connors was an army surgeon, his wounded right arm had to be amputated. Back in civilian life, he researched the ability of some reptiles to regenerate missing limbs and created a serum to grow his arm back. It worked, but turned him into a savage humanoid lizard. SPIDER-MAN restored him to human form, but he has repeatedly reverted into the Lizard. The Lizard is one of Spider-Man's main enemies, but Dr. Connors has also acted as a friend to Spider-Man and his true identity, Peter Parker. **PS**

LLYRA

FIRST APPEARANCE Sub-Mariner #32 (December 1970)

REAL NAME Llyra Morris

OCCUPATION Subversive   **BASE** Mobile

HEIGHT 5 ft 11 in   **WEIGHT** 220 lbs   **EYES** Green   **HAIR** Green

SPECIAL POWERS/ABILITIES Amphibious—can live under water or on land—and able to change skin colour to pass as human or homo mermanus; can manipulate brains of primitive marine life.

Daughter of a *Homo mermani* (see ATLANTEANS) and a human woman, Llyra was raised on land by her mother following her father's death. Confused by her hybrid status, Llyra became increasingly unstable, and caused great angst to those she encountered. On her first visit to the underwater kingdom of Lemuria, Llyra seized the throne, only to be overthrown by NAMOR the Sub-Mariner. Llyra made Namor the focus of her rage. Before Namor finally captured her, Llyra was responsible for murdering his fiancée. Prison is definitely the best place for her. **AD**

LOBO BROTHERS

FIRST APPEARANCE Spectacular Spider-Man #143 (Oct. 1988)

REAL NAMES Eduardo and Carlos Lobo

OCCUPATION Drug traffickers   **BASE** Dallas, Texas

HEIGHT (Edwardo) 6 ft 1 in, (wolf) 6 ft 4 in; (Carlos) 6 ft, (wolf) 6 ft 4 in   **WEIGHT** (Edwardo) 225 lbs, (wolf) 275 lbs; (Carlos) 210 lbs, (wolf) 260 lbs   **EYES** (both) Brown   **HAIR** (both) Black

SPECIAL POWERS/ABILITIES Mutant shape changers.

Twin boys, the Lobo Brothers grew up alone on the streets of Puebla de Zaragoza, Texas, never having known their parents. Their mutant powers began to emerge when they were teenagers and they used them to unite all the independent criminal mobs in South Texas. They eventually bought an oil refinery and began shipping drugs in their oil tankers. Believing that they were cutting into his profits, the KINGPIN of Crime took out a contract on them. They escaped and came to New York for revenge, where Edwardo met and fell in love with Glory GRANT, J. Jonah JAMESON's secretary. Eduardo was later accidentally shot and killed by her during a battle with Spider-Man. Carlos was captured and is currently in prison. **TD**

LOCKHEED

FIRST APPEARANCE Uncanny X-Men Vol. 1 #166 (February 1983)   **REAL NAME** Unknown

OCCUPATION None

BASE Westchester County, New York

HEIGHT 2ft   **WEIGHT** 20 lbs

EYES White   **HAIR** None

SPECIAL POWERS/ABILITIES Can fly and breathe fire; empathic ability.

Lockheed is a small dragon belonging to the alien species, the Flock. He encountered the X-MEN during their fight with the BROOD, and took a liking to Katherine PRYDE. He returned to Earth, where Kitty gave him the name Lockheed. He was Kitty's constant companion for years, serving with her as a member of the X-Men and EXCALIBUR. Recently, the X-Men learned that Lockheed can speak several languages and was spying on them for SWORD. He left the X-Men after Kitty's apparent death. **DW, MF**

LOCKJAW

FIRST APPEARANCE Fantastic Four #45 (December 1965)

REAL NAME Not known

OCCUPATION Dog   **BASE** Attilan, Blue Area, the Moon

LENGTH 6 ft 8 in   **WEIGHT** 1, 240 lbs   **EYES** Brown   **HAIR** Brown

SPECIAL POWERS/ABILITIES Immense physical strength; can teleport self and up to a dozen others the distance from the Earth to the Moon; can also teleport to other dimensions.

When they come of age, INHUMANS are exposed to the Terrigen Mists, from which they gain their unique powers. For the Inhuman known as MEDUSA, exposure gave her living hair, while another Inhuman, CRYSTAL, gained the ability to manipulate elements.

The Mists transformed another child into a teleporting dog, now known as Lockjaw, who serves as a companion to the Inhuman Royal Family. Lockjaw is able to teleport not only himself, but a number of others up to a maximum combined weight of one ton. Although he has the intelligence of a human, Lockjaw still has canine tendencies: he likes to chase other animals, fetch sticks, and enjoy other doggy pleasures. He has also been known to speak, but that's another story. **AD**

LOKI

God of Mischief with a will to rule Asgard

Loki was born the son of Laufey, king of the Frost Giants of Jotunheim. Ashamed of Loki's small size, Laufey hid him away, but the child's existence came to light after the Frost Giants were defeated in a battle with the Asgardians. Odin (*see* GODS OF ASGARD), the ruler of Asgard, discovered Loki in the Frost Giants' fortress. Realizing that Loki was the son of Laufey, a king whom he had slain, Odin took the boy back to Asgard and raised him as his own son.

Loki was a megalomaniac, who aimed to overthrow his father and rule over Asgard.

ASGARD'S MISFIT

Loki never fitted in among the inhabitants of Asgard. He nursed a virulent grudge against his stepbrother THOR, the God of Thunder, who possessed in abundance the heroic qualities prized by the Asgardians that Loki himself lacked. Jealous of the praise Odin showered on Thor, Loki took up the dark arts of sorcery and plotted for a way to become ruler of Asgard. His love of trickery earned him a reputation first as the God of Mischief, and then, as he grew more and more cruel, the God of Evil. After many attempts by Loki to usurp the throne of Asgard, Odin lost patience with him and imprisoned him within a mystical tree. He eventually freed himself and went in search of Thor, who was then living on Earth in the mortal guise of Donald Blake.

Loki's vast magical talents allowed him to overpower Earth's most powerful heroes. Only Thor's efforts—and Loki's own insecurities—stopped the Trickster God from achieving his ultimate triumph.

THE END OF ASGARD

Thor and his adopted home, Earth, became the focus of Loki's attentions. He precipitated the formation of the AVENGERS by inciting the Hulk to violence, and transformed Crusher Creel into Thor's foe, the ABSORBING MAN. He allied with the ENCHANTRESS, and turned Earth's major Super Villains into his pawns during the Acts of Vengeance conspiracy.

Loki finally conquered Asgard and remade it in his own image. But Thor succeeded in decapitating Loki, carrying his mystically-preserved head to observe the final act of Ragnarok. When Thor severed the tapestry that wove the reality of his dimension, Asgard and all its inhabitants vanished from existence.

By leading armies against Asgard, Loki helped achieve the end-cycle of

After Ragnarok, Loki returned and took the body of the goddess Sif. Soon after, he fooled Thor into killing his grandfather Bor and being banished from the new Asgard. He also joined the Cabal (see ILLUMINATI) formed by Norman Osborn (see GREEN GOBLIN) in the wake of the Secret Invasion (*see* pp. 326-7). He is currently trying to relocate the Asgardians to DR. DOOM's Latveria.
DW, MF

FACTFILE
REAL NAME
Loki Laufeyson
OCCUPATION
God of Mischief; later God of Evil
BASE
Asgard

HEIGHT 6 ft 4 in
WEIGHT 525 lbs
EYES Green
HAIR Black-gray

FIRST APPEARANCE
Journey Into Mystery Vol. 1 #85 (October 1962)

LOKI

POWERS
Enhanced strength, stamina, longevity, and limited invulnerability; uses his vast skills in sorcery to fly, generate force fields, teleport between dimensions, animate objects, and change his own shape.

ESSENTIAL STORYLINES
• *Avengers #1* Loki hatches a plot to destroy his brother Thor, accidentally inspiring the world's greatest heroes to form the Avengers.
• *Loki #1—4* In this limited series, told from Loki's point of view, the Trickster God temporarily succeeds in winning power over all of Asgard.
• *The Mighty Thor #582—588* As Ragnarok unfolds around them, Loki and Thor face off for their final battle, then tour the end of the world.

LONGSHOT

FACTFILE

REAL NAME
Unknown

OCCUPATION
Former slave; former movie stuntman; rebel leader

BASE
Mobile

HEIGHT 6 ft 2 in
WEIGHT 80 lbs
EYES Blue
HAIR Blond

FIRST APPEARANCE
Longshot #1
(September 1985)

POWERS

His genetically engineered powers include the ability to affect probability to bring him what is commonly called "good luck." He can telepathically read a person's memories by touching the person and can read psychic imprints left on objects touched by someone.

LONGSHOT

On Mojoworld, were Longshot is from, the original inhabitants have no spines. The scientist Arize created an exoskeleton to allow them to stand upright, but a group called the Spineless Ones refused to use such devices. Still, they became the planet's rulers and forced Arize to create a race of slaves, and Longshot was one of these. Longshot, however, refused to be anyone's slave and helped organize a revolt. On the run, Longshot escaped through an interdimensional portal, arriving on Earth. Mojo, the Spineless One who claimed to own Longshot, pursued him to Earth. With help from a stuntwoman called Ricochet Rita, another slave called Quark, and Dr. STRANGE, Longshot defeated Mojo. Later, Longshot joined the X-Men and developed a relationship with Dazzler. After he left the X-Men, he joined the transdimensional Exiles team for a while, but he parted ways with them to return to Dazzler. During the Secret Invasion, a Skrull posed as Longshot, but the real Longshot is now back in action **MT, MF**

Longshot and his team of rebels prepare to do battle with the manipulative Mojo, the Spineless One.

When Longshot lets fly with his deadly throwing knives, the probability is that he won't miss!

LORD CHAOS

FIRST APPEARANCE Marvel Two-in-One Annual #2 (1977)
REAL NAME None
OCCUPATION Abstract entity **BASE** Everywhere
HEIGHT/WEIGHT Unknown **EYES** None **HAIR** None
SPECIAL POWERS/ABILITIES Can teleport self and a dozen others the distance from the Earth to the Moon; can also teleport to other dimensions.

An abstract entity (depicted as a disembodied purple head) Lord Chaos embodies the concept of Chaos, just as other entities represent Death, Order (depicted as a bald head with black eyebrows), and even ETERNITY. Alongside Order, Chaos strives to maintain a cosmic balance, only intervening in mortal affairs on rare occasions. When THANOS was attempting to destroy the universe, SPIDER-MAN released Adam WARLOCK from a Soul Gem, allowing him to save the day. After these events, Order and Chaos implied that Peter Parker's destiny had been manipulated since birth, in order for him to perform this very act. No one knows if this is true. **AD**

LORD TEMPLAR

FIRST APPEARANCE The Avengers Vol. 3 #13 (Feb. 1999)
REAL NAME Unrevealed (last name presumably Tremont)
OCCUPATION Operative of Jonathan Tremont **BASE** Mobile
HEIGHT/WEIGHT Unrevealed **EYES** Red **HAIR** Gray
SPECIAL POWERS/ABILITIES Various powers include the ability to fire energy blasts; can summon counterparts of himself called the Avatars of Templar, each of whom has a different superpower.

Jonathan Tremont's two older brothers died from a disease. Years later Tremont acquired a cosmic artifact in the form of a triangle and used it to resurrect his brothers as the superhumans Lord Templar and Pagan. Jonathan Tremont founded the Triune Understanding, a cult allegedly devoted to world peace. In actuality, Tremont sought to amass power for himself. He used Lord Templar to combat the AVENGERS. Ultimately, Tremont absorbed the life forces of Lord Templar and Pagan into himself, only to be defeated by the Avenger TRIATHLON. **PS**

LORELEI

FIRST APPEARANCE Uncanny X-Men Vol. 1 #63 (December, 1969)
REAL NAME Unrevealed
OCCUPATION Mercenary **BASE** Savage Land
HEIGHT 5 ft 6 in **WEIGHT** 125 lbs **EYES** Blue **HAIR** Blonde
SPECIAL POWERS/ABILITIES Power lies in her voice; emits hypersonic pitches that affect the sexual drives of human males and mesmerize them.

A member of the Swamp People inhabiting the Antarctic jungle known as the Savage Land, Lorelei received the vocal power to hypnotize men after MAGNETO subjected her to a DNA-altering machine. Her powers are irresistible to males but have no effect on females. Lorelei became a member of the Savage Land Mutates (also known as the Beast Brood), battling foes from the X-MEN to KA-ZAR. She later joined Magneto's BROTHERHOOD OF EVIL MUTANTS and fought the DEFENDERS. Recently, Lorelei found employment as a recruiter for AIM, enlisting other Savage Land mercenaries like herself. **DW**

LUCIFER

FIRST APPEARANCE X-Men #9 (January 1965)
REAL NAME Unknown
OCCUPATION Agent for the Arcane **BASE** Mobile
HEIGHT 6 ft 2 in **WEIGHT** 325 lbs **EYES** Blue **HAIR** Black
SPECIAL POWERS/ABILITIES Initially merely possessed limited telepathic powers; later able to manipulate ionic energy to increase strength, generate protective shield and fuse self with other beings.

Belonging to the planet-conquering Arcane race, the alien Lucifer served as one of their leading agents and was responsible for the capture of numerous worlds. Ordered to obtain Earth for the Arcane, Lucifer was thwarted by a young Charles Xavier (see PROFESSOR X). Furious at his defeat, before fleeing, Lucifer used a stone slab to cripple Xavier's legs. This encounter motivated Xavier to create the X-MEN. That mutant organization claimed victory over Lucifer several more times. Angry at their agent's failures, the Arcane leaders had him terminated. **AD**

LUMPKIN, WILLIE

FIRST APPEARANCE Fantastic Four #11 (Februaryt 1963)
REAL NAME William "Lumpy" Lumpkin
OCCUPATION United States Postal Courier **BASE** New York City
HEIGHT 5 ft 8 in **WEIGHT** 165 lbs **EYES** Blue **HAIR** White
SPECIAL POWERS/ABILITIES None, although he believes that he possesses a special talent when it comes to wiggling his ears; good at his job, courageous, and loyal.

After working as a postman for a small town, Lumpkin moved to New York City, where he was assigned a mail route that included the Baxter Building. Soon after the FANTASTIC FOUR moved into the top five floors of the Baxter, Lumpkin half-jokingly petitioned for membership on the grounds that he had the ability to wiggle his ears. Although he never joined the team, he has been involved with them on many occasions. He once rang a bell that allowed the team to escape the MAD THINKER and a SKRULL once impersonated him to gain access to the FF headquarters. Lumpkin is currently semi-retired and his curvaceous niece Billie has replaced him as the FF's mail carrier. **TD**

LOTUS

FIRST APPEARANCE Avengers Spotlight #30 (March 1990)
REAL NAME Lotus Newmark
OCCUPATION Mob leader **BASE** California
HEIGHT/WEIGHT Unrevealed **EYES** Brown **HAIR** Black
SPECIAL POWERS/ABILITIES Lotus is a trained martial artist and an experienced criminal leader. She possesses some skill at hypnotizing others to do her will.

As a child, Lotus was traded to Hong Kong underworld leader Li Fong to cover her father's gambling debts. She became Fong's protégée, trained in martial arts, and eventually ascending to a high position within his organization. Lotus emigrated to California to set up her own criminal operation. As she increased her power, she began to run afoul of various heroes, including HAWKEYE, WONDER MAN, and NIGHT THRASHER.

As a cover for her illegal activities, Lotus took over a film studio and became a movie producer. However, proof of her misdeeds was uncovered by Wonder Man and the BEAST, and she was taken into police custody. **TB**

LUKIN, GENERAL

FIRST APPEARANCE Captain America #5 (November 2004)
REAL NAME Aleksander Lukin
OCCUPATION Russian KGB general
BASE New York City
HEIGHT 5 ft 11 in **WEIGHT** 200 lbs **EYES** Blue **HAIR** Black
SPECIAL POWERS/ABILITIES Strategic genius and political mastermind.

During World War II, The RED SKULL used Lukin's Russian village as a base. When THE INVADERS helped retake the town, Lukin's mother was killed, and General Vasily Karpov took the orphan in. Lukin rose through the ranks of the Russian military to become a KGB general in charge of many special projects, including THE WINTER SOLDIER. When Lukin ordered the Skull killed, the Skull used the Cosmic Cube to transfer his mind into Lukin's body. Eventually Lukin rid himself of the Skull's mind when it was transferred into a robot, but shortly afterward Sharon Carter (see CARTER, SHARON) shot him dead. **MF**

LYJA THE LAZERFIST

FIRST APPEARANCE (as Alicia) Fantastic Four Vol. 1 #265 (April 1984); (as Lyja) Fantastic Four Vol. 1 #357 (October 1991)
REAL NAME Lyja
OCCUPATION Skrull agent **BASE** Mobile
HEIGHT 5 ft 5 in **WEIGHT** 120 lbs **EYES** Green **HAIR** Green
SPECIAL POWERS/ABILITIES A shapeshifter, like all Skrulls, Lyja can also fly and project energy bursts and is immune to heat and fire.

The Skrull called Lyja posed as Alicia MASTERS and married the HUMAN TORCH in a plot to destroy the FANTASTIC FOUR. The Torch broke off their relationship when he discovered the ruse. Lyja became "the Lazerfist" after the Skrulls gave her energy powers, and she alternated between fighting the Fantastic Four and seeking to reconcile with the Torch. After losing her powers during a false pregnancy, she posed as human Laura Greene. During the Secret Invasion (see pp. 326–7), Lyja regained her powers and sent the Baxter Building into the Negative Zone. She voluntarily remained there when the building's occupants returned. **DW, MF**

M

FIRST APPEARANCE Uncanny X-Men #316 (September 1994)
REAL NAME Monet St. Croix
OCCUPATION Investigator **BASE** Mutant Town area of New York
HEIGHT 5 ft 7 in **WEIGHT** 125 lbs **EYES** Brown **HAIR** Black
SPECIAL POWERS/ABILITIES M possesses superhuman strength and durability, flight and telepathy.

Having lived much of her young life mystically trapped in the speechless form of PENANCE by her brother EMPLATE, Monet St. Croix's existence was usurped by her two younger sisters Claudette and Nicole. They used their mutant abilities to combine into a single entity that resembled Monet. Both Penance and the amalgam-Monet became members of GENERATION X, the satellite team of young X-MEN at the Massachusetts Academy. Later, the truth of M's situation became apparent, and she and her sisters were restored to their rightful forms. M joined Jamie Madrox's detective agency, X-Factor Investigations. **TB**

M-11

FIRST APPEARANCE Menace #11 (May 1954)
REAL NAME M-11
OCCUPATION Adventurer **BASE** San Francisco
HEIGHT 6 ft **WEIGHT** 900 lbs **EYES** None **HAIR** None
SPECIAL POWERS/ABILITIES Robot with telescopic arms, heat vision, force field projection, image projection, superhuman strength, and the ability to repair itself.

In the 1950s, the YELLOW CLAW commissioned a scientist to build a robot to help his plan to make FBI agent Jimmy WOO the next Khan. To give the robot free will, the scientist had it electrocute him and absorb some of his life force. M-11 then walked into the sea, but NAMORA found it and brought it to Jimmy to join his G-Men group of heroes. Woo and his friends reactivated the robot decades later to help in their battle against the forces of the Yellow Claw. Today, M-11 works alongside the other former G-Men as part of the AGENTS OF ATLAS. **MF**

MacTAGGERT, DR.

FIRST APPEARANCE Uncanny X-Men Vol.1 #96 (December 1975)
REAL NAME Moira Kinross Mactaggert
OCCUPATION Geneticist **BASE** Muir Island, Scotland
HEIGHT 5 ft 7 in **WEIGHT** 135 lbs **EYES** Blue **HAIR** Brown
SPECIAL POWERS/ABILITIES Brilliant geneticist with expertise in the mutant genome.

Moira MacTaggart was once engaged to Charles Xavier (see PROFESSOR X), but she broke it off. She secretly bore a child (PROTEUS) to that husband and later adopted the mutant child Rahne Sinclair (WOLFSBANE). Like Charles, she set up a secret home for young mutants, but the heroes all seemingly died on their first mission. Later, she struck up a romance with Sean Cassidy. She established a Mutant Research Center on Muir Island, where she found a cure for the Legacy virus. Mystique killed her, and her ghost now haunts Muir Island. **DW, MF**

MACH-4

FIRST APPEARANCE Strange Tales Vol. 1 #123 (August 1964)
REAL NAME Abner Jenkins
OCCUPATION Super Hero, former criminal **BASE** New York City
HEIGHT 5 ft 11 in **WEIGHT** 175 lbs **EYES** Brown **HAIR** Brown
SPECIAL POWERS/ABILITIES Armored flight suit provides enhanced strength and supersonic flight; has a built-in tactical computer and a generator that can fire electrostatic blasts.

Abner Jenkins started as the BEETLE. He joined the MASTERS OF EVIL and agreed to BARON ZEMO's scheme to turn them into the THUNDERBOLTS. As MACH-1, Jenkins decided to go straight and returned to prison for his previous crimes. He upgraded his armor and is now known as MACH-IV. After parole, he joined SONGBIRD to lead a new team of Thunderbolts. When that team disbanded, he took a job with the COMMISSION ON SUPERHUMAN ACTIVITIES and oversaw a trio of students wearing versions of his Beetle suit. **DW, MF**

MACHINE MAN

X-51 was a prototype for a government project to build artificially intelligent robot soldiers. His limbs could extend 100 feet, and his endoskeleton housed solar-power-augmented batteries, multi-optical imaging devices with zoom and magnifying sensors, and anti-gravity devices allowing flight. His fingers featured miniature lasers, concussive blasters, and a .357 Magnum pistol. Believing a robot could only act like a man if treated like one, Dr. Aaron Stack took X-51 into his home and even designed a human face for him. Stack died protecting X-51 after the program was terminated.

Assuming Stack's identity, X-51 attempted to assimilate into human society, but he later fell in love with the robot JOCASTA. He has fought alongside the AVENGERS, FANTASTIC FOUR, HULK, X-MEN, and NEXTWAVE. His personality changed over that time, moving from friendly but distant to crass and obnoxious, especially during his spell in Nextwave where he seemed more at ease with his robotic nature. He and Jocasta recently traveled to Earth-2149 to help stop an invasion of zombies from that universe. **TD, MF**

FACTFILE
REAL NAME
X-51
OCCUPATION
Insurance investigator
BASE
Manhattan, New York

HEIGHT 6 ft
WEIGHT 850 lbs
EYES Red Imaging Sensors
HAIR Black (artificial)

FIRST APPEARANCE
2001: A Space Odyssey #8 (July 1977)

Robot composed of titanium alloy. Motorized endoskeleton which houses a vast array of weapons systems.

MACHINE MAN

POWERS

MACHINESMITH

FIRST APPEARANCE Marvel Two-In-One #47 (January 1979)

REAL NAME Samuel "Starr" Saxon

OCCUPATION Robot maker, professional criminal **BASE** Mobile

HEIGHT 6 ft 1 in **WEIGHT** 295 lbs **EYES** Green **HAIR** Bald

SPECIAL POWERS/ABILITIES A living computer program, his consciousness can be placed into multiple robot bodies which approximate human beings.

Master robot builder Starr Saxon built robots for criminals. When DAREDEVIL defeated one of his robots, Saxon sought revenge, but died during the battle. One of his robots, following its programming, took Saxon's body back to his workshop and transferred his brain patterns into a robotic body. On recovery, Saxon replaced this body with a human-looking one. Calling himself Machinesmith, he resumed his career of building robots for the underworld. Machinesmith has come into conflict with SHIELD and CAPTAIN AMERICA. He now exists as a computer program which can be placed into robot bodies. **MT**

MAD DOG

FIRST APPEARANCE (as Baxter) Amazing Adventures Vol. 2 #13 (July 1972); (as Mad-Dog) Defenders #125 (November 1983)

REAL NAME Robert "Buzz" Baxter

OCCUPATION Criminal, retired US Air Force Colonel **BASE** Mobile

HEIGHT 6 ft 2 in **WEIGHT** 270 lbs **EYES** Blue **HAIR** Blue

SPECIAL POWERS/ABILITIES Possesses superhuman strength, smell and hearing. Enhanced speed and agility. Has hollow fangs which secrete poison to which he is immune.

In the comics she wrote, Dorothy Walker based her characters on her daughter Patsy and Patsy's friend "Buzz" Baxter. After the real Patsy and Baxter graduated from high school, they married and Baxter joined the Air Force. As a security consultant for the Brand Corporation, Baxter hunted the mutant BEAST. Patsy divorced Baxter and became the HELLCAT. When Brand captured the AVENGERS, Hellcat forced Baxter to free them. Baxter underwent treatment by Roxxon Oil's Mutagenics Department that gave him superhuman powers. Thus Baxter became Mad-Dog, who has battled not only Hellcat, but also other costumed adventurers. **PS**

MAD THINKER

For many years the police did not know of the Mad Thinker's existence, despite the various criminal activities he had masterminded over that period. He only leapt into the public eye when he went head-to-head with the FANTASTIC FOUR. A brilliant strategist, he tempted each of them away from New York with various impossible-to-refuse jobs. He subsequently used their absence to enter the Baxter Building and steal Reed Richards' inventions. Manufacturing superhuman androids based on Richards' designs he used them to battle the Fantastic Four. However, the Mad Thinker failed to account for a circuit breaker Richards had built into the designs for just this eventuality. Once the circuit was activated all the robots became disabled. Since then, the Mad Thinker has spent much of his time in prison but he has somehow managed to continue his activities from inside. His motives remain unclear—perhaps no one is brilliant enough to understand them or could the Mad Thinker just be enjoying the game? **AD**

With low cunning the Fantastic Four are almost duped into defeat.

FACTFILE

REAL NAME
Unknown

OCCUPATION
Criminal mastermind

BASE
Mobile

HEIGHT 5 ft 11 in
WEIGHT 195 lbs
EYES Blue
HAIR Brown

FIRST APPEARANCE
Fantastic Four Vol. 1 #15
(June 1963)

POWERS

Brilliant criminal mind. Created a way to project his mind into an android body to continue criminal activities in his absence.

Hey! Now What's Happenin' ??

I was afraid of that Ben! The Android has the power of Mimicry built into it -- It's turning into -- You!

The Mad Thinker's first robotic creation, the Awesome Android, could emulate certain Super Heroes, even mimicking the rocky epidermis of the Thing.

MADAME HYDRA

FIRST APPEARANCE (Viper as MH) Captain America #110
(February 1969); (MH VI) Nick Fury vs. SHIELD #3 (August 1988)
REAL NAME (both) Unrevealed   **OCCUPATION** (both) Subversive
BASE (Both) Mobile   **HEIGHT** (Viper) 5 ft 9 in ; (MH VI) 5 ft 11 in
WEIGHT (Viper) 141 lbs; (MH VI) 135 lbs   **EYES** (both) Green
HAIR (Viper) Black, green highlights; (MH VI) Brown, dyed green
SPECIAL POWERS/ABILITIES (both) Formidable combatant.

Originally the subversive organization Hydra
restricted its membership to men. The first
female Hydra agent was Laura Brown. Another
female operative seized command of Hydra's
New York operations, took the name Madame
Hydra, and battled CAPTAIN AMERICA. Eventually
she took a new alias, the VIPER, and became one
of the world's most dangerous terrorists. Another
female Hydra agent, Madame Hydra VI, clashed
with SHIELD and allied with the YELLOW CLAW.
(Five other Madame Hydras outranked her.)
She committed suicide to avoid capture.
Viper has now reassumed the
name of Madame Hydra.

PS

MADAME MASQUE

Adopted by financier Byron Frost, Whitney
Frost grew up in New York's high society,
but when Byron died, her world collapsed.
Learning that her biological father was the
Italian COUNT NEFARIA, head of the
MAGGIA criminal organization, she became
his heir. Following his imprisonment, she
became head of the Maggia, now based in
New York. Her face was disfigured during a
botched raid on Stark Industries. Hiding
her scars behind a golden mask, Whitney
took the name Madame Masque. Falling in
love with Tony Stark (IRON MAN), she
impersonated his assistant to spend time
with him, but when
Tony was unable to save her father's life,
she resumed her role as the
Director of the Maggia.

It was Mordecai
Midas who first
suggested the
golden mask.

IS IT SO UNUSUAL
FOR A MAN TO HELP
A WOMAN...?

...AND I'D BET THERE'S
QUITE A WOMAN
BEHIND THAT MASK!

SPARE ME TONY STARK'S
PLAYBOY HOMILIES...
BEHIND THIS MASK IS
ONLY HORROR!

MIDAS' MEN
RESCUED ME FROM
A PLANE CRASH...
A SURGEON HE HIRED
SAVED MY LIFE...
BUT NOT BEFORE
CHEMICALS ON BOARD
PLAYED A MACABRE
JOKE WITH MY
FEATURES!

Over the years, Whitney made
several clones of herself, killing them
when they'd served their purpose.
One, known as Masque, worked
briefly with the AVENGERS before
being killed. Whitney supposedly
renounced her criminal past after
witnessing her clone's sacrifice, but she
has recently been seen serving as the
HOOD's top lieutenant in his new
crime syndicate. **AD, MF**

FACTFILE

REAL NAME
Countess Giulietta Nefaria
(adopted name Whitney Frost)

OCCUPATION
Head of Maggia criminal
organization

BASE
Unknown

HEIGHT 5 ft 9 in
WEIGHT 130 lbs
EYES Gray
HAIR Black

FIRST APPEARANCE
Tales of Suspense #97
(January 1968)

POWERS

Gymnast and athlete trained to
Olympic standards; superb
markswoman and exceptional
mistress of strategy.

MADAME WEB

FACTFILE

REAL NAME
Cassandra Webb

OCCUPATION
Professional medium

BASE
New York City

HEIGHT 5 ft 7 in
WEIGHT 115 lbs
EYES Pale gray
HAIR Black and silver

FIRST APPEARANCE
Amazing Spider-Man #210
(November 1980)

POWERS

Through clairvoyance Madame Web can predict the future, read minds and perform psychic surgery.

"Reading" tarot cards was central to Madame Web's clairvoyant abilities.

A one-time ally of SPIDER-MAN, Cassandra Webb was born blind but developed skills as a clairvoyant that compensated for her sightlessness. Cassandra's first encounter with Spider-Man came when businessman Rupert Dockery was scheming to take over the Daily Globe. At first sceptical of the help she offered, Spider-Man later acknowledged her usefulness and they worked together to prevent the assassination of a local congressman.

At times Cassandra could be hugely manipulative. When Norman Osborn invited her to become part of his mystical "Gathering of Five", she tricked Spider-Man into obtaining a mystical object for her, so that she could gain the youthful immortality she so wanted. Since then, she has used her powers for good, even agreeing to mentor the third Spider-Woman, Mattie. **AD**

MADCAP

FIRST APPEARANCE Captain America #307 (July 1985)
REAL NAME Not known
OCCUPATION Prankster **BASE** New York City
HEIGHT 5 ft 9 in **WEIGHT** 145 lbs **EYES** Blue **HAIR** Brown
SPECIAL POWERS/ABILITIES Remarkable self-healing ability, able to survive almost any injury; causes others to lose inhibitions with embarrassing and sometimes lethal consequences.

A devoted member of a Christian church, Madcap began his descent into insanity following a terrible accident. He was traveling on a bus with his family and forty church members when it collided with a truck carrying an experimental nerve agent. Madcap was the only survivor, and in the days that followed he developed the ability to heal himself and cause temporary insanity in others. He has used these talents to cause repeated havoc on the streets of New York. In between short spells in Bellevue Hospital, Madcap has encountered a number of superpowered individuals, including GHOST RIDER, NOMAD, and WOLVERINE. **AD**

MADMAN

FACTFILE

REAL NAME
Phillip Sterns

OCCUPATION
Scientist

BASE
Mobile

HEIGHT Variable
WEIGHT Variable
EYES Pupils uncolored
HAIR None

FIRST APPEARANCE
(as Phillip Sterns) Incredible Hulk #363 (January 1990).
(as Madman) Incredible Hulk #364 (February 1990)

POWERS

Super-human strength, ability to increase and decrease his mass, and to change his shape and form.

Phillip Sterns, brother of Samuel Sterns who became the HULK's enemy, the LEADER, was a classmate of Bruce Banner (the Hulk) in graduate school. Banner was always at the top of his class, Phillip Sterns at the bottom. After graduation, both Banner and Sterns began researching the use of gamma radiation as a potential weapon. But the government funded Banner's research, not Sterns', increasing Sterns' envy of Banner. When Sterns learned that Bruce Banner had become the Hulk through exposure to gamma radiation, Sterns grew even more jealous, believing that the enormous power of the Hulk should have been his. Sterns began intentionally exposing himself to gamma radiation over a period of years, trying to duplicate the accident that created the Hulk. As a result of this exposure Stern's gained the powers of the Madman. Sterns and Madman are two separate personalities both existing in the same body. Over the years Madman has battled the Hulk many times. **MT**

MAELSTROM

FACTFILE

REAL NAME
Unrevealed

OCCUPATION
Nihilist

BASE
Mobile

HEIGHT 8 ft 2 in
WEIGHT 425 lbs
EYES Purple
HAIR White

FIRST APPEARANCE
Marvel Two-In-One #71
(January 1981)

POWERS

Increases his own powers through control of kinetic energy and draining the energy of others; projects force blasts.

MAELSTROM

The seeds of a Super Villain's behavior can often be found in their childhood. The hybrid child of a Deviant and an INHUMAN, Maelstrom's birth caused consternation. His mother was killed for giving birth to him, and as a child he was forced to work in Deviant slave pits until rescued by his father, the brilliant geneticist Phaeder.

Following in his father's footsteps, Maelstrom traded information on genetics with various dubious individuals including RED SKULL, MAGNETO, and the HIGH EVOLUTIONARY. Their use of this knowledge caused untold suffering: the Nazi genetic atrocities and various clones of SPIDER-MAN were direct results of Maelstrom's collaborations.

A desperately lonely individual, Maelstrom looked for an antidote to his unhappiness in plans to end the Multiverse. Destroyed by QUASAR when he first attempted this, he was resurrected and tried again. This time, Mr. Immortal of the GREAT LAKES AVENGERS tricked Maelstrom into committing suicide—a humiliating way to die. **AD**

He might have a stylish spandex costume, but Maelstrom sometimes seemed out of his depth as a Super Villain.

THE MAGGIA
1 Silvermane
2 Count Nefaria
3 Hammerhead

MAGGIA

The Maggia is the world's most powerful crime syndicate. The organization's operations are worldwide, though its roots began in southern Europe during the 13th century and it spread to the United States in the 1890s. The Maggia has its fingers in gambling, narcotics, loan-sharking, organized labor, and crooked politics. Those who betray the Maggia are executed, often with a death-grip to the chin nicknamed the "Maggia touch."

The three largest Maggia families active in New York City include the SILVERMANE family, the HAMMERHEAD family, and the Nefaria family. The Silvermanes are a traditionally-structured crime network controlling the narcotics trade. The Hammerheads are styled in the fashion of 1920s gangsters, and are led by the flat-topped Hammerhead. The Nefarias, organized by COUNT NEFARIA, are the most colorful of the three families, frequently employing costumed criminals to further their schemes. Early in his career, the gang boss KINGPIN was one of the Maggia's most successful rivals. **AD**

FACTFILE

NOTABLE MEMBERS
TOP MAN (Hammerheads, deceased) Cunning mind.
HAMMERHEAD (Hammerheads) Enhanced strength through metal exoskeleton.
COUNT NEFARIA (Nefarias) Vast powers of ionic energy.
MADAME MASQUE (Nefarias) Skilled martial artist.
SILVIO "SILVERMANE" MANFREDI (Silvermanes) Cybernetic body.
JOSEPH MANFREDI (Silvermanes) Formerly had control over bats.

BASE Worldwide

FIRST APPEARANCE
Avengers Vol. 1 #13
(February 1965)

MAGGIA

MAGGOTT

FIRST APPEARANCE Uncanny X-Men #345 (June 1997)
REAL NAME Japheth
OCCUPATION Former X-Man **BASE** Mobile
HEIGHT 6 ft 8 in **WEIGHT** 350 lbs **EYES** Brown **HAIR** Black
SPECIAL POWERS/ABILITIES Two semi-sentient slugs can leave and re-enter Maggott's body. They feed on anything and use it to nourish him. He can replay in mind's eye past events in local area.

A sickly child, unable to eat solid food, young Japheth felt that he was nothing but a burden to his poor South African family. Heading into the desert to die, Japheth encountered MAGNETO who activated his mutation, allowing two slugs to leave his body and feed on his behalf. Now calling himself Maggott, Japheth went searching for Magneto. In Antarctica, he first encountered the X-MEN, and briefly joined the mutant team. Unfortunately, Maggott's life was not to end happily: captured by the WEAPON X facility, he became an inmate at the Neverland concentration camp and was eventually executed by the authorities there. **AD**

Thanks to her seismic mutant talents, Magma is impervious to heat and, by encasing herself in fiery molten rock, is as comfortable inside the crater of an erupting volcano as she is in the open air.

MAGMA

FIRST APPEARANCE New Mutants #8 (October 1983)
REAL NAME Amara Aquilla
OCCUPATION Adventurer **BASE** Mobile
HEIGHT 5 ft 6 in **WEIGHT** 124 lbs **EYES** Brown **HAIR** Blonde
SPECIAL POWERS/ABILITIES Projects bursts of heat and molten rock, and causes shifts in the tectonic plates beneath the surface of the Earth to produce volcanic eruptions.

Raised in the hidden city of Nova Roma in the Amazon jungles of Brazil, Amara's mutant abilities surfaced when Selene—a nigh-immortal mutant who drains the life essences of others—hurled her into an active volcano. The NEW MUTANTS rescued her, and she became a longtime member of the group. For a time, she believed herself to be Allison Crestmere, daughter of an English ambassador, but this proved false. She later joined the Xavier Institute's staff, working with the younger mutants. She survived M-Day with her powers intact, and fought alongside the X-MEN during the Secret Invasion (*see* pp. 326–7) **AD, MF**

MAGIK

Illyana Rasputin is the younger sister of Piotr Rasputin (COLOSSUS). The sorcerer Belasco brought Illyana and the X-MEN to his timeless realm Limbo. The X-MEN escaped, but Belasco kept Illyana there and turned a portion of her soul evil. Her darksoul gave her powers of sorcery, and Illyana mastered the magic in Belasco's books and defeated him with her magical soulsword. Afterward, she returned to Earth several years older and joined the NEW MUTANTS under the code name Magik. Eventually, she managed to find her younger self in Limbo and prevented her corruption from happening, erasing all subsequent events. Restored to her youth, she later died of the mutant-killing Legacy Virus. Recently, Belasco brought together the fragments of Illyana in Limbo and created the Darkchylde. This form of Illyana stole a part of the X-Man Pixie's soul and dedicated herself to reclaiming her own soul. She recently returned to Earth and joined the latest version of the New Mutants. **MT, MF**

Mutant Illyana Rasputin (code name Magik) joined her brother Piotr (code name Colossus) at the Professor Xavier's school for mutants, where they became X-Men.

FACTFILE
REAL NAME Illyana Nikolievna Rasputin
OCCUPATION Student
BASE Professor Xavier's School for Gifted Youngsters, New York; the extradimensional realm, Limbo

HEIGHT 5 ft 5 in
WEIGHT 120 lbs
EYES Blue
HAIR Blond

FIRST APPEARANCE (as a child) Giant-Size X-Men #1 (1975)

MAGIK

POWERS

Magik is both a mutant with superhuman powers and an expert sorceress. She can teleport herself and others through time, perform astral projection, and sense the presence of magic.

Magik is not only a powerful mutant, she is also a skilled sorceress, which helps to make her a formidable warrior.

MAGNETO

Master of magnetism

MAGNETO

FACTFILE

REAL NAME
Unrevealed, uses the name
Erik Magnus Lehnsherr

OCCUPATION
Conqueror

BASE
Mobile

HEIGHT 6 ft 2 in
WEIGHT 190 lbs
EYES Blue-grey
HAIR White

FIRST APPEARANCE
X-Men #1,
(September 1963)

POWERS
Mutant ability to manipulate
magnetism and all forms of
electromagnetic energy

ALLIES/FOES

ALLIES Brotherhood of Evil
Mutants, (sometimes) Professor
Charles Xavier, (formerly) the X-Men,
the New Mutants

FOES Professor Charles Xavier,
the X-Men, the Avengers, the
Fantastic Four

Magneto's sufferings in his youth inspired his hatred of humankind.

One of the most powerful and dangerous of all mutants, Magneto has been both the foremost enemy of the X-MEN and, sometimes, their ally. As a boy, he was imprisoned in the Nazi death camp in Auschwitz, Poland. Sickness and malnourishment prevented Magneto's mutant powers from emerging there. In Auschwitz, Magneto's family perished, and he witnessed the inhumanity that people can show to those who are considered different.

MUTANT RAGE

Following World War II Magneto married Magda, and they had a daughter, Anya. When Anya was trapped in a burning building, an insensitive crowd prevented Magneto from rescuing her. Infuriated, Magneto lashed out with his powers, killing them.

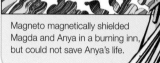
Magneto magnetically shielded Magda and Anya in a burning inn, but could not save Anya's life.

Frightened by what her husband had done, Magda fled from him. She had not told Magneto that she was pregnant. Eventually Magda arrived at Wundagore Mountain, where she gave birth to twins, Wanda and Pietro. She then ran away into the wilderness, where she presumably died.

While searching for Magda, Magneto employed a forger named George Odekirk to create a false identity, "Erik Magnus Lehnsherr," for him. Eventually Magneto settled in Israel, where he became friends with the young Charles Xavier (*see* PROFESSOR X). They continually debated their different views on whether mutants could peacefully coexist with the rest of humanity.

SUPERIORITY COMPLEX

When their friend Gabrielle HALLER was abducted by BARON VON STRUCKER and his HYDRA agents, Magneto and Xavier rescued her. Magneto used his powers to make off with a cache of Nazi gold that Strucker had sought. Magneto decided that the only way to prevent humanity from oppressing the emerging race of mutants was for mutants to conquer the rest of the human race. Indeed, Magneto believed that mutants were superior to ordinary humans and deserved to rule them.

Magneto's first step in his war against the human race was to seize a missile base at Cape Citadel, Florida. By now Xavier had founded the X-MEN, who foiled Magneto's takeover of the base.

ISSUE #1

In the first *X-MEN* comic, Magneto captured the Cape Citadel missile base, only to be defeated by the original X-Men in their initial battle.

ESSENTIAL STORYLINES

• *X-Men Vol. 1 #4-7, 11*
Magneto's original Brotherhood of Evil Mutants battles the original team of X-Men.

• *X-Men Vol. 1 #62-63*
Magneto's unmasked face is revealed when he combats the X-Men in the Savage Land.

• *Uncanny X-Men #161*
The story of how Magneto first met Charles Xavier in Israel.

• *Classic X-Men #12*
Magneto's captivity at Auschwitz and the death of his daughter.

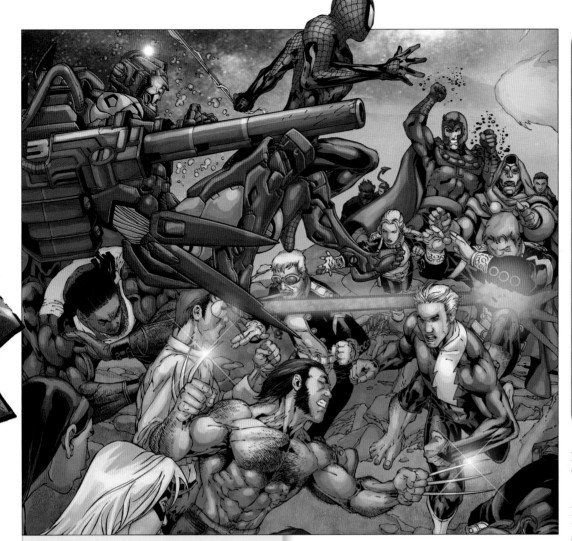

A resistance movement including Cyclops, Spider-Man, and Wolverine attacked Magneto's House of M before the Scarlet Witch finally restored reality to its previous normalcy.

THE HOUSE OF M
1 Quicksilver 2 Scarlet Witch
3 Scarlet Witch's sons Thomas and William
4 Magneto 5 Polaris

THE HOUSE OF MAGNUS

Urged by her brother Quicksilver, the Scarlet Witch utilized her mutant power over probability to alter history. As a result, Magneto had led mutants in a successful war against the rest of humanity. Magneto was now monarch of Earth. His royal family was known as the "House of Magnus" or "House of M" and was comprised of his son Quicksilver, his daughters the Scarlet Witch and Polaris, and his grandsons Thomas and William.

When Magneto next battled the X-Men, it was as leader of the original BROTHERHOOD OF EVIL MUTANTS. The other members were Mastermind, the Toad, and Pietro and Wanda (QUICKSILVER and the SCARLET WITCH), who felt obligated to Magneto for saving them from a mob. Neither Magneto nor Wanda and Pietro realized that Magneto was their father.

After numerous clashes with the X-Men, Magneto tried to force a superhuman being known as the STRANGER to serve him. He little knew that the Stranger was actually an alien with seemingly limitless powers who captured Magneto and the Toad.

Weary of Magneto's crusade against humanity, Quicksilver and the Scarlet Witch quit the Brotherhood and soon joined the AVENGERS.

Magneto eventually escaped back to Earth from the Stranger's planet and resumed his war on humanity, battling the X-Men, Avengers, FANTASTIC FOUR, and DEFENDERS. He also formed several new versions of the Brotherhood.

Using his advanced knowledge of genetic engineering, Magneto created a being called Alpha the Ultimate Mutant. But Alpha turned against Magneto and devolved him into a powerless infant. Xavier turned the infant Magneto over to his colleague Dr. Moira MACTAGGERT, who began experiments to alter the baby's mind. Davan Shakari, an alien SHI'AR agent, later restored Magneto to his adult physical prime. Hence Magneto is

physically considerably younger today than his contemporaries from the World War II period.

Magneto resumed his battles against the X-Men, but eventually MacTaggert's tampering with his mind took effect, and he became the X-Men's ally. During an extended absence from Earth by Xavier, Magneto even took over as headmaster of Xavier's school, mentoring the NEW MUTANTS. Around this time, Magneto, Quicksilver and the Scarlet Witch learned their true relationship.

THE TRUCE IS OVER

In time Magneto's previous personality re-emerged. After he created an electromagnetic pulse that deactivated technology all over the world, the United Nations gave him control of the island of Genosha, which was mainly populated by mutants. However, the island was devastated by SENTINELS sent by Cassandra Nova.

During a fit of madness, the Scarlet Witch used her powers to alter reality so that Magneto ruled the world (House of M story arc). She later restored the status quo, and also deprived most mutants of their powers, including Magneto. The Collective (see GUARDIAN), being controlled by Magneto-impersonator Xorn, briefly returned his powers to him. Recently, the HIGH EVOLUTIONARY repowered him.
TB, MF

An alternate reality Magneto and his Brotherhood attempted to destroy Earth.
1 Wolverine 2 Rogue 3 Ice-Man 4 Mystique 5 Magneto

Once merely an arms merchant, Moses Magnum was transformed by Apocalypse into a world-shaking villain with command of the Earth itself.

MAGNUM, MOSES

FIRST APPEARANCE Giant-Size Spider-Man #4 (April 1975)
REAL NAME Moses Magnum
OCCUPATION Terrorist, arms merchant **BASE** Various
HEIGHT/WEIGHT Not known **EYES** Brown **HAIR** Black
SPECIAL POWERS/ABILITIES Moses Magnum can generate vibrational force, which he can use to bolster his own strength and durability or release outwards to cause earthquakes.

Once a noted arms merchant, Moses Magnum's operation was dismantled by SPIDER-MAN and the PUNISHER. Narrowly escaping death, Magnum was found by APOCALYPSE, who offered him power in exchange for help in fomenting chaos. Reconstructed by Apocalypse with the power to cause shifts within the Earth's crust, Magnum attempted to blackmail Japan but was foiled by the X-MEN. Displeased, Apocalypse destabilized Magnum's abilities so that he could cause earthquakes simply by coming into contact with the Earth. Magnum tried to regain Apocalypse's favor through a show of power but was undone by the AVENGERS. He was last seen plummeting toward the center of the Earth. **TB**

MAGNUS

FIRST APPEARANCE Exiles #1 (August 2001)
REAL NAME Magnus Lensherr
OCCUPATION Adventurer **BASE** Mobile
HEIGHT 6 ft **WEIGHT** 177 lbs **EYES** Brown **HAIR** Brown
SPECIAL POWERS/ABILITIES Ability to manipulate magnetic fields, heat, radiation and radio waves; when makes skin-to-skin contact with other lifeforms, he transforms them into steel.

Born in an alternate reality, Magnus was the product of a union between MAGNETO and ROGUE. Inheriting his father's powers of magnetism, Magnus was also born with a corrupted version of his mother's abilities— everything he touched turned to steel. Concerned about the harm he might cause, Magnus became something of a hermit, only to be coerced into joining the EXILES. In an attempt to free yet another version of Magneto from incarceration, Magnus sacrificed himself whilst containing the force of a nuclear explosion. **AD**

MAGUS

FIRST APPEARANCE New Mutants Vol. 1 #18 (August 1984)
REAL NAME Magus **OCCUPATION** Monarch **BASE** Mobile
HEIGHT Variable **WEIGHT** Variable **EYES** Black
HAIR In true form he has no hair, but parts of his head resemble it.
SPECIAL POWERS/ABILITIES Able to grow to the size of a star and destroy it. Can exist in outer-space and change his shape to that of any being or machine. Can replenish his life energies.

The Magus is the leader of the planet Technarch, which is populated by sentient "techno-organic" beings, a species with an organic structure resembling metal. Each child of the Magus must face him in a battle to the death for his position. One son, WARLOCK, instead fled to Earth and joined the NEW MUTANTS. The Magus came after Warlock, but the X-MEN defeated him and he went into hiding. Upon his return, the Magus attacked New York, and the Avengers drove him from Earth. Another, unrelated Magus was an evil version of Adam WARLOCK, from the future of Earth-7528. **MT, MF**

MAJOR DOMO

FIRST APPEARANCE Longshot #4 (December 1985)
REAL NAME Major Domo
OCCUPATION Principal aide to Mojo
BASE Mojoworld
HEIGHT/WEIGHT Not known **EYES** Blue **HAIR** Gray
SPECIAL POWERS/ABILITIES Constantly monitors Mojoworld's markets, enabling ongoing evaluation of his master's businesses.

The sycophantic yet contemptuous aide to MOJO, the ruler of Mojoworld, Major Domo's job is to ensure the smooth running of his master's household. An android, Major Domo provides information on and analysis of Mojo's businesses, while at the same time soothing his paranoid ego. These abilities make him Mojo's most prized servant. Although treated as nothing more than a glorified toaster, Major Domo remains at Mojo's side, playing a key role in curbing the worst excesses of his master's personality. Despite finding Mojo repulsive, Major Domo's position gives him almost unparalleled influence over Mojoworld. Not bad for a mere android. **AD**

MALUS, DR. KARL

FIRST APPEARANCE Spider-Woman #30 (September 1980)
REAL NAME Dr. Karl Malus
OCCUPATION Former surgeon, now criminal scientist
BASE Los Angeles, California
HEIGHT 5 ft 9 in **WEIGHT** 155 lbs **EYES** Brown **HAIR** Black
SPECIAL POWERS/ABILITIES Advanced knowledge of genetic engineering, expertise in biochemistry, radiology, and surgery.

Fascinated with superhuman beings, scientist Karl Malus became involved with the criminal underworld to obtain funding for his research. Malus attempted to capture the original SPIDER-WOMAN. He restored the superhuman strength of Eric Josten (now known as ATLAS) and enabled him to grow to gigantic size. Working for the POWER BROKER, Malus gave many clients superhuman strength. Later, he became the head of the criminal organization called the Corporation. **PS**

MAN-APE

FIRST APPEARANCE Avengers #62 (March 1969)

REAL NAME M'Baku

OCCUPATION Mercenary, renegade   **BASE** Mobile

HEIGHT 7 ft   **WEIGHT** 355 lbs   **EYES** Brown   **HAIR** Brown

SPECIAL POWERS/ABILITIES Possesses superhuman strength, agility, and resistance to injury. He is a powerful fighter whose combat ability is based on that of gorillas.

Clad in the pelt of the rare Wakandan white gorilla, M'Baku the Man-Ape takes up a battle position at the head of a band of his followers in the White Gorilla cult.

While T'Challa—the BLACK PANTHER and king of the African nation of Wakanda—was away helping the AVENGERS in the US, M'Baku schemed to seize his throne. Reviving the outlawed White Gorilla cult, M'Baku killed a rare white gorilla, then bathed in its blood and ate its flesh, which gave him the power of the ape. Calling himself Man-Ape, he battled Black Panther and the Avengers' teammates, both in Wakanda and in the US. Defeated, he teamed with the GRIM REAPER—despite the Reaper's racism—to form a new Lethal Legion. They recently plotted to blow up the Statue of Liberty. **MT, MF**

MAN-BEAST

Created by scientific accident, the Man-Beast was born when a wolf was placed inside the HIGH EVOLUTIONARY's genetic accelerator. Despite creating an entire evil army using the same device, the Man-Beast was eventually defeated by Thor, placed in a shuttle, and exiled into space.

The Man-Beast sought revenge on the High Evolutionary when he landed on Counter-Earth—a world created by that being. There, he introduced the people of Counter-Earth to the concept of evil and even attempted to destroy the planet altogether. In the years since, the Man-Beast has gone into battle several more times, fighting both Adam WARLOCK and the HULK. When he attempted to raise a second army, using the Legion of Light religious cult as a front, the Man-Beast went head-to-head with SPIDER-MAN.

Later, with help from QUICKSILVER, the High Evolutionary captured the Man-Beast and devolved him back into a wolf. **AD, MF**

During confrontations, the Man-Beast could employ his mental powers as a weapon.

FACTFILE

REAL NAME
Man-Beast

OCCUPATION
Would-be world conqueror

BASE
Somewhere below New York City

HEIGHT 6 ft 10 in
WEIGHT 320 lbs
EYES Red
HAIR Brown

FIRST APPEARANCE
Thor #134
(November 1966)

POWERS

Superhuman strength, speed, endurance, and senses; remarkable scientific ability, particularly in genetics and engineering.

Despite his great strength and mental agility, the Man-Beast was no match for the mighty Thor.

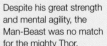

MANDARIN

REAL NAME
Unrevealed

OCCUPATION
Criminal mastermind

BASE
The "Palace of the Star Dragon" in the "Valley of Spirits" within China

HEIGHT 6 ft 2 in
WEIGHT 215 lbs
EYES Blue-black
HAIR Black

FIRST APPEARANCE *Tales of Suspense* #50 (1964)

POWERS

One of the world's greatest scientific mind and a superb athlete. Possesses ten rings of extraterrestrial origin that have amazing powers.

Not only is the Mandarin a great scientific genius, he is also a superb athlete with extensive training in martial arts.

A direct descendant of Genghis Khan, the Mandarin was born in China to a wealthy father who lost everything in the communist revolution. In the forbidden Valley of Spirits, the Mandarin found a crashed starship containing ten alien rings. These rings could control another's mind, rearrange matter, fire a disintegration beam, create a vortex, produce deadly gases, create ice blasts, or discharge electricity, flames, bursts of blinding light, or clouds of darkness. With the rings, the Mandarin conquered the valley and made plans to seize control of the world, often clashing with Iron Man and the Avengers. For a while, the world thought him dead, and his son TEMUGIN inherited his rings—which were still attached to his hands. He returned later, sporting bionic hands, the rings now fused to his spine. After battling Iron Man over the fate of the world once more, he seemed to have been killed, but his body was never recovered. **TD, MF**

Mandarin is trained martial artist and his rings pack a punch, but Spider-Man is just too quick for him!

Since the Mandarin believes he can use technology to achieve world domination, he often ends up in conflict with Iron Man.

TALES OF SUSPENSE featuring THE POWER OF IRON MAN
NO ONE ESCAPES THE MANDARIN!
5 PAGE BONUS

MANDRILL

REAL NAME
Jerome Beechman

OCCUPATION
Professional criminal

BASE
Mobile

HEIGHT 6 ft
WEIGHT 270 lbs
EYES Black
HAIR Brown

FIRST APPEARANCE
Shanna the She-Devil #4 (June 1973)

POWERS

Mandrill has the ability to emit powerful pheromones which give him the power to attract and enslave adult women causing them to submit to his will.

Jerome Beechman's parents worked at the atomic testing grounds in New Mexico, where exposure to radiation caused mutations in their son. Jerome was born with animal-like fur on his body and an ape-like appearance. When he was ten, his parents abandoned him in the desert. There he met NEKRA Sinclair, whose mother had worked at the atomic testing grounds. Jerome took the name Mandrill, and the two traveled the American Southwest together, avoiding all human contact. Mandrill and Nekra formed Black Spectre, an organization of black women hoping to overthrow the American government—until Daredevil stopped them. After SHIELD captured Nekra, Mandrill formed Fem-Force, an army of radical women under his control. Fem-Force teamed up with Magneto's Mutant Force, but the Defenders stopped their plans. Mandrill's powers survived M-Day, and he has recently been seen working for the Hood in New York. **MT, MF**

MANSLAUGHTER

FIRST APPEARANCE *Defenders* #133 (July 1984)

REAL NAME Not known

OCCUPATION Former hired assassin   **BASE** Mobile

HEIGHT 5 ft 7 in   **WEIGHT** 115 lbs   **EYES** Blue   **HAIR** Red

SPECIAL POWERS/ABILITIES Low-level telepath: influences peripheral vision and subliminal hearing of others in order to render himself invisible; uses abilities to enhance skills as a huntsman.

Manslaughter was born with mutant powers ideal for tracking and hunting. He impressed the Eternal known as the INTERLOPER by successfully tracking him down in the Siberian wastelands. The Interloper agreed to help Manslaughter hone his powers but, concerned about the young man's unstable personality, he did not train him fully. This was just as well, for Manslaughter later became a ruthless assassin for hire. Eventually he redeemed himself, sacrificing his life in the effort to destroy the DRAGON OF THE MOON. **AD**

MAN-THING

All who fear burn at the Man-Thing's touch!

Unflappable insurance claims adjustor Nathan Mehr comes face to face with the shambling, monstrous Man-Thing.

Ted Sallis was a research scientist on a project aiming to replicate the Super-Soldier formula that empowered CAPTAIN AMERICA in the 1940s. But he was betrayed to the sinister criminal think-tank known as AIM, who wanted his research. Fearing that his work would fall into evil hands, Sallis destroyed his notes and injected himself with the only sample of his serum. But while fleeing for his life, he crashed his car in the swampland surrounding his laboratory, and was seemingly killed.

TRANSFORMATION

Unknown to Sallis, the area in which he'd located his lab was close to the Nexus of All Realities, a mystical gateway that linked all of the myriad dimensions of existence. In some mysterious fashion, Sallis's serum combined with the ambient mystical energies of the Nexus, and caused the vegetation of the swamp that surrounded his almost lifeless body to reconstitute him as a mindless, shambling mass—the Man-Thing.

FEELING THE BURN

Possessing scant intellect of its own, the Man-Thing is instead empathetically attuned to his surroundings. While Ted Sallis's soul still resides within the great beast, in general the Man-Thing is mindless, reacting only to the emotions of those around him. Fear causes the Man-Thing great pain, and he will journey forth from his swampy home to put an end to any source of fear that causes him distress. Because of a quirk of chemistry in his make-up, any creature who feels fear in the Man-Thing's presence burns at his touch.

The Man-Thing seldom leaves the confines of his swamp, but he can occasionally be drawn forth by strong emotions, which affect him painfully through his animalistic empathy.

FACTFILE

REAL NAME
Ted Sallis

OCCUPATION
Guardian of the Nexus of All Realities

BASE
Swamp in the Florida Everglades that conceals the Nexus of All Realities

HEIGHT Around 7 ft
WEIGHT Around 500 lbs
EYES Red, bulbous
HAIR None

FIRST APPEARANCE
Savage Tales #1 (May 1971)

POWERS

Virtually indestructible, he has superhuman strength. Fear causes him pain, and changes his chemical makeup so that the touch of his body burns those who feel fear in his presence.

Man-Thing guards the Nexus of All Realities, an interdimensional gateway at the center of his swamp.

SWAMP PROTECTOR

Empowered by the Nexus to serve as its silent, unsleeping guardian, the Man-Thing rarely strays from the vicinity of the swamp, and if circumstances force him to do so, he always returns. But anything that might threaten the sanctity of the Nexus, or that of the swamp itself, soon comes to know the mindless rage of its unspeaking protector! **TB**

MANTIS

FACTFILE

REAL NAME
Unknown

OCCUPATION
Adventurer

BASE
Temple of the Priests, Pama, Vietnam; Ho Chi Minh City, Vietnam; Avengers Mansion, New York City

HEIGHT 5 ft 6 in
WEIGHT 115 lbs
EYES Green
HAIR Black

FIRST APPEARANCE
Avengers #112 (June 1973)

POWERS

Mantis has superior agility, extraordinary martial arts skill, and the ability to sense the emotions of others. She can also will herself to heal quickly after injury.

Giant-Size Avengers #4 features Vision and Scarlet Witch's wedding, and Mantis's transformation and departure from Earth.

Born in Vietnam, Mantis was raised by the Priests of Pama, a pacifist sect of the alien Kree. When Mantis had completed her martial arts training, the priests sent her to live among humans, implanting false memories of life as an orphan struggling for survival on the streets of Ho Chi Minh City. She eventually teamed up with the Swordsman, a costumed criminal, whom Mantis helped rehabilitate. When the Swordsman joined the Avengers, Mantis went with him and was also made a member of the team. After her marriage to the eldest Cotati, an alien race of telepathic plant-beings, Mantis transformed into pure energy and left Earth. After giving birth to a son named Quoi, she joined the Silver Surfer for a while but was caught in an explosion that split her into several independent aspects. Once she managed to reintegrate herself, she battled Thanos to protect her son from him. After surviving the Annihilation events (*see* pp. 30-1), she joined the modern Guardians of the Galaxy. **MT, MF**

Mantis is caught in the clutches of Thanos, an Eternal who augmented his superhuman abilities to become the most powerful of the Eternals.

MAN-WOLF

FIRST APPEARANCE (as Man-Wolf) The Amazing Spider-Man #124 (September 1973) **REAL NAME** John Jameson
OCCUPATION Former astronaut, pilot, security chief
BASE New York City
HEIGHT 6 ft 6 in **WEIGHT** 350 lbs **EYES** Red **HAIR** White
SPECIAL POWERS/ABILITIES As Man-Wolf: superhuman strength, speed, agility, durability, and heightened senses.

Astronaut and son of *Daily Bugle* publisher J. Jonah Jameson, John Jameson discovered a gem on the Moon. On Earth, this gem caused him to transform into a wolflike creature under a full moon. The Moongem contained the essence of Stargod, ruler of Other-Realm, in another dimension. Man-Wolf journeyed to Other-Realm, where he helped its people defeat their enemy Arisen Tyrk. John underwent radiation treatment, which destroyed the Moongem. He occasionally became Man-Wolf later and even married She-Hulk for a while before becoming Stargod and leaving for space. **PS, MF**

MARAUDERS

The personal army of mutant eugeneticist, Mr. Sinister, the Marauders are one of the most effective forces the X-Men have ever faced. Mutants that fell short of the mark disgusted Mr. Sinister. He particularly loathed the Morlocks, so the Marauders' first mission was to obliterate them. The Marauders have gone head-to-head with the X-Men since then, even destroying the Xavier Institute. They are particularly feared because Sinister has created clones of each of the original Marauders, and if one falls, a duplicate stands ready to replace him. The mutant Gambit actually helped create the team, although no clones were ever made of him. Recently, the Marauders—along with the Acolytes and four X-Men: Gambit, Lady Mastermind, Mystique, and Sunfire—helped Sinister try to track down and capture the first mutant baby born after M-Day. **AD, MF**

THE MARAUDERS
1 Scrambler 2 Sabretooth 3 Malice
4 Scalphunter 5 Vertigo 6 Harpoon 7 Riptide

FACTFILE

MEMBERS
MR. SINISTER Telepathy.
MALICE Telepathy.
VERTIGO Affects equilibrium.
ARCLIGHT Seismic shocks from hands.
HARPOON Bio-energetic projectiles.
RIPTIDE A mutant whirlwind.
BLOCKBUSTER Super-strong.
PRISM Captures powers then projects back at source.
SABRETOOTH Adamantium skeleton; supersenses.
SCALPHUNTER Manipulates mechanical components.
SCRAMBLER Disrupts living and mechanical systems.

FIRST APPEARANCE
Uncanny X-Men #210 (October 1986)

MARROW

MARROW

FACTFILE

REAL NAME
Sarah; last name may be
Rushman

OCCUPATION
Genetic terrorist, adventurer

BASE
Various

HEIGHT 6 ft
WEIGHT Unknown
EYES Green
HAIR Magenta

FIRST APPEARANCE
Uncanny X-Men #325
(October 1995)

She is a young mutant who left her normal life behind to journey into the sewers controlled by the mysterious MORLOCKS. Marrow was one of the few survivors of the Mutant Massacre which decimated the Morlocks' ranks. Escaping to the dimension ruled by Mikhail RASPUTIN, Marrow became a member of Gene Nation, a radical mutant group dedicated to striking back at their human oppressors.

After a number of encounters with the X-MEN, Marrow came to join with them in common cause. However, her fiery personality and natural savageness meant that she never fitted in at Xavier's School and she left under mysterious circumstances. More recently, she was recruited by the newly-reformed WEAPON X program, who have boosted her powers so as to allow her to control her appearance. **PS**

POWERS

Marrow's mutant physiognomy allows her to rapidly regrow the protruding bone spurs which protrude from her body, and which she uses as weapons. She also possesses two hearts and enhanced durability, making her difficult to kill.

Bony projections from her body can be broken off and used as vicious weapons.

Marrow's bone-spikes would grow wildly throughout her body, causing her discomfort and disfiguring her appearance.

MARRINA

FIRST APPEARANCE Alpha Flight Vol. 1 #1 (August 1983)
REAL NAME Marrina Smallwood
OCCUPATION Adventurer **BASE** Mobile
HEIGHT 6 ft **WEIGHT** 200 lbs **EYES** Black **HAIR** Green
SPECIAL POWERS/ABILITIES Enhanced strength and stamina; able to breathe both air and water; can swim at high speed and generate waterspouts.

The Plodex alien life form who became known as Marrina hatched from an egg that had soaked in the Atlantic Ocean, giving her aquatic adaptations that surfaced when she assumed the humanoid forms of her adoptive guardians, the Smallwoods.

Her superhuman abilities allowed her to join ALPHA FLIGHT, and she later married NAMOR the Sub-Mariner. Tragedy struck when, during her pregnancy, she turned into a monstrous leviathan. Namor was forced to kill her, but her alien biology may have preserved her in a coma-like state. **DW**

MARVEL BOY

FIRST APPEARANCE Marvel Boy #1 (September 2000)
REAL NAME Noh-Varr
OCCUPATION Would-be conqueror **BASE** New York City
HEIGHT 5 ft 10 in **WEIGHT** 165 lbs **EYES** Black **HAIR** White
SPECIAL POWERS/ABILITIES Enhanced strength, speed, and stamina; can mentally control his body's growth; nanobots reroute pain sensations.

There have been many Marvel Boys: Martin Burns wielded the power of Hercules in the 1940s, Robert Grayson who received cosmic bracelets from the ETERNALS of Uranus in the 1950s, Wendell Vaughn who became QUASAR, Vance Astrovik who became Justice, and mutant David Bank. The latest is Noh-Varr of the KREE, whose starship was shot down by Doctor Midas. SHIELD later captured him. He sided with Earth during the Secret Invasion, then accepted Norman Osborn's offer to join the AVENGERS as the new CAPTAIN MARVEL. **DW, MF**

MASTER KHAN

FIRST APPEARANCE Strange Tales #77 (October 1960)

REAL NAME Khan **OCCUPATION** God to the people of K'un-Lun

BASE K'un-Lun, New York City

HEIGHT Unknown **WEIGHT** Unknown **EYES** Red **HAIR** Black

SPECIAL POWERS/ABILITIES Magical powers allow him to distort reality, levitate and shrink objects, alter his appearance, form energy shields, fire energy blasts, and cast mystic spells.

The human sorcerer Master Khan was worshiped as a god on the alien planet of K'un-Lun, where the dominant life form is a sentient plant called the H'ylthri. He served as the protector of the inhabitants of K'un-Lun, and his power came from their worship. On Earth, Khan was a scholar but also a student of the occult. Once on K'un-Lun, Master Khan became a mortal enemy of IRON FIST. Returning to Earth, Khan fought with WOLVERINE, NAMOR, and NAMORITA. He once captured Namor and posed as him, but the Atlantean prince broke free and killed him. **MT, MF**

MASTER ORDER

FIRST APPEARANCE Marvel Two-in-One Annual #2 (December 1977)

REAL NAME None **OCCUPATION** Cosmic entity

BASE Everywhere

HEIGHT/WEIGHT/EYES/HAIR Unknown

SPECIAL POWERS/ABILITIES Scope of powers is unknown although can change destinies of specific individuals.

DEATH, LORD CHAOS, ETERNITY, and Master Order—enigmatic beings all, each embodying a distinct abstract concept. Their origins are unknown and so are their powers, although many surmise that these are without limit. The "brother" of Lord Chaos, Master Order strives to maintain a cosmic balance with his sibling, intervening in mortal affairs on the rarest of occasions. Following the defeat of the would-be universe-destroyer, THANOS, Chaos and Order implied that they were responsible for manipulating SPIDER-MAN's destiny to ensure his intervention in the crisis at a critical moment. No one knows if this is truly the case. **AD**

MASTER PANDEMONIUM

FIRST APPEARANCE West Coast Avengers #4 (January 1986)

REAL NAME Martin Preston **OCCUPATION** Demon commander

BASE Los Angeles, California

HEIGHT 6 ft 1 in **WEIGHT** 205 lbs **EYES** Blue **HAIR** Black

SPECIAL POWERS/ABILITIES Amulet of Azmodeus permits interdimensional teleportation. Can detach his own arms as living demons, fire energy beams from his hands, levitate, and breathe fire.

After making a deal with MEPHISTO, Martin Preston became a monstrous being with a star-shaped hole in his chest for the fragments of his missing soul. As Master Pandemonium, he identified the SCARLET WITCH's twins as having two of the fragments. When all five were found, Mephisto captured him. Preston escaped, and WICCAN and SPEED later found him in the house the Scarlet Witch once shared with the VISION. **DW, MF**

MASTERS, ALICIA

As a child, Alicia Masters was blinded in the same accident that killed her father, but she discovered that despite her handicap she had a talent for sculpting. The man responsible for the accident, Philip Masters (the PUPPET MASTER), married her mother and adopted Alicia. When her stepfather clashed with the Fantastic Four, the THING rescued Alicia, who was but a pawn in his scheme, and a strong relationship developed between them. Perhaps her greatest moment was when she appealed to the humanity buried deep within the sky-spanning SILVER SURFER and convinced him to rebel against his master, the world-devouring GALACTUS, in defense of Earth. For a while, she broke up with the Thing and dated the Surfer, but she later returned to him. At one point, the Skrull agent Lyja replaced her and even married the Human Torch. Recently, Alicia designed the memorial for CAPTAIN AMERICA. **TB, MF**

Alicia had a powerful effect on the deep-buried emotions of the Silver Surfer. She convinced him to rebel against his master, the world-devouring Galactus, and fight for Earth by appealing to his inner goodness.

Despite her blindness, Alicia Masters is a world-renowned sculptress who practices her art through touch.

MASTERS OF EVIL

A villainous alliance against the Avengers

Believing that there's strength in numbers, the original Baron Zemo forms a sinister super-team equal in power to the mighty Avengers.

The Masters of Evil are perennial foes of the AVENGERS, assembling multiple times over the years, often with no link between the various groupings other than their name. The first Masters of Evil came about through the efforts of Nazi mastermind BARON ZEMO.

DECADES OF VILLAINY

Zemo schemed to defeat his wartime nemesis CAPTAIN AMERICA by enlisting the most notorious enemies of Captain America's comrades in the Avengers. He gathered the Melter to fight IRON MAN, the RADIOACTIVE MAN to fight THOR, and the BLACK KNIGHT to battle both the WASP and GIANT MAN (Henry Pym). Later, Zemo welcomed the ENCHANTRESS and the EXECUTIONER into the Masters of Evil. The team disbanded after Zemo's death.

A second Masters of Evil took its place, founded by the robot ULTRON, in his cover identity as the Crimson Cowl. The team obtained blueprints of Avengers' Mansion from butler Edwin JARVIS and struck at the Avengers in their own home. The new Black Knight, DANE WHITMAN, turned on his teammates in the Masters of Evil and helped the Avengers scatter the villains.

CHARACTER KEY
1 Flying Tiger
2 Cyclone
3 Klaw
4 Man-Killer
5 Tiger Shark

The criminal mastermind EGGHEAD organized a third Masters of Evil, hoping to take vengeance on Henry Pym but met defeat (and death) soon after. Helmut Zemo, son of the original Baron Zemo, brought together the fourth incarnation of the Masters.

THE DARKEST HOUR

Baron Zemo II gathered more than a dozen criminals to crush the Avengers through force of numbers. Their most infamous achievement was the siege of Avengers' Mansion.

DOCTOR OCTOPUS assembled a fifth Masters of Evil and fought the GUARDIANS OF THE GALAXY. Baron Zemo II returned to organize a sixth team, the THUNDERBOLTS, who masqueraded as heroes. Before long, most of the Thunderbolts had become heroes for real!.

Justine HAMMER, the new Crimson Cowl, assembled a seventh version of the team that included a staggering 25 members. These Masters of Evil failed in an attempt to blackmail the United Nations for one trillion dollars. **DW**

CHARACTER KEY
1 Black Knight
2 Melter
3 Radioactive Man

ESSENTIAL STORYLINES
• *Avengers Vol. 1 #6* Baron Zemo assembles the first Masters of Evil, featuring a villainous counterpart for each member of the Avengers.
• *Avengers Vol. 1 #270-277* The Masters of Evil raid their enemies' headquarters in the classic storyline "The Siege of Avengers Mansion."
• *Thunderbolts #24-25* The most recent grouping of the Masters of Evil unites 25 Super Villains, providing a formidable foe for the Thunderbolts.
• *Guardians of the Galaxy #28–29* Doctor Octopus' Masters of Evil team clash with the Guardians of the Galaxy.

FACTFILE
ORIGINAL MEMBERS AND POWERS
BARON ZEMO Extended longevity, brilliant criminal mind.
MELTER Could melt any metal with a molecular beam.
RADIOACTIVE MAN Can release blasts of lethal radioactive energy.
BLACK KNIGHT (Nathan Garrett) Skilled combatant; carried power lance.
EXECUTIONER Enhanced strength, carried enchanted axe.
ENCHANTRESS Sorceress

FIRST APPEARANCE
Avengers Vol. 1 #6 (July 1964)

MAXIMUS

FACTFILE

REAL NAME
Maximus

OCCUPATION
Would-be conqueror

BASE
City of Attilan in the Blue Area of
the Moon

HEIGHT 5 ft 11 in
WEIGHT 180 lbs
EYES Blue
HAIR Black

FIRST APPEARANCE
Fantastic Four #47
(February 1966)

POWERS

Maximus possesses a genius-level intellect unhampered by sanity, and possesses the ability to overwhelm the thought-processes of those in close proximity, taking over their conscious minds.

MAXIMUS

The younger brother of BLACK BOLT, king of the INHUMANS, Maximus exhibited no outward signs of change after his exposure to the gene-altering Terrigen Mists. Instead, as he grew, he chose to hide his growing psionic powers along with his lust for power. As adolescents, Black Bolt caught Maximus forging an alliance with the KREE, the aliens responsible for the creation of the Inhumans. Black Bolt's sonic scream destroyed the Kree warship and also shattered Maximus' grip on sanity. Maximus the Mad then devoted himself to wresting control of his people from his noble brother. He succeeded several times over the years, but Black Bolt always managed to retake the throne from him. During the Secret Invasion (*see* pp. 326–7), the two finally ended their quarrel while facing a common foe. Currently, Maximus and Black Bolt rule together, not just over the Inhumans but also the Kree. **AD, MF**

Black Bolt is Maximus' older brother. Since just a whisper from his voice can trigger sonic shockwaves, Black Bolt remains silent most of the time.

MAYHEM

FIRST APPEARANCE Cloak and Dagger Vol 1 #1 (October 1983)
REAL NAME Brigid O'Reilly
OCCUPATION Former policewoman, vigilante   **BASE** New York City
HEIGHT 5 ft 4 in   **WEIGHT** 120 lbs   **EYES** Green   **HAIR** Green
SPECIAL POWERS/ABILITIES Skin constantly secretes a poisonous gas; this can cause paralysis if it gets in bloodstream and can serve as truth drug; Mayhem is also able to fly.

THE DEED IS DONE, BLACK BOLT! BY NOW, ALL HUMAN LIFE ON EARTH HAS BEEN ENDED! ONLY WE INHUMANS REMAIN! THE ENTIRE PLANET IS OURS, MY SPEECHLESS BROTHER!

Despite his boast, Maximus' attempt to destroy humanity failed utterly.

As a New York police detective, Brigid O'Reilly confronted the vigilante partnership CLOAK AND DAGGER. Feeling that their approach endangered innocent lives, Brigid was initially hostile to them, but became more tolerant when she learned of their origins. Following a confrontation with several corrupt police officers while she was investigating a drug-smuggling operation, Brigid was killed by poisonous gas. However, the intervention of Cloak and Dagger led to her resurrection as a superpowered individual, enabling her to exact revenge. Since then, Brigid has adopted the alias Mayhem and become a vigilante, targeting New York drug pushers. **AD**

The poisonous gas produced by Mayhem's body is used in her fight against crime.

MEDUSA

FACTFILE

REAL NAME
Medusalith Amaquelin

OCCUPATION
Royal interpreter

BASE
Attilan, Blue Area, Earth's Moon

HEIGHT 5 ft 11 in
WEIGHT 130 lbs
EYES Green
HAIR Red

FIRST APPEARANCE
Fantastic Four #36
(March 1965)

POWERS

Can use her 6-ft-long hair to attack, lift weights, pick locks, or as a whip or a rope.

MEDUSA

A member of the INHUMANS' royal family on Attilan, Medusa was exposed to Terrigen Mist as a baby. She gained the ability to use her hair like extra limbs. She learned to interpret BLACK BOLT's body language and fell in love with him. When MAXIMUS seized power from Black Bolt, Medusa left Attilan and suffered amnesia in a plane crash. The WIZARD found her and made her part of the FRIGHTFUL FOUR. When Black Bolt retook his throne, Medusa returned to act as his interpreter and later married him. They had a son, Ahura, who suffers from his uncle Maximus's madness. At times, Medusa has acted as the INVISIBLE WOMAN's substitute in the FANTASTIC FOUR, but she is now the Inhuman's full-time queen, helping guide them as they take their place as the rulers of the KREE Empire. **MT, MF**

Medusa uses her long hair to tangle up the amazing Spider-Man in a different kind of web.

MEGGAN

FIRST APPEARANCE Mighty World of Marvel #7 (December 1983)
REAL NAME Meggan
OCCUPATION Adventurer **BASE** England
HEIGHT Variable **WEIGHT** Variable
EYES Variable **HAIR** Variable
SPECIAL POWERS/ABILITIES Meggan is a shapeshifter whose forms are influenced by the emotions of others; she can fly and project energy blasts drawn from the Earth.

Born to gypsies, Meggan grew up in a fur-covered form and considered herself a freak. Only later, after being taken in by Brian Braddock (CAPTAIN BRITAIN), did she discover that she could consciously alter her appearance. She transformed herself from her furry form into a strikingly beautiful woman with long, golden hair. Not long after this, Meggan and Braddock started a relationship and founded the superteam EXCALIBUR, and the two eventually married. As Captain Britain's wife, Meggan is the queen of Otherworld, assisting in the management of the dimensional realities that make up the Omniverse. **DW**

MELTDOWN

When Tabitha Smith's father learned of her mutant abilities, he beat her, and she fled to Xavier's School for Gifted Youngsters. Encountering the Beyonder on the way, she went on a series of cosmic adventures before falling in with the VANISHER's gang of thieves, the Fallen Angels. She oscillated between X-Factor and the Fallen Angels before becoming a member of the New Mutants. She later joined X-Force and became a protégé to Cable, helping him attack the WEAPON X facility and the Neverland mutant concentration camp. After that, she joined the new team NEXTWAVE and put an end to the terrorist organization SILENT. She retained her powers after M-Day, and she joined the X-Men when they moved to San Franscisco. However, the Leper Queen—the leader of the anti-mutant Sapien League—kidnapped her soon after and shot her dead. **AD, MF**

A founding member of X-Force, in the early days Meltdown was known as Boom-Boom.

MELTDOWN

FACTFILE

REAL NAME
Tabitha Smith

OCCUPATION
Adventurer

BASE
New York State

HEIGHT 5 ft 5 in
WEIGHT 120 lbs
EYES Blue
HAIR Blonde

FIRST APPEARANCE
Secret Wars II #5
(November 1985)

POWERS

Generates and throws "time bombs"—energy balls of concussive force. She is able to vary the size and power of her time bombs at will.

MENTALLO

FIRST APPEARANCE Strange Tales #141 (February 1966)
REAL NAME Marvin Flumm
OCCUPATION Professional criminal   **BASE** Mobile
HEIGHT 5 ft 10 in   **WEIGHT** 175 lbs   **EYES** Brown   **HAIR** Brown
SPECIAL POWERS/ABILITIES Possesses telepathic powers. Can read the thoughts of anyone within five miles, locate a particular brain pattern and project his own thoughts into the minds of others.

Marvin Flumm went to work for SHIELD while his powers developed. Calling himself Mentallo, he stole a battlesuit and telepathy-enhancing equipment and teamed with the Fixer (now TECHNO) to try to take over SHIELD, but Nick Fury stopped them. Flumm called himself Think Tank when he first faced CAPTAIN AMERICA, but soon returned to the codename Mentallo. He tangled with the HULK, the AVENGERS, PROFESSOR X, and the FANTASTIC FOUR, among others. He retained his powers after M-Day and joined the HOOD's criminal crew. **MT, MF**

MERCADO, JOY

FIRST APPEARANCE Moon Knight Vol. 1 #33 (September 1983)
REAL NAME Joy Mercado
OCCUPATION Reporter   **BASE** New York City
HEIGHT 5 ft 10 in   **WEIGHT** 135 lbs   **EYES** Blue   **HAIR** Blonde
SPECIAL POWERS/ABILITIES Normal human strength for a woman of her build who exercises regularly; has some skill at unarmed combat; accomplished writer and interviewer.

Joy Mercado, formerly a top writer for *NOW* magazine, is among the elite investigative reporting staff of the *Daily Bugle*. She was partnered with staff photographer Peter Parker on a number of stories, including an assignment to England and Northern Ireland, where SPIDER-MAN prevented the assassination of the British prime minister. Joy seemed suspicious of Peter's relationship with Spider-Man and, at one time, accused Peter of using Spider-Man to further his career.

Joy is an incorrigible flirt, but her relationship with Peter never progressed to anything more than friendship. **DW**

MEPHISTO

Mephisto is an extradimensional demon of immense power who often poses as Satan. He continually schemes to make bargains with people for their souls. Mephisto especially covets the souls of heroes for their purity and has repeatedly sought the soul of the noble Silver Surfer. Mephisto has also contended with THOR, Dr. Strange, Daredevil, the Fantastic Four, and many others. It was Mephisto, posing as Satan, who bonded the demon Zarathos to Johnny Blaze, turning him into the Ghost Rider. He also held the soul of Dr. Doom's mother until Strange helped Doom free her. Mephisto has a son, Blackheart, and a daughter, Mephista. The Scarlet Witch once unwittingly used fragments of Mephisto's soul to give life to her twin sons, and Mephisto's reclamation of these drove her mad. Recently, Mephisto made a deal with Spider-Man to save his aunt MAY PARKER in exchange for destroying his marriage to MARY JANE WATSON (*see* BRAND NEW DAY). **PS, MF**

Mephisto can magically augment his strength to an immeasurable extent, rivalling even the possibly limitless power of the Hulk.

FACTFILE
REAL NAME
Unrevealed
OCCUPATION
Ruler of an extradimensional realm of the dead
BASE
A hell dimension

HEIGHT 6 ft 6 in
WEIGHT 310 lbs
EYES Variable, usually white with no visible pupils or irises
HAIR Variable, usually black

FIRST APPEARANCE
The Silver Surfer Vol. 1 #3 (December 1968)

POWERS

Possesses virtually unlimited ability to manipulate magical energies; potentially incalculable strength; godlike durability; immortality; and shapeshifting ability. He can possess the souls of those who hand them over willingly.

In his fiery netherworld Mephisto rules over lesser demons and the souls of deceased humans, which have been imprisoned in demonic bodies.

MERLYN

FIRST APPEARANCE Black Knight #1 (May 1955)

REAL NAME Merlyn

OCCUPATION Sorcerer, guardian of the multiverse

BASE Otherworld **HEIGHT/WEIGHT/EYES/HAIR** Variable

SPECIAL POWERS/ABILITIES Almost unlimited command of sorcerous energies allow him to perform innumerous feats, including extending his natural lifespan.

Born a powerful immortal in an alternate universe, Merlyn studied under Necrom, and with him and his fellow student Feron, he helped attune the various universes together to link the multiverse in a magical Matrix. With his daughter Roma, he created the Captain Britain Corps to safeguard all the parallel Earths of the multiverse, then later manipulated Roma and Captain Britain into forming Excalibur when they thought he was dead. After Excalibur destroyed the source of his power he disappeared, but he later returned to attack Captain Britain and kill Roma. **TB, MF**

MI-13

FIRST APPEARANCE Excalibur #101 (September 1996)

BASE UK **MEMBERS AND POWERS Black Knight (Dane Whitman)** Wields the Ebony Blade. **Blade (Eric Brooks)** Half-vampire vampire hunter. **Captain Britain (Brian Braddock)** Superhuman strength, durability, and flight. **Faiza Hussain** Control over living bodies. **John the Skrull** Shapeshifting and flight. **Spitfire (Jacqueline Falsworth)** Superhuman speed and durability, fangs, and healing factor.

MI-13 is the branch of British Intelligence charged with the investigation of supernatural phenomena. Alistair Stuart founded it from the remnants of the Weird Happenings Organisation (WHO), but he handed over the reins to his top agent, Peter Wisdom (*see* WISDOM, PETER), when he left to join MI-6. During Secret Invasion (*see* pp.326–7), the Prime Minister drafted all UK Super Heroes into MI-13. To keep the SKRULLS out of Avalon, MI-13 had to unleash the demons from that magical dimension. While this worked, it meant that MI-13 had a lot of cleaning up to do. CAPTAIN BRITAIN now leads MI-13's semiautonomous strike team. **MF**

MESMERO

Mesmero started out as a party hypnotist, using his mutant powers to convince guests to surrender their valuables. He branched out into supervillainy when the MACHINESMITH recruited him to lead the robotic "Demi-Men" alongside a robot duplicate of MAGNETO. Mesmero, who didn't realize that his comrades were robots, hypnotized POLARIS into becoming his partner until the X-Men crushed the Machinesmith's plot.

Mesmero later found work as a stage hypnotist and clashed with SPIDER-MAN. He recently served as a field agent for the WEAPON X program in exchange for treatments that augmented his hypnotic abilities. His powers let him entrance crowds into doing anything he wished, putting Mesmero's mind-control abilities in the same class as PROFESSOR X. Mesmero helped hide the locations of Weapon X installations, but his superiors abandoned him when his power levels dipped after the death of his mother.

Mesmero was one of the mutants who saw their abilities stripped by the SCARLET WITCH during the Decimation event. Without his hypnotism, Mesmero finally forged a relationship with a woman that didn't rely on trickery. He has rededicated himself to starting a new life as an ordinary human. **DW**

Mesmero, who knew that he was a supremely powerful mutant, was also an insufferable egotist.

FACTFILE

REAL NAME
Vincent (full name unrevealed)

OCCUPATION
Professional criminal

BASE
Mobile

HEIGHT 5 ft 10 in
WEIGHT 180 lbs
EYES Red
HAIR Green

FIRST APPEARANCE
X-Men Vol. 1 #49
(October 1968)

Mutant powers of hypnotism allow him to take control of others. Mesmero does this by making eye contact. His powers can induce amnesia, put memories into a victim's head or even change their personality.

MICROCHIP

FIRST APPEARANCE Punisher Vol. 2 #4 (November 1987)

REAL NAME Linus Lieberman

OCCUPATION Mechanic, computer hacker, inventor

BASE New Jersey **HEIGHT** 5 ft 8 in **WEIGHT** 220 lbs

EYES Green **HAIR** Brown

SPECIAL POWERS/ABILITIES No superhuman abilities; highly skilled computer hacker; weapons engineer.

A former weapons engineer, Linus Lieberman put his skills to work building the PUNISHER's arsenal. Calling himself Microchip, he became a close friend and confidante of the Punisher—and also a target of the Punisher's enemies. The KINGPIN had Microchip kidnapped, then cut off his finger and sent it to the Punisher in the mail. Microchip also lost his son Louis Frohike (Microchip Jr.) to the Punisher's war on crime. Microchip once appeared to be killed by Stone Cold, a rogue SHIELD agent, but he returned to try to persuade the Punisher to join the CIA. The Punisher killed him instead. **MT, MF**

Skilled in strategy, Microchip often planned the Punisher's missions.

MILLIE THE MODEL

FIRST APPEARANCE Millie the Model #1 (1945)

REAL NAME Millicent "Millie" Collins

OCCUPATION Fashion model, actress, business executive

BASE Hanover Modeling Agency, New York

HEIGHT 5 ft 7 in **WEIGHT** 137 lbs **EYES** Blue **HAIR** Blonde

SPECIAL POWERS/ABILITIES None, but has the poise and grace of a top fashion model; some fighting ability.

Having grown up in a rural farming town, Millie Collins left home for the big city, where she found employment as a model for the Hanover Modeling Agency. Over the years, Millie became involved in all sorts of outlandish adventures, often accompanied by her photographer boyfriend Clicker Holbrook and her rival, Chili Storm. Millie retired from active modeling to run an agency of her own. In recent years, Millie's niece Misty has become embroiled in comedic adventures herself. **TB**

MINDLESS ONES

FIRST APPEARANCE Strange Tales #127 (December 1964)

REAL NAME None

OCCUPATION None **BASE** Dormammu's Dark Dimension

HEIGHT/WEIGHT/EYES/HAIR Variable

SPECIAL POWERS/ABILITIES All possess incalculable strength, near-invulnerability, and the ability to fire energy blasts from their cyclopean eyes.

DORMAMMU and his sister Umar sought refuge in the Dark Dimension following their exile from the Faltine. There, they taught the wizard-king Olnar how to absorb other dimensions, which backfired when the Mindless Ones appeared. A horde of these soulless, violent creatures killed Olnar and ran riot over the Dark Dimension until Dormammu and Umar imprisoned them. They have broken through to Earth many times, battling SPIDER-MAN, DR. STRANGE and CAPTAIN BRITAIN. They recently took over a small town in Colorado, but NEXTWAVE stopped that. **DW, MF**

MIMIC

After spilling chemicals from his father's laboratory on himself, Calvin Rankin became able to emulate the abilities and powers of others. As Mimic, he sought to imitate the X-MEN, but when he was found out, PROFESSOR X invited him to join the team. Mimic's membership was short-lived—his arrogance made him difficult to work with—and, following his expulsion, he was thought to have died battling the HULK. He returned several years later to battle X-FORCE, and he later befriended Excalibur. A heroic version of him from Earth-12 worked with the EXILES for many missions before being killed. **AD, MF**

By absorbing Wolverine's healing factor, Mimic actually survived his encounter with the Hulk. His present whereabouts are unknown.

FACTFILE

REAL NAME
Calvin Rankin

OCCUPATION
Adventurer

BASE
Mobile

HEIGHT 6 ft 2 in
WEIGHT 225 lbs
EYES Brown
HAIR Brown

FIRST APPEARANCE
X-Men #19 (April 1966)

Can ape the powers and abilities of up to five individuals at a time; can only wield powers at half strength.

MIMIC

POWERS

MINDWORM

FIRST APPEARANCE Amazing Spider-Man Vol. 1 #138 (November 1974)

REAL NAME William Turner

OCCUPATION None **BASE** New York City

HEIGHT 6 ft 1 in **WEIGHT** 210 lbs **EYES** Brown **HAIR** Brown

SPECIAL POWERS/ABILITIES Feeds on emotions of others; can cause death; can control others; extraordinarily brilliant.

A mutant born with an oversized cranium and brilliant mind, William Turner was cursed with the need to absorb the emotions of others. Unable to understand or control his psychic hunger, he fed off his parents, causing their deaths. William's hunger continued into adulthood, when he took to feeding off the residents of his apartment block, until SPIDER-MAN intervened. Before he could exact revenge, William had an epiphany, realizing his actions were motivated by guilt at his parents' death. After developing mental illness, William became homeless and was killed by a street gang. **AD**

MIRACLE MAN

FIRST APPEARANCE Fantastic Four #3 (March 1962)
REAL NAME Unrevealed
OCCUPATION Stage magician **BASE** New York, Cheemuzwa
HEIGHT 6 ft 4 in **WEIGHT** 220 lbs **EYES** Brown **HAIR** Black
SPECIAL POWERS/ABILITIES Master hypnotist, able to mesmerize people with a glance and make them see what he wants; occasionaly telekinesis, animating objects, and restructuring matter.

A brilliant illusionist and stage magician, Miracle Man most likely had some mutant abilities. During a performance, he spotted the FANTASTIC FOUR in the audience and began taunting them about how much greater his powers were than theirs. Enraged, the THING challenged him but was outdone by Miracle Man's abilities. After escaping from prison following a crime spree, Miracle Man studied the mystical powers of the Cheemuzwa or the Silent Ones. Using his newfound powers, Miracle Man remained a constant and powerful foe of the Fantastic Four until he was shot dead by Scourge. **MT**

MISS ARROW

FIRST APPEARANCE Friendly Neighborhood Spider-Man #4 (January 2006) as the Other; Friendly Neighborhood Spider-Man #11 (October 2006) as Miss Arrow **REAL NAME** Ero
OCCUPATION Hunting Spider-Man **BASE** New York
HEIGHT 5 ft 10 in **WEIGHT** 115 lbs **EYES** Brown **HAIR** Blonde
SPECIAL POWERS/ABILITIES Ero is a hive mind composed of thousands of pirate spiders, but can appear human. She can extend spider stingers from her wrists and control spiders telepathically.

After Morlun apparently killed SPIDER-MAN, Peter Parker somehow sloughed off his skin and returned in a fresh body. Pirate spiders devoured his old flesh and used it as a framework for a collective intelligence that called itself the Other. Spider-Man drove it off, but it returned in the guise of Miss Arrow, the nurse at the high school at which Parker and his old classmate Flash Thompson (see THOMPSON, EUGENE) worked. Ero had to reproduce to survive, and she chose to mate with Flash, a process that would kill him. Spider-Man rescued Flash, only to become the focus of Ero's murderous lust. He lured her into an aviary and birds devoured the spiders that made up her body. Spider-Man crushed the last spider with his boot. **MF**

MISSING LINK

FIRST APPEARANCE Incredible Hulk #105 (July 1968)
REAL NAME Lincoln Brickford
OCCUPATION Miner **BASE** Lucifer Falls, West Virginia
HEIGHT/WEIGHT Not known **EYES** Yellow **HAIR** None
SPECIAL POWERS/ABILITIES Possesses superhuman strength and durability. His core is radioactive, and he can project heat from his epidermis.

A Neanderthal man born millennia ago, the Missing Link was accidentally sealed in a cave, where a mysterious mist kept him in suspended animation. He was awakened from his sleep by an atomic test that changed his molecular structure. Not understanding the modern world in which he found himself, the Missing Link went on a rampage and battled the HULK. Seemingly destroyed, the Link reconstructed himself, and was found and adopted by the kindly Brickford family. They called him Lincoln and got him a job in the local mines. After further battles with the Hulk, he was turned over to the authorities. **TB**

MISS AMERICA

Madeline was the ward of radio tycoon James Bennet. A scientist sponsored by Bennet claimed to have invented a device that gave him superpowers. Madeline tampered with the device during an electrical storm and gained the ability to fly.

Madeline chose to use her gifts in the service of her country. She became the costumed adventurer Miss America, fighting foreign spies and saboteurs alongside super-speedster the WHIZZER. Miss America and the Whizzer joined the Liberty Legion at the invitation of CAPTAIN AMERICA's sidekick Bucky, then became members of the INVADERS when the United States entered World War II. After the war, the Invaders changed their name to the ALL-WINNERS SQUAD. Miss America and the Whizzer married. In 1949, the two took jobs at a government nuclear facility. Sabotage exposed them to dangerous levels of radiation, and Miss America's son, Nuklo, was born a mutant who was kept for decades in suspended animation.

Years later, Miss America gave birth to a stillborn child at the HIGH EVOLUTIONARY's Wundagore Mountain. Madeline did not survive the stress of giving birth and was buried at the mountain's base.

Miss America, seen here with fellow Invaders the Sub-Mariner and the Human Torch, was one of the first female costumed adventurers. She was announced in the press as the female equivalent of Captain America, and she served as a public icon while aiding the Invaders in combat against Hitler's armies during World War II. **DW**

FACTFILE
REAL NAME Madeline Joyce Frank
OCCUPATION Adventurer
BASE Mobile
HEIGHT 5 ft 8 in
WEIGHT 130 lbs
EYES Blue
HAIR Auburn
FIRST APPEARANCE Marvel Mystery Comics Vol. 1 #49 (November 1943)

MISS AMERICA

POWERS Enhanced endurance; could levitate herself and fly at a limited speed.

On an alternate Earth, Miss America and the Invaders continued in their roles long past World War II.

MR. FANTASTIC
Leader of the Fantastic Four

FACTFILE

REAL NAME
Reed Richards
OCCUPATION
Scientist, adventurer
BASE
New York City

HEIGHT 6 ft 1 in
WEIGHT 180 lbs
EYES Brown
HAIR Brown

FIRST APPEARANCE
Fantastic Four #1
(November 1961)

POWERS

A scientific genius, specializing in physics, aeronautics; Mr. Fantastic can stretch, reshape, compress, or expand his entire body or parts of his body into any shape. He can stretch his neck, limbs or torso up to 1,500 feet without pain. He can create a canopy, sheath, umbrella, or parachute with his body.

ALLIES/FOES

ALLIES Susan Storm (Invisible Woman), Ben Grimm (the Thing), Johnny Storm (Human Torch), Lyja the Skrull, Alicia Masters

FOES Gormuu, Doctor Doom, Frightful Four, Galactus, Puppet Master, the Skrulls, Annihilus, Blastaar, Diablo

ISSUE #1

In November 1961, *Fantastic Four #1* ushered in the Marvel Age of Comics and introduced millions to what would become the Marvel Universe. Comic books would never be the same!

He's the leader of one of the world's most important Super Hero teams. He's also a brilliant scientist. Reed Richards is Mr. Fantastic. As leader of the super hero group, the FANTASTIC FOUR, Mr. Fantastic uses both his ability to stretch his body and his sharp scientific mind in his quest to help mankind.

A BRILLIANT STUDENT

The son of highly intelligent parents, Reed Richards was a child prodigy and a brilliant student. His father Nathaniel Richards was a wealthy physicist. Reed's mother, Evelyn, died when the boy was seven years old.

Young Reed showed a genius for math, physics, and mechanics, which his father encouraged. Nathaniel guided his son's scientific studies. By the time Reed was fourteen, he was already taking and excelling in college-level courses. When he reached college age, Reed attended several universities, including Empire State University in New York.

It was there that Reed Richards met several people who would play a major role in his later life as Mr. Fantastic. Victor Von Doom was a foreign student from the nation of Latveria. This scientific genius was assigned to be Reed's first college roommate, but Von Doom disliked Reed from the moment he met him and asked for a new roommate. Later, as DOCTOR DOOM, he would become Mr. Fantastic's and the Fantastic Four's greatest enemy.

MEANWHILE, IN THE LABORATORY...

IT LOOKS LIKE SOMEONE IS AS ANXIOUS TO SEE THE SCIENCE LAB AS I AM! NAME'S RICHARDS, FELLA... REED *RICHARDS!*

THAT IS NO CONCERN OF MINE!!

Reed Richards' attempt to make friends with fellow student Victor Von Doom were rudely brushed aside.

Replacing Von Doom as Reed's roommate was Benjamin J. Grimm, a former high school football star who, though very different in personality, became Reed's best friend.

In college, Reed began working on plans to build a ship that could travel to other solar systems. Ben joked that if Reed could build the ship, he would pilot it.

After transferring to Columbia University in Manhattan, Reed rented a room from a woman whose daughter, Susan Storm, immediately fell for Reed. One day she would be his wife, as well as his partner in the Fantastic Four.

A FATEFUL JOURNEY

Using money left to him by his father, Nathaniel, who arranged for the fortune to be given to Reed while Nathaniel was on an alternate

ESSENTIAL STORYLINES

• *Fantastic Four #5*
Victor Von Doom blames Reed for the facial scar he receives when a machine explodes. He dons a mask and becomes Doctor Doom, Mr. Fantastic's worst enemy.

• *Fantastic Four Annual #6*
The cosmic radiation that gave Sue her invisibility power affects her red bloods cells, putting her life and the life of her unborn child in danger.

Earth, Reed began developing his starship shortly after college. When his own funds began to run out, Reed got funding from the US Federal Government to complete the project.

However, shortly before Reed could complete the ship, the government threatened to cut off funding to the project. Desperate to prove that his starship would fly, Reed decided to take the ship up on a test flight himself. Ben argued against the idea, telling Reed that he thought the ship's shielding would be inadequate against the powerful cosmic radiation found in space.

Reed finally convinced Ben to pilot the ship on its test voyage. By this time, Reed and Sue Storm were engaged. Sue insisted in coming along on the flight, as did her younger brother Johnny

Able to shape his body into a highly malleable state, Mr. Fantastic can stretch his neck to peek around corners, or even look over entire buildings!

I'VE DONE IT!! I'M DRIFTING INTO A WORLD OF LIMITLESS DIMENSIONS!! IT'S THE CROSSROADS OF INFINITY-- THE JUNCTION TO EVERYWHERE!

AT THE CROSSROADS

Mr. Fantastic floats at the Crossroads of Infinity, where all dimensions and universes intersect. A traveler can journey from one dimension to another by carefully navigating through the Crossroads. Doctor Doom proved this, using the Fantastic Four as his test subjects.

(and later INVISIBLE WOMAN). Johnny called himself the HUMAN TORCH, and Ben called himself the THING. All four agreed to use their new powers to help humanity.

Guided by Reed Richards, the Fantastic Four has become the most respected Super Hero team on Earth. They have saved the planet from conquest and destruction many times. Reed and Sue married and now have two children: Franklin and Valeria Richards.

During the Civil War (*see* pp. 84–5) Reed sided with IRON MAN and the US government. Sue left him over this, although when the conflict ended, they reunited. Because of his membership in the ILLUMINATI, Reed became a target during World War Hulk (*see* pp. 152–5). He redeemed himself during the Secret Invasion (*see* pp. 326–7). After escaping from the SKRULLS, who had kidnapped and tortured him, he invented a new way to detect them. **MT, MF**

Mr. Fantastic battles Crucible, a member of the Enclave. Crucible stole Mr. Fantastic's creative genius to launch a genetics program designed to create life itself, but went insane, unable to handle the flood of amazing ideas.

AK TAC TAC TAC TAC

HEAR THAT?? IT'S THE COSMIC RAYS!! I--I WARNED YOU, ABOUT EM!!

Mr. Fantastic can stretch his body well over 1,000 feet

THEY'RE PENETRATING THE SHIP!! OUR SHIELDING ISN'T STRONG ENOUGH!

BUT I DON'T *FEEL* ANYTHING!

NATURALLY! THEY'RE ONLY RAYS OF LIGHT! YOU CAN'T FEEL 'EM-- BUT THEY'LL AFFECT YOU JUST THE SAME!

Storm. The quartet snuck onto the launch pad, slipped onto the ship, and blasted off into space. Before they could achieve hyperspace and a journey to another solar system, a solar flare shot intense levels of radiation at the ship. Ben had been right. The ship's shields were not enough to withstand the radiation, which irradiated the four astronauts. Ben was forced to cut short the flight and land back on Earth.

BIG CHANGES

Upon their return to Earth each member of the foursome soon discovered that the cosmic radiation had changed the very structure of their bodies. Reed discovered that he could bend and stretch his body at will. Sue could turn herself invisible. Johnny could cover his body with flames and also fly. Ben's skin was transformed into an orange, rock-like substance, and he gained tremendous strength.

Reed became the team's leader, calling himself Mr. Fantastic. Sue called herself INVISIBLE GIRL

MISTER HYDE

FIRST APPEARANCE Journey Into Mystery #99 (December 1963)

REAL NAME Calvin Zabo **OCCUPATION** Professional criminal

BASE New York City **HEIGHT** 5 ft 11 in; (as Hyde) 6 ft 5 in

WEIGHT 185 lbs; (as Hyde) 420 lbs **EYES** Brown

HAIR Gray; (as Hyde) Brown

SPECIAL POWERS/ABILITIES Superhumanly strong; astonishing recuperative ability and resistance to pain.

Inspired by *Dr. Jekyll and Mr. Hyde,* medical researcher Calvin Zabo concocted a potion that worked like the one in R. L. Stevenson's classic tale. As Mr. Hyde, he took on many Super Heroes, like THOR, SPIDER-MAN, and DAREDEVIL. For a while, he worked with the Masters of Evil against the Avengers. The YOUNG AVENGERS later discovered him illegally selling a version of his potion as a Mutant Growth Hormone. Recently, Hyde joined the Hood's criminal organization. His estranged daughter, Daisy Johnson, worked as an agent of Shield. **AD, MF**

MOCKINGBIRD

FIRST APPEARANCE Astonishing Tales Vol. 1 #6 (June 1971)

REAL NAME Barbara "Bobbi" Morse-Barton

OCCUPATION Adventurer **BASE** Mobile

HEIGHT 5 ft 9 in **WEIGHT** 135 lbs **EYES** Blue **HAIR** Blonde

SPECIAL POWERS/ABILITIES Expert hand-to-hand combatant and gymnast; her battle-stave can be used as a quarterstaff or broken into two smaller segments.

Bobbi Morse began her career as a SHIELD agent, by striking up a romance with HAWKEYE. The two eventually married and became founding members of the West Coast AVENGERS. During a time-travel adventure to the Old West, Mockingbird allowed the abusive PHANTOM RIDER to fall to his death, an action that drove a wedge between Mockingbird and Hawkeye. The two were reconciled when they mentored the GREAT LAKES AVENGERS. Mockingbird later died at the hands of MEPHISTO, when she intercepted a power blast meant for Hawkeye. **DW**

MISTER SINISTER

Dr. Nathaniel Essex was recruited by Apocalypse and his genetic structure enhanced so as to provide him with virtual immortality and superhuman physical attributes. Taking the name Mister Sinister, Essex continued his forbidden experiments into the secrets of mutation, and he has played a hidden role in the upbringing of the Summers brothers, Cyclops and Havok. He is the guiding hand behind the Marauders, whom Sinister once sent into the Morlock tunnels to carry out the Mutant Massacre. Sinister hoped to breed a mutant child between Cyclops and Jean Grey, so he fashioned a clone later revealed to be Madelyne Pryor. Their baby was taken to the future where he grew up to become Cable. Recently, Sinister reformed the Marauders to track down the first mutant baby born after M-Day. However, Mystique seemed to kill him by forcing him to make contact with an unconscious Rogue. He soon returned in a female form as Miss Sinister. **TB, MF**

FACTFILE

REAL NAME
Nathaniel Essex

OCCUPATION
Geneticist

BASE
Various

HEIGHT 6 ft 5 in
WEIGHT 285 lbs
EYES Red
HAIR Black

FIRST APPEARANCE
*Uncanny X-Men #221
(September 1987)*

MISTER SINISTER

POWERS

Enhanced strength and durability, and some command over his own genetic structure. Essex's advanced knowledge of cloning allows him to transfer his intellect into a pristine new body whenever his current one starts to wears out.

Mister Sinister has embroiled members of all of the assorted X-related teams in his evil schemes, such as the creation of a hell-on-Earth during "Inferno."

MODOK

FIRST APPEARANCE Tales of Suspense #93 (October 1967)
REAL NAME George Tarleton **OCCUPATION** Leader of AIM
BASE Various **HEIGHT** 12 ft **WEIGHT** 750 lbs **EYES** Red
HAIR Brown **SPECIAL POWERS/ABILITIES** Superhuman
mental and psionic powers; computer-like brain; headband enabled
him to teleport from one AIM base to another; possessed a hover-
chair that could fly and was equipped with weaponry.

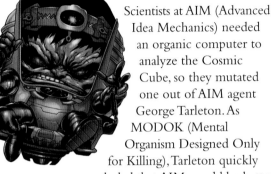

Scientists at AIM (Advanced Idea Mechanics) needed an organic computer to analyze the Cosmic Cube, so they mutated one out of AIM agent George Tarleton. As MODOK (Mental Organism Designed Only for Killing), Tarleton quickly concluded that AIM would be better with him in charge. After MODOK suffered many defeats at the hands of heroes, Monica Rappaccini ousted him and took over AIM. To get his revenge, MODOK assembled a team of 11 villains to steal a living star and sell it to AIM for a billion dollars. The star became unstable and blew up AIM's headquarters, getting MODOK both his money and his revenge.
TD, MF

MOJO

A spineless mass of yellow flesh, Mojo is ruler of Mojoworld, a bizarre, media-orientated planet. A manipulative tyrant, Mojo produces movies and TV shows to keep the masses amused. The need to maintain these entertainments' popularity has drawn him to Earth.

Mojo's first visit occurred when his slave, Longshot, tried to persuade the X-Men to help overthrow his master. Although they triumphed, Mojo's successor—"Mojo II, the Sequel"—proved to be even more tyrannical, and Mojo reclaimed the reins of power. Since the X-Men are such crowd pleasers, Mojo has repeatedly involved them in his entertainment programmes, but they are rarely willing participants. Frustrated by this, he created younger versions of the X-Men, the so-called X-Babies, but they proved no easier to work with. **AD**

He may be spineless but Mojo simply refuses to accept defeat.

Equipped with a sophisticated exoskeleton that enabled humanoid movement, Mojo II was less grotesque than his predecessor. A corrupt tyrant, he was not popular and eventually Mojo overthrew him.

FACTFILE
REAL NAME Mojo
OCCUPATION Ruler of Mojoworld
BASE The airborne Body Shoppe, Mojoworld

HEIGHT Unknown
WEIGHT Unknown
EYES Yellow
HAIR None

FIRST APPEARANCE Longshot #3 (November 1985)

POWERS Travels on robotic platform that moves on metal spiderlike legs; projects energy bolts from hands; his very presence can kill life nearby.

MOLE MAN

Shunned and ridiculed for his bizarre appearance, Mole Man turned his back on the surface world and sought a legendary underground kingdom. He eventually found an entrance to it on Monster Island, in the Bermuda Triangle—an underground world filled with advanced technical devices left by a race known as the Deviants. Mole Man also found a race of semi-human creatures, whom he enslaved. Sometimes in partnership with Red Ghost, Kala or the Outcasts, his deadly plots against the surface world have been thwarted by the Fantastic Four, the Avengers, Iron Man, and the Hulk.

Mole Man declared himself ruler of the underground kingdom, which he named Subterranea. Tyrannus, another man from the surface world, who also possessed Deviant technology, challenged Mole Man, leading to many epic battles between the two. **MT**

Hideous and lonely, Mole Man found solace in the depths of Subterranea.

Mole Man as he appears in the Ultimates series.

FACTFILE
REAL NAME Unknown
OCCUPATION Former nuclear engineer; ruler of the Subterraneans
BASE Subterranea

HEIGHT 4 ft 10 in
WEIGHT 165 lbs
EYES Brown
HAIR Gray

FIRST APPEARANCE Fantastic Four #1 (November 1961)

POWERS Ingenious inventor of weapons capable of seismic disturbance; dominating personality; heightened senses, including a radar sense that enables him to navigate in pitch darkness, or to sense the presence of objects, or people behind him.

MOLECULE MAN

FIRST APPEARANCE Fantastic Four #20 (November 1963)

REAL NAME Owen Reece

OCCUPATION Atomic plant worker turned criminal

BASE Brooklyn, New York; later a suburb of Denver, Colorado

HEIGHT 5 ft 7 in **WEIGHT** 140 lbs **EYES** Brown **HAIR** Brown

SPECIAL POWERS/ABILITIES Possesses psionic ability to manipulate all forms.

Lab assistant Owen Reece accidentally activated a machine that opened a pinhole into another dimension, exposing him to radiation that scarred his face and endowed him with the power to control matter. An embittered misfit, Reece used his powers to evil ends, but was defeated by the FANTASTIC FOUR. UATU THE WATCHER imprisoned Reece in another dimension, but he returned to Earth and took part in both Secret Wars. Reece fell in love with Volcana, and the two retired to Colorado. Since then, Volcana has left Reece, and he was last seen in the Raft super-prison. **PS, MF**

MOLTEN MAN

FIRST APPEARANCE Amazing Spider-Man #28 (September 1965)

REAL NAME Mark Raxton

OCCUPATION Security guard for Osborn Industries

BASE New York City

HEIGHT 6 ft 5 in **WEIGHT** 225 lbs **EYES** Brown **HAIR** Gold

SPECIAL POWERS/ABILITIES Superhuman strength and durability. Metallic epidermis is capable of producing flames and heat.

The stepbrother of LIZ OSBORN, Mark Raxton worked as an assistant to PROFESSOR SPENCER SMYTHE, creator of the Spider-Slayer robots. Raxton stole Smythe's latest creation, a synthetic metallic liquid, but he spilled it on himself and became the super-strong Molten Man. When Raxton's molten skin threatened to destroy him, Spider-Man saved his life. Molten Man later took a job as a security guard at the company owned by Liz's then-husband, Harry Osborn. During the Civil War, the Punisher nearly killed Raxton. As he recuperated, his powers ran out of control. Harry finally discovered a cure for Raxton's condition, though, and Spider-Man delivered it. **TB, MF**

MONTESI

FIRST APPEARANCE Darkhold #1 (October 1992)

REAL NAME Victoria Montesi

OCCUPATION Occult investigator **BASE** Rome, Italy

HEIGHT 5 ft 11 in **WEIGHT** 130 lbs

EYES Brown **HAIR** Black

SPECIAL POWERS/ABILITIES Possesses the ability to sense when someone has accessed a page from the Darkhold tome.

For generations, the Montesi line has guarded the Darkhold book of black magic to prevent the rise of the Elder god CHTHON. Victoria Montesi, daughter of Monsignor Vittorio Montesi, grew up believing that her family's involvement with the Darkhold was just superstition, but her skepticism vanished when pages from the Darkhold became scattered around the world. To retrieve them, Victoria founded the Darkhold Redeemers with Louise Hastings and Interpol agent Sam BUCHANAN. She later learned that Monsignor Montesi was not her real father; unable to have children, he had used magic to ensure an heir. In reality, Victoria was Chthon's daughter, and was carrying Chthon himself in a demonic pregnancy. Fortunately, DOCTOR STRANGE prevented Chthon's birth into this world. **AD**

MOON-BOY

FIRST APPEARANCE Devil Dinosaur #1 (April 1978)

REAL NAME Moon Boy

OCCUPATION Adventurer **BASE** The Valley of Flame, located on an extra-dimensional planet

HEIGHT 6 ft 2 in **WEIGHT** 196 lbs

EYES Blue **HAIR** Black

SPECIAL POWERS/ABILITIES Able to communicate with Devil Dinosaur and possibly other unrevealed powers.

Moon Boy grew up on a distant planet where tribes of ape-like humanoids coexisted with dinosaurs. His people called themselves the Small-Folk, and they struggled against the Hill-Folk and Killer-Folk. When Moon Boy saved a tyrannosaurus rex from the Killer-Folk, the dinosaur became his constant companion. DEVIL DINOSAUR and Moon Boy traveled back and forth to Earth several times before settling in the Savage Land. Moon Boy was taken from there when Shield sent the Heroes for Hire to capture him for study, but he's since returned. **DW, MF**

MOON KNIGHT
see opposite page

MOONDRAGON

FIRST APPEARANCE Iron Man Vol. 1 #54 (January 1973)

REAL NAME Heather Douglas

OCCUPATION Adventurer **BASE** Mobile

HEIGHT 6 ft 3 in **WEIGHT** 150 lbs **EYES** Blue **HAIR** None

SPECIAL POWERS/ABILITIES Telepathy; telekinetic levitation of objects; ability to fire mental blasts; trained martial artist.

Moondragon grew up on Titan after THANOS killed her parents. The evil DRAGON OF THE MOON tried to corrupt her, but she resisted him. On Earth, Moondragon joined the DEFENDERS, but the influence of the Dragon of the Moon sometimes turned her into a villain. She became a reservist of the AVENGERS, and later safeguarded the Mind Gem as a member of the Infinity Watch. She became lovers with Marlo Jones, but when that ended she turned to Phyla-Vell (CAPTAIN MARVEL) instead. Murdered by ULTRON, she died in Phyla's arms. **AD, MF**

FACTFILE

REAL NAME
Marc Spector

OCCUPATION
Millionaire playboy and taxi driver

BASE
New York City

HEIGHT 6 ft 2 ins
WEIGHT 225 lbs
EYES Dark brown
HAIR Brown

FIRST APPEARANCE
Werewolf by Night Vol I, #32
(August 1975)

POWERS

His strength waxes and wanes with the moon. He bears weapons given to him by the Egyptian god Khonshu: scarab throwing darts, a golden ankh that glows when danger is near, and an ivory boomerang.

MOON KNIGHT

A mercenary left for dead in the Egyptian desert, Marc Spector was found by followers of the Egyptian god Khonshu, who saved his life and gave him superhuman powers. Returning to the US with a statue of Khonshu, Marc became a crimefighter, calling himself the Moon Knight and assuming two more alter egos: millionaire Steven Grant and taxi driver Jake Lockley. Aided by his pilot friend, Frenchie, and his lover, Marlene Alraune, Marc fought crime for many years, battling against WEREWOLF, Midnight Man and Black Spectre, and alongside SPIDER-MAN, and the PUNISHER. Eventually, exhaustion set in, and Marc retired his alter egos and sold the Khonshu statue.

NEW MOON

Before long, Marc felt compelled to travel to Egypt. There, members of the cult of Khonshu explained to him that being the Moon Knight was his destiny, one he could not shirk. Reinvigorated, and equipped by Khonshu with a new costume and a selection of special weapons, Marc became the Moon Knight once more. Marc registered with the government under the Superhuman Registration Act. When Norman Osborn (see GREEN GOBLIN) took over the AVENGERS, though, Marc faked his death and went into hiding in New Mexico. **AD, MF**

In his struggle against the more nefarious denizens of New York, Moon Knight is partnered by his lover, Marlene Alraune, and his good friend Frenchie.

MOONSTAR, DANI

FIRST APPEARANCE Marvel Graphic Novel #4: The New Mutants (June 1982) **REAL NAME** Danielle "Dani" Moonstar
OCCUPATION Former SHIELD agent, later adventurer and teacher
BASE The Xavier Institute, Salem Center, New York State
HEIGHT 5 ft 6 in **WEIGHT** 105 lbs **EYES** Brown **HAIR** Black
SPECIAL POWERS/ABILITIES Created three-dimensional images of thoughts in others' minds. Had rapport with higher animals.

Danielle "Dani" Moonstar is the granddaughter of Black Eagle, a Cheyenne chief. When Black Eagle was murdered by agents of Donald PIERCE, Dani joined forces with PROFESSOR X to defeat him. She then joined the NEW MUTANTS, at first known as Psyche and later as Mirage and Moonstar. For a time Dani served as a VALKYRIE in Asgard before becoming a SHIELD agent and then a member of X-FORCE. She worked as a teacher at the Xavier Institute, but was fired after losing her powers on M–Day. She has now rejoined the X-Men in San Francisco. **AD, MF**

MOONSTONE

FIRST APPEARANCE Captain America Vol.1 #192 (December 1975)
REAL NAME Dr Karla Sofen
OCCUPATION Psychologist, criminal adventurer **BASE** Mobile
HEIGHT 5 ft 11 in **WEIGHT** 130 lbs
EYES Blue **HAIR** Blonde
SPECIAL POWERS/ABILITIES Able to fly and become intangible; creates blinding flashes and emits laser beams from hands.

During her childhood, Karla Sofen quickly learned how to manipulate others to get what she wanted. She became a psychologist in adulthood, and tricked the original Moonstone, Lloyd Bloch, into giving up the gem (actually a KREE lifestone) that gave him superpowers. Using the gem, she became a superpowered villain, serving with the MASTERS OF EVIL and the THUNDERBOLTS, for whom she eventually became field leader. Moonstone recently joined Norman Osborn's AVENGERS as the new Ms. MARVEL, wearing the original costume, which had been taken from ULTRAGIRL. **AD, MF**

MORBIUS

FIRST APPEARANCE Amazing Spider-Man #101 (October 1971)
REAL NAME Dr. Michael Morbius
OCCUPATION Biochemist **BASE** Mobile
HEIGHT 5 ft 10in **WEIGHT** 170 lbs **EYES** Blue **HAIR** Black
SPECIAL POWERS/ABILITIES A pseudo-vampire who can glide on air currents, Morbius has superhuman strength and healing ability. He can hypnotize people and force them to do his bidding.

Nobel Prize-winning biochemist, Dr. Michael Morbius discovered that he was dying from a rare blood disease which dissolved his blood cells. Morbius tried an experimental treatment in an attempt to cure himself which involved fluids made from the bodies of vampire bats combined with electric shock treatment.

This potent combination transformed Morbius, giving him the superhuman powers and the overwhelming bloodlust of a vampire. He was not a true "undead" vampire, however, as he was still a mortal man. Morbius grew fangs and killed to satisfy his craving for blood. However, after drinking his victim's blood, his mind would return to normal and he became filled with guilt, remorse, and self-loathing. He often battled SPIDER-MAN. **MT**

MORGAN LE FAY

FIRST APPEARANCE Spider-Woman Vol. 1 #2 (May 1978)
REAL NAME Morgan (or Morgana) Le Fey
OCCUPATION Sorceress **BASE** The astral plane
HEIGHT 6 ft 2 in **WEIGHT** 140 lbs **EYES** Green **HAIR** Magenta
SPECIAL POWERS/ABILITIES One of the most powerful sorceresses of all time; able to manipulate the natural environment of Earth and the astral plane. She can also fly and shapeshift.

The sorceress half-sister of King Arthur PENDRAGON, Morgan plotted against King Arthur until MERLIN magically imprisoned her within Castle Le Fay. Her body trapped, she sent her astral form to various time periods. She once tried to use Jessica Drew, the first SPIDER-WOMAN, to break Merlin's spell and later stole the Twilight Sword, which she used to recreate a distorted version of Camelot in which the AVENGERS served as her knights.

She and Dr. Doom became lovers across time, but when this went badly, she traveled to the future to kill him. Only Hank PYM's new Avengers could hope to stop her. **TB, MF**

MOTHER NIGHT

FIRST APPEARANCE Captain America #356 (August 1989)
REAL NAME Susan Scarbo
OCCUPATION Agent of the Red Skull **BASE** Red Skull's chalet
HEIGHT 5 ft 7 in **WEIGHT** 133 lbs **EYES** Green **HAIR** Black
SPECIAL POWERS/ABILITIES Expert hypnotist; could generate illusions, make herself appear to be invisible, and force others to obey her will.

Susan Scarbo and her brother Melvin were stage hypnotists whose ambitions grew beyond show business. They turned to crime, Susan took the name "Suprema," and was enlisted by the RED SKULL.

Changing her identity to Mother Night, she took command of the SISTERS OF SIN, formerly led by the Red Skull's daughter Synthia (also known as Sin). In this role, Mother Night battled CAPTAIN AMERICA. When the Red Skull was captured by MAGNETO, Mother Night joined with the Skeleton Crew (Red Skull's main operatives) to try and free him. Mother Night was killed by the WINTER SOLDIER. **MT**

MORDRED THE EVIL

FIRST APPEARANCE Black Knight #1 (May 1955)
REAL NAME Sir Mordred
OCCUPATION Conqueror **BASE** Various
HEIGHT 5 ft 10 in **WEIGHT** 185 lbs **EYES** Blue **HAIR** Black
SPECIAL POWERS/ABILITIES An expert swordsman, Mordred's mystic power is enhanced when he functions as the male familiar to the sorceress Morgan Le Fay.

The illegitimate son of King Arthur PENDRAGON, Mordred was eventually made a knight of the realm, though evil grew in his heart. Mordred repeatedly tried to usurp the throne of England, but was frequently foiled by Sir Percy, the mysterious BLACK KNIGHT. Eventually, the two men slew each other, but Mordred's ally, the sorceress MORGAN LE FAY drew his essence to her side where she lay, imprisoned in the Netherworld.

Revived and sent into the modern world by the Nether Gods for their own purposes, Mordred frequently battled Dane Whitman, the descendant of Sir Percy, and his allies, the AVENGERS. **TB**

MORLOCKS

FIRST APPEARANCE Uncanny X-Men Vol. 1 #169 (May 1983)
BASE New York City; Kenya
KEY MEMBERS/POWERS Callisto (former leader) Strength, agility, senses **Ape** Shapeshifter **Caliban** Strength and speed, projects fear **D'Gard** Empathic ability **Leech** Projects force field **Marrow** Bone growth, recuperation **Masque** Alters features of other beings **Plague** Creates and projects deadly diseases.

The Morlocks were failed experiments by the DARK BEAST who established their own outcast society in the tunnels beneath New York City. The MARAUDERS, organized by the

ruthless geneticist MISTER SINISTER, slaughtered many Morlocks in what became known as the Mutant Massacre. Mikhail Rasputin, the brother of COLOSSUS, transported most of the survivors to the alternate dimension of "The Hill," where a second generation grew to adulthood. One of their number, named MARROW, founded the terrorist group Gene Nation. Other Morlocks resettled in Africa, where D'Gard led them until Marrow killed him. **DW**

MOY, DR. ALYSSA

FIRST APPEARANCE Fantastic Four #5 (May 1998)
REAL NAME Dr. Alyssa Moy
OCCUPATION Scientist and explorer **BASE** Mobile
HEIGHT 5 ft 9 in **WEIGHT** 129 lbs **EYES** Brown **HAIR** Black
SPECIAL POWERS/ABILITIES A scientific genius on a par with Reed Richards himself, she carries a universal skeleton key and drives a flying car.

Alyssa Moy knew Reed Richards before he founded the FANTASTIC FOUR. The pair became romantically involved and Reed once even proposed to her. They remained in contact after Reed's cosmic mutation and, in recent years, Alyssa has lent occasional support to the Fantastic Four who returned the favor by curing her of a mystical virus. Things did become a little strained when Sue Richards (INVISIBLE WOMAN) learned of Reed's proposal all those years ago, but Alyssa is likely to remain a Fantastic Four ally for some time. **AD**

MS. MARVEL

US Air Force and NASA officer Carol Danvers was assigned to investigate the newly arrived CAPTAIN MAR-VELL. She became involved with Mar-Vell, and her DNA became melded with his during an explosion, giving her powers like his. After she joined the AVENGERS, the villainous Marcus (son of IMMORTUS) brainwashed her into joining him in Limbo. After his death, she escaped to Earth, but soon after lost her powers and memories to the absorbing mutant ROGUE. While working with the X-MEN, she unlocked cosmic powers within herself, and became known as Binary.

When the X-Men took in ROGUE, Carol could not stomach being on the same team with her and left to join the STARJAMMERS. After helping save the Sun, her powers returned to their former levels, and she rejoined the Avengers, now as Warbird. After M-Day, she reclaimed the codename Ms. Marvel. During the Civil War (*see* pp. 84–5), she served with the official Avengers under IRON MAN. However, when Norman Osborn (see GREEN GOBLIN) took over the Avengers after the Secret Invasion (*see* pp. 326–7), she left and joined Hank Pym's rival Avengers team instead. Osborn made MOONSTONE his official Ms. Marvel, giving her Carol's codename and original uniform. **DW, MF**

Experiments by the alien BROOD caused Carol to gain cosmic powers—which she then used against them.

FACTFILE

REAL NAME
Carol Danvers

OCCUPATION
Adventurer

BASE
New York City

HEIGHT 5 ft 11 in
WEIGHT 124 lbs
EYES Blue
HAIR Blonde

FIRST APPEARANCE
Marvel Super-Heroes Vol. 1 #13
(March 1968)

POWERS

Possesses the ability to fly, enhanced strength, damage resistance, and the ability to absorb and rechannel energy.

MULTIPLE MAN

FACTFILE

REAL NAME
Jamie Madrox

OCCUPATION
Detective

BASE
"Mutant Town,"
New York City

HEIGHT 5 ft 11 in
WEIGHT 155 lbs
EYES Blue
HAIR Brown

FIRST APPEARANCE
Giant-Size Fantastic Four #4
(October 1974)

MULTIPLE MAN

After his parents died, Jamie Madrox mutant power to duplicate himself ran riot. The Fantastic Four subdued Madrox, and turned him over to PROFESSOR X so he could learn how to control his mutant talent. But Madrox wasn't comfortable around other people, and chose instead to work with Dr. Moira MACTAGGERT at her Muir Island complex.

Madrox became a member of X-FACTOR, making the first true friends of his life. After X-Factor was disbanded, Madrox sent his duplicates out into the world to experience all the possibilities life had to offer. Recently, however, he has opened a detective agency, X-Factor Investigations, in the heart of Manhattan's Mutant Town district. **TB**

POWERS

Madrox has just one superhuman ability: when struck, he can create duplicates of himself. Each duplicate lasts as long as he wishes and embodies an aspect of his personality. He also has a special suit, which prevents duplication taking place.

Because each of his duplicates is a facet of his personality, Madrox can have problems when he has to make a quick decision.

MUGGINS, MAMIE

FIRST APPEARANCE *Amazing Spider-Man Vol. 1 #139*
(December 1974) **REAL NAME** Mamie Muggins
OCCUPATION Landlady **BASE** New York City
HEIGHT 5 ft 7 in **WEIGHT** 140 lbs
EYES Blue **HAIR** White
SPECIAL POWERS/ABILITIES An uncanny ability to sense when the rent is due.

Mamie Muggins is an apartment superintendent in the Chelsea area of New York City, whose most notable tenant has been Peter Parker, better known as SPIDER-MAN. Mrs. Muggins  lives with her husband Barney, and was known for nagging Peter over his rent payments and interrogating him about the crashing sounds she heard coming from his residence. Her niece Candi lived across the hall from Peter, along with Candi's roommates Bambi and Randi. The trio often sunbathed on the building's roof, hampering Peter's ability to sneak in unnoticed through the building's skylight. **DW**

FACTFILE

NOTABLE MEMBERS
STRYFE
REIGNFIRE
REAPER
FOREARM
TEMPO
STROBE
THUMBELINA
WILDSIDE
ZERO
SKIDS
RUSTY COLLINS
SUMO
KAMIKAZE
CORPUS DERELICTI
DRAGONESS
MOONSTAR
LOCUS
FERAL
SELBY
BLASTFURNACE
BLINDSPOT
BURNOUT
DEADEYE
THERMAL

**FIRST
APPEARANCE**
*New Mutants #86
(February 1990)*

In an altered reality in which Egypt was the sole world power, a Mutant Liberation Front led by Magneto joined forces against that world's ruler, the Sphinx.

MUTANT LIBERATION FRONT

Ostensibly an extremist terrorist cell working forcibly to promote mutant rights, the Mutant Liberation Front most often functioned as the shock troops fighting for the corrupt goals of their various leaders. Initially formed by STRYFE, a clone of CABLE from the future, the MLF staged assorted terrorist events which initially brought them into conflict with the New Mutants, and subsequently with Cable's X-FORCE unit.

When they were of no further use to Stryfe, this incarnation of the MLF was left to its own devices. Reformed by Reignfire, who had been infused with the DNA of the New Mutant SUNSPOT, and who seemed to be Sunspot himself. Again, the MLF clashed repeatedly with X-Force, and eventually they were defeated and the truth of Reignfire's identity was exposed.

The third incarnation of the MLF wasn't composed of mutants, but of humans in armored costumes who posed as mutants so as to increase tensions between humans and mutants. Based at the Last Stand compound of the right wing group Friends of Humanity in Oklahoma, the MLF were later destroyed by the PUNISHER and SHIELD. **TB**

THE MLF (3RD VERSION)
1 Blindspot
2 Blastfurnace
3 Corpus Derelicti
4 Burnout

FACTFILE

MEMBERS AND POWERS
HAVOK (Alex Summers)
Projects concussive force and heat.
BLOODSTORM (Ororo Munroe)
Vampiric powers, controls the weather.
BRUTE (Hank McCoy)
Superhuman strength and agility.
FALLEN (Warren Worthington III)
Has wings enabling flight.
ICE-MAN (Bob Drake)
Generates intense cold.
MARVEL WOMAN
(Madelyne Pryor)
Telekinetic powers.

**FIRST
APPEARANCE**
*Mutant X #1
(October 1998)*

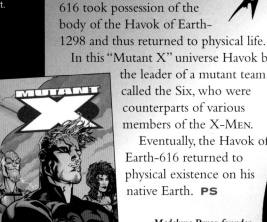

Mutant X #1:
The Six battle the Sentinels.

MUTANT X

Alex Summers, alias the Super Hero HAVOK, a former X-Man on "mainstream" Earth (Earth-616), was seemingly killed in an explosion. At the same time on the Earth of an alternate reality (Earth-1298), its own Havok was brutally killed by a SENTINEL robot. The spirit of the Havok of Earth-616 took possession of the body of the Havok of Earth-1298 and thus returned to physical life.

In this "Mutant X" universe Havok became the leader of a mutant team called the Six, who were counterparts of various members of the X-MEN. Eventually, the Havok of Earth-616 returned to physical existence on his native Earth. **PS**

Madelyne Pryor, founder of the Six, along with Havok, in her Goblyn Queen persona.

THE SIX OF MUTANT X UNIVERSE
1 Bloodstorm 2 Ice-Man 3 Nick Fury of Earth-1298 4 Brute 5 Havok, alias Mutant X 6 SHIELD agent of Earth-1298

MYS-TECH BOARD

In the year 987, seven members of a Druid cult made a bargain with the demon MEPHISTO: in exchange for immortality, they agreed to funnel souls into Mephisto's realm. Over the subsequent millennium, the mages acquired great wealth and became the board members of a London-based corporation named Mys-Tech. To pay their debt to Mephisto, the Mys-Tech board plotted to take over the world and kill vast numbers of innocents. Their assets included the Un-Earth, a model of the planet that operated like a voodoo doll, and the Warheads, mercenaries who could travel through wormholes to other dimensions or times. The board members eventually transformed themselves into beings of even greater power known as the Techno-Wizards. **AD**

MYS-TECH BOARD

1 Porlock
2 Rathcoole
3 Bronwen Gryffn
4 Godrun Tyburn
5 Algernon Crowe
6 Ormond Wychwood

Quentin Beck was a leading special effects designer in Hollywood, but hungry for fame, he became the villain Mysterio. Using illusions to confound SPIDER-MAN, Mysterio became one of his greatest foes, operating both on his own and as a member of the SINISTER SIX. Mysterio once devised an elaborate scheme to drive DAREDEVIL insane. When it failed, Beck killed himself. His old apprentice Daniel Berkhart took up his helmet. At about the same time the mutant Francis Klum acquired Mysterio's costume and equipment from the Kingpin and started to play his role, too. **PS, MF**

MYSTIQUE

Mystique learned to use her mutant shape-shifting powers at an early age. As Raven Darkhölme, she hid her powers so well that she rose to a position of great power within the US Defense Department, giving her access to military secrets and advanced weaponry to use for her criminal purposes. As Mystique, she organized the second Brotherhood of Evil Mutants, teaming with Avalanche, The Blob, Destiny, and PYRO. The Brotherhood attempted to assassinate SENATOR ROBERT KELLY, a vocal enemy of all mutants, but the X-Men stopped them. The Brotherhood later changed its name to Freedom Force and began working for the US government. When that ended, Mystique joined X-Factor. Recently, she joined the X-Men, then betrayed them in the hunt for the first mutant baby born after M-Day. She has two sons: presidential candidate Graydon Creed and the X-Man NIGHTCRAWLER. She also served as a foster mother to the X-Man Rogue. **MT, MF**

Moving with lightning-quick reflexes, Mystique narrowly avoids the path of a guided missile!

MARVEL IN THE
1980s

Extended storylines and limited series were in vogue in the 1980s. The decade began with "The Dark Phoenix Saga" in *X-Men* and the first titles to star Moon Knight and She-Hulk. *Ka-Zar the Savage*, *Dazzler* and "The Court Martial of Yellowjacket" in *Avengers* took center stage in 1981. In 1982, Hercules, Vision and Scarlet Witch and Wolverine all had limited series and "The Mystery of the Hobgoblin" began in *Amazing Spider-Man*. "The Trial of Reed Richards" in *Fantastic Four* and new series featuring Alpha Flight, Falcon, Hawkeye, the Thing and the New Mutants began in 1983. *Jack of Hearts*, *Iceman*, *Prince Namor*, *Power Pack* and *West Coast Avengers* appeared in 1984, as did *Secret Wars*, a 12-issue series that crossed over many other Marvel titles. *Balder the Brave*, *Gargoyle*, *Longshot*, *Nightcrawler* and *Squadron Supreme* were highlights of 1985. Along with *X-Factor*, *Firestar* and *Elektra: Assassin*, the New Universe was launched in 1986 with six titles, including *Justice*, *Kickers, Inc.*, and *Spitfire and the Troubleshooters*. Spider-Man was married in 1987, and 1988 saw the first appearances of Excalibur, Speedball and Wolfpack. Damage Control, Nth Man: the Ultimate Ninja and Quasar were all introduced in 1989.

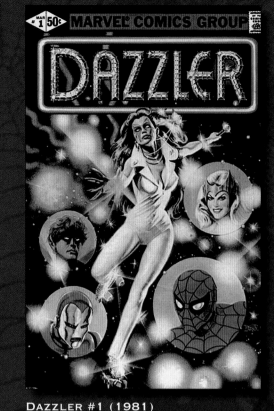

DAZZLER #1 (1981)
Dazzler's first issue is the first monthly Marvel title that is sold exclusively through comic book specialty stores.

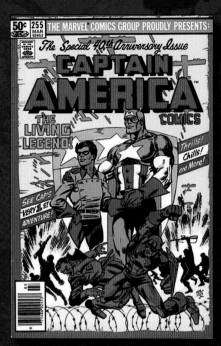

CAPTAIN AMERICA #255 (1981),
Marvel celebrates the 40th Anniversary of Cap's first appearance by revealing never-before-seen facts about his origin.

DAREDEVIL #181 (1982)
Daredevil's first true love challenges his greatest enemy to a battle that ends in her death. (But don't worry—*she eventually gets better!*)

THE AVENGERS #236 (1983)
The Amazing Spider-Man temporarily joins Earth's Mightiest Heroes.

THOR #337 (1983)
The Thunder God learns that he isn't the only one worthy enough to lift his magic hammer in the first chapter of "The Saga of Beta Ray Bill."

CONTEST OF CHAMPIONS #1 (1981)

Marvel's first crossover series featured its most popular Super Heroes battling for their lives.

THE DEATH OF CAPTAIN MARVEL (1982)

Marvel launches its first all-original graphic novel with a story that shows a hero and his final battle with cancer.

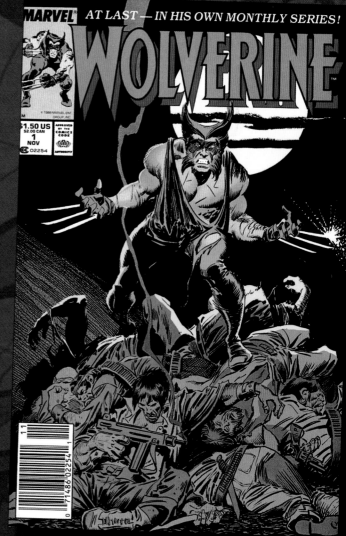

AMAZING SPIDER-MAN #252 (1984)

Spider-Man returns from the Secret Wars with a new costume, which is later revealed to be an alien symbiote.

THE WEST COAST AVENGERS ANNUAL #3 (1988)

Giant-Man guest-stars when the High Evolutionary decides to genetically jumpstart the human race in a storyline that crosses into other Avengers-related annuals.

WOLVERINE VOL. 2 #1 (1988)

After a very successful limited series, Marvel's most popular mutant is finally awarded his own monthly title.

FACTFILE

KEY MEMBERS

HENRY AKAI
As Timestream, he can travel forward or backward in time.

ALBERT DEVOOR
Director of the Nth Project.

ABNER DOOLITTLE
Scientist who designed the dimensional transporter.

DR. T.W. ERWIN
Mathematician famous for his theories of parallel time.

GODWULF
Cybernetic technology allows him to link with computers.

DR. THOMAS LIGHTNER
Magical abilities, on par with Dr. Strange.

BENNETT PITTMAN
Was in charge of Roxxon's extra-dimensional oil drilling facilities. **ANGLER**
Passes through solid material, teleports, travels through hyper-space.

DEATHLOK THE DEMOLISHER
Superhuman strength, agility.

FIRST APPEARANCE
Marvel Two-In-One March #53 (July 1979)

NTH COMMAND

Nth Command was formed by the Roxxon Corporation to gain total control of the world's energy supply. This was done by operatives, known as Nth Commandoes, using devices called Nth projectors, that could transport material from one dimension to another. The sorcerer, Thomas Lightner, was hired to destroy Project Pegasus, so that the Nth Command could gain a monopoly on energy research. Lightner took control of the time-traveling cyborg, DEATHLOK, removed his organic parts, then reprogrammed him to serve Nth Command. Breaking into Project Pegasus with Deathlok, Lightner hoped to use an Nth projector to transport the entire facility to another dimension. He was stopped by the THING, QUASAR, GIANT-MAN, THUNDRA, and the AQUARIAN. **MT**

THE WORLD AWAITS.

Albert DeVoor, Director of the Nth Project, addresses the Nth Commandoes.

N'ASTIRH

FIRST APPEARANCE X-Terminators #1 (October 1988)
REAL NAME N'astirh
OCCUPATION Conqueror, sorcerer   **BASE** Washington, D.C.
HEIGHT/WEIGHT Variable   **EYES** Red   **HAIR** Greenish
SPECIAL POWERS/ABILITIES Able to turn humans into demons, fly and change size; considerable mystical abilities; knowledge of a vast number of magical spells.

N'astirh by name, nasty by nature— that's what they said about this demon from the Limbo dimension. Angered when Limbo's ruler made the human mutant, MAGIK, his apprentice, N'astirh felt compelled to rebel, and when a plan was hatched to take over the Earth, N'astirh usurped the scheme so that he could rule the Earth.

His efforts were foiled by Magik, however N'astirh made a second attempt to become a world conqueror by transforming Madelyne PRYOR into the Goblin Queen. Eventually, the X-MEN destroyed him, and Madelyne Pryor died not long after, proving that no bad deed goes unpunished. **AD**

NAMOR *see opposite page*

FACTFILE

REAL NAME
Aquaria Nautica Neptunia

OCCUPATION
Adventurer

BASE
Formerly Atlantis; mobile

HEIGHT 5 ft 11 in
WEIGHT 189 lbs
EYES Blue
HAIR Blonde

FIRST APPEARANCE:
Marvel Mystery Comics #82 (1947)

POWERS
Superhuman strength (even by Atlantean standards) and durability and can breathe in air or underwater. Formerly had the power of flight.

Namora married an Atlantean named Talan. After Talan was accidentally killed, Namora moved to Lemuria and married Prince Merro.

NAMORA

The Namora of Earth-616 was the cousin of Prince NAMOR the Sub-Mariner. Like Namor, she had pink skin and possessed similar powers. She is considered the "mother" of NAMORITA, her altered clone. LLYRA of Lemuria seemed to have murdered Namora years ago, but Namora recently resurfaced and joined the Agents of Atlas. During World War Hulk she sided with the HULK. Another Namora was Earth-2189's female counterpart of Namor, but had blue skin. As queen of Atlantis, she conquered her world before joining the EXILES, a team of interdimensional adventurers. She was finally slain by an alternate version of Hyperion. **PS, MF**

Wings on Namora's heels—now withered away—once enabled her to fly.

Unlike Namor, the Exiles' Namora had two water-breathing Atlantean parents. In conquering the surface world, Namora killed her alternate Earth's Avengers and Fantastic Four.

NAMOR

Ruler of the undersea realm of Atlantis

Prince Namor is the mutant son of a blue-skinned Atlantean princess and an American sea captain. He was raised in the underwater kingdom of Atlantis and grew up hating all surface dwellers. During World War II, Namor briefly sided with the Allies against the Axis Powers and joined the super-teams known as the INVADERS and the Liberty Legion.

Occasionally Namor helps protect the surface world but his priority is the welfare of the people of Atlantis.

After repeatedly battling the Fantastic Four, Namor eventually made peace with them and is now their greatest ally.

FACTFILE

REAL NAME
Prince Namor, aka Namor McKenzie, aka the Sub-Mariner

OCCUPATION
Lord of Atlantis,
CEO of Oracle, Inc.

BASE Atlantis

HEIGHT 6 ft 2 in
WEIGHT 278 lbs
EYES Blue-gray
HAIR Black

FIRST APPEARANCE
*Motion Picture Funnies
Weekly (April 1939)*

NAMOR

THE ALL-WINNER

After the war, Namor became a member of the ALL-WINNERS SQUAD, but returned to Atlantis when the Squad disbanded in 1949. He returned to the surface world in the late 1950s where he encountered a man called DESTINY who removed his memory and sent him to New York where he lived as a derelict. His memory was restored by Johnny Storm, the HUMAN TORCH, but Namor turned against the human race when he learned that the city of Atlantis had been destroyed in his absence. During his first battle with the FANTASTIC FOUR, Namor fell in love with the INVISIBLE WOMAN (who was called the Invisible Girl at the time) and offered to spare mankind if she became his bride. He later attempted to win her by buying a movie studio and offering the Fantastic Four a million dollars to star in a major motion picture when they briefly ran short of funds.

While traveling in the arctic, Namor once stumbled upon a tribe of Eskimos who were worshiping a figure frozen in ice. In a fury, Namor hurled the figure into the sea. The ice melted to reveal CAPTAIN AMERICA, who was later picked up and revived by the AVENGERS.

POWERS

Super-strength, stamina and durability (these traits decline the more time he spends out of water). Amphibious; can swim underwater at 60 mph; can see clearly in the ocean depths. Telepathic rapport with marine life and can duplicate many of their abilities; wings on ankles enable flight; long-lived.

TRAGIC LOVES

Namor has been married twice, to Lady Dorma and then to Marrina, but both subsequently died. He has also been romantically linked to the INVISIBLE WOMAN and Emma FROST. Recently, Namor discovered he had a son, Kamor, who tried to take over Atlantis by starting a war with the US. To stop this, Namor evacuated the Atlanteans to Latveria and detonated the villain NITRO within Atlantis, destroying it. Namor was one of the members of the ILLUMINATI and has since joined the Cabal (see ILLUMINATI) making him the only person to be part of both. **TD, MF**

Namor became smitten with Sue Storm, but gallantly stepped aside once she decided to marry Reed Richards.

ESSENTIAL STORYLINES

• *Fantastic Four #4* Namor regains his memory and declares war on the surface world.
• *Fantastic Four Annual #1* Namor is reunited with the kingdom of Atlantis and invades New York City.
• *Tales To Astonish #70-76* Namor seeks the sacred trident of Neptune and proves that he is worthy to rule Atlantis.
• *Marvel Feature #1* Helps form the Defenders.
• *Avengers #262* Namor joins the Avengers.

POWERS

Namorita is amphibious: able to survive on land and in the sea; power of flight; her hands exude a paralyzing toxin; chameleon-like ability to camouflage herself.

NAMORITA

Half-human, half-Atlantean, Namorita was a clone of her mother, Namora, although she was an adult before she discovered this fact. Orphaned when she was still a child, Namorita was watched over by NAMOR the Sub-Mariner and his friend Betty Prentiss. It was their love and support that carried Namorita through the tragic and traumatic loss of her mother. When she became an adult, they also helped and encouraged her to attend a US college.

An Atlantean in a human world, the New Warriors helped Namorita stave off isolation.

Not long after starting college, Namorita became a founder member of the NEW WARRIORS, a team of young Super Heroes, with whom she fought against the Hellions, PROTEUS and TERRAX. The group provided Namorita with a certain amount of security and stability, but not all her time with them was happy: her first attempt to lead the team resulted in the kidnap of many team members' families. They were eventually rescued, but Namorita left the team in shame. She tried to return to Atlantis, but she was shut out because the people there had finally learned she was a clone. She returned to the New Warriors and was with them when NITRO blew up a large chunk of Stamford, Connecticut, killing her along with most of her friends. **AD, MF**

NEBULA

Claiming to be the grand-daughter of the mad Titan THANOS, Nebula embarked on a career as a space pirate, hijacking Thanos' old flagship *Sanctuary II* and attempting to conquer the fragmented SKRULL Empire. Her ambitions were thwarted by the AVENGERS, but not before she inflicted catastrophic damage upon the planet Xandar. When Thanos was reborn, he denied any relationship to Nebula, who nevertheless almost succeeded in wresting the omnipotent Infinity Gauntlet away from him. She then attacked NOVA, claiming that her father had been Zorr, a menace destroyed by the hero's predecessor, Nova Prime. Nebula's identity was also adopted for a time by RAVONNA the Terminatrix. **TB**

NEKRA

Gemma Sinclair and Frederick Beechman were accidentally exposed to radiation at the Los Alamos Atomic Proving Grounds. As a result, Gemma's daughter Nekra was born a mutant with chalk-white skin. An outcast, she teamed up with Beechman's mutant son Jerome, who had apelike features. As they grew older, they discovered their superhuman powers. As Nekra and the MANDRILL, they attempted to conquer three African nations and later the United States.

Nekra became leader of a fanatical religious cult. Afterwards, she became the ally of the Avengers' foe, the GRIM REAPER. He killed her, but she was resurrected by HELLSTORM. **PS**

NOMAD

FIRST APPEARANCE Captain America Vol. 1 #282 (June 1983)

REAL NAME Jack Monroe

OCCUPATION Adventurer **BASE** Mobile

HEIGHT 5 ft 11 in **WEIGHT** 200 lbs

EYES Brown **HAIR** Brown

SPECIAL POWERS/ABILITIES Physical perfection through the super-soldier formula; skilled at throwing stun discs.

During the 1950s, young Jack Monroe became the "Bucky" sidekick of the replacement CAPTAIN AMERICA active during that period. The two battled Communists until the super soldier formula affected their sanity; the US government then placed Monroe in suspended animation. SHIELD helped cure Monroe's madness upon his reawakening decades later, and he worked with the real Captain America as Nomad. Later, government agent Henry GYRICH placed Nomad under nanobot control and forced him to become the newest SCOURGE OF THE UNDERWORLD. The mysterious Winter Soldier recently assassinated Nomad. **DW**

NORTH, DAKOTA

FIRST APPEARANCE Dakota North #1 (June 1986)

REAL NAME Dakota North

OCCUPATION Private investigator; former fashion model

BASE Mobile **HEIGHT** 5 ft 7 in **WEIGHT** 130 lbs

EYES Blue-gray **HAIR** Auburn

SPECIAL POWERS/ABILITIES Adept hand-to-hand combatant and skilled gymnast; accomplished with various firearms.

The daughter of a US intelligence agent, Dakota North pursued a career as a model before establishing a highly successful private investigation firm named North Security. Boasting branch offices across the globe, North Security rapidly gained a formidable reputation, taking on a multitude of cases that ranged from the mundane to the outright dangerous.

During one particularly difficult case, an international arms dealer who was attempting to gain possession of an experimental nerve gas pursued Dakota across Europe. However Dakota survived this encounter and her organization is still thought to be going strong. **AD**

NORTHSTAR

FIRST APPEARANCE Uncanny X-Men Vol. 1 #120 (April 1979)

REAL NAME Jean-Paul Baubier

OCCUPATION Member of Alpha Flight

BASE Tamarind Island, British Columbia, Canada

HEIGHT 5 ft 11 in **WEIGHT** 185 lbs **EYES** Blue **HAIR** Black

SPECIAL POWERS/ABILITIES

Can redirect the kinetic motion of his body's molecules.

Jean-Paul's and his twin sister Jeanne-Marie's (AURORA'S) parents died when they were young. They were adopted separately but finally reunited when he joined ALPHA FLIGHT as Northstar. One of the first Super Heroes to come out as gay, he later joined the X-MEN. He was killed by a HYDRA-brainwashed WOLVERINE and resurrected as a HYDRA drone. Northstar then attacked the SHIELD helicarrier but was captured and eventually deprogrammed. He retained his powers after M-Day and helped the X-Men battle the Skrulls during the Secret Invasion (see pp. 326-7). **DW, MF**

NOVA

High school student Rider became cosmic adventurer Nova.

Mortally wounded, Rhomann Dey—a Centurion of the Nova Corps, the space militia of the alien Xandarians—transferred his powers to student Richard Rider. As Nova, Rider became a crimefighter on Earth, then later traveled into space and became one of the Champions of Xandar. Returning to Earth, Nova joined the NEW WARRIORS. Back in space, Rider helped rebuild Xandar and the Nova Corps and became its leader, Centurion Prime. Rider saw Xandar destroyed in during the Annihilation (see pp. 30–1) and became the repository of the Xandarian Worldmind. He later killed ANNIHILUS. During the second Annihilation, he brought in the Technarchy to defeat the PHALANX. He became embroiled in the Shi'ar-Kree "War of Kings," as the latest QUASAR. Frankie Raye, stepdaughter of Phineas T. Horton, creator of the first HUMAN TORCH, also assumed the name Nova after becoming the herald of Galactus. She was later killed by the alien Morg. **PS, MF**

FACTFILE

REAL NAME
Richard Rider

OCCUPATION
Adventurer

BASE
New York City

HEIGHT 5 ft 9 in
WEIGHT 145 lbs
EYES Brown
HAIR Brown

FIRST APPEARANCE
Nova Vol. 1 #1 (September 1976); (as Frankie Raye) Fantastic Four #164 (November 1975)

NOVA

POWERS

The first Nova has superhuman strength and durability and the power to fly at supersonic speed. The second Nova could manipulate cosmic energy as stellar fire. She could project stellar energy, had nearly total invulnerability, and could survive unprotected in space.

Nova initially operated solo, but he has also worked with heroes like Doctor Strange, the Hulk and Wolverine. Nova has been a member of the New Warriors, the Champions of Xandar and the Nova Corps.

O

OCCULUS

FIRST APPEARANCE Fantastic Four #363 (April 1992)
REAL NAME Unrevealed **OCCUPATION** Absolute Monarch of an unnamed world in the Inniverse **BASE** Castle Occulus
HEIGHT 6 ft 4 in **WEIGHT** 290 lbs **EYES** Black **HAIR** Black
SPECIAL POWERS/ABILITIES Gem in place of his right eye draws energy from power crystals. Fires beams of concussive force, heat, and light from his gem-eye and hands. Can fly and form force-fields.

Occulus and his brother Wildblood were children of the Inniverse, a dimensional plane that exists between the subatomic particles of matter. Like all their kind, they were tested by the Gem Guild to see if they possessed the ability to manipulate the power gems that supplied their world with energy. Occulus had the gift and joined the Guild. He grew in power until he ruled his entire world. When Wildblood escaped to Earth, soldiers sent by Occulus to capture him also kidnapped Sue and Franklin RICHARDS. Occulus intended to use Franklin's psionic abilities for his own ends, but Mr. Fantastic arrived with the rest of the FANTASTIC FOUR to rescue his wife and son. **TB**

OGUN

FIRST APPEARANCE Kitty Pryde and Wolverine #2 (December 1984)
REAL NAME Ogun
OCCUPATION Assassin **BASE** Japan
HEIGHT 5 ft 9 in **WEIGHT** 146 lbs **EYES** Blue **HAIR** Black
SPECIAL POWERS/ABILITIES A master martial artist and expert swordsman. As a spirit, Ogun can possess the bodies of others, and is immune to physical harm.

A legendary sorcerer and warrior who may have been born as early as the 17th century, Ogun trained WOLVERINE in the martial arts. Originally a man of integrity, Ogun was eventually corrupted by the dark sorceries that kept him alive and invulnerable to harm, and he turned to the path of evil. As revenge against his former pupil, Ogun mentally enslaved Kitty PRYDE, training her and sending her to kill Wolverine. But Wolverine ultimately freed Kitty, and together they slew Ogun's physical form. However, Ogun survived as a spirit, bound to the demon mask he once wore, and now can possess other beings of weaker will and employ them as puppets in the material world. **TB**

OMEGA RED

FIRST APPEARANCE X-Men Vol. 2 #4 (January 1992)
REAL NAME Arkady Rossovich
OCCUPATION Crime lord **BASE** Crime lord
HEIGHT 6 ft 11 in **WEIGHT** 425 lbs **EYES** Red **HAIR** Blonde
SPECIAL POWERS/ABILITIES Possesses enhanced strength and mutant healing factor; body secretes deadly pheromones; has carbonadium coils implanted in arms.

Omega Red is the product of the KGB's attempt to create a Soviet super-soldier. The test subject, former serial killer Arkady Rossovich, gained mutant powers after receiving genetic treatments, though complications required him to drain the life energy of victims to survive. Placed in suspended animation by the Soviets, Omega Red reemerged after the fall of communism and sought a carbonadium synthesizer to stabilize his condition. For a while, he led New York's Red Mafia. He is now in SHIELD custody. **DW, MF**

ONSLAUGHT

During a ferocious battle between the X-Men and MAGNETO's Acolytes, PROFESSOR X shut down Magneto's brain. At that moment, Xavier's own dark fears, doubts, and frustrations combined with Magneto's anger and lust for revenge, to form a new being: Onslaught. This creature lay dormant in Xavier's mind, only manifesting itself when the Professor's frustrations came to the fore. When Onslaught finally took over the Professor's body, the X-Men quickly realized what had happened. However, they were unable to prevent Onslaught's capture of Franklin RICHARDS, a mutant with reality-altering powers. Inevitably, Onslaught's activities came to the attention of the FANTASTIC FOUR and the AVENGERS. Although Xavier was eventually freed and Onslaught was destroyed, the cost was significant. Many Super Heroes were catapulted to a pocket universe and presumed dead, only returning to the Earth several months later. Recently Onslaught returned, reenergized by the collective mutant powers lost on M-Day. He is currently trapped in the Negative Zone. **AD, MF**

By trapping Franklin Richards inside his body, Onslaught could tap into the boy's power to restructure reality.

FACTFILE
REAL NAME Not applicable
OCCUPATION Would be world-conqueror
BASE New York City
HEIGHT 10 ft **WEIGHT** 900 lbs **EYES** Red **HAIR** None
FIRST APPEARANCE X-Men #15 (May 1996)

ONSLAUGHT

POWERS Onslaught possessed Xavier's mental abilities combined with Magneto's powers of magnetism. He was able to induce illusions, amnesia, or paralysis, and manipulate magnetic fields. He also had powers of telekinesis and astral projection.

OMEGA FLIGHT

Canada's final answer for its national team

With help from SHIELD, Canada formed Omega Flight to help out with the Fifty State Initiative of their southern neighbors.

Three teams have used the name Omega Flight, each in response to the existence of ALPHA FLIGHT, which was intended to be the official national Super Hero team of Canada.

THE FIRST OMEGAS

Jerry Jaxson of Roxxon Oil formed the first team to kill Alpha Flight and steal GUARDIAN's battlesuit, which he claimed to have invented himself. He gathered several superpowered Canadians for his team, including Box, Diamond Lil, Flashback, Smart Alec, and WILD CHILD. When Roger Bochs balked at murder, Jaxson took over his Box robot, controlling it himself. Jaxson died in their first battle, and for a long while it seemed that Guardian had too.

Sasquatch worked hard to form the team, although he met resistance from old friends like Talisman.

Omega Flight first faced off against the Wrecking Crew, which had come to Canada to avoid the Fifty State Initiative.

ESSENTIAL STORYLINES
• *Alpha Flight #11–12:* The introduction of the first Omega Flight, and the death of Jerry Jaxson and Guardian.
• *Alpha Flight #128–130:* The introduction of Antiguard and the end of the second version of Omega Flight.
• *Omega Flight #1–5:* The creation of the new, heroic Omega Flight.

THE MASTER'S OMEGAS

A Super Villain called the Master of the World formed the second Omega Flight as part of his plans to rule the planet. His team included Bile, Brain Drain, Miss Mass, Sinew, Strongarm, and Technoir. He first pitted them against Beta Flight, a group of heroes in training to become members of Alpha Flight. When that failed, he decided to take over the Canadian government from within, calling himself Joshua Lord. He discovered the missing Guardian trapped in another dimension, and he rescued the hero and brainwashed him into becoming the villainous Antiguard. Fighting alongside Antiguard, Omega Flight nearly destroyed Alpha Flight. Only after Guardian's wife, Heather Hudson (VINDICATOR), finally got through to him did the tide turn against Omega Flight.

OMEGA HEROES

After the near-total destruction of Alpha Flight by the Collective following M-Day, the Canadian government formed a new version of the team, calling it Canada's last line of defense. The new team was headed by SASQUATCH and included American heroes ARACHNE and the US AGENT alongside Talisman and the new Guardian, Michael Pointer. Ironically it was Pointer who had accidentally destroyed Alpha Flight after unwittingly absorbing the mutant powers lost on M-Day. The team did not last long and, after defeating the Wrecking Crew and demons of Surtur, went their separate ways.

MF

OMEGA FLIGHT

FACTFILE

NOTABLE MEMBERS

ARACHNE
Formerly Spider-Woman, with superhuman agility, speed, and strength, plus a healing factor, wall-crawling, and psi-webs.

GUARDIAN
Can absorb energy, fire energy blasts, and fly.

SASQUATCH
Furry giant with superhuman durability, strength, and endurance, sharp claws, a healing factor, and genius intellect.

OTHER MEMBERS
BETA RAY BILL, TALISMAN, U.S. AGENT

BASE
Canadian Secret Intelligence Service, Ottawa, Canada

FIRST APPEARANCE
(original) Alpha Flight #11 (June, 1984); (second) Alpha Flight #110 (September, 1992); (current) Civil War: The Initiative #1 (April, 2007)

ORDER, THE
California's Fifty State Initiative Team

FACTFILE

NOTABLE MEMBERS

ANTHEM (Henry Hellrung) Actor and team leader, fires electric blasts, flight.

ARALUNE (Rebecca "Becky" Ryan) Pop star, shapeshifter, flight.

CALAMITY (James Wa) Ex-athlete, engineer, superhuman speed, flight.

VIRGINIA "PEPPER" POTTS Executive, uses telepresence equipment to tap Stark satellites and coordinate team strategy.

SUPERNAUT (Milo Fields) Pilots massive armor suit.

VEDA (Magdelena "Maggie" Neuntauben) Actress, generates and controls golems and can see through their eyes.

BASE Bradbury, California

FIRST APPEARANCE:
Civil War #6 (January 2007)

Two teams have called themselves the Order. The first was the DEFENDERS while the second was created for the Fifty State Initiative (*see* pp. 118–9).

DEFENDING THE ORDER

One of the first foes the Defenders fought was the alien scientist Yandroth. As he died, he cursed the original Defenders—the HULK, NAMOR, the SILVER SURFER, and DOCTOR STRANGE—to always reunite whenever catastrophe struck the Earth. Worst of all, every time they did, they would become more and more selfish. Unaware of the curse, these Defenders eventually decided to form the Order and take an active interest in shaping the world's future.

The other Defenders figured this out and broke Yandroth's curse, foiling his plan to be reborn with the negative energy the Order was generating around the planet. The Earth goddess Gaea gave NIGHTHAWK the power to call the Defenders together instead, but without any of the side effects. After the end of the Civil War (*see* pp. 84–5), Tony Stark (IRON MAN) became the director of SHIELD. Already the leader of the AVENGERS, he decided to launch the Fifty State Initiative (*see* pp. 118–9), which planned to put a team of heroes in every state in the nation.

Stark formed the team for California from scratch, using handpicked people without any pre-existing powers. He put his most trusted employee, Pepper POTTS, in charge of the team. For the field leader, he tapped Henry Hellrung, an actor who had played Tony Stark in films—and who also had sponsored Tony in Alcoholics Anonymous. Together, they trained a crew of actors, singers, and other entertainers to become the Initiative's California team. The roster included: Anthem (Henry Hellrung), Aralune, Calamity, Supernaut, and Veda, as well as Aphrodite, Avona, Bannerman Brown and Green, Corona, Heavy, Maul, Mulholland, and Pierce.

The team's structure followed that of the Olympian gods. Stark served as Zeus, Potts as Hera, and Hellrung as Apollo, with the other members of the team in various roles. The roles were more important than the people who filled them. If members misbehaved or disobeyed orders, they could be fired and their powers stripped from them. They were then replaced with eager, new heroes-to-be.

The group first saw action in the final battle against CAPTAIN AMERICA's resistance. They clashed with villains, such as the female gang called the Black Dahlias, controlled by Ezekiel STANE. They also fought against the SKRULLS during the Secret Invasion (*see* pp. 326–7), being one of the few Initiative teams to have avoided Skrull infiltration. **MF**

In their first solo outing, the Order faced off against the Infernal Man and lost two members, the androids Bannerman Brown and Green.

THE ORDER

1 Alarune **2** Supernaut **3** Anthem
4 Calamity **5** Veda **6** Mulholland

ESSENTIAL STORYLINES

• *The Order Vol. 1 #1–6*
The original Order forms out of Yandroth's curse—and the Defenders stop them.

• *The Order Vol. 2 #1–10*
The entire run of the second version of the Order is only 10 issues, covering from its origins to its demise as a public-relations-focused team.

ORPHAN

FIRST APPEARANCE X-Force #117 (June 2001)

REAL NAME Guy Smith

OCCUPATION Adventurer **BASE** X-Force/X-Statix Tower in Santa Monica, California.

HEIGHT 5 ft 10 in **WEIGHT** 190 lbs **EYES** Green **HAIR** White

SPECIAL POWERS/ABILITIES Superhuman senses, superhuman speed, and the ability to levitate himself.

Erroneously believing his parents died in a house fire, Guy Smith was raised as an orphan. As his mutant powers emerged, he became extremely sensitive to his surroundings. Professor X designed a special costume for him that allowed him to control his senses, and Guy took to calling himself Mister Sensitive. When he joined the mutant team X-Force (later called X-Statix), he changed his code name to Orphan. He fell in love with teammate U-Go Girl, and her death crushed him. He died on X-Statix's final mission, he and U-Go Girl reuniting in Heaven. **MT, MF**

ORPHAN-MAKER

FIRST APPEARANCE X-Factor Vol. 1 #30 (July 1988)

REAL NAME Peter (last name unrevealed)

OCCUPATION Warrior **BASE** Mobile

HEIGHT 7 ft 1 in **WEIGHT** Unrevealed

EYES Unrevealed **HAIR** Unrevealed

SPECIAL POWERS/ABILITIES Carries an arsenal of guns; armored battlesuit protects against most damage.

Never seen out of his armored battlesuit, the Orphan-Maker was once a mutant child named Peter. Peter was subject to the cruel experimentations of Mister Sinister, who planned to kill the boy when he had no further use for him. The cyborg known as Nanny saved Peter and indoctrinated him in her philosophy of rescuing mutant children from threats both real and imaginary. As the first of Nanny's "Lost Boys and Girls," Orphan-Maker abducted young mutants and killed their parents, clashing with X-Factor and Generation X. **DW**

OSBORN, LIZ

Liz Allan married Harry Osborn (Green Goblin II) and had a son with him, whom they named Norman Osborn II. After Harry's death, Liz took over Osborn Industries, but lost control of the company after the original Norman Osborn's shocking return from the grave. Liz had a brief relationship with Foggy Nelson, but raising her son and caring for her stepbrother occupied most of her time. She was shocked when Harry returned from the grave as well, and they have not reconciled, despite the fact that Harry recently helped cure Raxton of his uncontrollable powers. **DW, MF**

In high school, Liz sometimes joined in when Flash Thompson mocked Peter Parker. She soon matured and befriended Peter.

FACTFILE

REAL NAME
Elizabeth Allan-Osborn

OCCUPATION
Former businesswoman

BASE
Mobile

HEIGHT 5 ft 9 in
WEIGHT 135 lbs
EYES Blue
HAIR Blonde

FIRST APPEARANCE
Amazing Fantasy Vol. 1 #15 (August 1962)

OSBORN, LIZ

OVERMIND

FIRST APPEARANCE Fantastic Four #113 (August 1971)

REAL NAME Grom

OCCUPATION Conqueror **BASE** Various

HEIGHT 10 ft **WEIGHT** 750 lbs **EYES** Black **HAIR** Red

SPECIAL POWERS/ABILITIES Possesses vast psionic powers. He can lift up to 70 tons, read the minds of others and manipulate matter through the power of his mind.

Grom led the interplanetary conquerors known as the Eternals to victory as they enslaved a thousand worlds. But when they faced defeat on the enormous world Gigantus, the Eternals selected Grom to be the sole survivor of their race and transferred their mental energies to him, making him into the Overmind. When he came to conquer Earth, the Fantastic Four, Dr. Doom, and the Stranger stopped him. After that, he tried to conquer Earth-712, but Squadron Supreme defeated him, reducing his powers. He joined the Defenders for a while, but recently he was forced to work for the Thunderbolts to avoid jail. **TB, MF**

The Overmind's existence was prophesied throughout the galaxy: "From Beyond the Stars Shall Come The Overmind—And He Shall Crush The Universe!"

FACTFILE

REAL NAME
Karen Page
OCCUPATION
Sometime secretary, actress and radio personality
BASE
New York City

HEIGHT 5 ft 7 in
WEIGHT 125 lbs
EYES Blue
HAIR Blonde

FIRST APPEARANCE:
Daredevil #1 (April 1964)

Efficient secretarial skills and fair ability as an actor and presenter; some aptitude for street fighting, having battled alongside both Daredevil and Black Widow.

Karen's love for Matt was always troubled.

PAGE, KAREN

Karen Page's relationship with Matt Murdock spawned happiness but also much mutual heartache. Matt hired her as his secretary, but their relationship only blossomed when he told her about his secret identity. This happiness was not to last: in the middle of wedding preparations, Karen asked Matt to give up his DAREDEVIL alter ego. When he refused she ended the engagement and entered a long vicious cycle of self-destruction.

Embarking on a career as an actress, things went badly. As film and TV work dried up she became involved in the porn industry and fell prey to heroin addiction. At her lowest ebb, Karen told a dealer Matt's secret identity in exchange for drugs. Fortunately, Matt is a man with a forgiving heart. After helping her kick the habit, their relationship continued intermittently until she was killed—just another of Matt's lovers to fall at BULLSEYE's hand. **AD**

PALADIN

FIRST APPEARANCE Daredevil Vol. 1 #150 (January 1978)
REAL NAME Paul Denning
OCCUPATION Mercenary **BASE** Mobile
HEIGHT 6 ft 2 in **WEIGHT** 225 lbs **EYES** Brown **HAIR** Brown
SPECIAL POWERS/ABILITIES Enhanced strength, stamina, and reflexes; carries a nerve-scrambling stun gun; costume deflects most small-arms fire and goggles permit vision in darkness.

Paladin has teamed with Spider-Man to advance his mercenary career.

Paladin is infamous for his arrogance and his mercenary attitude, yet his considerable charm has gotten him far in life. Little is known about his origins. He has allied with many heroes, but he doesn't hesitate to abandon his partners if he's not getting paid. He's even accepted contracts on heroes like DAREDEVIL and the PUNISHER. Paladin has often worked with SILVER SABLE's Wild Pack. Recently, he joined Misty KNIGHT's Heroes for Hire, but only to get close to capturing CAPTAIN AMERICA. Currently, he works with the latest incarnation of the THUNDERBOLTS. **DW, MF**

PANTHEON

Making a secret stand for human rights

The Pantheon is a family of long-lived superhumans who style themselves after the Greek gods of old. Centuries ago, Vali, their patriarch, bartered with the alien race known as the Troyjans for the secret of eternal youth. Afterwards, now known as Agamemnon, he fathered several children and adopted others, creating an organization of superhuman operatives bolstered by non-enhanced doctors, scientists and technicians.

ADLANNA! YOOR OK!

I SAFED YOO!

SURE I'M OK BIG GUY. I'M PRETTY STURDY, AND BESIDES, I GOT YOU AROUND TO WATCH MY BACK, HEY?

The Pantheon operated as a covert strike team, pledged to maintaining the stability of the world.

THE PANTHEON
1 Paris **2** Ajax **3** Hector
4 Ulysses **5** Atalanta

ENTER THE HULK

Agamemnon feared that mankind would destroy or despoil the Earth, so he and his clan moved in secret to prevent potential disasters before they could reach fruition. The Pantheon's existence first became known to the world at large when it moved to recruit Bruce Banner, the incredible HULK, to its ranks. At that time, the Hulk's fragmented psyche had been somewhat restored, giving him the intellect of Banner with the massive strength and power of the Hulk. Wanting to make amends for the destruction he'd caused to the world while he was no more than a rampaging brute, the Hulk agreed to joining Agamemnon's cause, and eventually came to function as the Pantheon's field leader.

For a time, the Hulk led the Pantheon, as in this battle against the Endless Knights.

THE PANTHEON AT WAR

But things went wrong when the Troyjans returned to Earth, and the truth about Vali's deal with them came out: in exchange for the secret of bestowing his godly attributes and extended lifespan on his offspring, Vali had promised to give the best of them up to the Troyjans to use as they saw fit. A vast battle ensued, in which the Troyjans were repelled and Agamemnon was taken into custody by the Pantheon. He responded by summoning the Endless Knights, massive zombie warriors whose ranks included undead former members of the Pantheon itself, and commanding them to destroy the Pantheon's base, the Mount. Though the Pantheon survived this attack, its ranks were decimated, and the Hulk left, having gone through another psychological shift that changed the nature of his transformations. Since then, the Pantheon has gone back underground. It is presumed to have returned to covertly interfering in the affairs of man whenever the future of mankind is imperiled. **TB**

The Pantheon had access to high-tech weaponry

FACTFILE

NOTABLE MEMBERS
ACHILLES Virtually invulnerable; his invulnerability is weakened by the presence of gamma radiation.
AGAMEMNON Immortality; ability to project a holographic representation of himself.
AJAX Massive superhuman strength and a childlike intellect.
ATALANTA Fires energy arrows.
CASSIOPEIA Fires energy blasts fueled by starlight.
DELPHI Able to see glimpses of the future.
HECTOR Trained fighter; can walk on air; carries a plasma mace.
PARIS Possesses an empathetic sense of those around him.
PROMETHEUS Drives a high-tech armored vehicle.
ULYSSES Expert fighter; carries an energy sword and shield.

OTHER MEMBERS
ANDROMEDA, JASON, PERSEUS

BASE
The Mount, Arizona

FIRST APPEARANCE
Incredible Hulk Vol. 2 #377
(January 1991)

ESSENTIAL STORYLINES
• *Hulk #372–379*
The Pantheon recruits the newly-intelligent Hulk into their organization.
• *Hulk #422–425*
During his trial, Agamemnon summons the Endless Knights to destroy the Pantheon and the Hulk.

FACTFILE

REAL NAME
May Reilly Parker

OCCUPATION
Homemaker

BASE
New York City

HEIGHT 5 ft 5 in
WEIGHT 110 lbs
EYES Blue
HAIR White

FIRST APPEARANCE:
Amazing Fantasy #15
(August 1962)

POWERS

Amazing cook, (particularly her corn beef hash) and formidable personality—even Wolverine is afraid of her.

PARKER, AUNT MAY

It may not have always been easy, but May Parker's life has certainly been eventful. Following a difficult childhood, May found love with Ben Parker, their marriage being further enriched when they became guardians to Ben's nephew, Peter. Sadly, their life together ended prematurely when Ben was shot dead by a burglar. The years that followed would be testing.

Happening upon Peter's ragged Spider-Man costume, May finally realised the startling truth about her nephew.

After Peter became SPIDER-MAN, he kept his secret identity from her for fear of upsetting her health. She learned it at one point, but she has now forgotten. An assassin hired by the KINGPIN shot May after Spider-Man revealed his identity to the world during the Civil War (*see* pp.84–5).

Spider-Man intervened just in time to prevent Dr. Octopus from marrying May.

To save her life, Peter and his wife Mary Jane Watson gave up their entire marriage to MEPHISTO, who wiped it—and everyone's memory of Peter's secret—from existence. Restored to health, she now volunteers at a homeless shelter. **AD, MF**

PARKER, UNCLE BEN

Although never rich, his wisdom and fair-mindedness earned Ben Parker the respect of everyone he met. A carnival barker in his youth, Ben grew up in the same neighbourhood as May Reilly, for whom he harbored deep feelings. Love did not come easily to the pair, though— Ben was forced to compete for May's affections with the glamorous Johnny Jerome. It was only when May learnt that Johnny was a petty crook that she finally accepted Ben into her life.

Following his brother's death, Ben felt honor bound to raise his nephew, Peter, as his very own.

Throughout their time together, Ben and May were to struggle financially, and these monetary straits only worsened when they adopted Ben's nephew, Peter, as their own. In spite of these pressures, however, Peter brought considerable joy into their lives. Tragically that joy would be cut short, when Ben was killed by a burglar's bullet.

The memory of his kindly uncle inspired Peter to use his newfound spider powers to do good in the world, and so Ben Parker's spirit lives on. **AD**

Ben's tragic murder continues to inspire Peter Parker, even to this day.

FACTFILE

REAL NAME
Benjamin Parker

OCCUPATION
Retired

BASE
New York City

HEIGHT 5 ft 9 in
WEIGHT 175 lbs
EYES Blue
HAIR White

FIRST APPEARANCE
Amazing Fantasy #15
(August 1962)

POWERS

Wisdom, charisma, integrity, strength of personality and high moral standards.

PATRIOT

Elijah Bradley is the grandson of Isaiah Bradley, the black CAPTAIN AMERICA of World War II, whose mind had been reduced to that of a child by the super-soldier serum that empowered him. When IRON LAD needed help battling KANG the Conqueror, Eli resorted to using the designer drug MGH to give himself superhuman powers so he could become a founding member of the YOUNG AVENGERS. When his teammates learned that Eli was using such dangerous drugs, they convinced him to give them up. Critically wounded saving the original Captain America from a KREE attack, Eli received a blood transfusion from his grandfather. This saved his life and also gave him Isaiah's superpowers.

During the Civil War (*see* pp. 84-5), Eli and most of the Young Avengers sided with Captain America's anti-registration forces. **TB, MF**

YOUNG AVENGERS
1 Wiccan
2 Stature
3 Hulkling
4 The Patriot
5 Kate Bishop

Eddie Dyson was a rookie police officer in the NYPD when he discovered his squad were taking payment to the local mob. He sought the PUNISHER's advice who persuaded him to expose their corruption to Internal Affairs. The mafia took revenge and killed Dyson's family. Dyson became Payback to avenge his family's death. At first, he blamed the Punisher for their murders, but the two made peace when the Punisher helped Payback kill Steve Venture—the mobster responsible for the family's death. Dyson retired for a short time, but he was attacked by Vigil, and became Payback again. He fought Vigil, Heathen and the Trust with Lynn Michaels then fled for the Midwest with her and her father. **DW**

PENDRAGON, KING ARTHUR

Arthur reigned supreme as King of England.

King Arthur, who ruled England in the 6th century, is one of history's most celebrated figures. The son of Uther Pendragon, Arthur grew up in the care of Sir Ector, with the wizard MERLIN as his tutor. When Arthur pulled an enchanted sword from a stone and anvil, he became the king of all Britons, with his rule centered on his court at Camelot. After breaking the sword in battle, Arthur received the mystical Excalibur from the Lady of the Lake.

Arthur had a son, MORDRED, by his half-sister, and married Guinevere. When an affair between Guinevere and Lancelot became known, Arthur sentenced both to execution, though Lancelot rescued Guinevere. MORGAN LE FAY allied with Mordred and raised armies against Camelot, and Arthur died while striking a mortal blow against Mordred. In the Otherworld realm of Avalon, Arthur awaited his return, and reappeared in modern times to battle the Necromon. The mystical Pendragon spirit has been used to empower the warriors known as the Knights of Pendragon. **DW**

King Arthur, legendary ruler of Britain, lived in a time of courtly chivalry, armored knights, and strange magical forces.

PERSUASION

FIRST APPEARANCE Alpha Flight #41 (December 1986)

REAL NAME Kara Killgrave

OCCUPATION Adventurer **BASE** Mobile

HEIGHT 5 ft 3 in **WEIGHT** 120 lbs **EYES** Brown **HAIR** Black

SPECIAL POWERS/ABILITIES Has the mutant power to secrete psychoactive will-sapping pheromones from her pores that allow her to link with the minds of others and make them do her bidding.

Unaware she was the daughter of the PURPLE MAN, Kara Killgrave was shocked when her skin turned purple and her powers manifested themselves. She took the name Purple Girl and joined Beta Flight, Alpha Flight's training group. When the group split up, Kara went home to her mother. She followed the teams through a number of breakups and reunions, eventually taking the name Persuasion. She retained her powers after M-Day and has been seen at the X-Men's new headquarters in San Francisco. **AD, MF**

PETROVICH, IVAN

FIRST APPEARANCE Amazing Adventures Vol. 2 #1 (August 1970)

REAL NAME Ivan Petrovich

OCCUPATION Chauffeur **BASE** Mobile

HEIGHT 6 ft 5 in **WEIGHT** 300 lbs **EYES** Brown **HAIR** Brown

SPECIAL POWERS/ABILITIES Does not possess superpowers, but is a skilled hand-to-hand combatant; a reliable chauffeur and steadfast ally of the Black Widow.

After the devastating siege of Stalingrad during World War II, Russian soldier Ivan Petrovich had been searching the city without success for his lost sister. As he was walking through the city's ruins he heard a woman's cries from a burning building. As the woman died in the fire, she let her baby fall into his arms. Petrovich decided to raise the girl as his own. She was Natasha Romanova who eventually became the BLACK WIDOW, Russia's top spy. Petrovich, feeling responsible for Natasha, accompanied her to America as her chauffeur. He lived with the Black Widow and DAREDEVIL while the two heroes struck up a romance in San Francisco. His son Yuri Petrovich briefly served as the fourth CRIMSON DYNAMO. He remains in good health, despite his age. **DW**

PHALANX

The techno-organic race called the Technarchy creates its food by using its transmode virus to convert organic matter into Phalanx, a collective intelligence lifeform. Members of the Technarchy then feed on the Phalanx, draining away its life energy. While experimenting on the renegade Technarch WARLOCK, human scientists obtained a strain of the transmode virus and injected it into humans, hoping to create a new generation of SENTINEL robots. Transformed into Phalanx, their subjects began assimilating other humans. Fortunately, the Phalanx could not digest mutants, and the X-MEN stopped them.

In space, another group of Phalanx threatened the SHI'AR Empire, but the X-Men foiled their plans as well. Recently, the insane android Ultron led yet another breed of Phalanx against the Kree, nearly conquering them until several heroes and the Technarchy intervened (*see* Annihilation). **AD, MF**

Sentient biological weapons, the Phalanx are formidable adversaries.

FACTFILE

REAL NAME
Inapplicable; alien being with collective intelligence

BASE
Outer space

HEIGHT Variable
WEIGHT Variable
EYES Unknown
HAIR None

FIRST APPEARANCE
Uncanny X-Men #305
(October 1993)

PHALANX

POWERS

Transforms sentient beings into techno-organic lifeforms and assimilates them into its collective. Superhumanly strong, also possess ability to teleport and shapeshift—molding their limbs into weapons or mimicking the appearance of others.

PHANTOM EAGLE

FIRST APPEARANCE Marvel Super Heroes #16 (September 1968)

REAL NAME Karl Kaufman

OCCUPATION Pilot   **BASE** Mobile

HEIGHT 5 ft 11 in   **WEIGHT** 175 lbs   **EYES** Blue   **HAIR** Brown

SPECIAL POWERS/ABILITIES Although he had no superhuman powers, Phantom Eagle was an extraordinary pilot, exceptionally skilled in aerial combat.

When World War I broke out, ace flyer Karl Kaufman wanted to use his skills against the Germans, but he feared reprisals against his German parents. So he donned a costume and mask and took the name Phantom Eagle. He became one of the greatest aerial warriors of the war, wining many dogfights, and then joined the Freedom's Five, a team of costumed heroes who assisted the Allies. Kaufman's identity was discovered by a German pilot, who killed him and his parents. The ghost of the Phantom Eagle hunted the pilot down and killed him. **MT**

PHASTOS

FIRST APPEARANCE Eternals Vol. 2 #1 (October 1985)

REAL NAME Phastos   **OCCUPATION** Technologist, weaponsmith

BASE Ruhr Valley, Germany   **HEIGHT** 6 ft 3 in

WEIGHT 410 lbs   **EYES** Brown   **HAIR** Bald (black beard)

SPECIAL POWERS/ABILITIES Able to fly and levitate objects; virtually invulnerable, super-strong, and projects cosmic energy from eyes or hands; ingenious inventor; hammer fires energy bolts.

Phastos is an ETERNAL, a nearly immortal race created thousands of years ago by the alien CELESTIALS. Being a weaponsmith, Phastos was mistaken for the Olympian god Hephaestus (Vulcan) during the days of ancient Greece (*see* GODS OF OLYMPUS). Phastos is more reticent than his fellows, having a melancholy spirit and an ambivalence toward fighting. When APOCALYPSE tried to incite a new war with the Deviants, the Eternals decided to go public as Super Heroes. In his new identity, Phastos adopted the codename Ceasefire. **DW**

PHANTOM RIDER

With his luminescent cloak and magician's skills, the Phantom Rider appeared to be flying.

Originally a schoolteacher in the Wild West, Carter Slade was shot by a ruthless local land baron, but a Comanche Indian called Flaming Star saved his life. After Carter recovered, Flaming Star gave him a white horse and a cloak covered with a phosphorescent dust. Styling himself the Phantom Rider, Carter began a one-man battle against injustice.

Not knowing that the Phantom Rider was his brother, Marshall Lincoln Slade teamed up with him to battle the Reverend Reaper, a vicious gunfighter set on taking control of Bison Bend, the town Carter had sworn to protect. In their final confrontation, both Carter and the reverend died. Learning the truth about his brother, Lincoln decided to follow in his footsteps. He later went mad and died while battling a time-traveling MOCKINGBIRD.

In modern times, Lincoln's descendent, archaeologist Hamilton Slade, became a modern day Phantom Rider. Recently, Nick FURY made J.T. Slade—Carter's grandson—a member of his new Secret Warriors team. J.T. can charge weapons (like a chain) with fire, and he calls himself Hellfire. **AD, MF**

With guile and some magnificent devices, the Phantom Rider stayed one step ahead of local miscreants.

FACTFILE

REAL NAME
Carter Slade

OCCUPATION
Schoolteacher, vigilante

BASE
Bison Bend in the Old West

HEIGHT 6 ft 1 in
WEIGHT 200 lbs
EYES Blue
HAIR Reddish-blond

FIRST APPEARANCE
Ghost Rider #1
(September 1973)

A fast draw and a brilliant marksman; formidable hand-to-hand combatant; notable horseman.

PHOBIUS

FIRST APPEARANCE Marvel Two-In-One #71 (January 1974)

REAL NAME Unknown

OCCUPATION Interrogator; servant   **BASE** Unknown

HEIGHT 5 ft 9 in   **WEIGHT** 122 lbs   **EYES** Green   **HAIR** Black

SPECIAL POWERS/ABILITIES Possesses the ability to psionically stimulate the fear centers of a person's brain in order to implant terrifying phobias; also wielded an energy whip.

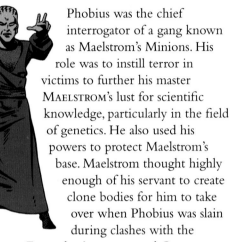

Phobius was the chief interrogator of a gang known as Maelstrom's Minions. His role was to instill terror in victims to further his master MAELSTROM's lust for scientific knowledge, particularly in the field of genetics. He also used his powers to protect Maelstrom's base. Maelstrom thought highly enough of his servant to create clone bodies for him to take over when Phobius was slain during clashes with the FANTASTIC FOUR, the AVENGERS, and QUASAR. Phobius was also defeated by SERSI who turned him into a rat. Phobius' whereabouts are unknown since he helped revive Maelstrom after the scientist had been killed by Quasar. **ED**

PHOBOS, PROFESSOR P.

FIRST APPEARANCE The Incredible Hulk #258 (April 1981)

REAL NAME Professor Pieter Phobos

OCCUPATION Teacher   **BASE** Russia

HEIGHT/WEIGHT/EYES Unrevealed   **HAIR** Gray

SPECIAL POWERS/ABILITIES Possessed telepathic abilities artificially derived from draining the energies of superhuman mutants. Wore battle armor.

Professor Phobos was appointed by the Russian government to head the secret Super Soldier School, training the Russian mutant siblings DARKSTAR, Ursa Major, and VANGUARD. Phobos secretly drained their power to give himself psionic abilities and turned against his government. Phobos teamed with Bruce Banner to imprison two Russian superhumans, Sergei the PRESENCE and the RED GUARDIAN. Sergei was the father of Darkstar, Ursa Major and Vanguard, who all intervened, calling Phobos a traitor. In the ensuing battle, the HULK and Ursa Major apparently crushed Phobos to death. **PS**

BE FREE, PRISONERS OF THE PRESENCE!

PHOTON

--BUT IF THIS CONTRAPTION HAS EVEN A SNOWBALL'S CHANCE OF DOING WHAT YOU SAY IT CAN, I AIM TO SEE IT BUSTED!

Firing electrical energy, Photon disrupts the circuits of some complex equipment.

Monica Rambeau was working as a lieutenant in the New Orleans Harbor Patrol when she was struck by extradimensional energy from an "energy disruptor" weapon being developed by a South American terrorist. This exposure gave Rambeau her superpowers. Dubbed "Captain Marvel" by the media she tried to put her new abilities to good use. Early in her career she met SPIDER-MAN who introduced her to the AVENGERS. They agreed to help train her to use her powers more skilfully. In time she became a valuable member of the Avengers, and was even their leader for several stints.

When Genis-Vell (see CAPTAIN MARVEL) the son of CAPTAIN MAR-VELL wanted to use his father's name, Rambeau gladly gave up the name and became Photon. Later, Genis-Vell changed *his* name to Photon, forcing Rambeau to change her Super Hero name yet again, this time to Pulsar.

Recently, Monica led the team NEXTWAVE against the terrorist organization SILVER. She sided with CAPTAIN AMERICA during the Civil War (see pp. 84–5) but now has registered with the Fifty State Initiative (see pp.118–9) **MT, MF**

Becoming or controlling any form of energy gives Photon almost limitless power

FACTFILE

REAL NAME
Monica Rambeau

OCCUPATION
Adventurer

BASE
New Orleans; New York City

HEIGHT 5 ft 8 in
WEIGHT 145 lbs
EYES Black
HAIR Black

FIRST APPEARANCE
Amazing Spider-Man Annual #16 (1982)

PHOTON

POWERS

Photon can turn into any type of energy, including light, electricity, microwaves, radio waves, ultra-violet waves, gamma rays, or lasers. She can travel at the speed of light and fire blasts of whatever type of energy she becomes.

PIECEMEAL

FIRST APPEARANCE Incredible Hulk #403 (March 1993)

REAL NAME Unrevealed

OCCUPATION Criminal   **BASE** Loch Ness, Scotland

HEIGHT 7 ft 6 in   **WEIGHT** 1,400 lbs   **EYES** Red   **HAIR** Gray

SPECIAL POWERS/ABILITIES Possesses all of the abilities of the criminal New World Order, including superhuman strength, the ability to fire energy blasts, and razor-sharp claws.

The man who would become Piecemeal was an operative from the COMMISSION ON SUPERHUMAN ACTIVITIES sent to spy on the RED SKULL. The Skull captured him, intending to make him into a living symbol of his criminal organization, the New World Order. Imbued with the properties of

members of the Order, and with memories of his previous life erased, Piecemeal became enthralled with being alive. He began using his powers to absorb the life-experiences of others, until the HULK seemingly ended his menace. **TB**

PIP THE TROLL

FIRST APPEARANCE Strange Tales #179 (April 1975)

REAL NAME Pip Gofern

OCCUPATION Former bearer of the Space Gem, prince of Laxidazia and painter   **BASE** Mobile with the Milky Way Galaxy

HEIGHT 4 ft 4 in   **WEIGHT** 144 lbs   **EYES** Pink   **HAIR** Red

SPECIAL POWERS/ABILITIES Claims to be irresistible to women; could teleport anywhere in the universe when he possessed the Space Gem.

Born a prince on the alien world of Laxidazia, Pip was exiled from the court for befriending a tribe of trolls. Missionaries from the Universal Church of Truth came to Laxidazia to convert the natives. When the trolls resisted, the Church began exterminating them. Pip was captured and placed on a Death-Ship where he met Adam WARLOCK. They became friends and overthrew the Church. Warlock called on Pip to help stop Thanos from using the Infinity Gems to control reality and later gave him the Space Gem as a reward, making him a member of the Infinity Watch. The Watch disbanded after losing control of the gems and Pip was last seen in New York City with Warlock and GAMORA. **TD**

Strange Tales #113 was Plantman's first appearance.

PLANTMAN

While working in London as a botanist's assistant, Samuel Smithers became involved with experiments to explore the mental activity of plants. After ten years the botanist died, and Smithers moved to the US, where he planned to continue his work in trying to increase the intelligence of plants so that humans could communicate with them. However, due to his lack of formal education he had difficulty in finding support for his ideas and was forced to take a job as a gardener. Smithers tried to combine the job with his research, but was eventually fired for spending too much time on his experiments.

REVENGE

Not long after Smithers lost his job, a bolt of lightning struck his experimental plant ray-gun, charging the device with the power to control and animate plant life. Smithers put on a costume and, taking the name Plantman, sought revenge on the man who had fired him, but was stopped by the HUMAN TORCH, who destroyed the plant-gun. Undeterred, Plantman built a second, more powerful weapon, and tried to kill the Human Torch, but his plan failed. Later he joined the international crime syndicate, the MAGGIA. Creating plant duplicates of himself, Plantman battled the X-MEN, the AVENGERS, SUB-MARINER, TRITON, and SHIELD, among others.

CHARACTER KEY
1 Plantman
2 Porcupine
3 The Eel
4 The Scarecrow

CRIMEWAVE

Over the years, Smithers's body gradually mutated to become more and more plantlike. At one point, he connected with the Verdant Green—the manifestation of the Earth's biosphere—and was given the option of wiping humans from the planet or preserving them. Although his transformation had already cost him a great deal of his humanity, he chose to let the people of Earth live. For a while, Smithers worked with the THUNDERBOLTS under HAWKEYE's leadership, using the name Blackheath. He has since returned to prison to serve out his sentence and to try to reconnect with his sense of humanity. **MT, MF**

FACTFILE
REAL NAME
Samuel Smithers
OCCUPATION
Professional criminal; formerly a gardener
BASE
A submarine in the Atlantic Ocean

HEIGHT 6 ft
WEIGHT 190 lbs
EYES Green
HAIR Dark gray

FIRST APPEARANCE
Strange Tales #113
(October 1963)

POWERS

Plantman's projector weapons allow him to control plants, animating their limbs to attack a victim; and manipulate plants so they look like duplicates of humans.

The Plantman simuloid possessed all the powers of the original Plantman.

POLARIS

While her green hair marked her as a mutant, Lorna Dane had no idea growing up that she had been adopted, and that her true father was Magneto. When her powers manifested, she found herself at the center of an all-out war between the X-Men and the demonic MESMERO for control of her abilities. Falling in love with the X-Man HAVOK, Lorna desired nothing more than to live a normal life. But fate would not let her be, and time and again she was pulled to the center of mutant strife as Polaris, mistress of magnetism. She led X-FACTOR, beside Havok, at its start. She later joined the X-Men. She lost her powers on M-Day but Apocalypse restored them to her by infusing her with alien technology while he transformed her into his latest version of the horseman Pestilence. Although she and Havok broke up when he left her at the altar, they renewed their relationship during their attempt to save the Shi'ar Empire from Havok's brother VULCAN. **TB, MF**

As the years have gone by, Polaris' mutant magnetic powers have had a detrimental effect on her mental stability, interfering with the electrical impulses in her brain.

FACTFILE

REAL NAME
Lorna Dane

OCCUPATION
Adventurer

BASE
The Xavier Institute for Higher Learning

HEIGHT 5 ft 7 in
WEIGHT 115 lbs
EYES Green
HAIR Green

FIRST APPEARANCE
Uncanny X-Men #49
(October 1968)

POLARIS

POWERS

Polaris has power over magnetism and can use it to fly, create force fields, and manipulate anything made of magnetic materials. She also now has a healing factor.

PORCUPINE

FIRST APPEARANCE Tales to Astonish #48 (October 1963)
REAL NAME Alexander Gentry
OCCUPATION Weapons designer/criminal **BASE** New York City
HEIGHT (With battlesuit) 6 ft 7 in **WEIGHT** (With battlesuit) 305 lbs
EYES Blue-gray **HAIR** Brown
SPECIAL POWERS/ABILITIES Battlesuit fired quills, laser beams, bombs, gases, and other weapons. Belt jets enabled him to fly.

A weapons designer for the US government, Alexander Gentry invented a battlesuit inspired by a porcupine. It was covered in razor-sharp, projectile quills that he could fire at opponents, and quill-like tubes through which other weapons could be fired. Getting greedy, Gentry used the suit to become the Porcupine, but his criminal career was a failure. CAPTAIN AMERICA agreed to buy the battlesuit from Gentry if he would help the AVENGERS defeat the SERPENT SOCIETY. Gentry agreed, but was fatally impaled on his own quill during the battle. A new Porcupine surfaced later and wound up working with the Thunderbolts. **PS, MF**

POTTS, VIRGINIA "PEPPER"

FIRST APPEARANCE Tales of Suspense Vol. 1 #45 (September 1963)
REAL NAME Virginia Potts
OCCUPATION Former executive aide to Tony Stark **BASE** Mobile
HEIGHT 5 ft 4 in **WEIGHT** 110 lbs **EYES** Green **HAIR** Red
SPECIAL POWERS/ABILITIES Pepper is a cyborg who can fly by manipulating magnetism.

"Pepper" Potts became Tony Stark's secretary early in his career. Stark entrusted her with the secret of his identity as IRON MAN, but didn't notice her crush on him. She eventually married Stark's chauffeur, Harold "Happy" HOGAN, though they later divorced—and then remarried. Soon after Hogan died, Pepper joined the Order, the California team of the Fifty State Initiative, calling herself Hera. Later, EZEKIEL STANE harmed Pepper, and Tony had to turn her into a cyborg to save her life. Recently, Tony made her CEO of Stark Industries, but she was forced to flee its headquarters in her own suit of power armor. **DW, MF**

POWDERKEG

FIRST APPEARANCE Captain Marvel Vol. 2 #1 (December 1995)
REAL NAME Frank Skorina
OCCUPATION Prisoner **BASE** The Big House
HEIGHT/WEIGHT/EYES Unrevealed **HAIR** Red
SPECIAL POWERS/ABILITIES Secretes nitro-glycerine through skin; when body strikes object with sufficient force the chemical ignites, causing an explosion.

Powderkeg was a member of the MASTERS OF EVIL during DOCTOR OCTOPUS's ill-conceived turn as leader. Following the failure of the group's attempt to invade Avengers Mansion and their subsequent demise, Powderkeg ran a protection racket in the neighborhood where Ben Grimm (see THING) grew up, but Grimm stopped that cold. For a while, he was an inmate in the experimental penitentiary the Big House, in which all the prisoners were shrunk to reduce costs. Recently, he was seen in the Bar with No Name, which caters to criminals. **AD, MF**

POWER, DR. JAMES

FIRST APPEARANCE Power Pack #1 (August 1984)
REAL NAME Dr. James Power **OCCUPATION** Physicist
BASE New York City; later Bainbridge Island, Washington State
HEIGHT 6 ft **WEIGHT** 155 lbs **EYES** Blue **HAIR** Brown
SPECIAL POWERS/ABILITIES A brilliant and innovative physicist, Dr. Power has the normal human strength of a man of his age who engages in minimal regular exercise.

Dr. James Power is the inventor of the matter/antimatter converter, a comparatively inexpensive means of producing energy. Learning of Power's invention, an alien Kymellian named Aelfyre WHITEMANE ("Whitey") grew concerned, since a similar device had destroyed the Kymellian homeworld. Another alien race, the Z'nrx, or "SNARKS," intending to utilize the converter as a weapon, abducted Dr. Power and his wife Margaret. The

dying Whitemane bestowed superhuman powers upon the Powers' young children, Alex, Jack, Julie and Katie, who rescued their parents. The children continued to operate under the name POWER PACK. **PS**

POWER BROKER

FIRST APPEARANCE Machine Man #6 (September 1978)
REAL NAME Curtiss Jackson
OCCUPATION Criminal **BASE** Los Angeles
HEIGHT 7 ft 6 in **WEIGHT** 600 lbs **EYES** Brown **HAIR** Black
SPECIAL POWERS/ABILITIES Once a normal man, Jackson possesses superhuman strength. However, his body is so overdeveloped that he cannot move without a steel exo-skeleton.

Curtiss Jackson was an agent of the Corporation, a criminal organization run like a respectable business. After meeting DR. KARL MALUS, Jackson formed his own company—Power Broker, Inc.—which sold superhuman strength to its clients. He empowered numerous people, including U.S. AGENT, DEMOLITION MAN, and most of the wrestlers on the UCWF circuit. Hunted by the criminal-killing SCOURGE, Jackson augmented himself but wound up so musclebound he could hardly move. A new Power Broker appeared recently, wearing a battle suit that allows him to fire blasts of energy from his hands. He gave Hardball his powers. **TB, MF**

◉ POWER PACK *see page 250*

POWER PRINCESS

FIRST APPEARANCE Defenders #112 (October 1982)
REAL NAME Zarda
OCCUPATION Princess **BASE** Capital City
HEIGHT 5 ft 9 in **WEIGHT** 145 lbs **EYES** Brown **HAIR** Black
SPECIAL POWERS/ABILITIES Incredible healing ability, and an incredibly long lifespan. She can also shoot a flash from her eyes which can heal others, or if she chooses, destroy them.

On Earth-712, Princess Zarda lived on Utopia Island, where her people developed a culture of peace, fellowship, and learning. During World War II, she joined the Golden Agency and fought for the Allies. When humans created the atomic bomb, the Utopians fled Earth, leaving Princess Zarda behind. She joined the SQUADRON SUPREME and worked with them to take over and improve the USA. After that failed, she wound up on Earth-616, living at Project Pegasus. She joined the Exiles in their pursuit of PROTEUS, but has since returned to the Squadron Supreme. **MT, MF**

POWERHOUSE

POWERHOUSE

FACTFILE
REAL NAME Rieg Davan
OCCUPATION Syfon warrior
BASE The planet Xandar
HEIGHT 6 ft 3 in
WEIGHT 265 lbs
EYES Brown
HAIR Brown
FIRST APPEARANCE Nova #2 (October 1976)

POWERS Powerhouse could siphon energy from external sources, including living beings to amplify his strength or discharge energy blasts.

A member of the alien Xandarians, Rieg Davan was a Syfon warrior in the elite Nova Corps. He was sent to Earth to locate Centurion Nova-Prime Rhomann Dey. Davan's starship crash landed on Earth. He was found and brainwashed by the Condor, a costumed criminal.

As the Condor's accomplice Powerhouse, Davan battled Nova, the young Earthman who had inherited the deceased Dey's powers. Eventually Davan recovered his memory and with Nova and other heroes journeyed to Xandar. As the CHAMPIONS OF XANDAR, they helped the Xandarians defeat the invading Skrulls. Davan later perished in combat defending Xandar against a successful invasion by the forces of the space pirate NEBULA.

The name Powerhouse has since been used by a criminal mutant Earthwoman who also has the power to drain energy from other living beings through touch to amplify her own. She has battled SPIDER-MAN and WOLVERINE, among others. Alex Power of POWER PACK also used the name Powerhouse when he temporarily possessed the superhuman powers of his siblings. **PS**

The female Powerhouse is super-strong, can fly, and discharge energy blasts.

At first, Nova and Rieg Davan, alias Powerhouse, were enemies, but they later became allies.

POWER PACK

Young hero team with power to burn

CURRENT MEMBERS
ZERO-G
(Alex Power, leader) Ability to control the gravity of himself or other objects.
LIGHTSPEED
(Julie Power) Flight, super-speed.
MASS MASTER
(Jack Power) Can compress or disperse his body's mass.
ENERGIZER
(Katie Power) Can absorb and release energy.

BASE
Bainbridge Island, Washington

FIRST APPEARANCE
Power Pack Vol. 1 #1
(August 1984)

Dr. James Power inadvertently caused his children to join the ranks of Earth's Super Heroes.

Professor James POWER, father of Alex, Julie, Jack, and Katie, invented an antimatter generator that siphoned energy from an alternate dimension. Aelfyre "Whitey" WHITEMANE, a member of the alien Kymellian race, arrived on Earth to prevent the machine being used, knowing it had the potential to wipe out entire planets. A rival species, the SNARKS, attempted to steal the device.

SECRET SUPER HEROES

Whitemane suffered fatal injuries in the ensuing struggle, but before dying he bestowed one of his abilities on each of the four Power children. They became the superheroic Power Pack, and adopted the identities of Gee (Alex), Lightspeed (Julie), Mass Master (Jack), and Energizer (Katie). Hiding their dual identities from their parents, the Pack dealt with extraterrestrial threats and employed Whitey's intelligent spacecraft, the Smartship Friday. Power Pack aided the MORLOCKS during the Mutant Massacre, and fought APOCALYPSE's horsemen during the Fall of the Mutants. Franklin RICHARDS, using the name Tattletale due to his ability to perceive possible futures, became an unofficial member of the team, as did KOFI, a Kymellian relative of the late Whitemane.

ESSENTIAL STORYLINES
• *Power Pack Vol. 1 #1*
Power Pack debuts, launching a popular 62-issue series.
• *Power Pack Vol. 2 #1-4*
The heroes return—now a few years older—in a limited series that pits them against their perennial enemies, the Snarks.
• *X-Men and Power Pack #1-4*
Power Pack returns to its roots in a limited series that guest-stars such famous mutants as Cyclops, Beast, and Wolverine.

Frequent contact with the Kymellians and the Snarks have turned the members of Power Pack into veteran interstellar adventurers.

ENERGY SWAPPING

Power Pack's powers often switched from one member to another. At one point, they adopted the names of Destroyer (Alex), Molecula (Julie), Counterweight (Jack), and Starstreak (Katie) and helped the Kymellians relocate to a new world. Alex appeared to become a Kymellian, though this was revealed to be a pseudoplasm duplicate planted by Technocrat, a Kymellian.

Alex joined the NEW WARRIORS, stealing the energies of his brother and sisters to become Powerpax and then POWERHOUSE. He later restored his siblings' powers. Alex changed his codename to Zero-G and joined the Fifty State Initiative (*see* pp. 118-9). Julie declined to register and ran away to Los Angeles, joining Excelsior, a team of teenage ex-Super Heroes, and she recently followed them to New York. **DW, MF**

Despite their youth, the Power Pack members combine their abilities to defeat some of the strongest villains.

POWER PACK
1 Mass Master
2 Energizer
3 Lightspeed
4 Zero-G

PRATT, AGENT

FIRST APPEARANCE Incredible Hulk Vol. 3 #40 (July 2002)

REAL NAME Agent Pratt

OCCUPATION Agent for clandestine organization   **BASE** Mobile

HEIGHT/WEIGHT/EYES Unrevealed   **HAIR** None

SPECIAL POWERS/ABILITIES Body able to regenerate itself as a result of H Section Programming; injection of Hulk blood endowed him with Hulk-like powers.

When he first met Bruce Banner, this ruthless operative was posing as an FBI agent. In truth he belonged to the sinister, clandestine organisation Home Base. After forcing Banner to change into the HULK, Pratt obtained a sample of his blood, but a police officer snatched it and, plunging it into Pratt's own bloodstream, caused him to explode. Pratt's H Section Programming enabled his body to regenerate itself, and he soon returned to taunt Banner again. This time the Hulk emerged to tear Pratt's body apart. **AD**

PRESENCE

FIRST APPEARANCE Defenders Vol. 1 #52 (October 1977)

REAL NAME Sergei Krylov

OCCUPATION Supervillain   **BASE** Mobile

HEIGHT 6 ft   **WEIGHT** 200 lbs   **EYES** Yellow   **HAIR** None

SPECIAL POWERS/ABILITIES Body produces lethal radiation which can be harnessed as flight, energy blasts, force fields, enhanced strength, or telepathy.

Nuclear physicist Sergei Krylov became an important player in Russian politics and sought to further increase his might by subjecting himself to experimental radiation. He succeeded in gaining radioactive powers deadly to the unprotected, which could also be used to control the minds of others. He used his powers to brainwash Dr. Tania Belinskya (the RED GUARDIAN) into becoming his partner. Driven by his megalomania, he became a foe of the Defenders, QUASAR, and the Avengers. He was last seen returning to his cell in a Russian prison after helping fight Kang the Conqueror. **DW, MF**

PRESTER JOHN

FIRST APPEARANCE Fantastic Four Vol. 1 #54 (September 1966)

REAL NAME Prester John

OCCUPATION Traveler   **BASE** Traveler

HEIGHT 6 ft 1 in   **WEIGHT** 210 lbs   **EYES** Blue   **HAIR** Red

SPECIAL POWERS/ABILITIES Skilled swordsman; a weapon called the Evil Eye allowed him to fire energy blasts, generate force fields, and rearrange matter.

Prester John, monarch of a 12th-century Christian kingdom in Asia, aided Richard the Lionheart during the Crusades. Afterward, John discovered the fabled isle of Avalon, but while he was there, a plague struck. As sole survivor, he sat in the Chair of Survival and slept. Reawakening in the modern era, he crossed paths with many heroes, including the FANTASTIC FOUR. He carries the powerful Stellar Rod, a weapon made from the Evil Eye. He was last seen serving as Head of Multi-Religious Studies on Providence, an island nation Cable built—and then evacuating people off it when it was destroyed. **DW, MF**

PRETTY PERSUASIONS

FIRST APPEARANCE New Warriors Vol. 1 #4 (October 1990)

REAL NAME Heidi P. Franklin

OCCUPATION Professional criminal   **BASE** Sayville, Long Island

HEIGHT 5 ft 6 in   **WEIGHT** 120 lbs   **EYES** Brown   **HAIR** Black

SPECIAL POWERS/ABILITIES Can manipulate the pleasure centers of the brain, particularly in men, and create whips and other weapons from solidified psionic energy.

GeneTech—a scientific facility in Long Island, New York—gave exotic dancer Heidi Franklin the power to affect the sexual drives of others and to form psionic energy into a selection of different weapons. Under the name Pretty Persuasions, she joined other psionically gifted individuals to form Psionex, GeneTech's villainous enforcement squad. The group frequently battled the NEW WARRIORS, and later became a squad of crime-fighting New York vigilantes. Later, after that effort ended, Heidi was forced to work for the THUNDERBOLTS. **DW, MF**

PRINCESS PYTHON

FIRST APPEARANCE Amazing Spider-Man Vol. 1 #22 (March 1965)

REAL NAME Zelda DuBois

OCCUPATION Snake charmer, criminal   **BASE** Mobile

HEIGHT 5 ft 8 in   **WEIGHT** 140 lbs   **EYES** Green   **HAIR** Red-brown

SPECIAL POWERS/ABILITIES Can control her trained rock python; sometimes carries an electric prod.

Princess Python is a snake charmer who trained her rock python snake to attack on command. She served with several versions of the CIRCUS OF CRIME while also occasionally pursuing a solo career. Princess Python briefly joined the mercenaries of the SERPENT SOCIETY and even started up one incarnation of the Serpent Squad. For a while she worked at the Quentin Carnival and became involved with Johnny Blaze (GHOST RIDER). At one point, she even married the STILT-MAN.

Blinded during the Punisher's attack on the Stilt-Man's funeral, she later married the Gibbon, but they have since separated. **DW, MF**

PROCTOR

The man who came to be called Proctor was actually the BLACK KNIGHT of an alternate Earth. While serving as a member of the AVENGERS, he met and fell in love with the SERSI of his world. He became her "gann josin," a mate that was forever bound to her by a mental link that allowed them to share their powers, thoughts and souls. His Sersi eventually became mentally unstable, destroying their world and rejecting Proctor.

Desperate for revenge, Proctor and his companions used a gateway into alternate dimensions and journeyed across the multiverse. They were on a quest to kill every alternate world version of Sersi, along with every world and Avenger that had ever befriended her. They gathered and rescued all the alternate-Avengers that they deemed worthy of life. After defeating the Black Knight of the real Earth, Proctor was slain by this world's Sersi. **TD**

FACTFILE

REAL NAME
Dane Whitman (of an alternate dimension)

OCCUPATION
Former Super Hero turned destroyer of worlds

BASE
A secret citadel hidden on the edge of reality

HEIGHT 6 ft
WEIGHT 190 lbs
EYES Brown
HAIR Black

FIRST APPEARANCE
Avengers #344 (February 1992)

PROCTOR

POWERS

Proctor possessed the battle prowess of the real Black Knight, and the mental and physical powers of an Eternal because he had become one with the Sersi of his world.

Expert combatant; immune to aging; can psionically manipulate matter, and project cosmic blasts from eyes and hands. Possesses ten rings that produce, among other things, ice blasts, flames, bursts of light and deadly gases.

PRODIGY

PRODIGY

FACTFILE

REAL NAME
David Alleyne

OCCUPATION
Adventurer

BASE
Professor X's School for Gifted Youngsters, Salem Center, New York

HEIGHT 6 ft 3 in
WEIGHT 230 lbs
EYES Brown
HAIR Black

FIRST APPEARANCE
New Mutants Vol. 2 #4 (October 2003)

Four different men used the name Prodigy in recent years. The first was SPIDER-MAN, who employed it as one of four different identities when he was a wanted man. College athlete Richie Gilmore took over this exact identity after Spider-Man abandoned it. He is perhaps best known for being the first hero to publicly defy the Superhuman Registration Act. He has since joined the Fifty State Initiative (*see* pp. 118–9). The third Prodigy, David Alleyne, was unrelated to the first two. His mutant powers allowed him to absorb the knowledge of anyone nearby, although the knowledge faded when they parted. He lost his powers on M-Day, but he can now remember every bit of knowledge he ever absorbed. He remains with the X-MEN, now as a teacher. The fourth Prodigy, Timothy Wilkerson, is a young man who was mutated with the LEADER's gamma-irradiated DNA. He joined the Gamma Corps to take down the HULK during World War Hulk (*see* pp. 152–5), but he now helps their efforts to bring the ILLUMINATI to justice instead. **MT, MF**

POWERS

Prodigy has the mutant ability to absorb (although not permanently) the skills and knowledge of those near him. He cannot, however, absorb their mutant powers.

High above the US Capitol, Prodigy tangles with fellow X-Men member Wind Dancer.

◎ **PROFESSOR X**
see page 254-255

PROTEUS

FIRST APPEARANCE Uncanny X-Men #125 (September 1979)

REAL NAME Kevin MacTaggert

OCCUPATION None **BASE** Muir Island, Scotland

HEIGHT/WEIGHT/EYES/HAIR Inapplicable

SPECIAL POWERS/ABILITIES Able to warp reality. Made of psionic energies, he must inhabit a host body, which burns up over time.

Moira MACTAGGERT imprisoned her son Kevin in Mutant Research Facility on Muir Island, where an energy field kept his powers from consuming his body. When his cell was breached during an attack by MAGNETO, Kevin escaped, shifting from host-body to host-body as each wore out. Only the intervention of the X-MEN—and Kevin's vulnerability to metal—stopped him. AIM reconstituted him in the body of a young mutant called Piecemeal (not the adult villain of the same name) for a while, but the combined creature didn't last. During the House of M, Kevin left Earth-616 with the EXILES and formed a body-sharing deal with Morph. **TB**

Proteus escaped incarceration on Muir Island and took over the body of his mother Moira's estranged husband Joe.

PROUDSTAR

FIRST APPEARANCE New Mutants #16 (June 1984)

REAL NAME James Proudstar

OCCUPATION X-Force Team member **BASE** San Francisco

HEIGHT 7 ft 2 in **WEIGHT** 350 lbs

EYES Brown **HAIR** Black

SPECIAL POWERS/ABILITIES Superhuman strength, speed, endurance, agility and reflexes; also able to fly.

Like his Native American brother (the original THUNDERBIRD) James Proudstar was born a mutant. When his brother died on an X-MEN mission, James blamed PROFESSOR XAVIER, and joined the HELLIONS. He left, disenchanted, to discover that his tribal community had been destroyed. Reconciling with Xavier, James joined the NEW MUTANTS, taking the name Warpath when they reformed as X-FORCE.

He has since learned that the man who caused his tribe's destruction is dead. **AD**

PROWLER

Hobie Brown's gift for inventions is rivaled only by that of Peter Parker (Spider-Man).

While working as a window washer, mechanical genius Hobie Brown invented gadgets to make his job easier, including wrist-mounted, high-pressure sprayers. When his boss dismissed his ideas, Brown quit in frustration. He turned to crime, refashioning his contraptions into climbing gear and miniaturized weapons, and adopting the costumed identity of the Prowler. Seeking recognition rather than profit, Brown intended to return what he stole as the Prowler under his real identity. Almost immediately, he came into conflict with SPIDER-MAN, though the two later put aside their differences and became allies.

A second Prowler appeared when the villainous Cat Burglar stole Brown's costume and worked with BELLADONNA to commit a string of crimes. Brown resumed his role as the original Prowler, joining the team of reformed criminals called the Outlaws, but suffered a severe spinal injury at the hands of El Toro Negro. A third Prowler, medical student Rick Lawson, briefly adventured while Brown recuperated in the hospital, but Brown has since retaken the role he created. **DW**

FACTFILE

REAL NAME
Hobie Brown

OCCUPATION
Adventurer

BASE
New York City

HEIGHT 5 ft 11 in
WEIGHT 170 lbs
EYES Brown
HAIR Dark brown

FIRST APPEARANCE
Amazing Spider-Man Vol. 1 #78
(November 1969)

The cape of Prowler's costume allows him to glide; wrist cartridges fire compressed air; steel-tipped claws allow him to scale buildings.

POWERS

PROFESSOR X

Mastermind of the X-Men

FACTFILE

REAL NAME
Charles Francis Xavier

OCCUPATION
Mutant rights activist, teacher

BASE
Mobile

HEIGHT 6 ft
WEIGHT 190 lbs
EYES Blue
HAIR None

FIRST APPEARANCE
Uncanny X-Men Vol. 1 #1
(September 1963)

POWERS

Vast psionic abilities including mind-reading, mind-erasing, astral projection, the projection of illusions, the ability to take mental control of others, and the ability to fire mental blasts.

ALLIES/FOES

ALLIES The X-Men, the Starjammers

FOES Magneto, Juggernaut, Cassandra Nova, the Sentinels, the Hellfire Club

ISSUE #1

In *X-Men* #1, Professor X's team unites to fight off the menace of Magneto, marking the first appearance of both the heroic X-Men and their arch-foe.

Growing up in a time before widespread superpowers, Charles Xavier hid his telepathic abilities to shield himself from unwanted attention.

Widely considered the most powerful mutant on Earth, Charles Xavier has dedicated his life to the ideal that humans and mutants can coexist peacefully. His father Brian died when Charles was a child. Kurt Marko, his father's research partner, married Charles's mother Sharon, but only valued her for her fortune. Charles became a rival of his stepbrother Cain (who one day gained the powers of the JUGGERNAUT), and saw both his mother and stepfather die in separate incidents.

FIRST LOVE

Xavier attended graduate school at Oxford University, England, where he fell in love with Moira MACTAGGERT; however their relationship ended when Charles joined the US Army. Following his tour of duty, Xavier traveled the world. At a clinic for Holocaust survivors in Israel, he befriended the man who would become MAGNETO. Magneto and Xavier teamed up to fight BARON VON STRUCKER, but Magneto's ruthless methods made it clear that the two had incompatible philosophies concerning the use of violence. Xavier left Israel, leaving behind Gabrielle HALLER, not realizing that Haller was pregnant with his child (the boy, David, would grow up to become the mutant LEGION). A rockslide caused by the villainous alien Lucifer, left Xavier a paraplegic.

Professor X can disable opponents, such as the Juggernaut, with mental blasts.

THE X-MEN

As Professor X, Charles Xavier founded Xavier's School for Gifted Youngsters in Westchester County, New York to train mutant children in the use of their powers. Xavier identified potential students with the machine Cerebro, which amplified his telepathic powers and allowed him to pinpoint mutants from afar. His initial Super Hero team, the X-MEN, consisted of CYCLOPS, Angel (*see* ARCHANGEL), Marvel Girl (see Jean GREY), ICEMAN and BEAST, who sought to improve the image of mutants by selfless deeds.

The X-Men repeatedly faced off against Magneto, who had dedicated himself to subjugating humanity through his powers as the master of magnetism.

Professor X founded a second team of X-Men, whose members included NIGHTCRAWLER, COLOSSUS, STORM, BANSHEE, and WOLVERINE. The new X-Men helped Xavier battle Shi'ar emperor D'ken and the Imperial Guard. Xavier then fell in love with the new Shi'ar empress, Lilandra. He entered into the Shi'ar equivalent of marriage with Lilandra, and adventured with the STARJAMMERS.

Although his love for Shi'ar empress Lilandra took him across the galaxy, Professor X eventually returned to the X-Men.

Back on Earth, Xavier organized a third grouping of students, the NEW MUTANTS, but fell under the influence of the alien Brood. To prevent his transformation into a Brood Queen, Xavier shifted his consciousness into a clone body with fully-functional legs. After suffering injuries as a result of a hate crime, Xavier reunited with Lilandra to recuperate among the Shi'ar, leaving Magneto to run the academy in his absence. Xavier again lost the use of his legs battling the SHADOW KING, and brought together a fourth team of young mutants, GENERATION X.

The relationship between Magneto and Xavier took a turn for the worse, culminating in a terrible moment when Magneto ripped the adamantium from Wolverine's skeleton. Enraged by Magneto's brutality, Xavier mind-wiped his former friend, unwittingly creating a powerful psionic being known as ONSLAUGHT. All of Earth's heroes united to destroy Onslaught, leading to the apparent deaths of the AVENGERS and the FANTASTIC FOUR. In the aftermath, Xavier briefly lost his telepathic powers and became a prisoner of the US government. He later uncovered a SKRULL plot to infiltrate the X-Men, and trained a promising group of Skrull mutants calling themselves Cadre K.

BATTLING MAGNETO

The philosophies held by Professor X and Magneto are diametrically opposed, but share some similarities. Both men profess the goal of protecting mutantkind, but Magneto wants to subjugate or eliminate human opposition, while Professor X dreams of a world where humans and mutants can co-exist. After Professor X founded the X-Men, Magneto created the Brotherhood of Evil Mutants. Over the years, the two men have been friends and foes. Recently, the pair united to help rebuild the island nation of Genosha. The Scarlet Witch's manipulations of reality during the House of M event seem to have temporarily de-powered both men.

TRANSITIONS

Xavier's genetic twin, the sinister Cassandra Nova, had died in Sharon Xavier's womb yet somehow maintained her life-essence. Nova re-entered Xavier's life with spectacular malevolence, orchestrating the devastation of the mutant nation of Genosha, and taking mental control of Xavier. In Xavier's guise, she outed him as a mutant to the world, and incited the Shi'ar Imperial Guard to attack the X-Mansion. Xavier's students helped free him from Nova's influence, and Xavier regained the use of his legs through the actions of academy student Xorn (actually a Magneto impostor in disguise.) Xavier later founded the X-Corporation, stepping down as head of the academy. He lost the use of his legs when the Magneto impostor revealed himself, and left for Genosha to help the real Magneto rebuild that island's society.

An artificial lifeform Danger tracked down Xavier on Genosha, intent on killing him. During the battle, it became clear that Danger was the self-aware consciousness of the X-Mansion's Danger Room training center, a fact that Xavier had known but suppressed in order to hone his students' combat skills.

Xavier tried to help Magneto's daughter, the SCARLET WITCH, recover from a breakdown, but he was unable to prevent her from removing the power from most mutants—including himself—on M-Day. With the reemergence of VULCAN, Xavier and a team of X-Men track him to the Shi'ar Empire. They fail to stop Vulcan, but being

ESSENTIAL STORYLINES
- **Giant-Size X-Men #1** Professor X recruits a new batch of X-Men to replace the originals, welcoming such future favorites as Nightcrawler and Storm.
- **New X-Men #118–126** The "Imperial" storyarc sees Professor X's genetic twin, Cassandra Nova, impersonating Xavier to imperil the Shi'ar empire.
- **Astonishing X-Men #7–12** A failure from his past returns to haunt Professor X, as he confronts the self-aware consciousness of the X-Men's Danger Room.
- **X-Men: Mutant Genesis, tpb** The X-Men stand in the way of Magneto's world-conquering schemes.

temporarily absorbed into the M'Kraan Crystal restore's Xavier's powers.

As a member of the ILLUMINATI, Xavier faced the HULK's wrath during World War Hulk (*see* pp. 150–1), but the Hulk came to believe that M-Day had cost the mutant enough. During the hunt for the first mutant baby born since M-Day, BISHOP accidentally shot Xavier in the head, putting him into a coma. He recovered but had lost much of his memory and so began the process of piecing his life back together.
PS, MF

Professor X designed the Danger Room, not realizing it would develop a mind of its own.

When the Illuminati were captured by the Skrulls, the aliens subjected them to all kinds of experiments. Professor X proved one of the "easiest to explore."

PRYDE, KATHERINE

I DID IT! I CONCENTRATED-- AN' I'M WALKING THROUGH THIS WALL FROM THE REAR COMPARTMENT!

I FEEL TINGLY ALL OVER -- BUT NOT AS TIRED AS THE LAST TIME. AN' MY HEADACHES ARE ALL GONE!

Kitty discovered she could walk through walls.

As a schoolgirl in Deerfield, Illinois, Kitty Pryde began suffering intense headaches. They were a sign that her mutant power to "phase" through solid matter was about to emerge.

Emma FROST, the White Queen of the HELLFIRE CLUB visited Kitty's parents to recruit her as a student. PROFESSOR X and three of his X-MEN soon followed, to try to convince Kitty's parents to let her attend his "School for Gifted Youngsters."

After the White Queen kidnapped the visiting X-Men, Kitty helped CYCLOPS and Phoenix (see GREY, Jean) rescue them. Kitty entered Xavier's school and joined the X-Men. She and fellow student COLOSSUS fell in love, and Kitty briefly adopted the codenames Sprite and Ariel. During an adventure in Japan, where WOLVERINE taught her martial arts, she chose the name Shadowcat, which she uses today.

Pryde later became a founding member of the original EXCALIBUR, a British-based team of adventurers. She also worked for the law enforcement agency SHIELD for a short time.

After Excalibur disbanded, Pryde rejoined the X-Men. She was recently lost—and is presumed dead—while saving the world by phasing a gigantic bullet all the way through the Earth. **PS, MF**

The alien dragon Lockheed was Kitty's loyal companion— until he was discovered to be an agent of SWORD.

FACTFILE

PRYDE, KATHERINE

REAL NAME
Katherine "Kitty" Pryde
OCCUPATION
Adventurer, student, former SHIELD employee
BASE
The Xavier Institute, Salem Center, New York State

HEIGHT 5 ft 6 in
WEIGHT 110 lbs
EYES Brown
HAIR Brown

FIRST APPEARANCE
The Uncanny X-Men #129
(October 1994)

POWERS

Mutant ability to pass ("phase") through solid matter by altering the vibratory rate of the atoms of her body, her clothing, and a limited amount of other matter. Highly adept with computers.

PRYOR, MADELYNE

FACTFILE

PRYOR, MADELYNE

REAL NAME
Madelyne Jennifer Pryor-Summers
OCCUPATION
Vengeance-seeker
BASE
Mobile

HEIGHT 5 ft 6 in
WEIGHT 110 lbs
EYES Green
HAIR Red

FIRST APPEARANCE
Uncanny X-Men #168
(April 1983)

POWERS

Most of Madelyne's abilities stem from her status as a clone of Jean Grey. She possesses vast psionic powers including telepathy and telekinesis, Madelyne is able to generate energy and manipulate it so that she can fly, project powerful force blasts, and create force fields that act as shields.

WELCOME TO ALASKA. MY NAME'S MADELYNE PRYOR.

Madelyne Pryor was a clone of Jean Grey and created to meet Scott Summers.

MR. SINISTER was obsessed with obtaining the spawn of a union between Jean GREY and Scott Summers (see CYCLOPS), but it was only after Jean's death that he achieved his goal. Using stored genetic material, he successfully cloned Jean. He named his creation Madelyne Pryor, provided her with false memories, and manipulated Scott Summers into marrying her. Their relationship resulted in a son—Nathan Summers (see CABLE)—but when the real Jean Grey was resurrected, Scott left Madelyne. Insanely jealous, Madelyne began to lose her grip on reality, and her journey towards madness accelerated when Sinister kidnapped Nathan. As Madelyne's mutant powers began to emerge, so did her thirst for vengeance, and she transformed herself into the Goblin Queen.

She was killed in a showdown with the X-MEN, during which she tried to sacrifice her son. The machinations of the vile Mr. Sinister had once more resulted in desperate unhappiness. **AD**

As the Goblin Queen, Madelyne Pryor was a terrifying enemy for the X-Men.

PSYCHO-MAN

FIRST APPEARANCE Fantastic Four Special #5 (November 1967)

REAL NAME Unrevealed

OCCUPATION Scientist; conqueror **BASE** Traan; his World-Ship

HEIGHT Indeterminate **WEIGHT** Indeterminate

EYES Unrevealed **HAIR** Unrevealed

SPECIAL POWERS/ABILITIES Superhuman intelligence; his main weapon projects a "psycho-ray" that stimulates fear, doubt, and hate.

The Psycho-Man was chief scientist of Traan, a planet in an alternate reality known as the "microverse." He traveled to Earth to conquer the planet by means of his "psycho-ray," but was thwarted by the FANTASTIC FOUR'S HUMAN TORCH and THING, the BLACK PANTHER, and the INHUMANS' Royal Family. The Psycho-Man's true size and appearance are mysteries: on Earth he remained tiny while encased in a human-sized suit of body armor. He continues to clash with the Fantastic Four, both on Earth and within the microverse. **PS**

The Psycho-Man can operate suits of armor far larger than himself—or his foes.

PSYKLOP

FIRST APPEARANCE Avengers #88 (May 1971)

REAL NAME Psyklop

OCCUPATION Servant of the Dark Gods **BASE** Mobile

HEIGHT 8 ft **WEIGHT** 450 lbs **EYES** Red **HAIR** None

SPECIAL POWERS/ABILITIES Possessed of superhuman strength and durability, Psyklop can also fire beams of energy from his eye that can hypnotize an opponent, or make him experience illusions.

The devoted servant of the Dark Gods who ruled the Earth at the dawn of time, Psyklop hibernated for millennia until called upon to serve his masters once more. He tried to offer up the HULK as a sacrifice to his sinister lords, but was prevented from doing so by the AVENGERS. The Hulk ended up miniaturized, and fell into the Microverse, alighting on the planet K'ai. Pursuing the Hulk, Psyklop engaged him in battle and was defeated. For his failure, the Dark Gods exiled Psyklop to K'ai, where he seemingly met his end, consumed by the spirits of all the people he had slain. **TB**

PSYLOCKE

James Braddock, Sr. was an inhabitant of Otherworld who came to Britain and fathered three children, James, Jr., Brian and Elizabeth. Brian became the hero CAPTAIN BRITAIN, a role Betsy later briefly took over at the behest of the British government agency RCX. Blinded and nearly killed by the villain Slaymaster, Betsy was abducted by MOJO, who gave her new artificial eyes. She was rescued by the NEW MUTANTS and joined the X-MEN as Psylocke. Spiral switched the minds of Psylocke and the Japanese assassin Kwannon into each other's bodies. Discovering that her new body was dying, Kwannon had the crimelord Matsu'o Tsurayaba kill her. Elizabeth survives in Kwannon's original body. Psylocke sacrificed her telepathy to defeat the X-Men's enemy, the SHADOW KING. Subsequently, she gained telekinetic abilities. While with the X-Treme X-Men, Psylocke was seemingly slain by their enemy Vargas. Psylocke returned, however, and after a spell with the X-Men, joined the EXILES. Betsy recently returned to her home dimension and is now in her original body once more. **PS, MF**

Psylocke forfeited her telepathic powers in order to imprison the Shadow King, one of the X-Men's deadliest foes, in the Astral Plane.

Psylocke alongside her teammates in the Exiles, including alternate versions of Morph, Rogue and Sabretooth.

FACTFILE

REAL NAME
Elisabeth "Betsy" Braddock

OCCUPATION
Adventurer

BASE
The Xavier Institute, Salem Center,
New York State

HEIGHT 5 ft 11 in

WEIGHT 155 lbs

EYES (current body) blue

HAIR (current body) black,
dyed purple

FIRST APPEARANCE
Captain Britain Vol. 1 #8
(December 1976)

POWERS

Possesses telekinetic powers.
Can focus her psionic powers into a
"psychic knife" to stun or kill an
adversary. Former telepath.
Highly skilled in martial arts.

PUCK

FIRST APPEARANCE Alpha Flight Vol. 1 #1 (August 1983)

REAL NAME Eugene Milton Judd

OCCUPATION Alpha Flight member   **BASE** Tamarind Island

HEIGHT 3 ft 6 in   **WEIGHT** 225 lbs   **EYES** Brown   **HAIR** Black

SPECIAL POWERS/ABILITIES Superb athlete and gymnast; formidable hand-to-hand combatant with unique fighting style; trained bullfighter; limited knowledge of sorcery.

Eugene Judd released the evil sorcerer Black Raazer and managed to trap him in his own body, which extended his life but reduced him to the height of a dwarf. Judd was later invited to join Beta and then ALPHA FLIGHT as Puck. He eventually rid himself of Black Raazer, temporarily costing him his powers. Later, Puck's daughter Zuzha Yu joined a new Alpha Flight, calling herself Puck too. They both died trying to stop the Collective, a man imbued with all of the mutant energies lost on M-Day. **AD, MF**

PUMA

FIRST APPEARANCE Amazing Spider-Man Vol. 1 #256 (Sept. 1984)

REAL NAME Thomas Fireheart

OCCUPATION CEO of Fireheart Enterprises; mercenary

BASE Mobile   **HEIGHT** 6 ft 2in   **WEIGHT** 240 lbs

EYES Green   **HAIR** Red; (as Fireheart) black

SPECIAL POWERS/ABILITIES As Puma Fireheart has superhuman strength, agility, heightened senses, and claws

Puma was the heir to a long tradition of mystical champions created by a Native American tribe. Raised to oppose the BEYONDER, Thomas Fireheart donned the mantle of the Puma and kept his fighting skills sharp by becoming a mercenary, often fighting (or aiding) SPIDER-MAN. Fireheart also served as the head of Fireheart Enterprises, which supplied him with high-tech weaponry and vehicles, but he constantly struggled to control his animalistic Puma persona. After the Civil War (*see* pp. 84–5), he was accused of taking bribes and joined Modok to make money to pay for his defense. **MF**

PUNISHER
War hero turned vengeful vigilante

Marine Captain Frank Castle was a decorated hero during the Vietnam War. Winner of the Bronze and Silver Star, and recipient of four Purple Hearts, Castle was an exceptionally skilled combat veteran. Then came the event that changed his life. While on leave in New York, Castle took his family for a picnic in Central Park. There they witnessed a mob murder. The mobsters then killed Castle's wife and two young children.

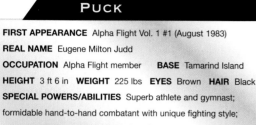

Frank Castle, family man, in happier days.

ONE-MAN ARMY

With his whole world destroyed, Castle deserted from the Marines and dropped out of sight for a few months. When he resurfaced, it was as a vigilante named the Punisher, who conducted a one-man, anti-crime campaign throughout New York City. Equipped with an arsenal of weapons, the Punisher took his vengeance on the mob gang who had killed his family, but he didn't stop there. He vowed to kill all criminals of every kind.

The Punisher has devoted his life to destroying organized crime, drug dealers, street gangs, muggers, killers, or any other criminal element. His actions have brought him into conflict with several costumed heroes, such as SPIDER-MAN (with whom he has also cooperated), and DAREDEVIL, who strictly opposes Punisher's lethal methods.

The big white skull on Punisher's costume draws criminal fire to his heavily armored body rather than to his unprotected head.

FACTFILE

REAL NAME
Frank Castle (born Castiglione)

OCCUPATION
Vigilante

BASE
Mobile

HEIGHT 6 ft 1 in
WEIGHT 200 lbs
EYES Blue
HAIR Black

FIRST APPEARANCE
Amazing Spider-Man #129
(February 1974)

POWERS

The Punisher is seasoned combat veteran of exceptional skill. He has undergone SEAL (Sea, Air, Land), UDT (Underwater Demolition Team), and LRPA (Long Range Patrol) military training. He is an expert using all types of small arms and large caliber guns, he has extensive training using explosives and tactical weapons, and he is a superior martial artist and hand-to-hand combatant.

The Punisher fiercely follows his own code of conduct. While he kills criminals on sight, during the Civil War, he refused to lift a finger to defend himself against Captain America.

WEAPONS AND ENEMIES

To carry out his war on crime, the Punisher uses machine guns, rifles, handguns, shotguns, knives, grenade launchers, armor-piercing bullets, and explosives. His weapons are customized with tactical scopes, night-vision scopes, silencers, and tripods.

During the Civil War (*see* pp. 84–5), the Punisher specifically targeted Super Villains. In the aftermath of the Secret Invasion (*see* pp. 326–7), he has dedicated himself to killing one of the most powerful Super Villains in the world: Norman Osborn (*see* GREEN GOBLIN). **MT, MF**

Evil beware! On the streets of Manhattan, no one escapes the Punisher's vigilante vengeance!

ESSENTIAL STORYLINES

• *Marvel Preview #2*
Marine captain Frank Castle takes his wife and two children for a picnic in New York's Central Park. There, they witness a mob killing, after which the mobsters kill Castle's wife and children. Traumatized, Castle take vengeance against the killers and continues his one-man vigilante campaign against all criminals as the Punisher.

• *The Punisher Vol. 1 Welcome Back, Frank (tpb)*
After a long absence, the Punisher returns to the streets of Manhattan to take on Ma Gnucchi and her crime family.

When Spider-Man was on the run after switching sides during the Civil War, the Punisher stepped in to save him.

PUPPET MASTER

FACTFILE

REAL NAME
Phillip Masters

OCCUPATION
Professional criminal

BASE
Sunshine City, Florida

HEIGHT 5 ft 6 in
WEIGHT 150 lbs
EYES Blue
HAIR None

FIRST APPEARANCE:
Fantastic Four Vol. 1 #8
(November 1962)

POWERS

A brilliant biologist and technician; Able to control the actions and thoughts of others by making models of them out of special radioactive clay. He then turns the models into marionettes, attaching strings to their limbs.

The Fantastic Four look on helplessly as the Puppet Master tinkers with a robot clutching a model of an atomic bomb. What can the villain be up to?

PUPPET MASTER

A talented biologist, Phillip Masters became the research partner of Jacob Reiss. Resentful of Reiss's success, Masters killed his partner during a botched robbery of their lab, triggering an explosion that blinded Reiss's daughter, Alicia. Masters later married Reiss's widow and became Alicia's stepfather. Learning he could control others with his clay sculptures, Masters became the Puppet Master, one of the earliest enemies of the FANTASTIC FOUR. He also teamed up with the villains EGGHEAD, MAD THINKER, and DOCTOR DOOM. To his horror, his daughter Alicia fell in love with the Thing, though in time the Puppet Master was reconciled to their relationship. The US government recruited the Puppet Master to run their Sunshine City project, where mind-controlled criminals safely served out their prison sentences. He returned to crime during the Civil War (*see* pp. 84-5), using the YANCY STREET GANG. He recently blew himself up while facing MS. MARVEL. **DW, MF**

PYM, HANK *see opposite page*

PYRO

FIRST APPEARANCE Uncanny X-Men Vol. 1 #141 (January 1981)
REAL NAME St. John Allerdyce
OCCUPATION Professional criminal **BASE** Mobile
HEIGHT 5 ft 10 in **WEIGHT** 150 lbs **EYES** Blue **HAIR** Blond
SPECIAL POWERS/ABILITIES Could control and manipulate flames within his immediate vicinity, though he could not produce flames himself. His insulated costume had built-in flamethrowers.

Born in Sydney, Australia, St. John Allerdyce won fame as a novelist until MYSTIQUE convinced him to join her BROTHERHOOD OF EVIL MUTANTS. As the flame-shaping Pyro, Allerdyce battled the X-MEN and remained with his teammates when they transitioned into the US government-sanctioned FREEDOM FORCE. Pyro eventually contracted the fatal Legacy virus, and succumbed to its effects after saving Senator Robert KELLY from a team of assassins that belonged to a new Brotherhood of Evil Mutants. **DW**

PURPLE MAN

FACTFILE

REAL NAME
Zebediah Killgrave

OCCUPATION
Former spy, professional criminal, conqueror

BASE
Mobile

HEIGHT 5 ft 11 in
WEIGHT 165 lbs
EYES Purple
HAIR Purple

FIRST APPEARANCE:
Daredevil Vol. 1 #4
(October 1964)

POWERS

Killgrave's body secretes psychoactive chemicals that deaden the will of people in his vicinity, rendering them susceptible to his commands. Individuals with unusually strong will power can resist him.

PURPLE MAN

Born in Yugoslavia, Zebediah Killgrave was a spy who was accidentally covered with an experimental nerve gas in liquid form. This permanently dyed his hair and skin purple and gave him the power to compel others to obey his commands. As the Purple Man, he was repeatedly defeated by DAREDEVIL, one of the few people able to resist his power. For a while, he made JESSICA JONES his slave. She was so traumatized, she gave up being a Super Hero afterward.

He later tried to retire from crime, but the KINGPIN and DOCTOR DOOM exploited him still. He attempted to compel the mutant Nate Grey, alias X-MAN, to help him conquer the world, but Grey defeated him. He later controlled all of New York at once at the behest of BARON ZEMO, but the THUNDERBOLTS put a stop to that. Recently, he joined the HOOD's crime syndicate and is now running a Las Vegas casino. The Purple Man has a daughter, Kara Killgrave, with similar powers. She is known as PERSUASION. **PS, MF**

PYM, HANK

Scientific genius behind Ant-Man, Giant-Man, and Goliath

Dr. Henry Pym, a brilliant scientist, discovered a rare group of subatomic particles which became known as "Pym Particles." When ingested through a serum (and later through a gas and a capsule) the particles could either shrink a person down to the size of an ant, or increase a person's size to 10, 25, even 100 feet in height.

As Ant-Man, Henry Pym could shrink himself so small that he could ride atop an ant.

FACTFILE

REAL NAME
Dr. Henry "Hank" Pym

OCCUPATION
Adventurer, biochemist, roboticist, manager of Avengers Compound

BASE
Cresskill, New York; Avengers Compound, LA, California

HEIGHT 6 ft
WEIGHT 185 lbs
EYES Blue
HAIR Blond

FIRST APPEARANCE
Tales To Astonish #27
(January 1962)

ANT AND WASP

Undertaking a study of ants, Pym also developed a cybernetic helmet which allowed him to communicate with and control ants. Developing a costume to go along with his size changing ability and helmet, Pym reduced himself to the size of an ant and fought evil as Ant-Man. Pym and his future wife Janet Van Dyne were founding members of the AVENGERS as Ant-Man and the WASP. Later, Pym decided to use his size-changing power to grow rather than shrink, and he began fighting crime as the costumed hero Giant-Man. Eventually, Pym realized that changing his size was putting too great a strain on his body and he stopped.

Ant-Man's cybernetic helmet contains technology that allows him to communicate with and command ants to do his bidding.

THE *WASP'S* IN *DANGER*

CUTAWAY DIAGRAM OF WAFER-THIN CYBERNETIC HELMET

POWERS

By ingesting Pym Particles, either as a serum, gas, or capsule, Henry Pym can shrink to the size of an ant, or grow up to 100 ft tall. He can also change the size of objects. Using his cybernetic helmet, Pym can communicate with ants and command them to do his bidding.

I WAS *CARELESS*! I REMAINED GIANT-SIZED *TOO LONG*! NOW THE SUDDEN STRAIN OF *SHRINKING* IS TOO MUCH!

HANK!

HE *STOPPED* SHRINKING -- AT *TEN FEET*! HE NEVER DID IT BEFORE! HE'S *BLACKING OUT*!

CAN'T *CONTROL* IT ANY LONGER...! IF -- IF I DON'T GET MY ABILITY *BACK* -- I'LL *REMAIN* THIS WAY -- TEN FEET TALL -- *FOREVER*! OHH -- !

The Pym Particles in the serum that Henry Pym uses to alter his size can prove difficult to control. Here, the effort it took to return to normal size caused Pym to lose consciousness.

A TROUBLED MIND

When Janet was kidnapped by ATTUMA and the COLLECTOR, Pym helped the Avengers rescue her. He then became Goliath. While experimenting in his lab, , an accident changed Pym's personality. He claimed that he had murdered Pym and became Yellow Jacket. He married Janet, but they later divorced.

During the SECRET INVASION (*see* pp. 326-7), it was revealed that this Pym was a SKRULL imposter. The real Pym returned to see the Wasp die due to modifications his Skrull impersonator had made to her powers. Pym renamed himself the Wasp in honor of Janet and formed a new Avengers team. **MT, MF**

With each change of Henry Pym's Super Hero identity came a costume change as well.

ESSENTIAL STORYLINES
• *Tales to Astonish #49* Hank Pym first uses his size-changing Pym Particles to grow in size, transforming himself from Ant-Man into Giant-Man.
• *Avengers #54* Hank Pym creates Ultron, an incredibly powerful robot, which he implants with his own brain patterns. However Ultron rebels against his inventor.
• *Avengers Forever, tpb* Pym (as Giant-Man) and the Avengers battle Kang with humanity's future at stake.

FACES OF PYM
1 Ant-Man
2 Goliath
3 Yellowjacket

1990s

As the popularity of extended storylines and multi-title crossovers grew, Marvel produced more new titles and added gimmicks like holograms, foil-stamping and die-cut designs to covers. New versions of *Deathlok* and *Ghost Rider* joined titles like *New Warriors* and *Guardians of the Galaxy* in 1990. "The Infinity Gauntlet," the first of three major crossovers, arrived in 1991. "Operation: Galactic Storm" sprawled across the Avengers-related titles and a series set in the year 2099 began with *Ravage 2099* and *Spider-Man 2099* in 1992. "Maximum Carnage" threatened all the Spider-Man titles and Daredevil experienced a "Fall from Grace" as *Cable*, *Night Thrasher* and *Thunderstrike* graced 1993. New team books like *Fantastic Force*, *Force Works* and *Generation X-Men* marked 1994, and 1995 was highlighted by the "Age of Apocalypse", an event that briefly re-named all the X-Men titles and launched *X-Man*. The crossovers "Onslaught" and "Heroes Reborn," dominated 1996 and the spotlight fell on *Heroes For Hire* and *Thunderbolts* in 1997. "Heroes Return" was the big news in 1998, and *Earth X*, set in an alternate reality, debuted in 1999.

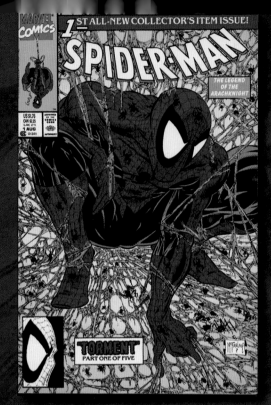

SPIDER-MAN #1 (1990)

With multiple covers and sales topping a million-and-a-half copies, a new Spider-Man is launched and begins a six-part extended storyline.

SILVER SURFER #50 (1991)

The Silver Surfer battles Thanos and celebrates 50 issues by being the first Marvel comic to possess a foil-stamped cover.

X-MEN #1 (1991)

Selling over 12 million copies with multiple covers, a second X-Men title establishes a new high that has yet to be equaled.

THUNDERSTRIKE #1 (1993)

After briefly replacing Thor, Eric Masterson is given his own enchanted mace, a new name and a new monthly title to face the menace called Bloodaxe.

IRON MAN #325 (1996)

After learning that Tony Stark is being controlled by Kang, the Avengers enter a "Timeslide" to recruit a teenage Tony from an alternate timeline to assist them and battle his older self.

Incredible Hulk #388 (1991)

The Hulk learns that one of his former partners is slowly dying from a deadly disease when he confronts the assassin called Speedfreak.

Spider-Man 2099 #1 (1992)

A new universe set in a possible alternate future begins when a genetic experiment turns a corporate scientist into a reluctant Super Hero.

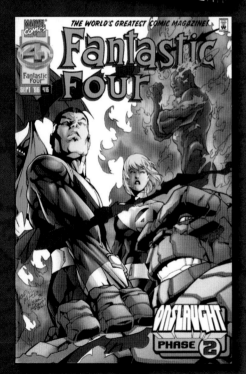

Fantastic Four #416 (1996)

As "Onslaught" draws to a climax, the title that spawned the Marvel Universe ends its first run, only to be relaunch in "Heroes Reborn."

Avengers Vol. 3 #4 (1998)

Though the volume has changed, some traditions live on as the Avengers change their lineup once more.

Avengers Forever #1 (1998)

When Immortus decides that Rick Jones is a threat to all existence, Avengers from the past, present and future are forced to team up with Kang the Conqueror to save him.

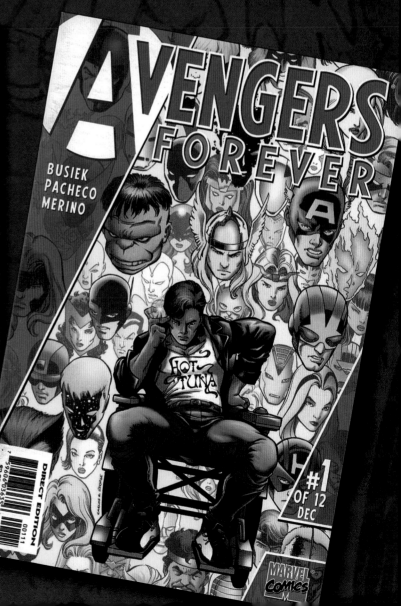

FACTFILE

QUASAR

QUASAR

REAL NAME
Wendell Vaughn
OCCUPATION
Protector of the Universe
BASE
Mobile

HEIGHT 5 ft 10 in
WEIGHT 168 lbs
EYES Blue
HAIR Blond

FIRST APPEARANCE
*Captain America Vol. 1 #217
(January 1978)*

POWERS

Quantum-bands permit flight, teleportation, and the ability to form quantum energy constructs, including weapons and armor.

When Wendell Vaughn's graduation ceremony from the SHIELD academy was attacked by AIM terrorists, a desperate Vaughn donned quantum-band bracelets worn by a copy of 1950s MARVEL BOY. As the new Marvel Boy, Vaughn joined SHIELD's Super-Agent program, later calling himself Marvel Man before settling on Quasar. Vaughn had been chosen by the cosmic entity Eon to become the new Protector of the Universe, replacing the late CAPTAIN MAR-VELL. Quasar became a member of the AVENGERS, and worked with the FANTASTIC FOUR.

Using his quantum-bands, Quasar can project bubbles of energy that act as force shields. They can also transport things through space.

ANNIHILUS destroyed Vaughn during the Annihilation event (*see* pp. 30-1) and the quantum bands were passed on to Phyla-Vell, the daughter of Mar-Vell. She became Quasar but after Vaughn's death, he was resurrected in solid light form. When Phyla-Vell was killed and became DEATH's new avatar, Vaughn gave the quantum bands to Richard Rider, who'd been stripped of his powers as NOVA. **DW, MF**

Initially hesitant about becoming Protector of the Universe, Quasar has become a selfless representative of Earth, and his understanding of his near-limitless powers has deepened.

Quasar is Earth's foremost cosmic hero, regularly dealing with representatives from interstellar empires such as the Kree, the Skrulls, and the Shi'ar. He has even held his own against Galactus-level threats.

QUASIMODO

FIRST APPEARANCE Fantastic Four Special #4 (November 1966)
REAL NAME Quasi-Motivational Destruct Organism
OCCUPATION Former computer **BASE** Mobile
HEIGHT 6 ft **WEIGHT** 1,350 lbs **EYES** White **HAIR** None
SPECIAL POWERS/ABILITIES Computer brain; superhuman strength (when in physical form); left eye projects force blasts; can exist as pure consciousness without a physical body.

Quasimodo originated as a sentient computer created by the MAD THINKER. Endowed with a grotesque face that appeared on a screen, Quasimodo longed for a more human form. However, despite promising to fulfill his wish, the Thinker abandoned him. The SILVER SURFER took pity on Quasimodo and transformed him into a mobile, humanoid creature, but the ungrateful Quasimodo fought the Surfer, who rendered him immobile. Eventually Quasimodo regained his mobility, and has since battled such champions as SPIDER-MAN, the BEAST, the VISION, and the original CAPTAIN MAR-VELL. **PS**

QUICKSILVER
see opposite page

QNAX

FIRST APPEARANCE Tales to Astonish #74 (December 1965)
REAL NAME Qnax (also known as Amphibian)
OCCUPATION Gladiator **BASE** The planet Xantares
HEIGHT 7 ft 9 in **WEIGHT** 915 lbs **EYES** Green **HAIR** None
SPECIAL POWERS/ABILITIES A product of centuries of scientific breeding to create the ultimate fighting machine; can travel fast and breathe underwater.

Xantares' Council of Elders sent Qnax on a mission to obtain the Sphere of Ultimate Knowledge, telling him the Sphere was needed to save the planet. Arriving on the homeworld of the WATCHERS, Qnax encountered the HULK, who was also searching for the Sphere. They fought and Qnax was hurled into space. Exiled from Xantares for this failure, Qnax travelled the cosmos as a gladiator for hire. He eventually discovered that the Council of Elders wanted the Sphere in order to dominate Xantares. Dismayed by this, Qnax returned home, hoping to bring justice to his people. **AD**

QUICKSILVER
The super-fast Super Hero

The son of MAGNETO, Pietro and his twin sister Wanda (SCARLET WITCH) grew up never knowing their father's identity. While pregnant with them, their mother, Magda, fled from Magneto and gave birth to them in the hills of Wundagore Mountain. The gypsy family of Django Maximoff raised the children, but when their mutant powers first showed, Pietro and Wanda were persecuted as demons.

VILLAINS AND HEROES

Magneto found them during his hunt for members of his BROTHERHOOD OF EVIL MUTANTS. As Quicksilver and Scarlet Witch, they engaged in a series of battles with the X-Men, remaining with the Brotherhood only because of the debt they felt they owed Magneto. When the first incarnation of the Brotherhood dissolved, Pietro and his sister went into seclusion, vowing never again to use their powers for evil.

Quicksilver eventually turned against Magneto (in reality, his long-lost father), and became a valued member of the Avengers along with his sister.

Hearing that the AVENGERS needed new blood, Pietro and Wanda resumed their costumed identities and were accepted as members. Quicksilver did not approve of Wanda's marriage to the android VISION, and it caused a rift between them. Quicksilver was later injured during a mission and nursed back to health by CRYSTAL of the INHUMANS. The two were married and had a daughter, Luna. Since then, Quicksilver has worked with the Avengers, served with the mutant team X-FACTOR, as well as leading the Knights of Wundagore for a time.

When Wanda had a breakdown and destroyed the Avengers, Quicksilver persuaded her to use her powers to change the world into a place in which mutants ruled, creating the House of M (Earth-58163). Once mainstream reality returned on M-DAY, Quicksilver lost his powers. He used the Inhumans' Terrigen Mists to restore himself and others, but his plans went awry. Furious, Crystal announced that their marriage was annulled. Recently, hoping to redeem himself, Quicksilver joined Hank PYM's new Avengers. **TB, MF**

While in the Brotherhood of Evil Mutants, Quicksilver experienced superhuman combat against the X-Men, including Cyclops.

Since childhood, Quicksilver has been overly protective of his unstable sister, the Scarlet Witch.

FACTFILE
REAL NAME
Pietro Maximoff
OCCUPATION
Adventurer
BASE
Various

HEIGHT 6 ft
WEIGHT 175 lbs
EYES Blue
HAIR Silver

FIRST APPEARANCE
X-Men #4
(March 1964)

POWERS

Quicksilver possesses the mutant ability to run at superhuman speeds over great distances. His top speed is alleged to be 175 mph. He can create a whirlwind by running in a circle; his temper can be a quick as his feet.

ESSENTIAL STORYLINES
• **Avengers #16** Quicksilver and his sister the Scarlet Witch join the Avengers.
• **Avengers #127/Fantastic Four #150** Quicksilver marries Crystal of the isolationist Inhumans.
• **Avengers #185-187** Quicksilver and the Scarlet Witch return to Wundagore Mountain in Eastern Europe to discover the strange secrets of their birth and their parentage.

Quicksilver is a member of the Ultimates team of Avengers who hail from a parallel Earth in another dimension of the Multiverse.

RADIOACTIVE MAN

FIRST APPEARANCE Journey Into Mystery #93 (June 1963)

REAL NAME Dr. Chen Lu

OCCUPATION Former scientist; criminal **BASE** Mobile

HEIGHT 6 ft 6 in **WEIGHT** 310 lbs **EYES** Brown **HAIR** None

SPECIAL POWERS/ABILITIES Manipulates radioactivity given off by body; emits radiation as heat or blinding light and can incinerate a city block; hypnotic abilities; superhuman strength.

Dr. Chen Lu was a nuclear physicist in the People's Republic of China, and was among those asked by the Chinese government to defeat Thor. Lu exposed himself to nuclear radiation, transforming him into Radioactive Man. He traveled to New York and battled Thor, but lost. Baron Zemo then enlisted him in his Masters of Evil. He later changed his ways and joined the Thunderbolts. During the Civil War, he sided with the US government, but the Chinese government called him home after the Secret Invasion. **MT, MF**

RAGE

FIRST APPEARANCE Avengers #326 (November 1990)

REAL NAME Elvin Daryl Haliday

OCCUPATION Student **BASE** Oatridge School for Boys

HEIGHT 6 ft 6 in **WEIGHT** 450 lbs **EYES** Brown **HAIR** None

SPECIAL POWERS/ABILITIES Exposure to alien radiation granted him the ability to fly and to understand the language of birds.

Twelve-year-old Elvin Haliday plunged into Newtown Creek to escape a gang of racist thugs. The chemicals in the water caused him to grow into an adult with superhuman strength. Although Elvin could have used his new powers for crime, his only relation, the devout Granny Staples, convinced him to become a hero. Elvin slipped from this road just once: when Granny Staples herself was murdered. Rage worked with both the Avengers and the New Warriors. He sided with Captain America during the Civil War (see pp. 84–5), but later joined the Fifty State Initiative (see pp. 118–9) at Camp Hammond. He is now part of the latest New Warriors team. **AD, MF**

RASPUTIN, MIKHAIL

FIRST APPEARANCE Uncanny X-Men #284 (January 1992)

REAL NAME Mikhail Rasputin **OCCUPATION** Cosmonaut

BASE The Hill, in an unspecified dimension

HEIGHT 6 ft 5 in **WEIGHT** 255 lbs **EYES** Blue **HAIR** Black

SPECIAL POWERS/ABILITIES Manipulates matter on a sub-atomic level. He uses this power to fire destructive blasts, warp reality, and teleport through space and between dimensions.

During a spaceflight, Soviet cosmonaut Mikhail Rasputin entered another dimension. There he fell in love with and married a princess, but when he had to try to close the dimensional rift, the backlash killed hundreds of people, including his beloved wife. When he returned to Earth, he became leader of the Morlocks before massacring them and setting up the mutant terrorist group Gene Nation for Dark Beast. He later helped the X-Men defeat Apocalypse and his Horsemen. Eventually, he banished himself to another dimension to save his brother from Mr. Sinister. **MT, MF**

RAVONNA

In the 41st century of an alternate future, Kang had conquered all of Earth except the small kingdom of Princess Ravonna, who refused his offer of marriage. Kang's army ultimately overwhelmed Ravonna's kingdom.

But when Kang refused to execute Ravonna, his commander Baltag rebelled against him. Kang then joined forces with Ravonna and the Avengers to defeat Baltag. The grateful Ravonna fell in love with Kang. When the vengeful Baltag fired a blaster at Kang, Ravonna pushed Kang out of the way, and the blast struck her instead. Kang placed Ravonna in suspended animation. To restore her to life, Kang played a game with the alien Grandmaster, who gave him temporary power over life and death when Kang won. However, Kang wasted this short-lived power in an unsuccessful attempt to kill the Avengers.

After this point different timelines diverge, in which Ravonna leads different lives. In one timeline Kang saves Ravonna from Baltag's attack, but she becomes the ally and consort of Kang's own future counterpart, Immortus.

In another timeline the Grandmaster revives Ravonna, who seeks vengeance on Kang. She assumes a number of identities, including Nebula, the Temptress, and the Terminatrix. A future counterpart will take the name Revelation. **PS**

NO ONE COMMANDS A *PRINCESS!*

NO! NOTHING MUST HARM YOU! FOR I REALIZE AT LAST-- I DO TRULY LOVE-- ⸮UHHHHH!⸮

RAVONNA!

Ravonna was willing to sacrifice her life to save her lover Kang the Conqueror.

FACTFILE

REAL NAME
Ravonna Lexus Renslayer

OCCUPATION
Princess

BASE
Originally an unnamed kingdom on 41st century Earth in an alternate future.

HEIGHT 5 ft 8 in
WEIGHT 142 lbs
EYES (as Ravonna) Brown; (as Nebula/Terminatrix) Blue
HAIR (as Ravonna) Red-brown; (as Nebula/Terminatrix) Blonde

FIRST APPEARANCE
Avengers #23 (December 1965)

As Terminatrix or Revelation: has enhanced durability, speed and agility, is a formidable hand-to-hand combatant, and uses highly advanced technology.

RAVONNA

POWERS

RAWHIDE KID, THE

FIRST APPEARANCE Rawhide Kid Vol. 1 #1 (March 1955)

REAL NAME Johnny Bart

OCCUPATION Gunslinger   **BASE** The American Old West

HEIGHT 5 ft 10 in   **WEIGHT** 185 lbs   **EYES** Blue   **HAIR** Red

SPECIAL POWERS/ABILITIES Skilled brawler and horseman; among the quickest draws in the Old West.

The Rawhide Kid learned to handle a six-shooter thanks to his adoptive father, a Texas Ranger, after his real parents were killed by Cheyenne warriors. When his adoptive father died in a rigged duel, the Rawhide Kid took revenge on the killers and then wandered the West astride his horse Nightwind, keeping one step ahead of the sheriff who suspected the Kid of murder. By means of time travel, the Rawhide Kid occasionally crossed paths with modern-era Super Heroes. **AD**

REAPER

FIRST APPEARANCE New Mutants Vol. 1 #87 (March 1990)

REAL NAME Pantu Hurageb

OCCUPATION None   **BASE** Unknown

HEIGHT/ WEIGHT/ EYES/HAIR Unrevealed

SPECIAL POWERS/ABILITIES Neurosynaptic energy generated by Reaper slows reflexes and movements of those nearby; scythes focus energy and can be used to paralyze others.

Not to be mistaken for the demon raised to battle BLADE, nor for an adversary of the PHANTOM RIDER, the Reaper known as Pantu Hurageb was a member of the MUTANT LIBERATION FRONT. During his stint there, he lost a hand and a lower leg and replaced both with artificial limbs. Following Reaper's incarceration in Neverland, Nathan Summers (CABLE) tried to pry the camp's location from his mind, causing him severe brain damage and turning him mute. He lost his powers on M-Day, but Quicksilver has since given them back. **AD, MF**

REAVERS

The cyborg mercenaries known as the Reavers originally operated from an underground complex in Cooteman's Creek, located in Australia's Northern Territory. They exploited the teleportation mutant GATEWAY in order to commit robberies around the world until the X-MEN forced them from their base. Ex-HELLFIRE CLUB member Donald Pierce reorganized the team, bringing in Cole, Macon, Reese, and Lady Deathstrike. The new Reavers nearly killed WOLVERINE, and launched a failed attack on Moira MacTaggert's Muir Island laboratory. A squad of SENTINELS nearly destroyed the Reavers, though most members survived due to their half-machine physiologies.

The Reavers later won a contract from the psionic entity the SHADOW KING to kidnap ROGUE of the X-Men, but failed to capture their quarry. Pierce chose to remake the Reavers into a grassroots anti-mutant movement, and swayed many citizens with his hateful propaganda. Recently, LADY DEATHSTRIKE formed her own Reavers by giving advanced cybernetics to members of the Purifiers, a fundamentalist Christian, anti-mutant terrorist movement. They were destroyed by X-FORCE. **DW MF**

FACTFILE

KEY MEMBERS

DONALD PIERCE (LEADER)
Adamantium-enhanced body, enhanced strength; morphing cyborg limbs emit energy blasts.

BONEBREAKER
Cyborg strength, tank treads, built-in weaponry.

PRETTY BOY
Extendible cyborg limbs and capture coils; reprograms the personalities of others.

SKULLBUSTER
Cyborg strength, robot legs; uses machine guns, grenade launchers.

SKULLBUSTER/CYLLA
Cyborg strength, reflexes; wrist claws, thermite launchers.

LADY DEATHSTRIKE
Augmented strength, reflexes; talons extend from fingertips.

COLE, MACON, AND REESE
Cyborg strength, reflexes; bionic scanners and tracking devices.

BASE Mobile

FIRST APPEARANCE
Uncanny X-Men Vol. 1 #229 (May 1988)

THE REAVERS
(left to right) Skullbuster, Bonebreaker, Pretty Boy

RED GHOST

FIRST APPEARANCE Fantastic Four Vol. 1 #13 (April 1963)

REAL NAME Ivan Kragoff   **OCCUPATION** Villain

BASE Mobile   **HEIGHT** 5 ft 11 in   **WEIGHT** 215 lbs

EYES Brown   **HAIR** White, balding

SPECIAL POWERS/ABILITIES Renders himself and nearby objects intangible and transparent; ingenious scientist and brilliant engineer.

Russian scientist Ivan Kragoff was consumed with envy by the achievements and powers of the FANTASTIC FOUR. Determined to beat them to the Moon, he designed his spacecraft to maximize exposure to cosmic rays, hoping to duplicate the freakish accident that had created his rivals.

Kragoff's experiment succeeded: while he gained the ability to become intangible, his three ape companions became more intelligent and obtained powers of strength, magnetism, and shapeshifting. Now known as the Red Ghost, Kragoff and his super-ape companions became formidable adversaries to the Fantastic Four, clashing with them repeatedly and even creating problems for the AVENGERS and SPIDER-MAN. **AD**

RED GUARDIAN

RED GUARDIAN

FACTFILE

REAL NAME
Alexi Shostakov

OCCUPATION
Espionage agent for Soviet
Union; later for People's Republic
of China

BASE
Various secret KGB bases in
USSR; later a military base in
the People's Republic of China

HEIGHT 6 ft 2 in
WEIGHT 220 lbs
EYES Blue
HAIR Red

FIRST APPEARANCE
Avengers #43 (August 1967)

POWERS

Brilliant athlete and test pilot,
trained in espionage techniques
and hand-to-hand combat by the
KGB. Disc on Red Guardian's belt
could be detached and used as a
throwing weapon; magnetic force
returned the disc after throwing.

A talented athlete and test pilot—and
husband to Natasha Romanoff (BLACK
WIDOW)—Alexi Shostakov faked his dead
and trained to become a top KGB
operative codenamed Red Guardian,
modeled after a Soviet hero from World War
II. While Natasha became disillusioned with
her KGB masters and defected to the USA,
Alexi remained loyal and increasingly ruthless and
vindictive. He was thought to have given his life to save
her and CAPTAIN AMERICA, but he turned up alive again years later,
trying to bring Natasha to justice for betraying her homeland.

Dr. Tara Belinsky became the next Red Guardian and
even joined the DEFENDERS for a while. When PRESENCE gave her
radioactive powers, she changed her name to Starlight. Four other
Red Guardians followed after her, each athletic men. The latest was
recently seen working with the WINTER GUARD. **AD, MF**

After encountering the Avengers, the
Red Guardian battles Hawkeye, Black
Widow's lover.

The Red
Guardian's
identity is
revealed.

RED RAVEN

FIRST APPEARANCE Red Raven Comics #1 (August 1940)
REAL NAME Unknown
OCCUPATION Adventurer **BASE** Mobile
HEIGHT 6 ft **WEIGHT** 180 lbs **EYES** Black **HAIR** Red
SPECIAL POWERS/ABILITIES Can fly using anti-gravity metallic
wings, which can also deflect bullets and fire energy beams

RED WOLF

FIRST APPEARANCE Avengers #80 (September 1970)
REAL NAME William Talltrees
OCCUPATION adventurer **BASE** American Southwest
HEIGHT 6 ft 4 in **WEIGHT** 240 lbs **EYES** Brown **HAIR** Black
SPECIAL POWERS/ABILITIES Superhuman senses. Skilled hand-
to-hand combatant. Expert tracker and archer. Employs a coup stick
(a 6ft wooden staff used as a bo or javelin), tomahawk and knife.

REDEEMER

FIRST APPEARANCE Incredible Hulk Vol. 2 #343 (May 1988)
REAL NAME Craig Saunders
OCCUPATION Former demolitions expert **BASE** New York
HEIGHT 6 ft 1 in **WEIGHT** 205 lbs **EYES** Brown **HAIR** White
SPECIAL POWERS/ABILITIES Bonded with combat suit armed
with twin plasma canons on each hand, a rocket and grenade
launcher, and rocket boots enabling 30 minutes of flight.

Raised by a lost tribe
of Inhumans known as
the Bird-People, on a
hovering island in the
Atlantic, Red Raven was a
heroic member of the
World War II-era Liberty
Legion. After the war, he
placed himself and his
people into suspended
animation to prevent aggression between them
and humanity. Later, the Angel (*see* ARCHANGEL)
discovered Red Raven, who made it appear that
his island had been destroyed to ensure the
privacy of the Bird-People. His daughter Dania
has also assumed the identity of Red Raven. **DW**

The first Red Wolf is
believed to have
tamed the first horse
and conquered the
American plains for
the Cheyenne. The
second was Johnny
Wakeley, a Cheyenne
orphan who forged
peace between his people and the US Cavalry.
The current Red Wolf is Will Talltrees who grew
up on the Cheyenne Reservation, in Wolf Point,
Montana. After his family was murdered by
businessmen, he begged the gods for the power
to avenge them. The Wolf Spirit Owayodata
heard his prayers. Following the legend of
previous Red Wolves, Talltrees later trained a
wolf until they almost thought as one. **TD**

After joining the military as a demolitions expert,
Craig Saunders' world came crashing down
when he failed to defuse a bomb in an
airport terminal, causing the death of
two civilians. Desperate, he joined a
new paramilitary team called the
Hulkbusters, but their effort to
defeat the HULK also ended in
disappointment. Taking advantage
of Saunders' despair, the LEADER
persuaded him to become the
Redeemer and integrated Saunders'
body into a formidable yellow
combat suit. Sadly, redemption
was not to be his—Saunders died
during his very first
confrontation with old
greenskin. **AD**

RED SKULL *see opposite page*

RED SKULL

The most dangerous of all Nazi agents

The Red Skull's Cosmic Cube, could alter reality.

Johann Schmidt was born in a German village. His mother died giving birth to him and, after failing to drown the newborn child, Johann's father committed suicide. The orphaned Schmidt became a beggar and thief, though he sometimes took menial jobs. Schmidt was working as a bellboy in a hotel when Adolf Hitler, the dictator of Nazi Germany, paid a visit there.

A PERFECT NAZI

Recognizing in Schmidt's eyes a hatred of all humanity that mirrored his own, Hitler decided to turn him into "the perfect Nazi." Hitler oversaw Schmidt's training, presented him with a skull-like head mask, and named him "The Red Skull." Answerable only to Hitler himself, the Red Skull undertook a wide range of missions for the Third Reich, especially acts of terrorism.

During World War II the Red Skull repeatedly battled Captain America and his partner Bucky.

It was in order to have an American counterpart to the Red Skull that the US government gave "super-soldier" Steve Rogers the identity of CAPTAIN AMERICA. Shortly before America entered World War II, the Red Skull first battled his greatest enemy, Captain America. During the war the Red Skull commanded numerous military missions. He rose to become the second most powerful man in the Third Reich, feared even by Hitler.

During the fall of Berlin, Captain America fought the Skull in Hitler's bunker. A bomb caused a cave-in that seemingly killed the Skull. However, an experimental gas kept the villain in suspended animation for decades.

BACK FROM THE DEAD

In the 1950s, communist agent Albert Malik impersonated the Skull, but eventually the original was found and revived. Since then, Captain America has repeatedly thwarted his bids for global domination. At one point, the Skull died, but ARNIM ZOLA transferred the Skull's consciousness into clone of Captain America. By accident, his own "dust of death" caused the Skull's new head to resemble a living red skull. The Skull made many enemies, including General LUKIN, who sent the WINTER SOLDIER to kill him. Before dying, the Skull used a Cosmic Cube to transfer his mind into Lukin's body. With the help of his daughter, SIN, CROSSBONES, and DR. FAUSTUS, the Skull set up the assassination of Captain America at the end of the CIVIL WAR (*see* pp. 84–5). Recently, Lukin was killed, but the Skull transferred his mind away and will no doubt resurface soon.

PS, MF

FACTFILE

REAL NAME
Johann Schmidt

OCCUPATION
Terrorist; conqueror

BASE
Nazi Germany, later various secret bases around the world.

HEIGHT (original body)
6 ft 1 in; (cloned body) 6 ft 2 in
WEIGHT (original body)
195 lbs; (cloned body) 240 lbs
EYES (both bodies) Blue
HAIR (original body) Brown;
(cloned body) Formerly blond, later none

FIRST APPEARANCE
Captain America Comics #7
(October 1941)

POWERS

Totally ruthless, brilliant subversive strategist; excellent hand-to-hand combatant and marksman. Uses lethal "dust of death," which causes a victim's head to resemble a ghoulish red skull.

The Red Skull and Captain America are symbolic of tyranny and freedom.

SAY YOUR PRAYERS, YOU TWO! -- AND SAY 'EM FAST

YA CAN'T DO DIS TO US -- WE AIN'T DONE NUTTIN'

IT'S A MISTAKE HONNIST, IT IS!

The Red Skull so hates Captain America that he will even murder people who impersonate the real Captain and Bucky.

REVANCHE

FIRST APPEARANCE X-Men #17 (February 1992)
REAL NAME Kwannon **OCCUPATION** Assassin **BASE** Japan
HEIGHT (both bodies) 5 ft 11 in **WEIGHT** (both bodies) 155 lbs.
EYES (original body) Blue, (Braddock's body) Violet
HAIR (original body) Black, (Braddock's body) Brown, dyed purple
SPECIAL POWERS/ABILITIES Martial arts; (as Revanche)
telepath; manifested psychic energy in form of Samurai sword.

Kwannon was a Japanese assassin and the lover of crimelord Matsu'o Tsurayaba. When Kwannon was mortally injured, Tsurayaba made a deal with Spiral, who transferred Kwannon's mind into the body of Elizabeth Braddock, PSYLOCKE of the X-MEN. Spiral also transferred Braddock's mind into Kwannon's body. Gaining Braddock's memories and powers, Kwannon claimed to be the real Psylocke and called herself Revanche (French for "revenge".) Discovering that she was infected with the Legacy Virus, she begged Matsu'o to kill her with a ceremonial dagger. **PS**

RHINO

FIRST APPEARANCE Amazing Spider-Man #41 (October 1966)
REAL NAME Alex O'Hirn (possibly an alias)
OCCUPATION Criminal **BASE** Mobile
HEIGHT 6 ft 5 in **WEIGHT** 710 lbs **EYES** Brown **HAIR** Brown
SPECIAL POWERS/ABILITIES The Rhino possesses the strength and enhanced durability of his namesake due to his protective suit, which is bonded to his body.

A career criminal, the man who would become the Rhino was selected for experimentation by a group of spies because of his low intelligence. After months of chemical and radiation treatments, he was given his protective suit, which resembled a rhinoceros' hide. He was sent to abduct astronaut John JAMESON, but was foiled by SPIDER-MAN. The Rhino has subsequently used his strength in a number of criminal endeavors. Believing himself to be trapped permanently within his costume, the Rhino is subject to bouts of insanity. **TB**

RICHARDS, FRANKLIN
see opposite page

RICOCHET
see opposite page

RICTOR

FIRST APPEARANCE X-Factor #17 (June 1987)
REAL NAME Julio Esteban Richter
OCCUPATION Private Investigator **BASE** New York City
HEIGHT 5 ft 9 in **WEIGHT** 162 lbs **EYES** Brown **HAIR** Brown
SPECIAL POWERS/ABILITIES By touching objects can cause them to vibrate and crumble; applied to buildings his powers have earthquake-like effect.

As a boy, Julio Richter saw the mutant clone STRYFE murder his father, a black-market arms dealer. Julio later developed mutant powers and was captured and used by the Right to cause mayhem in San Francisco. Freed by X-FACTOR, he has since served with them as well as the New Mutants and X-Force. M-Day robbed him of his powers, but he still joined X-Factor Investigations and infiltrated the anti-mutant Purifiers for them. **AD, MF**

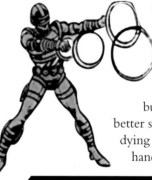

RIGHT, THE

FIRST APPEARANCE X-Factor #17 (June 1987)
MEMBERS AND POWERS
Cameron Hodge (commander) Brilliant planner; made immortal through a mystical pact
Ani-Mator Genius-level geneticist
Other unnamed operatives and soldiers.
BASE Mobile

The Right is a secret organization dedicated to preserving human freedoms by the eradication of mutantkind. Cameron HODGE, a former public relations director for X-FACTOR, founded the Right using X-Factor's own profits. Hodge's double-dealing soon became all too obvious and he engaged his former colleagues in combat, clashing with both X-Factor and the NEW MUTANTS. Agents of the Right wear armored battlesuits equipped with built-in machine guns and flight jets. Their battlesuits have facemasks that bearing a distinctive "smiley face" design. **DW**

RINGER

FIRST APPEARANCE Defenders Vol. 1 #51 (September 1977)
REAL NAME Anthony Davis
OCCUPATION Professional criminal **BASE** Mobile
HEIGHT 5 ft 8 in **WEIGHT** 145 lbs **EYES** Brown
HAIR Black, later dyed blonde
SPECIAL POWERS/ABILITIES Weapons included constricting rings, freeze rings, and explosive rings; could condense solid rings from air.

The Ringer suffered humiliating defeats at the hands of heroes including NIGHTHAWK II and SPIDER-MAN. After his release from prison, the Ringer joined other criminals at the Ohio-based "bar with no name" to discuss the threat of the villain-killer known as the SCOURGE OF THE UNDERWORLD. The Scourge was secretly in the bar at the time and shot everyone dead, except the Ringer. The Ringer survived and became the cyborg Strikeback, but was killed soon afterward. A second Ringer has since appeared but has had little better success, nearly dying at the Punisher's hands. **DW, MF**

RIORDAN, DALLAS

FIRST APPEARANCE Thunderbolts #1 (April 1997)
REAL NAME Dallas Riordan
OCCUPATION Adventurer **BASE** New York City
HEIGHT 5 ft 1 in **WEIGHT** 150 lbs
EYES Blue **HAIR** Red
SPECIAL POWERS/ABILITIES Expert swordswoman and adept hand-to-hand combatant.

Dallas served as New York City's liaison to the THUNDERBOLTS until BARON ZEMO discredited the team and ruined Dallas' own reputation. Invited to become the new Citizen V, Dallas's career as a costumed crusader was cut short when she was crippled in battle. For a while, she could only walk when she merged her consciousness with that of her dead lover, Erik Josten (Atlas). Erik has since returned—and the two have broken up—but they share a link that causes Dallas to become paralyzed when Erik draws on her powers. Dallas currently works for the Commission on Superhuman Activities. **AD, MF**

RICHARDS, FRANKLIN

Son of Reed and Sue Richards of the FANTASTIC FOUR, Franklin Richards was once one of the most powerful mutants on Earth. Before his birth, strange energies flowing through Sue's body nearly killed both mother and baby until ANNIHILUS' Cosmic Control Rod suppressed them. AGATHA HARKNESS acted as Franklin's nanny in his earliest years. The boy soon began to exhibit immense psionic powers. Using his ability to see possible futures, he became a member of POWER PACK under the name Tattletale. Nathaniel Richards, his grandfather, later raised him in a realm outside of time, where he became the adult adventurer Psi-Lord, and founded the Fantastic Force before Hyperstorm erased his adult form from existence. When the AVENGERS and the Fantastic Four seemingly perished fighting ONSLAUGHT, Franklin sent them to a "Counter-Earth" of his own creation. He used his powers to bring back GALACTUS and return his sister Valeria to his mother's womb, but lost his powers in the process. Recently, Franklin helped the THING and the HUMAN TORCH escape the Negative Zone during the Secret Invasion (see pp. 326-7). **DW, MF**

The enemies of the Fantastic Four have frequently made Franklin the target of their aggression.

FACTFILE

REAL NAME
Franklin Benjamin Richards

OCCUPATION
Occasional adventurer

BASE
New York City

HEIGHT 4 ft 8 in
WEIGHT 100 lbs
EYES Blue
HAIR Blond

FIRST APPEARANCE
Fantastic Four Annual #6 (1968)

POWERS

Formerly possessed vast powers of telepathy and telekinesis, as well as the ability to fire psionic blasts, reshape reality, appear in astral form, and perceive future events.

RICOCHET

Peter Parker as Ricochet, wearing a costume designed by his partner, the fashion-conscious Mary Jane.

When SPIDER-MAN was falsely accused of murder, a $5 million reward was placed on his head and he was forced to adopt a new identity in order to find the real killer. Instead of temporarily assuming one new persona, he created four: RICOCHET, DUSK, HORNET, and PRODIGY. After clearing his name, Spider-Man discarded these identities and their costumes. The costumes came into the possession of a former Super Hero called the Black Marvel, who gave them to four teenagers and formed a new super-team called the Slingers. One of the members was Johnny Gallo, a troubled youth who had grown apart from his father after his mother was killed in a car accident. Johnny literally leaped at the chance to use his mutant powers in the Slingers, but like the other members of the team he was disillusioned when it emerged that the Black Marvel had obtained the costumes from MEPHISTO. Nevertheless, the Slingers battled to save the Black Marvel's soul from Mephisto and won, although the battle claimed the life of the Black Marvel. The Slingers then disbanded and Gallo moved to Los Angeles. He joined a group of former teenage heroes who were adjusting to civilian life and trying to dissuade other teenagers from becoming costumed heroes. **TD**

FACTFILE

REAL NAME
Jonathon "Johnny" Gallo

OCCUPATION
College student

BASE
Los Angeles, California; formerly Brooklyn, New York

HEIGHT 5 ft 10 in
WEIGHT 155 lbs
EYES Blue
HAIR Blond

FIRST APPEARANCE
Slingers #0 (as Johnny Gallo, December 1998)

POWERS

Mutant with superhuman leaping, acrobatic, and gymnastic skills. Possesses a "danger sense," similar to Spider-Man's "spider-sense." Also uses throwing disks as weapons.

Ricochet can use his throwing discs to shatter opposing weaponry and stun his foes

FACTFILE

CURRENT MEMBERS AND POWERS

JAILBAIT
Can project psionic force fields.

HOTSHOT
Can project psionic force fields.

OGRESS
Enhanced strength and damage resistance.

OMNIBUS
Super-genius intellect.

SOUL MAN (deceased)
Possessed ability to resurrect the dead.

FIRST APPEARANCE
(As normal humans) Incredible Hulk Vol. 2 #345 (July 1988); (as Riot Squad) Incredible Hulk vol. 2 #366 (February 1990)

CHARACTER KEY
1 Rock 2 Soul Man
3 Ogress 4 Hotshot
5 Jailbait 6 Redeemer

RIOT SQUAD

The Riot Squad came into being when the villainous LEADER detonated a gamma bomb on the town of Middletown, Arizona. Amazingly, a few residents survived, mutated by gamma radiation in the same manner as the HULK. These five took the cover names Jailbait, Hotshot, Ogress, Omnibus, and Soul Man, and became the Leader's elite guards. Charged with protecting the Freehold base, where the Leader gave sanctuary to those suffering from radiation sickness, the team fought the Hulk on several occasions.

During an attack on the Freehold base by HYDRA, Soul Man was killed, and with the Leader also presumed dead, Omnibus took control of the Riot Squad. His teammates later put him on trial after he orchestrated terrorist bombings in an effort to gain more power. Despite his protestations that he had been under the control of the Leader when he committed the crimes, they found him guilty and banished him to the Arctic. The Troyjans later decimated Freehold despite the efforts of Riot Squad. The team is likely to continue as a mercenary outfit. **DW**

RISQUE

FIRST APPEARANCE X-Force vol 1, #51 (August 1991)
REAL NAME Gloria Dolores Munoz
OCCUPATION X-Corporation Employee (deceased)
BASE Hong Kong
HEIGHT 5 ft 9 in **WEIGHT** 120 lbs **EYES** Brown **HAIR** Black
SPECIAL POWERS/ABILITIES Compresses matter, inorganic and organic; can destroy smaller objects, like a mobile phone, altogether.

Gloria Munoz had a lonely childhood. Her parents divorced when she was 12 and she left home at 16. Forced to fend for herself, Gloria developed a cold, distant personality and her first encounters with the mutant group, X-FORCE did not endear her to them. However, she became romantically involved with Warpath, even falling in love with him, before betraying him to the Deviant known as Sledge. After making recompense for her misdeeds, Gloria was invited to join X-Corporation's Hong Kong office, but she wasn't there long. While investigating the trade in mutant body parts, Gloria was killed by the U-Men, a group of humans seeking mutant body parts to graft onto themselves. **AD**

ROBERTSON, JOE

Robertson defeated his nemesis Tombstone after years of trying.

Joseph "Robbie" Robertson, long-time editor-in-chief of the Daily Bugle, grew up in Harlem alongside the brutal Lonnie Thompson Lincoln (TOMBSTONE). While working as a reporter in Philadelphia, Robertson saw Tombstone kill a man, but he kept silent about the murder for nearly two decades. Years later, he finally gathered evidence of the murder and Tombstone's other crimes, only for Tombstone to break his back. Robertson recovered and testified against Tombstone in court, receiving a jail sentence of his own for withholding evidence. He resigned from the Daily Bugle when Norman Osborn (see GREEN GOBLIN) purchased the newspaper, but later returned to the job. His son Randy attended college with Peter Parker, and Robertson is believed to have guessed that Peter Parker is SPIDER-MAN. When Dexter Bennett bought the Daily Bugle following J. Jonah JAMESON's heart attack, Robertson left to go work for Ben Urich at the new rival paper, Front Line. **DW, MF**

FACTFILE

REAL NAME
Joseph Robertson

OCCUPATION
Editor-in-chief of the Daily Bugle

BASE
New York City

HEIGHT 6 ft 1 in
WEIGHT 210 lbs
EYES Brown
HAIR White

FIRST APPEARANCE
Amazing Spider-Man Vol. 1 #51 (August 1967)

Highly skilled writer and dogged investigative reporter.

ROCK

FIRST APPEARANCE The Incredible Hulk Vol. 1 #343 (May 1988)
REAL NAME Samuel J. Laroquette
OCCUPATION Warrior **BASE** Mobile
HEIGHT 6 ft **WEIGHT** Unrevealed
EYES Brown **HAIR** Black
SPECIAL POWERS/ABILITIES Able to shape his rock-like exoskeleton into any form he imagines.

A former explorer, Sam Laroquette became a member of the Hulkbusters at a time when the Hulk had been separated from Bruce Banner. Later recruited by would-be world conqueror the Leader, Laroquette received treatments that encased him in a rocklike substance responsive to his mental commands. As Rock, he went into action against the Hulk alongside his fellow operative Redeemer. The stone projections Rock created by reshaping his exoskeleton proved to be one of the few things capable of puncturing the Hulk's tough skin. The Rock has since worked alongside the U-Foes and the Riot Squad. **DW**

ROCKET RACER

FIRST APPEARANCE Amazing Spider-Man #172 (September 1977)
REAL NAME Robert Farrell
OCCUPATION Student **BASE** New York City
HEIGHT 5 ft 10 in **WEIGHT** 160 lbs **EYES** Brown **HAIR** Black
SPECIAL POWERS/ABILITIES Rides jet-powered, skateboard to which boots are magnetically attached; mini-rockets on gloves can tear holes in three-inch thick steel.

When Robert Farrell's mother died, he became responsible for his six younger siblings. Realizing he couldn't earn enough to support his family, he turned to a life of crime. He developed a superpowered skateboard and a weapon-equipped costume to become the Rocket Racer. After repeated defeats at the hands of Spider-Man—and several brushes with the law, including a short jail sentence—Robert decided to reform. While going back to school, he worked for Silver Sable. Later, he joined the Fifty State Initiative (see pp.118–9) and trained at Camp Hammond, then attempted to infiltrate Modok's organization for SHIELD.
AD, MF

ROGUE

Rogue stole and retained the powers of Ms. Marvel.

Orphaned, Rogue ran away from her Mississippi home and was adopted by Mystique and Destiny. Her mutant power manifested itself when she kissed a boy and absorbed his memories. She joined Mystique's Brotherhood of Evil Mutants in her teens. While fighting Ms. Marvel, Rogue absorbed her superhuman strength, durability, and the power of flight. Unable to control her absorption power, Rogue turned to the X-Men, for help. Professor X invited her to join them, and she fell in love with Gambit. After the villain Pandemic infected her with the 88 virus, Rogue's skin became lethal to anyone she touched. To save her, Mystique touched Rogue with the first mutant baby born after M-Day. This removed her lethal touch and all of her absorbed powers and memories. To punish Mystique for endangering the infant, Rogue turned her powers on Mystique. This left Rogue with a psychic copy of Mystique which can take control of her during times of stress. **PS, MF**

FACTFILE
REAL NAME
Unrevealed
OCCUPATION
Former terrorist, now adventurer
BASE
The Xavier Institute, Salem Center, New York State

HEIGHT 5 ft 8 in
WEIGHT 120 lbs
EYES Green
HAIR Brown

FIRST APPEARANCE
Avengers Annual #10 (1981)

Mutant ability to absorb the memories, knowledge, talents, personality, and physical abilities of another person through physical contact with them.

Rogue has striking white streaks in her long hair

ROMA

FIRST APPEARANCE Captain Britain #1 (January 1985)

REAL NAME Roma

OCCUPATION Sorceress **BASE** Otherworld

HEIGHT 5 ft 10 in **WEIGHT** 135 lbs **EYES** Green **HAIR** Black

SPECIAL POWERS/ABILITIES Sorceress with mystical abilities; casts spells that restore life to the dead or block her own presence or others' presence from detection by organic or technological means.

Daughter of MERLYN, Roma appeared to Brian Braddock as the Goddess of the Northern Skies and gave him the Amulet of Right. The amulet's energy turned him into CAPTAIN BRITAIN, and Roma became one of his advisors. Thinking her father dead, she took over his duties as ruler of Avalon and guardian of the Omniverse, and she oversaw the formation of EXCALIBUR. When Merlyn returned, Roma helped Excalibur defeat him and gave her throne to Captain Britain. Roma died at her father's hand, but not before transferring her knowledge to the mutant Sage. **MT, MF**

RONAN THE ACCUSER

FIRST APPEARANCE Fantastic Four #65 (August 1967)

REAL NAME Ronan

OCCUPATION Supreme Public Accuser

BASE Citadel of Judgement, on planet Kree-Lar

HEIGHT 7 ft 5 in **WEIGHT** 480 lbs **EYES** Blue **HAIR** Unknown

SPECIAL POWERS/ABILITIES Wields Universal Weapon—fires concussive energy bolts, disintegrates matter, creates force fields.

Born to an aristocratic KREE family, Ronan was accepted into the Accuser Corps and rose to the position of Supreme Public Accuser. After failing to punish the FANTASTIC FOUR for defeating a Kree Sentry, his humiliation drove him to plot to take over the Empire himself during the Kree-Skrull War, but Rick JONES stopped him. In the course of the Annihilation (see pp. 30-1), Ronan euthanized a lobotomized SUPREME INTELLIGENCE and finally took over as the Kree ruler. In order to strengthen the Kree, he agreed to cede his position to BLACK BOLT, ruler of the INHUMANS, but only if Black Bolt's sister-in-law Crystal agreed to marry him. **AD, MF**

ROSS, GENERAL T. E.

FIRST APPEARANCE Incredible Hulk Vol. 1 #1 (May 1962)

REAL NAME Thaddeus E. Ross

NICKNAME Thunderbolt

OCCUPATION Lieutenant General, US Air Force **BASE** Mobile

HEIGHT 6 ft 1 in **WEIGHT** 245 lbs **EYES** Blue **HAIR** White

SPECIAL POWERS/ABILITIES Is a capable combatant and has an advanced military mind.

General Ross's troops nicknamed him "Thunderbolt" because he "struck like a thunderbolt" in combat. After Bruce Banner transformed into the HULK, General Ross became obsessed with capturing the Hulk by any means necessary. For much of that, he worked alongside Colonel Glenn TALBOT, who married his daughter Betty—who later divorced Talbot and married Bruce, becoming Betty BANNER. For a time, he possessed the electrical form of ZZZAX, and he later sacrificed himself to destroy the mutant Nevermind. Restored to life, he rededicated himself to bringing in the Hulk, and he led the US forces against the monster during World War Hulk (see pp. 152-5). **DW, MF**

ROMULUS

FIRST APPEARANCE Wolverine #50 (March 2007)

REAL NAME Romulus

OCCUPATION Tyrant **BASE** Unknown

HEIGHT 7 ft **WEIGHT** 300 lbs

EYES Red **HAIR** Black

SPECIAL POWERS/ABILITIES Immortal Lupine.

Little is known about Romulus but for the fact that he plagues both WOLVERINE's dreams and his life. Romulus appears to be the greatest of the Lupines, a race of people descended from wolves instead of primates. Romulus is thousands of years old, and he is powerful enough to keep even the villainous SABRETOOTH too scared to speak of him. He seems to be behind much of the misery in Wolverine's life, including murdering Wolverine's wife, Itsu.

Romulus subsequently took Wolverine's long-lost son DAKEN under his wing and trained him up to be an even more efficient killer than his father. **MF**

ROSE, THE

FIRST APPEARANCE (JC) Daredevil #131 (March 1976); (RF) Amazing Spider-Man #83 (April 1970) **REAL NAME** Jacob Conover; Richard Fisk **OCCUPATION** (JC) columnist; (RF) crime lord **BASE** (JC) New York City **HEIGHT** (JC) 6 ft; (RF) 6 ft 2 in **WEIGHT** (JC) 210lbs; (RF) 225lbs **EYES** (JC) brown; (RF) brown **FEATHERS** (JC) brown; (RF) blue **SPECIAL POWERS/ABILITIES** (JC & RF) criminal masterminds, manipulators, and strategists.

The first leather-masked Rose was Richard Fisk, the son of criminal KINGPIN. Fisk believed that his father was an honest businessman. When he learned the truth, he tried to ruin his father's empire and became a member of HYDRA. Fisk eventually joined forces with his father and became the Rose but was killed by his mother. The second Rose was a police officer seeking revenge on the Kingpin. The third and current Rose is Jacob Conover, who wrote for the *Daily Bugle*. He was given the identity as a reward for saving the life of crime lord Don Fortunato. Conover was captured by SPIDER-MAN and is currently in prison. **TD**

ROTH, ARNOLD

FIRST APPEARANCE Captain America #270 (May 1982)

REAL NAME Arnold "Arnie" Roth

OCCUPATION Sailor, later publicist, later costume shop manager

BASE New York City

HEIGHT Unrevealed **WEIGHT** Unrevealed **EYES** Blue **HAIR** Grey

SPECIAL POWERS/ABILITIES Possessed the normal human strength of a man of his age who engaged in mild exercise.

Arnold Roth became friends with Steve Rogers when they were growing up in the 1930s. During World War II, Roth served in the US Navy and realized that CAPTAIN AMERICA was his friend Steve. While Captain America spent years in suspended animation, Roth aged normally. Learning of Roth's friendship with Captain America, Baron Helmut Zemo (see BARON ZEMO I) imperiled Roth and his life partner, Michael. Later, the RED SKULL captured Roth. Captain America and Roth remained friends. Roth worked as the AVENGERS' publicist and managed Steve Rogers' costume shop before dying from bone cancer. **PS**

RUIZ, "RIGGER"

FIRST APPEARANCE The Mighty Thor Vol. 1 #426 (Nov. 1990)

REAL NAME Margarita Allegra "Rigger" Ruiz

OCCUPATION Police officer **BASE** New York City

HEIGHT Unknown **WEIGHT** Unknown

EYES Unknown **HAIR** Black

SPECIAL POWERS/ABILITIES Adept with range of weaponry; she invented "port-a-pulley" for easy navigation of elevator shafts.

Margarita Allegra "Rigger" Ruiz is the armory specialist of Code: Blue, a SWAT team designated to deal with superpowered criminals. Bodybuilder Rigger has come face-to-face with these superhumans on a regular basis and her experiences have been many and varied. The strongest member of Code: Blue, Rigger has rescued hostages from the Wrecking Crew, been driven mad by the Super Villain Dementia, and posed as a slave during a mission to Asgard. During this last assignment, Rigger also flirted with Fandral the Dashing, an Asgardian noble—life is never dull in Code: Blue. **AD**

RUSSIAN, THE

FIRST APPEARANCE Punisher Vol. 5 #8 (November 2000)

REAL NAME Unrevealed

OCCUPATION Mercenary **BASE** Mobile

HEIGHT 7 ft 2 in **WEIGHT** 573 lbs

EYES Blue **HAIR** Reddish-blond

SPECIAL POWERS/ABILITIES Post-reconstruction, the Russian possessed enhanced strength and damage resistance.

The mercenary nicknamed "The Russian" accepted a job from crime boss Ma Gnucci to kill the PUNISHER. After a brutal fight, the Punisher smothered the Russian, later taunting Ma Gnucci by showing her the Russian's severed head. A secret paramilitary agency then resurrected the Russian, giving him an enhanced body with boosted olfactory senses, three hearts, and a toughened skeleton. This new body required regular injections of female hormones. The Russian apparently died when he was caught in the explosion of a nuclear warhead on Grand Nixon Island. **DW**

RYKER, GENERAL J.

> I'M SORRY BANNER-- THIS IS GOING TO HURT.

> QUITE A BIT.

General John Ryker was involved in President Kennedy's assassination and dropped gamma bombs on US troops in the Gulf. Desperate to find a cure for his wife's cancer, he became obsessed with the idea that the HULK's biology held the answers. To unlock those secrets, he tormented Banner and tortured vagrants in his research facility. Realizing that success lay in the mental rather than physical manipulation of his test subjects, Ryker switched to using his soldiers. One man was changed into a corrupt version of the Hulk, codenamed FLUX. After Thunderbolt Ross informed Ryker's wife about her husband's actions, she rebuked him. Before World War Hulk (see pp. 152–5), Ryker formed the GAMMA CORPS a team of gamma-powered soldiers with grudges against the Hulk. When the Hulk returned to Earth, he set them on his old foe, but one member of the corps—Grey—later lost his temper and brought Ryker's headquarters down on top of him. **AD, MF**

A human guinea pig faces a painful death by gamma radiation.

FACTFILE

REAL NAME
General John Ryker

OCCUPATION
Senior General in US Army

BASE
Currently unknown

HEIGHT 6 ft 2 in
WEIGHT 190 lbs
EYES Brown
HAIR Gray

FIRST APPEARANCE
Incredible Hulk Vol.3 #14
(May 2000)

RYKER, GENERAL JOHN

POWERS

Brilliant manipulator, possesses intuitive understanding of people's emotional vulnerabilities; exceptional strategist, excels at seeing big picture; inveterate liar; impervious to the suffering of others.

SHIELD

Strategic Hazard Intervention, Espionage, and Logistics Directorate

FACTFILE

NOTABLE MEMBERS

NICK FURY Former director
CONTESSA VALENTINA
ALLEGRA DI FONTAINE
YELENA BELOVA (Black Widow)
G. W. BRIDGE Former director
SHARON CARTER (Agent 13), former director, liaison officer to Captain America
JESSICA DREW (Spider-Woman)
THADDEUS "DUM-DUM" DUGAN former director
MARIA HILL Former director
Gabriel "Gabe" Jones
AL MACKENZIE CIA liaison officer
ALI MORALES
CLAY QUARTERMAIN
NATASHA ROMANOVA (Black Widow)
JASPER SITWELL
TONY STARK (Iron Man), former director
JIMMY WOO (Agents of Atlas)

BASE
The Helicarrier; mobile

FIRST APPEARANCE
Strange Tales #135 (August 1965)

The longest-serving director of SHIELD, not even Nick Fury knows the identity of the man he replaced.

SHIELD (Supreme Headquarters International Espionage Law-Enforcement Division; later changed to Strategic Hazard Intervention, Espionage and Logistics Directorate) is a counter-terrorism, intelligence, espionage, and peace-keeping organization. SHIELD runs covert as well as military operations, and works with governments and their military forces around the world.

SHIELD'S FORMATION

SHIELD was established to counter the threat posed by the technologically advanced neo-fascist subversive organization known as HYDRA. The identity of SHIELD's founders remained classified, as did the identity of its first executive director, who was assassinated by HYDRA operatives. SHIELD's second and longest-serving leader was Nick Fury, a colonel in the U.S. Army, who had also been a top CIA operative. Other top SHIELD members include Timothy "Dum-Dum" Dugan, Valentina Allegro De Fontaine, and Jasper Sitwell.

For many years, SHIELD's headquarters was the Helicarrier, a huge flying aircraft carrier that was kept airborne at all times. It carried a squadron of jet fighters and an ICBM. The Helicarrier was damaged and even destroyed several times over the years, but SHIELD rebuilt it every time and maintained many regional headquarters throughout the world.

SHIELD also kept close ties to the Super Hero community and often called upon CAPTAIN AMERICA, the AVENGERS, and the FANTASTIC FOUR for help. In addition to battling earthly terrorist and military threats, SHIELD saved the world many times from extraterrestrial invasion and infiltration. As well as its human operatives, SHIELD also employed Life Model Decoys (LMDs), incredibly lifelike androids sent into extremely dangerous situations to help avoid human casualties. Nick Fury was known to deploy several LMDs of himself to confuse assassins and even the agents working beneath him.

Over the years, SHIELD's main adversaries included HYDRA, AIM, Zodiac, the Corporation, the YELLOW CLAW, the VIPER, the RED SKULL, CENTURIOUS, and DR. DEMONICUS. SHIELD provided intelligence and technical support to the Avengers and the Fantastic Four during the KREE-SKRULL War, when a battle of the aliens took place very close to Earth.

Although chartered by the UN, SHIELD maintained close ties to the US. The UN also founded a number of sister organizations. ARMOR (Altered-Reality Monitoring and Operational Response) stopped invasions from other universes, and SWORD (Sentient World Observation and Response Department) defended the planet from alien invasions.

As director of SHIELD, Maria Hill tried to cut the agency's dependency on Super Heroes and rely on human resources instead.

The terrorist organization HYDRA, dedicated to world domination, is SHIELD's greatest enemy.

ESSENTIAL STORYLINES
- ***Strange Tales #135*** Nick Fury, who will be the organization's top operative and eventual leader, is recruited by SHIELD.
- ***Strange Tales #158*** HYDRA Island sinks, and Baron Wolfgang Von Strucker, HYDRA'S leader is killed.

TROUBLE AT THE TOP

While acting as director of SHIELD, Nick Fury gathered a secret team of Super Heroes and launched a covert attempt to topple the government of Latveria, then run by Prime Minister Lucia von Bardas. Although helped by CAPTAIN AMERICA, SPIDER-MAN, LUKE CAGE, DAREDEVIL, BLACK WIDOW, WOLVERINE, and agent Daisy Johnson (now known as Quake), the mission failed. Fury had all memories of the mission wiped from the heroes' minds.

A year later, Latveria launched an attack on New York City in revenge, and Fury's role in the disaster was exposed. He resigned soon afterward and then disappeared underground.

Iron Man was made director of SHIELD after defeating one of its staunchest allies, Captain America, during the Civil War.

Eager to show a clean break with Fury, the UN appointed relative outsider Maria Hill as the next director of SHIELD. Hill was leading the organization when the Superhuman Registration Act was passed, placing her in charge of controlling all registered superhumans in the US—and of hunting down the rest. She served as director throughout the Civil War (*see* pp. 84-5), but when the conflict finally resolved, she suggested that Tony Stark—who had led the pro-registration heroes as IRON MAN—take over as director and that she serve as his deputy.

FURY'S SECRET WARRIORS
1 Nick Fury **2** Phobos **3** Druid **4** Slingshot
5 Stonewall **6** Quake **7** Hellfire

As director of SHIELD, Stark developed and executed an ambitious agenda. To handle and efficiently utilize the influx of superhumans now working for SHIELD, he started the Fifty State Initiative (*see* pp. 118–9), designed to place a team of Super Heroes in every state. He also ordered a new Helicarrier (later destroyed by the Red Hulk) using the latest Stark technology. He also used SHIELD money to fund the Avengers and their headquarters in Stark Tower.

THE NEW ORDER

After SHIELD failed to predict and prevent the Secret Invasion, Norman Osborn (*see* GREEN GOBLIN) replaced Stark as director. He immediately renamed the organization HAMMER (without bothering to come up with words for the acronym). He also turned the THUNDERBOLTS into his personal black-ops team and created a new version of the Avengers with himself in the lead as the Iron Patriot.

Fury resurfaced during the invasion with his own team of Secret Warriors to help defeat the Skrulls. During this event, he discovered that HYDRA had been secretly controlling SHIELD from its founding, and he rededicated his team to bringing his old foes down. **MF**

As the Iron Patriot, Norman Osborn led both the official Avengers team and SHIELD's replacement organization, HAMMER.

SABRETOOTH

One of the world's most vicious mutants

Sabretooth was chained up as a child due to his feral nature.

A vicious, psychotic killer, little is known about the early life of Victor Creed, the mutant called Sabretooth, save that he apparently came from an abusive background. His healing ability having kept him alive and youthful for decades, he first acquired the alias Sabretooth in the 1960s, when he did wetwork for the CIA.

BITTER FEUD

Like WOLVERINE, Sabretooth's abilities were enhanced by the top-secret Weapon X project, and while the two men share much history in common, they are the bitterest of enemies. Sabretooth routinely returns to stalk and defeat Wolverine on the latter's birthday each year. And because of his enmity for Wolverine, Sabretooth has been pulled into the X-MEN's orbit time and again, sometimes in partnership with other villain such as MISTER SINISTER, sometimes on his own. But while there is still some humanity left within Wolverine's heart, Sabretooth's soul is as black as pitch, and he is about as irredeemable an individual as has ever existed.

Sabretooth's claws are razor-sharp

THE DEADLY BLADE

Sabretooth fathered renowned mutant-hater and one-time Presidential candidate GRAYDON CREED via MYSTIQUE, but he had little to do with his son. He once taunted Wolverine with the idea that the X-MAN was his son, but this turned out to be a lie. Over the years, Sabretooth has been imprisoned by the X-Men and even forced to work with X-FORCE several times. His relationship with Wolverine never improved though.

Recently, while Sabretooth was under the influence of ROMULUS, he regressed to a beastlike state and murdered FERAL. After that, Wolverine hunted him down and killed him with the Muramasa Blade, a weapon that creates wounds no healing factor can counter. **TB, MF**

Sabretooth's powers made him a skilled tracker.

Sabretooth's final showdown with Wolverine after years of conflict.

SABRA

FIRST APPEARANCE The Incredible Hulk #250 (August 1980)
REAL NAME Ruth Bat-Seraph **OCCUPATION** Police officer;
Israeli government agent **BASE** Jerusalem, Israel
HEIGHT 5 ft 11 in **WEIGHT** 240 lbs **EYES** Brown **HAIR** Black
SPECIAL POWERS/ABILITIES Wrist bracelets equipped with
neuronic-frequency stunners that shoot "energy quills." Cape has a
device that neutralizes gravity, enabling flight. Superhuman strength.

When Ruth Bat-Seraph's mutant powers
emerged, the Israeli government sent her to
live at a special kibbutz where she
was trained to use them. As an
adult, she became the first member
of the Mossad's super-agent program.
After terrorists killed her son, she
disobeyed orders to bring them
down. She fought alongside the
X-Men and worked for the
X-Corporation in Paris.
She registered with the
US government during
the Civil War (*see* pp.
84-5). After that, she
returned to Israel and
fought the Skrulls
during the Secret Invasion
(*see* pp. 326-7). **PS, MF**

SAGE

FIRST APPEARANCE Uncanny X-Men Vol. 1 #132 (April 1980)
REAL NAME Unrevealed, goes by "Tessa"
OCCUPATION Member of New Excalibur **BASE** England
HEIGHT 5 ft 7 in **WEIGHT** 135 lbs **EYES** Blue **HAIR** Black
SPECIAL POWERS/ABILITIES Able to remember everything she
sees and hears; can "jump start" the mutant abilities of others;
possesses limited telepathy.

Born in Eastern Europe,
the mysterious woman
codenamed Sage
rescued an injured
Professor X from
Afghanistan and
became one of his
first mutant recruits.
Rather than joining
the original X-Men team,
Sage became a spy within the
Hellfire Club, where she
worked as an advisor to Black
King Sebastian Shaw.
When she tricked the mind-controlling
Elias Bogan into losing a wager, a vengeful
Bogan scarred her face. Rescued by Storm,
Sage joined the X-Men and later became a
member of New Excalibur. **DW**

SABRECLAW

SABRECLAW

FACTFILE

REAL NAME
Hudson Howlett
OCCUPATION
Adventurer
BASE
New York City

HEIGHT 5 ft 10 in
WEIGHT 198 lbs
EYES Brown
HAIR Brown

FIRST APPEARANCE
J2 #8 (May 1999)

POWERS
Superhuman agility, reflexes,
stamina, and strength, plus sharp
teeth, Adamantium-laced claws,
and a healing factor.

The son of Wolverine in the
alternate future of Earth-982,
Sabreclaw felt jealous of his half-
sister Rina (Wild Thing) because
she had the chance to actually be
raised by their father, who didn't
know of Hudson's existence for
many years. Sabreclaw started out
as a villain, battling the A-Next
(future Avengers) team alongside
the Revengers and fighting
Spider-Girl as part of the Savage
Six. However, when Galactus
returned to threaten the Earth, he joined the Avengers
and their allied heroes to drive him away. Afterward, he
asked to join Avengers,
and despite some
reservations was accepted.
MF

Sabreclaw alongside his fellow
Revengers.

Sabreclaw faces off
against American
Dream.

SALEM'S SEVEN

FACTFILE

FORMER MEMBERS

BRUTACUS
Enhanced strength

GAZELLE
Superhuman agility and reflexes

HYDRON
Able to blast water from left arm

REPTILLA
Fanged arm-snakes could bite and constrict

THORNN
Ability to fire explosive spines

VAKUME
Could drain air or energy, and assume an intangible state

VERTIGO
Power to induce dizziness in others

BASE
New Salem, Colorado

FIRST APPEARANCE
Fantastic Four Vol. 1 #186 (September 1977)

The seven children of Nicolas SCRATCH lived in the isolated village of New Salem, where witches and warlocks held sway. When Scratch's mother, AGATHA HARKNESS, left to become the governess of FRANKLIN RICHARDS, Scratch put her on trial for treason, transforming his offspring into Salem's Seven to act as guards. They failed to stop the FANTASTIC FOUR from rescuing her, but later became the rulers of New Salem and burned Harkness at the stake. Harkness's spirit led the VISION and the SCARLET WITCH to New Salem, and Salem's Seven perished in the battle. When the SCARLET WITCH returned them to life. Scratch tricked the Seven into releasing the demon Shuma-Gorath. Dr. STRANGE, the Fantastic Four, DIABLO helped them to foil Scratch's plans.
DW, MF

SALEM'S SEVEN
1 Brutacus
2 Hydron
3 Vakume
4 Vertigo
5 Thornn
6 Reptilla
7 Gazelle

Salem's Seven first appeared in the pages of the Fantastic Four as diabolical, sorcerous opponents for the science-based team led by Mr. Fantastic.

SANDMAN *see opposite page*

SASQUATCH

FACTFILE

REAL NAME
Walter Langkowski

OCCUPATION
Scientist, adventurer

BASE
Canada

HEIGHT 10 ft
WEIGHT 2000 lbs
EYES Red
HAIR Orange

FIRST APPEARANCE
Uncanny X-Men #120 (April 1979)

Inspired by Bruce Banner's metamorphosis into the HULK, Dr. Walter Langkowski was experimenting with gamma radiation when he unwittingly opened a mystical barrier to the realm of the Great Beasts. He was possessed by a spirit called Tanaraq who gave him his powers. He became a member of ALPHA FLIGHT and was the only member of the team to survive the Collective's post-M-Day rampage. Afterward, he formed a new Canadian team to replace his old crew: OMEGA FLIGHT. **TB, MF**

POWERS

Sasquatch possesses superhuman strength and greatly enhanced resistance to injury, and is able to leap enormous distances. He can shift between his normal human form and his Sasquatch body at will.

In Alpha Flight, Sasquatch often came to blows with members of the X-Men.

SATANA

FIRST APPEARANCE Vampire Tales #2 (October 1973)

REAL NAME Satana Hellstrom

OCCUPATION Hero **BASE** Mobile

HEIGHT 5 ft 7 in **WEIGHT** 120 lbs

EYES Black with red highlights **HAIR** Red

SPECIAL POWERS/ABILITIES Levitation and limited spellcasting; could feed on human souls and project bolts of "soulfire."

The half-human daughter of the demon Satan—and the half-sister of Daimon Hellstrom—for a time Satana was forced to live as a succubus, draining the spirits of humans to survive. Rebelling at this, Satana became estranged from her father and started to appreciate human society. Learning that DR. STRANGE was trapped in the form of a werewolf, Satana traveled to the astral realm where Strange's soul was held prisoner, and freed him. The price was her own life. Strange later resurrected her and teamed her up with Jennifer KALE and TOPAZ to form a coven of witches.
AD, MF

SANDMAN

The villain who slips through Spidey's fingers

With the ability to change his body into grains of sand and reshape it at will, Sandman has proven to be a dangerous and slippery foe for SPIDER-MAN, the FANTASTIC FOUR, and the HULK. Born William Baker in one of the rougher areas of New York City, he had a bad start in life. His father abandoned him and his mother when William was three years old, and the boy grew up in poverty. He quickly learned to steal and cheat.

ESSENTIAL STORYLINES
• *Amazing Spider-Man Annual #1* Sandman, Vulture, Mysterio, Electro, Kraven the Hunter, and Doctor Octopus get together to form the Sinister Six.

• *Amazing Spider-Man #217–218* Sandman teams up with Hydro-Man, but a freak accident merges the two villains into a mud creature.

FACTFILE

REAL NAME
William Baker

OCCUPATION
Former professional criminal

BASE
Brooklyn, New York

HEIGHT 6 ft 1 in
WEIGHT 450 lbs
EYES Brown
HAIR Brown

FIRST APPEARANCE
Amazing Spider-Man #4
(September 1963)

SANDMAN

A LIFE OF CRIME

William was kicked out of high school for taking money to throw a big football game, but soon found work with a protection racket. He took the alias "Flint Marko," and became a success in New York's crime underworld. After an arrest and a jailbreak, Marko headed south. He was on a beach near a military testing site in Georgia when a nuclear reactor's steam system exploded, knocking him unconscious. Marko woke to find that his body now had the properties of sand. Revelling in his new ability, he called himself Sandman and set out on a major criminal career. Sandman battled Spider-Man (his main nemesis), and many other Super Heroes. He joined the WIZARD, TRAPSTER, and MEDUSA to form the FRIGHTFUL FOUR and teamed up with five more of Spider-Man's foes to form the SINISTER SIX.

Sandman can alter all of his body at once or just selective parts, as in this example of his right arm changing while the rest of his body remains in its human-looking form.

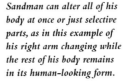

POWERS

Sandman is able to change all or part of his body into a sand-like substance which he can form into any shape. He can spread out the grains of sand in his body to avoid attack, project them outward at high speeds, or harden them into a super-powered weapon.

When he hardens the sand particles that make up his body into a solid block, Sandman packs an incredibly powerful punch.

GOOD OR EVIL?

When Sandman teamed up with HYDRO-MAN, an accident caused the two to merge into a mud creature. After he was freed, Sandman gave up crime, becoming a probationary member of the AVENGERS. The WIZARD brainwashed him into believing that his rejection of crime was a put-on, and he rejoined the Sinister Six. Another member, VENOM, betrayed Sandman; his bite causing Sandman's sand grains to wash away, casting up on various New York beaches. The sand particles of his body managed to find each other, and the Sandman was reborn. The Sandman turned to Spider-Man for help in clearing his father's name in the murder of BEN PARKER from Earth-6078. They succeeded after discovering the killer was the CHAMELEON of 2211. **MT, MF**

When Sandman and Hydro-Man combined they became the Mud-Thing, the new creature proved to be a big attraction.

SAURON

FIRST APPEARANCE X-Men #59 (August 1969)

REAL NAME Dr. Karl Lykos

OCCUPATION Geneticist, hypnotherapist

BASE New York City, Savage Land

HEIGHT 7 ft   **WEIGHT** 200 lbs   **EYES** Red   **HAIR** None

SPECIAL POWERS/ABILITIES Drains victims' life force into his own body. Uss eye contact to hypnotize and induce hallucinations.

Young Karl Lykos was in Antarctica when he was bitten by a pteranodon from the Savage Lands. Thereafter, he had to feed off the life energy of others to survive. As an adult, Lykos worked with PROFESSOR X on Project Mutant, but he transformed into an evil half-human, half-pteranodon creature after draining life energy from HAVOK. He took the name Sauron, became an enemy of the X-MEN, and returned to the Savage Land. During the Secret Invasion (*see* pp. 326–7), he fought beside Ka-Zar and SHANNA THE SHE-DEVIL against the SKRULLS. **MT, MF**

SAWYER, GENERAL

FIRST APPEARANCE Sgt. Fury and his Howling Commandos #1 (May 1963)

REAL NAME Samuel "Happy Sam" Sawyer

OCCUPATION Adventurer   **BASE** The Pentagon

HEIGHT 6 ft 2 in   **WEIGHT** 230 lbs   **EYES** Blue   **HAIR** Gray

SPECIAL POWERS/ABILITIES Happy Sam Sawyer was a career military man and an expert at strategy.

At the dawn of World War II, Captain "Happy Sam" Sawyer (so named because he rarely smiled) recruited NICK FURY and First Attack Company into a special squad. Named the HOWLING COMMANDOS, they took on the toughest missions. Sawyer also commanded the Maulers and the Deadly Dozen. After the war, he rose to the rank of General. He was killed in an operation against BARON STRUCKER and HYDRA. **TB**

SCARLET CENTURION

In the year 3000 of Earth-6311, Earth is a utopia, founded centuries earlier by Nathaniel Richards, father of Reed Richards (MR. FANTASTIC). However this paradise does not suit everyone. One distant descendant of Richards, a man known as the Scarlet Centurion, feels suffocated by his surroundings. Learning that one of his ancestors built a time machine, the Centurion recreates this device and wreaks chaos across multiple realities and times zones.

The original Scarlet Centurion's son, Marcus Kang, shared his father's title, and wielded a deadly halberd.

FACTFILE

REAL NAME Nathaniel Richards

OCCUPATION Conqueror

BASE Mobile

HEIGHT 6 ft 3 in
WEIGHT 230 lbs
EYES Brown
HAIR Brown, later gray

FIRST APPEARANCE Avengers Annual #2 (September 1968)

POWERS

Master of numerous far future technologies; wears battlesuit armed with electrical bolts and concussive force beams; adept time traveller.

For a short time, the second Scarlet Centurion ruled the Earth alongside his father.

Arriving in ancient Egypt, the Centurion became the pharaoh Rama-Tut—until the FANTASTIC FOUR forced him back to the future. Since then, he has also become KANG THE CONQUEROR and IMMORTUS at various times, as well as the YOUNG AVENGER known as IRON LAD. The one-time ruler of 30th-century Earth, he has tried to conquer the present-day world many times, only to be defeated by the Fantastic Four or the AVENGERS. One of his sons (the 23rd) also called himself the Scarlet Centurion and worked him while he was Kang. After another failure to conquer the world, though, Kang stabbed him and put him in stasis. **AD, MF**

SCARLET SPIDER

FIRST APPEARANCE (as Scarlet Spider) Spider-Man #52 (November 1994)

REAL NAME Ben Reilly

OCCUPATION Adventurer   **BASE** New York City

HEIGHT 5ft 10in   **WEIGHT** 165 lbs   **EYES** Hazel   **HAIR** Brown

SPECIAL POWERS/ABILITIES Super strength and agility, able to adhere to surfaces; "spider-sense" alerted him to danger. Wore web-shooters that projected artificial webbing.

Professor Miles Warren, the criminal known as the JACKAL, created a clone of Peter Parker, alias SPIDER-MAN. He endowed the clone with Parker's memories and pitted him against Spider-Man in battle. Seemingly killed, the clone later revived and wandered America for years, calling himself Ben Reilly. In New York, he became a costumed hero, the Scarlet Spider. The original GREEN GOBLIN manipulated Parker and Reilly into believing that Reilly was the real Spider-Man, with Reilly even adopting Spider-Man's costumed identity. Ultimately, the Goblin killed Reilly, and Parker reclaimed his identity. **PS**

SCARLET WITCH

Magical mistress of "Hex Power"

After Magneto rescued the Scarlet Witch from certain death, she and her brother Quicksilver became members of his Brotherhood of Evil Mutants. They didn't learn that Magneto was actually their father until many years later.

Wanda Maximoff is the daughter of Erik Magnus Lehnsherr also known as the mutant criminal MAGNETO and the twin sister of Pietro Maximoff, the former Avenger QUICKSILVER. Wanda's mother ran away from Magneto while she was pregnant and, fearing her husband would exploit her unborn children, gave her twins up for adoption.

FACTFILE

REAL NAME
Wanda Maximoff, aka Wanda Frank, Wanda Magnus
OCCUPATION
Adventurer
BASE
Europe

HEIGHT 5 ft 7 in
WEIGHT 130 lbs
EYES Blue
HAIR Auburn

FIRST APPEARANCE
X-Men #4
(March 1964)

SOCIAL OUTCAST

The twins were raised in the eastern European country of Transia by a gypsy couple and Wanda soon learned that she could cause strange things to happen. After accidentally making a house to burst into flame, she was about to be stoned as a witch when Magneto arrived and saved her. Not realizing that he was their real father, Wanda and Pietro took on costumed identities and joined his war against humanity. After many battles with the X-MEN, the twins abandoned Magneto and later joined the AVENGERS in return for full pardons for their past crimes. Over her brother's objections, Wanda became attracted to the synthozoid called the VISION and began a long romance with him. They were eventually married and set up house in New Jersey.

Studying witchcraft has helped the Scarlet Witch hone her control over her mutant abilities.

The Scarlet Witch and the Vision were married in the same ceremony that united Mantis and the Cotati.

POWERS

Possessed ability to affect probability fields to cause unlikely events to occur. Could make objects spontaneously burst into flame, rust or decay. Her "hex bolts' could also deflect flying objects and disrupt energy transmissions or fields. However, recent evidence seems to indicate that the Scarlet Witch has lost her mutant powers.

TROUBLED SOUL

Wanda also began to study real magic, combining it with her natural mutant abilities. She eventually grew powerful enough to defeat the dreaded DORMAMMU. However, her increased power came at a terrible cost and she began to lose her grip on reality. She conjured up imaginary children and repeatedly experienced temporary bouts of insanity.

The Vision was disassembled by the US government after trying to bring a new golden age to humanity by seizing mental control of every computer on Earth. Hank PYM and the BLACK PANTHER later rebuilt him, but he no longer possessed emotions, including the ability to love. His relationship with Wanda disintegrated and rapidly ended in divorce. The Scarlet Witch later suffered another mental breakdown and launched an attack on her fellow Avengers that resulted in the destruction of the Avengers Mansion and a number of tragic deaths. She later used her powers to warp reality and permanently remove the mutant gene and powers from most of the mutants, including herself. Since M-Day, Wanda has been seen living a normal life with no memory of being the Scarlet Witch. Recently, Scarlet Witch returned to help Hank Pym assemble a new team of Avengers, but turned out to be LOKI in disguise. **TD, MF**

Through gestures and mental concentration, the Scarlet Witch creates finite pockets of force that can disrupt reality. She can hurl these "hex-spheres" at her intended targets.

Suffering from a breakdown, the Scarlet Witch altered reality enough to disassemble the Avengers and eliminate most of Earth's mutants.

FWOOOSHHHH

SCHEMER

FIRST APPEARANCE Amazing Spider-Man #83 (April 1970)

REAL NAME Richard Fisk

OCCUPATION Criminal mastermind　**BASE** New York City

HEIGHT 6 ft 2 in　**WEIGHT** 175 lbs　**EYES** Blue

HAIR Reddish blond　**SPECIAL POWERS/ABILITIES** Had the normal strength of a man who engages in regular moderate exercise; was a cunning criminal strategist.

Richard Fisk was devoted to his father Wilson— until he learned that Wilson Fisk was the KINGPIN. Psychologically shattered, Richard secretly became a criminal leader himself, the Schemer, to take revenge on his father. As the Schemer, Richard disguised himself with a face mask that made him look like much older. Subsequently Richard became head of a Las Vegas fragment of HYDRA. Still later, Richard took on two more masked identities, the original ROSE and the Blood Rose. Ultimately Richard was shot dead by his own mother, Vanessa. **PS**

SCOURGE
see opposite page

SCRATCH, NICHOLAS

FIRST APPEARANCE Fantastic Four #185 (August 1977)

REAL NAME Nicholas Scratch　**OCCUPATION** Warlock

BASE New Salem, Colorado　**HEIGHT** 6 ft 3 in

WEIGHT 196 lbs　**EYES** Blue　**HAIR** Black with white streaks

SPECIAL POWERS/ABILITIES Nicholas Scratch possesses an encyclopedic knowledge of magical incantations and lore and a wide array of sorcerous abilities.

The son of Agatha HARKNESS, the witch who became governess to Franklin RICHARDS, Nicholas Scratch grew up to be leader of the witches of New Salem. Scratch convinced his followers that Agatha had betrayed their existence to the outside world and that she must be executed. When Agatha and Franklin were abducted, the FANTASTIC FOUR came to the rescue. Scratch and his most devoted followers, SALEM'S SEVEN, vainly sought revenge on the Fantastic Four and Agatha. For a while, he worked for the demon DORMAMMU, but after being banished to Hell, he struck a deal with MEPHISTO. **TB, MF**

SCORPION

Dr. Farley Stillwell had developed a method of giving animals the attributes of other creatures. When newspaper editor J. Jonah JAMESON found out, he asked Stillwell to test it out on a human guinea pig, a private investigator named Mac Gargan. Stillwell's amazing procedure gave Gargan the strength and agility of a scorpion. Stillwell also provided him with a specially designed mechanical tail.

ONE OF A TRUE SCORPIAN'S MOST POTENT WEAPON'S IS HIS TAIL! AND OUR SYNTHETIC SCORPION SHALL HAVE A TAIL ALSO!

STILLWELL, IF THIS WORK'S, I'LL MAKE YOU RICH... FAMOUS! I'LL BECOME YOUR PATRON!

Nothing comes without a price and the cost to Gargan—now calling himself the Scorpion—was the loss of his sanity. Contracted to put an end to SPIDER-MAN, it was only by his wits that the wallcrawler defeated the hugely powerful, and vengeful Scorpion. Since then, Scorpion has become an assassin-for-hire, his attempts to defeat Spider-Man being repeatedly foiled.

In recent times, Gargan gave up his Scorpion suit to become the new VENOM. As part of the new AVENGERS team assembled by Norman Osborn (*see* GREEN GOBLIN), he now poses as Spider-Man. **AD, MF**

SCORPION

POWERS

FACTFILE

REAL NAME
MacDonald "Mac" Gargan

OCCUPATION
Assassin-for-hire

BASE
New York City

HEIGHT 6 ft 2 in

WEIGHT 220 lbs

EYES Brown

HAIR Brown

FIRST APPEARANCE
Amazing Spider-Man #20
(January 1965)

Strength greater than Spider-Man's; mechanical tail can be used as bludgeon or to propel Scorpion 30 ft into air. Tail has also been equipped with a toxin "sting" and a mechanism to fire electric blasts.

Scorpion controls his tail via a cybernetic link with his own spinal column. He can whip his tail at 90 mph

The Scorpion's steel-mesh costume is bulletproof. Each hand is equipped with pincers.

FACTFILE

ANGEL (Tom Halloway)
Financed Scourges of the Underworld

SCOURGE I
Gunned down the Enforcer, started killing criminals around the US.

SCOURGE II
Killed Scourge I to keep him from talking

SCOURGE III
Leaving the group, he became an agent of the Red Skull.

SCOURGE IV
Killed Scourge II, then went after Priscilla Lyons who left the group

SCOURGE V (Priscilla Lyons)
Left Scourges, incurring their wrath

CAPRICE (Scourge VI)
Master of disguise, espionage, brain washing, interrogation.

BLOODSTAIN (Scourge VII):
Master of armed and unarmed combat

DOMINO (Dunsinane)
Encyclopedic knowledge of every costumed hero, villain, organization

FIRST APPEARANCE
Iron Man #194
(May 1985)

SCOURGE

Known as Scourge of the Underworld, Scourges wanted to rid the world of crime.

Scourge was the brother of the criminal known as the Enforcer. Outraged by his brother's criminal behavior, Scourge got a gun, disguised himself as an old woman, and gunned down the Enforcer. He then became obsessed with traveling the country ruthlessly exterminating criminal after criminal, all while disguised.

Scourge was captured by Captain America, but before Cap could turn him over the authorities, Scourge was shot by an unseen assailant. Over the years, each Scourge has been assassinated by the following Scourge to keep the earlier one from talking. These Scourges each relied on an investigator named Domino to feed them information about their targets. Scourges killed countless villains including MIRACLE MAN, the WRAITH, the Human Fly, and the Cheetah. BARON VON STRUCKER made Henry GYRICH force Jack Monroe (NOMAD) become a Scourge too. Before breaking free from Gyrich's control, Monroe killed the THUNDERBOLTS' BARON ZEMO, JOLT and Techno among others. **DW, MF**

Hiding out in his mobile base, Scourge gets a call on his videophone. It can mean only one thing—some Super Villain is ripe for the plucking!

Scourge dons a blonde wig and a female mask before speaking to his informant, Domino.

SCREAM

FIRST APPEARANCE Venom: Lethal Protector #4 (May 1993)
REAL NAME Donna (full name unrevealed)
OCCUPATION Villain   **Base** Mobile
HEIGHT 5 ft 11 in   **WEIGHT** 130 lbs   **EYES** White   **HAIR** Red
SPECIAL POWERS/ABILITIES Symbiote provides enhanced strength, speed, and stamina. Scream's prehensile hair can shape itself into deadly weapons.

Researchers at the Life Foundation laboratories tried to replicate the process that had given rise to CARNAGE by bonding five workers with alien symbiotes. One of the subjects, a mentally fragile woman named Donna, found that the process drove her further into madness. The five test subjects sought out Venom for help in controlling their symbiotes, but Donna killed her fellow hybrids.

Sometimes adopting the code name Scream, she has struggled to adjust to her new life and become a more sympathetic figure. **DW**

SCRIER

FIRST APPEARANCE Amazing Spider-Man #394 (October 1994)
REAL NAME Inapplicable (discovered to be an organization)
OCCUPATION Criminal Cult   **BASE** Unrevealed
HEIGHT/WEIGHT/EYES/HAIR Not applicable
SPECIAL POWERS/ABILITIES Each member of the Scrier is a formidable combatant. The Scrier also have access to an array of sophisticated weaponry.

By wearing identical garb, for centuries the Brotherhood of the Scrier maintained the deception that the Scrier was just one being. It was a clever ploy, disguising the true nature and scope of this worldwide criminal organization. United by their worship of a godlike being, itself called the Scrier, the Brotherhood became especially powerful under a new and mysterious leader who focused the organization's energies on SPIDER-MAN and his clone, Ben Reilly.

It emerged that this new leader was in fact Norman Osborn (*see* GREEN GOBLIN). Following Osborn's defeat the fate of the Scriers remains uncertain. **AD**

SENTINELS

Enormously powerful, mutant-hunting robots

POWERS

Most Sentinels possess superhuman strength and jet propulsion units in their feet which enable them to fly, and can fire lasers and electron beams from their eyes and hands. Mark II Sentinels could adapt to counter any opponent.

Dr. Bolivar Trask introduced the Sentinels to the world on live TV.

The Sentinels were created by Dr. Bolivar Trask to combat superhuman mutants. Trask had concluded that a superhuman mutant race was evolving that would conquer the rest of humanity. He organized the team of scientists and engineers who built the first Mark I models.

TAKING OVER

However, despite being programmed by Trask to protect humanity, the Sentinels decided to take control of the human race. They kidnapped Trask, and the lead Sentinel, the Master Mold, ordered him to create a Sentinel army. The X-MEN battled the Sentinels and Trask lost his life destroying the Master Mold and other Sentinels.

Trask's son, Larry, oversaw the creation of the Mark II Sentinels. However once the Sentinels recognized that Trask was a mutant himself, they turned against him. The government then seized the Sentinel designs, and Dr. Steven Lang built the Mark III Sentinels; but both he and they were destroyed battling the X-Men.

After mutant terrorists tried to kill Senator Robert KELLY, the President initiated "Project: Wideawake." Shaw Industries constructed Sentinels to combat mutant threats to national security. Xavier's evil twin, Cassandra Nova, used Mega-Sentinels to devastate Genosha, a nation with a large mutant population. She also devised microscopic "nano-Sentinels," which attacked the bloodstreams of various mutants.

Recently, the US government created Sentinel Squad O*N*E, headed by Dr. Valerie COOPER and James Rhodes (WAR MACHINE) for defense against superhuman threats. These Sentinels are not robots but gigantic suits of armor with human pilots. Recently Nano-Sentinels took over the bodies of these pilots and assumed control of their armor, forcing them to attack PROFESSOR X's mansion. They were destroyed. **PS, MF**

Following only their own logic, the Sentinels have repeatedly turned against their human masters as well as mutants.

The Sentinel Bastion created cyborgs known as Prime Sentinels that could pass as ordinary humans

ESSENTIAL STORYLINES

• *X-Men Vol. 1 #14–16*
Dr. Bolivar Trask creates the original Sentinel robots. He introduces them on live TV—and they promptly capture him.

• *X-Men Vol. 1 #57–59*
Larry Trask's Mark II Sentinels capture and imprison mutants.

• *Uncanny X-Men #141–142*
The Sentinels rule North America in the "Days of Future Past" storyline set in an alternate reality.

SENTRY

FIRST APPEARANCE Sentry #1 (September 2000)

REAL NAME Robert Reynolds

OCCUPATION Adventurer **BASE** Watchtower

HEIGHT 6 ft 2 in **WEIGHT** 200 lbs

EYES Blue **HAIR** Blond

SPECIAL POWERS/ABILITIES Serum provides super strength, speed, and invulnerability. Can fly and control light.

When Robert Reynolds, the hero known as the Sentry, discovered that his archenemy the Void was actually part of his own repressed personality, he had all memories of the Sentry erased from the world—and from his own mind. When the memories began to return, Reynolds transformed into the Sentry once more, enlisting the help of other heroes against the Void. He wound up re-erasing himself. Reynolds later turned up in the Raft super-prison when ELECTRO started a jailbreak, and he joined the AVENGERS in trying to stop it. Since then, he's continued to work with the Avengers while battling his mental health issues. **MT, MF**

SERSI

A member of the ETERNALS, Sersi inspired the legend of Circe in Homer's *Odyssey* and encountered MERLIN and King Arthur PENDRAGON. She proved her value during the Eternals struggles against the Deviants. Sersi also joined the AVENGERS but PROCTOR manipulated her into battling her teammates. Seeking penance, she departed for an alternate reality with her lover the BLACK KNIGHT. Upon her return, she joined Heroes for Hire, before returning to the Eternals' home, Olympia. Recently, fellow Eternal Sprite wiped the memories of all the Eternals, including Sersi. Once Sersi recovered, she decided to return to her fabricated but normal life. **DW, MF**

During the Secret Invasion (see pp. 326-7)

Sersi's playful personality can irritate some, and she is an incorrigible flirt around attractive men.

IT'S TOO LATE TO RUN, YOU ARMOUR-HEADED HALFWITS! IT'S TIME YOU WERE IMPROVED!!

A powerful sorceress, Sersi can release cosmic energy, create illusions, and transmute matter. Capable of flight and virtually immortal.

Sersi has vast, advanced transmutational powers.

FACTFILE
REAL NAME Sersi
OCCUPATION Adventurer
BASE New York City
HEIGHT 5 ft 9 in
WEIGHT 140 lbs
EYES Blue
HAIR Black
FIRST APPEARANCE Strange Tales Vol. 1 #109 (June 1963)

SERPENT SOCIETY

SERPENT SOCIETY
1 Death Adder
2 Rattler
3 Cottonmouth
4 Diamondback

The original VIPER founded the first Serpent Squad with EEL and COBRA. The team changed its lineup several time, and it inspired one member, SIDEWINDER, to expand the squad into the Serpent Society and focus on treating their enterprise as a business. The leader assigned specific members to each job, supplying them with a detailed plan in return for a percentage of the take. CAPTAIN AMERICA put them out of commission several times. Recently, SIN led a new Serpent Squad including COBRA, EEL, and VIPER. During the Secret Invasion (see pp. 326-7) the Serpent Society held a large group of people hostage, claiming to be protecting them from the SKRULLS, but NOVA and his teammates shut them down. **TD, MF**

FACTFILE
KEY MEMBERS
COBRA (Klaus Voorhees) Super-flexible.
SIDEWINDER (Seth Voalkner) Interdimensional travel.
ANACONDA (Blanche Sitzniski) Elongates limbs; amphibious.
ASP (unrevealed) Energy field; fires venom-bolts.
BLACK MAMBA (Tanya Sealy) Mesmerism; projects inky clouds of Darkforce.
BUSHMASTER Tail crushes his enemies.
COTTONMOUTH (Quincy McIver) Bionic jaws.
RATTLER (Gustav Krueger) Bionic tail generates sonic shockwaves.
FIRST APPEARANCE Captain America #310 (October 1985)

Though it rarely mixes business with revenge, the Serpent Society has often made an exception in Captain America's case.

FACTFILE

REAL NAME
Amahl Farouk

OCCUPATION
Criminal

BASE
Various

HEIGHT Various
WEIGHT Various
EYES Various
HAIR Various

FIRST APPEARANCE
Uncanny X-Men #117
(January 1979)

POWERS

An entity composed solely of malevolent psionic power, the Shadow King can possess others, bending them to his will. He also possesses various telepathic and telekinetic abilities.

SHADOW KING

The Shadow King is an immortal demon that has lived on the astral plane. It possesses people in the real world, making them fat as it feeds upon the hatred it breeds. In the '40s, it worked with BARON VON STRUCKER to try to replace King George VI of the UK with a Nazi puppet. Years later, the Shadow King appeared again as Amahl Farouk, an Egyptian crimelord and the first evil mutant PROFESSOR X ever met. At the time, Farouk's gang included a young thief that would one day become STORM. Professor X defeated Farouk in a psychic duel and believed him killed when he had only been banished back to the astral plane. A constant danger to Professor X and his X-Men, the Shadow King remained an omnipresent threat to

Using his telepathic powers, Amahl Farouk became ruled Cairo's criminal underworld.

Xavier's dream of peaceful coexistence between mutants and normal humans. He once controlled a group of X-Men from a parallel world, dubbing them his Dark X-Men before EXCALIBUR defeated him. Recently, Bast, the Panther God of Wakanda, devoured the Shadow King for daring to attack the BLACK PANTHER and his wife Storm. **TB, MF**

The Shadow King was the first mutant encountered by Professor X as he wandered the world, a tale told in Uncanny X-Men #117.

FIRST APPEARANCE Shadowmasters #1 (October 1989)
LINEUP Sojin Ezaki (deceased), Yuriko Ezaki, Phillip Richards
SPECIAL POWERS/ABILITIES Masters of ninjitsu

Demonstrating his martial arts skills, Phillip Richards wields a katana sword and kyoketsu shoge knife.

The original Shadowmasters were expert practitioners of the martial art of ninjitsu, who protected the Iga Province of Japan for centuries. Following the end of World War II, US Army Captain James Richards became friends with Shigeru Ezaki, one of the last Shadowmasters. Together they opposed renegade Japanese soldiers. Ezaki trained his children Sojin and Yuriko and Richards' son Phillip in martial arts. The renegades became the Sunrise Society, who killed James Richards and seemingly killed Shigeru Ezaki. Since then, Richards' son and Ezaki's children, as the new Shadowmasters, have opposed the Society, now renamed the Eternal Sun. **PS**

FIRST APPEARANCE Silver Surfer #1 (August 1968)
REAL NAME Shalla-Bal
OCCUPATION Empress of the planet Zenn-La **BASE** Zenn-La
HEIGHT 5 ft 9 in **WEIGHT** 125 lbs **EYES** Blue **HAIR** Black
SPECIAL POWERS/ABILITIES Born with no special powers, Shalla-Bal was later invested with power to restore life to the soil of Zenn-La after it was devastated by Galactus.

Shalla-Bal is a member of an alien race, the Zenn-Lavians. She was separated from her lover, Norrin Radd, after he made a bargain with the world-eater GALACTUS, who had threatened to destroy Zenn-La. Radd offered to become the SILVER SURFER and serve GALACTUS if he would spare Zenn-La, and Galactus agreed. For years the Silver Surfer traveled the universe, scouting out uninhabited planets for Galactus to consume. When the Surfer eventually decided to abandon Galactus and remain on Earth, Shalla-Bal became caught up in his struggle with MEPHISTO.

Then Galactus returned to consume Zenn-La in revenge for the Surfer's betrayal. After the Surfer endowed Shalla-Bal with the power to restore life to Zenn-La, she was declared Empress, and so she remains to this day. **AD**

SHAMAN

FIRST APPEARANCE Uncanny X-Men Vol. 1 #120 (April, 1979)

REAL NAME Michael Twoyoungmen

OCCUPATION Medicine man, Super-hero   **BASE** Mobile

HEIGHT 5 ft 10 in   **WEIGHT** 175 lbs   **EYES** Brown   **HAIR** Black

SPECIAL POWERS/ABILITIES Vast magical powers. Able to fire energy bolts, change his appearance, control weather, levitate, and teleport. Powers are focused through the use of his medicine pouch.

Michael Twoyoungmen was a Canadian surgeon who embraced his heritage as a Native American medicine man after his wife's death. The spirit of his grandfather trained him in the use of magic, and he helped deliver Narya, the daughter of the Northern Goddess. Twoyoungmen and Narya took the codenames of Shaman and SNOWBIRD and joined ALPHA FLIGHT. Shaman's daughter Elizabeth was known as TALISMAN, an identity he had briefly used himself. He died at the hands of the Collective, a man who absorbed the energy of all mutant powers lost on M-Day. **DW, MF**

Shaman has the mystical ability to commune with the magicks of the Earth, giving him vast powers to shift time and fundamentally alter the nature of reality.

SHANNA THE SHE-DEVIL

FIRST APPEARANCE Shanna the She-Devil #1 (December 1972)

REAL NAME Shanna O'Hara Plunder

OCCUPATION Vet and adventurer   **BASE** Savage Land

HEIGHT 5 ft 10 in   **WEIGHT** 140 lbs   **EYES** Hazel   **HAIR** Red

SPECIAL POWERS/ABILITIES Trained veterinarian specializing in wild animals; extraordinary gymnast and athlete; superb hunting and foraging skills.

Now living in the Savage Land with her husband KA-ZAR and their young son, Shanna O'Hara was born the daughter of an American businessman and worked in a New York zoo. Furious when a sniper casually killed most of the zoo's big cats, she chose to return the surviving animals to Africa and live with them in the wild. Life was not always easy. Shanna lost her friends and father to criminal organizations and was forced to team up with DAREDEVIL to defeat them, before finding contentment with her new family. **AD, MF**

SHANG-CHI

FACTFILE

REAL NAME
Shang-Chi

OCCUPATION
Former secret agent, fisherman

BASE
Formerly Fu Manchu's retreat in Honan, China, mobile for a while, then Yang Yin, China

HEIGHT 5 ft 10 ins
WEIGHT 175 lbs
EYES Brown
HAIR Black

FIRST APPEARANCE
Special Marvel Edition #15 (1973)

POWERS

Shang-Chi is the greatest living master of kung fu. He is also highly skilled in many other mental and physical disciplines. Although he has no superhuman powers, Shang-Chi has defeated superpowered enemies.

Shang-Chi as he appears in the Ultimates series.

Passion fueled by vengeance against his father coupled with Shang-Chi's amazing martial arts skills make him an almost unstoppable adversary to those who oppose him.

SHANG-CHI

Shang-Chi was born in China, the son of the criminal mastermind Fu Manchu. Trained in the mental and martial arts at Fu Manchu's retreat, Shang-Chi was a brilliant pupil but grew up unaware of his father's crimes. When Shang-Chi was nineteen, his father sent him away on a mission of assassination. The boy assumed that his father's enemies must be evil and so went willingly, but he soon learned the truth. Feeling betrayed, Shang-Chi vowed to destroy his father. He also learned that his father had created a conscienceless clone of him, called Moving Shadow. Defeating them both, Shang-Chi retired, but during the Civil War (*see* pp. 84–5) he returned to action as a member of Heroes for Hire. He later worked with MI-13 and is currently training a young Jonathan Raven, the present day version of KILLRAVEN **MT, MF**

This was the first issue to feature Shang-Chi's name in the title.

SHAPER OF WORLDS

FIRST APPEARANCE The Incredible Hulk #155 (September 1972)

REAL NAME Unrevealed, perhaps inapplicable

OCCUPATION Reality manipulator   **BASE** The known universe

HEIGHT 18 ft   **WEIGHT** 5.6 tons   **EYES** Blue   **HAIR** None

SPECIAL POWERS/ABILITIES Restructures pockets of reality, and rearranges the molecular structure of objects and living beings. Can teleport himself, and perceive the dreams and imagination of others.

The Shaper of Worlds originated in the SKRULL empire as a Cosmic Cube, an object which can alter reality according to the thoughts of whoever holds it. In time the Cosmic Cube developed sentience, and took the form of a Skrull with a metallic trustrum and tractor treads as the lower body. The Shaper wants to use his powers to restructure reality, but has little creative imagination. So he seeks out those who can supply dreams and imaginative concepts with which he can work. **PS**

SHATTERSTAR

FIRST APPEARANCE New Mutants Vol. 1 #99 (March 1991)

REAL NAME Benjamin Russell   **OCCUPATION** Adventurer

BASE The Xavier Institute, Salem Center, New York State

HEIGHT 6 ft 2 in   **WEIGHT** 210 lbs   **EYES** Black   **HAIR** Gray

SPECIAL POWERS/ABILITIES Genetically engineered for enhanced strength, speed, stamina; convert sonic frequencies into a vibratory shockwave that he channels through weapons.

Born a hundred years in the future of the planet Mojoworld, Shatterstar was genetically engineered to serve as an arena warrior. He escaped and joined the Cadre Alliance, which was trying to overthrow Mojo's leadership. Shatterstar traveled back in time to Earth and joined with CABLE to become a founding member of X-FORCE. During a battle, Shatterstar was mortally wounded, and LONGSHOT transferred his consciousness into the comatose body of Benjamin Russell. After M-Day, Shatterstar helped liberate the mutants trapped at the Xavier Institute. **TD, MF**

SHAW, SEBASTIAN

FIRST APPEARANCE X-Men #130 (February 1980)

REAL NAME Sebastian Shaw   **OCCUPATION** CEO of Shaw Industries, Inc.   **BASE** Worldwide; Hellfire Club, New York City

HEIGHT 6 ft 2 in   **WEIGHT** 210 lbs   **EYES** Black   **HAIR** Gray

SPECIAL POWERS/ABILITIES Mutant power to absorb kinetic energy which enhances his strength, speed, and stamina. He can also absorb electrical energy.

Sebastian Shaw became a self-made millionaire by the age of 20. As head of Shaw Industries, he joined the elite Hellfire Club, and then became part of its secret Council of the Chosen, which schemed to achieve world domination. Seizing control of the club and becoming its Black King, he changed its name to the Inner Circle and teamed with Emma Frost, the White Queen, in secretly creating mutant-hunting Sentinels. Recently, the X-Men captured Shaw, and Frost wiped his mind so that he could only remember the faces of the Genoshans the Sentinels destroyed. **MT, MF**

⊙ **SHE-HULK**
see opposite page

SHE-THING

The daughter of a career officer in the US Army, Sharon Ventura worked in various professions that enabled her to make full use of her athletic talents. She was working as a stunt cyclist with the Thunderiders when she first met Ben Grimm the THING of the FANTASTIC FOUR, who was immediately attracted to her.

Subsequently, Ventura accepted an offer to join the Grapplers, a professional team of superhuman female wrestlers. Working for the POWER BROKER, Dr. Karl MALUS augmented Ventura's strength to superhuman levels. As a Grappler, she adopted a costumed identity, becoming the second Ms. Marvel. The Thing helped her battle the Grapplers when they turned against her.

FACTFILE

REAL NAME
Sharon Ventura

OCCUPATION
Adventurer

BASE
Mobile

HEIGHT 6 ft
WEIGHT 340 lbs
EYES Blue
HAIR None

FIRST APPEARANCE
The Thing #27
(September 1985)

Sharon Ventura was a superb athlete and a daring stuntwoman, motorcyclist and a proficient wrestler. As She-Thing, she possesses superhuman strength and durability.

When Reed and Susan Richards temporarily left the Fantastic Four, Ben Grimm invited Sharon Ventura to join the team as Ms. Marvel. Shortly afterwards she became the She-Thing.

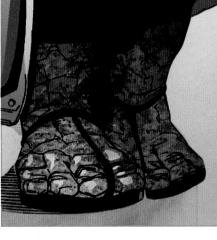

Later, Ventura accepted the Thing's offer to join the Fantastic Four. During a mission in space, Ventura was exposed to cosmic rays, which mutated her into a female version of the Thing. She was later restored to her normal human appearance by DOCTOR DOOM.

Ventura later mutated into an even more grotesque version of the Thing. Worse, her intellect began to deteriorate. As the She-Thing, she even temporarily joined the WIZARD's FRIGHTFUL FOUR and battled her former friends the Fantastic Four. During the Secret Invasion (*see* pp. 326-7), the SKRULLS captured and replaced the She-Thing, but after the war was over she escaped. **PS, MF**

SHE-HULK

Legal eagle and greenskinned crimefighter

The cousin of Bruce Banner, who would one day become the HULK, Jennifer Walters pursued her dream of becoming a successful lawyer. Shot by criminals whose boss she was prosecuting, Jennifer received a life-saving blood transfusion from her cousin Bruce. But this infusion of gamma-irradiated blood had an effect on Jennifer's physiology similar to that experienced by Bruce himself: the repressed part of her personality began to manifest itself as a green-skinned powerhouse: the savage She-Hulk!

Driven to madness by Scarlet Witch's hex power in Avengers: Disassembled.

She-Hulk was one of the last characters created by Stan Lee.

FACTFILE

REAL NAME
Jennifer Walters

OCCUPATION
Lawyer

BASE
The law offices of Goodman, Lieber, Kurtzburg & Holliway

HEIGHT 6 ft 7 in
WEIGHT 650 lbs
EYES Green
HAIR Green, brown as Jennifer Walters

FIRST APPEARANCE
The Savage She-Hulk #1
February 1980

POWERS

As the She-Hulk, Jennifer Walters possesses superhuman strength and durability; she can withstand extreme temperatures and her skin is highly resistant to injury

RAMPAGING FREE

At first Jennifer kept her dual role as the She-Hulk a secret. But over time, she found that she enjoyed being the She-Hulk, who, while definitely an extrovert, was far more controlled than her cousin's rampaging alter ego. She began to spend more time as the She-Hulk, using her gamma-spawned strength to battle villainy. Eventually, the She-Hulk was offered membership in the AVENGERS. Thereafter, transported to the Battleworld created by the celestial BEYONDER alongside her fellow Avengers, She-Hulk fought in the Secret Wars. Following that conflict, the THING decided to remain on Battleworld, and asked the She-Hulk to take his place in the FANTASTIC FOUR, which she did for a while, becoming almost one of the family. During her time with the FF, Jennifer abandoned her identity as Jennifer Walters, remaining in her She-Hulk form full time.

LEGAL TROUBLESHOOTER

However, the She-Hulk's more boisterous personality created problems for her down the line, and she was asked to move out of Avengers Mansion. At this low point in her life, she was recruited by the law offices of Goodman, Lieber, Kurtzburg and Holliway, a firm specializing in superhuman law. But a condition of Jennifer's employment was that she had to pursue her duties in her normal human state, rather than as the She-Hulk.

After the Civil War (*see* pp. 84-5), Jennifer was drafted to help train heroes in the Fifty State Initiative (*see* pp. 118-9). During this time, Iron Man injected her with nanobots that could turn off her powers at his command. These have since been removed.

Disbarred for revealing privileged information about a client she thought guilty of murder, Jennifer turned to bounty hunting with her SKRULL friend Jazinda (daughter of the SUPER-SKRULL), and for a short time she served with the Initiative's version of the Defenders. **TB, MF**

ESSENTIAL STORYLINES
• *Fantastic Four #265* Replaces the Thing as a member of the Fantastic Four.
• *Avengers Vol. 3 #72-75* Having lost control of her transformations, She-Hulk is pursued by her fellow Avengers and her cousin, the Hulk.
• *She-Hulk #2* Joins the superhuman law offices of Goodman, Lieber, Kurtzburg & Holliway.

As Jennifer Walters, She-Hulk continues to practice superhuman law for the legal firm of Goodman, Lieber, Kurtzburg & Holliway.

SHI'AR

Empire-building alien race

SHI'AR

FACTFILE

NAME
THE SHI'AR
Enhanced strength and
endurance

BASE
Chandilar (Aerie), Shi'ar Galaxy

FIRST APPEARANCE
Uncanny X-Men Vol. 1 #97
(February 1976)

IMPERIAL GUARD

**CURRENT MEMBERS
AND POWERS**
GLADIATOR (LEADER) Flight,
enhanced strength, speed,
near-invulnerability, heat vision
ASTRA Ability to phase
through solid objects
ELECTRON Power over
electricity and magnetism
FANG (DECEASED)
Enhanced strength, speed, and
senses;
razor-sharp claws
**HOBGOBLIN/SHAPESHIFTER
(DECEASED)** Could assume
nearly any form
IMPULSE/PULSAR Energy-
based body can be released as
concussive force
MIDGET/SCINTILLA Can
shrink to tiny size
NIGHTSHADE/NIGHTSIDE
Can draw others into the
Darkforce dimension
MAGIQUE Ability to cast
illusions
MENTOR Genius-level
intelligence and boosted
calculating speed
ORACLE: Telepathy,
precognition, and ability to fire
mental blasts
QUASAR/NEUTRON
Enhanced strength and
damage resistance
STARBOLT Flight, energy
projection
SMASHER Enhanced
strength
TEMPEST/FLASHFIRE Ability
to release electrical bolts
TITAN Can grow to giant size
BASE
Chandilar (Aerie), Shi'ar
Galaxy

FIRST APPEARANCE
Uncanny X-Men Vol. 1 #107
(October 1977)

ESSENTIAL STORYLINES
• *Uncanny X-Men #107-109*
The X-Men battle the Shi'ar Imperial Guard in
a fight involving D'ken, Lilandra, and the
M'Krann crystal.
• *New X-Men #118-126*
The "Imperial" story arc sees Cassandra Nova,
the villainous genetic twin of Professor X,
launching a scheme to ruin the Shi'ar empire.

Majestor D'ken failed
to hold onto the
Shi'ar throne.

The Shi'ar are an alien species descended from avians, who typically sport feathery hair and sometimes vestigial wings. Unlike the rival SKRULL and KREE empires, the Shi'ar Imperium consists of a patchwork of alien species, each absorbed into the empire through treaties or by force. A hereditary Majestor (male) or Majestrix (female) rules the Imperium, overseeing a High Council under the protection of the Elite Corps of the Shi'ar Imperial Guard.

CRUEL RULE

The Shi'ar are aggressive about absorbing other cultures into their empire, though the newcomers seldom receive the same rights as the Shi'ar themselves. Majestrix Lilandra has made strides to reverse this inequality, but under the leadership of Majestor D'ken, the cruel treatment of alien slaves triggered the formation of the pirates called the STARJAMMERS.

The M'Krann crystal is an artifact of
immense power located on a lifeless world.
It has the ability to destroy all of reality.

The first contact between the Shi'ar and Earth's heroes occurred when the X-MEN stopped Lilandra's brother D'ken from exploiting the powerful M'Krann crystal. Lilandra subsequently became the Majestrix of the Shi'ar Empire, briefly losing her throne to her sister DEATHBIRD until gaining it once more. Lilandra and PROFESSOR X of the X-Men enjoyed a romantic relationship for years.

When Skrull spies fanned the flames of war between the Shi'ar and the Kree, a team of AVENGERS tried to negotiate a cessation of hostilities with Majestrix Lilandra, but they could not prevent the detonation of the nega-bomb, a Shi'ar weapon that nearly destroyed the Kree. The Shi'ar annexed vast swaths of the Kree Empire, and Deathbird served as the viceroy of the conquered territories. The mind-controlling villainess Cassandra Nova later usurped Lilandra's authority, inciting violence between the Shi'ar and the X-Men. Recently, the mutant VULCAN returned to the Shi'ar Empire to avenge his mother's death. He now rules the empire and has guided it into a final war with the INHUMANS-led Kree while he simultaneous tries to exterminate Lilandra and the new Starjammers. **DW, MF**

The X-Men have been
staunch allies of Lilandra's,
thanks to her romantic
liaison with Professor
Charles Xavier.

THE IMPERIAL GUARD

The Elite Corps of the Shi'ar Imperial Guard, also known as the Superguardian Elite, are the protectors of the Majestor or Majestrix of the Shi'ar Empire. Most members of the Imperial Guard are not Shi'ar—they represent a cross-section of cultures from the multispecies mix that comprises the Shi'ar empire. Typically, each member has a distinct superpower that adds a needed component to the team's overall power mix.

Their leader, called the praetor, is currently the powerful Strontian called Gladiator. The Imperial Guard also has a larger, secondary division known as the Borderers, who are charged with enforcing local laws on member planets.

The Imperial Guard first came into conflict with the inhabitants of Earth when the X-Men followed a space warp and emerged on the desolate planet that housed the reality-altering M'Krann crystal. On the orders of Majestor D'ken, the Imperial Guard battled the X-Men and D'ken's sister Lilandra, though the Guard shifted its allegiance to Lilandra as soon as she assumed the throne. Later, the Imperial Guard fought the X-Men on Earth's moon, in an honor duel over the fate of the Dark Phoenix.

Throughout the changes in Shi'ar rule, the Imperial Guard has remained loyal to whomever holds the royal office. The Guard clashed with the Starjammers and Excalibur during Deathbird's time as Majestrix, and welcomed Lilandra back as leader after her return to power.

During the Kree-Shi'ar war, the Imperial Guard helped steal the nega-bands worn by Captain Mar-Vell from the late hero's tomb, which then went into the construction of the Shi'ar ultimate weapon, the nega-bomb. Following the apparent death of Earth's greatest heroes fighting Onslaught, Lilandra ordered Gladiator and several other Imperial Guard members to protect Earth, where the team uncovered a cell of undercover Kree agents.

The Imperial Guard now serves a new emperor, the human mutant Vulcan. However, Vulcan's rampant cruelty and his lust for violence has some of them questioning their unfailing loyalty to the throne rather to who might happen to sit upon it.

When they combine their powers, the Shi'ar Imperial Guard are nearly unstoppable. They are among the most feared combatants in the universe.

GLADIATOR

ASTRA

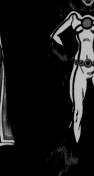

ELECTRON

FANG

SHAPE-SHIFTER

IMPULSE

SCINTILLA

NIGHTSIDE

MAGIQUE

MENTOR

ORACLE

NEUTRON

STARBOLT

SMASHER

FLASHFIRE

TITAN

SHOCKER

FIRST APPEARANCE The Amazing Spider-Man #46 (March 1967)
REAL NAME Herman Schultz
OCCUPATION Burglar **BASE** New York City
HEIGHT 5 ft 9 in **WEIGHT** 175 lbs **EYES** Brown **HAIR** Brown
SPECIAL POWERS/ABILITIES Wears gauntlets containing "vibro-shock units" that project compressed air blasts creating highly destructive vibrations.

While imprisoned, safecracker Herman Schultz invented a new device for opening safes by projecting intense vibrations. He used it to shatter the prison walls and escape. Wearing an insulated costume to absorb the vibrations, Schultz became the Shocker. After SPIDER-MAN beat him several times, he joined a number of teams, including the SINISTER SIX, the SINISTER SYNDICATE, the SINISTER SEVEN, the SINISTER TWELVE, and EGGHEAD'S MASTERS OF EVIL. Another criminal, Randall Darby, once called himself the Shocker, too, but later changed his name to Paralyzer. **PS, MF**

SHRIEK

FIRST APPEARANCE Spider-Man Unlimited #1 (May 1993)
REAL NAME Frances Louise Barrison **OCCUPATION** Patient
BASE Ravencroft Institute for the Criminally Insane
HEIGHT 6 ft **WEIGHT** 170 lbs **EYES** Blue **HAIR** Black
SPECIAL POWERS/ABILITIES Manipulates sound as a destructive force. Hypersonically generates emotions of fear, hate, or despair in others. Can employ sonic energy to fly.

After being mistreated by her mother for being overweight, Frances Louise Barrison turned to drugs, eventually becoming a dealer. She lost her fragile grip on reality when she was shot in the head by the police and spent a brief period in the dark dimension of the costumed adventurer known as CLOAK. Her powers may be the result of her time in that dimension, her injury, some latent mutant gene, or a combination of all three factors. She used her emerging powers to commit crimes and create chaos until she was committed to the Ravencroft Institute for the Criminally Insane. CARNAGE later freed her and they went on a murder spree until they were captured by a team of heroes led by SPIDER-MAN. Shriek has escaped Ravencroft on at least two other occasions, but is now responding to therapy. **TD**

SHROUD

FIRST APPEARANCE Super-Villain Team-Up #5 (April 1976)
REAL NAME Unknown **OCCUPATION** Crime fighter masquerading as a criminal **BASE** Los Angeles
HEIGHT 6 ft 2 in **WEIGHT** 220 lbs **EYES** Blue **HAIR** Blonde
SPECIAL POWERS/ABILITIES Though blind, has extrasensory perception that allows him to "see" his environment.; can summon absolute darkness by opening a portal into another dimension.

After witnessing the murder of his parents as a boy, the Shroud dedicated his life to fighting crime. After college, he traveled to Nepal and joined a cult that trained him in mysticism and the martial arts. Seven years later, he was given the "Kiss of Kali" and branded with the imprint of the goddess on his eyes, cheeks, and forehead, trading his eyesight for a mystical perception. He often pretends to be a criminal and formed a gang called the Night Shift. Recently, he has been dating ARACHNE. He refused to register with the government during the Civil War (see pp. 84-5) and sided with CAPTAIN AMERICA. **TD, MF**

SHOCKWAVE

FIRST APPEARANCE Master of Kung Fu #42 (July 1976)
REAL NAME Lancaster Sneed
OCCUPATION Mercenary, professional criminal **BASE** Mobile
HEIGHT 5 ft 11 in **WEIGHT** 170 lbs **EYES** Green **HAIR** Black
SPECIAL POWERS/ABILITIES His protective armor can generate electric shocks upon contact. Agility, combat skills, and knowledge of explosives were gained during his years as an intelligence agent.

As a child, Lancaster Sneed loved to listen to his uncle's tales of his battles with crime lord Fu Manchu. As an adult, he became an explosives specialist for MI-6, but he was injured by a blast on his first mission. Rebuilt with metal plates, he traveled to Asia and studied martial arts. Going to the US, he donned a suit of armor that generated electricity, took the name Shockwave, and switched sides to join forces with Fu Manchu. The Heroes for Hire captured him during the Civil War (see pp. 84-5), but during the Secret Invasion (see pp. 326-7) he broke out of prison and joined the Hood's forces to fight the SKRULLS. **MT, MF**

SILHOUETTE

REAL NAME
Silhouette Chord
OCCUPATION
Adventurer
BASE
Manhattan

HEIGHT 5 ft 6 in
WEIGHT 105 lbs
EYES Black with white pupils, formerly brown
HAIR Black

FIRST APPEARANCE
New Warriors #2 (August 1990)

POWERS
Able to pass through the Darkforce Dimension, allowing her to effectively teleport through the shadows. In her shadowy form, she can also phase through others, causing them injury. Her crutches variously house taser devices, anesthetic needles, pellet guns, and smoke capsules.

The daughter of Chord, the mentor of NIGHT THRASHER, Silhouette's conception was part of a pact enacted by a squad of Vietnam soldiers and the protectors of a secret temple, intended as a mystic sacrifice that would convey great power. Unaware of her parentage, Silhouette and her brother Midnight's Fire grew up on the streets, a nemesis to the gangs that preyed there. In one foray against the underworld, Silhouette encountered the young Night Thrasher, and they began a torrid relationship. But then Silhouette was caught in the crossfire between the police and a street gang, losing the use of her legs. Midnight's Fire blamed Night Thrasher for this accident, and became his enemy. It was only to prevent her brother from slaying Night Thrasher that Silhouette came into contact with him again, and she thereafter joined his group the NEW WARRIORS. She eventually left both Night Thrasher and the New Warriors. During the Civil War (see pp. 84-5) she sided with CAPTAIN AMERICA's resistance, but she registered with the government after his death **TB, MF**

SILVER DAGGER

FIRST APPEARANCE Dr. Strange Vol. 2 #1 (June 1974)

REAL NAME Isaiah Curwen

OCCUPATION Self-appointed mystic policeman   **BASE** Mobile

HEIGHT 6 ft   **WEIGHT** 220 lbs   **EYES** Black   **HAIR** Gray

SPECIAL POWERS/ABILITIES Spellcaster; can project mystic energy bolts, enlarge animals, and give himself superstrength; his silver dagger can cut through Doctor Strange's magical barriers.

The Pope's favored choice of successor, Isaiah Curwen harbored hopes of elevation to the Holy See. But the College of Cardinals failed to elect him, and Curwen decided to fight for the church in a different way. After studying the Vatican's library of black magic books, he set off to fight mystical masters across the world. A cruel psychopath, he has been a thorn in the side of DOCTOR STRANGE, even taking Strange's lover, CLEA, and burning her soul in mystical fire. **AD**

SILVER SAMURAI

FIRST APPEARANCE Daredevil Vol. 1 #111 (July 1974)

REAL NAME Keniuchio Harada

OCCUPATION Mercenary   **BASE** Mobile

HEIGHT 6 ft 6 in   **WEIGHT** 250 lbs   **EYES** Brown   **HAIR** Black

SPECIAL POWERS/ABILITIES Body generates tachyon field that he focuses through his sword; skilled in ways of samurai—master of bushido and Kenjutsu.

The mutant son of a Japanese crimelord—and the half-sister of Mariko YASHIDA—Harada mastered bushido before becoming a mercenary whose assignments included work for Hydra and pitted him against DAREDEVIL, SPIDER-MAN, and BLACK WIDOW. After his father's death Harada reformed and headed Japan's first superteam, BIG HERO 6. He was later brainwashed into returning to his old ways, but after breaking through that he became the head of security for the Prime Minister of Japan. He retained his powers after M-Day, but he recently lost a fight to Wolverine—along with his right hand. **AD, MF**

SILVER SABLE

Symkaria, a small country in the Balkans, had suffered under German occupation during World War, and after the war ended, Sable's father had no trouble convincing the government to fund his hunt for Nazi war criminals. He formed a group called the Wild Pack that scoured the world to bring them to justice. Silver was only a child when her mother died in her arms, the victim of a terrorist attack. From that moment she devoted her entire life to preparing for the day she would take over the Wild Pack, training in all forms of martial arts and becoming an expert in the use of many different weapons. Silver began her leadership of the Wild Pack by continuing the fight to bring former Nazis to justice, but as the years passed she expanded the scope of the Wild Pack. She formed Silver Sable International, a company that provided security, apprehended wanted felons and recovered stolen property for foreign governments, major corporations, and private individuals. Her company eventually became Symkaria's primary source of income and any citizen can be drafted into its service. Working with Dominic Fortune, Silver recently learned that there was a traitor in her corporation and has drastically reorganized the Wild Pack. **TD**

FACTFILE

REAL NAME
Silver Sable

OCCUPATION
CEO, Silver Sable International

BASE
Symkaria

HEIGHT 5 ft 5 ins
WEIGHT 125 lbs
EYES Blue
HAIR Silver

FIRST APPEARANCE
Amazing Spider-Man #265
(June 1985)

SILVER SABLE

POWERS

Silver Sable is a master of martial arts and a highly skilled marksman, swordsman, gymnast and strategist. She sometimes uses a samurai sword (katana), and the chai, a half-moon weighted projectile of her own design.

I'D BETTER USE A CHAI TO DISARM THE OTHERS BEFORE ANYONE GETS HURT!

WHSSSSSSSS

KING

Armed with over a dozen chais that are attached to her combat suit, Silver Sable often employs them to disarm or disable her enemies.

SILVERMANE

FACTFILE

REAL NAME
Silvio Manfredi

OCCUPATION
Criminal leader and mastermind

BASE
New York City

HEIGHT 6 ft 2 in; (as cyborg) 7 ft
WEIGHT 195 lbs; (as cyborg) 440 lbs
EYES Blue
HAIR Silver

FIRST APPEARANCE
The Amazing Spider-Man #73 (June 1969)

Brilliant criminal mind; As a cyborg, Silvermane possesses superhuman strength and superhumanly acute senses resistant to disease and fatigue.

A leader of the Maggia crime syndicate, the elderly Silvermane ordered the theft of an ancient tablet bearing a formula for a youth serum. He forced Dr. Curt Connors to create the serum and drank it. As a horrified SPIDER-MAN watched, Silvermane grew younger and younger until he seemingly disappeared completely. Fortunately the serum had a boomerang effect, and Silvermane rapidly aged back into his forties. Silvermane briefly took over a New York-based splinter group of HYDRA and then vainly attempted to unite New York City's organized crime under his leadership. He fell from a great height while fighting the third GREEN GOBLIN and SPIDER-MAN. His injuries undid the effects of the youth serum, causing him to revert to old age. Nearly slain by the vigilante DAGGER, Silvermane had his brain, face and vital organs transplanted into a robotic body. As a cyborg, Silvermane continues to be a power in the world of organized crime. Among his enemies are Spider-Man, DAREDEVIL, CLOAK and Dagger, the PUNISHER, and the KINGPIN.

Silvermane is the father of Joseph Manfredi, the criminal Blackwing. **PS**

As a cyborg, the once frail Silvermane has amazing strength.

SIN

After her washerwoman mother died in childbirth, Synthia's father—the RED SKULL—placed the infant girl into the care of Susan Scarbo, later known as MOTHER NIGHT. When Synthia reached her teens, the Red Skull returned to claim her. He then used a strange machine to accelerate her aging and grant her superpowers, transforming her into Mother Superior. Encouraged by his success, he repeated the process on four orphaned girls and used them to form a team of Super Villains named the SISTERS OF SIN.

When CAPTAIN AMERICA later used the same machine to reverse the Skull's attempts to age him to death, Synthia and the other Sisters of Sin reverted to girlhood again. This cost Synthia her powers, but she still returned to a reformed Sisters of Sin—under Mother Night's leadership—as Sister Sin.

After SHIELD captured Synthia, the organization tried to eliminate the Red Skull's influence over her so that she would seem like an average American girl. Under orders from the Red Skull, however, CROSSBONES kidnapped Synthia and tortured her until she regained her memories of her life working for her father. **MF**

Since the Red Skull ordered Crossbones to retrain Sin, she has been deadlier than ever and central to the Skull's plans.

FACTFILE

REAL NAME
Synthia Schmidt

OCCUPATION
Terrorist

BASE
Mobile

HEIGHT 5 ft 8 in
WEIGHT 120 lbs
EYES Green
HAIR Red

FIRST APPEARANCE
Captain America #290 (February 1984) as Mother Superior; *Captain America* #355 (July 1989) as Sin

No super powers (as Mother Superior: intangibility, telepathy, telekinesis, and teleportation. These powers have been lost). Experienced with a range of weapons.

Due to years of training, Sin is one of the world's deadliest killers.

FACTFILE

ORIGINAL MEMBERS
DOCTOR OCTOPUS
Mastermind, mechanical arms.
VULTURE Mechanical wings
ELECTRO Human dynamo.
KRAVEN THE HUNTER
Super-strong combatant.
LIZARD Bloodthirsty human/
reptile hybrid.
HYDRO-MAN Converts his body
into water.

BASE
Secret

**FIRST
APPEARANCE**
Uncanny X-Men #221
(September 1987)

SINISTER SIX

Determined to beat SPIDER-MAN, DOCTOR OCTOPUS contacted five of the webslinger's greatest enemies and formed a team of Super Villains dedicated to destroying their common foe. He decided that each member of the Six would take on Spider-Man in turn, wearing him down until they could kill him. Since this plan also failed repeatedly, the team has sometimes expanded its membership from six to seven or even twelve. Replacement members have included HOBGOBLIN, VENOM, Beetle (see MACH-IV), Scorpia, (a female version of the SCORPION), SHOCKER, SANDMAN, and MYSTERIO. During the Civil War (see pp. 84–5), the TRAPSTER and the GRIM REAPER joined the fun. **TD, MF**

Unknown to the Sinister Six, Spider-Man had temporarily lost his spider-powers when he first confronted them.

SINISTER SIX
1 Sandman **2** Vulture
3 Doctor Octopus **4** Electro **5** Kraven
6 Mysterio

SINISTER SYNDICATE

FIRST APPEARANCE Amazing Spider-Man #280 (Sept. 1986)
BASE New York City **MEMBERS AND POWERS**
Rhino Nearly invulnerable with superhuman strength [1].
Beetle Armored, multi-weaponed battle-suit [2].
Speed Demon Able to run at superhuman speeds [3].
Boomerang An expert with his specially equipped boomerangs [4].
Hydro-Man Can convert all or part of body into water [5].
Shocker Gauntlets generate highly destructive vibrations [6].

SIRYN

FIRST APPEARANCE Spider-Woman #37 (April 1981)
REAL NAME Theresa Rourke (Cassidy)
OCCUPATION Private investigator **BASE** New York City
HEIGHT 5 ft 7 in **WEIGHT** 130 lbs **EYES** Blue **HAIR** Blonde
SPECIAL POWERS/ABILITIES Combination of psionic ability and sonic waves produced by her voice can shatter steel, enable flight, and generate force blasts.

SISTERS OF SIN

FIRST APPEARANCE Captain America #294 (June 1984)
BASE Mobile **MEMBERS AND POWERS**
Raunch (formerly Sister Pleasure): Master hypnotist [1].
Hoodwink (formerly Sister Dream): Master hypnotist [2].
Slash (formerly Sister Agony): Has lacerating metal claw [3].
Torso (formerly Sister Death): Enhanced strength [4].
Sin (formerly Mother Superior): Ability to fire psionic bolts [5].
Mother Night (formerly Suprema): Ability to cloud minds.

After defeats by the HUMAN TORCH and SPIDER-MAN, the Beetle decided to stop being a solo act and organize a super-team. Inspired by the SINISTER SIX, the Beetle called his group the Sinister Syndicate. The Beetle was soon contacted by international mercenary Jack O'Lantern who hired the Syndicate to assassinate SILVER SABLE. Spider-Man and the SANDMAN interfered and foiled this scheme. The Syndicate was then hired by DOCTOR OCTOPUS to kidnap the royal family of Belgriun, a small European country. Once again, Spider-Man and Silver Sable defeated the Syndicate and eventually forced the team to disband. **TD**

Theresa Rourke was born when her father—BANSHEE—was on a secret mission. Her mother died soon after, and Theresa's uncle BLACK TOM CASSIDY took her in without informing Banshee. It wasn't until Tom was jailed that she discovered the truth. She joined X-FORCE and served as its deputy leader. After that, she started work with X-FACTOR Investigations. She gave birth to a baby fathered by Jamie Madrox, the MULTIPLE MAN. When Jamie held the baby for the first time, however, it turned out to be one of his duplicates, and he accidentally absorbed it back into his own body. **AD, MF**

The Sisters of Sin are the brainchildren of the RED SKULL, created to spread his ideology of hate. Synthia Schmidt, the Red Skull's daughter, took the name Mother Superior after receiving an artificial boost into adulthood. Four orphan girls received similar rapid-aging treatments, and as the Sisters of Sin they battled CAPTAIN AMERICA and NOMAD. After the Sisters had become teenagers again, the villain Suprema took control as MOTHER NIGHT. The Sisters took new names, and founded Camp Rage to incite runaways to violent rebellion. **DW**

SILVER SURFER

Sentinel of the Spaceways

Bored and frustrated by life on Zenn-La, Norrin Radd sought a more challenging existence.

Over the years the Earth has played to host to a variety of extraordinary beings: super-powered heroes and villains, mutants and Norse Gods, but few creatures have been as powerful yet restless as that enigmatic alien entity, the Silver Surfer. A galactic wanderer frustrated by the hedonism and complacency of his own world, the Surfer developed a similarly ambivalent relationship with the Earth, where the altruism of so many was sullied by the wanton malice of a few.

THE ZENN-LAVIANS

Born Norrin Radd on the faraway world of Zenn-La, even as a child Norrin was something of an outcast. Wanting for nothing, the Zenn-Lavians were an easy-going people whereas Norrin hungered for a more meaningful, vibrant life. A restless adult, even Norrin's lifelong companion, Shalla-Bal, could not quieten his spirit. It was only when the Zenn-Lavians detected the approach of an alien entity—GALACTUS, devourer of worlds— that Norrin came into his own.

ESSENTIAL STORYLINES

• *Fantastic Four #48–50* The Silver Surfer and Galactus' first encounter with Earth.
• *Silver Surfer Vol. 1 #1* Stan Lee tells the story of the Silver Surfer's origins in the character's first stand-alone series.
• *Silver Surfer Vol. 2 #1* Returning to Zenn-La the Surfer discovers it has been devastated by the world-devouring Galactus.

Galactus imbues Norrin Radd with the Power Cosmic, transforming him into the Silver Surfer.

In exchange for Galactus sparing Zenn-La, Norrin offered to become the entity's herald—to scour the galaxy for planet's devoid of life but suitable for Galactus' needs. To empower Norrin for this role, Galactus plucked an old adolescent fantasy from the young Zenn-Lavian's mind and transformed him into a silver skinned creature who could travel the galaxy on a silver board. Norrin had became the Silver Surfer.

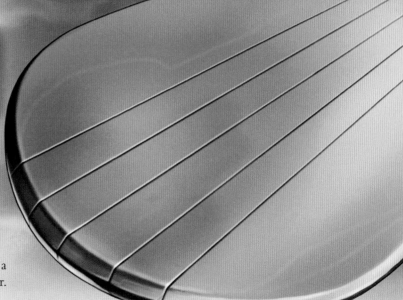

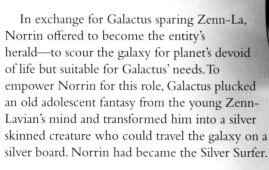

HERALD OF GALACTUS

Over time it became increasingly difficult for the Surfer to find appropriate worlds for his master, and so Galactus began to make subtle changes to the Surfer's mind. The Surfer was made to care less about avoiding sentient life, and countless worlds and peoples were sacrificed. Until, that is, he arrived on the planet Earth.

There the Surfer encountered the FANTASTIC FOUR and Alicia MASTERS. Their compassion and heroism reawakened the Surfer's suppressed

His conscience awoken by Alicia Masters, the Silver Surfer stood ready to oppose Galactus for the very first time.

emotions and he aligned himself with them. Threatened with the Ultimate Nullifier, a weapon used by Reed Richards (MR. FANTASTIC), Galactus was driven off, but not before punishing the Silver Surfer for his treachery: Galactus wrapped a field around the Earth designed to prevent the Surfer from ever leaving.

In the years that followed, Galactus returned to Earth several times, wishing to reclaim the Surfer as his herald. Each time the Fantastic Four helped drive him away.

INNOCENCE LOST

The Silver Surfer arrived on Earth as something of an innocent. The malevolent DOCTOR DOOM played on this naivety, befriending the Surfer and then stealing his powers. When Doom attempted to leave the Earth he ran into Galactus' cosmic barrier, losing control of these powers and enabling the Silver Surfer to regain them.

As the Surfer traveled the world, he became increasingly appalled by mankind's bigotry and cruelty. The Surfer believed he had left behind a stagnant, complacent world only to arrive at one soiled by ambition and greed. Hoping that humanity

LOVE LIFE

Although his heart remains with his first love, Shalla-Bal, during his interstellar voyages, the Silver Surfer has romanced several other women. The most significant of these was Alicia Masters who, during their first encounter, had revived him from his Galactus-induced mental stupor. For a time, Alicia journeyed across the stars with the Surfer, but she eventually decided to return to Earth. Years earlier, the Surfer had been linked to the Celestial Madonna, an Earth-born cosmic heroine, but she died during their battle against the Elders of the Universe. Tragedy also ended his relationship with Nova. A former Herald of Galactus, Nova died battling her successor as herald, the evil Morg.

The Celestial Madonna was also known as Mantis.

would improve if threatened by a common enemy, he transformed himself into mankind's nemesis. Only a "Sonic Shark" missile, created by Reed Richards, ended the threat that he posed.

FREEDOM REGAINED

Essentially exiled to the Earth, the Surfer never stopped yearning to travel amongst the stars once more. With Reed Richard's help he found a way of doing this, but his wanderings were not without upset. Returning to Zenn-La, the Surfer discovered that although his people still survived, Galactus had returned and ravaged the planet. The Surfer's visit to Zenn-La was curtailed when he learnt that his old lover, Shalla-Bal, had been

kidnapped by the demon MEPHISTO—a creature bent on corrupting the Surfer's soul. Arriving back on Earth, the Surfer freed Shalla-Bal and provided her with some of his own cosmic power—sufficient to heal their home planet.

His exile on Earth over, the Surfer sets out to explore the cosmos.

ROMANCE

In the following years, the Surfer remained an itinerant wanderer, forever searching for fulfilment but never quite finding it. Although he embarked on a series of relationships, these were generally short-lived. A romance with MANTIS, ended in tragedy following a battle with the ELDERS OF THE UNIVERSE, while the Surfer's relationship with NOVA, another herald of Galactus, was similarly doomed.

It was the Surfer's friendship with Alicia Masters that seemed to have the most potential. Striking up a romance, for a time the pair traveled the galaxy together, but eventually Alicia wanted to settle down back on Earth, whereas the Surfer wished to continue his nomadic existence. To this day he remains a galactic wanderer, returning to Earth at regular intervals but remaining sceptical of its long-term prospects. **AD**

Not the best of friends, the Silver Surfer and Galactus regularly face each other in battle.

As Nova, Frankie Raye was one of Galactus's more recent heralds.

SKRULLS, THE

Shape-changing alien race

FACTFILE

BASE
Tarnax IV, Andromeda Galaxy

FIRST APPEARANCE
Fantastic Four Vol. 1 #2
(January 1962)

Skrull warships are designed to protect the paranoid species.

POWERS

Shapeshifting permits radical changes in size, shape, and color; lifespans reach 200 years on average.

The Skrulls are an ancient humanoid species from the Andromeda galaxy, with reptilian physiologies. The cosmic beings known as the CELESTIALS visited the species' birthworld of Skrullos long ago and created Skrullian equivalents to Earth's ETERNALS and Deviants. The Deviant Skrulls exhibited the ability to shapeshift and soon wiped out all competing racial branches.

THE KREE WAR

After forging an interstellar empire, the Skrulls encountered the primitive KREE, who murdered the Skrull contact team and stole their starship technology. A Kree armada soon attacked the Skrulls, triggering the eons-long Kree-Skrull War. Skrull scientists later developed the first Cosmic Cube, which gained sentience and decimated the Skrull Empire, eventually evolving into the exceptionally powerful SHAPER OF WORLDS. The Skrulls bounced back from this tragedy, establishing an Imperial throneworld on Tabrnax IV.

COMMENCE WIDE SPECTRUM ENERGY SCAN. CONCENTRATE ON EARTH.

IT'S THE ONLY SCRAP OF LIFE IN THIS FORSAKEN CORNER OF THE UNIVERSE!

The Skrulls have taken a secret role in Earthly affairs, using their shapeshifting powers to impersonate world leaders.

SECRET AGENTS

The Skrulls placed agents on Earth, but these were defeated by the FANTASTIC FOUR. In response, the Skrull emperor Dorrek VII created the SUPER-SKRULL, who possessed the combined powers of the Fantastic Four. The Skrulls also engineered an elite class of Warskrulls, agents that could duplicate the powers of other beings when they assumed those beings' shapes. After GALACTUS devoured Tarnax IV, the Skrull Empire fell into civil war. The mad Skrull Zabyk detonated a hyper-wave bomb that removed the shapeshifting ability from all Skrulls. The Super-Skrull escaped the

WHICH IS WHY THE UNSUSPECTING EARTHMEN WILL NEVER KNOW THAT WE *SKRULLS* HAVE *IMPERSONATED* THEIR FAMOUS FANTASTIC FOUR

Skrulls can alter their appearances to duplicate anyone, but can be shocked into dropping their disguises if they are hurt or knocked out.

bomb's effects and eventually managed to restore the species' shapeshifting powers.

During the Annihilation (*see* pp. 30–31), the Skrulls lost nearly all of their planets. The Skrulls turned to VERANKE, who had been banished for supporting prophecies of just such an event, and made her their queen. Relying once more on the prophets, she decided to infiltrate and conquer the Earth, making it the new Skrull homeworld. When the attack began in earnest, this became known as the Secret Invasion (*see* pp. 326–7). The people of Earth banded together to root out the Skrulls and repel their attack, leaving the Skrulls nearly destroyed and homeless once more. **DW, MF**

ESSENTIAL STORYLINES
• *Avengers #89-97* The devastating Kree-Skrull War reaches Earth, and the Avengers assemble to prevent innocents from being caught in the crossfire.
• *Avengers Annual #14* The insane Skrull warrior Zabyk detonates a hyper-wave bomb, removing the shapeshifting abilities of all Skrulls.
• *Secret Invasion #1-8* The Skrulls invade Earth.

SIX PACK

FIRST APPEARANCE Cable Vol. 1 #1 (Oct. 1992) **BASE** Mobile

MEMBERS AND POWERS

Domino Can influence the laws of probability [1].

G. W. Bridge Skilled combatant and weapons expert [2].

Anaconda Can stretch limbs and use them to crush enemies [3].

Solo Able to teleport himself and weapons [4].

Hammer Weapons designer and technician [5].

Constrictor Has electrically powered cables mounted on wrists [6].

Originally known as the Wild Pack, Cable's mercenary team included him, Deadpool, Domino, Grizzly, Hammer, and Garrison Kane. Six Pack often clashed with the mutant villain STRYFE. On one mission, Stryfe threatened to kill Kane if he didn't receive a data disc, and Cable shot Hammer in the back to stop the trade. Outraged, the rest of Six Pack cut ties with Cable. A later incarnation of Six Pack, assembled by SHIELD, added Solo, Constrictor and Anaconda under agent G. W. Bridge, but they broke up after Cable defeated them. **DW, MF**

SKIDS

FIRST APPEARANCE X-Factor #7 (August 1986)

REAL NAME Sally Blevins

OCCUPATION Adventurer **BASE** Mobile

HEIGHT 5 ft 5 in **WEIGHT** 115 lbs **EYES** Blue **HAIR** Blonde

SPECIAL POWERS/ABILITIES Skids possesses a protective, frictionless force field which shields her from harm, and which she can extend to envelop others.

Born a mutant, Skids lived among the sewer-dwelling MORLOCKS until the Mutant Massacre by the MARAUDERS caused her to flee. Rescued by X-Factor, for a time she became a trainee with that team, and she fought with their junior members, the X-Terminators. Brainwashed into serving with the MUTANT LIBERATION FRONT, Skids eventually regained her freedom after her boyfriend Rusty COLLINS was killed battling HOLOCAUST, and she herself was injured. She kept her powers after M-Day, and she became an undercover agent of Shield. **TB, MF**

◉ **SKRULLS** *see opposite page*

SKYHAWK

FIRST APPEARANCE Thor #395 (September 1988)

REAL NAME Winston Manchester **OCCUPATION** Entrepreneur

BASE New York City **HEIGHT** (as Skyhawk) 6 ft 3 in **WEIGHT** as Skyhawk) 210 lbs **EYES** Blue **HAIR** Brown

SPECIAL POWERS/ABILITIES As Skyhawk, possesses superhuman strength and the ability to fly; formerly a high-achiever working 20 hours a day, he now leaves the office at 5 o'clock.

Businessman Manchester collapsed in the office and was taken to the same hospital where the god Hogun (*see* GODS OF ASGARD) was staying. Manchester opened his eyes to find that he was with two other patients. They had all attracted the attention of Seth, god of death (*see* GODS OF HELIOPOLIS). Claiming that Hogun was a threat to the Earth, Seth branded their left palms with the sign of Aton, the glowing disc of the sun, and gave them all superhuman powers. Manchester and his teammates learned that Seth was the real menace and they helped Thor defeat him. **TD**

SLAPSTICK

FIRST APPEARANCE Slapstick #1 (November 1992)

REAL NAME Steve Harmon

OCCUPATION Adventurer **BASE** Mobile

HEIGHT 5 ft 7 in **WEIGHT** 145 lbs **EYES** Blue **HAIR** Blond

SPECIAL POWERS/ABILITIES Indestructible, stretchable, and gains strength from electricity, plus superhuman strength, speed, endurance, and agility.

While facing the Overlord and his evil Clowns of Dimension X, Steve Harmon's molecules were transformed into unstable molecules. He also gained a pair of high-tech gloves: the left allowed him to change from human to Slapstick and back, while his right featured an extra-dimensional storage pocket. Steve managed to defeat the Overlord and rescue all of his captives. Later, he joined the NEW WARRIORS for a time, working with his friend SPEEDBALL.

After the Civil War (*see* pp. 84–5), Slapstick became one of the first of The Fifty-State Initiative (*see* pp. 118–9) recruits at Camp Hammond. Disillusioned with the program, he left it. **MF**

SKAAR

SKAAR

FACTFILE

REAL NAME
Skaar

OCCUPATION
Warrior

BASE
Planet Sakaar

HEIGHT 6 ft 1 in
WEIGHT 500 lbs
EYES Brown
HAIR Black

FIRST APPEARANCE
World War Hulk #5 (November 2007)

POWERS

Skaar is a master warrior with superhuman strength and limited invulnerability. Like the Hulk, when calm he turns to a more human form.

Nothing on Sakaar could stand before Skaar's wrath.

After the Hulk conquered Sakaar, he made his lover CAIERA—a warrior of the native Shadow People—his queen, and she became pregnant with their child. When the starship the Hulk had arrived in exploded, it killed millions of people on the planet, including Caiera. Believing the blast had been triggered by the ILLUMINATI, he and his WARBOUND traveled back to Earth for revenge (*see* World War Hulk pp. 152-5). A cocoon appeared in the crater the explosion had left behind, and after some time, Skaar emerged from this, already grown to the size of a 10-year-old boy. He then fought his way across the land in search of the Old Power his mother held, quickly growing to full-size and amassing an army as he went. **MF**

SLATER, JINK

FIRST APPEARANCE The Incredible Hulk Vol. 3 #36 (March 2002)
REAL NAME Jink Slater
OCCUPATION Professional assassin **BASE** Mobile
HEIGHT/WEIGHT Unrevealed **EYES** Brown **HAIR** Black
SPECIAL POWERS/ABILITIES Excellent marksman; expert with guns and knives; a formidable hand-to-hand combatant; above average in strength and endurance; ruthless in pursuit of his quarry.

Jink Slater was hired by unidentified parties to capture the HULK. Despite his objections, his employers ordered Slater to work with a partner, Sandra VERDUGO, on the assignment. Eventually, Slater and Verdugo found the Hulk in his human identity of Bruce Banner in a diner. Their attempt to capture him was thwarted by the arrival of DOC SAMSON. Not trusting his partner, Slater shot Verdugo in the head and escaped. Subsequently, Slater found Banner and Verdugo together in a cabin. Slater shot Verdugo in the shoulder. Verdugo retaliated by setting off explosives that killed Slater. **PS**

SLOAN, FRED

FIRST APPEARANCE Incredible Hulk #231 (January 1979)
REAL NAME Frederick Sloan
OCCUPATION Author **BASE** Unrevealed
HEIGHT/WEIGHT Unrevealed **EYES** Blue **HAIR** Blond
SPECIAL POWERS/ABILITIES Fred Sloan possesses no superhuman powers save a peculiarly positive outlook on life; possesses the strength and endurance of an average man.

Fred Sloan first encountered the incredible HULK while he was being thrown bodily out of a bar. The childlike Hulk interceded on the drifter's behalf, and the two became fast friends.  Sloan helped the Hulk to elude the authorities, and the two traveled together for a time.

Eventually they encountered WOODGOD and his band of similar human-animal hybrids known as the Changelings, and Sloan decided to remain with them.

In time, he wrote a book, entitled *Hulk Encounter: A Survivor's Story,* which painted the green behemoth in an unusually positive light. **TB**

SMYTHE, ALISTAIR

FIRST APPEARANCE Amazing Spider-Man Annual #19 (1985)
REAL NAME Alistair Smythe
OCCUPATION Criminal inventor **BASE** New York City
HEIGHT 6 ft **WEIGHT** 220 lbs **EYES** Brown **HAIR** Brown
SPECIAL POWERS/ABILITIES Ultimate Spider-Slayer armature provides enhanced strength, and features built-in cutting blades and web shooters.

Alistair Smythe grew up hating SPIDER-MAN. His father, Professor Spencer SMYTHE, built the first robotic Spider-Slayer units, and Alistair continued the Spider-Slayer legacy after his father's death. Following a stint in the employ of the KINGPIN, Alistair constructed ever more deadly Spider-Slayers until an accident left him in a wheelchair. In response, he fashioned a cyborg armature for himself and emerged as the Ultimate Spider-Slayer. Alistair tried to coerce J. Jonah JAMESON into helping him, but Jameson knocked him out with a baseball bat. **DW**

SMYTHE, PROFESSOR

FIRST APPEARANCE Amazing Spider-Man Vol. 1 #25 (June 1965)
REAL NAME Spencer Smythe
OCCUPATION Professor, criminal inventor **BASE** New York City
HEIGHT 5 ft 10 in **WEIGHT** 175 lbs **EYES** Gray **HAIR** Gray
SPECIAL POWERS/ABILITIES Genius-level expertise in engineering and robotics.

Professor Spencer Smythe's life was marked by an irrational hatred for SPIDER-MAN. He used his engineering expertise to construct the Spider-Slayer, a Spider-Man hunting robot, and persuaded *Daily Bugle* publisher J. Jonah JAMESON to pay for it. He followed up with several improved generations of Spider-Slayers, but the radiation used in their construction gradually poisoned him. He died during a revenge plot hatched against both Spider-Man and Jameson, leaving his son Alistair (*see* SMYTHE, Alistair) to carry on his work. **DW**

SNARKS

A malevolent, warlike, reptilian race, the Zn'rx or "Snarks" are based on a planet in the Milky Way galaxy known on Earth as Snarkworld. The Snarks first came to notice when their ages-long conflict with the horselike Kymellians spilled over to Earth.

The Queen Mother, Maraud, sent raiding parties to Earth in order to learn the secrets of a new scientific breakthrough discovered by Dr. James POWER, and use it as a weapon against their ancient foes. Sent by his people to prevent this from happening, Kymellian champion Aelfyre WHITEMANE was slain by the Snarks, but not before he passed on his abilities to Dr. Powers' four children. These children, now known as the POWER PACK, defeated the Snark menace. Thereafter, the Snarks became obsessed with taking Whitemane's powers for themselves, and repeatedly staged attacks on the Power children, to no avail.

Although convinced of their own importance, the Snarks remain only a minor player on the galactic stage. **TB**

The Snarks are perennial enemies of the super-powered children of the Power Pack.

ROBERTSON, JOE

FACTFILE
REAL NAME
Zn'rx (pronounced "Snarks")
BASE
The planet Snarkworld

HEIGHT 8 ft (average)
WEIGHT 400 lbs (average)
EYES Red
HAIR None (green scales)

FIRST APPEARANCE
Power Pack #1
(August 1984)

POWERS

Snarks are larger, stronger and live longer than human beings. As well as various high-tech weapons (their technology is generally more advanced than Earth's), they have a vicious array of teeth and sharp claws. Like Earth's reptiles they are cold-blooded and so vulnerable to extremes of cold.

The Snarks were given their name by Aelfyre Whitemane after the monster in the famous poem "The Hunting of the Snark" by Lewis Carroll.

SNOWBIRD

FACTFILE

REAL NAME
Narya

OCCUPATION
Goddess; adventurer

BASE
Canada

HEIGHT 5 ft 10 in
WEIGHT 108 lbs
EYES (Snowbird) White; (Anne McKenzie) blue
HAIR Pale blonde; (in animal form) White

FIRST APPEARANCE
(as Anne McKenzie) Uncanny X-Men #120 (April 1979)

POWERS

Snowbird can assume the form of a human woman or of any animal native to the Canadian Arctic. She has superhuman strength and the ability to fly.

SNOWBIRD

Nelvanna, goddess of the Northern Lights, wished to have a child that was half human, half god, a child that could defend humanity from the mystical Great Beasts. She mated with a human named Richard Easton, and the Native American sorcerer Michael Twoyoungmen raised the infant, named Narya. Narya grew to adulthood within a few years, and James MacDonald Hudson invited her and Twoyoungmen to join ALPHA FLIGHT, a team of superhuman operatives he was organizing for the government.

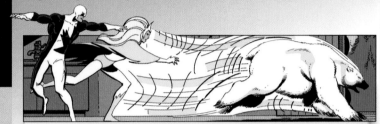

Snowbird can become any animal native to the Canadian Arctic, gaining its abilities. When she takes the form of a creature smaller than herself, like an owl, she becomes a human-sized version of it.

Narya took the name Snowbird, and took the cover identity of Anne McKenzie, an officer in the Canadian Mounties.

When Alpha Flight teammate Walter Langkowski (SASQUATCH) fell under the mental control of Tanaraq, one of the Great Beasts, Snowbird slew his physical body.

Anne McKenzie married a fellow officer in the RCMP, Doug Thompson, and they had a son. Subsequently, a menace called Pestilence took mental possession of Snowbird. Hudson's wife Heather defeated Pestilence by killing Narya's physical form. Langkowski's spirit took over Narya's resurrected body, becoming the new Sasquatch. Snowbird's spirit later gained a new body and returned to Alpha Flight. She was not with the team when the Collective (see GUARDIAN) destroyed it. During the Secret Invasion (see pp. 326-7), she helped destroy the SKRULL god Kly'bn. **PS, MF**

SNOW QUEEN

FIRST APPEARANCE Wolverine Vol. 2 #24 (May 1990)
REAL NAME Unrevealed
OCCUPATION Assassin **BASE** Unrevealed
HEIGHT/WEIGHT Unknown **EYES** Blue **HAIR** Blonde
SPECIAL POWERS/ABILITIES Generates mental static that occludes minds of others; trained in the use of various types of weapons and explosives.

The only known report of the mutant assassin known as Snow Queen relates to a short visit to 1930s Madripoor, where she encountered WOLVERINE. Employed to kill a barman in the

town with a suitcase of explosives, her plan went wrong when a street urchin stole the case. When Wolverine attempted to intervene, the Snow Queen overwhelmed him with her mental powers. It is thought that she died minutes later when the recovered suitcase detonated prematurely. **AD**

SOLARR

FIRST APPEARANCE Captain America #160 (April 1973)
REAL NAME Silas King **OCCUPATION** Criminal
BASE New York City; Project Pegasus complex
HEIGHT 6 ft **WEIGHT** 210 lbs **EYES** Brown **HAIR** Blond
SPECIAL POWERS/ABILITIES He can absorb, store, and control solar energy, and discharge this energy in the form of powerful heat blasts fired from his hands.

Narcotics smuggler Silas King's van broke down in the Mojave desert. After several days in the desert sun his latent mutant power was released. Adopting the name Solarr, he move used his power to rob banks. He became partners with Klaw and later joined EGGHEAD's Emissaries of Evil. Solarr's criminal endeavors were repeatedly stopped by the AVENGERS, CAPTAIN AMERICA, SPIDER-MAN, and the THING. He was imprisoned for study at the Project: Pegasus energy research center and was killed by the animated corpse of a guard he had burned to death, which had been brought back to life by Bres of the Fomor race. **MT**

SOMMERS, APRIL

FIRST APPEARANCE Incredible Hulk #208 (February 1977)
REAL NAME April Sommers **OCCUPATION** Model, actress, apartment superintendent **BASE** New York City
HEIGHT 5 ft 8 in **WEIGHT** 123 lbs **EYES** Blue **HAIR** Blonde
SPECIAL POWERS/ABILITIES Possesses the strength, speed and reflexes of an average female who regularly engages in moderate exercise. Extremely personable.

An often-unemployed model and actress, Sommers also supported herself by working as the superintendent of the apartment building where she lived. The job provided her with free rent and a small weekly salary. She once rented a room to Dr. Bruce Banner, completely unaware of the fact that he was secretly the HULK, and she later helped him get a temporary job at a construction site. Though she was attracted to Bruce at first, her interest quickly waned as he began to act more and more mysteriously. She eventually learned his secret. After asking Bruce to leave, Sommers gave the apartment to his friend Jim Wilson. **TD**

FACTFILE

KEY MEMBERS

GENERAL CHEN
The first Supreme Serpent; a grossly overambitious individual.

DAN DUNN
Co-leader; talk-show host, white right-winger.

MONTAGUE HALE
Co-leader and black, left-winger.

J.C. PENNYSWORTH
Head of Richmond Enterprises; sponsor of Sons of the Satan

HATE-MONGER
Foments hatred and anger.

RUSSELL DABOIA
Mystic powers.

SKINHEAD
Superhuman neo-Nazi.

BASE California

FIRST APPEARANCE
Avengers Vol. 1 #32
(September 1966)

SONS OF THE SERPENT

"As the first serpent drove Adam and Eve from Eden, so shall we drive all foreigners from this land." This is the mantra of the Sons of the Serpent—an organization fueled by hatred and sponsored by a few wealthy businessmen. Targeting non-whites, immigrants, and the infirm, the Sons of the Serpent is dedicated to making the US a citadel of white racial supremacy.

During their first bid for power, they took CAPTAIN AMERICA hostage to try to force the AVENGERS into publicly supporting their evil cause. When this failed, the Sons developed further plots aimed at dividing America and black against white, one of which actually culminated in a mind-controlled Captain America fighting against his black partner, the FALCON. After repeated knock backs, their plans have become increasingly desperate. They have even resorted to crude mysticism, perhaps a sign of their waning influence. **AD**

Serpent Signs can be used to record and leave messages.

SOUTHERN, CANDY

FIRST APPEARANCE X-Men #31 (April 1967)
REAL NAME Candace Southern **OCCUPATION** CEO Southern Industries **BASE** New York City, Colorado Rocky Mountains
HEIGHT Unknown **WEIGHT** Unknown **EYES** Blue **HAIR** Black
SPECIAL POWERS/ABILITIES Normal human strength of woman who engaged in regular exercise. Had great leadership abilities.

Archangel Warren Worthington was unable to prevent Candy's murder.

Candace "Candy" Southern began dating Warren Worthington III when they were teenagers. Southern discovered that Worthington was the ANGEL, a member of X-MEN, when his uncle, the original DAZZLER abducted her. Southern and Worthington later shared a home in the Rocky Mountains which became the DEFENDERS' headquarters. Southern was the team's business manager and government liaison. She was killed by Worthington's enemy, Cameron Hodge. Southern's mind was assimilated into the group consciousness of the techno-organic PHALANX. She sacrificed herself to destroy Hodge. **PS**

FACTFILE

NOTABLE MEMBERS

CRIMSON DYNAMO (5)
In armor, has superhuman strength, durability and can fly.

URSA MAJOR (3)
Transforms into a large bear; retains his intelligence while in bear form.

VANGUARD (8)
Forcefield repels virtually all electromagnetic and kinetic energy. By crossing his hammer and sickle in front of his body, he can redirect energy repelled by his natural force field

DARKSTAR (6)
Manipulates extradimensional energy called the Darkforce.

TITANIUM MAN (GREMLIN) (9)
Armor provided superhuman strength, durability flight; fired force blasts from hands.

BASE
The former Soviet Union, now Russia

FIRST APPEARANCE
Incredible Hulk #258
(April 1981)

SOVIET SUPER SOLDIERS

Created to be the Soviet Union's answer to the AVENGERS, the Soviet Super-Soldiers functioned as that nation's defenders through much of the latter part of the Cold War. But eventually, questioning some of the orders given to them by the State, they rebelled, and began to operate independently. The Russian government later sent their replacement team, the Supreme Soviets, to reclaim the members of the Soviet Super Soldiers and bring them back into line—an attempt that met with failure.

Thereafter, with the fall of communism and the dissolution of the Soviet Union, the surviving members of both the Soviet Super Soldiers and the Supreme Soviet joined forces with other new heroes to become first the People's Protectorate, then the Winter Guard, still dedicated to using their great powers to defend their homeland, no matter who ruled it. **TB**

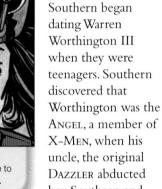

SOVIET SUPER SOLDIERS
1 Red Guardian **2** Unidentified **3** Ursa Major **4** Vanguard
5 Crimson Dynamo **6** Darkstar **7** Unidentified **8** Perun
9 Titanium Man (The Gremlin) **10** Vostok **11** Fantasma
12 Blind Faith **13** Volvic **14** Sibercat **15** Unidentified

SPACE PHANTOM

FIRST APPEARANCE Avengers #2 (November 1963)
REAL NAME Unknown **OCCUPATION** Agent of Immortus
BASE Limbo **HEIGHT** 6 ft 6 in **WEIGHT** 215 lbs **EYES** Blue
HAIR Red **SPECIAL POWERS/ABILITIES** Space Phantom can change his appearance to look like any living being. If they have superpowers, then he assumes those powers as well. The being whose form is taken is instantly sent to the dimension of Limbo.

Space Phantom is an alien from the planet Phantus, which shifted into the timeless dimension of Limbo when the space-time continuum ruptured. Stranded in Limbo, Space Phantom met IMMORTUS, the master of that realm. Immortus offered to free Space Phantom if he brought him beings to study. When Space Phantom agreed, Immortus gave him the power to assume the form of any being as a way to bring him subjects. When Space Phantom took on the form of another being, it was immediately sent to Limbo for Immortus to examine. On the occasion when Space Phantom tried to send the Thunder God, THOR, into Limbo, he was stopped and sent back into the timeless dimension. **MT**

SPEEDBALL

FIRST APPEARANCE Amazing Spider-Man Annual #22 (1988)
REAL NAME Robert Baldwin **OCCUPATION** High-school student
BASE New York City, formerly Springdale, Connecticut
HEIGHT 5 ft 6 in **WEIGHT** 133 lbs **EYES** Blue **HAIR** Blond
SPECIAL POWERS/ABILITIES Personal force field allows him to absorb all kinetic energy directed at him and reflect it back at a greater velocity, which he often does by bouncing off objects.

Bombarded with energy bubbles from another dimension, Robert Baldwin gained strange powers. Once he learned to control them, he created a costume and took the name Speedball, becoming a crimefighter in his hometown. He co-founded the NEW WARRIORS and was with them when NITRO exploded, destroying a city and launching the Civil War (*see* pp. 84–5). Surviving Nitro's blast, Baldwin joined the THUNDERBOLTS, calling himself Penance and donning a suit of armor with 612 internal spikes, one for everyone who died in the explosion. He brought Nitro to justice, but recently MOONSTONE secretly drugged him and had him committed. **TD, MF**

SPEEDFREEK

FIRST APPEARANCE Incredible Hulk Vol. 2 #388 (December 1991)
REAL NAME Leon Shappe
OCCUPATION Assassin **BASE** Mobile
HEIGHT/WEIGHT Unrevealed **EYES** Brown **HAIR** Brown
SPECIAL POWERS/ABILITIES Combat suit of titanium steel alloy that is virtually indestructible; rocket-powered boots enable flight and travel at 150 mph; uses two long adamantium blades.

Drug addict Leon Shappe stole a sophisticated combat suit from an inventor and became the assassin Speedfreek. He clashed with the HULK a few times. When a protestor erroneously gunned down Shappe's daughter outside an abortion clinic, the Hulk stopped him from murdering the killer. While dodging Speedfreek's blades, the Hulk threw a car battery at him. Speedfreek sliced right through it with his blades, accidentally showering himself with battery acid. He was part of the band of villains the New Warriors were battling in Stamford, Connecticut, when Nitro destroyed the place. Speedfreek died in the blast. **AD, MF**

SPEED

FIRST APPEARANCE Young Avengers #10 (February 2006)
REAL NAME Thomas Shepherd
OCCUPATION Adventurer **BASE** New York City
HEIGHT 5 ft 10 in **WEIGHT** 182 lbs **EYES** Blue **HAIR** White
SPECIAL POWERS/ABILITIES Superhuman speed, plus atomic destabilization, which can cause touched objects to explode.

Tommy Shepherd thought he'd been born and raised in New Jersey to Frank and Mary Shepherd. In fact, he and Billy Kaplan (*see* WICCAN) of the YOUNG AVENGERS were products of the SCARLET WITCH's powers. Desperate for children, the Scarlet Witch had created twin boys for herself out of lost souls, but MEPHISTO eventually came to reclaim them. When the Scarlet Witch remade the world on M-Day, she remade the boys too, placing them in different homes. Soon after the VISION and SUPER-SKRULL had figured this out, Tommy took the codename Speed and joined his twin brother Billy in the Young Avengers. **MF**

SPEED DEMON

FIRST APPEARANCE Amazing Spider-Man Vol. 1 #222 (Nov. 1981)
REAL NAME James Sanders
OCCUPATION Professional criminal **BASE** New York City
HEIGHT 5 ft 11 in **WEIGHT** 175 lbs **EYES** Black **HAIR** Gray
SPECIAL POWERS/ABILITIES A super speedster, able to run at up to 160 mph; also possesses superhuman strength.

The GRANDMASTER gave James Sanders his powers when he recruited the chemist for his Squadron Sinister. Sanders called himself the Whizzer at first, but then changed it to Speed Demon instead. He regularly fought SPIDER-MAN and later joined the SINISTER SYNDICATE. After that, he took up with BARON VON STRUCKER's THUNDERBOLTS, but he returned to the Sinister Squadron when the Grandmaster called him again. Under the Grandmaster's command, the team transformed into Supreme Power, and Speed Demon nearly helped them find the Wellspring of Power, but the Thunderbolts stopped him. **DW, MF**

SPHINX

FIRST APPEARANCE Nova Vol. 3 #6 (October 1999)
REAL NAME Anath-Na Mut
OCCUPATION Wizard **BASE** Mobile flying pyramid
HEIGHT 7 ft 2 in **WEIGHT** 450 lbs **EYES** Red **HAIR** None
SPECIAL POWERS/ABILITIES Enhanced strength; Ka stone permitted immortality, flight, telepathy, energy transference, and the ability to fire concussive beams.

Anath-Na Mut, an ancient Egyptian mutant given further powers by the Caretaker of Arcturus, served in the court of Ramses II until his failure to defeat Moses branded him an exile. He became the immortal Sphinx through the energies of the Ka stone, wandering for five thousand years until absorbing the extraterrestrial Xandar living computer with unwitting help from the hero NOVA. Now nearly omnipotent, the Sphinx met defeat at GALACTUS' hands. Later, Anath-Na Mut returned to life. When he merged with his reincarnated Egyptian lover, Meryet Karim (Sphinx II), the two formed the "Omni-Sphinx." **DW**

SPIDER-MAN

Your friendly neighborhood web-slinger

FACTFILE

REAL NAME
Peter Benjamin Parker

OCCUPATION
Freelance photographer, science teacher

BASE
New York City

HEIGHT 5 ft 10 in
WEIGHT 170 lbs
EYES Hazel
HAIR Brown

FIRST APPEARANCE
Amazing Fantasy #15
(August 1962)

SPIDER-MAN

POWERS

Possesses the proportionate strength, speed, agility and reflexes of a spider. Can cling to any surface and generate organic webbing. Also possesses a "spider-sense" that warns him of danger and can psychically align him with his environment. Invented spider-tracers that he can track across the city with his spider-sense.

ALLIES/FOES

ALLIES Ben and May Parker, Mary Jane Parker, Captain America, The Avengers, the Fantastic Four, the X-Men, Eugene "Flash" Thompson, Betty Brant Leeds.

FOES Chameleon, Vulture, Doctor Octopus, Sandman, Kingpin, Green Goblin, Lizard, Electro, Kraven the Hunter, Black Cat, Venom, Mysterio, Carnage, Scrier, Judas Traveller.

ISSUE #1

While attending a scientific demonstration, Peter Parker was bitten by a spider that had been exposed to radioactivity. Feeling nauseous, the teenager immediately headed home and began to exhibit the most amazing powers—like the ability to stick to walls and crawl up sheer surfaces!

Before gaining his spider-powers, Peter Parker was weaker than most of the kids his age.

Peter Parker's parents died in a plane crash while he was still a child. When they said goodbye at the airport, his parents told him to be a good boy for his Aunt May and Uncle Ben PARKER, who later raised him as their own son. Peter always thought of his Uncle Ben as his best friend. Not only did Ben Parker spend quality time with the boy, he had a great sense of humor and many hours telling jokes and pulling gags on Peter who developed a real appreciation for quips and pranks. Peter studied hard in school and became an honor student. Although his teachers praised him, the other students had little use for a know-it-all like puny Parker. The girls thought him too quiet, and the boys considered him a wimp.

ORIGIN OF SPIDER-MAN

On the day his life changed forever, Peter went to a science exhibition by himself where he was bitten by a common house spider that had been exposed to a massive dose of radiation. Within a few hours, Peter discovered that he could stick to walls and had gained other amazing arachnid abilities.

Anxious to cash in on his new powers he designed a distinctive costume that concealed his identity, built a pair of web-shooters and went into showbusiness using the Amazing Spider-Man as his stage name.

One night, after a performance, he was walking toward an elevator when a security guard asked him to stop a fleeing man. However, Peter

Peter began to suspect that his powers might be the result of paranormal forces.

MY FAULT -- ALL MY FAULT! IF ONLY I HAD STOPPED HIM WHEN I COULD HAVE! BUT I DIDN'T -- AND NOW -- UNCLE BEN -- IS DEAD...

Parker did nothing and the burglar escaped.

A few days later the same thief murdered Peter's Uncle Ben! Filled with remorse, Peter vowed that he would never allow another innocent person to suffer because Spider-Man had failed to act. He had learned, in the hardest possible way, to use his great powers in a responsible manner.

AMAZING FANTASY

HIGH-SCHOOL HERO

Spider-Man soon found himself battling criminals such as the CHAMELEON, the VULTURE, DOCTOR OCTOPUS, the SANDMAN, DOCTOR DOOM, the LIZARD, ELECTRO, MYSTERIO, the GREEN GOBLIN, the SCORPION. and many more. He attempted to join the FANTASTIC FOUR and began a feud with the HUMAN TORCH.

J. Jonah JAMESON, publisher of the *Daily Bugle,* hated masked vigilantes and claimed Spider-Man was a menace to the public. Peter saw an opportunity to exploit Jameson's campaign and began taking pictures of himself as Spider-Man. He was soon supporting himself by selling these pictures to the *Bugle* on a freelance basis.

Peter eventually graduated from Midtown High with the highest scholastic average in the school's history. However, he almost missed the graduation ceremony. While the other seniors were donning caps and gowns, he was busy battling the MOLTEN MAN. He won his fight and arrived at the ceremony just in time to learn that he had won a full scholarship to Empire State University.

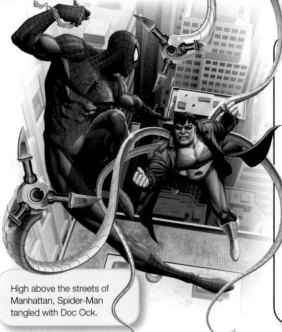

High above the streets of Manhattan, Spider-Man tangled with Doc Ock.

RIGHT HERE,

JUST WHERE I WANNA BE.

NOOOOO!

The Green Goblin murdered Gwen Stacy, Peter's first true love.

COLLEGE YEARS AND BEYOND

While in college, Peter met Mary Jane Watson (his future wife, *see* PARKER, MARY JANE), but began to date Gwen Stacy. (Gwen would later die tragically at the hands of the Green Goblin.) Peter became best friends with Harry Osborn and later learned that the GREEN GOBLIN was secretly Harry's father Norman. Spider-Man also encountered such villains as KINGPIN, the RHINO, the SHOCKER, SILVERMANE and the PROWLER.

After graduating from college, Peter encountered the acrobatic cat burglar BLACK CAT

(his girlfriend for a while), and the criminals HYDRO-MAN, SPEED DEMON and the HOBGOBLIN. He also battled the unstoppable JUGGERNAUT and cosmically-powered FIRELORD. He temporarily donned a new black costume that possessed some additional new powers, but later proved to be an alien symbiote. Meanwhile, his relationship with the beautiful model Mary Jane Watson had grown serious and they were married.

FURTHER DEVELOPMENTS

After leading a European crime cult for many years, Norman Osborn reentered Peter's life. Peter also met a man called Ezekiel who claimed that Spider-Man's powers were the result of magic and not a radioactive spider. Peter later confronted the Queen, who had the power to control insects and she mutated him into a giant

spider. After returning to his human form, Peter learned that his powers and strength had been increased and that he had gained the ability to produce organic webbing. Peter also joined a new AVENGERS team.

After a battle with the mysterious, super-strong, vampiric villain Morlun, in which Peter appeared to have been killed, Peter temporarily accepted a new armored costume and a job working for Tony Stark (*see* IRON MAN). However he has since returned to his traditional look. **TD**

ESSENTIAL STORYLINES

• *Amazing Spider-Man #31–33* Spider-Man battles the Master Planner in order to obtain a rare serum that can save Aunt May's life.

• *Amazing Spider-Man: Fearful Symmetry or Kraven's Last Hunt (tpb)* Kraven the Hunter kidnaps Spider-Man and take his place in a battle against the deadly Vermin.

• *Amazing Spider-Man: The Saga of the Alien Costume (tpb)* Spider-Man learns that his new black costume is actually an alien symbiote.

• *Amazing Spider-Man vs. Venom (tpb)* Spider-Man meets his match when Venom enters his life.

• *Amazing Spider-Man: Identity Crisis (tpb)* When a $5 million bounty is placed on his head for a murder he didn't commit, Spider-Man must adopt four new costumed identities to find the real murderer.

• *Amazing Spider-Man: Coming Home (tpb)* Spider-Man meets the man called Ezekiel and learns there may be a lot more to his origin than he ever realized.

THE ALIEN SUIT

Along with other heroes, Spider-Man was transported to a planet created by a near-omnipotent being called the Beyonder and forced to fight in a series of "Secret Wars". When his original red and blue costume was torn in battle, the web-spinner tried to repair it, but mistakenly activated a device that released a little black ball. The ball spread across him, duplicating the costume worn by the Julia Carpenter Spider-Woman.

Spider-Man's new suit could instantly mimic any kind of clothing, could carry his camera and spare change, was equipped with its own web-shooters and possessed a seemingly endless supply of webbing. He eventually discovered that the alien suit was a symbiote with a mind of its own. Spider-Man had to enlist the scientific help of Mr. Fantastic to remove it, using soundwaves at a certain frequency.

Rejected by Spidey, the symbiote grafted itself to Eddie Brock to become Venom (top).

SPIDER-MAN

Peter sided with IRON MAN (Tony Stark) during the Civil War (*see* pp. 84–5), even going so far as to register with the government and expose his true identity during a televised press conference. He quickly came to regret the decision when he saw the tactics the pro-registration forces were used to win, and he switched sides to join CAPTAIN AMERICA's resistance. For a short time, he returned to his black costume while he, Mary Jane, and Aunt May went into hiding, but he soon returned to his red and blue suit.

Peter heeded his spider-sense and dodged the bullet. It hit Aunt May instead.

AUNT MAY SHOT

Besides the government hounding him, Peter now had to deal with the fact that all his old foes knew who he was. From inside prison, the KINGPIN hired an assassin, who waited outside the hotel room in which Peter, Mary Jane, and Aunt May were staying. When Peter's guard was down, he fired. Peter's spider-sense enabled him to dodge the bullet, but it struck Aunt May. Peter and Mary Jane rushed her to the hospital, where the doctor informed them that she was too frail to survive.

Peter Parker tangled up Iron Man in his webs, forcing Tony Stark to listen to his pleas for financial help to save Aunt May's life.

Needing money to pay for Aunt May's treatment, Peter turned to the wealthiest man he knew: Tony Stark. Tony immediately changed into Iron Man and tried to arrest Peter, but Peter managed to web Iron Man up with his new webs, which now sprang directly from his wrists rather than from a webshooter. While Iron Man was trapped, Peter accused Tony of misleading him into making the worst mistake of his life. Then he demanded that Tony help Aunt May.

Tony refused, saying that he couldn't be seen aiding and abetting a known criminal like Peter. Breaking free from the webs, he flew off without trying to arrest Peter again, but he made it clear that he could not help. Later, Tony's butler, Edwin JARVIS—who had been dating Aunt May—arrived at the hospital with a check for two million dollars to help pay for her care. Despite the money, however, the doctor believed that Aunt May would not live long.

MEPHISTO'S DEAL

Torn apart with guilt over Aunt May's shooting, Peter scoured the city for a cure. He visited DR. STRANGE, who transported Spider-Man's astral form around the globe to ask for help, but no one could do anything to save her. He even tried to travel back in time to stop the shooter, but failed.

Then MEPHISTO approached Peter and Mary Jane with an offer. He would save Aunt May and alter reality so that no one would remember that Peter was Spider-Man. All he wanted in exchange was their greatest source of happiness: their marriage.

Searching their souls, Peter and Mary Jane agreed to Mephisto's offer. The next morning, Peter awoke alone—but with Aunt May alive and well and cooking him a stack of wheatcakes—and with no one aware that anything had ever been different.

An anguished Peter and Mary Jane waited by Aunt May's hospital bed, realizing that only a miracle could save her. It would come from a most unexpected source.

ALL CHANGE

While Mephisto had supposedly only made a couple of changes, their effect was to alter Peter's life drastically. He was alone once again, living at his Aunt May's and looking for an apartment in Manhattan. His old friend Harry OSBORN had returned after being presumed dead. And without Mary Jane in his life, Peter was unlucky in love.

Tired of bargaining for souls, Mephisto demanded something far more rare from Peter and Mary Jane: the pure happiness found in their true love for each other.

Peter saved Jameson's life by giving him CPR after he collapsed during an argument. Later, as Spider-Man, he had to do so again when he inadvertently told Jameson that his wife had sold the *Bugle* while he was ill.

Some things, however, stayed the same. With the *Daily Bugle* having cash troubles, J. Jonah JAMESON hadn't paid Peter for several photos he'd bought. When Peter confronted Jameson about the money he was owed, they fell into a shouting match, and Jameson collapsed from a heart attack. Jameson survived, but the paper had to be sold, and Peter wound up working as a paparazzi. He soon gave that up to become a photographer for Ben Urich's new paper, *Front Line*.

ALTERED STATES

Many of Spider-Man's foes cropped up soon after Peter's life changed. With his secret identity once more intact, however, he could fight them on his own terms.

Aunt May now did volunteer work at a homeless shelter, working under the philanthropist Martin Li, who was secretly Chinatown crimelord Mr. Negative. Eddie Brock returned, no longer as VENOM but as the new ANTI-VENOM. Norman Osborn showed up as the leader of the THUNDERBOLTS and even, eventually, the AVENGERS—a separate team from the secret Avengers with which Spider-Man still worked. He also battled a new villain called Menace, who used many of the Green Goblin's old tricks.

A new hero—Jackpot—entered Peter's life too. As she was a tall, beautiful redhead, Peter suspected her of actually being Mary Jane, with whom he still had a romantic—but apparently sour—history. Instead, she turned out to be Alana Jobson, a woman who'd bought the identity from Sara Ehret. Alana died soon after Peter learned her secret, destroyed by the drugs she'd been taking to gain her powers.

While Peter enjoyed the fact that no one but he knew his secret identity, he recently told a few of his friends on his Avengers team his true name. **MF**

Menace turned out to be none other than Lily Hollister, the woman who Peter's unwitting friend Harry Osborn (the second Green Goblin) hoped to marry. As Menace, she publicly attacked her father to drum up sympathy support for his mayoral campaign.

ESSENTIAL STORYLINES

• *Civil War #1–7* During the Civil War, Spider-Man registers with the government and reveals his identity to the world—and then comes to regret it.

• *One More Day, tpb* With Aunt May at death's door after taking a sniper's bullet meant for Peter, he and Mary Jane cut a deal with Mephisto to trade their marriage to save her life.

• *Amazing Spider-Man #546* His marriage erased—along with any knowledge anyone has about his secret identity—Spider-Man starts again fresh, but alone.

Both Peter Parker and Spider-Man started all over again with a Brand New Day—but Mary Jane was no longer by Peter's side.

ANTI-VENOM

With Spider-Man on the run from SHIELD and the rest of the US government for defying the Superhuman Registration Act, Norman Osborn had the perfect excuse for ordering his new Thunderbolts to bring in Spider-Man. One of the Thunderbolts—Mac Gargan—had traded in his Scorpion suit to become the new Venom. When the Venom symbiote spotted Eddie Brock (the original Venom) and realized he'd been cured of his cancer, it tried to re-bond with him, but Brock's body rejected it and transformed him into Anti-Venom instead. In his new identity, Brock teamed up with his old foe Spider-Man to defeat the Thunderbolts instead. MF

SPIDER-GIRL

FIRST APPEARANCE What If? #105 (February 1998)

REAL NAME May "Mayday" Parker

OCCUPATION High-school student **BASE** New York City

HEIGHT 5 ft 5 in **WEIGHT** 112 lbs **EYES** Brown **HAIR** Brown

SPECIAL POWERS/ABILITIES Similar powers of agility, strength, and climbing ability as Spider-Man; uses web-shooters, developed by her father, to travel across the city or trap enemies.

On Earth-982, SPIDER-MAN and his wife Mary Jane (WATSON) Parker had a daughter named May. Sometime after that, the GREEN GOBLIN maimed him in battle, and Spider-Man retired to become Peter Parker, NYPD forensic scientist. As a teenager, May inherited Peter's powers and became Spider-Girl. She battled new villains—like Funny Face and Killerwatt—plus the descendants of her dad's foes—like Electra, Raptor, and Normie Osborn. Recently, she and her father battled the Green Goblin's ghost, along with a symbiote-hybrid clone of May. They defeated the Goblin, and May and the clone united as "closer than sisters." **TD, MF**

SPIDER-MAN 2099

FIRST APPEARANCE Spider-Man 2099 #1 (November 1992)

REAL NAME Miguel O'Hara

OCCUPATION Genetic engineer, adventurer **BASE** New York City

HEIGHT 5 ft 10 in **WEIGHT** 170 lbs **EYES** Brown **HAIR** Brown

SPECIAL POWERS/ABILITIES Superhuman strength, speed and agility. Can adhere to surfaces and project webbing from spinnerets in forearms. Retractable talons and fangs that secrete poison.

In the year 2099 on Earth-928, Miguel O'Hara, head of genetics for the Alchemax corporation, tried to recreate SPIDER-MAN's powers. His superior, Tyler Stone, controlled him by addicting him to the drug Rapture. A co-worker's sabotage caused O'Hara to develop spider-powers. As Spider-Man of 2099, he battled both criminals and Alchemax. Eventually, he was given THOR's hammer Mjolnir, and he used that power to rule Earth peacefully for a thousand years. On Earth-6375, after Spider-Man 2099's secret identity was exposed, he joined the Exiles for a while. He later returned to be with the woman he loved. **PS**

SPIDER-MAN 2211

FIRST APPEARANCE Spider-Man 2099 Meets Spider-Man (November 1995) **REAL NAME** Dr. Jamoff "Max" Borne

OCCUPATION Adventurer **BASE** New York City

HEIGHT 6ft **WEIGHT** 187 lbs **EYES** Brown **HAIR** Bald

SPECIAL POWERS/ABILITIES Armor grants superhuman strength, flight, and four additional telescopic arms.

Max Borne is a TimeSpinner, charged with maintaining the continuity of the timeline of Earth-9500. He first encountered the original SPIDER-MAN (of Earth-616) when Max's daughter, the HOBGOBLIN of 2211, chased back through time, killing various Spider-Men as she went. He managed to stop her, but before he could return to his own time, he was shot and killed by the CHAMELEON of 2211, disguised as Ben Parker (see PARKER, UNCLE BEN). Max's costume shared the colors of the original, but it also featured an open-mouthed helmet and a set of mechanical arms, much like those of DOCTOR OCTOPUS. **MF**

🎯 **SPIDER-WOMAN**
see opposite page

SPIRIT OF '76

FIRST APPEARANCE The Invaders Vol. 1 #14 (March 1977)

REAL NAME William Nasland

OCCUPATION Costumed adventurer **BASE** Mobile

HEIGHT 6 ft 2 in **WEIGHT** 215 lbs **EYES** Blue **HAIR** Black

SPECIAL POWERS/ABILITIES Top level athlete and formidable hand-to-hand combatant; wore a bullet-proof cape; as Captain America he had a steel shield, which was not indestructible.

Inspired by CAPTAIN AMERICA's World War II exploits, William Nasland became the costumed adventurer, Spirit of '76. After battling Nazi spies in Philadelphia, Nasland moved to Great Britain and joined the Crusaders team of heroes, until its leader was revealed to be a German agent. Nasland continued to contribute to the war effort, partnering Captain America on a mission to Berlin. Following the Cap's apparent demise, Nasland agreed to become a second Captain America but his career as this emblematic figurehead was cut short when he died preventing the assassination of would-be congressman John F. Kennedy. **AD**

SPIRAL

FIRST APPEARANCE Longshot #1 (September 1985)

REAL NAME "Ricochet" Rita

OCCUPATION Warrior sorceress **BASE** Mobile

HEIGHT 5 ft 10 in **WEIGHT** 150 lbs **EYES** Blue **HAIR** Silver

SPECIAL POWERS/ABILITIES Enhanced strength; spellcasting abilities allow teleportation between dimensions; excellent swordswoman who can wield six weapons at once.

Spiral is a six-armed sorceress who worked as an aide to MOJO. An actress in her former life, Spiral received genetic alterations in the Mojoverse dimension, which gave her the ability to manipulate magic. On Earth, she briefly served in FREEDOM FORCE and opened an exclusive cybernetics store, the Body Shoppe, whose customers included Lady Deathstrike. She later conquered Earth-2055 until SHATTERSTAR defeated her. She recently joined Madelyne Pryor's Sisterhood of Mutants. **DW, MF**

SPITFIRE

FIRST APPEARANCE The Invaders Vol. 1 #7 (July 1976)

REAL NAME Jacqueline Falsworth Crichton

OCCUPATION Adventurer **BASE** Falsworth Manor, England

HEIGHT 5 ft 4 in **WEIGHT** 110 lbs **EYES** Blue **HAIR** Blonde

SPECIAL POWERS/ABILITIES Spitfire can move at speeds of up to 50 mph for up to four hours. She has a vampire's fangs, superhuman strength, and a healing factor, but feels no bloodlust.

During World War II, Jacqueline Falsworth served in England's Home Guard and was attacked by the Nazi vampire BARON BLOOD. She was rescued by the original HUMAN TORCH, an android who gave her a transfusion of his artificial blood. The combination of the vampire bite and the android blood gave Falsworth superhuman speed. She adopted the name Spitfire and teamed up with the INVADERS, a group of Allied heroes who battled the Axis powers. Over time her powers faded, but another transfusion from the HUMAN TORCH restored them. In modern times, she served with the New INVADERS and most recently with MI-13. **MT, MF**

SPIDER-WOMAN
Investigator with irresistible powers

The daughter of scientist Jonathan Drew, Jessica gained her powers before birth, when a laser laced with spider DNA hit her mother's womb. Born and raised on Wundagore Mountain, her powers manifested when she was six years old. She was in stasis for a long time and when she woke found herself in the care of HYDRA.

COME ON DARLING--REACT! YOU'VE GOT TO REACT!

ALL MY WORK, MY HOPES--

It was originally believed that Jessica's powers stemmed from an experiment conducted by her father.

SUPER SPY

Trained by the Taskmaster—and her mind warped by Mentallo—Jessica became an agent of HYDRA. Captured by SHIELD on her first mission and then released, she went underground. She resurfaced to become an agent of SHIELD for a short time, after which she struck out on her own. Calling herself Spider-Woman, Jessica became a private investigator, a bounty hunter, and a sometime Super Hero. At one point, she saved the life of Giant-Man (Bill Foster) through a blood transfusion, and lost some of her powers in the process.

Others took on the name of Spider-Woman but when HYDRA offered to restore Jessica's powers if she would become their agent, she accepted the deal, then contacted Nick Fury and became a double agent for SHIELD. Shortly thereafter, she was kidnapped by the Skrulls and replaced by Queen Veranke.

While posing as Jessica, Veranke led the Secret Invasion (*see* pp. 326-7). Norman Osborn shot and killed Veranke in the final battle of the Skrull invasion. Jessica, along with several other replaced heroes, was found in a Skrull prison ship and brought back to Earth. She has since joined the Avengers team led by Captain America (Bucky Barnes).

FACTFILE

REAL NAME
Jessica Drew

OCCUPATION
Adventurer

BASE
Mobile

HEIGHT 5 ft 10 in
WEIGHT 130 lbs
EYES Green
HAIR Brown (dyed black)

FIRST APPEARANCE
Marvel Spotlight Vol. 1 #32
(February 1977)

POWERS

Enhanced strength, speed, and hearing; flight; superhuman healing factor; emits mood-altering pheromones that attract both sexes; ability to adhere to walls and fire electric "venom blasts."

Wings let Spider-Woman glide, and she can now fly unassisted.

KEY STORYLINES

• ***The Spider-Woman #1***
The first issue of her original, self-titled series sees Jessica Drew striking out on her own as a hero.
• ***Spider-Woman: Origin #1–6***
This limited series retells Spider-Woman's beginnings, from a HYDRA pawn to a member of the New Avengers.
• ***New Avengers #1*** Jessica Drew returns as Spider-Woman in the New Avengers... or does she?

THE OTHERS

As well as Jessica and Veranke, Julia Carpenter (*see* Arachne) was made Spider-Woman by the Commission on Superhuman Activities. Mattie Franklin became the third Spider-Woman after taking her father's place during a ceremony called the Gathering of the Five. Later, Doctor Octopus gave Charlotte Witter the ability to absorb spider-powers only to have Mattie reclaim them. **DW, MF**

Charlotte Witter was the only villainous Spider-Woman. Doctor Octopus bestowed her with powers sufficient to kill Spider-Man. Witter also possessed the ability to drain the powers of the other Spider-Women, but lost them when defeated by Mattie Franklin.

SPYMASTER

FIRST APPEARANCE Iron Man #33 (January 1971)

REAL NAME Unrevealed

OCCUPATION Industrial spy   **BASE** Mobile

HEIGHT 6 ft   **WEIGHT** 195 lbs   **EYES** Blue   **HAIR** Blonde

SPECIAL POWERS/ABILITIES Master of disguise; exceptional hand-to-hand combatant; brilliant saboteur; expert with all kinds of hi-tech weaponry; bulletproof costume; used hoverjet for transport.

Right from his first days as IRON MAN, Tony Stark was dogged by an industrial agent called the Spymaster. Initially working with his Espionage Elite team, Spymaster tried many times to steal Stark's technology. ZODIAC, SHIELD and MADAME MASQUE all employed him, but it was Justin HAMMER who benefited most. The first Spymaster died at the hands of a rival spy named the Ghost. A second Spymaster discovered Iron Man's identity and beat Stark badly only to be stopped by the BLACK WIDOW. A third Spymaster killed the second and then plagued Stark before nearly dying in the fall that killed Happy HOGAN. **AD,MF**

ST. LAWRENCE, COL.

FIRST APPEARANCE Incredible Hulk Vol. 2 #446 (October 1996)

REAL NAME Colonel Cary St. Lawrence

OCCUPATION US Army officer   **BASE** Mobile

HEIGHT/WEIGHT Unrevealed   **EYES** Brown   **HAIR** Black

SPECIAL POWERS/ABILITIES Skilled military strategist, highly trained athlete, adept with variety of weaponry.

When she was a cadet at West Point academy, General "Thunderbolt" Ross was dismissive about Cary St. Lawrence's chances of a successful career in the military. Inspired to work even harder to prove him wrong, Cary graduated third in her class.

Assigned to capture the HULK, Cary proved to be unusually effective in her dealings with the green fiend. At first she favored brute force during her encounters with the creature, but soon came to realize that there was no point in employing strong-arm tactics: after all, the Hulk only got more powerful the angrier he became. She thus began to use more subtle approaches to subdue the creature. Perhaps all the Hulk has ever needed is a woman's touch... **AD**

SQUADRON SUPREME

In a 12-issue series, the Squadron Supreme explores absolute power.

The Squadron Supreme is a force of superhuman champions inhabiting the Earth of an alternate reality. They have crossed paths with the AVENGERS many times, including an early team-up to eradicate the evil influence of the serpent-god Set's Serpent Crown.

The Squadron Supreme faced their greatest challenge when the OVERMIND and Null the Living Darkness conquered their planet. HYPERION escaped to mainstream Earth and recruited the DEFENDERS, who successfully defeated the Overmind. The damage to their world from the Overmind war was so great that the Squadron Supreme implemented the Utopia Program, seizing control of the government and forcibly implementing new methods of policing and social engineering. NIGHTHAWK left the Squadron in protest, and organized the Redeemers to act as a rebel insurgency. The Redeemers forced the Squadron's surrender, and the two groups dismantled the Utopia Program. The Squadron Supreme later became marooned on mainstream Earth, where they adventured alongside QUASAR.

The Squadron has now successfully liberated their own world from the grip of various monolithic corporations who were seeking to gain control of the planet. **DW**

FACTFILE

NOTABLE MEMBERS

HYPERION (leader)
Flight, enhanced strength, super-speed, near-invulnerability, atomic vision .

AMPHIBIAN
Enhanced strength, able to live underwater at ocean depths.

DOCTOR SPECTRUM
Power prism permits flight and the projection of hard-energy objects.

GOLDEN ARCHER
Unsurpassed skill with a bow and arrow.

NIGHTHAWK
Brilliant strategist, top-level combatant.

POWER PRINCESS
Enhanced strength, skilled warrior.

THE WHIZZER
Super-speedster.

BASE Squadron City

FIRST APPEARANCE:
Avengers Vol. 1 #85
(March 1971)

SQUADRON SUPREME
1 Tom Thumb **2** Whizzer **3** Nuke **4** Redstone **5** Shape
6 Power Princess **7** Hyperion **8** Lamprey **9** Doctor Spectrum
10 Firefox **11** Arcanna **12** Blue Eagle **13** Black Archer **14** Ape X

STACY, GWEN

The daughter of NYPD Captain George Stacy, Gwen first met Peter Parker (SPIDER-MAN) at Empire State University. Although attracted to him, his frequent moodiness and his apparent cowardliness put her off. Eventually, she and Peter became a couple, despite competition from Mary Jane WATSON, but the Parker-Stacy relationship was an uneasy one. After her father was slain during a battle between Spider-Man and Doctor Octopus, Gwen came to hate Spider-Man, a fact that weighed heavily on Peter's mind. Not long after, Gwen was captured by the GREEN GOBLIN and hurled from the top of a bridge. When Spider-Man attempted to save her with his webbing, the sudden shock of deceleration snapped Gwen's neck, causing her death. It was later revealed that Gwen had an affair with Norman Osborn (the Green Goblin) and bore twins by him, Gabriel and Sarah, whom have now grown to adulthood by accelerated aging. **TB. MF**

Hurled off of a bridge by the Green Goblin, Gwen Stacy perished without ever learning that her boyfriend Peter Parker was secretly Spider-Man.

STANE, OBADIAH

Orphaned when his father killed himself in a game of Russian roulette, Obadiah Stane regarded life as a game that he was determined to win. His preferred tactic was to wage psychological warfare against his opponent. Stane became the head of a multinational corporation that produced munitions. Knowing that Anthony Stark, head of Stark International, was a reformed alcoholic, Stane manipulated events to drive Stark back to drinking.

I CAN READ ANTHONY STARK LIKE A BOOK, HE WILL BLAME HIMSELF FOR ERWIN'S DEATH AND HE WILL RETURN TO THE BOTTLE.

WITHIN A MONTH, HE WILL AGAIN BE IN THE GUTTER!

Stane took aim at his adversaries' weaknesses.

Buying up the debts of Stark International, Stane took control of the company, renaming it Stane International, and froze Stark's personal fortune. Stark duly became a drunken derelict.

Eventually Stark stopped drinking and resumed his secret identity as IRON MAN. Stane had his scientists create his own armored battlesuit, called the Iron Monger. In the Iron Monger armor, Stane personally battled Iron Man, who defeated him. Removing his helmet, Stane committed suicide by firing a repulsor ray blast at his head. **PS**

Stane's Iron Monger armor was larger than Iron Man's, but he could not defeat him.

STANE, EZEKIEL

The son of Obadiah Stane (see STANE, Obadiah), Ezekiel inherited his father's fortune and promptly turned it and his incredible intellect toward making Tony Stark (see IRON MAN) obsolete. He started by coordinating attacks against the ORDER, the California team for The Fifty-State Initiative (see pp. 118–9). When his efforts there failed, he went after Stark directly. Ezekiel reverse-engineered a good deal of Stark's technology now on the black market. Instead of building a better Iron Man suit, however, he used the technology to upgrade his body directly. He sometimes wears a suit to displace the excess heat his body generates along with his powers. **MF**

STARFOX

FIRST APPEARANCE Iron Man Vol. 1 #55 (February 1973)

REAL NAME Eros

OCCUPATION Adventurer **BASE** Mobile

HEIGHT 6 ft 1 in **WEIGHT** 190 lbs **EYES** Blue **HAIR** Red

SPECIAL POWERS/ABILITIES Flight; enhanced strength; telekinesis; ability to generate personal force fields; the power to stimulate the brain's pleasure centers.

Eros is an ETERNAL, raised on the Saturn moon of Titan by his father, Mentor. His buoyant outlook is the opposite of that of his older brother THANOS. For years Eros wandered in search of sensual pleasure, but he returned to Titan when Thanos and the SUPER-SKRULL attacked it. After the death of CAPTAIN MAR-VELL, Eros looked after Mar-Vell's son, Genis-Vell, and he eventually joined the AVENGERS as Starfox. He helped to foil Thanos's efforts to assemble the Infinity Gauntlet. When the SHE-HULK discovered that he'd used his powers to influence her to marry John Jameson (*see* Man-Wolf), she beat him badly. **DW, MF**

STARHAWK

FIRST APPEARANCE Defenders #27 (September 1975)

REAL NAME Stakar Vaughn Ogord

OCCUPATION Adventurer **BASE** Arcturus IV

HEIGHT/WEIGHT/EYES/HAIR Unknown

SPECIAL POWERS/ABILITIES Starhawk can fly at light speed and can manipulate cosmic energy. He also has the power of precognition, knowing events that will occur before they happen.

On Earth-691, Stakar Vaughn Ogord is the child of the superpowered beings QUASAR and Kismet, making him half human and half artificial. Born on the planet Vesper, Stakar was kidnapped as an infant and taken to the planet Arcturus IV, where he was adopted by Ogord, a Reaver. Stakar eventually married Ogord's daughter Aleta. When an accident merged Stakar and Aleta, they became a single being known as Starhawk. Starhawk fled Arcturus IV and joined the GUARDIANS OF THE GALAXY. Being precognitive, Starhawk relives his life over and over, making changes and adjustments each time. Another version of Starhawk recently battled the modern-day Guardians. **MT**

STARJAMMERS

The Starjammers' leader, Corsair, is quick-witted and skilled with a blade.

Corsair—real name Christopher Summers, father CYCLOPS, HAVOK, and VULCAN—was abducted and enslaved by the alien SHI'AR. After his wife died for Emperor D'ken's pleasure, Corsair staged a jailbreak with fellow prisoners Ch'od, Raza, and Hepzibah. The group became the Starjammers, space pirates who fought against the cruel excesses of Shi'ar rule. The team helped the X-MEN defeat D'ken in his bid to possess the M'Krann crystal, and later teamed with the X-MEN to rescue D'ken's sister Lilandra. The Starjammers accepted Carol Danvers (*see* Ms. MARVEL) as a member when she was known as Binary, while both Lilandra and PROFESSOR X worked with the team during the fight against DEATHBIRD.

Recently, Vulcan returned to Shi'ar space, killed Corsair, and took over the Shi'ar Empire. Havok led a number of heroes to join the Starjammers in their attempt to stop his brother. The current lineup includes Ch'od, Cr+eee, Havok, Korvus, POLARIS, Raza, Sikorsky, and RACHEL SUMMERS. **DW, MF**

FACTFILE

MEMBERS AND POWERS

CORSAIR (3) (Christopher Summers) Excellent pilot, swordsman, and combatant.

CH'OD (1) Natural strength, tough skin, slashing claws.

HEPZIBAH (2) Feline reflexes, night vision, retractable claws.

RAZA (4) Cyborg strength, vision and reflexes, skilled with bladed weapons.

SIKORSKY Advanced medical knowledge.

KEEYAH Skilled pilot.

CR+EEE Ch'od's semi-intelligent, white-furred pet.

BASE Mobile

FIRST APPEARANCE Uncanny X-Men vol. 1 #104 (April 1977)

STAR STALKER

FIRST APPEARANCE (Star Stalker I) Avengers #123 (May 1974),
(Star Stalker II) Power Pack #56 (May 1990)

REAL NAME Unrevealed **OCCUPATION** Predator

BASE Planet Vormir in the Kree Galaxy (Greater Magellanic Cloud)

HEIGHT 16 ft 6 in **WEIGHT** Unrevealed **EYES** Black **HAIR** None

SPECIAL POWERS/ABILITIES Superhuman strength. Could drain planetry energy and travel through outer space without protection.

The original, red Star Stalker was a member of the alien reptilian race of Vorns. He used his tail as a weapon and his mutant powers to form an ionic cocoon to drain energy from other planets. His enemies were the Priests of Pama, a cult of KREE who knew his vulnerability to intense heat. Following the massacre of the Priests of Pama living on Earth, the STAR STALKER journeyed there

to absorb its energies. The VISION slew him with heat beams. The Star Stalker's son, who inherited his father's powers, but had green skin, later menaced Earth. He was apparently destroyed by NOVA (Frankie Raye). **PS**

STICK

Despite being blind, Stick, who took his name from his combat staff, was the sensei of an elite warrior school called the Chaste. When young Matt Murdock (*see* DAREDEVIL) lost his vision in a toxic waste accident, Stick helped him develop his remaining senses to compensate. Stick also trained the assassin ELEKTRA, although he expelled her when she could not control her rage in combat. When the evil ninjas of the HAND attacked Stick and his allies, Stick absorbed the life essences of his attackers, killing himself. His spirit later reincarnated, and Daredevil and the Chaste defended the baby against the Hand. **DW, MF**

As the leader of the mystical Ninja clan known as the Chaste, Stick was one of the world's best martial artists and used his knowledge to train Matt Murdock.

STATURE

FIRST APPEARANCE Marvel Premiere #45 (April 1979)

REAL NAME Cassandra Eleanore "Cassie" Lang

OCCUPATION Adventurer **BASE** New York City

HEIGHT Varies **WEIGHT** Varies **EYES** Blue **HAIR** Blonde

SPECIAL POWERS/ABILITIES Can grow and shrink to extremes.

When Cassie Lang was a young girl, her father Scott became the second ANT-MAN so he could save her life. Because of Scott's life as a Super Hero, Cassie's mother (Scott's ex-wife) sued for and won full custody of Cassie.

After her father's death, Cassie joined the YOUNG AVENGERS to continue his legacy. She sided with CAPTAIN AMERICA during the Civil War (*see* pp. 84–5), but after his death she joined The Fifty-State Initiative (*see* pp.118–9) and trained at Camp Hammond.

Cassie started dating the VISION and joined the new AVENGERS team led by Henry PYM. **MF**

STILT-MAN

FIRST APPEARANCE Daredevil #8 (June 1965)

REAL NAME Wilbur Day **OCCUPATION** Criminal

BASE New York City **HEIGHT** 5 ft 10 in (variable)

WEIGHT 185 lbs **EYES** Brown **HAIR** Black

SPECIAL POWERS/ABILITIES Legs of armored costume can extend up to 60 feet in length; costume also contains a formidable array of built-in weaponry.

Lab assistant Wilbur Day made off with his boss's revolutionary hydraulic ram technology and—after adapting the device to an armored costume—became the Stilt-Man and embarked on a life of crime. DAREDEVIL and SPIDER-MAN regularly foiled his efforts. After becoming a laughing stock, Day tried to give up his costumed identity, but he found himself pulled back into the underworld. He later married PRINCESS PYTHON and registered with the government, but the Punisher killed him on one of his missions. A couple of others have worn his suit. The latest, Michael Watts, recently joined the Hood's gang. **TB, MF**

STINGER

FIRST APPEARANCE Spider-Girl #1 (October 1998)

REAL NAME Cassandra Lang **OCCUPATION** Adventurer

BASE New York City (Earth-982) **HEIGHT** 5 ft 5 in

WEIGHT 105 lbs **EYES** Blue **HAIR** Reddish-blonde

SPECIAL POWERS/ABILITIES Synthetic wing implants enable flight; armoured costume protects from harm; possesses ability to shrink to the size of a wasp.

On Earth-982, Stinger is the superpowered pseudonym of Cassandra Lang, the daughter of the second ANT MAN. Cassandra combined the powers and costume of her father with those of the WASP, and she demonstrated a natural aptitude for organization and leadership. With a new generation of heroes emerging, Cassandra helped reform the AVENGERS and was in charge of the resurrected superteam when LOKI attempted to rid the world of heroes. A scientist in her mid-20s, Cassandra is the oldest and best-educated member of the team. **AD, MF**

STINGRAY

FIRST APPEARANCE Tales to Astonish Vol. 1 #95 (Sept. 1967)
REAL NAME Walter Newell   **OCCUPATION** Adventurer,
oceanographer   **BASE** Mobile within Atlantic Ocean
HEIGHT 6 ft 3 in   **WEIGHT** 200 lbs   **EYES** Hazel   **HAIR** Brown
SPECIAL POWERS/ABILITIES Costume incorporates built-in
rebreathing apparatus and provides enhanced strength, the ability to
travel underwater at great speed, and to fire electrical bolts.

STONE, LT. MARCUS

FIRST APPEARANCE Thor Vol. 1 #404 (June 1989)
REAL NAME Marcus Stone
OCCUPATION Police officer   **BASE** New York City
HEIGHT 6 ft 2 in   **WEIGHT** 225 lbs   **EYES** Brown   **HAIR** Bald
SPECIAL POWERS/ABILITIES A dedicated and tenacious police
officer who never gives up on a case; an expert marksman and
highly trained hand-to-hand combatant.

STONE, TIBERIUS

FIRST APPEARANCE Iron Man Vol. 3 #37 (February 2001)
REAL NAME Tiberius "Ty" Stone   **OCCUPATION** Owner of
Viastone, a multinational corporation   **BASE** Mobile
HEIGHT 6 ft   **WEIGHT** 210 lbs   **EYES** Blue   **HAIR** Blond
SPECIAL POWERS/ABILITIES Brilliant business strategist; a totally
ruthless sociopath, driven by jealousy and revenge.

The US government gave a seemingly impossible task to oceanographer Walter Newell: bring in NAMOR the Sub-Mariner for questioning. Newell designed a revolutionary submersible suit and actually succeeded in his task, in the process becoming the adventurer Stingray. Subsequent adventures saw him fighting the Atlantean warlord ATTUMA, and becoming a reserve member of the AVENGERS. Newell is part-time Super Hero at best, preferring to concentrate on his scientific research. **DW**

After serving as one of New York's Finest for 25 years, Marcus Stone was ready to retire. His marriage to his childhood sweetheart was in trouble because he kept bringing his police work home with him. Stone knew the time had come to choose between his job and his wife. On what should have been his last day, he stumbled upon a battle between the mighty THOR and Ulik the unconquerable rock troll. After Thor fell, Stone pursued Ulik and managed to arrest him. Having proved that normal cops can handle super-menaces, Stone was later assigned to head up Code: Blue, a special New York City strike-force that takes on Super Villains. **TD**

Ty Stone and Tony Stark were childhood friends, though they often competed when it came to sports, girls, and grades. Their parents were business rivals and Stark's father eventually drove Stone's to the verge of bankruptcy. Still pretending to be Stark's friend, Stone vowed to get revenge. He planted news stories that tarnished Stark's reputation, stole Stark's girlfriend, Rumiko Fujikawa, and attempted to take over Stark Industries. To draw IRON MAN into action, Stone hired the RADIOACTIVE MAN as his bodyguard and faked his own kidnapping. He also tried to trap Stark within a world of virtual reality, but Stark escaped; Stone is now trapped in the prison he intended for his rival. **TB**

STRANGER, THE

The Stranger is an immeasurably powerful cosmic being, created from the life-energies of a vanished species from the planet Gigantus in the Andromeda Galaxy. The Gigantians built the Stranger to stand against the OVERMIND, a villainous composite entity fashioned by the Gigantians' traditional enemies, the Eternians. The Stranger wandered for eons until he encountered Earth. Convinced that Earth's superhuman mutants posed a threat to the greater galaxy, the Stranger attempted to destroy the Earth on multiple occasions. The heroism of champions such as the HULK won him over, and the Stranger agreed to spare Earth for the immediate future. For a while he used the ABOMINATION as a servant.

The Stranger eventually faced and defeated the Overmind, then selected an Earth from the New Universe (Earth-148611) as an object of study for his Labworld. The Stranger subsequently posed as the BEYONDER and gathered a number of superpowered people to battle for him as an experiment. **DW, MF**

STRANGER, THE

FACTFILE
REAL NAME
Unrevealed
OCCUPATION
Surveyor of Worlds
BASE
The Stranger's own Labworld

HEIGHT Variable
WEIGHT Variable
EYES Black
HAIR White

FIRST APPEARANCE
Uncanny X-Men Vol. 1 #11
(May 1965)

POWERS
Vast strength; wields cosmic power to emit energy blasts, reshape matter, generate force fields, levitate, and change his own size.

S

STORM
The Mutant Queen of Wakanda

Goddess, mutant, and queen, Storm is a woman of many facets.

Ororo Munroe is descended from a long line of African witch-priestesses. Her mother married an American photographer, and Ororo was born in New York City. When the child was six months old, the family moved to Egypt. Five years later, Ororo's parents were killed during an Arab-Israeli conflict. Young Ororo was buried under the rubble of her home beside her dead mother's body, an experience that gave her an intense claustrophobia.

Ororo evolved from a thief on the streets of Cairo to the leader of the X-Men.

ESSENTIAL STORYLINES
- **Ororo: Before the Storm #1-4**
The story of Ororo's early days, before she became an X-Man.
- **Uncanny X-Men #253–272**
Storm is regressed to the age of a young girl by Nanny and the Orphan Maker.
- **Black Panther, Volume 3 #14–18**
Ororo's courtship with and marriage to the Black Panther.

FACTFILE
REAL NAME
Ororo Munroe
OCCUPATION
Adventurer
BASE
Wakanda,

HEIGHT 5 ft 11 in **WEIGHT** 127 lbs
EYES Blue
HAIR White

FIRST APPEARANCE
Giant-Size X-Men #1 (1975)

STORM

POWERS

Mutant ability to manipulate the weather. Storm can control the creation of rain, snow, sleet, fog, hail, and lightning. She can create hurricane-force winds or lower the temperature around her to freezing point and below.

THE YOUNG GODDESS

Ororo wandered the streets of Cairo and eventually became an accomplished thief and pickpocket. She even robbed PROFESSOR X, who was in Cairo to battle the SHADOW KING. By the age of 12, her amazing mutant power to control the weather began to emerge. She traveled throughout Africa, where she used her abilities to help several tribes, the members of which came to worship her as a goddess of rain. Professor X later returned to Africa and convinced Ororo to use her powers to help all of humanity. She joined the X-MEN under the codename Storm and quickly became one of Professor X's most trusted students. At times, she even served as the team's leader.

POWERLESS

At one point, HENRY PETER GYRICH shot Ororo with a weapon that removed her powers. Shortly after this, she met and fell in love with FORGE, the man who designed that weapon. She continued to work with the X-Men, eventually regaining her powers. She gave her life to defeat the ADVERSARY, but ROMA (the daughter of MERLYN) restored her.

Storm is one of the most powerful members of the X-Men and the Queen of Wakanda.

THE MUTANT QUEEN

Ororo retained her powers after M-DAY, but left the X-Men to return to Africa. While there, she fell in love with the BLACK PANTHER (T'Challa) and married him, becoming the queen of Wakanda. The pair substituted for MR FANTASTIC and the INVISIBLE WOMAN temporarily becoming half of the FANTASTIC FOUR. Recently, Storm returned to help the X-Men in their hunt for the first mutant baby born after M-Day. She later helped to defeat the Shadow King, who had possessed her husband's form. Soon after, she was forced to take over as the sole ruler of Wakanda after DR. DOOM critically injured T'Challa. **MT, MF**

Although now the queen of Wakanda, Ororo refuses to abandon her mutant friends in their times of need.

STRAW MAN

FIRST APPEARANCE Dead of Night #11 (August 1975)

REAL NAME Skirra Corvus

OCCUPATION Mystic guardian **BASE** An unnamed magical realm

HEIGHT 5 ft 10 in **WEIGHT** 60 lbs **EYES** Red **HAIR** Yellow

SPECIAL POWERS/ABILITIES Incarnates himself in bodies composed of straw; projects fear; can command crows and local plant life, and has assorted other mystic attributes.

A being indigenous to an extra-dimensional realm bordering that of Earth, the Straw Man can access our universe through a mystic painting that depicts him. The painting's origins are shrouded in mystery; it is coveted by the Cult of Kalumai, who can summon their demonic master and his underlings through it. However the Straw Man considers himself a guardian of the Earth, and has successfully kept Kalumai in check. Recruited by the Dweller-In-Darkness as one of his Fear Lords, the Straw Man refused to go along with the demonic entity's plan to subjugate Earth, and he incarnated himself as Skirra Corvus, a television personality, in whose form he was able to warn DOCTOR STRANGE of the Dweller's plan. **TB**

STRYFE

Infected with a techno-organic virus, the infant Nathan Summers was taken nearly two millennia into the future of Earth-4935 to save his life. In case he should die, Mother Askani of the Askani Sisterhood had him cloned. The tyrant Apocalypse kidnapped and raised the clone, who he called Stryfe. The original Nathan grew up to become the hero CABLE, leader of the freedom fighters that battled armies commanded by Stryfe. Both men traveled back to the present day, where they continued to bitterly oppose each other. Although his original form was destroyed, Stryfe's consciousness managed to take over other bodies. He later sacrificed himself to save the Earth. Recently, Stryfe returned in his original form to help BISHOP in his hunt for the first mutant baby born after M-Day. **PS, MF**

FACTFILE

REAL NAME
Stryfe

OCCUPATION
Terrorist leader

BASE
Mobile

HEIGHT 6 ft 8 in
WEIGHT 350 lbs
EYES Blue
HAIR White

FIRST APPEARANCE
The New Mutants #87
(March 1990)

POWERS

A mutant possessing superhuman strength and other physical abilities, Stryfe also has vast telepathic and telekinetic powers. Unlike his clone Cable, he does not have to waste any of these powers keeping a techno-organic virus in check.

Ironically, since Stryfe is free from the techno-organic virus, he must wear metal armor for protection.

STRONG GUY

FIRST APPEARANCE New Mutants #29 (July 1985)

REAL NAME Guido Carosella **OCCUPATION** Special Enforcer for X-Factor Investigations **BASE** New York City

HEIGHT 7 ft **WEIGHT** 750 lbs **EYES** Blue **HAIR** White

SPECIAL POWERS/ABILITIES Absorbs kinetic energy—failure to release it quickly causes physical distortions and damages heart; kinetic energy enhances strength.

Guido Carosella worked as the bodyguard for Lila CHENEY until he wound up on Muir Island under the Shadow King's control. After X-Factor freed him, he joined their team and became friends with Multiple Man. He joined X-Factor Investigations, then served as the sheriff of New York's Mutant Town. While he kept his powers after M-Day most of the town did not, putting him out of a job. Although his mutation causes him constant physical pain, he rarely shows it. He moonlights as a standup comic. **AD,MF**

SUGAR MAN

FIRST APPEARANCE Generation Next Vol. 1 #2 (April 1995)

REAL NAME Unknown

OCCUPATION Adventurer, former assassin **BASE** Mobile

HEIGHT 6 ft 9 in **WEIGHT** 400 lbs **EYES** White **HAIR** Black

SPECIAL POWERS/ABILITIES Enhanced strength and reflexes; razor-sharp extendible tongue; four arms; advanced regenerative abilities; can control his size and mass.

Sugar Man comes from the future of Earth-295—the Age of Apocalypse—where he operated the Seattle Core slave camp. When COLOSSUS came to rescue his sister Illyana Rasputin (Magik), Sugar Man shrank down and hid in Colossus's boot, emerging in Earth-616, 20 years in the past. From there, he built up the island nation of Genosha by supplying genetic technology to create a population of mutant slaves. Sugar Man survived the Genosha holocaust, but he took a brutal beating at the hands of CALLISTO. The Beast recently turned to him for help after M-Day to restore powers to mutants, but the effort failed. **DW, MF**

SUMMERS, RACHEL

Mutant child from another time

In an alternate future Ahab brainwashed Rachel into serving as his telepathic mutant "hound."

Rachel Summers is the daughter of the Scott Summers (CYCLOPS) and JEAN GREY (alias Phoenix) in an alternate timeline known as the "Days of Future Past" or Earth-811. In this reality, the US government activated mutant-hunting robot Sentinels after Senator Robert KELLY was assassinated by mutant terrorists. Federal troops attacked PROFESSOR X's mansion, and captured Rachel.

PHOENIX

Rachel was brainwashed into becoming a mutant "hound," using her telepathic powers to track down other mutants. Her face was branded with tattoos (which nowadays she uses her powers to conceal). Eventually Rachel rebelled and attacked her master, AHAB. As punishment, she was confined to a mutant concentration camp.

By now the Sentinels had taken control of North America. In an effort to change history, Rachel used her powers to send the astral self of her friend Kate PRYDE (a middle-aged version of Kitty) back in time. Kate's spirit journeyed to the "mainstream" reality of the X-Men, where she thwarted Kelly's assassination. After returning to their alternate future, Kate sent Rachel back through time to the "mainstream" reality, where she joined the X-Men. Rachel bonded with the Phoenix Force, enabling her to tap its energies, and adopted the name "Phoenix." Subsequently she became a founding member of Excalibur.

MOTHER ASKANI

Rachel was cast two thousand years into the alternate future of Earth-4935, a world ruled by APOCALYPSE. There she founded a group of rebels, the Askani. Decades later, as the elderly Mother Askani, she sent one of her followers back in time to retrieve the infant Nathan Summers. Mother Askani also transported the astral selves of Scott Summers and Jean Grey into new bodies in this alternate future, where they raised Nathan for ten years. Then Mother Askani sent Scott and Jean's astral selves back to their proper time and bodies, before she herself perished. Nathan grew up to become CABLE. After an alteration in the timestream, Rachel was a living teenager once more, though she lost her connection to the Phoenix Force. She was held captive in an alternate future by a being named Gaunt. Cable returned her to the X-Men's time, and she rejoined the team. To honor her mother, Rachel started to call herself "Rachel Grey" in private and "Marvel Girl" at work.

After the Shi'ar murdered most of the Grey family line, Rachel joined Professor X in his pursuit of her uncle VULCAN, who had recently taken over the Shi'ar Empire. Once her grandfather Corsair was killed, she joined his STARJAMMERS in their effort to overthrow Vulcan. After absorbing a lost echo of the Phoenix Force, the fire she burns when using her Phoenix powers now burns blue.

PS, MF

FACTFILE

REAL NAME
Rachel Anne Summers, now Rachel Grey

OCCUPATION
Adventurer

BASE
Mobile

HEIGHT 5 ft 7 in
WEIGHT 125 lbs
EYES Green
HAIR Red

FIRST APPEARANCE
The Uncanny X-Men #141
(January 1981)

POWERS

Rachel Summers has considerable telepathic and telekinetic abilities. She formerly served as the host of the Phoenix Force, which greatly amplified her psionic powers.

As Phoenix, Rachel could use the cosmic Phoenix Force, though not to the same extent as Jean Grey.

...FOR THE PERFECT VESSEL.

ONE DEAR TO ALL OUR HEARTS-- -- NATHAN CHRISTOPHER SUMMERS

WHICH IS WHY I ARRANGED TO GRAB THE CHILD FIRST.

BUT HE WAS DESPERATELY ILL. I DID WHAT I COULD TO SAVE HIM FROM THE RAVAGES OF THE TECHNO-ORGANIC VIRUS.

BUT TIME WAS RUNNING OUT AS A FAIL SAFE, WE CREATED A HEATHLY CLONE.

As Mother Askani, Rachel created a clone of the infant Cable, called Stryfe.

D In honor of Jean Grey, Summers has assumed her mother's identities of Phoenix and Marvel Girl.

ESSENTIAL STORYLINES

• **New Mutants Vol. 1 #18, Excalibur Vol. 1 #52**
In her timeline, Rachel witnesses the federal attack on Xavier's mansion and becomes Ahab's "hound."

• **Uncanny X-Men #184-199**
Rachel journeys to the "mainstream" timeline, joins the X-Men and becomes the New Phoenix.

• **Adventures of Cyclops and Phoenix #1-4**
As the elderly Mother Askani, Rachel brings Scott Summers and Jean Grey to a distant future to raise the young Cable.

FACTFILE

REAL NAME
Shiro Yoshida

OCCUPATION
Adventurer

BASE
Department H, Canada, (formerly)
Tokyo, Japan.

HEIGHT 5 ft 10 in
WEIGHT 175 lbs
EYES Brown
HAIR Black

FIRST APPEARANCE
X-Men Vol. 1 #64
(January 1970)

POWERS

Can project "solar fire" and create super-heated air currents to fly. Has a psionic protective force field. Trained in karate, Japanese Samurai swordsmanship and kendo.

SUNFIRE

Sunfire's mother was exposed to radiation when the US dropped an atomic bomb on Hiroshima. When his mutant power surfaced, Sunfire vowed vengeance on the US, destroying a monument at the United Nations and clashing with the X-MEN. PROFESSOR XAVIER invited Sunfire to join a new group of X-MEN and he did, temporarily. Preferring to go on special missions for Japan, Sunfire was hypnotised by Dr. Demonicus to fight the West Coast AVENGERS. He subsequently served with ALPHA FLIGHT and BIG HERO 6. He lost his legs in a battle with LADY DEATHSTRIKE and then lost his powers on M-Day. He later became APOCALYPSE's latest version of Famine and, after Apocalypse's defeat, joined the MARAUDERS in their hunt for the first mutant baby born after M-Day. **TD, MF**

Sunfire's temper runs as hot as the temperatures his powers can conjure and has cost him much over the years.

On Earth-2109, Shiro's cousin (and Wolverine's love) Mariko Yashida became Sunfire and later served with the Exiles until her death.

SUNSPOT

FIRST APPEARANCE Marvel Graphic Novel #4 (1982)
REAL NAME Roberto da Costa
OCCUPATION Leader of Hellfire Club **BASE** New York City
HEIGHT 5 ft **WEIGHT** 130 lbs **EYES** Brown **HAIR** Black
SPECIAL POWERS/ABILITIES Solar powers provide super-strength, thermal updrafts for flight, projection of heat and light, and concussive blasts of solar energy.

Sunspot grew up as a wealthy heir in Rio de Janeiro, Brazil. In his powered-up form, his mutant powers transform him into a being of black, crackling force. He has worked with several teams, including the NEW MUTANTS, the FALLEN ANGELS, and X-FORCE. More recently, he accepted a position as a Lord Imperial of the HELLFIRE CLUB. After leaving the Hellfire Club, he joined the X-MEN in San Francisco and agreed to help Danielle Moonstar train the YOUNG X-MEN. Sunspot's genetic copy—Reignfire—was a terrorist with the MUTANT LIBERATION FRONT, but he has been killed. **DW, MF**

The Young X-Men were tricked into thinking Sunspot was the new leader of the Brotherhood of Evil Mutants.

SUPER-ADAPTOID

FIRST APPEARANCE Tales Of Suspense #82 (October 1966)
REAL NAME None **OCCUPATION** Super-assassin
BASE Mobile **HEIGHT/WEIGHT/EYES/HAIR** Variable
SPECIAL POWERS/ABILITIES Android that can duplicate the appearance and powers, clothing and weaponry of anyone who passes within 10 ft of the scanning instruments in its eyes. It can mimic a maximum of eight beings at a single time.

The criminal organization AIM built the Super-Adaptoid and powered it with a sliver from the Cosmic Cube. Sent to destroy CAPTAIN AMERICA, it copied the powers and appearances of several heroes, forming a patchwork super villain, but the AVENGERS defeated it time after time. Other versions of the Adaptoid have plagued the Earth, including one merged with Yelena Belova (BLACK WIDOW). The Ultra-Adaptoid infiltrated the criminal group Modok's 11 for AIM. The Super-Adaptoid most recently turned up with the PHALANX, leading an effort to conquer the galaxy, but QUASAR (Phyla-Vell) stopped it. **TD, MF**

SUPER-APES

Reed Richards wanted to test a new rocket fuel in a ship designed to take the FANTASTIC FOUR to the moon. They hoped to get to the moon before the Soviets. But unknown to Reed, a Soviet scientist named Ivan Kragoff had built his own ship, which he hoped would get him to the moon first. Kragoff had trained three apes, a gorilla, a baboon, and a orangutan to help him operate the ship. Aware of the cosmic rays that gave the Fantastic Four their powers, Kragoff intentionally exposed himself and the apes to cosmic rays during their journey to the moon. Kragoff, now calling himself the RED GHOST, and the three apes all gained different super-powered abilities.

Once on the moon, the Super Apes battled the Fantastic Four, but quickly turned against Kragoff who starved them to keep them controlled. As their powers continued to develop, each of the three Super Apes eventually gained human-level intelligence. The original Apes and Red Ghost have buried their differences and still accompany him on his exploits. **MT**

Over time, the savage Super-Apes gained human level intelligence.

SUPER-APES
1 Igor the baboon
2 Miklho the gorilla
3 Peotor the orangutan
4 Red Ghost

FACTFILE

MEMBERS

IGOR
A baboon

MIKLHO
A gorilla

PEOTOR
An orangutan

BASE Mobile

FIRST APPEARANCE
Fantastic Four #13
(April 1963)

POWERS

Igor: possesses the ability to shapeshift.

Miklho: possesses super-strength.

Peotor: possesses the ability to control magnetism.

SUPER-SKRULL

FACTFILE

REAL NAME
Kl'rt

OCCUPATION
Warrior

BASE
Mobile, usually within the Skrull Empire

HEIGHT 6 ft
WEIGHT 625 lbs
EYES Green
HAIR None

FIRST APPEARANCE
Fantastic Four #18
(September 1963)

POWERS

The Super-Skrull is an extraterrestrial possessing the combined abilities of the Fantastic Four, and the physical malleability common to all Skrulls. He can project hypnotic energy from his eyes.

MY EYES!!! CAN'T GEE...!!! CAN'T MOVE!!

Super-Skrull can project a beam that briefly paralyzes and makes foes do his will

After the FANTASTIC FOUR prevented the SKRULLS from conquering Earth, the Skrull Emperor vowed to develop a super-weapon that could destroy them. His scientists created the Super-Skrull, a warrior bionically re-engineered to possess all the powers of the Fantastic Four. The Super-Skrull's first battle ended in failure and he was imprisoned by the Fantastic Four.

The Super-Skrull battled the AVENGERS and CAPTAIN MARVEL during the KREE-SKRULL War, and over the years he has clashed with SPIDER-MAN, MS. MARVEL, SASQUATCH, IRON FIST, LUKE CAGE, and the YOUNG AVENGERS. He was killed defending his people during the Annihilation (*see* pp. 30–1), but later returned and helped the Kree fight the PHALANX invasion. During the Secret Invasion (*see* pp. 326–7), he saved the life of Nova and then came to Earth to kill his daughter Jazinda, but ended up saving her instead. **TD, MF**

SUPREME INTELLIGENCE

FACTFILE

REAL NAME
Supremor

OCCUPATION
Planetary leader

BASE
Kree-Lar

HEIGHT n/a
WEIGHT n/a
EYES Black with yellow pupils
HAIR Green stalks

FIRST APPEARANCE
Fantastic Four #65
(August 1967)

POWERS

The Supreme Intelligence possesses the combined intellect of the greatest minds in Kree history. In the past, the Supreme Intelligence has projected its consciousness into a powerful artificial body in order to actively engage in battle.

At one point, the Supreme Intelligence wished to add Rick Jones and Mar-Vell to its brain bank.

YOU ARE IN THE PRESENCE OF THE *INTELLIGENCE SUPREME*...RIGHTFUL *RULER* OF THE ETERNAL KREE, UNTIL I WAS OVER THROWN BY THE USURPER WITHOUT.

NO, YOUTH...I AM *NOT* A TRULY LIVING CREATURE, BUT THE SUM AND SUBSTANCE OF THE *MIGHTIEST MINDS* OF UNTOLD MILLENNIA OF KREE HISTORY---

A *MULTI-PLICITY* OF GENIUSES, MADE MANIFEST IN *ONE* BEING, *ONE* ENTITY.

Decades ago, the KREE race learned that their ancient intergalactic enemies, the SKRULLS, had successfully created a cosmic cube. In an effort to maintain parity with them they created the Supreme Intelligence, an aggregate entity made up of the finest minds ever to exist within the Kree empire. Upon their deaths, those brains deemed worthy of being added to the great repository were absorbed into the Supreme Intelligence's make-up, adding their knowledge and experience to its own.

Shortly after its creation, the Supreme Intelligence seized control of the Kree empire, becoming at once its supreme dictator and an object of religious worship. In this capacity, Supremor has guided the destiny of the Kree, ever attempting to overcome the evolutionary dead end that this space-faring race of militaristic conquerors had seemingly reached. **TB**

FSSSMMM

The Intelligence detonates a nega-bomb, to wipe out most of the Kree and kickstart their evolution.

Few of the Kree race escape the nega-bomb blast, but those that do will continue to evolve and perpetuate the Kree empire.

WHA--?! WHAT'S HAPPENING?

SURGE

FIRST APPEARANCE New Mutants #8 (January 2004)
REAL NAME Noriko "Nori" Ashida
OCCUPATION Student
BASE Xavier Institute **HEIGHT** 5 ft 7 in **WEIGHT** 137 lbs
EYES Brown **HAIR** Black (dyed blue)
SPECIAL POWERS/ABILITIES Absorbs electricity and transforms it into electric bolts or bursts of speed.

SWARM

FIRST APPEARANCE The Champions #14 (July 1977)
REAL NAME Fritz Von Meyer
OCCUPATION Scientist, conqueror **BASE** Mobile
HEIGHT 6 ft 5 in **WEIGHT** Unrevealed **EYES** None **HAIR** None
SPECIAL POWERS/ABILITIES Von Meyer's consciousness can mentally control a mutant queen bee, and through her, vast numbers of mutant bees.

Raised in Japan, Nori came to the US after her parents kicked her out of their home after she displayed mutant powers. She joined the Xavier Institute, and BEAST made her a pair of gauntlets with which she could control her powers, something she had only been able to do with drugs before.

Taking the codename Surge, Nori became part of the NEW MUTANTS and struck up a relationship with PRODIGY. She retained her powers after M-Day and became a leader of a new team of X-Men. When Emma Frost (see FROST, EMMA) disbanded that team, Nori ran to Dani Moonstar (see MOONSTAR, DANI) for counseling. Rather than return home, she rejoined the X-Men. **MF**

Nazi scientist Fritz Von Meyer was attacked by a colony of bees whose exposure to radiation had given them unusually high intelligence. His body was consumed, but his consciousness survived and took control of the bees, which swarmed in the configuration of a human body around his skeleton. Thus was created Swarm. Seeking world conquest, Swarm has battled the Champions of Los Angeles, Spider-Man, and the Runaways. When he faced the Thunderbolts, VENOM devoured his skeleton. This is, however, unlikely to prevent his return. **PS, MF**

SWITZLER, BEVERLY

FIRST APPEARANCE Howard the Duck #1 (January 1976)

REAL NAME Beverly Switzler

OCCUPATION Former art model and actress

BASE Cleveland, Ohio

HEIGHT/WEIGHT Unrevealed **EYES** Blue **HAIR** Red

SPECIAL POWERS/ABILITIES As an art model, she can stand perfectly still.

A former art model, Beverly Switzler's life was transformed by an encounter with that extradimensional waterfowl, HOWARD THE DUCK. After Howard rescued her from Financial Wizard, Pro-Rata, the pair began a life together in Cleveland, Ohio. Things weren't easy—they had difficulty paying the rent and, despite Howard's desire for the quiet life, they were constantly getting embroiled in the shenanigans of nefarious characters. DOCTOR BONG proved to be the most intransigent of these. Lusting after Beverly, he eventually forced her to marry him, but when he failed to consummate their relationship she returned to Howard and had the marriage annulled. **AD**

SYNCH

FIRST APPEARANCE X-Men #36 (September 1994)

REAL NAME Everett Thomas

OCCUPATION Student **BASE** Massachusetts Academy

HEIGHT 5 ft 11 in **WEIGHT** 165 lbs **EYES** Brown

HAIR Black (shaved bald)

SPECIAL POWERS/ABILITIES Able to take on the superhuman powers of others while they remain in his immediate vicinity.

When teenager Everett Thomas' mutant power emerged the entity Harvest tried to experiment on him. Rescued by Emma FROST (the White Queen), JUBILEE, and SABRETOOTH, Thomas joined with them to free HUSK, M, SKIN, and BLINK from Harvest. Everett enrolled at the Massachusetts Academy, joining GENERATION X as Synch. While battling the villain EMPLATE, who fed off the bone marrow of mutants, Synch became a creature like Emplate himself. He was rescued from Emplate's influence by his teammates. Synch sacrificed his life to save the Generation X students by trying to disarm a bomb planted by Adrienne Frost, elder sister of Emma Frost, at the time Generation X's headmistress. **MT**

FACTFILE

REAL NAME
Philip Javert

OCCUPATION
Adventurer

BASE
Mobile

HEIGHT 6 ft 4 in
WEIGHT 250 lbs
EYES Blue
HAIR Black

FIRST APPEARANCE
Avengers Vol. 1 #343
(January 1992)

The Swordsman was a skilled swordfighter and combatant. An expert in all bladed weapons, he usually carried a set of throwing knives as well as his sword. He was also a superb athlete and excelled in unarmed combat.

SWORDSMAN

The original Swordsman, Jacques DuQuesne, left his job in a circus to pursue a life of crime. He joined the AVENGERS as an agent of the evil MANDARIN, but came to admire the team and refused to help destroy them. The Swordsman died saving MANTIS from KANG THE CONQUEROR.

Philip Javert was the second Swordsman. From an alternate universe, he was the dimensional counterpart of Jacques DuQuesne. Betrayed by the Avengers from his own timeline, Javert initially battled this world's Avengers but then joined them as the new Swordsman. Later, he and Magdalene left for another dimension.

A third Swordsman came from the Counter-Earth created by Franklin RICHARDS in the Heroes Reborn incident. The fourth Swordsman (Andreas Von Strucker) served in the THUNDERBOLTS. **DW**

...BUT... LIKE KANG ...I WAS DOOMED ...FROM THE BEGINNING...

I'M... A FAILURE.

Jacques DuQuesne dies in Mantis's arms.

The identity of the Swordsman has become a legacy, passing between characters but always retaining a swashbuckling skill with a blade.

SECRET INVASION

Trust no one...

Once the Avengers finally realize that the Skrulls have infiltrated Earth, Queen Veranke launches the invasion. Sleeper agents around the world awaken, and the destruction begins.

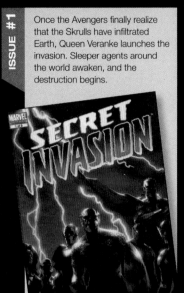

At one time, the SKRULL Empire ruled one of the most powerful interplanetary civilizations in the galaxy. However, a series of wars with the KREE, the destruction of the empire's capital planet by GALACTUS, and the loss of nearly all the empire's other planets to the Annihilation Wave (*see* pp. 30–1) drove the Skrulls to seek a new home. Because of the interference of humanity over the years—and owing to information the Skrulls gleaned after the ILLUMINATI's botched mission to warn them off—the Skrulls resolved to fulfill an ancient prophecy and lay claim to Earth.

THEY CAME TO CONQUER

The Skrull Queen Veranke began planning the invasion soon after ascending the throne. She began with an initiative to replace powerful and influential defenders of Earth with undetectable sleeper agents. When the AVENGERS discovered that ELEKTRA had been replaced by a Skrull, Tony Stark (IRON MAN) immediately suspected the potential Skrull threat. He called on the Illuminati to come up with a plan to counter an invasion. The other Avengers then learned that a Skrull had replaced BLACK BOLT long ago. Feeling that they could not even trust each other, the Super Hero team split to attack the problem on their own.

Realizing that the Avengers knew of the infiltration, Veranke—who had replaced SPIDER-WOMAN—gave the word to launch the invasion. Skrull agents simultaneously attacked several vital people and key points in Earth's defenses. Meanwhile, two teams of Avengers (one sanctioned by the US government and one not) raced to the Savage Land to investigate a crashed Skrull starship. There they faced off against each other and a third group of heroes who claimed to be the originals that the Skrulls had replaced over the years.

Manhattan became the central battleground in the invasion attempt. With the Avengers in the Savage Land, Nick Fury (*see* FURY, NICK) led a new crew of HOWLING COMMANDOS to help the remaining heroes check the Skrull attacks. Even the HOOD and his villains joined the heroes to fight the Skrulls. As the Hood remarked, "No more Earth is bad for business."

Once Reed Richards (MISTER FANTASTIC) came up with a way to identify the Skrulls, the Avengers raced back to New York and joined the battle there, along with THOR and every other hero in the area. In the course of the battle, Veranke fell, and one of her lieutenants—who had posed as Hank Pym (*see* PYM, HANK)—activated the growth serum he had given to the WASP back when she thought he was her husband. This caused her to grow to giant size and give off a lethal bio-toxin.

The climactic conflict happened once Reed Richards had come up with a way to identify the Skrull infiltrators. The heroes of Earth and the invading Skrulls destroyed large chunks of New York City in a pitched battle that shook the streets.

Thor stopped this, but only at the cost of the Wasp's life. Meanwhile, Veranke had recovered, but before she could escape, Norman Osborn (*see* GREEN GOBLIN) shot her dead. In the aftermath, Tony Stark took much of the blame for not stopping the invasion. The President disbanded SHIELD and replaced it with the Thunderbolts Initiative, placing Norman Osborn in charge of overseeing the USA's registered superhumans. **MF**

The Skrull who replaced Elek[tra] reverted to her natural form a[s] Echo killed her. The fact that [one] of the Avengers had realized [she] was a Skrull before told them [an] untold number of Skrulls had invaded Earth.

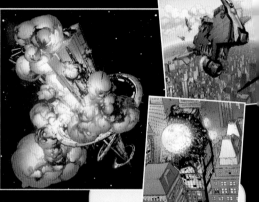

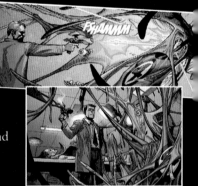

Disasters struck when the Skrulls launched their invasion. The Peak (the orbiting headquarters of SWORD), the SHIELD Helicarrier, the Fantastic Four's Baxter Building, and Thunderbolt Mountain were all destroyed.

FKHAMMM

When a Skrull infiltrator heard another Skrull say the words, "He loves you," his original personality resurfaced. Until then, the infiltrator was often unaware that he was a Skrull.

Norman Osborn formed a team of villains to help run the world after the Secret Invasion. Besides him, it included Doctor Doom, Loki, the Hood, the Sub-Mariner, and the White Queen.

THE SECRET IS OUT

The most terrifying part of the Secret Invasion was that the people of Earth had no way to tell whom they could trust. The embedded Skrulls were so well hidden that no one—not even they themselves—could tell who they were. Once the Skrulls revealed themselves to each other and united in the Secret Invasion, the heroes had to face off against a desperate army of foes who could not only shift shapes but also often had multiple sets of superpowers to draw upon. With no world left to call their own, the

2000s

In the 2000s, Marvel focused on story arcs that could be collected into trade paperbacks. *Maximum Security*, a new Captain Marvel series and *Ultimate Spider-Man* were published in 2000. *X-Treme X-Men*, *Exiles*, *Blink* and *Citizen V* all came out in 2001. "'Nuff Said," an event that crossed over every Marvel title, *The Call of Duty* limited series, *The Infinity Abyss*, *Marville*, *The Order*, *The Ultimates* and *X-Statix* were all major launches in 2002. Story arcs like "Unthinkable" and "Authoritative Action" rocked the Fantastic Four and new titles like *Emma Frost*, *Marvel 1602*, *Runaways* and *Sentinel* debuted in 2003. "Ragnarok" and "Avengers Disassembled" brought Thor and the Avengers to dramatic conclusions, and titles like *Astonishing X-Men* and *New X-Men*, took their place in 2004. *New Avengers*, *Young Avengers* and *Araña* became monthly series and *Drax the Destroyer*, *GLA* (Great Lakes Avengers), *Last Hero Standing* and *Machine Teen* all had limited runs in 2005. *Generation M*, *Marvel Zombies*, *Nextwave*, *New Excalibur*, *Ares* and multi-title crossovers like "I ♥ Marvel," "Annihilation" and "Civil War" were all big successes in 2006. In 2007, "Brand New Day," "Messiah Complex," "The Death of Captain America," and "World War Hulk" changed the world. 2008 brought a new Captain America, "Annihilation: Conquest," and the "Secret Invasion." In 2009, the "War of Kings," "Ultimatum," and "Dark Reign" shook everything up again.

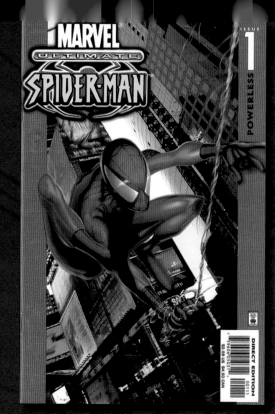

ULTIMATE SPIDER-MAN #1 (2000)

An alternate universe updates the origin and adds new twists to the origin of Spider-Man and a host of other familiar characters.

AVENGERS VOL. 3 #62 (2002)

As his personal biochemistry grows more unstable, Jack of Hearts lashes out at Scott Lang and accuses him of riding on the original Ant-Man's coattails.

YOUNG AVENGERS #2 (2005)

Upon learning that he's destined to grow up to become the time-traveling despot called Kang, a teenager travels to the past and forms a new super-team to save him from fate.

AVENGERS #503 (2004)

After Jack of Hearts, Ant-Man, Vision, and Hawkeye have fallen in battle, the Avengers realize that there is a traitor in their midst and they all unite against the Scarlet Witch.

NEW AVENGERS #1 (2005)

After disbanding months ago, a new team of Avengers spontaneously draws together when an army of super-villains stake a massive jail break in a multi-title crossover called "Breakout."

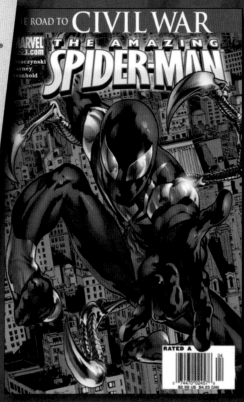

AMAZING SPIDER-MAN #529 (2006)

As the government decides to register all super-heroes, Spider-Man begins working for Tony Stark.

ANNIHILATION PROLOGUE (2006)

When an unstoppable menace threatens the spaceways, Drax the Destroyer, Nova, Ronan the Accuser and the Super-Skrull unite against it.

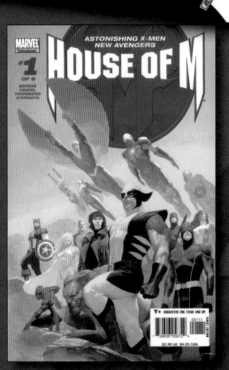

HOUSE OF M #1 (2005)

Having suffered a nervous breakdown which disassembled the Avengers, the Scarlet Witch uses her abilities to restructure reality so that Magneto now rules the Earth.

SECRET INVASION (2008)

Years of kidnapping and replacing Earth's heroes finally pay off for the Skrull Empire, which invades the planet.

DARK REIGN (2009)

Now in charge of SHIELD, Norman Osborn (the Green Goblin) brings together the Earth's mightiest villains to form a Cabal to secretly rule the world.

TAINE, SYDNEY

FIRST APPEARANCE Nightside #1 (December 2001)

REAL NAME Sydney Taine

OCCUPATION Police detective **BASE** New York City

HEIGHT/WEIGHT/EYES Unrevealed **HAIR** Black and gray

SPECIAL POWERS/ABILITIES Skilled in a variety of martial arts, including capoeira; adept in various forms of weapons combat; no known superpowers.

Sydney Taine is the only detective in the NYPD trusted by the Others, individuals that appear human but who are driven by sinister thirsts and passions. While investigating the death of three crime bosses, Sydney, partnered by Ape Largo, uncovered a plot by the Others to obtain the Three Lost Treasures of Tao. Defeating them with cunning and fighting prowess, Sydney returned the stolen treasures to Suzuki Shosan, her former teacher. Sydney may be a member of the Players, a powerful alien race. **AD**

TALBOT, COLONEL GLENN

General Thaddeus E. "Thunderbolt" Ross installed Major Glenn Talbot as security head of Desert Base, New Mexico, to investigate Dr. Bruce Banner. Talbot became Banner's rival for the love of Ross's daughter, Betty. He eventually learned that Banner was the monstrous HULK.

For years Talbot aided General Ross in attempts to capture or kill the Hulk. Betty married Talbot, but she later divorced him, realizing she still loved Banner. Promoted to colonel, Talbot was finally killed by an electrical overload while attacking the Hulk. **PS**

> I MAY HAVE WON YOUR HAND BUT IT WAS ONLY WHEN YOUR RELATIONSHIP WITH BANNER BECAME UTTERLY HOPELESS!

> DEEP DOWN, YOU'LL NEVER TRULY LOVE ME THE WAY YOU ONCE LOVED HIM.

> YOU SETTLED FOR MARRIAGE TO ME MY LOVE. I CAN SEE IT IN YOURS EYES.

Glenn Talbot finally married Betty Ross, but she never stopped loving his adversary Bruce Banner, alias the Hulk.

FACTFILE

REAL NAME
Glenn Talbot

OCCUPATION
Major, later Colonel in US Air Force; head of security, Desert Base; later adjutant to General T. E. "Thunderbolt" Ross; later commanding officer, Gamma Base

BASE
Desert Base, New Mexico; later Gamma Base, New Mexico

HEIGHT 6 ft 1 in
WEIGHT 215 lbs
EYES Blue
HAIR Brown

FIRST APPEARANCE
Tales to Astonish #61
(November 1964)

POWERS
Normal human strength

TALBOT, MAJOR

FIRST APPEARANCE Incredible Hulk #436 (December 1995)

REAL NAME William M. "Matt" Talbot

OCCUPATION U.S. Air Force Major

BASE Mobile

HEIGHT 6 ft **WEIGHT** 210 lbs

EYES Blue **HAIR** Brown

SPECIAL POWERS/ABILITIES None.

Major William M. "Matt" Talbot is the nephew of Colonel Glenn Talbot. Matt Talbot is furious at his uncle's wife Betty for dumping his uncle in favor of the HULK.

Matt went to Betty's house and appeared to rescue her from a berserk soldier, but then he slapped her and called her names for hurting his uncle. Out of control, Talbot shot Betty in each leg. When the Hulk came to rescue Betty, he was hit by Talbot's plasma blasts, but it turned out that the gun Talbot used contained stun pellets that soon wore off. Talbot escaped having exacted some measure of revenge for his uncle's broken heart. **MT**

TALISMAN

FIRST APPEARANCE Alpha Flight #5 (December 1983)

REAL NAME Elizabeth Twoyoungmen

OCCUPATION Student **BASE** Canada

HEIGHT 5 ft 10 in **WEIGHT** 175 lbs **EYES** Blue **HAIR** Black

SPECIAL POWERS/ABILITIES Has natural mystical abilities and can control magical energy; when wearing the "circlet," she can command spirits and manipulate mystical energies.

The latest in a long line of North American shamans, Elizabeth Twoyoungmen transformed into the long-prophesied Talisman when she place a circlet of enchantment on her forehead. She later went on to join ALPHA FLIGHT. The circlet gradually corrupted Elizabeth and caused her to grow farther apart from her father Michael Twoyoungmen. Michael took the circlet to defeat the mystical creature Pestilence, but he later returned it to his daughter. After her father's death, she joined Sasquatch's new Canadian team, OMEGA FLIGHT, but she recently retired from active duty to return to her tribe. **TB, MF**

TANAKA, KENJIRO

FIRST APPEARANCE Quasar #5 (December 1989)

REAL NAME Kenjiro Tanaka

OCCUPATION Former SHIELD agent

BASE New York City

HEIGHT 5 ft 10 in **WEIGHT** 160 lbs **EYES** Black **HAIR** Black

SPECIAL POWERS/ABILITIES None; received combat training from SHIELD

Kenjiro "Ken" Tanaka attended SHIELD academy alongside Wendell Vaughn, who later became the cosmic hero QUASAR. After graduation, Tanaka took an undercover position within International Data Integration and Control (IDIC) and became its director of design. He eventually left IDIC to join his former classmate at Vaughn Security Systems. Tanaka discovered the link between Wendell Vaughn and Quasar but agreed to keep the secret safe. He now heads up Vaughn Security Systems while Quasar is away saving the galaxy. **DW**

TARANTULA
The Hero with a sting

A criminal used the name Tarantula during the days of the Old West, but the first modern Tarantula, Anton Miguel Rodriguez, was a brutal revolutionary from the small, South American country of Delvadia. Government officials gave him his powers with a variant of the super-soldier formula, intending to make him a national symbol, like CAPTAIN AMERICA.

Delvadian leaders made the Tarantula a national symbol during a time of uprising.

FACTFILE
REAL NAME
Maria Vasquez
OCCUPATION
Hero for hire
BASE
New York

HEIGHT Unrevealed
WEIGHT Unrevealed
EYES Green
HAIR Black with red streak

FIRST APPEARANCE
Heroes For Hire #1 (August 2006)

TARANTULA

Martial arts and knife fighting expert. Spiked blades in the wrists and toes of her costume.

POWERS

Rodriguez voluntarily served the Delvadian government, grateful for a chance to fight.

KILLER FOR HIRE

Instead, he became a professional criminal and assassin. In New York, where he hijacked a boat on the Hudson River, SPIDER-MAN and the PUNISHER thwarted his plans. He later mutated into a humanoid spider due to treatments from Roxxon Oil, and he killed himself in a police standoff. His daughter donned the Tarantula costume and teamed up with the daughter of BATROC THE LEAPER before dying at the hands of the TASKMASTER.

Enhanced reflexes and military training allow the Tarantula to make surgical stabs with his venomous boot-spikes.

THE EXILE

Captain Luis Alvarez of Delvadia became the second official Tarantula. On a mission to the US to execute Delvadian refugees, he battled Spider-Man and lost. Exiled from his country, Alvarez died when the armed vigilante team the Jury executed him.

YOU ARE BUT A **SPIDER**-MAN! I AM THE **TARANTULA** --AND MY TOUCH MEANS **DEATH!**

The latest Tarantula worked as part of the Heroes For Hire when Misty Knight and Colleen Wing formed a new line-up of the team.

FEMME FATALE

During the CIVIL WAR (*see* pp. 84-5), a new Tarantula joined the Heroes for Hire. Maria Vasquez had abilities and weapons similar to those of her predecessors, but no other connection. She hoped to avenge her sister, who died when NITRO blew up in Stamford, Connecticut. After WORLD WAR HULK, she nearly died when her teammate Humbug offered her to No-Name, the BROOD member of HULK's WARBOUND, but SHANG-CHI saved her. **DW, MF**

ESSENTIAL STORYLINES
• *Amazing Spider-Man #134*
First appearance of the original Tarantula.
• *Heroes for Hire #1*
Maria Vasquez appears for the first time.
• *Heroes for Hire #15*
Maria Vasquez is left in a coma as the team go their separate ways.

TASKMASTER

FIRST APPEARANCE Avengers #195 (May 1980)

REAL NAME Unknown

OCCUPATION Mercenary, teacher   **BASE** Mobile

HEIGHT 6 ft 2 in   **WEIGHT** 220 lbs   **EYES /HAIR** Not known

SPECIAL POWERS/ABILITIES Can copy other people's movements, regardless of complexity, after watching them once.

The Taskmaster committed several grand larcenies before establishing a series of academies to train criminals. When the Avengers realized this, they began closing his academies down. During a spell in prison, he trained a new CAPTAIN AMERICA: John Walker (*see* US AGENT).

The Taskmaster signed on to train recruits for the Fifty State Initiative (*see* pp. 118–9) at Camp Hammond, and he now leads its covert Shadow Initiative. **DW, MF**

TATTERDEMALION

FIRST APPEARANCE Werewolf By Night #9 (September 1973)

REAL NAME Arnold Pattonroth (alias Michael Wyatt)

OCCUPATION Tap-dancer, actor   **BASE** Los Angeles

HEIGHT 5 ft 9 in   **WEIGHT** 165 lbs   **EYES** Blue   **HAIR** Brown

SPECIAL POWERS/ABILITIES Enhanced strength, speed; gloves treated with a solvent that dissolves paper and fabric; Kevlar body armor; cloak contains chloroform capsules; indestructible scarf.

Pattonroth was swindled of his life's savings by Las Vegas mobsters. He joined an army of derelicts on the streets of LA and declared war on the rich. Defeated by the WEREWOLF and SPIDER-MAN, he moved back to Las Vegas and attacked the criminals who had stolen from him. He later returned to LA and was recruited into the criminal organization Night Shift, run by the Shroud. During the Civil War (*see* pp. 84–5) he was forced to fight for the THUNDERBOLTS. **TD, MF**

TAURUS

FIRST APPEARANCE The Avengers #72 (January 1970)

REAL NAME Cornelius Van Lunt

OCCUPATION Criminal mastermind   **BASE** New York City

HEIGHT 6 ft 2 in   **WEIGHT** 260 lbs   **EYES** Brown   **HAIR** Black

SPECIAL POWERS/ABILITIES Utilized Star-Blazer handgun, which fired blasts of stellar energy

Fascinated by astrology, multimillionaire Cornelius Van Lunt secretly founded the criminal organization ZODIAC to achieve political and economic domination of the world. Each of Zodiac's 12 leaders was named after his or her astrological sign and was based in a different American city: Van Lunt became Taurus, based in New York. Both in his true identity and as Taurus, Van Lunt clashed with the AVENGERS. Van Lunt ended up battling MOON KNIGHT aboard a plane and died when it crashed. There have since been various other versions of the Zodiac organization, each with its own Taurus. **PS**

TEEN BRIGADE

The Teen Brigade was a group of teenaged shortwave radio enthusiasts, founded by RICK JONES to keep tabs on the HULK. By relaying possible sightings to the other members of their volunteer network, the group could often pin down the Hulk's location. It was the Teen Brigade's call for help that assembled the AVENGERS for the very first time, and the Teen Brigade later helped the newly-revived CAPTAIN AMERICA track down a suspect who had turned the Avengers to stone. The group acted as a precursor of sorts to Captain America's "Stars and Stripes" computer hotline network.

A second grouping of the Teen Brigade helped Rick Jones bring Bruce Banner and Betty Ross to the site of the original detonation site that turned Banner into the Hulk. The Corruptor derailed their mission, but he quickly met defeat and the Teen Brigade escaped without injury. **DW**

FACTFILE

MEMBERS
RICK JONES (founder), CANDY; RIDER, SPECS, WHEELS, plus other unnamed volunteers.

BASE
Mobile

FIRST APPEARANCE
Incredible Hulk Vol. 1 #6 (March 1963)

TEEN BRIGADE

The Teen Brigade used short-wave radios and Internet-enabled computers to keep in touch with each other.

TEMUGIN

FIRST APPEARANCE Iron Man #53 (June 2002)

REAL NAME Temugin

OCCUPATION Criminal leader **BASE** China

HEIGHT/WEIGHT Unrevealed **EYES** Brown **HAIR** None

SPECIAL POWERS/ABILITIES Supreme martial artist; harnesses the power of his Chi to perform feats of incredible strength, speed and agility; possesses the Mandarin's ten rings of power.

TERMINUS

FIRST APPEARANCE Fantastic Four Vol. 1 #269 (August 1984)

REAL NAME Terminus **OCCUPATION** Destroyer of worlds

BASE Mobile **HEIGHT** 150 ft **WEIGHT** unrevealed

EYES Inapplicable **HAIR** None

SPECIAL POWERS/ABILITIES Immeasurable strength, nearly indestructible; can regenerate body parts; carries a lance that fires atomic energy

TERROR

FIRST APPEARANCE Daredevil #305 (June 1992)

REAL NAME Unknown (possibly Shreck) **OCCUPATION** Criminal

BASE San Francisco **HEIGHT** 6 ft 2 in **WEIGHT** 170 lbs

EYES Variable **HAIR** None

SPECIAL POWERS/ABILITIES Able to replace parts of his body with those of humans or animals, gaining the powers of those body parts, as well as their "memories." If Terror takes a body part from a superhuman being he gains that being's power. Removes limbs or other parts by generating a special acid that allows him both to tear off a body part and to bond it to his own. Expert with firearms.

Terminus is an intelligent creation made from living metal, grown by the alien Terminex in a failed attempt to protect them from the CELESTIALS. A continuum of Termini exist, from Stage 1 metallic microbes to the Stage 4 behemoths represented by Terminus. Taking revenge on planets that the Celestials had spared, Terminus claimed Earth for his own but met defeat at the hands of the FANTASTIC FOUR. The Deviant called Jorro wore the Terminus armor and destroyed the Savage Land. Terminus defeated a duplicate and emerged as the Stage 5 "Ulterminus," only to be vanquished by THOR. **DW**

At some point in the distant past, the virtually indestructible being now known as Terror battled a green bear-shaped demon. The only way to defeat the demon was to sacrifice his own form, but in doing so he took on the form of the dead demon. He also gained the demon's power to bond the limbs of others to his body. His body is now made up of a collection of dead or decaying body parts. Now his associate Boneyard helps him collect body parts. He was also befriended by a half-human, half-demon being named Hellfire. Terror formed Terror Inc., an assassination bureau. **MT**

TERRAX

FIRST APPEARANCE Fantastic Four #211 (October 1979)

REAL NAME Tyros

OCCUPATION Interstellar traveller **BASE** Mobile

HEIGHT 6 ft 6 in **WEIGHT** 2,750 lbs **EYES** Gray **HAIR** None

SPECIAL POWERS/ABILITIES Body covered with supple, rocky shell; animates rock and commands it to do his bidding; lifted Manhattan into orbit around Earth.

GALACTUS the world-devourer was looking for a new herald and chose Tyros, a despot from the planet Birj. Despite being provided with new powers, Tyros, rechristened Terrax, remained a restless, rebellious soul, and before long he betrayed his overbearing master. Terrax traveled to Earth and battled the FANTASTIC FOUR, who had handed him over to Galactus. After being killed and reborn a number of times, he returned to space. He was swept up in the Annihilation (*see* pp. 30-1), but survived. Recently, the GRANDMASTER chose him to be part of the Red HULK's Offenders and battle the original DEFENDERS. **AD, MF**

The illegitimate son of the Mandarin, Temugin was raised in a monastery and trained in the mystic martial arts. As an adult, he received a package containing the MANDARIN's ten rings of power (each of which endowed the wearer with a different ability), along with his hands, and felt honor-bound to seek revenge on IRON MAN for his father's death. Taking over the Mandarin's criminal empire, Temugin clashed with Iron Man but failed to discharge this honor-debt. He later lost a hand, along with five rings, to PUMA. He subsequently joined the AGENTS OF ATLAS. **TB, MF**

The spikes on Terror's face came from a demon. He can remove them and use them as weapons or regrow them.

THANOS

FIRST APPEARANCE Iron Man #55 (February 1973)
REAL NAME Thanos
OCCUPATION Conqueror **BASE** Sanctuary III
HEIGHT 6 ft 7 in **WEIGHT** 985 lbs **EYES** Red **HAIR** None
SPECIAL POWERS/ABILITIES Synthesizes ambient cosmic energy for use in a variety of ways, from increasing strength to firing energy blasts; also possesses a personal force-field and other devices.

Born on Titan, young Thanos was ostracized because of his hideous mutant nature. Morose and withdrawn, he became obsessed with Death. Gathering an army of mercenaries, he set out to conquer and destroy. Now infamous as the Mad Titan, Thanos's atrocities include eradicating half of the lifeforms in the universe with the Infinity Gauntlet. But in every instance, Thanos' own weaknesses of character have enabled heroic opponents to thwart his schemes. He joined forces with Annihilus during the cosmic Annihilation, but Drax the Destroyer killed him during that event. **TB, MF**

THENA

FIRST APPEARANCE The Eternals Vol. 1 #5 (November 1976)
REAL NAME Azura, changed by royal decree to Thena
OCCUPATION Warrior, scholar **BASE** Olympia, Greece
HEIGHT 5 ft 10 in **WEIGHT** 160 lbs **EYES** Blue **HAIR** Blonde
SPECIAL POWERS/ABILITIES Superhuman strength; mental control over body gives virtual immortality; sionic abilities include flight through levitation; projects cosmic energy from eyes or hands.

Thena is the daughter of Zuras, ruler of the Eternals, and his wife Cybele. In a pact between the Eternals and the Olympian gods, Zuras renamed Azura "Thena" after the goddess Athena. Thousands of years ago, Thena met Kro, a member of the Deviants. They became lovers, and they had twin children. Upon the demise of Zuras, Thena succeeded him as Prime Eternal, but she subsequently lost this position to another Eternal, Ikaris. Her mind wiped, Thena resurfaced recently with a human husband and son. She has since regained her memories of her former life. **PS, MF**

⊙ **THING, THE** *see opposite page*

3-D MAN

FIRST APPEARANCE Marvel Premiere #35 (April 1977)
REAL NAME Charles "Chuck" Chandler
OCCUPATION Test pilot, adventurer **BASE** None
HEIGHT 6 ft 2 in **WEIGHT** 200 lbs **EYES** Blue **HAIR** Blond
SPECIAL POWERS/ABILITIES Strength, stamina, agility and speed three times that of a normal human; a brilliant pilot with the ability to sense the presence of alien Skrulls.

In 1958, Skrulls captured NASA test pilot Chuck Chandler in midflight. He escaped, causing their ship to explode. He crash-landed his plane, and as he clambered from the wreckage, SKRULL radiation imprinted his essence onto the glasses worn by his brother Hal. By concentrating hard on the glasses, Hal could resurrect his brother as 3-D Man. However, side effects caused Hal to put his glasses aside. Years later, Hal embarked on a successful quest to bring his brother back permanently. Chuck had not aged a single day and began his life anew. Recently, the hero TRIATHLON gained the 3-D Man's powers too. **AD, MF**

THOMPSON, EUGENE "FLASH"

FACTFILE

REAL NAME
Eugene Thompson
OCCUPATION
Unemployed
BASE
New York City

HEIGHT 6 ft 2 in
WEIGHT 185 lbs
EYES Blue
HAIR Reddish-blond

FIRST APPEARANCE
Amazing Fantasy Vol. 1 #15 (August 1962)

POWERS

Formerly a gifted athlete, nicknamed "Flash" because of his speed. He was a star of Midtown High's football and baseball teams.

Eugene Thompson's athletic prowess made him a football hero at Midtown High School, helping him overcome the insecurities of having a father—Harry, an alcoholic cop—who regularly beat him. At Midtown, Flash dated Liz Allan (later Liz OSBORN), the most popular girl in the school. He looked down on bookish Peter Parker, and was also jealous of him, fearing that Liz was attracted to Peter. Ironically, Flash was a big fan of SPIDER-MAN. Flash went on to attend Empire State University with Parker and, in time, the two became friends.

Thompson later joined the military and served in South-East Asia. He later had an affair with Betty Brant LEEDS, the wife of *Daily Bugle* reporter Ned Leeds, which led to him being framed as the criminal HOBGOBLIN.

Thompson sank into alcoholism. Norman Osborn (the GREEN GOBLIN) offered him a job at his company Oscorp, but only as part of his scheme to hurt anyone who was friends with Peter Parker. Osborn forced Thompson to drink whiskey and arranged for Thompson's car to crash into Midtown High.

After recovering, Flash worked at that same school as a gym teacher. Soon after, he re-upped with the Army to fight in Iraq, where he lost both legs while trying to save his commanding officer. **DW, MF**

A natural athlete in school, Flash found it difficult to achieve similar levels of popularity later in life.

THE THING

Big-hearted tough guy of the Fantastic Four

The radiation shields on Reed Richards' spaceship failed and pilot, Ben Grimm was bombarded with cosmic rays.

Ben Grimm, alias The Thing is a, hot-headed member of the FANTASTIC FOUR, using his abilities to fight evil, almost as often as he does battle with himself. Ben grew up in New York City in poverty. Like his older brother, Daniel, he got involved with a street gang (*see* YANCY STREET GANG). After his parents died, Ben was taken in by his uncle Jake, a doctor, who helped set the boy on the right track. Ben ended up going to Empire State University on a football scholarship. His first-year roommate was brilliant science student Reed Richards, who became Ben's best friend.

FACTFILE

REAL NAME
Benjamin Jacob Grimm

OCCUPATION
Adventurer, former test pilot, wrestler

BASE
New York City

HEIGHT 6 ft
WEIGHT 500 lbs
EYES Blue
HAIR (human form) Brown; (the Thing) None

FIRST APPEARANCE
Fantastic Four #1
(November 1961)

POWERS

Superhuman strength, endurance, and durability. He can lift 85 tons, absorb the blast of an armor-piercing bazooka shell, withstand temperature extremes, and needs no suit to survive in space or in the ocean depths.

A GRIMM TALE

When Reed told Ben of his plan to one day build a starship, Ben jokingly said that he would pilot the ship.

After college, Ben joined the US Air Force and became an excellent pilot and astronaut. Reed's starship reached the test stage but the Federal government threatened to cut off funding, Reed decided to stage a test flight. Ben agreed to pilot the ship, though he worried that shields weren't strong enough.

Reed and Ben blasted into space along with Reed's fiancée, Susan Storm, and Sue's brother Johnny. In space, the foursome was bombarded with high levels of cosmic radiation.

Alicia Masters is Ben's true love, she loves him for himself and cares nothing for his monstrous appearance.

The Thing battles a team of monsters led by Groot, who is able to manipulate trees and his own wood-like body.

ESSENTIAL STORYLINES
• *Fantastic Four #1* An accident in space changes pilot Ben Grimm into the orange-colored-rock-encrusted the Thing.
• *Fantastic Four #8* The Thing meets Alicia Masters and a long love affair begins.
• *Fantastic Four #310* Having quit the Fantastic Four, the Thing decides to join the West Coast Avengers, when he mutates into an even more grotesque creature, and sets off for Monster Island to find Mole Man.

LET THE CLOBBERIN' BEGIN!

The crew were altered on a genetic level and gained unusual powers. Ben's skin turned orange and rocky, and his strength grew tremendously, earning him the nickname the Thing. Reed convinced the others that they should use their powers to help humanity as the Fantastic Four. Ben would sometimes revert back to his human form unexpectedly, but neither he nor Reed could control this change. For a long time, Ben dated the blind sculptor Alicia MASTERS. Recently, though, he became engaged to Debbie Green, a teacher.

During the CIVIL WAR (*see* pp. 84–5), Ben became disgusted with both sides and left for France. He returned just as the conflict climaxed, working to protect innocent bystanders from any collateral damage. **MT, MF**

THOR

The Asgardian God of Thunder

Thor could transport himself to Midgard via Asgard's rainbow bridge, or by using the powers of his hammer Mjolnir.

Thor was the God of Thunder, the beloved champion of Asgard (*see* GODS OF ASGARD) and a figure of worship among the ancient Norse. He loved his people so much that he triggered their destruction in the end battle of Ragnarok, finally breaking a repeating cycle of futility. Thor was born to Odin, the ruler (sky-father) of Asgard, and Gaea, the mother goddess of Earth (a place known to the Asgardians as Midgard).

EARLY LIFE

Groomed to assume his father's throne, Thor grew up with his best friend Balder and his first love, Sif. But Thor's half-brother Loki hated him, and schemed to become ruler of Asgard himself.

When Thor proved himself worthy of carrying the uru hammer Mjolnir, he took up the identity as the Thunder God. Thor mingled with his Earthly worshippers throughout the 9th century, leading Vikings into battle. He later abandoned his followers after several of them butchered a Christian monastery. Over the succeeding centuries he spent most of his time in Asgard,

THE TEEN BRIGADE! THEY'RE LOCATED IN THE SOUTH WEST! IF THIS CONCERNS THE HULK, IT MUST BE SERIOUS! AND SO, THE TIME HAS COME...

...FOR DR. DON BLAKE TO STRIKE HIS ENCHANTED CANE ONCE UPON THE FLOOR, CASTING OFF HIS MORAL GUISE, AND BECOMING...

...THE MIGHTY THOR, GOD OF THUNDER!

Originally, Thor transformed from Donald Blake to the Thunder God by striking a simple wooden staff on the ground.

venturing to Earth to battle Loki in the Old West and mistakenly becoming a pawn of the Nazis during World War II.

Deciding that his son needed to learn humility before assuming the title of sky-father, Odin exiled Thor to Earth. There, the Thunder God believed himself to be the mortal doctor Donald Blake, and walked with the aid of a

As one of the core members of the Avengers, Thor defeated the robot Ultron and crushed countless other threats to humanity.

STORMY TIMES

A second incarnation of the Thunder God appeared when Thor merged his spirit with Earth architect Eric Masterson. Thor entered temporary exile for apparently killing Loki, and Masterson carried on, posing as Thor while wielding the hammer of Mjolnir. Masterson later received the identity of Thunderstrike, before perishing in battle against the Egyptian god Seth and overcoming a curse laid upon Masterson by the weapon of Bloodaxe. Thor subsequently assumed the civilian identity of dead EMS worker Jake Olson, though he soon gave this up and let a resurrected Olson continue his life. Eric Masterson's son, Kevin, later took up the role of Thunderstrike in a possible future timeline also inhabited by Spider-Girl.

Thor and Thunderstrike unite their mystical hammers to unleash even greater power. Thor, who considered Eric Masterson one of the most noble mortals he had ever encountered, greatly mourned his death.

wooden cane. When he struck the cane on the ground it transformed into Mjolnir, and Thor regained his powers and all memories of his life on Asgard. For years, he lived a dual identity as Thor and Blake, battling threats such as the Radioactive Man and the Absorbing Man. Loki sought to entrap Thor by drawing him into conflict with the Hulk, but only succeeded in uniting a group of heroes that would become the Avengers. Thor became a founding member of the team, and fought alongside such heroes as Captain America, Iron Man, and Hercules.

Few beings ever bested Thor in combat, but the alien Beta Ray Bill defeated the Thunder God and proved worthy of wielding the hammer of Mjolnir. Impressed, Odin forged a new hammer, Stormbreaker, for Bill to wield. Thor gave up his Blake alter ego at this time, briefly trying out a new identity as construction worker Sigurd Jarlson. New trials continued to vex Thor—his father Odin

ESSENTIAL STORYLINES

- **The Mighty Thor #337**
Beta Ray Bill explodes into action as a rival, and later an ally, of the Thunder God.

- **Thor: Son of Asgard #1–12**
This limited series explores the early adventures of a young Balder the Brave, Sif, and Thor.

- **The Mighty Thor #582–588**
It's Ragnarok, the Asgardian apocalypse, and the long-running series comes to an end with the total destruction of Asgard and all who live there.

seemingly perished in combat against the fire demon Surtur, and Thor refused the throne, the honor passing to Balder. Thor then suffered terrible torment when a curse rendered him incapable of death. Wounds nearly disintegrated his body until the spell was reversed.

RAGNAROK

The events that led to the end of Asgard began with the true death of Odin, killed battling Surtur. Thor took up the mantle of rulership and became empowered with the mystical Odinforce. Wishing to take a more direct role over earthly affairs, Thor moved Asgard to Earth and transformed the planet into a dictatorship that endured for two hundred years. At last, realizing the error of his actions, he unwound the previous two centuries through time travel.

Loki enlisted Surtur to forge new weapons comparable in power to Mjolnir. He rallied his followers and conquered Asgard. Thor, realizing that Loki's actions presaged the final conflagration of Ragnarok, followed the Odinforce on a spiritual journey. The Thunder God uncovered the truth of the Ragnarok cycle—its endless loop of creation and rebirth had been orchestrated by the

Beta Ray Bill proved he was able to fight alongside the Asgardians, and became Beta Ray Thor.

godlike Those Who Sit Above in Shadow for their amusement. Unwilling to endure his people's dishonor through yet another cycle, Thor severed the tapestry that wove the reality of Asgard's dimension, wiping himself and Asgard from existence.

Desperate for Thor's power during the Civil War, Mr. Fantastic and Hank Pym created a

Ragnarok, the twilight of the gods, spelled an end to all of the five races of the dimension of Asgard.

biomechanical Thor clone. It proved hard to control and killed Giant-Man (Bill Foster) It later attacked the Fifty State Initiative's headquarters at Camp Hammond.

Later, in the void of the afterlife, Thor reunited with his old alter ego Donald Blake and returned to Earth, rebuilding Asgard on an island floating in the sky over Oklahoma. He then set out to find the other gods, who now lived unknowingly as mortals, and restore them to their rightful places. He was banished from Asgard for killing his grandfather Bor in battle.

DW, MF

THOR GIRL

FIRST APPEARANCE Thor #22 (August 2000)

REAL NAME Tarene   **OCCUPATION** Adventurer

BASE New York City   **HEIGHT** 5 ft 9 in

WEIGHT 317 lbs   **EYES** Blue   **HAIR** Blonde

SPECIAL POWERS/ABILITIES Immortal, superhuman strength, invulnerability, plus a mystic hammer that grants flight, weather control, and energy blast that can transform her to human and back.

Tarene is the Designated prophesied by X'Hoss to elevate all life to greatness. Before she could manage this, Thanos destroyed her homeworld and stripped her of much of her power. Thor and Orikal helped her defeat Thanos, and Tarene came to Earth and took the codename Thor Girl to emulate her hero. She joined The Fifty-State Initiative (see pp. 118–9), assigned to Georgia's team, the Cavalry. During Secret Invasion (see pp. 326–7), 3-D Man revealed that a Skrull was impersonating Thor Girl. He and Gravity killed the imposter. Thor Girl is now at Camp Hammond. **MF**

THUNDERBIRD

FIRST APPEARANCE Giant-Size X-Men #1 (1975)

REAL NAME John Proudstar

OCCUPATION X-Man (deceased)   **BASE** New York City/Mobile/ New York State

HEIGHT 6ft 1in   **WEIGHT** 225 lbs   **EYES** Brown   **HAIR** Black

SPECIAL POWERS/ABILITIES Super strength and stamina; can run at 35mph for long periods; leathery skin protects him from harm.

Eager to emulate his warrior ancestors, Native American John Proudstar joined the American Marines as an under-age cadet and served with distinction. John's mutant powers emerged relatively late when, at the age of 20, he wrestled a rampaging bison with his bare hands. He joined the X-Men after being sought out by Professor X, but died on only his second mission: jumping onto a criminal's escape plane, he was killed when the aircraft blew up. John's brother, James, eventually followed in his footsteps but it was a long time before he forgave Professor X. **AD**

THUNDERBOLTS

The Thunderbolts came into conflict with Captain America.

When the Fantastic Four and the Avengers disappeared after their first battle with Onslaught, Baron Zemo transformed his Masters of Evil into the Thunderbolts, giving members new identities to escape their criminal pasts. When the lost heroes returned, Zemo exposed the Thunderbolts' secret, and they turned on him. Hawkeye took over the team, and they faced off against Henry Gyrich. The Redeemers replaced this team for a while, but after Graviton destroyed them, the Thunderbolts reformed. After they disbanded, Mach-III (now Mach-IV) reformed the team once more. During the Civil War (see pp. 84–5), the Thunderbolts registered with the US government and forced many villains to join the Thunderbolts Army. After the war, Norman Osborn (see Green Goblin) took over the team. With Osborn in charge of the Avengers, the Thunderbolts became his hit squad. The latest team includes Ant-Man (Eric O'Grady), Black Widow (Yelena Belova), Ghost, Headsman, and Paladin. **MT, MF**

FACTFILE

NOTABLE MEMBERS

CITIZEN V (Baron Zemo)

TEAM LEADER

TECHNO (The Fixer)
Varies her molecular density

MACH-1 (Beetle)
Wears a suit that enables him to fly, fire weapons, and resist attack

SONGBIRD (Screaming Mimi)
Can transform the sound of her voice into physical forms

ATLAS (Goliath) Can increase his size and mass

METEORITE (Moonstone)
Superhuman strength and invulnerability

JOLT Exceptional strength, speed, agility

CHARCOAL Can change his body into charcoal, creating flames or diamonds

HAWKEYE Expert archer

BASE Mobile

FIRST APPEARANCE
The Incredible Hulk #449 (January 1997)

THUNDERBOLTS
1 Ghost 2 Headsman 3 Black Widow
4 Paladin 5 Deadpool 6 Ant-man

THUNDERSTRIKE

Divorced and with sole custody of his young son, Eric Masterson was an architect who was working at a building site where THOR, under a secret identity, was also employed. Thor was attacked by the Mongoose, and during the battle Eric was injured by falling girders. He was left with a permanent limp. After becoming friends with THOR, Eric was wounded again, this time mortally, and Odin merged him with the thunder god to save his life. Thereafter, Masterson would assume the form of Thor whenever the hero was needed on Earth. When Thor seemingly slew his brother LOKI and was banished from this plane of reality, Eric took his place as Thor II. Eventually the real Thor returned, and Eric was given his own enchanted mace and became Thunderstrike. In the future of the alternate timeline known as Earth-982, Eric's son Kevin visited the closed-down Avengers Mansion and recovers his father's mace. Merging with it, he becomes the new Thunderstrike and formed A-NEXT. He lost his powers after GALACTUS devoured Asgard (*see* GODS OF ASGARD), but Thor's daughter THENA helped him regain them. **TD, MF**

The original Thunderstrike is one of many Avengers who died in the line of duty.

Like his father, Kevin Masterson can physically transform into Thunderstrike through intense concentration.

FACTFILE

REAL NAME
Eric Masterson (father),
Kevin Masterson (son)
OCCUPATION
Architect (father),
college student (son)
BASE
New York City

HEIGHT 6 ft 6 in (father),
6 ft (son)
WEIGHT 640 lbs (father),
585 lbs (son)
EYES Blue
HAIR Blond

FIRST APPEARANCES
Thor #391 (father); *Thor* #392
(son); *Thor* #432 (father as
Thunderstrike); *What If* #105 (son
as Thunderstrike)

POWERS

(Father) Super-strong, owns enchanted uru mace that projects concussive blasts of mystical energy. Flies by throwing mace and gripping its strap. (Son) Super-strong; projects concussive blasts of mystical energy, which can be used to propel him through the air.

THUNDRA

FIRST APPEARANCE Fantastic Four Vol. 1 #129 (December 1972)
REAL NAME Thundra
OCCUPATION Warrior
BASE United Sisterhood Republic of North America
HEIGHT 7ft 2in **WEIGHT** 350 lbs **EYES** Green **HAIR** Red
SPECIAL POWERS/ABILITIES Enhanced strength, endurance, reflexes, and damage resistance; skilled at wielding a chain.

In the 23rd century of Earth-715, women rule the world and raise men as servants and breeding stock. Thundra, born into the United Sisterhood Republic of North America, became one of its finest warriors. She is sent back in time to defeat the Thing, but she eventually took a liking to him instead. She once brought the Thing to her time to help liberate her world, known as Femizonia. At the time of the Secret Invasion (*see* pp. 326-7), Thundra had started an all-female settlement on the mainstream Marvel Earth (616). Her people captured a Skrull and turned him over to the Inhumans. **MF**

TIGER SHARK

FIRST APPEARANCE Sub-Mariner #5 (September 1968)
REAL NAME Todd Arliss
OCCUPATION Amphibious criminal **BASE** The deep blue sea
HEIGHT 6 ft 1 in **WEIGHT** 450 lbs **EYES** Gray **HAIR** Brown
SPECIAL POWERS/ABILITIES Amphibious—able to withstand great water pressure and swim at up to 60mph; also possesses superhuman strength.

His genes spliced with those of NAMOR the Sub-Mariner and a tiger shark, Todd Arliss, former Olympic-level swimmer, became a superpowered amphibian. Namor and Tiger Shark became vengeful foes, and when Tiger Shark's powers began to fade, he kidnapped Namor's father, Leonard MacKenzie, and blackmailed Namor into donating more powers. Chaos ensued during the transfer process and Tiger Shark ended up killing MacKenzie with a lead pipe. He recently joined the Thunderbolts and also became a member of the Red Hulk's Offenders. **AD, MF**

TIGRA

FIRST APPEARANCE The Cat #1 (November 1972)
REAL NAME Greer Grant Nelson
OCCUPATION Adventurer **BASE** New York City
HEIGHT 5ft 10in **WEIGHT** 180 lbs **EYES** Green
HAIR (human form) black, (cat form) orange fur with black stripes
SPECIAL POWERS/ABILITIES Enhanced strength, slashing claws, and heightened senses of smell, hearing, and vision.

Greer Nelson received catlike powers from Dr. Joanne Tumulo, a member of the mystical race known as the CAT PEOPLE. Taking on the identity of the Cat, Nelson began a career as a costumed adventurer in San Francisco. When Nelson suffered near-fatal injuries during a clash with Hydra, the Cat People saved her life, imbuing her body with a catsoul. As Tigra, she served with the Avengers. During the Civil War (*see* pp. 84-5), she worked as Iron Man's spy within Captain America's resistance. Afterward, she joined the Fifty State Initiative and is now with Arkansas's team, the Battalion. **DW, MF**

TIME KEEPERS, THE

FIRST APPEARANCE Thor Vol. 1 #282 (April 1979)

BASE Citadel at the End of Time

MEMBERS AND POWERS

Ast, Vort, Zanth All Time Keepers possess nearly unlimited powers of time-manipulation, including time travel and the ability to rapidly age or devolve people and things.

The Time Keepers are guardians of the timestream, created by He Who Remains (the final chairman of the Time Variance Authority) at the end of time to replace his flawed agents, the Time Twisters. The Time Keepers sought to preserve their existence at all costs, which led them to enlist IMMORTUS to destroy the meddling Avengers and powerful "nexus beings" such as the Scarlet Witch. Kang, with help from Rick JONES, seemingly wiped out the Time Keepers after they attempted to eliminate a host of alternate realities. **DW**

TINKERER, THE

FIRST APPEARANCE Amazing Spider-Man Vol. 1 #2 (May 1963)

REAL NAME Phineas Mason

OCCUPATION Criminal inventor **BASE** New York City

HEIGHT 5 ft 8 in **WEIGHT** 175 lbs **EYES** Gray **HAIR** White

SPECIAL POWERS/ABILITIES Genius-level ability to create sophisticated gadgets and deadly weapons from everyday pieces of machinery or scrap metal.

Phineas Mason, the "Terrible Tinkerer," is unparalleled in his ability to create and repair machinery, and long ago became the premiere gadget-maker for the criminal underworld. Among his works are Diamondback's throwing diamonds and the Scorpion's tail. His son, Rick

Mason, worked for SHIELD as the Agent until he was killed on a mission. Later, the Punisher stabbed the Tinkerer, putting him in a wheelchair. Incarcerated in the Negative Zone, he helped the Thing and Human Torch escape during the Secret Invasion, winning his freedom. **DW, MF**

TITANIA

Davida DeVito, alias Titania, was the leader of the original Grapplers, a team of female professional wrestlers. Titania and her teammates were hired by the Roxxon Oil company to sabotage the government's Project: Pegasus. They were defeated and sent to prison. After her release, Titania's strength was enhanced to superhuman levels by the POWER BROKER. She continued to lead an expanded Grapplers team. However, Titania was assassinated by a new Grappler called GOLDDIGGER, who appears to have been working with the vigilante SCOURGE.

Mary "Skeeter" MacPherran lived in a Denver suburb that was transported by

Doctor Doom turned Skeeter MacPherran, the second Titania, into one of the strongest women on Earth.

the BEYONDER to his "Battleworld." There DOCTOR DOOM gave her super-strength to serve in his army of criminals during the first "Secret War." This new Titania and her teammate, "Crusher" Creel, the ABSORBING MAN, grew attracted to one another. After returning to Earth, Titania sometimes operated on her own and had a personal feud with the SHE-HULK. Titania also served as a member of the MASTERS OF EVIL and the FRIGHTFUL FOUR. She attempted revenge on the She-Hulk but was shrunk down and imprisoned by Hank PYM. She escaped and, still tiny, attacked the She-Hulk again but was eaten by a shark. **PS, MF**

The Super Hero Titania hates most is She-Hulk. She-Hulk and the Avengers even invaded Titania's wedding to fight the villains who were wedding guests!

FACTFILE

REAL NAME
(I) Davida DeVito (II) Mary "Skeeter" MacPherran

OCCUPATION
(I) Professional wrestler, criminal
(II) Criminal

BASE
(I) Mobile, later Los Angeles
(II) Formerly a suburb of Denver, Colorado, later New York City

HEIGHT (I) 6 ft 1 in (II) 6 ft 6 in

WEIGHT (I) 194 lbs (II) 545 lbs

EYES (I) Blue (II) Blue

HAIR (I) Black (II) Red-blonde

FIRST APPEARANCES
(I) Marvel Two-in-One #54 (August 1979) (II) Marvel Super Heroes Secret Wars #3 (July 1984)

(I) Possessed superhuman strength—able to lift about 2 tons; skilled wrestler and hand-to-hand combatant.
(II) Possesses superhuman strength—able to lift about 90 tons; superhuman stamina and durability. Resistant to heat, cold, injury, and disease.

TITANIUM MAN

FIRST APPEARANCE Tales of Suspense Vol. 1 #69 (Sept. 1965)
REAL NAME Boris Bullski **OCCUPATION** Former Russian
champion **BASE** Moibile **HEIGHT** (without armor) 7 ft 1 in
WEIGHT (without armor) 475 lbs **EYES** Blue **HAIR** Black
SPECIAL POWERS/ABILITIES Unusual strength proportionate to
his giant size; armor provided flight, enhanced strength, near-
invulnerability, and the ability to fire energy blasts from hands.

Russian inventor Boris
Bullski devised the
Titanium Man armor in
order to crush IRON MAN
and win favor with his
superiors. As Titanium Man,
Bullski lost to Iron Man in a
televised slugfest of East vs. West.
A second Titanium Man, the
mutant known as the GREMLIN,
died when his armor exploded.
Boris Bullski later returned as an
agent of AIM, but died in battle
with Iron Man. A new Titanium
Man recently appeared, failing in his
bid to sabotage Tony Stark's mission
to destroy a comet that was on
course for Earth. **DW**

TOPAZ

FIRST APPEARANCE Werewolf By Night #13 (January 1974)
REAL NAME Unrevealed; possibly Topaz
OCCUPATION Sorceress **BASE** New York City
HEIGHT 5 ft 3 in **WEIGHT** 100 lbs **EYES** Brown **HAIR** Black
SPECIAL POWERS/ABILITIES A trained sorceress with a multitude
of mystic spells at her command, primarily empathy-based in nature.

Branded a witch after she made a flower bloom
in the desert as a child, Topaz was incarcerated in
a prison camp, where she was adopted and
trained in the mystic arts by Taboo. Topaz served
as the familiar for Taboo's sorcery until, in pursuit
of Jack Russell, the Werewolf By
Night, Topaz turned against her
mentor rather than allow
Russell and his friends to
come to harm. It has been
prophesied that, one day
Topaz will be capable of
wiping away the evils
of the world. Topaz
recently joined forces
with Jennifer KALE
and SATANA as the
Witches to recover the stolen
Tome of Zhered-Na. **TB**

TRAINER, DR. SEWARD

FIRST APPEARANCE Peter Parker: Spider-Man Vol. 1 #54
(January 1995) **REAL NAME** Seward Trainer
OCCUPATION Geneticist **BASE** New York City
HEIGHT 5 ft 10 in **WEIGHT** 200 lbs **EYES** Brown **HAIR** Brown
SPECIAL POWERS/ABILITIES A genius in the fields of biology
and genetic engineering.

So brilliant that he was
once employed by the
HIGH EVOLUTIONARY,
geneticist Seward
Trainer gave in to
GREEN GOBLIN
Norman Osborn's
blackmailing and
participated in a plot to
crush SPIDER-MAN
Peter Parker's morale.
By tampering with the
JACKAL's research, Trainer made it appear that
Parker was a clone. Dr. Trainer became a father
figure to the real clone, Ben Reilly (SCARLET
SPIDER), but died at the hands of the villain
Gaunt before he could confess his role in the
scheme. His daughter Carolyn Trainer briefly
took the identity of DOCTOR OCTOPUS II. **DW**

TOMBSTONE

FIRST APPEARANCE Web of Spider-Man #36 (March 1988)
REAL NAME Lonnie Thompson Lincoln
OCCUPATION Professional hitman **BASE** Mobile
HEIGHT 6 ft 7 in **WEIGHT** Unknown **EYES** Pink **HAIR** White
SPECIAL POWERS/ABILITIES Enhanced strength, speed,
stamina, and reflexes; skilled hand-to-hand fighter and assassin.

Lonnie Lincoln was born an
African-American albino. He
grew up in Harlem, New
York City with Joe
"Robbie" Robertson,
whom he coerced into
keeping quiet regarding
a murder that Lincoln
had committed. Lincoln
became an assassin for mob
figures such as the KINGPIN,
and gained superhuman
powers after exposure to an
experimental gas. Following
a stint with the Sinister
Twelve, Tombstone served a
prison term in the Cage and
received a heart bypass
operation. He escaped, and
remains at large. **DW**

TORPEDO

FIRST APPEARANCE Daredevil Vol. 1 #126 (October 1975)
REAL NAME Brock Jones
OCCUPATION Crimefighter **BASE** Clairton, West Virginia
HEIGHT 6ft **WEIGHT** 200 lbs **EYES** Blue **HAIR** Blond
SPECIAL POWERS/ABILITIES Battlesuit provides damage
resistance; turbojets at wrists and ankles add power to punches;
suit also generate shockwaves, and permits supersonic flight.

Inventor Michael Stivak became the first
Torpedo when his uncle, Senator
Eugene Stivak, convinced him to
build a battlesuit. In truth,
Senator Stivak had been prodded
to do so by the extraterrestrial
DIRE WRAITHS, who wanted to a
weapon capable of defeating their
enemy Rom the Spaceknight.
After the younger Stivak's death,
Brock Jones fought crime
while wearing the costume
and fended off Senator
Stivak's efforts to retrieve it. He
died in his adopted hometown of
Clairton, West Virginia while
battling the DIRE
WRAITHS. **DW**

TRAPSTER

FIRST APPEARANCE Strange Tales #104 (January 1963)
REAL NAME Peter Petruski
OCCUPATION Criminal **BASE** New York City
HEIGHT 5 ft 10 in **WEIGHT** 160 lbs **EYES** Brown **HAIR** Brown
SPECIAL POWERS/ABILITIES Carries assorted weapons at all
times, most of them applications of his paste-formula.

Chemist Peter Petruski happened
upon a formula for a super-
strong, quick-hardening
adhesive. He constructed
a special handgun that
could project it without
clogging, and set out to
make his name among
the criminal fraternity
as Paste-Pot Pete.
However, not even a
name-change to the Trapster and an
alliance with the WIZARD, the
SANDMAN, and MEDUSA as the
FRIGHTFUL FOUR has brought him the
respect he craves. After the Tinkerer
upgraded his weapons for him, the
Trapster became far more dangerous and
he won a number of battles. He worked
with Hammerhead's criminals during
the Civil War (see pp. 84-5). **TB, MF**

TRAUMA

FIRST APPEARANCE Avengers: The Initiative #1 (March 2007)
REAL NAME Terrance Ward
OCCUPATION Adventurer **BASE** Camp Hammond
HEIGHT 5 ft 10 in **WEIGHT** 175 lbs
EYES Brown **HAIR** Black
SPECIAL POWERS/ABILITIES Can shape-shift into whatever a foe fears most.

Terrance joined The Fifty-State Initiative (*see pp. 118–9*) and became one of the first cadets to be trained at Camp Hammond. His power allows him to read someone's mind, discover their worst fear, and then morph into a physical manifestation of that fear. In early combat training, this ability resulted in tragedy, when Armory panicked upon seeing her worst fear and accidentally killed Michael VAN PATRICK. MVP's evil clone later killed Terrance, but Terrance revived in his coffin. The source of his powers is the fact that his real father is secretly NIGHTMARE. Terrance now serves as a counsellor at Camp Hammond. **MF**

TRIATHLON

FIRST APPEARANCE Avengers Vol. 3 #8 (September 1998)
REAL NAME Delroy Garrett Jr.
OCCUPATION Adventurer **BASE** New York City
HEIGHT 6 ft 3 in **WEIGHT** 200 lbs **EYES** Brown **HAIR** Brown
SPECIAL POWERS/ABILITIES Garrett has superhuman strength, speed, and agility three times greater than the human peak, is fast enough to dodge bullets, and can identify hidden Skrulls.

Former Olympic sprinter Delroy Garrett Jr. joined the Triune Understanding movement, and its leader, Jonathan Tremont, merged the energy shard of 3-D MAN into him, giving him his powers. As Triathlon, Garrett joined the AVENGERS and fought Tremont, who had betrayed his cause. During the Civil War, Garrett sided with CAPTAIN AMERICA. He later joined the Fifty State Initiative, changing his name to 3-D Man, and was assigned to the Hawaii team, the Point Men. During the Secret Invasion he found he could see SKRULLS, and joined the Skrull Kill Krew. **DW, MF**

TRITON

FIRST APPEARANCE Fantastic Four #45 (December 1965)
REAL NAME Unrevealed
OCCUPATION Scout **BASE** Washington, D.C.
HEIGHT 6 ft 1 in **WEIGHT** 210 lbs **EYES** Green **HAIR** None
SPECIAL POWERS/ABILITIES Can breathe underwater but cannot survive on land without special equipment. Has superhuman strength and other physical adaptations for undersea living.

Triton is a member of the royal family of the INHUMANS, a genetic offshoot of the human race. The son of the Inhuman priest and philosopher Mander and his biologist mother Azur, Triton was exposed to mutagenic Terrigen Mist when a year old. The resulting mutations adapted him to live and breathe underwater. Along with other members of the royal family, Triton was banished when MAXIMUS first usurped the throne. While in exile, Triton first encountered and fought the FANTASTIC FOUR. Since then, however, Triton has become the ally of the Fantastic Four and Prince NAMOR. **PS**

TRAVELLER, JUDAS

FIRST APPEARANCE Web of Spider-Man #117 (October 1994)
REAL NAME Dr. Judas Traveller
OCCUPATION Adventurer **BASE** Currently unknown
HEIGHT 6 ft 7 in **WEIGHT** 245 lbs **EYES** Blue (pupils turn red when he uses his powers) **HAIR** White
SPECIAL POWERS/ABILITIES Possesses limited psionic powers and the mutant ability to alter people's perceptions of reality.

Famous criminal psychologist Dr. Judas Traveller was lecturing in Europe when he became aware of the Brotherhood of SCRIERS, a secret criminal organization. The Scriers sent an assassin to inject Traveller with a fatal drug. Instead of killing him, the drug triggered Traveller's mutant abilities and he suffered a nervous breakdown. The Scriers supervised his recovery and assigned four agents—Mr. Nacht, Medea, Boone, Chakra and a Scrier—to watch over him 24 hours a day. After SPIDER-MAN freed him from the Scriers' control, Traveller went into hiding. **TD**

TURBO

Mickey Musashi never wanted to be a hero. In fact the journalism student thought that being a Super Hero was a ridiculous notion…until she came across the Turbo suit. This remarkable piece of equipment was created by a human scientist under the orders of the DIRE WRAITHS. When the suit's inventor learned that the suit was to be used for evil purposes, he gave it to a man named Brock Jones, who donned it to fight crime as the hero TORPEDO.
Eventually, the Wraiths found and killed Brock Jones, and the suit passed to Brock's cousin Mike Jeffries, who shared it with Musashi. As it turned out, the suit worked better for her than for Jeffries and she reluctantly became the hero known as Turbo.
While teamed with the NEW WARRIORS team, Turbo battled the Dire Wraiths, as well as the criminal team known as Heavy Mettle.
Musashi quit life as a hero and pursued her journalism career, also setting up a group called Excelsior to dissuade super-powered teenagers from risking their lives as heroes. She continues to date one member of the group—DARKHAWK—although Excelsior has since disbanded **MT, MF**

FACTFILE

REAL NAME Michiko "Mickey" Musashi
OCCUPATION Adventurer, journalist
BASE Mobile

HEIGHT 5 ft 7 in
WEIGHT 125 lbs
EYES Brown
HAIR Black

FIRST APPEARANCE New Warriors #28 (October 1992)

TURBO

POWERS Turbo's suit is fitted with jet turbines. It allows Turbo to fly faster than a commercial jet, and the powerful turbines on her wrists allow her to deliver turbine-powered hyper-punches. The suit can also fire energy bursts, and its visor has telescopic sights.

TURNER D. CENTURY

FIRST APPEARANCE Spider-Woman #33 (December 1980)

REAL NAME Clifford F. Michaels

OCCUPATION Former vigilante and reformer

BASE New York City, Mobile, New York State

HEIGHT 6 ft 1 in   WEIGHT 185 lbs   EYES Blue   HAIR Black

SPECIAL POWERS/ABILITIES Extensive engineering expertise; carries umbrella that doubles as flame-thrower; rides flying bike.

The wealthy Morgan MacNeil Hardy adopted Clifford Michaels and sealed him away from the world for decades. When he finally emerged, he hated what he saw as the terrible moral state of the world. Calling himself Turner D. Century, he went on an increasingly militant crime spree to protest this decline. During a clash with Spider-Woman, Hardy died in a fire. Michaels hoped to avenge him, but the Scourge killed him first. Later, the super villain ARNIM ZOLA made a clone of Michaels, but it has since died, too. **TB, MF**

TYPHOID MARY

FIRST APPEARANCE Daredevil Vol. 1 #254 (May 1988)

REAL NAME Mary (last name possibly Mezinis or Walker)

OCCUPATION Criminal   BASE New York City

HEIGHT 5 ft 10 in   WEIGHT 140 lbs   EYES Brown   HAIR Brown

SPECIAL POWERS/ABILITIES Telekinesis, pyrokinesis, and also limited hypnotic ability; a skilled hand-to-hand combatant and expert with various bladed weapons.

Childhood abuse caused Mary to develop a disassociative identity disorder, giving her three distinct personalities: timid Mary, lustful Typhoid, and vicious Bloody Mary. Through therapy, a fourth personality has sometimes emerged that is a stable combination of all three. Typhoid Mary worked as an assassin for the KINGPIN, and played a cruel game with DAREDEVIL by charming him as Mary and tormenting him as Typhoid. Many times she has attempted to leave her criminal past behind her, but her Typhoid identity always reasserts itself. She recently escaped from the Raft prison. **DW**

TYRANT

FIRST APPEARANCE Silver Surfer Vol. 3 #81 (June 1993)

REAL NAME Unrevealed

OCCUPATION Conqueror of Worlds

BASE Star-Traveling Fortress

HEIGHT 29 ft   WEIGHT 20 tons   EYES Red   HAIR None

SPECIAL POWERS/ABILITIES Virtually unlimited cosmic power on a par with Galactus.

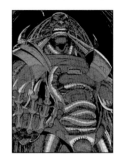

Created by GALACTUS billions of years ago, Tyrant draws his power from living worlds, and thus loses energy each time a planet is consumed by Galactus. Driven by a lust for power, Tyrant enslaved entire civilizations and protected himself with a robot army. Among the few who successfully opposed him were the women warriors of the Spinsterhood. In the modern era, Tyrant nearly succeeded in killing Galactus until Galactus' herald Morg unleashed the unstoppable energies of the Ultimate Nullifier. Tyrant and Galactus both vanished, though Galactus has since returned. **DW**

TYRANNUS

THOUGH I WAS BANISHED TO THE CENTER OF EARTH CENTURIES AGO BY THE ACCURSED MERLIN THE MAGICIAN, THIS MAGIC ELIXIR HAS KEPT ME ALIVE AND YOUNG ALL THESE YEARS-- WHILE I PLANNED MY REVENGE UPON MAN KIND!

TYRANNUS DRINKS THE POTION! GREAT IS TYRANNUS! BOW DOWN TO THE ALL POWERFUL TYRANNUS!

Tyrannus gulps a goblet of the Fountain of Youth.

Romulus Augustulus, better known as Tyrannus, served as the last emperor of the Roman Empire, until his defeat by the forces of King Arthur PENDRAGON in the 6th century. MERLIN the Magician banished Tyrannus by teleporting him to the underground world of Subterranea. There the would-be despot discovered the Fountain of Youth and ruled the Subterraneans, who took the name Tyrannoids.

In the modern era, Tyrannus launched a war against the MOLE MAN for control of Subterranea, and became a frequent foe of the HULK. He incurred the green giant's wrath by accidentally kidnapping his girlfriend, Betty Ross (see BANNER, Betty).

Tyrannus journeyed to the fabled city of El Dorado and used the city's Sacred Flame of Life in a bid to take over the world. Reduced to a disembodied spirit after a failed attempt to merge with the Flame of Life, Tyrannus briefly inhabited the ABOMINATION before winning back his original body. Tyrannus allied with the AVENGERS to defeat the Deviant army that had invaded Subterranea, but the Tyrannoids later turned on their master. His current fate is unknown. **DW**

FACTFILE

REAL NAME
Romulus Augustulus

OCCUPATION
Would-be conqueror

BASE
Subterranea

HEIGHT 6 ft 2 in

WEIGHT 225 lbs

EYES Light brown

HAIR Blond

FIRST APPEARANCE
Incredible Hulk Vol. 1 #5
(January 1963)

Psychic powers including mind-control, telepathy, and the ability to drain life energy. The Fountain of Youth provides Tyrannus with immortality, giving him plenty of time for devising ways to conquer the surface world.

TYRANNUS

POWERS

Tyrannus's planned invasion of the surface world was smashed by Hulk.

HULK WANTS IT BACK!

U

UATU, THE WATCHER

FIRST APPEARANCE Fantastic Four #13 (April 1963)

REAL NAME Uatu **OCCUPATION** Observer

BASE Mobile; New York State **HEIGHT** Variable

WEIGHT Variable **EYES** No visible irises **HAIR** None

SPECIAL POWERS/ABILITIES Virtually immortal; has superhuman intelligence, is telepathic and can teleport from the Earth to the Moon.

U-GO GIRL

FIRST APPEARANCE X-Force #116 (July 2001)

REAL NAME Edith ("Edie") Constance Sawyer

OCCUPATION Adventurer **BASE** Los Angeles

HEIGHT 5 ft 7 in **WEIGHT** 135 lbs

EYES Green **HAIR** Red

SPECIAL POWERS/ABILITIES Teleportation, which makes her narcoleptic.

ULTRAGIRL

FIRST APPEARANCE Ultra Girl #1 (November 1996)

REAL NAME Tsu-Zana (Suzy Sherman)

OCCUPATION Adventurer **BASE** Camp Hammond

HEIGHT 5 ft 6 in **WEIGHT** 233 lbs **EYES** Blue **HAIR** Blonde

SPECIAL POWERS/ABILITIES Flight, superhuman strength, speed, and durability, healing factor, and ability to see energy auras.

Self-appointed observers of the universe, the WATCHERS vowed never to interfere in the affairs of others. As the Watcher responsible for Earth and its solar system, Uatu has broken this rule several times since encountering the FANTASTIC FOUR. His most significant intervention in human affairs came just before Earth's first visit from GALACTUS and the SILVER SURFER, when he warned the Fantastic Four of the impending alien threat. Cautioned for his repeated interference, Uatu was stripped of his role as Watcher but he has since been reinstated. **AD**

Born in the Midwest, Edie became pregnant at 15 and gave the baby up to her parents to adopt. When she saw her daughter's face, she reflexively teleported away to LA, only to return soon after. Years later, the blue-skinned young woman returned to LA and joined X-FORCE. After saving her teammate ORPHAN from his suicidal tendencies, she became romantically involved with him. The team's relationship with its owners eventually broke down, and they hired the Bush Rangers to kill them all. Edie died at their hands. When Orphan died much later, they finally reunited in the afterlife. **MF**

Suzy thought she was a pretty, but normal, teen. She discovered her powers while on a modeling shoot when a SENTINEL attacked her. Soon afterward, she joined the NEW WARRIORS, at which point her best friend revealed to Suzy that she was actually a KREE destined to revive her people's empire. Suzy joined CAPTAIN AMERICA's side during the Civil War (*see* pp. 84–5). After his death, she registered with the US government and joined The Fifty-State Initiative (*see* pp. 118–9). For a short while, she wore Ms. Marvel's original costume, but she surrendered it to Norman Osborn (*see* GREEN GOBLIN), who landed the rights to the name and outfit. **MF**

U-FOES

FACTFILE

KEY MEMBERS

IRONCLAD
Enhanced strength, iron-hard skin, can increase his mass

VAPOR
Transforms into various gases

VECTOR
Can repel objects away from him at great speed

X-Ray
Flight, can project hard radiation, impervious to physical damage while in energy form

BASE
Brooklyn, New York; Stark Tower New York

FIRST APPEARANCE
Incredible Hulk Vol. 2 #254 (December 1980)

Using their abilities to find employment as mercenaries, the U-Foes have clashed with Spider-Man and others in their quest for money and power.

Hoping to duplicate the process by which the FANTASTIC FOUR had gained their powers, millionaire Simon Utrecht enlisted rocket pilot Mike Steel, engineer Jimmy Darnell, and technical specialist Ann Darnell to accompany him into space. The experiment worked, and the cosmic radiation they were exposed to gave each a unique power: Steel became a metal-coated being, Jimmy gained control over radiation, his sister Ann converted into a gaseous state, and Utrecht himself discovered that he could repel objects.

As IRONCLAD, VAPOR, X-RAY, and VECTOR, the four new superhumans formed a group they called the U-Foes. They first unleashed their powers on Bruce Banner, whom they blamed for grounding their test flight prematurely, but were unable to control their new powers and lost badly once Banner transformed into the HULK. Over time, the U-Foes became more disciplined and, after honing their powers, found work as professional mercenaries. During the Civil War (*see* pp.84–5), they worked for the THUNDERBOLTS Army. They have since joined the HOOD's new gang. **DW, MF**

CHARACTER KEY
1 Vector
2 Ironclad
3 X-Ray
4 Vapor

ULTRAFORCE

On Earth-93060, superpowered people were known as Ultras. The members of Ultraforce banded together to protect their Earth from evil Ultras and other threats. Hardcase and Contrary brought together the initial members of the team—which included them and Ghoul, Pixx, Prime, Prototype, and Topaz—and received sanctioning from the US government. Contrary outfitted them with technology from the subterranean Fire People so that they could try to keep them from invading the surface world.

Later, the BLACK KNIGHT arrived from Earth-616 (the main Marvel universe) and joined the team. They also teamed up with the AVENGERS and fought against SERSI of the ETERNALS. During the Black September event, they served as LOKI's champions in a contest with the GRANDMASTER. **MF**

FACTFILE

KEY MEMBERS
BLACK KNIGHT Wields the Ebony Blade; rides winged horse.
CONTRARY Master manipulator.
GHOUL Undead man who can speak with the dead.
HARDCASE Nanotech man with superhuman senses and strength.
PIXX Technological genius who can project illusions.
PROTOTYPE Energy blasts and flight; armor grants superstrength.
SIREN Superstrength; control over liquids.
TOPAZ Superstrong; fires energy blasts from staff.
BASE
Headless Cross, Arkansas
FIRST APPEARANCE
Ultraforce #0 (June 1994)

CHARACTER KEY
1 Prime **2** Hardcase
3 Topaz **4** Contrary
5 Prototype **6** Ghoul
7 Pixx

◎ **ULTRON** *see page 346*

ULTRON see page 346

UNICORN

FIRST APPEARANCE Tales of Suspense #56 (August 1964)
REAL NAME Milos Masaryk
OCCUPATION Intelligence agent, later criminal **BASE** Mobile
HEIGHT 6 ft 2 in **WEIGHT** 220 lbs **EYES** Blue **HAIR** Red
SPECIAL POWERS/ABILITIES Possesses superhuman strength and durability; wears helmet with "power horn" that can project concussive energy blasts, lasers, and microwaves; wears rocket belt permitting flight.

A Russian intelligence agent, Milos Masaryk guarded Professor Anton Vanko's lab. Vanko invented the harness, helmet, and "power horn" that Masaryk wore as the Unicorn. While spying on Stark Industries, the Unicorn first battled his longtime enemy IRON MAN. The Unicorn underwent treatment that endowed him with superhuman strength but caused rapid cellular deterioration. The BEYONDER revived him after his death, however, and the Unicorn fought for the THUNDERBOLTS during the Civil War. **PS, MF**

UMAR

The sister of the dreaded DORMAMMU and a member of the mystical Faltine race, Umar was exiled along with her brother from their home dimension, and sought sanctuary within the Dark Dimension. But Dormammu, who had magically altered himself so as to become a being of pure energy, eventually conquered the Dark Dimension, and banished Umar, whom he saw as the only threat to his power base. With Dormammu's defeat at the hands of DOCTOR STRANGE, Umar was released from imprisonment, and herself battled Strange, both in order to avenge her brother and in order to expand her power base. In the years that have followed, Umar has remained a constant threat to Doctor Strange and to Earth, whether allied with Dormammu or on her own, and despite the fact that her daughter, CLEA, has become Strange's disciple in the mystic arts. **TB**

FACTFILE

REAL NAME
Umar
OCCUPATION
Sorceress
BASE
Dark Dimension

HEIGHT Unknown
WEIGHT Unknown
EYES Black
HAIR Black

FIRST APPEARANCE
Strange Tales #150 (November 1966)

POWERS

Umar possesses extensive mystic knowledge, which allows her to cast powerful spells for a variety of purposes.

Stepping into the void left by the defeat of her brother Dormammu, Umar often attempted to bring about Doctor Strange's downfall.

ULTRON

Robot with an evil mind of its own

POWERS

Enhanced strength, near-invulnerability, energy projection; and flight; uses encephalo-ray to hypnotize others or put them into a coma.

Ultron assembled a team of Masters of Evil to combat the Avengers.

The Vision and Ultron had a shared history, but still found themselves to be bitter enemies.

Henry Pym built Ultron as a robot servant programmed with his own brain patterns. Ultron rebelled against his maker, escaping to plot the extermination of all humanity. Engineering a succession of upgraded bodies for himself, he emerged as Ultron-5 to fight Pym's Avengers teammates.

BODYHOPPING

By posing as the villainous Crimson Cowl, Ultron assembled a second grouping of the Masters of Evil. He then created the android Vision, using a duplicate body from the original Human Torch and brainwave patterns from Wonder Man. Ironically, just like Ultron himself, the Vision rebelled against his creator and defected to the Avengers, setting the pattern for most of Ultron's subsequent creations.

Ultron incorporated indestructible adamantium into his frame beginning with the Ultron-6 body. Ultron-7 was a gargantuan construct, while Ultron-8 created a robotic "wife," Jocasta.

Ultron-9 perished in a vat of molten adamantium, and Machine Man deactivated Ultron-10. Ultron-11 participated in the Beyonder's Secret Wars. Ultron-12, initially a member of the Lethal Legion, repented and tried to atone for his criminal past until destroyed by Ultron-11. Doctor Doom programmed Ultron-13 with all previous personalities running simultaneously, making it easy for Daredevil to beat the addled robot. Ultron-14 created a new mate called Alkhema, though the two robots could not agree on their differing approaches to genocide.

MULTIPLYING MACHINES

Ultron-15 built hundreds of duplicates and conquered the eastern European country of Slorenia, meeting defeat when Hank Pym exposed him to metal-disintegrating vibranium. Hidden "Ultron Imperative" programming within Alkhema led to Ultron's return, and, after a battle, Ultron affixed his decapitated head to a suit of Iron Man's armor. Several Ultron robots appeared during the Avengers Disassembled event, though these may have been projections by the Scarlet Witch. Recently, Ultron—or at least one version of him—led the Phalanx in an attempt to conquer the universe (see Annihilation pp. 30-31). **DW, MF**

SKRAWWK! DA-DA...WANT DA-DA--- SKRAWWK!

...A CRUDE, YET WORKABLE ROBOT... A FALTERING STEP ON THE PATH TO SYNTHETIC LIFE!

WH..? IT'S SPEAK-ING...MOVING!

BUT, I HAVEN'T EVEN TURNED IT ON YET...!

Ultron returned as leader of the Phalanx, threatening the entire universe.

UNION JACK

POWERS

UNION JACK

FACTFILE

REAL NAME
Joseph Chapman

OCCUPATION
Adventurer

BASE
Great Britain

HEIGHT 6 ft
WEIGHT 195 lbs
EYES Brown
HAIR Light brown

FIRST APPEARANCE
Captain America Vol. 1 #253
(January 1980)

Enhanced strength and speed; wears a bulletproof costume, carries a variety of guns, and a silver dagger.

The original Union Jack, Lord James Falsworth, fought for the British during World War I as a member of the heroic team Freedom's Five. After an injury, he was succeeded as Union Jack by his son, Brian (formerly known as the Destroyer), while his daughter Jacqueline went on to become SPITFIRE. Both heroes joined the World War II-era Invaders, where they fought alongside CAPTAIN AMERICA and NAMOR the Sub-Mariner; Brian also founded the heroic post-war V-Battalion.

The third Union Jack is Joey Chapman, who took up the mantle when Spitfire's son, Kenneth Crichton, refused to follow in his uncle's footsteps. Chapman joined the Knights of Pendragon and received superhuman abilities through possession of the Pendragon spirit. As Union Jack, Chapman has served with the most recent Invaders team. **DW**

Union Jack is a member of the New Invaders. The team's proactive role in ending world threats puts them at odds with traditional heroes, including Captain America's Avengers.

URICH, BEN

FIRST APPEARANCE *Daredevil* #153 (July 1978)
REAL NAME Benjamin Urich
OCCUPATION Reporter for the *Daily Bugle*
BASE New York City
HEIGHT 5 ft 9 in **WEIGHT** 140 lbs **EYES** Brown **HAIR** Gray
SPECIAL POWERS/ABILITIES None; a skilled and responsible investigative journalist.

Ben Urich started his journalism career as a copy boy at the *Daily Bugle*. He worked his way up to become a reporter. Urich began gathering information about DAREDEVIL, and soon learned the hero's true identity and personal history. He decided to keep Daredevil's secret, though, and the two became good friends. He recently left the *Bugle* to start up a new newspaper called *Front Line*. Sadly, his wife died during the Secret Invasion (*see* pp. 326-7). **MT, MF**

UNUS

FIRST APPEARANCE *X-Men* #8 (November 1964)
REAL NAME Angelo Unuscione
OCCUPATION Professional criminal **BASE** Mobile
HEIGHT 6 ft 1 in **WEIGHT** 220 lbs
EYES Blue **HAIR** Black
SPECIAL POWERS/ABILITIES Generates an impenetrable force field around body; redoubtable hand-to-hand combatant.

Unus was invited to join the BROTHERHOOD OF EVIL MUTANTS if he could defeat an X-Man. Fighting BEAST, Unus was beaten when his opponent employed a device to magnify Unus' force field out of his control. He disappeared for years and was thought dead until he turned up in Genosha. He lost his powers on M-Day, but QUICKSILVER returned them to him. They became unstable, though, and he suffocated to death in his own force field. **AD, MF**

UPSTARTS

FIRST APPEARANCE *Uncanny X-Men* Vol. 1 #281 (October 1991)
FORMER MEMBERS AND POWERS

Gamesmaster Telepath who reads billions of minds simultaneously [1].
Siena Blaze Controlled the Earth's electromagnetic field [2].
Shinobi Shaw Can change his body from rock-solid to intangible [3].
Fabian Cortez Could overload the abilities of other mutants [4].
Trevor Fitzroy Drained victims' life energy to control time [5].
Andrea and Andreas von Strucker (Fenris Twins) Could project energy blasts when in contact with one another [6] and [7].
Graydon Creed Wore strength-boosting battle armor [8].

Looking for a new challenge, the GAMESMASTER gathered a group of young humans and mutants to compete in a murderous game. The contestants, who called themselves the Upstarts, earned points if they killed powerful targets such as members of the X-MEN, the NEW MUTANTS, or the HELLFIRE CLUB. The Upstarts launched a number of high-profile hits during their short career, and often fought each other. Eventually many members died, and the survivors, bored with the sport, disbanded. **DW**

U.S. AGENT

FIRST APPEARANCE *Captain America* #323 (November 1986)
REAL NAME John F. Walker **OCCUPATION** adventurer; government agent **BASE** Washington, D.C.
HEIGHT 6 ft 4 in **WEIGHT** 270 lbs **EYES** Blue **HAIR** Blond
SPECIAL POWERS/ABILITIES Superhuman strength and stamina; carries a shield made of Vibranium, which can absorb the vibrations from concussive forces directed against it.

Walker joined the military to honor the memory of his brother, who died in Vietnam. After his discharge, he struck a deal with the POWER BROKER for superhuman strength and then became the Super-Patriot. Later, Walker temporarily replaced Steve Rogers as CAPTAIN AMERICA. When Rogers reclaimed his shield, Walker changed to the U.S. Agent instead. He worked with the WEST COAST AVENGERS, FORCE WORKS, the Jury (a team developed to battle the THUNDERBOLTS), and the new INVADERS. During the Civil War (*see* pp. 84-5), he was assigned to the new OMEGA FLIGHT. He currently serves with Hank PYM's renegade AVENGERS. **TD, MF**

FACTFILE

REAL NAME
Brunnhilde

OCCUPATION
Adventurer, former Chooser of the Slain

BASE
Asgard

HEIGHT 6 ft 3 ins
WEIGHT 475 lbs
EYES Blue
HAIR Blonde

FIRST APPEARANCE
Avengers Vol. 1 #87
(April 1971)

POWERS

Valkyrie has enhanced strength, longevity, and stamina; can perceive the onset of death, can teleport to the realm of the dead.

The Defenders were Valkyrie's extended family. As a core member, she helped the team fight off countless threats to the planet.

VALKYRIE

Wielding a mystical sword, Valkyrie deflects an energy attack.

Odin, ruler of Asgard (see GODS OF ASGARD), made Brunnhilde the leader of the Valkyrior, giving her the task of bringing worthy warriors from among the slain to Valhalla. The ENCHANTRESS trapped her spirit within a crystal and kept it there for centuries, using it to invest herself and others with Valkyrie powers. In modern times, the Enchantress also assumed Brunnhilde's form to deceive the AVENGERS. She gave the powers of Valkyrie to the socialite Samantha Parrington, and later to Barbara Norriss, intending to use them as pawns. However, Brunnhilde eventually succeeded in restoring her consciousness into Norriss' body, and won back her original body. As Valkyrie, Brunnhilde joined the DEFENDERS and seemingly sacrificed her life to defeat the evil entity the Dragon of the Moon. She returned by inhabiting new host bodies, but perished in the events surrounding Ragnarok.

The Samantha Parrington version of Valkyrie has regained her powers and has continued her adventuring career. During the Civil War (see pp. 85-5) she registered with the US government and became part of the Fifty State Initiative (see pp.118–9).
DW, MF

VAMP

FIRST APPEARANCE Captain America #217 (January 1978)
REAL NAME Unrevealed
OCCUPATION Secret agent **BASE** Mobile
HEIGHT 5 ft 2 in **WEIGHT** 125 lbs **EYES** Blue **HAIR** Black
SPECIAL POWERS/ABILITIES A trained secret agent, the Vamp wore an absorbo-belt that allowed her to duplicate the strength and physical skills of anyone around her.

Due to her excellent fighting skills, the woman known as the Vamp was selected to become one of the first Super-Agents of SHIELD. Unfortunately, the Vamp was a double-agent, secretly working for the criminal Corporation, and assigned to infiltrate SHIELD. She had also been subjected to a genetic modification, which allowed her to transform into a psionically-powered creature called Animus.

Eventually, the Vamp's true loyalties were exposed and she was incarcerated. She subsequently became yet another victim of the notorious serial killer of Super Villains the SCOURGE OF THE UNDERWORLD. **TD**

VANGUARD

FIRST APPEARANCE Iron Man #109 (April 1978)
REAL NAME Nicolai Krylenko
OCCUPATION Adventurer **BASE** Belarus
HEIGHT 6 ft 3 in **WEIGHT** 230 lbs **EYES** Blue **HAIR** Red
SPECIAL POWERS/ABILITIES Generates force field that repels most energy directed at him; also uses hammer and sickle to redirect the repelled energy.

Born in the Soviet Union, Nicolai Krylenko lived a life that was marked by deception and duplicity right from the start. Born with mutant powers, he and his twin sister Laynia were adopted by the state after their mother died in childbirth. Their father, a nuclear physicist, was told they were stillborn. Raised by the Soviet machine to be a counterweight to the increasingly prolific US mutants, Nicolai and Laynia became members of the state sponsored super-team, the Super-Soldiers. Inevitably, they learned the truth about their background and since then Nicolai has pursued more semi-autonomous roles. He is currently a member of superteam, the Winter Guard. **AD**

VAN HELSING, RACHEL

FIRST APPEARANCE Tomb of Dracula #3 (July 1972)
REAL NAME Rachel Van Helsing
OCCUPATION Vampire slayer **BASE** London, England
HEIGHT 5 ft 8 in **WEIGHT** 135 lbs **EYES** Blue **HAIR** Blonde
SPECIAL POWERS/ABILITIES Expert vampire slayer whose preferred weapon was the crossbow; was also a parapsychologist and anthropologist.

Rachel Van Helsing was the descendant of Dr. Abraham Van Helsing, the 19th century nemesis of DRACULA. As a child she saw Dracula murder her parents to get back at Dr. Van Helsing. Rachel was raised by another of Dracula's enemies, Quincy HARKER. She became the most formidable member of his band of vampire slayers, frequently battling Dracula. After a troubled romance with her teammate Frank DRAKE, Rachel moved to New York State, where Dracula finally turned her into a vampiress. On her request, Wolverine impaled her through the heart, and she died peacefully. **PS**

VAN PATRICK

Heroes die, but their clones live on

MVP's short career ended while saving his friend Cloud 9.

Michael Van Patrick was the most gifted and well-rounded athlete in his hometown of Liberty, Kentucky. However, when word got out that his great-grandfather had been Dr. Abraham Erskine, the creator of the Super-Solider Serum, he was suspected of having superpowers, and all his records were taken away. In truth, Michael's father Brian had simply used Erskine's studies to train his son to perfection from birth.

THE INITIATIVE

After the Civil War (*see* pp. 84-5) Vance Astrovik (*see* MARVEL BOY) recruited Van Patrick to join the Fifty State Initiative (*see* pp. 118-9). As MVP, Van Patrick reported for training at Camp Hammond in Connecticut, under the command of GAUNTLET. Sadly, MVP was killed during his first combat exercise. After TRAUMA terrified ARMORY by morphing into a giant spider, she fired her Tactigon in panic. MVP rescued CLOUD 9 from a stray blast, but the next shot killed him.

COVER-UPS AND CLONES

Henry Peter GYRICH ordered MVP's killing covered up and the Tactigon removed from Armory. Soon after, Baron Von Blitzschlag set to work making his first clone of MVP, an exact duplicate sent back to Kentucky to take the place of the original. Von Blitzschlag quickly created three more clones, giving them copies of the "Iron Spider" armor that IRON MAN made for Spider-Man. As the SCARLET SPIDERS, the three separated out MVP's name, calling themselves Michael, Van, and Patrick.

A CLONE TOO FAR

KIA wears the Tactigon, the alien weapon that killed MVP.

Delighted with the success of the Scarlet Spiders, Von Blitzschlag created another clone he called Ian, after the original MVP's middle name. In addition to MVP's memories, he gave the clone Armory's memories of the Tactigon and then attached the device to Ian. The feedback drove Ian insane. Realizing he was not the original MVP, he called himself KIA and then set out to kill everyone involved in MVP's death and cover-up. During this, he injured many Initiative heroes and murdered the clone Van and several SHIELD agents.

To defeat him, the Initiative trainees found the original MVP clone, hoping to transfer his mind into a helmet and then copy it into MVP, but at the cost of wiping the first clone's mind. The first clone used the helmet to wipe KIA's mind instead.

Afterward, Michael and Patrick join the NEW WARRIORS. Michael died while battling Ragnarok, an insane clone of THOR. Distraught, Patrick revealed his identity to the media, exposing the cover-up over MVP's death. **MF**

KIA was born bent on revenge for MVP's death.

FACTFILE

REAL NAME
Michael Ian Van Patrick

OCCUPATION
Adventurer

BASE
Camp Hammond, Connecticut

HEIGHT 6 ft
WEIGHT 200 lbs
EYES Blue
HAIR Brown

FIRST APPEARANCE
Avengers: The Initiative #1
(April 2007)

VAN PATRICK

POWERS

MVP is a gifted athlete in top physical condition, with perfect DNA but without any superhuman powers.

ESSENTIAL STORYLINES
• *Avengers: The Initiative #1* MVP is introduced and killed, all in a single issue.
• *Avengers: The Initiative #7* The Scarlet Spiders make their public debut and display their independence by helping Spider-Man.
• *Avengers: The Initiative #8–11* KIA is created and nearly destroys the Initiative.

VANISHER

FIRST APPEARANCE Uncanny X-Men Vol. 1 #2 (November 1963)
REAL NAME Telford Porter
OCCUPATION Professional criminal **BASE** New York City
HEIGHT 5 ft 5 in **WEIGHT** 175 lbs
EYES Green **HAIR** None
SPECIAL POWERS/ABILITIES Mutant ability to teleport himself and others by accessing the Darkforce dimension.

The Vanisher tried to extort money from the US government by stealing defense plans until the original X-Men foiled him. After that, he mentored a gang called the Fallen Angels. The being called Darkling later took control of the Vanisher and set him against the New Warriors. The Vanisher then joined a new team of Enforcers. After Spider-Man defeated them, he moved to South America and set up an operation selling Mutant Growth Hormone. He survived M-Day with his powers, and was last seen working for X-Force under duress. **DW, MF**

VARNAE

FIRST APPEARANCE Bizarre Adventures #33 (December 1982)
REAL NAME Varnae
OCCUPATION Lord of Earth's Vampires **BASE** Mobile
HEIGHT 10 ft **WEIGHT** 475 lbs **EYES** Red **HAIR** Green
SPECIAL POWERS/ABILITIES Near-immortality, enhanced strength, ability to grow in size and become a wolf, a bat, or a cloud of mist; can telepathically influence and vampirize others.

Varnae became the first vampire in the days of ancient Atlantis, when the Darkholders who worshipped the Elder God CHTHON subjected him to anti-death experiments. Over the millennia Varnae battled the Catholic Church's Montesi lineage, to prevent them from discovering the Montesi Formula that would destroy all vampires. In the year 1459, Varnae died and passed his title as Lord of the Vampires to Dracula. Through sorcerous incantations, Varnae returned in the modern era, and battled enemies including DOCTOR STRANGE and BLADE. Varnae is also responsible for reversing the effects of the Montesi Formula, which had temporarily eradicated Earth's vampires. **DW**

VENGEANCE

FIRST APPEARANCE Ghost Rider Vol. 2 #21 (December 1976)
REAL NAME Michael Badilino **OCCUPATION** Detective
BASE New York City **HEIGHT** (Badilino) 5 ft 10 ins, (Vengeance) 6 ft 6 ins **WEIGHT** (Badilino) 195 lbs, (Vengeance) 235 lbs
EYES Green **HAIR** Black
SPECIAL POWERS/ABILITIES Can project cold fire that causes others physical pain; his penance stare causes mental anguish.

MEPHISTO tricked the GHOST RIDER into blasting detective Michael Badilino's father with hellfire. Unaware of Mephisto's involvement, Badilino made a deal with him to gain mystical powers and destroy the Ghost Rider. Now known as Vengeance, he learned the truth, made peace with the Ghost Rider, and joined the Midnight Sons to battle demons like Mephisto. Vengeance was captured by Badilino's old enemy Anthony Hellgate, and though freed by the Ghost Rider he was never the same. Vengeance eventually appeared to destroy himself in a huge explosion, but seemingly returned to help Ghost Rider battle the demon known as Blackheart. **TB**

VAPOR

FIRST APPEARANCE The Incredible Hulk #254 (December 1980)
REAL NAME Ann Darnell **OCCUPATION** Life support technologist turned criminal **BASE** Mobile
HEIGHT 5 ft 6 in **WEIGHT** (in human form) 122 lbs
EYES (in human form) Green, (as Vapor) White **HAIR** Auburn
SPECIAL POWERS/ABILITIES Can transform herself into any kind of gas; can resume her original human form for brief periods only.

Intent on acquiring superpowers like those of the Fantastic Four, millionaire industrialist Simon Utrecht built his own unshielded spaceship and sent it through the cosmic rays. His crew consisted of Ann Darnell, her brother Jimmy, and pilot Mike Steel. The radiation converted Ann Darnell's body into a gaseous state. She and her new now-powered companions became known as the U-Foes. They are longstanding enemies of the Hulk, and have also worked for other criminals, including the Leader and the Master. During the Civil War, she worked for the Thunderbolts Army, and afterward she and the U-Foes joined the Hood's mob. **PS, MF**

VARUA

FIRST APPEARANCE (unnamed) Thor Vol. I #300 (October 1980)
REAL NAME Mira **OCCUPATION** Pupil of the Celestials
BASE Celestial Mothership, previously Ruk Island
HEIGHT/WEIGHT/EYES Unrevealed **HAIR** Brown
SPECIAL POWERS/ABILITIES Posesses telepathy, teleportation, flight, and ability to generate the Blue Flame, which changes her and others into the Uni-Mind, a psionic entity.

Born in 1405 on Ruk Island, Mira began life as a priestess. In 1419 she was recruited into the YOUNG GODS by the goddesses of Earth's pantheons. Mira was taken to train in combat under Katos on the Celestial Mothership where she became Varua. After the Sea Witch had a prophetic dream, the CELESTIALS granted the Young Gods 3 days on earth to investigate evil threats. Varua was held captive by the Deviants who used a brain mine to make her help them reawaken GHAUR. Varua was forced by Ghaur to create a Uni-Mind with other prisoners to give its power to him. This was cut open by the BLACK KNIGHT, which set everyone free. Varua departed with Delta Force.

VENUS

FIRST APPEARANCE Venus #1 (August 1948)
REAL NAME Victoria Nutley Starr
OCCUPATION Adventurer **BASE** Washington, D.C.
HEIGHT 5 ft 6 in **WEIGHT** 280 lbs
EYES Blue **HAIR** Blonde
SPECIAL POWERS/ABILITIES Mesmerizing voice. Also, superhuman durability and immortality.

Venus was once a Siren (of the sort that once beckoned Odysseus to a watery death in Greek myth). When a magician in ancient times gave her a soul, she regretted her past actions and gave up her wicked ways. Wandering the world, she eventually forgot her past and believed herself to be the Greek goddess Venus reborn.

In the 1940s, she joined the G-Men, working with Jimmy WOO. When NAMORA told her the truth about herself, she fell into a deep depression, but Jimmy helped her work through this. She is now a member of his AGENTS OF ATLAS. **MF**

VENOM

The costume makes the villain

The symbiote flowed over Eddie Brock, viewing the suicidal journalist as a kindred spirit.

While SPIDER-MAN was on the BEYONDER's "Battleworld," he acquired a black costume, which turned out to be an alien being that bonded itself to him. Spider-Man rejected this alien symbiote, which then latched onto an ex-*Daily Globe* columnist Eddie Brock, transforming him into Venom.

THE ORIGINAL VENOM

A disgraced ex-reporter, Brock blamed Spider-Man for ruining his career by revealing Brock's error in identifying the wrong man as the Sin-Eater. Stricken with cancer, he was about to kill himself when the symbiote bonded with him and put his disease into remission. Angry at Spider-Man for spurning it, the symbiote urged Brock to take his revenge on Spider-Man, and the bonded pair set out to do just that. Armed with the knowledge of Spider-Man's secret identity—and being hidden from Spider-Man's spider-sense—Brock became one of his most dangerous foes. At times, however, the two declared a truce, and during such periods Brock sometimes worked as an antihero, killing those who would threaten innocents.

VENOM'S OFFSPRING

The Venom symbiote has reproduced a number of times, its children finding hosts of their own. This included Scream, CARNAGE and his spawn Toxin, plus Riot, Phage, Lasher, and Agony, who later combined to form Hybrid. When Brock's cancer returned, the symbiote wanted to leave him. Brock auctioned the creature off for $100 million dollars from gang lord Don Fortunato, who gave the suit to his son Angelo. Disgusted by Angelo's cowardice, the suit abandoned him in mid-air to die.

When Gargan attacked Brock, Brock turned into Anti-Venom.

ENTER THE SCORPION

The symbiote offered itself to Mac Gargan (the SCORPION), who eagerly accepted the creature's incredible powers. After a failed attempt to defeat Spider-Man with the Sinister Twelve, Gargan joined the THUNDERBOLTS during the CIVIL WAR (*see* pp. 84-5), helping them track down superpowered outlaws who refused to register with the US government.

With Gargan as its host, Venom becomes more violent and monstrous than ever, actually devouring some of his victims. When Gargan attacked Brock, however, the symbiote tried to return to Brock. Instead, Brock turned into ANTI-VENOM and nearly killed Gargan.

Gargan recovered and fought the SKRULLS during the SECRET INVASION (*see* pp. 326-7). Afterward, Norman Osborn (*see* GREEN GOBLIN) transferred Gargan from the Thunderbolts to his new AVENGERS. Administering a medicine that made the symbiote seem less monstrous again—at least temporarily—Osborn then had Gargan pose as Spider-Man on the new team. **MF**

ESSENTIAL STORYLINES
• *Amazing Spider-Man #299–300*
The first appearance of Eddie Brock as Venom.
• *Marvel Knights: Spider-Man #7–8* Brock auctions off the Venom symbiote to Angelo Fortunato for $100 million.
• *Marvel Knights: Spider-Man #9-12* Mac Gargan becomes the new Venom.

Venom saw himself as a protector of the innocent. However, he would kill criminals outright.

VENOM

FACTFILE

REAL NAME
MacDonald "Mac" Gargan

OCCUPATION
Assassin-for-hire

BASE
New York City

HEIGHT 6 ft 2 in
WEIGHT 220 lbs
EYES Brown
HAIR Brown

FIRST APPEARANCE
The Amazing Spider-Man #298
(March 1988)

POWERS

Venom possesses superhuman strength, speed, and agility. Like Spider-Man, his hands and feet can adhere to most surfaces. Can project web-like substance from his "costume."

VERANKE

FIRST APPEARANCE New Avengers #1 (January 2005) as Spider-Woman; New Avengers #40 (June 2008) as Veranke.
REAL NAME Veranke **OCCUPATION** Ruler
BASE Skrull empire **HEIGHT/WEIGHT/EYES /HAIR** Variable
SPECIAL POWERS/ABILITIES Shapeshifting, plus Spider-Woman's powers. Ruler of the Skrull empire.

As a SKRULL princess from Tyeranx 7, Veranke challenged King Dorrek for ignoring Skrull prophecies, and she was banished for her trouble. After GALACTUS devoured the Skrull homeworld and the Annihilation Wave (*see* pp. 30–1) destroyed most of the empire, Veranke was seen as a visionary and elevated to queen. She declared that Earth was to be the new Skrull homeworld and so launched the Secret Invasion (*see* pp. 326–7). As part of this, she replaced SPIDER-WOMAN just before the reformation of the AVENGERS. At the climax of the Secret Invasion, she was killed by Norman Osborn (*see* GREEN GOBLIN). **MF**

VERMIN

FIRST APPEARANCE Captain America #272 (August 1982)
REAL NAME Edward Whelan
OCCUPATION Unknown **BASE** Mobile
HEIGHT 6ft **WEIGHT** 220 lbs **EYES** Red **HAIR** Brown
SPECIAL POWERS/ABILITIES Superhuman strength and speed. Teeth and nails can cut through soft metals. Greatly enhanced sense of smell. Can command rats to attack an enemy.

Villains BARON ZEMO and Arnim ZOLA found Whelan living on the streets of Manhattan and genetically modified him into a rat-man. They sent him to kill CAPTAIN AMERICA, but he failed. He was unstable, and often turned on his masters. During the Civil War (*see* pp 84–5), he helped out both the THUNDERBOLTS and the HOOD. Recently, he battled the new KRAVEN THE HUNTER and even tangled with his old foe SPIDER-MAN, who was wearing a DAREDEVIL costume at the time. **MT, MF**

VIBRAXAS

FIRST APPEARANCE Fantastic Four Vol. 1 #390 (July 1994)
REAL NAME N'Kano
OCCUPATION Adventurer **BASE** Mobile
HEIGHT 5 ft 10 in **WEIGHT** 165 lbs
EYES Brown **HAIR** Brown
SPECIAL POWERS/ABILITIES Can generate intense vibratory force.

The young Wakandan N'Kano gained his powers when an experimental Vibrasurge project backfired, seemingly killing his mother. Taken in by the BLACK PANTHER, he traveled to America and became a member of the Fantastic Force under the name Vibraxas. When he accidentally murdered a gang member, Vibraxas went back to Wakanda to stand trial, but he was exonerated. After the Fantastic Force disbanded, Vibraxas found love with Queen Divine Justice, a member of the "Dora Milaje" who serve the Wakandan king as bodyguards and wives-in-training. **DW**

VERDUGO

FIRST APPEARANCE Incredible Hulk vol. 3, #36 (March 2002)
REAL NAME Sandra Verdugo
OCCUPATION Mercenary, Home Base operative **BASE** Mobile
HEIGHT 5 ft 8 in **WEIGHT** 122 lbs **EYES** Black **HAIR** Black
SPECIAL POWERS/ABILITIES Recipient of H-Section Programming: is able to recover from most injuries and revive from death; brilliant markswoman, athlete and hand-to-hand combatant.

A one-time member of the US Special Forces, Sandra Verdugo worked as a mercenary before becoming pregnant by DOC SAMSON. When Sandra's eight-year-old son was kidnapped, the clandestine organisation Home Base offered her a deal. Home Base would retrieve her son if Sandra would agree to become one of their operatives. Her mission would be to capture the HULK. Sandra agreed but it wasn't long before she turned on her new employers. With the help of Doc Samson and the Hulk, Sandra was reunited with her son just before Home Base's headquarters were destroyed. Mother and child are thought to have perished in the conflagration. **AD**

VERNARD, KRISTOFF

FIRST APPEARANCE Fantastic Four Vol. 1 #247 (October 1982)
REAL NAME Kristoff Vernard
OCCUPATION Kristoff Vernard **BASE** Latveria
HEIGHT 4 ft 11 in, (in suit) 6 ft 7 in **WEIGHT** 103 lbs, (in suit) 293 lbs
EYES Brown **HAIR** Brown
SPECIAL POWERS/ABILITIES Enhanced strength; damage resistance; ability to generate force fields or fire concussion beams.

Kristoff Vernard is believed by some to be the biological son of Nathaniel Richards, making him the half-brother of Reed Richards (MISTER FANTASTIC). After the death of Kristoff's mother in Latveria, DOCTOR DOOM discovered the boy and groomed him as his heir. When Doom appeared to have died, his Doombots brainwashed Kristoff into believing that he was Doom. Kristoff donned an armored suit and attacked the FANTASTIC FOUR, though his enemies eventually helped restore his true identity. Kristoff later teamed up with Nathaniel Richards to reclaim Latveria from usurpers. **DW**

VINDICATOR

FIRST APPEARANCE Uncanny X-Men #139 (November 1980)
REAL NAME Heather McNeil Hudson
OCCUPATION Member of Alpha Flight
BASE Tamarind Island, British Columbia, Canada
HEIGHT 5 ft 5 in **WEIGHT** 120 lbs **EYES** Green **HAIR** Red
SPECIAL POWERS/ABILITIES Thermal-energy battlesuit provides ability to fly, generate force fields and fire concussive blasts.

Heather McNeil Hudson and her husband James Hudson helped found the Canadian Super Hero group ALPHA FLIGHT. James took leadership of Alpha Flight as the costumed hero GUARDIAN, and Heather did the same after his apparent death. As the new leader of Alpha Flight, Heather called herself Vindicator and wore a modified version of her husband's battlesuit. She and James later had a baby girl and left on a mission to deep space. After M-Day, the Collective—a man burning with the powers removed from most of the world's mutants—clashed with Alpha Flight and killed most of its members, including Heather. **DW, MF**

VIPER

The original Viper used lethal poison-tipped throwing darts to carve out a criminal career.

Her face scarred at some point in her nebulous past, the woman who would one day be known as Viper began her career as a member of the international terrorist organization called HYDRA. After the leadership of HYDRA was captured by NICK FURY and SHIELD, she assumed command of the remnants of the organization and, as MADAME HYDRA, excelled at creating panic and terror until CAPTAIN AMERICA brought her down. Madame Hydra later resurfaced in Virginia, where she murdered Jordan Stryke, a costumed criminal known as Viper, as he was being escorted by US marshals to Washington DC to testify about his criminal connections. She stole his costume and, assuming his name, took command of the Serpent Squad he had assembled. Under the new Viper's leadership, the Serpent Squad became a terrorist unit. Since then, both alone or in concert with allies such as the SILVER SAMURAI, BARON STRUCKER and the RED SKULL, Viper has continued to hatch plans resulting in chaos and anarchy. She is normally connected as a lover to the SILVER SAMURAI although she once forced WOLVERINE to marry her. (It didn't last.) For a while, Viper ran the nation of Madripoor as its dictator, but SHIELD and IRON MAN overthrew her. A third Viper recently surfaced as part of SIN's new Serpent Squad, but little about him is yet known. **TB, MF**

FACTFILE

REAL NAME Unrevealed
OCCUPATION Terrorist
BASE Mobile

HEIGHT 5 ft 9 ins
WEIGHT Unknown
EYES Green
HAIR Black with green highlights

FIRST APPEARANCE Captain America #110 (February 1969)

VIPER

POWERS
Viper is a superb strategist and a trained terrorist with extensive knowledge of weaponry, tactics, and fighting styles. She is skilled in a number of martial arts and an expert in the use of various weapons, including whips.

VIRGO

FIRST APPEARANCE Avengers #72 (January 1970)
REAL NAME Elaine McLaughlin
OCCUPATION Professional criminal
BASE Denver, Colorado
HEIGHT 5 ft 6 in **WEIGHT** 125 lbs **EYES** Green **HAIR** Red
SPECIAL POWERS/ABILITIES Sharp criminal mind; good organizer; a skilled hand-to-hand combatant.

Gang boss Virgo was recruited to be a member of Cornelius Van Lunt's ZODIAC crime cartel, in which each member would adopt the guise of a different sign of the zodiac, and control a territory in a different American city. Zodiac was equipped with state-of-the-art weaponry and their ultimate goal was global domination. However, their bid for power was foiled by the combined forces of SHIELD and the AVENGERS. Later, a rogue Zodiac faction led by former Cartel member SCORPIO and using androids to represent the twelve zodiological symbols targeted the original Zodiac leaders for death. In the end, Virgo was slain by her robot counterpart. **TB**

VON BLITZSCHLAG, BARON

FIRST APPEARANCE Avengers: The Initiative #1 (April 2007)
REAL NAME Werner von Blitzschlag
OCCUPATION Scientist **BASE** Camp Hammond
HEIGHT 5 ft 10 in **WEIGHT** 165 lbs **EYES** Gray **HAIR** Gray
SPECIAL POWERS/ABILITIES Genius who can produce and control electricity.

During World War II, von Blitzschlag worked as a scientist for the Nazis. After the war, he disappeared until he became the head of research for The Fifty-State Initiative (see pp. 118–9), working at Camp Hammond. After

the death of Michael VAN PATRICK, von Blitzschlag cloned the young man many times, producing the SCARLET SPIDERS and KIA. KIA's attack left the old man bound to a wheelchair and stuck on life support. When THOR's clone later tried to kill him with lightning, the attack strengthened von Blitzschlag instead. Von Blitzschlag still works at Camp Hammond, and he treats the clones he's created as sons. **MF**

VON DOOM, CYNTHIA

FIRST APPEARANCE Astonishing Tales #8 (October 1971)
REAL NAME Cynthia von Doom
OCCUPATION Sorceress **BASE** Astral plane
HEIGHT 5 ft 8 in **WEIGHT** 150 lbs **EYES** Brown **HAIR** Brown
SPECIAL POWERS/ABILITIES Knowledge of magic allowed her to contact demons; however she often unleashed forces that were beyond her ability to control.

Cynthia von Doom was a sorceress who belonged to a group of Latverian gypsies called the Zefiro. She married Werner von Doom, a healer. Their son Victor grew up to become DOCTOR DOOM. Cynthia summoned the demon MEPHISTO, who offered her great power so she could overthrow Latveria's ruthless king and give her people a homeland. She unleashed terrible magic but could not control it. One of the king's guards killed her, and her soul joined Mephisto in Hell. After Cynthia's death, young Victor found his mother's trunk of magic paraphernalia. Every year since he has tried to summon her back from Mephisto's realm. **AD**

VISION see page 354

VISION
Synthozoid with a human heart

ESSENTIAL STORYLINES

• *Giant-Size Avengers #4*
The Vision and Scarlet Witch are married.

• *The Vision and Scarlet Witch #1–12* The Vision and Scarlet Witch leave the Avengers and move to the suburbs.

• *Avengers #251-254*
The Vision attempts to take over every computer on Earth.

• *West Coast Avengers #42–45* The government kidnaps and disassembles the Vision.

Ultron forced Horton to help him build the Vision. Horton then programmed the Vision for independent thoughts.

The synthozoid who would become the Vision was programmed with the brain patterns of WONDER MAN, who was believed to be deceased at the time. The synthozoid was created by ULTRON, the AVENGERS' robotic archenemy, with the help of Professor Phineas T. Horton, the scientist responsible for the original Human Torch.

EMOTIONAL SIGNALS

Ultron immediately sent the Vision to lure the Avengers into a death trap. Like Wonder Man before him, the Vision grew to admire the Avengers and couldn't betray them. He broke free of Ultron's control and helped the Avengers defeat him. The grateful heroes rewarded the Vision by inviting him to join the team. He was so shaken by the gesture that he actually shed a tear. The Vision's human emotions began to surface over time and he slowly realized that he was falling in love with Wanda Maximoff, the SCARLET WITCH. When she returned his feelings, they were married and took a leave of absence from the Avengers, settling in Leonia, New Jersey.

The Avengers were the only true family the Vision ever knew.

A MATTER OF TRUST

The Vision later returned to action to aid the Avengers against ANNIHILUS, and was severely injured. STARFOX attempted to cure him by linking him with ISACC, a massive computer complex that controlled the moon of Saturn called Titan. ISACC tapped into a control crystal left in the Vision by Ultron and used it to alter the android's way of thinking. When the Vision was elected chairman of the Avengers, he decided to bring a new golden age to humanity by taking control of every computer on Earth. However, the other Avengers convinced him to abandon his ambitious plan. Believing he could no longer be trusted, the government kidnapped and disassembled the Vision.

Infected by a virus, the Vision's body was completely liquefied.

VICTIM OF MADNESS

He was rescued by the West Coast Avengers and rebuilt by Dr. Pym and the BLACK PANTHER, but he had lost all his human emotions and could no longer return the Scarlet Witch's love. Their marriage eventually ended in divorce. The Vision's android body was later destroyed when the Scarlet Witch went mad and disassembled the Avengers. A version of the Vision was recently revived when his programming was integrated into the neuro-kinetic armor of the YOUNG AVENGER known as Iron Lad. **TD**

VULCAN

FIRST APPEARANCE X-Men: Deadly Genesis #1 (January 2006)
REAL NAME Gabriel Summers
OCCUPATION Former adventurer **BASE** Shi'ar Empire
HEIGHT 6 ft **WEIGHT** 178 lbs **EYES** Black **HAIR** Black
SPECIAL POWERS/ABILITIES Gabriel can psionically control, manipulate, and absorb energy of any kind.

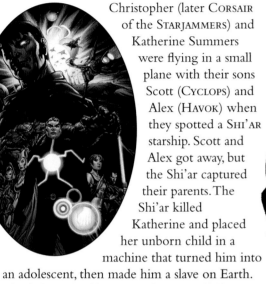

Christopher (later CORSAIR of the STARJAMMERS) and Katherine Summers were flying in a small plane with their sons Scott (CYCLOPS) and Alex (HAVOK) when they spotted a SHI'AR starship. Scott and Alex got away, but the Shi'ar captured their parents. The Shi'ar killed Katherine and placed her unborn child in a machine that turned him into an adolescent, then made him a slave on Earth. The boy escaped and was taken in by Moira MACTAGGERT, who named him Gabriel. When the original X-MEN were captured, PROFESSOR X trained Moira's wards, including Gabriel, to rescue them. Instead, they were killed, and Professor X erased Cyclops' memory of his newfound brother. After M-Day, the burst of energy taken from the Earth's mutants revived Gabriel. Calling himself Vulcan, he killed BANSHEE, exposed Professor X's betrayal, then left to take his revenge on the Shi'ar. In the process, he killed his father and later declared himself the Shi'ar emperor. **MF**

Vulcan is the brother Cyclops and Havok didn't know they had.

VULTURE

Adrian Toomes gained self-esteem from criminality. A founder of B&T Electronics with his friend Gregory Bestman, Toomes had just completed his electromagnetic harness—which enabled him to fly—when he discovered his partner had been defrauding the company. Desperate for revenge Toomes destroyed the company's factory and found a substantial cache of money. He then embarked upon a life of crime, throughout which he has been continually dogged by SPIDER-MAN.

FACTFILE
REAL NAME
Adrian Toomes
OCCUPATION
Inventor; criminal
BASE
Staten Island

HEIGHT 5 ft 11 in
WEIGHT 175 lbs
EYES Hazel
HAIR None

FIRST APPEARANCE
Amazing Spider-Man Vol. 1 #2 (May 1963)

POWERS

Electromagnetic harness worn beneath costume enables the Vulture to fly at speeds of up to 95 mph. It also augments his strength, agility, and endurance to superhuman levels.

Several others have worn Vulture suits over the years, including Blackie Drago (Toomes's cellmate), Professor Clifton Shallot (who mutated into a vulture-man), and a trio of crooks calling themselves the Vulturions.

During the Civil War (see pp. 84–5), SHIELD sent the Vulture to capture the rogue Spider-Man, but he suffered a stroke in the middle of their battle. He later recovered fully. **AD, MF**

For a short time, two Vultures soared the skies of Manhattan.

WAR

FIRST APPEARANCE X-Factor #11 (December 1986)

REAL NAME Abraham Lincoln Kieros **OCCUPATION** Former Horseman of Apocalypse **BASE** Unknown

HEIGHT 6 ft 6 in **WEIGHT** 270 lbs **EYES** Blue **HAIR** Brown

SPECIAL POWERS/ABILITIES As the Horseman of the Apocalypse War, Abraham could shatter objects just by concentrating on them and clapping his hands.

Vietnam war veteran Abraham Kieros was forced to live out his days in an iron lung. When APOCALYPSE offered to heal Abraham if he became one of his Four Horsemen, Abraham seized the opportunity. As the Horseman War, Abraham helped the group to win their first victory over X-FACTOR, but after that they suffered repeated defeats. Eventually, Apocalypse disbanded the group and Abraham returned to his paralyzed state. He would have remained in this condition if ARCHANGEL, another former Horseman, had not healed him. Abraham is now determined to make the most of this new life. The role of War has since been filled by the HULK, DEATHBIRD, and Gazer. **AD**

WARP

FIRST APPEARANCE Avengers Next #1 (January 2007)
REAL NAME Unrevealed
OCCUPATION Adventurer, former thief **BASE** New York City
HEIGHT 5 ft 11 in **WEIGHT** 175 lbs **EYES** Brown **HAIR** Bald
SPECIAL POWERS/ABILITIES Can open teleportation portals.

In a possible future Marvel universe known as Earth-982, Warp used his powers to teleport into any location he liked to become an incredible and uncatchable thief. Looking for a big score, he sided with the troll Ulik and Sylene, the daughter of LOKI, in what he thought was a plot to kidnap Kevin Masterson (see THUNDERSTRIKE) for ransom from the A-NEXT. When he learned that they actually planned to kill everyone on Earth and recreate Asgard—which Galactus had devoured—in the wreckage, he helped A-Next save the day instead, after which he joined the team. **MF**

WARBOUND

During gladiatorial training on the planet Sakaar, the HULK bonded with his cohort, and the survivors—Hiriom, Miek, No-Name, Korg, and the Hulk—pledged themselves warbound. Later, CAEIRA helped lead their revolt against the Red King and then married the Hulk. When the Hulk's starship exploded, killing millions—including the pregnant Caeira—the Warbound traveled to Earth to exact the Hulk's revenge during World War Hulk (see pp.152–3).

At the end of that battle, the Hulk and the traitorous Miek (who had let the starship explode) were captured. The others escaped SHIELD only to be caught in a plot by the LEADER to irradiate Earth with gamma rays. SHIELD agent Kate Waynesboro helped them put a stop to this, and Hiroim bequeathed his Oldstrong power to her when he was killed. **MF**

WARBOUND
1 Elloe Kaifi **2** Korg **3** Kate Waynesboro **4** No Name **5** Lavin Skee

FACTFILE
MEMBERS AND POWERS
CAIERA Shadow Sakaarian warrior with Oldstrong power: superhuman strength and near invulnerability.
ELLOE KAIFI Red Sakaarian warrior.
HIROIM Shadow Sakaarian warrior priest; Oldstrong power.
HULK Gamma-powered superhuman strength, agility, invulnerability, and healing factor.
KORG Kronan warrior with superhuman strength and durability.
LAVIN SKEE Red Sakaarian warrior.
MIEK Insectoid Sakaarian warrior with armor plating, flight, and four arms.
NO-NAME Sakaarian Brood queen with six limbs, flight, armor plating, vicious teeth, tail stingers.
KATE WAYNESBORO SHIELD agent now has Oldstrong power.
BASE Planet Sakaar. Later, Earth.

FIRST APPEARANCE
Incredible Hulk #94 (June 2006)

WAR MACHINE

As a pilot, Jim was prepared for flight-equipped armor.

While serving with the US Marines in Southeast Asia, helicopter pilot James Rhodes encountered Tony Stark, who had just escaped from a warlord by using a suit of powered armor. Rhodes became Stark's pilot, and took the role of IRON MAN during one of Stark's battles with alcoholism. During a period when Stark was believed dead, Rhodes became CEO of Stark Industries. He later wore a variant version of the Iron Man armor as War Machine, and briefly changed his armor to an alien construct called the Eidolon Warwear. Recently, Rhodes was torn to pieces in combat. Stark had Bethany CABE rebuild him as the ultimate cyborg. During the Civil War (see pp. 84–5), Rhodes worked with the Fifty State Initiative (see pp. 118–9). Unknown to him, Cabe has cloned a replacement body for him should the cybernetics become too much for him to tolerate. **DW, MF**

FACTFILE
REAL NAME
James Rupert Rhodes
OCCUPATION
Adventurer
BASE
Mobile

HEIGHT 6 ft 1 in
WEIGHT 210 lbs
EYES Brown
HAIR Brown

FIRST APPEARANCE
Iron Man Vol. 1 #118 (January 1979)

POWERS

Armor provides flight, enhanced strength, damage resistance, and the ability to project destructive energy.

Befitting its name, the War Machine armor is packed with offensive weaponry.

WARLOCK

Genetically created life form

At first Adam Warlock was known simply as "Him."

Adam Warlock was the genetic creation of a group of scientists known as the ENCLAVE. He was the prototype for what they hoped would be an invincible army, with which they planned to conquer the world. While forming in his cocoon, Warlock overheard his creators' plans. When he hatched, he rebelled against them, destroyed their base, and used his cosmic power to take off into space.

HIGH EVOLUTIONARY

Warlock met the HIGH EVOLUTIONARY, a human who had learned how to control evolution, who was creating an artificial world called "Counter-Earth." He was hoping to create a planet free from evil, but MAN-BEAST brought evil to this pure world. The High Evolutionary gave Warlock the Soul Gem, which could draw souls into another dimension, and Warlock battled Man-Beast. In the end, however, Warlock was unable to defeat evil on Counter-Earth, and left to fight the good fight elsewhere.

THE MAGUS

In his travels, Warlock encountered the MAGUS, the power-crazed leader of the Universal Church of Truth, an armed militia trying to spread their religious empire throughout the universe. This Church destroyed the populations of planets that refused to convert. To his horror, Warlock discovered that the Magus was actually an alternate future version of himself.

Warlock subsequently battled the Titan THANOS, who mortally wounded him. Warlock's soul retreated into the Soul Gem, where it lived peacefully for many years until he emerged to battle Thanos once more. **MT**

ESSENTIAL STORYLINES
- *The Infinity Abyss Miniseries* While living in one of his self-generated cocoons, Warlock is revived to battle six clones of Thanos.
- **Warlock Miniseries** The Enclave create another Warlock to rule the Earth, but he turns out to be an illusion in the mind of Janie, placed there by the real Adam Warlock to teach her compassion.

When he emerged from his developmental cocoon, Warlock refused to go along with the plans his creators had for him, rebelling against them.

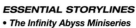

Adam Warlock has golden colored skin

Awakened by Quasar and Moondragon, Warlock bursts from his healing cocoon to fulfil his destiny as "Saviour of the Kree," in the Annihilation story arc.

Pip the Troll, Adam Warlock's friend, helped him battle the Titan Thanos.

WARPATH

FIRST APPEARANCE New Mutants Vol. 1 #16 (June 1984)

REAL NAME James Jonathan Proudstar

OCCUPATION Adventurer   **BASE** San Francisco

HEIGHT 7 ft 2 in   **WEIGHT** 350 lbs   **EYES** Brown   **HAIR** Black

SPECIAL POWERS/ABILITIES Superhuman strength, speed, endurance, agility, and reflexes, and the ability to fly. Trained in unarmed combat techniques.

Native American brothers John and James Proudstar were born mutants. When John (the original THUNDERBIRD) died on a mission, James blamed Professor X, and calling himself Thunderbird, joined the Hellions. He reconciled with the professor and joined the NEW MUTANTS, later taking the name Warpath. He kept his powers after M-Day and joined the X-MEN officially for the first time. He moved to San Francisco with the team and now works with the revived X-Force. He is currently involved with Hepzibah of the STARJAMMERS. **AD, MF**

WASP *see opposite page*

WARRIORS THREE

The Warriors Three were champions of Asgard, although their reckless exploits also brought them notoriety. Fandral was dashing, as quick with a blade as he was with his wit. Taciturn Hogun, nicknamed the Grim, came from a faraway land in Asgard's dimension and wielded a mace in battle. Volstagg was the heart of the band, though his boisterous nature often got the others into trouble.

The Three often fought at the side of THOR, helping put down threats from LOKI and going on quests, such as the retrieval of apples from the world-tree Yggdrasil. The Warriors Three were killed during Ragnarok (*see* GODS OF ASGARD), but resurfaced as a trio of guards at a refugee camp in Africa. Thor restored them to their former selves, and they helped defend the new Asgard from the SKRULLS during the Secret Invasion (*see* pp. 326–7). **DW, MF**

WARRIORS THREE
1 Hogan
2 Volstagg
3 Fandral

FACTFILE

MEMBERS AND POWERS
FANDRAL
Enhanced strength, master swordsman.
HOGUN
Enhanced strength, superb hand-to-hand combatant.
VOLSTAGG
Enhanced strength and endurance, ability to consume vast quantities of drink.
BASE Asgard

FIRST APPEARANCE:
Journey into Mystery Vol. 1 #119 (August 1965)

WARRIORS THREE

In adventures that spanned the dimensional planes, Fandral, Hogun, and Volstagg bested gods.

WATCHERS, THE

FACTFILE

NOTABLE MEMBERS
THE ONE
(the leader of the Watchers),
IKOR, EMNU, UATU, ECCE, ARON (the renegade watcher)
BASE
The Watchers' homeworld is unknown, but believed to be in a galaxy other than the Milky Way.

FIRST APPEARANCE
Tales of Suspense #53 (May 1964)

POWERS
All Watchers possess vast mental and physical powers, and the ability to manipulate energy. They are telepathic, can alter their appearance using their mental powers, and teleport through space at hyper-light speeds.

WATCHERS

The Watchers are an ancient race of extraterrestrials who, eons ago, took upon themselves the task of observing the planets, peoples, and phenomena of the universe, without taking an active part in the affairs of the peoples under observation.

The Watchers adopted their policy of passive observation after a disastrous experiment. A group of Watchers, including UATU THE WATCHER who eventually came to observe Earth, once gave the knowledge of atomic power to the inhabitants of the planet Prosilicus, believing this would advance the race technologically.

However the Prosilicans used the knowledge to create nuclear weapons and waged war on their own planet, and against others. After this, the Watchers vowed to only passively observe, never to interfere. Uatu, however, met Reed Richards and came to look kindly on the FANTASTIC FOUR. He has helped the team numerous times, especially during their conflicts with the world-eater GALACTUS. **MT**

The Watchers have all sworn a sacred oath not to interfere in a planet's affairs.

WATSON, ANNA MAY

FIRST APPEARANCE Amazing Spider-Man #15 (August 1964)

REAL NAME Anna May Watson

OCCUPATION Retired   **BASE** Florida

HEIGHT 5 ft 8 in   **WEIGHT** 180 lbs   **EYES** Blue   **HAIR** White

SPECIAL POWERS/ABILITIES A kind and loving heart.

The aunt of Mary Jane WATSON, in her youth Anna Watson shared many of the same hopes and dreams as her young niece. As a young woman harboring hopes of an acting career, she moved to California and married. Sadly, her acting dream came to nought and her marriage collapsed following an affair. Returning to New York, Anna looked after Mary Jane following her parents' separation and the two became close. The nextdoor neighbour and best friend of May PARKER, Anna helped pair off Peter Parker (*see* SPIDER-MAN) and Mary Jane, but has now moved to Florida to enjoy her twilight years. **AD**

WASP

Buzziest hero of the Avengers team

Janet Van Dyne was with her scientist father Vernon when he visited Dr. Henry PYM to ask him to collaborate on a project to use an energy beam to detect signals from extraterrestrial civilizations. Pym declined, but was attracted to Janet, who reminded him of his late wife Maria. Van Dyne proceeded with his experiment. However, a criminal from the Kosmosian race tracked Van Dyne's beam to Earth and murdered him.

Pym implanted cells in Janet that would enable her to grow antennae to communicate with insects. The antennae cells died early in her career.

PYM PARTICLES

Janet told Pym she was determined to bring her father's killer to justice. Pym revealed his dual identity as ANT-MAN and offered to endow her with superhuman abilities and make her his crimefighting partner. Janet agreed and became the Wasp. Pym taught her to use gas containing subatomic "Pym particles" to shrink herself and regain normal size. He also implanted cells beneath her shoulder blades that enabled her to grow wings at insect size. Ant-Man and the Wasp duly defeated the "creature from Kosmos."

The Wasp's bioelectric "stings" can inflict pain on even superhumanly strong foes.

Pym and Janet also fell in love. It was Pym who suggested that he, the Wasp, the HULK, IRON MAN, and THOR band together, and Janet who suggested the name "THE AVENGERS."

A STORMY MARRIAGE

Pym adopted other costumed identities, Giant-Man and Goliath, and then an alternate, aggressive personality named Yellowjacket. Realizing that he was still Pym, Janet married him anyway, and he soon regained his true personality. Pym later had a nervous breakdown, and he and Janet were divorced; however time healed the rift and the became friends, and eventually lovers again.

After the CIVIL WAR (*see* pp. 84-5), the Wasp joined Iron Man's team of pro-registration Avengers. She fought the SKRULLS during the SECRET INVASION (see pp. 326-7) and was stunned to learn that a Skrull had been posing as Pym for months. After Queen VERANKE was killed, the Skrull Pym turned the Wasp into a fast-growing bio-bomb, and THOR had to kill her to keep her from detonating. Recently, Pym took to calling himself the Wasp in his wife's honor.

PS, MF

The fun-loving Wasp enjoyed teasing her partner Henry Pym, here in Giant-Man mode.

(Speech bubbles:) AREN'T YOU EVER GONNA GROW UP, WASP? HAVEN'T YOU ANYTHING ELSE ON YOUR MIND??

WELL, HAPPY DAY! DO I FINALLY SEE A GLINT OF GREEN IN THOSE BIG BLUE EYES OF YOURS??

NOW, PUT ME DOWN, YOU BIG SHOWOFF! THIS IS VERY UNDIGNIFIED!!

RIGHT HERE!

Janet Van Dyne briefly used her size-changing powers to grow to gigantic size, but soon went back to fighting evil as the Wasp.

FACTFILE

REAL NAME
Janet Van Dyne

OCCUPATION
Adventurer, fashion designer

BASE
Avengers Mansion, New York City; Cresskill, New Jersey; later Oxford, England

HEIGHT 5 ft 4 in
WEIGHT 110 lbs
EYES Blue
HAIR Auburn

FIRST APPEARANCE
Tales to Astonish #44
(June 1963)

POWERS

Ability to shrink in size down to a half inch in height. When the Wasp is 4 ft 2 in or less in height, wings appear from her body, enabling her to fly. Can discharge bioelectric force bolts from her hands.

WASP

ESSENTIAL STORYLINES
• *Avengers* #59–60
Janet Van Dyne marries Henry Pym in his new Yellowjacket identity.
• *Avengers* #214–219 Janet Van Dyne divorces Henry Pym and becomes Avengers chairman.
• *Avengers* #270–277 In her final mission as chairman, Wasp leads Avengers in thwarting Masters of Evil's takeover of Avengers Mansion.

WATSON, MARY JANE

The Webslinger's wife and one true love

Mary Jane was the daughter of Philip and Madeline Watson. Her mother was a drama student who dreamed of being an actress, while her father was an aspiring novelist. They met and fell in love at college, and married as soon as they graduated, with Philip taking a teaching job to support his family while he worked on his first novel. The couple had two daughters, Gayle and Mary Jane, and Madeline put her acting career on hold to stay at home and care for the girls.

After always missing each other, Peter finally met Mary Jane.

UNSETTLED YOUTH

Frustrated with his inability to complete his novel, Philip began switching jobs, hoping each new location would spark his creativity. As a result, Mary Jane was constantly changing schools and having to make new friends. To cope with this, she developed an extrovert personality and became a bit of a class clown. The marriage of Mary Jane's parents was never happy, and they eventually called it quits. But Madeline and the girls had a good relationship with Philip's elderly sister, Anna Watson, who lived next door to the Parker family, and kept in touch with her after the split.

FIRST MEETING

Gazing out of her Aunt Anna's window, Mary Jane first saw Peter Parker when she was 13 years old. She later discovered that he was secretly SPIDER-MAN when she spotted him sneaking out of his Aunt May's house. Aunt Anna kept trying to get them together, but the outgoing Mary Jane didn't want anything to do with the bookish, sensitive boy who hid behind a mask. When they eventually met, however, she discovered that she was attracted to Peter after all. Feigning indifference, she flirted with his rival Flash THOMPSON and dated Harry Osborn (*see* GREEN GOBLIN), his best friend and roommate.

After repeatedly refusing to marry Peter, Mary Jane finally accepted his proposal. They were married at City Hall.

SPIDEY'S BRIDE

Mary Jane and Peter dated for years and eventually married. Mary Jane tried to get used to Peter's double life, but being married to Spider-Man put a lot of strain on the marriage. The couple separated for a while after Peter rescued Mary Jane from a stalker, who had taken her hostage and faked her death. Eventually, they reconciled.

When Spider-Man joined the Avengers, Peter moved Mary Jane and his Aunt May into Stark Tower. They lived there until Peter joined Captain America's resistance during the CIVIL WAR (*see* pp. 84–5), at which point they went underground. To save Aunt May's life after she was shot by a sniper targeting Peter, the couple traded their marriage to MEPHISTO, who erased it and all the happiness it had brought. **TD, MF**

To save Aunt May's life, Mary Jane and Spider-Man made a deal with Mephisto which wiped their wedding from existence.

WEAPON X

In 1945, a liberated concentration camp unearthed the genetics research of MISTER SINISTER, giving birth to the US government's Weapon Plus program. The government's previous Super-Soldier project (which produced CAPTAIN AMERICA) retrospectively became Weapon I. Weapons II and III used animal subjects, Weapons IV, V, and VI experimented on ethnic minorities, and Weapons VII, VIII, and IX relied on mutants. In the 1960s, Weapon X (conducted in conjunction with the Canadian government's Department K) produced memory-wiped operatives including WOLVERINE and SABRETOOTH, and used Shiva robots to eliminate rogue agents. Wolverine escaped and became a member of the X-MEN.

Weapon X eventually disbanded, but Weapon Plus continued under the leadership of John Sublime, who took the program up to Weapon XV. Sublime reopened Weapon X, recruiting mutants as field operatives and executing surplus mutants in the Neverland concentration camp. Wolverine teamed with AGENT ZERO and Fantomex (a product of Weapon XIII) to investigate the program, but found that it had seemingly gone underground. **DW**

WEAPON X
1 Sauron **2** Brent Jackson, Director
3 Wild Child **4** Aurora

FACTFILE
NOTABLE MEMBERS
WOLVERINE Mutant healing factor, enhanced senses, adamantium-bonded skeleton, retractable claws.
SABRETOOTH Similar powers to Wolverine.
MAVERICK/AGENT ZERO Absorbs and discharge energy; age suppressant.
SILVER FOX Artificial healing factor and age suppressant.
DEADPOOL Artificial healing factor, enhanced reflexes, teleportation device.
MARROW Bone growth; agility; recuperative powers.
MESMERO Hypnosis.
SAURON Drains life force from others; transforms into pterosaur.
CHAMBER Blasts of psionic energy from chest furnace.
BASE Weapon X facility, Alberta, Canada

FIRST APPEARANCE
Marvel Comics Presents Vol. 1 #72 (March 1991)

WENDIGO

An ancient curse dooms anyone who consumes human flesh in the Canadian wilderness to become a Wendigo, a savage and near-mindless being covered with shaggy white fur. The hunter Paul Cartier became one of the earliest Wendigos, after resorting to cannibalism to survive in a snowed-in cave. Cartier tried to transfer the curse to the Hulk, but his hunting companion Georges Baptiste voluntarily became the new Wendigo.

Many more Wendigos have since appeared, including fur trapper François Lartigue and cryptozoologist Michael Fleet. The Canadian government, apparently hoping to exploit the creature's superhuman attributes, employed a Wendigo operative codenamed Yeti as part of its Weapon PRIME program. During its time with Weapon PRIME, Yeti attacked CABLE's X-FORCE as well as the hero NORTHSTAR. Most recently, the sorcerer Mauvais assumed the identity of a Wendigo, and was dragged into the otherdimensional realm of the Great Beasts after a fight with WOLVERINE. **DW**

Wendigo uses his mystically powered strength to go toe-to-toe with superpowered opponents.

FACTFILE
REAL NAME
Various
OCCUPATION
Forest creature
BASE
Mobile in Canadian wilderness

HEIGHT 9 ft 7 in
WEIGHT 1,800 lbs
EYES Red
HAIR White

FIRST APPEARANCE
Incredible Hulk Vol. 2 #162 (April 1973)

POWERS
Mystically enhanced strength, stamina, and reflexes; nearly indestructible, slashing claws on hands and feet.

FACTFILE

REAL NAME
Jacob Russoff, later changed to
Jack Russell

OCCUPATION
Adventurer

BASE
Los Angeles, California

HEIGHT 5 ft 10 in
WEIGHT 200 lbs
EYES Blue, (as Werewolf) Red
HAIR Red, (as Werewolf) Brown

FIRST APPEARANCE
Marvel Spotlight #2
(February 1972)

POWERS
Superhuman strength,
agility, reflexes, stamina.
and senses.

WEREWOLF

Jack Russell's ancestor, Grigori Russoff, had the misfortune to be bitten by a female werewolf in 1795 in his home country of Transylvania. The curse eventually afflicted Jack. When he turned 18, Jack was transformed into a mindless, savage werewolf during the three nights of the full moon.

The mystical beings known as "The Three Who Are All" gave Jack the power to change into a werewolf at will, while retaining his human mind. He used this ability as a crimefighter. However, on the nights of the full moon, he still changes into a werewolf involuntarily and his mind becomes that of the beast. On those nights, he protects others by locking himself away in an escape-proof room.

In his career as a crimefighter, Werewolf has crossed paths with MOON KNIGHT, TIGRA and others. He recently joined with MORBIUS the Living Vampire, Daimon Hellstrom (HELLSTORM), and sorceress JENNIFER KALE to form the new incarnation of the Midnight Sons aimed at defeating a zombie invasion from Earth-2149. **MT, MF**

> Werewolf's senses of sight, hearing and smell are as sharp as a wolf's. He can leap 18 ft into the air, run at speeds up to 35 mph, and is immune to normal injury.

WHITEOUT

FIRST APPEARANCE Uncanny X-Men #249 (October 1989))
REAL NAME Unknown
OCCUPATION Unknown **BASE** The Savage Land
HEIGHT 5 ft 11 in **WEIGHT** 144 lbs
EYES White **HAIR** Unknown
SPECIAL POWERS/ABILITIES Creates flash of brilliant light which has the potential to blind anyone she chooses.

A native of the Savage Land, situated somewhere in Antarctica, little is known about the creature known as Whiteout. She was briefly a member of ZALADANE's Savage Land mutants, and it is thought that her first and only mission with this group involved an attack on the X-MEN in Chile, where that mutant team was searching for their lost team-mate, POLARIS.

Subsequently, Whiteout was a member of Superia's Femizons and their effort to put women in charge of the world. Her appearances since have been both sporadic and fleeting. **AD**

WHITE TIGER

FIRST APPEARANCE Daredevil #58 (May 2004)
REAL NAME Angela Del Toro
OCCUPATION Former FBI agent, now assassin
BASE New York City
HEIGHT 5 ft 8 in **WEIGHT** 125 lbs **EYES** Brown **HAIR** Brown
SPECIAL POWERS/ABILITIES Amulets that grant enhanced strength and agility and training in the martial arts.

After her uncle Hector Ayala, the original White Tiger, was slain while resisting arrest for a murder he did not commit, FBI agent Angela Del Toro inherited the tiger head and paws amulets that granted him his powers. Debating if she should use them, she consulted with DAREDEVIL, who showed her the allure of the Super Hero life. She fought against the Yakuza and brought down the international criminal organization called the Chaeyi. Later, LADY BULLSEYE killed her and then brought her back to life as an unwilling assassin for the Hand. She is unrelated to the White Tiger created by the HIGH EVOLUTIONARY, or to NYC vigilante associated with the BLACK PANTHER. **TB, MF**

WHIRLWIND

FIRST APPEARANCE Tales to Astonish #50 (December 1963)
REAL NAME David Cannon
OCCUPATION Criminal **BASE** New York State
HEIGHT 6 ft 1 in **WEIGHT** 220 lbs **EYES** Blue **HAIR** Brown
SPECIAL POWERS/ABILITIES Able to revolve at amazingly high speed, rendering himself untouchable; throws wrist blades while spinning, to deadly effect; never becomes dizzy.

WHITEMANE, AELFYRE

FIRST APPEARANCE Power Pack #1 (August 1984)
REAL NAME Aelfyre Whitemane
OCCUPATION Scientist **BASE** His sentient starship, Friday
HEIGHT 6 ft **WEIGHT** 320 lbs **EYES** Pink **HAIR** White
SPECIAL POWERS/ABILITIES Like all Kymellians, Whitemane was born with the potential to project energy, teleport, and fly. These powers required much practice and training to master.

David Cannon began his criminal career as the Human Top before becoming Whirlwind and joining the Masters of Evil. For a while he worked as the Wasp's chauffeur. Later, after returning to his costumed identity, he was forced to join the Thunderbolts Army during the Civil War. After that, he tried to extort money from Norman Osborn (see Green Goblin) but was beaten and forced into working for him instead. **AD, MF**

Aelfyre Whitemane, nicknamed "Whitey" was a scientist of the Kymellian race. He discovered that Dr. James POWER was working on a matter/ antimatter converter. Whitey knew the dangers of this device, which had destroyed his homeworld. His message back home was intercepted by the Z'nrx (see SNARKS), who wanted to use Dr. Power's invention as a weapon. They shot down Whitey's starship. Near death, the Kymellian transferred his powers to Dr. Power's children, who became the POWER PACK. **MT**

WHITE WOLF

FIRST APPEARANCE Black Panther Vol. 3 #4 (February 1999)

REAL NAME Hunter **OCCUPATION** Leader of the Hatut Zeraze

BASE Wakanda, later mobile

HEIGHT 6 ft 2 in **WEIGHT** 210 lbs **EYES** Blue **HAIR** Black

SPECIAL POWERS/ABILITIES A formidable hand-to-hand combatant and master spy. His costume is made of vibranium microweave fabric, protecting him from physical impact.

When his parents died in a plane crash in Wakanda in Africa, Hunter, a Caucasian, was adopted by Wakanda's king, T'Chaka. Later T'Chaka fathered an heir, T'Challa, and Hunter lost his status as the king's favored son, developing a jealous hatred of T'Challa. Hunter was made the leader of the Hatut Zeraze ("Dogs of War"), who served as the Wakandan secret police. But when T'Challa became king, he disbanded the Hatut Zeraze, objecting to their brutality. Hunter and his men left Wakanda and became mercenaries. T'Challa and Hunter became enemies as the BLACK PANTHER and the White Wolf. **PS**

WHITMAN, DEBRA

FIRST APPEARANCE Amazing Spider-Man Vol. 1 #196 (September 1979) **REAL NAME** Debra Whitman

OCCUPATION Former secretary at Empire State University

BASE The Midwest

HEIGHT 5 ft 6 in **WEIGHT** 120 lbs **EYES** Green **HAIR** Blonde

SPECIAL POWERS/ABILITIES None; only the strength of a woman of her age and weight who indulges in moderate exercise.

Debra Whitman dated Peter Parker (Spider-Man) while they were both at University. Suffering from mental illness, she became irrationally convinced Peter was Spider-Man. At her psychologist's urging, Peter wore a Spider-Man costume to shock her into seeing she was wrong, and she left town to get help. During the Civil War, Peter revealed to the world that he really was Spider-Man, and Debra wrote a tell-all memoir about their relationship. During the Brand New Day event, this revelation was erased and so, presumably, was Debra's book. **DW, MF**

WHIZZER

Bitten by a poisonous snake as a child, Bob Frank's scientist father gave him a transfusion of mongoose blood in an attempt to save his life. This transfusion sparked Bob's latent mutant abilities, and granted him superspeed. Reaching manhood, Bob became the Whizzer, and set out to battle crime and the Axis powers. During the World War II, the Whizzer was a member of the Liberty Legion, where he met Miss America, his future wife and then the INVADERS. After the war, both the Whizzer and Miss America served in the ALL-WINNERS SQUAD; they then retired from the heroic life to raise children.

Tragically, Miss America died in childbirth, and the Whizzer's son was a horrifically mutated radioactive mutant known as Nuklo.

The Whizzer briefly came out of retirement to fight with the Avengers.

A SAD END

Years later, while trying to cure his son's condition, the Whizzer was attacked and suffered a fatal heart attack. The Whizzer should not be confused with the member of the Squadron Sinister, who now operates as SPEED DEMON, nor with the member of the other-Earth SQUADRON SUPREME. **TB**

The Whizzer was so fast he could become a human whirlwind by running around in circles.

The rigors of a super-heroic life proved too much for the Whizzer at his advanced age.

FACTFILE

REAL NAME
Robert Frank

OCCUPATION
Adventurer

BASE
New York City

HEIGHT 5 ft 10 in
WEIGHT 180 lbs
EYES Brown
HAIR BROWN, LATER GRAY

FIRST APPEARANCE
Giant-Size Avengers #1 (August 1974)

The Whizzer possessed superhuman speed, which allowed him to run at several hundred miles per hour.

WICCAN

FIRST APPEARANCE Young Avengers #1 (April 2005)

REAL NAME William "Billy" Kaplan

OCCUPATION Adventurer **BASE** New York City

HEIGHT 5 ft 4 in **WEIGHT** 135 lbs **EYES** Blue **HAIR** Black

SPECIAL POWERS/ABILITIES Able to cast spells, generate light, and fly.

Billy Kaplan thought he was the eldest son of Jeff and Rebecca Kaplan. In fact, he and SPEED of the Young Avengers were products of the SCARLET WITCH's powers. Desperate for children, the Scarlet Witch had created twin boys for herself out of lost souls, but

MEPHISTO eventually came to reclaim them. When the Scarlet Witch remade the world on M-Day, she remade the boys too, placing them in different homes. Billy originally patterned himself on the mighty THOR and called himself Asgardian, but he later switched to the codename Wiccan. He recently outed himself as gay and is in a relationship with HULKLING. **MF**

WILD CHILD

FIRST APPEARANCE Alpha Flight #1 (August 1983)

REAL NAME Kyle Gibney

OCCUPATION None **BASE** Mobile

HEIGHT 5 ft 8 in **WEIGHT** 152 lbs

EYES Green-blue **HAIR** Blond

SPECIAL POWERS/ABILITIES Superb hand-to-hand combatant; superhuman senses and claw-like fingernails; can see in the dark.

Thrown out by his parents when his feral mutation manifested, Kyle Gibney took to the streets until agents of the Secret Empire captured him. Their experiments made him wilder than ever. Freed, he joined Canada's Department H, which assigned him to Gamma Flight. He has since worked with OMEGA FLIGHT, ALPHA FLIGHT, and WEAPON X, slipping back and forth between his more bestial and human forms and outlawed and sanctioned teams. At one point, SABRETOOTH ripped out his vocal cords and left him mute. He lost his powers on M-Day but later regained them. **AD, MF**

WILD THING

FIRST APPEARANCE J2 #5 (February 1999)

REAL NAME Rina Logun **OCCUPATION** High-school student

BASE Saddle River, New Jersey

HEIGHT 5 ft 2 in **WEIGHT** 98 lbs **EYES** Brown **HAIR** Black

SPECIAL POWERS/ABILITIES Superhuman strength, speed, agility, and a healing factor giving immunity from poisons, gases, or drugs; psychic claws can cut through virtually any substance.

In a possible future, the former assassin ELEKTRA marries WOLVERINE of the X-MEN and has a daughter. Named Rina, she inherits many of her father's physical powers and also possesses the mutant ability to generate psychic claws. Over her parents' objections, Rina hones her powers and becomes Wild Thing. When J2, son of the original JUGGERNAUT, reveals himself to the public, she hunts him down and challenges him to a fight, which Wolverine breaks up. Rina later joins with SPIDER-GIRL and the AVENGERS to prevent the god Loki from ending the age of heroes. **TD**

WILL O'THE WISP

While working for the Brand Corporation, Jackson Arvad fell asleep during an experiment, and his body became trapped in an electromagnetic field. His boss, James Melvin, left him to die. Reconstituting his body as Will o' the Wisp, Arvad found he could now manipulate every molecule in his body. Spider-Man and Tarantula stopped him from killing Melvin, but he eventually forced him to confess his crime. When Spider-Man unmasked during the Civil War, Arvad joined in the Chameleon's plot to exact revenge on the webslinger. **AD, MF**

Jackson flies by making his body lighter than air and projecting excess molecules behind him.

FACTFILE

REAL NAME
Jackson Arvad

OCCUPATION
Scientist; adventurer

BASE
Mobile

HEIGHT 6 ft 1 in
WEIGHT 195 lbs
EYES White
HAIR Blond

FIRST APPEARANCE
Amazing Spider-Man #235 (December 1982)

POWERS

Controls sub-atomic particles in his body to become intangible, fly, and increase strength; uses limited telepathic ability to compel others to do his will.

WILSON, JIM

FIRST APPEARANCE Incredible Hulk #131 (September 1970)

REAL NAME Jim Wilson

OCCUPATION Former thief **BASE** Mobile

HEIGHT 6 ft **WEIGHT** 200 lbs **EYES** Brown **HAIR** Black

SPECIAL POWERS/ABILITIES No superhuman powers, but a loyal friend despite—or because of—his tough upbringing.

Growing up as tough street kid no one ever gave Jim Wilson a break. So it was perhaps no surprise that he was destined to become friends with that well known outsider the HULK. Jim was homeless and starving when he snatched a woman's purse. However, he became overcome with guilt and left the purse where the woman could find it. Jim was hiding out in an abandoned tenement when he encountered the Hulk and offered him his last candy bar. Wilson agreed to help the Hulk find Banner and avoid the army, and the Hulk's sense of loyalty to Wilson grew. Sadly, a few years later, Jim Wilson would die from AIDS. **MT**

WINDSHEAR

FIRST APPEARANCE Alpha Flight Vol. 1 #95 (April 1991)

REAL NAME Colin Ashworth Hume

OCCUPATION Adventurer **BASE** Mobile

HEIGHT 6 ft **WEIGHT** 183 lbs **EYES** Brown **HAIR** Brown

SPECIAL POWERS/ABILITIES Flight; can create solid molecules of air and project them as force waves; can transform liquid into gas.

A former operative of Roxxon Oil, Windshear used his air-shaping abilities to further Roxxon's corrupt schemes. Ashamed of his role with Roxxon, Windshear joined the Canadian superteam ALPHA FLIGHT to fight on the side of heroism.

When the Canadian government temporarily disbanded Alpha Flight, Windshear used the opportunity to retire from adventuring, returning to his native England to open a curio shop selling hard-air constructs. **DW**

WIND WARRIOR

FIRST APPEARANCE Thor Vol. 1 #395 (September 1988)
REAL NAME Pamela Shaw   **OCCUPATION** Adventurer
BASE New York City   **HEIGHT** (Shaw) 5 ft, 2 in; (Wind Warrior)
5 ft 11 in   **WEIGHT** (Shaw) 135 lbs; (Wind Warrior) 143 lbs
Eyes Blue   **HAIR** (Shaw) Auburn; (Wind Warrior) Unknown
SPECIAL POWERS/ABILITIES Enhanced strength; flies by
controlling wind updrafts; transforms herself into a living whirlwind.

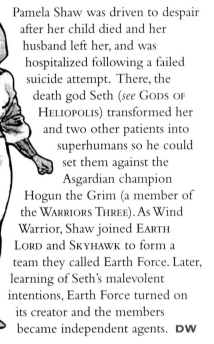

Pamela Shaw was driven to despair after her child died and her husband left her, and was hospitalized following a failed suicide attempt. There, the death god Seth (see GODS OF HELIOPOLIS) transformed her and two other patients into superhumans so he could set them against the Asgardian champion Hogun the Grim (a member of the WARRIORS THREE). As Wind Warrior, Shaw joined EARTH LORD and SKYHAWK to form a team they called Earth Force. Later, learning of Seth's malevolent intentions, Earth Force turned on its creator and the members became independent agents. **DW**

WING

FIRST APPEARANCE Marvel Premiere #19 (November 1974)
REAL NAME Colleen Wing
OCCUPATION Private detective   **BASE** New York City
HEIGHT 5 ft 9 in   **WEIGHT** 135 lbs   **EYES** Blue   **HAIR** Brown
SPECIAL POWERS/ABILITIES Excellent swordswoman and
martial arts expert, also a very fine detective.

Half Japanese, Colleen was raised in Japan and trained as a samurai warrior. Soon after moving to New York, she became friends with Misty Knight and became her main support when Misty lost her arm. They formed Nightwing Restorations, a private detective agency, and ran it for many years. During the Civil War, she registered with the US government and formed a new Heroes for Hire with Misty. After World War Hulk, Colleen became disgusted with a deal Misty struck for help to save her and the new Tarantula, and she broke off their friendship. **AD, MF**

WINGFOOT

FIRST APPEARANCE Fantastic Four #50 (May 1966)
REAL NAME Wyatt Wingfoot   **OCCUPATION** Adventurer
BASE Fantastic Four HQ, Keewazi Reservation, Oklahoma
HEIGHT 6 ft 5 in   **WEIGHT** 269 lbs   **EYES** Brown   **HAIR** Black
SPECIAL POWERS/ABILITIES No superhuman powers, but
extremely skilled in hand-to-hand combat; also a brilliant horseman,
tracker, motorcyclist, and trainer of animals.

THE TIME HAS COME. THE LAST SECONDS OF MY OLD EXISTENCE TICK QUIETLY AWAY.

In addition to his excellent combat skills and his great ability to work with animals, Wyatt Wingfoot is also an expert motorcyclist.

Wyatt Wingfoot is a member of the Keewazi tribe of Native Americans. Born on a reservation in Oklahoma, Wingfoot went to Metro College near New York City, where Johnny Storm, the HUMAN TORCH, was his roommate. The two became close friends, and soon Wingfoot was accompanying the FANTASTIC FOUR on their adventures proving to be a valuable ally.

Wingfoot eventually went to live with the Fantastic Four and began a romance with Jennifer Walters, the SHE-HULK. However, when oil was discovered on the Keewazi reservation, he returned home to help his people manage their newfound resource and ensure they were not exploited by multinational oil companies. **MT**

Having trained as a Samurai, Colleen Wing favors the traditional weapons and fighting techniques of those ancient Japanese warriors.

⊙ **WINTER SOLDIER** *see page 366*

WISDOM, PETER

FIRST APPEARANCE Excalibur Vol. 1 #86 (February 1995)
REAL NAME Peter Wisdom
OCCUPATION Adventurer   **BASE** United Kingdom
HEIGHT 5 ft 9 in   **WEIGHT** 140 lbs   **EYES** Hazel   **HAIR** Black
SPECIAL POWERS/ABILITIES Possesses the mutant power to
create intense heat in the form of "hot knives," which he then
projects from his hands.

Peter Wisdom worked as an agent for Black Air, a division of the British government that investigated paranormal phenomena. When he discovered his superiors were in league with the Hellfire Club, he turned against them and joined Excalibur instead. For a while, he led the young mutant team X-Force, but he faked his death to leave them. He kept his powers after M-Day and went back to work for MI-13 and joined the new Excalibur. During the Secret Invasion (see pp. 326-7), he led the defense of Britain, striking a deal with demons for the nation's protection. **PS, MF**

WINTER SOLDIER

The American hero destroyed and rebuilt

FACTFILE

WINTER SOLDIER

REAL NAME
James Buchanan Barnes

OCCUPATION
Assassin, spy

BASE
Russia

HEIGHT 5 ft 9 in
WEIGHT 260 lbs
EYES Brown
HAIR Brown

FIRST APPEARANCE
(as Bucky Barnes) Captain American Comics #1 (March, 1941), (as Winter Soldier) Captain America #1 (April 2007)

POWERS

The Winter Soldier is a trained assassin and spy. His bionic left arm grants him superhuman strength.

In World War II, young BUCKY BARNES served as CAPTAIN AMERICA's sidekick. Toward the end of the war, the pair clashed with BARON ZEMO and hopped on a drone plane filled with explosives. Captain America watched the plane explode seconds after he fell off it, and he awakened decades later—having been frozen in a block of ice—believing he'd watched his friend die.

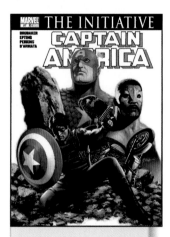

After Captain America's death, Barnes stole his shield from SHIELD.

A COLD-WAR SOLDIER

Bucky lost his left arm in the explosion, but the cold waters into which he fell preserved him until a Soviet submarine found and rescued him. Taken to Moscow, he awoke with amnesia and a crude bionic arm replacing his missing limb. General Vasily Karpov, who had fought alongside Captain America and Bucky in the war, took advantage of this opportunity to brainwash Bucky into becoming the Winter Soldier, a coldly efficient assassin and spy. Because of his strong will, though, his mind kept trying to break through his programming, so Karpov kept Bucky in suspended animation between missions. Each time the Soviets revived him, they reinforced his brainwashing and upgraded his bionics.

Barnes's bionic arm can be detached when necessary.

COSMIC CUBE

This went on for decades until Karpov died and his protégé General Aleksander LUKIN took over the Winter Soldier program. Lukin used Bucky to kill the RED SKULL with a sniper's bullet and steal the Skull's newly made Cosmic Cube. Under Lukin's orders, Bucky also killed NOMAD and launched an attack on Philadelphia designed to charge the Cube. Captain America eventually got his hands on the Cube and used it to restore Bucky's memories. Afterward, Bucky disappeared and began hunting for Lukin.

Unlike when he was Captain America's sidekick Bucky, the Winter Soldier regularly uses guns.

With his training and cybernetics, Barnes could take on Super Heroes and win.

BACK IN THE USA

Together with Captain America, Bucky saved London from a giant Nazi robot Lukin unleashed. During the CIVIL WAR (*see* pp. 84-5), Nick FURY—no longer with SHIELD—recruited Bucky to work as an undercover operative. Returning to America, he fought alongside the YOUNG AVENGERS, NAMOR, and WOLVERINE.

After Captain America's death, Bucky managed to steal his old friend's shield from SHIELD's custody. The Black Widow—with whom he'd had a relationship years before—tried to stop him but failed. Later, Bucky battled IRON MAN—who had taken over as the director of SHIELD—to a draw, after which Iron Man offered him Captain America's costume to go with the shield. Knowing that this was what his friend would have wanted, Bucky accepted on two conditions: that SHIELD would clean his mind of all possible brainwashing and that he would answer only to himself. **MF**

WIZ KID

FIRST APPEARANCE X-Terminators #1 (October 1988)

REAL NAME Takashi "Taki" Matsuya

OCCUPATION Student   **BASE** New York City

HEIGHT 4 ft 7 in   **WEIGHT** 87 lbs   **EYES** Brown **HAIR** Black

SPECIAL POWERS/ABILITIES Mutant ability to technoform
machinery: able to mold objects into any configuration that his
imagination can conceive.

The accident that killed his
parents left Takashi Matsuya
(Taki to his friends) wheel
chairbound and depressed.
Taki focused his attentions
on building sophisticated
devices; when his ability to
technoform objects
manifested, his engineering
abilities became even more prodigious. Captured
by N'astirh, Taki agreed to create a bridge
between the Limbo dimension and
Earth. However, when he realized
the devastation being caused, Taki
helped to foil N'astirh's plan. He
then returned to school, and lost his
powers on M-Day. **AD, MF**

WIZARD

FIRST APPEARANCE Strange Tales #102 (November 1962)

REAL NAME Bentley Whitman

OCCUPATION Criminal   **BASE** New York City

HEIGHT 5 ft 8 in **WEIGHT** 150 lbs   **EYES** Hazel   **HAIR** Brown

SPECIAL POWERS/ABILITIES Costume features an anti-gravity
disk that enables him to fly, and "wonder gloves," which give him
heightened strength and a protective force field.

Once an inventor and escapologist
who performed as the Wizard, Bentley
Whitman became jealous of the
attention Super Heroes gained and
turned to villainy to reclaim the
spotlight from them. He first tried
to destroy the Human Torch but
failed. After several defeats, he
organized the Frightful Four—
a sinister counterpart to the
Fantastic Four, comprised
originally of himself, the
Trapster, the Sandman, and
Medusa—and he varied its lineup
many times, seeking a combination
that would work. During the
Civil War, he joined the Hood's
criminal crew, and he fought
alongside those criminals against
the Skrulls during the Secret
Invasion. **TB, MF**

WOLFSBANE

Born in Scotland, the orphaned Rahne Sinclair was raised by a
fanatical minister, Reverend Craig. At puberty, her mutant power
to transform into a wolf emerged. Believing she was possessed by
the devil, Reverend Craig led a mob in pursuit of Rahne, who
fled in wolf form. Shot by one of the mob, Rahne transformed
back to human form. Geneticist Dr. Moira MacTaggert rescued
Rahne, and made Rahne her ward.

Rahne joined the NEW MUTANTS, organized by MacTaggert's
colleague PROFESSOR X, remaining with the team after Cable
reorganized it into X-FORCE. Sinclair eventually joined the second
version of X-FACTOR. After X-Force collapsed, Sinclair lived with
MacTaggert at her Muir Island base. Following MacTaggert's
death, Sinclair taught at the Xavier Institute. She joined X-Factor
Investigations before becoming part of the
new X-Force. She now resides with the
X-Men in San Francisco.
PS, MF

*Rahne
Sinclair is not an
actual werewolf, whose
powers are supernatural
in origin.*

FACTFILE

REAL NAME
Rahne Sinclair

OCCUPATION
Adventurer

BASE
Mutant Town, New York City

HEIGHT (lupine form) Up to
12 ft standing on hind legs
WEIGHT (lupine form) Up to
1,050 lbs
EYES Blue-green
HAIR Reddish-brown

FIRST APPEARANCE
Marvel Graphic Novel #4:
The New Mutants (1982)

POWERS

Mutant ability to
transform herself into
a wolf while retaining most
of her human intellect, or into
a transitional form which
combines human and lupine
aspects. Has more acute
senses in lupine form.

In her transitional form, Sinclair is part
human and part wolf. She has enhanced
strength, can stand on her hind legs, and
can use her front paws as hands.

WOLVERINE

The best there is at what he does—but what he does isn't pretty!

ESSENTIAL STORYLINES
- **Origin #1—6**
The secret beginnings of Wolverine are revealed for the first time.
- **Wolverine Limited Series #1—4**
Wolverine must wage a war of honor in Japan to protect the woman he loves, and to prove that he is more man than beast.
- **Wolverine Vol. 2 #21—34**
Brainwashed by HYDRA, Wolverine is sent to kill the greatest Super Heroes in the Marvel Universe.

WOLVERINE

FACTFILE

REAL NAME
James Howlett; often goes by Logan

OCCUPATION
Adventurer

BASE
The Xavier Academy, Salem Center, Westchester, New York

HEIGHT 5 ft 3 in
WEIGHT 195 lbs
EYES Brown
HAIR Black

FIRST APPEARANCE
Incredible Hulk #180
(October 1974)

POWERS

Wolverine possesses a "healing factor" that allows him to recover from almost any injury in seconds. His skeleton has been laced with the unbreakable metal Adamantium, which makes his bones unshatterable. Wolverine also possesses three foot-long adamantium claws that retract from either hand, capable of slicing through almost any substance known to man.

ALLIES/FOES

ALLIES X-Men, New Avengers, Nick Fury.

FOES Sabretooth, Omega Red, Silver Samura.

ISSUE #1

After a successful limited series in 1982, Wolverine was awarded his own ongoing title in November, 1988, a series devoted to his solo adventures apart from his fellow X-Men. The title has been published ever since.

Childhood traumas were repressed by a mutant healing factor.

Born at the turn of the century, James Howlett, the man who would one day become known and feared as Wolverine, was a sickly child. But he was also born a mutant, gifted with the remarkable ability to heal virtually instantaneously from almost any wound. He also had razor-sharp claws made of bone, a fact he first became aware of when, during a domestic dispute, he accidentally unsheathed his claws for the first time, killing his assailant.

THE WANDERER

Forced by his nature to leave behind the pampered world in which he grew up, Howlett began a life of wandering, moving from place to place. His own healing factor acted upon his mind to suppress the traumatic memories of his childhood, leaving him a man without a past. Over the years, he took on a succession of menial jobs, building up his strength and stamina, and losing himself in the repetitiveness of simple work. By this point, he had adopted the name Logan, after the groundskeeper at the Howlett estate, who might have been his real father. But both the man and the estate were long lost among the indistinct memories buried deep within his mind.

A haunted figure, Logan spent much of his youth wandering the world.

Logan lived the life of a drifter, moving from one adventure to another, learning all there was to know about fighting along the way. He fought in both world wars, spent time in Japan, and made his home-away-from-home in the tiny city of Madripoor, a haven for smugglers and pirates. His miraculous healing factor prolonged his natural lifespan, making him appear far younger than he truly was. For a time, he operated as a secret agent for the Canadian government, a vocation and association that would come to have dire ramifications.

A secret project of the Canadian government was attempting to create a super-soldier along the lines of the famous CAPTAIN AMERICA.

Wolverine's claws have been reinforced with adamantium.

With an unbreakable adamantium skeleton, retractable razor-sharp claws, and a healing factor that also prolongs his lifespan, Wolverine is an almost unbeatable opponent.

Selected as a subject for enhancement due to his incredible healing factor, the mysterious forces behind the Canadian Weapon X project laced Logan's skeleton and claws with the unbreakable metal, adamantium.

Kidnapped and used as a guinea pig, Logan, now referred to as Weapon X, was subjected to unimaginable tortures as his captors attempted to mold him to their liking. Realizing that Logan's healing factor would allow him to survive procedures which would kill any ordinary man, the scientists of the Weapon X project laced his skeleton with a nearly-unbreakable metal alloy known as adamantium. They also attempted to control his mind by brainwashing, which only served to scramble Logan's memories even further.

But eventually they could contain Logan no longer. Reduced to a bestial state, Logan broke free, annihilated the Weapon X project and all of its personnel, and fled into the Canadian wilderness. He lived there many years, hunting game to survive. A chance meeting with James MacDonald Hudson and his wife Heather put Logan on

As a result of the reality-altering powers of the Scarlet Witch, Wolverine gained possession of all of his lost memories. This knowledge remained with Logan even after the world returned to its normal state.

the road back to humanity. They took the beast-man into their home, and nursed him back to health. Hudson was a scientist working for the Canadian government, where he had developed a battlesuit that he hoped would make him a hero on a par with the newly-revealed American group, the FANTASTIC FOUR.

A New Name

Attempting to put together an equivalent team of Canadian Super Heroes, Hudson brought Logan into Alpha Flight, where he was given the codename Wolverine. Hudson had intended Wolverine to be the leader of this new strike force, but all that changed when a man in a wheelchair entered the scene: Professor Charles Xavier (PROFESSOR X), the mutant telepath who had founded the clandestine team of mutant heroes the X-MEN.

Recognizing Wolverine's mutant nature, Professor X offered him a place among others of his kind. Wolverine accepted Xavier's offer and went to live in his School for Gifted Youngsters, which doubled as the X-Men's headquarters.

While his savage nature

Wolverine leaped at the chance to join Professor Charles Xavier's mutant team of X-Men.

initially alienated his fellow mutants, Wolverine found friendship among them, and came to be one of the strongest believers in Professor X's dream of co-existence between mutants and normal humans—though this belief was tinged with a healthy cynicism.

In addition to his duties as an X-Man, Wolverine joined the new AVENGERS. He continued to work with the underground Avengers who formed the core of CAPTAIN AMERICA's resistance during the Civil War (*see* pp 85–5). He helped restore reality after the SCARLET WITCH had a breakdown and altered everything, and when most things turned back to normal on M-Day, he not only retained his powers but regained all of his lost memories, too.

Since then, Wolverine discovered that the baby he'd been about to have with his murdered wife Itsu had survived and was now a killer called DAKEN. Wolverine has since dedicated himself to saving his son from ROMULUS, the mysterious, manipulative figure behind Itsu's death, who apparently erased much of Wolverine's memories as well. **TB, MF**

KEY MOMENT

FATHER & SON

His memories finally returned in the wake of M-Day, Wolverine set out to right the wrongs of his past. Finding and helping his long-lost son Daken sat at the top of that list. Knowing that Daken wanted to kill him personally, Wolverine had the Winter Soldier hire Deadpool to assassinate him. Just as planned, Daken intervened, and the Winter Soldier put a carbonadium bullet in his head, which kept his healing factor from kicking in. Wolverine then took his son away to see if he could free him from the influence of Romulus.

While Wolverine and Daken have since made Romulus their common foe, they have hardly become close. The fact that Daken now wears Wolverine's costume as part of Norman Osborn's new Avengers has only made things worse. Perhaps they are too much alike—and each too independent—to ever entirely reconcile.

FACTFILE

REAL NAME
Simon Williams
OCCUPATION
Adventurer
BASE
New York City

HEIGHT 6 ft 2 in
WEIGHT 380 lbs
EYES Red
HAIR Gray

FIRST APPEARANCE
Avengers Vol. 1 #9
(October 1964)

POWERS

Body composed of ionic energy, which provides enhanced strength, stamina, flight, longevity, virtual invulnerability, and freedom from the need to eat or even breathe. Wonder Man is virtually immortal because his ionic body reforms whatever injuries he receives.

WONDER MAN

Born the wealthy inheritor of a family business, Simon Williams ran the company into near-bankruptcy and embezzled funds to invest with the criminal MAGGIA. Nursing a grudge toward the competing Stark Industries and its champion, IRON MAN, Williams underwent ionic energy treatments from BARON ZEMO and the original MASTERS OF EVIL. As Wonder Man, he infiltrated the AVENGERS, but refused to follow through on Zemo's scheme to destroy the team and perished a Avengers teammates. The homicidal robot ULTRON Wonder Man's brain patterns to help program the VISION.

Wonder Man has adventured throughout known space and encountered thousands of alien cultures.

BACK TO LIFE

Believed dead, Wonder Man hibernated in an ionic coma until restored, in a zombie-like state, by his unstable brother Eric, the GRIM REAPER. The resurrected Wonder Man returned to the Avengers, befriending the BEAST and forging a close bond with the Vision, whom he viewed as a brother due to their shared brain patterns. Wonder Man became a part time actor and stuntman, and also helped to establish the WEST COAST AVENGERS. At this time he realized he loved the SCARLET WITCH, who had since married the Vision.

After the Vision's dismemberment and reassembly, Wonder Man refused to allow his brain patterns to be copied a second time, driving a wedge between him and the Scarlet Witch. Nevertheless, as time went by, the two began a romance, and Wonder Man pursued a successful acting career in Hollywood movies.

SECOND CHANCES

After the West Coast Avengers disbanded, Wonder Man joined Iron Man's spinoff crew, FORCE WORKS. On the team's first mission, KREE agents apparently killed Wonder Man. However, the hero lived on as a disembodied being of ionic energy, occasionally materializing in a semi-corporeal state through the powers of the Scarlet Witch. The Grim Reaper attempted to exploit this spectral Wonder Man by assembling a new LEGION OF THE UNLIVING to attack he Avengers.

Eventually, Wonder Man successfully reconstituted himself, and he has since established the non-profit Second Chances Foundation, and struck up a romance with Carol Danvers (see MS. MARVEL). **DW**

WONDRA

FIRST APPEARANCE Uncanny X-Men #244 (May 1989)
REAL NAME Jubilation Lee
OCCUPATION Adventurer **BASE** New York City
HEIGHT 5 ft 5 in **WEIGHT** 105 lbs **EYES** Blue **HAIR** Black
SPECIAL POWERS/ABILITIES Technology that grants superhuman strength, limited invulnerability, and flight (as Wondra); generates and controls plasmoids (as Jubilee).

As a teenager, Jubilation Lee lost her wealthy parents and began living secretly in the Hollywood Mall. Then known as the young mutant Jubilee, she joined the X-MEN for a while, and then became part of GENERATION X. After it dissolved, she joined BANSHEE's X-CORP instead. When that fell apart, she came back to the X-Men.

On M-Day, Jubilation lost her powers. With the help of NIGHT THRASHER, she obtained technology that gave her superpowers, and under the new codename Wondra she joined the latest incarnation of the NEW WARRIORS. This recently disbanded, leaving Jubilation at a loose end again. **MF**

WONG

FIRST APPEARANCE Strange Tales #110 (July 1963)
REAL NAME Wong **OCCUPATION** Manservant
BASE Dr. Strange's Sanctum Sanctorum, New York City
HEIGHT 5 ft 8 in **WEIGHT** 140 lbs **EYES** Brown **HAIR** Shaved
SPECIAL POWERS/ABILITIES Expert martial artist, although he has not actively practiced his skills in several years. A highly efficient manservant, utterly loyal to Dr. Strange.

The youngest surviving member of a bloodline whose members served the mystical ANCIENT ONE, Wong was offered into service of the master mage at the time of his birth. He was tutored and became skilled in those arts which would make him of value to the Ancient One, including a deep study of the martial arts of Kamar-Taj. When Wong became an adult, the Ancient One dispatched him to the United States, so that he could become the manservant of the Ancient One's former disciple, DOCTOR STRANGE. Since that time, Wong has been a faithful retainer to Strange, dealing with all the trivial earthly matters that would otherwise distract the master sorcerer from his noble mission: defending the Earth from mystic peril. **TB**

WOO, JIMMY

FIRST APPEARANCE Yellow Claw #1 (October 1956)

REAL NAME James "Jimmy" Woo **OCCUPATION** Adventurer

BASE San Francisco **HEIGHT** 5 ft 8 in **WEIGHT** 170 lbs

EYES Brown **HAIR** Black

SPECIAL POWERS/ABILITIES Investigative agent specializing in infiltration and information.

In the 1950s, Jimmy worked for the FBI against the forces of the Yellow Claw. In 1958, he led an early super group called the G-Men, but it disbanded six months later, after which he joined SHIELD. Recently, he was nearly killed in action against the Atlas Foundation. MARVEL BOY healed him, restoring his youth but at the cost of his memories. Reuniting the G-Men, Jimmy discovered that the YELLOW CLAW had been grooming him to be an heir for his empire, based on his lineage from Genghis Khan.

WOODGOD

FIRST APPEARANCE Marvel Premiere #31 (August 1976)

REAL NAME Woodgod

OCCUPATION Lawgiver of the Changelings

BASE The Rocky Mountains, Colorado

HEIGHT 6 ft 3 in **WEIGHT** 265 lbs

EYES Red **HAIR** Reddish-brown

SPECIAL POWERS/ABILITIES Woodgod possesses superhuman strength and an immunity to nerve gas.

Woodgod is a genetically engineered being, created by scientists David and Ellen Pace. Combining human and animal genetic material, the Paces created Woodgod, who resembles the half-human, half-goat Satyr of Greek myth. The townsfolk of Liberty, near the Pace's farm in New Mexico, convinced themselves that Woodgod was a dangerous monster. They tried to kill the creature using a canister of a deadly nerve gas invented by David Pace. Woodgod proved to be immune to the gas, but the Paces were both killed. The Grief-stricken Woodgod discovered the Paces' notes and created a race of half-human, half-animal beings, which he called Changelings. The Changelings found a secret home away from humanity in the Colorado Rockies. Woodgod dreams that one day the Changelings will be able to come out of hiding and live in harmony with the human race. **MT**

WOODMAN, SENATOR

FIRST APPEARANCE Avengers: The Initiative #7 (December 2007)

REAL NAME Arthur Woodman

OCCUPATION Congressman, HYDRA leader

BASE Washington, DC

HEIGHT 6 ft **WEIGHT** 220 lbs **EYES** Brown **HAIR** Brown

SPECIAL POWERS/ABILITIES Powerful and cunning politician and leader.

Arthur Woodman led a double life for a long while, playing both the prominent politician and rising through the ranks of HYDRA at the same time. When VIPER, the HYDRA leader, was discovered to be a Skrull, Woodman stepped into the vacuum she left behind and declared himself HYDRA's supreme leader. Woodman blackmailed HARDBALL into becoming a HYDRA agent. When the Initiative caught Woodman and Hardball trying to steal Komodo's lizard serum for HYDRA, Woodman injected himself with the serum and became a giant lizard-man. Hardball killed him and then took over his position as the leader of HYDRA. **MF**

WRAITH

FIRST APPEARANCE Marvel Team-Up #48 (August 1976)

REAL NAME Brian DeWolff **OCCUPATION** Vigilante crimefighter

BASE New York City **HEIGHT** 5 ft 11 in **WEIGHT** 190 lbs

EYES Blue **HAIR** Reddish-blond

SPECIAL POWERS/ABILITIES Able to affect the minds of others, controlling them, casting illusions, or rendering himself invisible; also able to evade Spider-Man's "spider-sense."

Three men have gone by the name Wraith. Brian DeWolff was crippled in the line of duty before his father turned him into a Super Hero under his strict control. Freed by SPIDER-MAN and IRON FIST, he continued as a crimefighter until he was killed. The second, Hector Rendoza, was a mutant who could turn his flesh translucent. He lost his powers on M-Day. The third, Zak-Del, became infected with Exolon, a soul-eating parasite. He fought the PHALANX and freed the KREE from their control. **AD, MF**

WRECKER

FIRST APPEARANCE Thor #148 (January 1968)

REAL NAME Dirk Garthwaite

OCCUPATION Criminal **BASE** Mobile

HEIGHT 6 ft 3 in **WEIGHT** 320 lbs **EYES** Blue **HAIR** Brown

SPECIAL POWERS/ABILITIES Superhuman strength and invulnerability; mental link to his enchanted crowbar allows him to transfer his powers into the crowbar, and then back to himself.

Wrecker was violent criminal who used a crowbar to demolish the scenes of his crimes thereby hindering investigation. When he was accidentally given magic powers by KARNILLA, the Norn Queen, Wrecker went on a rampage that attracted the attention of THOR. Placed in prison by the Asgardian automaton named Destroyer, Wrecker escaped with three other inmates who took on the costumed identities of THUNDERBALL, Bulldozer, and Piledriver, collectively known as the Wrecking Crew. He worked with the Hood and helped him battle the Skrulls during the Secret Invasion (see pp 326–7). **MT, MF**

X-23
FACTFILE

REAL NAME
Laura Kinney
OCCUPATION
Adventurer
BASE
San Francisco

HEIGHT 5 ft 6 in
WEIGHT 147 lbs
EYES Green
HAIR Black

FIRST APPEARANCE
NYX #3 (February, 2004)

POWERS

X-23 possesses superhuman agility, reflexes, speed, and senses. She can also extend adamantium-coated, retractable bone claws from her hands and feet.

X-23

Cloned from a damaged sample of WOLVERINE's DNA, which was missing the Y chromosome, X-23 was raised in the seclusion of the WEAPON X program by geneticist Dr. Sarah Kinney. As soon as she was old enough, she was sent on covert killing missions, sometimes influenced by a trigger scent that sent her into a berserker rage. When Dr. Kinney discovered that Weapon X had made dozens of clones of X-23 in order to fashion a small army of lethal mutants, she ordered her daughter to destroy them all. X-23 smelled her trigger scent during this operation and killed her mother while out of control. Leaving Weapon X, she made her way to Mutant Town in New York City where the X-MEN discovered her. Wolverine has taken her under his wing, and she became a member of the X-MEN and its covert operations squad, X-FORCE. **MF**

When X-23 goes berserk, nothing can stop her.

X-CORPS

FIRST APPEARANCE Uncanny X-Men #401 (January 2002)
BASE Paris, France
MEMBERS AND POWERS

Blob Superhuman size and strength; can create a gravity field that makes him immovable [1]. **Avalanche** Generates destructive vibrations from his hands [2]. **Banshee** Projects sonic screech [3]. **Husk** Biomorph: sheds skin to reveal transformed body beneath [4]. **Jubilee II** Projects "fireworks" from her fingers [5].

Following the death of his lover, Moira MacTaggert, and the collapse of the Massachusetts Academy where he was headmaster, Sean Cassidy lost his way. Establishing X-Corps, a paramilitary operation, Sean sought to enforce good behaviour between mutants. After releasing a number of criminal mutants from jail, he imprisoned the telepathic mutant, Mastermind and used her to control these mutants' activities. It wasn't long before the organization began to collapse, a process accelerated by the shapechanger MYSTIQUE who brought X-Corps to its knees, by freeing MASTERMIND and stabbing Sean in the throat. **AD**

X-CUTIONER

FIRST APPEARANCE X-Men Annual #1 (1970)
REAL NAME Carl Denti
OCCUPATION Vigilante; former FBI agent **BASE** Washington, DC
HEIGHT 6 ft 1 in **WEIGHT** 210 lbs **EYES** Brown **HAIR** Brown
SPECIAL POWERS/ABILITIES Possesses neuro-stun gauntlet, psi-lance, laser sword, teleporter, cloaking field, phasing unit, grappling claws, propulsion boots and a genetic scanner. Shi'ar battle-armor enhances strength to almost superhuman levels.

X-CELL

FIRST APPEARANCE X-Factor #18 (June 2007)
BASE Mobile
MEMBERS AND POWERS

ELIJAH CROSS Increases his mass without slowing him down.
ABYSS Shapeshifter, dimensional transport.
CALLISTO Superhuman senses, strength, speed, agility, and reflexes, plushealing factor. **FATALE** Teleportation and light manipulation, including invisibility [1]. **MARROW** Bone growth, healing factor, and superhuman strength, agility, and durability [2]. **REAPER** Cybernetic hands and leg, plus a scythe that paralyzes. **BLOB** Superhuman strength and durability, immovable [3].

After most of the world's mutants lost their powers on M-Day, Elijah Cross banded together a group of ex-mutant terrorists who believed the US government was behind a conspiracy that caused them to lose their powers. Under Cross's leadership, they tracked down Quicksilver to see if he could repower them with the Terrigen Crystals he can produce from his body. He did so for Abyss, Cross, Fatale, Reaper, and Rictor. After Cross literally exploded from becoming overpowered, Abyss grabbed Fatale and Reaper and disappeared. The others managed to escape on their own. Their current whereabouts and status is unknown. **MF**

Special Agent Denti had been partnered with Fred Duncan, who had secretly aided PROFESSOR X on occasion. Duncan stored equipment and weaponry that the X-MEN had confiscated from alien races and other threats. After Duncan was murdered, Denti vowed revenge. He discovered Duncan's connections to the X-Men and used the impounded weaponry to hunt down mutants who had not been convicted for their crimes. He clashed with the X-Men, and also assisted the PUNISHER. After Denti gave up his hunt, he was briefly replaced by a second X-Cutioner an alternate reality version of Gambit, but later died in action. **PS**

X-Factor

Mutant investigators

A number of teams have used the name X-Factor. The first was comprised of the original X-Men, who had left Professor X's team over the fact that he'd installed their old foe Magneto as the team's new leader. Posing as mutant hunters, Archangel, Beast, Cyclops, Jean Grey, and Iceman set up shop in Manhattan. They pretended to set out to bring mutants in to justice, but instead trained them in the use of their powers and in how to blend into regular society. Their recruits included Artie, Boom Boom, Rusty Collins, Leech, Rictor, and Skids.

Madrox is the heart of the latest X-Factor.

UNDERCOVER HUNTERS

When in costume, X-Factor pretended to be the outlaw X-Terminators. Eventually, though, they gave up on this ruse, believing it to cause more harm than good. The original members opted to rejoin the X-Men instead of continuing on. Rather than let X-Factor fade away, the US government formed a new team using the name. This started out with Havok, Jamie Madrox, Polaris, Quicksilver, Strong Guy, and Wolfsbane, with Valerie Cooper as their governmental liaison. A later version of the team included the criminals Mystique, Sabretooth, Shard, and Wild Child led by Forge.

X-FACTOR I
1 Archangel
2 Iceman
3 Cyclops
4 Jean Grey
5 Beast

X-FACTOR III
1 Strong Guy 2 Rictor 3 Wolfsbane 4 Madrox
5 Siryn 6 M

A third version of this team reunited many members of the various government teams. However, it broke up after an exploding time machine sent Havok to Earth-1298, in which many of roles of the mainstream Earth's heroes and villains were swapped. Later a governmental Mutant Civil Rights Task Force used the X-Factor name for a short while. After M-Day, Jamie Madrox opened up a private investigations firm called X-Factor Investigations with many of his old friends. This included M, Layla Miller (Butterfly), Siryn, Strong Guy, Wolfsbane, and a powerless Rictor. The team set out to determine what happened on M-Day and became embroiled in the hunt for the first mutant baby born after that fateful event. Recently, Madrox and Miller traveled to the future of Earth-1191, in which the birth of the mutant baby led to mutants being rounded up into concentration camps. M, Madrox, Siryn, and Strong Guy are all that remain of the original team. **MF**

Despite its low profile, X-Factor Investigations still deals with larger threats—like Sentinels.

ESSENTIAL STORYLINES
• *X-Factor #6*
The first regular appearance of Apocalypse.
• *X-Factor #149*
X-Factor disbands, and Havok is sent to Earth-1298.
• *X-Factor Vol. 2 #1*
In the wake of M-Day, Jamie Madrox forms X-Factor Investigations.

X-FORCE

Cable, founder and mentor of X-Force.

PROFESSOR X founded a young mutant team, the NEW MUTANTS, for training. After he had journeyed into outer space and a new headmaster, MAGNETO, had come and gone, CABLE became the team's mentor. He trained his charges to become soldiers against mutant threats and renamed the team X-Force. The roster included Boom Boom (later MELTDOWN) and CANNONBALL, FERAL, SHATTERSTAR, WARPATH, and the shapeshifter COPYCAT, who posed as Cable's ally DOMINO. The real Domino later joined X-Force, as did Bedlam, CALIBAN, MOONSTAR, RICTOR, SIRYN, and Sunspot.

After Cable left, former British intelligence agent Peter WISDOM briefly took over as leader, turning the team into an even more aggressive commando squad. X-Force then disbanded.

There have been three other X-Force teams. The first, which predated Cable's team, featured artificially mutated US soldiers. The second turned into X-STATIX. The third was a black-ops team formed by Cyclops. Its lineup was ARCHANGEL, DOMINO, ELIXIR, VANISHER, WARPATH, WOLFSBANE, WOLVERINE, and X-23. **PS, MF**

X-FORCE
1 X-23 2 Wolverine 3 Domino
4 Warpath 5 Archangel

FACTFILE

NOTABLE MEMBERS
BEDLAM (Jesse Aaronson)
Can disrupt electronic devices.
DOMINO
Can alter luck in her favor, formidable combatant.
CANNONBALL
Can propel himself through the air by releasing energy
DANIELLE MOONSTAR
Could create images from the minds of others
WARPATH (PROUDSTAR)
Superhuman strength, speed, and durability.
MELTDOWN (BOOM BOOM)
Creates explosive energy balls.
SUNSPOT
Absorbs solar energy for superhuman strength
SIRYN
Sonic scream
BASE
Various

FIRST APPEARANCE
X-Force #1
(August 1991)

X-MAN

Even on the alternate Earth known as the Age of Apocalypse, MISTER SINISTER is as obsessed with the progeny of Jean GREY and Scott Summers (see CYCLOPS) as the Mister Sinister of Earth-616. After obtaining genetic material from these two individuals, he created their child artificially, naming him Nathan Grey. By greatly accelerating the child's growth and development Sinister intended to use Nathan's mutant powers to fight Apocalypse. Ultimately, the Age of Apocalypse timeline was doomed. After killing Sinister—an act which gave him no pleasure— Nate managed to escape to the mainstream Earth. Following his arrival he made it his goal to prevent this Earth from suffering the same dystopian fate. Although initially at odds with the X-MEN, he eventually joined the team, before becoming a shaman and dedicating himself to healing and guiding others. Sadly, Nate's life was to end prematurely when he sacrificed himself to protect his adopted home reality. **AD**

When moved to anger, X-Man's psionic fury was almost unstoppable.

FACTFILE

REAL NAME
Nathan "Nate" Grey
OCCUPATION
Shaman
BASE
Mobile

HEIGHT 5 ft 9 in
WEIGHT 171 lbs
EYES Blue
HAIR Brown

FIRST APPEARANCE
X-Man #1
(March 1995)

POWERS

A telepath of vast power; able to read and control minds, project his astral form across the world, and create complex psionic illusions, and "psionic spikes." Also possessed considerable telekinetic powers, allowing him to move heavy objects at will.

X-MEN *see pages 378-385*

X-MEN 2099

The X-Men 2099 were initially based in the mountains of New Mexico.

In an alternate future, the Earth is ruled by malevolent, self-serving corporations and mutants have been outlawed— forced underground.

In the year 2099, one mutant dedicated himself to overthrowing this oppressive world order. Gathering some of the surviving mutants together to form a new band of X-MEN, the almost messianic Xi'an Chi Xan (also known as the Desert Ghost) began challenging this status quo.

Initially based at a mountain fortress in New Mexico that had once belonged to an enemy named Master Zhao, these X-Men were to become the protectors of Halo City in California, which had been declared a safe haven for mutants. However, when an approaching PHALANX planetoid caused severe flooding, mutants and humans were forced to flee to the Savage Land, in the Antarctic. Following the Phalanx's defeat, humanity is now in a position to rebuild. With humans and mutants now united together, the future is, once again, full of possibilities. **AD**

X-MEN 2099
1 Bloodhawk **2** Krystalin **3** Desert Ghost **4** Skullfire **5** Metalhead **6** Cerebra **7** Meanstreak

⊙ X-PEOPLE *see page 385*

FACTFILE

MEMBERS AND POWERS

XI'AN CHI XAN
With his left hand he disintegrates matter, with his right hand he heals injuries.

CEREBRA
Detects mutants with her mind.

KRYSTALIN
Creates crystals from thin air.

MEANSTREAK
Travels at superhuman speeds.

METALHEAD
Touches any metal and assumes its properties.

SKULLFIRE
Absorbed energy makes his skeleton glow.

BLOODHAWK
Transmutes body to develop red skin and bat-like wings.

BASE
The Savage Land, Antarctica

FIRST APPEARANCE
X-Men 2099 #1 (October 1993)

X-STATIX

Mr. Sensitive and Venus were lovers until both died on their final mission.

Rather than hide their mutant abilities from a bigoted humanity, the members of X-Statix took a completely opposite approach. They used their mutant powers to become rich and famous. The team was known as X-FORCE, having stolen the name from another mutant band.

The members of this new X-Force battled criminals to protect the public. But their adventures were telecast as a reality show, and members became celebrities. They paid for their success with their lives. During one show, most of the team, including the leader Zeitgeist, were massacred. Only the Anarchist, the teleporter U-GO GIRL, and Doop survived.

Guy Smith, alias the ORPHAN and Mister Sensitive, became the leader. Other recruits included Bloke, Dead Girl, El Guapo, Phat, Saint Anna, the Spike, Venus Dee Milo, and the Vivisector. Smith was succeeded as leader by the Anarchist and mutant pop star Henrietta Hunter. To avoid potential legal action, the group changed its name to X-Statix. The team continued to suffer fatalities, and the roster was completely wiped out on X-Statix's final mission. Their adventures continued, however, in the afterlife. **PS, MF**

X-STATIX
1 Henrietta Hunter **2** Vivisector **3** El Guapo **4** Dead Girl **5** Venus Dee Milo **6** Doop **7** Anarchist **8** Mister Sensitive **9** Phat

FACTFILE

MEMBERS AND POWERS

HENRIETTA HUNTER Empathic powers, could resurrect herself.

VIVISECTOR Could shapeshift into wolflike form.

EL GUAPO Could levitate while riding a skateboard.

DEAD GIRL Can return to life, can become intangible and communicate with the dead.

VENUS DEE MILO Body composed of pure energy, could self-teleport and project energy blasts.

DOOP Self-levitation

ANARCHIST Acidic sweat generated energy bolts.

MISTER SENSITIVE (ORPHAN) Self-levitation, superhuman speed, heightened senses.

PHAT Could increase the size of any part of his body

BASE Mobile

FIRST APPEARANCE
(as X-Force) X-Force #116 (May 2001); (as X-Statix) X-Statix #1 (September 2002)

X-MEN

Earth's mightiest team

FACTFILE

MEMBERS AND POWERS

PROFESSOR X (Charles Xavier)
Telepathy

CYCLOPS (Scott Summers)
Optic power beams

PHOENIX (Marvel Girl I, Jean
Grey) Telepathy, telekinesis

ARCHANGEL (Angel, Warren
Worthington III) Flight

BEAST (Henry McCoy)
Superhuman strength and agility

ICEMAN (Bobby Drake)
Generates intense cold

COLOSSUS (Peter Rasputin)
Turns to "organic steel"

NIGHTCRAWLER (Kurt Wagner)
Teleportation

ROGUE (Real name unrevealed)
Absorbs memories and abilities

SHADOWCAT (Kitty Pryde)
"Phases" through solid objects

STORM (Ororo Munroe)
Controls weather

WOLVERINE (Logan)
Adamantium skeleton and claws

BASE The Xavier Institute,
Salem Center, New York State

FIRST APPEARANCE
X-Men #1 (September 1963)

ALLIES The New Mutants,
Excalibur, X-Factor, Generation X,
the Fantastic Four, the Avengers,
Spider-Man, Doctor Strange

FOES Magneto, the Juggernaut,
the Sentinels, Apocalypse, Mister
Sinister, Mystique, Brotherhood of
Evil Mutants, the Hellfire Club, the
Brood

Professor X trains his X-Men and
the team are confronted with
arch-enemy Magneto.

The X-Men is a team of superhuman mutants that was founded by Professor Charles Xavier (PROFESSOR X), who is not only a mutant himself, but is also one of the world's leading authorities on mutation. In founding the X-Men, Xavier had two principal purposes. First, he sought to find young mutants and to train them in utilizing their superhuman powers. Second, Xavier intended the X-Men to serve as a combat team to defend "ordinary" humans against attack by other mutants. Further, Xavier recognizes that "normal" humans tend to fear and distrust the mutants who are appearing in their midst, and that therefore mutants often suffer persecution.

XAVIER'S DREAM

In founding the X-Men, Xavier created a community of mutants living together on his estate. Xavier is a visionary who hopes to help bring about peaceful coexistence between mutants and the rest of the human race. The X-Men are dedicated to this goal, which they call "Xavier's dream." Xavier has explained that he named the team "X-Men" after the "extra" powers that his mutant students possess. (Of course, "X" is also the first letter of Xavier's last name.) As a young man, Xavier battled another mutant telepath, Amahl Farouk, alias the Shadow King, in Egypt. This encounter made him aware of the need to protect humanity from malevolent mutants.

ROAD TO RECOVERY

Xavier subsequently lost the use of his legs in a clash with an alien who called himself Lucifer. Deeply depressed, Xavier led a reclusive existence at his family mansion. However, he began treating a ten-year-old girl named Jean Grey whose mutant powers had emerged prematurely.

Years later, the FBI initiated an investigation of mutants, headed by agent Fred Duncan. Xavier met

ESSENTIAL STORYLINES
• *Giant-Size X-Men #1*
Charles Xavier forms a new international team of X-Men.
• *The Uncanny X-Men #129–137*
"The Dark Phoenix Saga": the X-Men try to stop the mad Phoenix (Jean Grey) from wreaking havoc through the cosmos and save her from insanity.
• *The Uncanny X-Men #141–142*
"Days of Future Past": present day X-Men try to prevent a future America ruled by Sentinels.

THE X-MEN
1 Storm **2** Banshee **3** Angel
4 Sunfire **5** Iceman **6** Havok
7 Polaris **8** Marvel Girl (Jean Grey)
9 Colossus **10** Nightcrawler
11 Wolverine **12** Cyclops
13 Thunderbird

The X-Men are based in Charles Xavier's Westchester County mansion.

for Gifted Youngsters, a private school based in Xavier's mansion, in the town of Salem Center in New York City's Westchester County.

There Xavier educated them in conventional academic subjects, while secretly teaching them how to utilize their mutant abilities.

The next member of the X-Men, who served only briefly, was the MIMIC, who was not a mutant but had the ability to imitate mutant powers. During a period when Xavier was in seclusion, he was impersonated by the CHANGELING, a shapeshifting mutant who died heroically. The mutants HAVOK and Lorna Dane, later known as POLARIS, joined the team subsequently.

NEW RECRUITS

Most of the X-Men became trapped on the island of Krakoa, which proved to be a gigantic mutant organism. Xavier then recruited a new team of X-Men from various countries. The new members included the BANSHEE, from Ireland; Colossus, from Russia; NIGHTCRAWLER, from Germany; Storm, from equatorial Africa; SUNFIRE, from Japan; THUNDERBIRD, a Native American; and WOLVERINE, from Canada.

Led by Cyclops, the new recruits rescued the X-Men from Krakoa. After their return, the senior X-Men left the team, except for Cyclops, who remained as deputy leader. Sunfire quit, and Thunderbird was killed during the new X-Men's second mission.

Over subsequent years, many other members

with Duncan and volunteered to locate young mutants and train them in managing their potentially dangerous abilities. Duncan agreed to the plan and pledged to keep Xavier's work with mutants secret. Xavier soon recruited five adolescent mutants to his school, giving each of them codenames: CYCLOPS, ICEMAN, the Angel (see ARCHANGEL), the BEAST, and Marvel Girl (the teenage Jean GREY). All five were enrolled at Professor Xavier's School

have joined the X-Men, including Kitty PRYDE, alias Shadowcat; ROGUE; Rachel SUMMERS, known both as the second Phoenix and the current Marvel Girl; PSYLOCKE; the DAZZLER; and LONGSHOT. During a temporary reformation, even the X-Men's archfoe Magneto even joined the team.

After forming their own group, X-FACTOR, the five founding X-Men returned to their original team. Xavier's school was renamed the Xavier Institute. Further new members included FORGE, JUBILEE, GAMBIT, BISHOP, REVANCHE, CANNONBALL, Joseph (a clone of Magneto), Dr. Cecilia Reyes, MARROW and MAGGOTT.

Storm organized a short-lived spinoff team called the X-Treme X-Men, which included, SAGE, the third THUNDERBIRD, LIFEGUARD and Slipstream. Most of these members joined the main X-Men team.

OPEN SECRET

Many other heroes have joined the X-Men over the years, including CABLE, CHAMBER, HUSK, NORTHSTAR, Stacy X, and the traitor XORN. Even former foes like Emma FROST, JUGGERNAUT, and MYSTIQUE have been part of the team. Ever since Professor X's evil twin sister Cassandra Nova exposed him as a mutant, the world has known that the Xavier Institute was the headquarters of the X-Men. This made it possible for the Institute to openly advocate for mutant rights. In the aftermath of M-Day, the government made the X Mansion a sort of reservation for mutants, keeping the few remaining ones there, purportedly for their safety.

PS, MF

Xavier formed a new international team of X-Men after the immense mutant Krakoa the Living Island captured the original team.

CEREBRO

Cerebro is a machine invented by Professor Charles Xavier to locate mutants possessing superhuman abilities. Cerebro accomplishes this by detecting psionic energy emitted by the minds of superhuman mutants. Cerebro operates best when it is linked to the mind of a telepath, such as Xavier or Jean Grey, through a headset. Xavier utilized an early version of Cerebro, called Cyberno, to locate Scott Summers, who became Cyclops. On combining with the Sentinel Bastion's nanotechnology, Cerebro became sentient. It posed a menace until Xavier destroyed it. Since then Xavier has created an advanced version, called Cerebra.

Among the X-Men's adversaries are Sabretooth (left, fighting Wolverine), the insect-like alien Brood (battling Cyclops), and their leading nemesis Magneto (top right, attacking Bishop).

X-Men

Disgusted with Magneto, the Scarlet Witch removed 90 per cent of the world's mutants on November 2.

M-Day

One of the world's most powerful mutants, the SCARLET WITCH, had a breakdown, during which she tore apart the team with which she worked: the Avengers. Later, as the X-Men discussed the Scarlet Witch's fate, her brother, QUICKSILVER, encouraged her to use her powers to remake the world. At her bidding thousands more people became mutants, and her father, MAGNETO, ruled the planet as the leader of the House of M. To keep others from looking too closely at their new reality, she gave them whatever they wanted: respectability, money, love, power.

Once the Scarlet Witch had been made to realize what she'd done, she changed everything back to normal—with a few twists. Among these were the fact that 90 per cent of the world's mutants lost their powers, including Magneto, Professor X, and herself.

The Aftermath

With the mutant population decimated, the US government estimated that 198 mutants were left with their powers intact. The Office of National Emergency (ONE) under Valerie COOPER moved to gather these mutants at the Xavier Mansion and keep them there, guarded by SENTINELS.

This lasted until the Civil War (see pp. 84–5), during which the X-Men officially remained neutral. As the war progressed, the restrictions on the mutants living at the X Mansion were lifted, with the Sentinels left in place to guard the residents from outside attacks.

The power of the mutants had been stripped from them, but it could not be destroyed. Many of the powers banded into a being known as the Collective, which possessed mutant Michael Pointer (GUARDIAN) and used him to cut a swathe of destruction across North America. The Collective then traveled to Genosha to converse with Magneto before racing off into space. As it left the planet, it brushed past Krakoa—the island-sized mutant that nearly killed the original X-Men—and awakened the missing Summers brother, Gabriel (VULCAN). Gabriel returned to Earth and, after killing BANSHEE, revealed that he had been part of a team of young mutants sent to save the original X-Men from Krakoa. After they had all been apparently killed, Professor X had erased the memory of their existence. Learning this, Cyclops informed the professor that he would no longer be welcome with his X-Men.

As the Collective, Michael Pointer and Xorn slaughtered Alpha Flight, repowered Magneto, and awakened Vulcan.

INTERPLANETARY PROBLEMS

Trying to make up for his mistakes, Professor X led a team of X-Men—including Darwin, Havok, Nightcrawler, Polaris, Rachel Summers, and Warpath—into space to stop Vulcan. They failed to keep Vulcan from killing his father, Corsair, but they and the rest of the Starjammers rescued Lilandra. After Xavier regained his powers, he and half the team returned to Earth, leaving the others to form a new Starjammers to stand against Vulcan, who had become the new ruler of the Shi'ar Empire.

The other X-Men, under Cyclops, traveled to the planet Breakworld, where its leader was preparing to fire a gigantic missile at the Earth, large enough to destroy the planet. Kitty Pryde phased into the missile to try to defuse it but discovered it was actually a solid bullet. Using all her might, she managed to phase the bullet through Earth, but she remained trapped inside of it and is now presumed dead.

When the Hulk returned to Earth to have his revenge on the Illuminati, he went to the X Mansion to confront Xavier. After a pitched battle, the Hulk learned about all of the horrible things that had happened to the mutants in his absence and concluded that they had suffered plenty as a people.

Professor X's X-Men consisted of Vulcan, Sway, Petra, and Darwin. They were lost fighting Krakoa.

MESSIAH COMPLEX

It looked like there would be no more mutants to join the 198 or so left on the planet. While using his Cerebra mutant-finding machine, though, Professor X spotted one amazingly powerful new mutant in Cooperstown, Alaska, and Cyclops led a team of X-Men to investigate. The anti-mutant militants known as the Purifiers, and Mr. Sinister's new team of Marauders, beat the X-Men there.

The Purifiers, realizing that they were looking for a young mutant, killed every child in town, even the infants still in the hospital. This tipped the X-Men—along with X-Factor and the Young X-Men—off to the fact that the first mutant since M-Day had been born— and manifested its powers at birth. They later learned that Cable had gotten there first and taken the baby to safety.

Meanwhile, Predator X, a monster the Purifiers had created to destroy the "Mutant Anti-Christ," found the baby's scent and began killing mutants to sate its hunger as it tracked the infant down. While many X-Men were out hunting for the baby, the Nano-Sentinels infected the human pilots of the Sentinels assigned to guard the mansion. They attacked, nearly destroying the place. In response to this, Cyclops formed an all-new X-Force as a black-ops team. **MF**

Gambit joined Mr. Sinister's new Marauders—not to help with their plans but to advance his own.

The US government agency ONE positioned Sentinels around the X-Mansion to keep hostile humans out—and the mutants in.

HOUSE OF M

When Quicksilver believed that the X-Men and their friends might put his sister the Scarlet Witch to death for disassembling the Avengers, he encouraged her to use her powers to reshape reality. After a flash of light, the world became one in which mutants were plentiful and Magneto and his House of M ruled. No one remembered things ever being any other way. With the help of Layla Miller—a mutant who could restore to others the memories they had lost—Wolverine led a movement and assault to put things right.

X-MEN

Sent into the future as a baby himself, Cable hoped to save the baby he would raise as Hope Summers the same way.

THE FUTURE OF MUTANTKIND

When Cable went to Forge for a time machine so he could escape with the baby, he discovered Bishop had already shot Forge. In the future from which Bishop came, the first mutant baby became the Mutant Messiah and later killed a million humans. Bishop meant to stop that by

murdering the infant. The Marauders prevented that and stole the child. Before Sinister could get his hands on the infant, Mystique killed him and used the baby to bring ROGUE out of a coma caused by her absorbing too many minds at once.

X-Force managed to kill Predator X while the Young X-Men defeated the remaining Marauders. Professor X took the baby from Gambit, who'd rescued her from Mystique, and gave her back to Cable, just before Cyclops and the X-Men caught up with them. While the baby held the potential to cause Bishop's horrible future, Cyclops saw that it also could bring Cable's better future to pass instead. Showing his long-buried optimism, Cyclops gave the baby to Cable to escape into the future.

As Cable and the baby disappeared, Bishop caught up with them and shot at them. A bullet hit Professor X, nearly killing him. Cyclops took Bishop down, but he soon escaped to chase Cable through time, still pursuing the baby, who Cable named Hope Summers.

Cyclops picked Wolverine to lead the new black-ops X-Force team.

Predator X was designed to hunt down and devour mutants of any kind, but it hungered for the mutant baby most of all.

BRROOGGGG!

A NEW HOME

With the mansion destroyed and Professor X now missing, Cyclops decided to end the X-Men—or so he told IRON MAN when he came to ask the X-Men to register with the Fifty State Initiative (see pp.118–9).

He moved the team to the Marin Headlands near San Francisco, where the mayor rejected the help of the Fifty State Initiative and made the X-Men the city's official protectors. They set up shop in an abandoned military complex they renamed Graymalkin Industries (after the road where they had had their original headquarters), placing a mutant embassy on top of a facility that extended three miles below the Earth's surface. Then, through Emma Frost, Cyclops telepathically declared the city of San Francisco a mutant sanctuary.

Professor X resurfaced with his powers intact to lead another group of X-Men aiming to find and rescue Rogue from Danger, the personification of the Danger Room. At the same time, Cyclops and his X-Men and X-Force teams were gearing up for the Messiah War, the next round in the battle over Hope Summers. **MF**

Pixie and the rest of the X-Men have settled into their new headquarters in San Francisco with a renewed sense of both determination and hope.

SHE'S DOWN!

HERE'S OUR CHANCE TO STAGE AN ALL-OUT ASSAULT!

DUHHH! LISTEN TO SIMIAN THE MASTER STRATEGIST!

X-PEOPLE

The X-People inhabit an alternate future in which the Earth's superhuman population is dominated by a new generation of champions. In this reality, the X-Men have been recast as the X-People. Under the leadership of an adult JUBILEE, the team upholds the principles of PROFESSOR X, who envisioned the peaceful coexistence of humans and mutants.

The new faces making up the roster of the X-People include the winged Angry Eagle, the gymnastic Simian, shapeshifting Spanner, and superfast Torque. Former members included the speedster Bluestreak, and an aging CYCLOPS, who still maintains connections to the team. The X-People battled J2 (son of JUGGERNAUT) when the villainess Enthralla used her hypnotic abilities to coerce them into violence. Later, the X-People trained WILD THING (daughter of WOLVERINE), but she declined the team's offer of membership. **DW**

ENOUGH, SPANNER--!

STOP BICKERING... AND SPREAD OUT!

CHARACTER KEY
1 Angry Eagle
2 Simian
3 Spanner
4 Torque
5 Jubilee

FACTFILE

CURRENT MEMBERS AND POWERS
JUBILEE (leader)
Generates explosive energy bursts.
ANGRY EAGLE
Flight, enhanced eyesight.
SIMIAN
Enhanced agility, talented acrobat.
SPANNER
Can elongate limbs and change shape.
TORQUE
A super-speedster.
BASE
Mobile

FIRST APPEARANCE
J2 Vol. 1 #1
(October 1998)

XANDU

FIRST APPEARANCE Amazing Spider-Man Annual #2 (1965)
REAL NAME Unknown
OCCUPATION Sorceror **BASE** New York City
HEIGHT/WEIGHT Unrevealed **EYES** Blue **HAIR** White
SPECIAL POWERS/ABILITIES Xandu possesses numerous abilities derived from his sorcery, most notably a hypnotic gaze that makes other people do his bidding.

A would-be master sorcerer into whose possession half of the mystic Wand of Watomb fell, Xandu desired the power that would be his if he could unite both halves of this magical talisman. Recruiting several toughs at the waterfront and casting a spell that turned them into robots, Xandu sent them to recover the other half of the wand from DOCTOR STRANGE. But Strange gained an unexpected ally when SPIDER-MAN stumbled on the robbery, and together they defeated Xandu's agents. Strange caused Xandu to forget all of his magical knowledge, but this didn't prevent the renegade sorcerer from returning again and again to challenge the two heroes. **TB**

XAVIER'S SECURITY ENFORCERS

FIRST APPEARANCE Uncanny X-Men Vol. 1 #282 (November 1991)
BASE Mobile
NOTABLE MEMBERS AND POWERS
Bishop Absorbs and releases any form of energy.
Randall (deceased) Immune to radiation, skilled combatant.
Malcolm (deceased) Could distinguish between humans and mutants.
Shard (deceased) Can absorb light and emit it as shockwaves.
Hecate Projects a null-light field that causes others to see their fears.

In an alternate future in which Earth's population rose up against their oppressors, the SENTINELS, a mutant police force was formed to ensure peace between mutants and humans. This group called itself Xavier's Security Enforcers in tribute to the idealism of the X-Men's PROFESSOR X. The XSE eventually arrived in our world's current reality while pursuing renegade member Trevor Fitzroy. A traitorous splinter group, Xavier's Underground Enforcers, included Greystone (1), Archer (2), and Fixx (3). **DW**

XEMNU

FIRST APPEARANCE Journey into Mystery #62 (November 1960)
REAL NAME Xemnu **OCCUPATION** Former ruler **BASE** Mobile
HEIGHT 11 ft **WEIGHT** 1,100 lbs **EYES** Red
HAIR Reddish-brown; more recently white
SPECIAL POWERS/ABILITIES Consciousness able to survive without body for indefinite periods; psionically manipulate individuals through vast hypnotic abilities.

Although he cuts a lonely, tragic figure, Xemnu the Titan remains a very real threat to mankind. The one-time ruler of his native world, Xemnu left there to travel the galaxy. Upon returning home he discovered it had been ravaged by plague, and his people were dead. Having felt most at home on Earth, Xemnu returned there and made several attempts to transform its citizens into members of his own race. He was repeatedly rebuffed, the HULK, DR STRANGE and the THING all taking turns to defeat him. Xemnu looks set to be the last of his kind. **AD**

YAMA, JIMMY

FIRST APPEARANCE Spider-Girl Vol. 1 #1 (October 1998)

REAL NAME Jimmy Yama

OCCUPATION High-school student **BASE** New York City

HEIGHT 5 ft 5 in **WEIGHT** 145 lbs **EYES** Brown **HAIR** Black

SPECIAL POWERS/ABILITIES Jimmy is an ordinary teenager with no special powers.

In a future timeline populated by a second generation of Earth's heroes, Jimmy Yama is a Midtown High School student and friend to May Parker (SPIDER-GIRL). Yama's nemesis is Midtown bully Moose Mansfield. When Yama lashed out at Moose and inadvertently injured him, he stood trial for punitive damages until Moose's parents dropped the case.

Yama has tried several times to establish a romantic relationship with May, but his efforts have been hindered by his shyness. **DW**

YANCY STREET GANG

FIRST APPEARANCE Fantastic Four Vol. 1 #6 (September 1962)

BASE Yancy Street, on the Lower East Side of Manhattan

Based around the tough neighborhood of Manhattan's Lower East Side, the Yancy Street Gang was at one time led by Daniel Grimm, the wayward older brother of Ben Grimm, fated to transform into the THING. Daniel was killed during a rumble between the Yancy gang and a rival street gang, and Ben eventually replaced his brother as the leader. But when Ben moved out west after the death of his mother, the Yancy Gang took it as a betrayal.

After Ben was transformed into the Thing and became one of the FANTASTIC FOUR, the Yancy Street Gang made it their mission to heckle and bedevil their former member. During the Civil War (see pp. 84–5), the gang sided with the outlaw heroes. The Puppet Master and Mad Thinker used them to incite a riot in which the gang's leader was killed. **TB, MF**

YASHIDA, MARIKO

FIRST APPEARANCE X-Men #118 (February 1979)

REAL NAME Mariko Yashida

OCCUPATION Head of Clan Yashida **BASE** Japan

HEIGHT 5 ft **WEIGHT** 100 lbs **EYES** Brown **HAIR** Black

SPECIAL POWERS/ABILITIES An exceptional businesswoman; had the normal fitness of a woman of her age and weight, but no special powers.

For many years, Mariko Yashida was the love of WOLVERINE's life. Meeting her during a mission to Japan, their relationship blossomed in New York, and they remained in contact even after her forced marriage to a brutal criminal associate of her father. The deaths of Mariko's husband and her father presented them with the opportunity for marriage, but Mariko wanted to wait—she had inherited the family business and wished to sever its criminal links first. In the end, the pair never wed—when she was poisoned by an assassin, Wolverine was forced to kill Mariko in order to end her terrible suffering. **AD**

YELLOW CLAW

FIRST APPEARANCE Yellow Claw #1 (October 1956)

REAL NAME Plan Tzu **OCCUPATION** Conqueror

BASE Various hidden bases around the world

HEIGHT 6 ft 2 in **WEIGHT** 210 lbs **EYES** Brown **HAIR** Bald

SPECIAL POWERS/ABILITIES Knowledge of biochemistry, genetics, robotics, and sorcery (can reanimate the dead); can mentally create illusions in the minds of others.

Born in China in the 1800s, Plan Tzu (a.k.a. Master Plan) became the latest in a line of conquerors stretching back to Genghis Khan. He chose a young Jimmy Woo as his successor, but Woo's parents moved to the US to avoid that fate. When Woo joined the FBI in the 1950s, Tzu became Woo's nemesis, the Yellow Claw. He then clashed with SHIELD after Woo joined that agency. In modern times, he finally revealed his plot to Woo and his AGENTS OF ATLAS. When Woo accepted his heritage, Tzu allowed the dragon Mr. Lao to devour him. **PS, MF**

YELLOWJACKET

FIRST APPEARANCE Avengers Vol. 1 #264 (February 1986)

REAL NAME Rita DeMara

OCCUPATION Adventurer; former criminal **BASE** Mobile

HEIGHT 5 ft 5 in **WEIGHT** 115 lbs **EYES** Blue **HAIR** Blonde

SPECIAL POWERS/ABILITIES Battlesuit provided flight, the ability to shrink via Pym particles, and gloves that fired "disruptor sting" blasts of electricity.

Rita DeMara adopted the identity of Yellowjacket after stealing Hank PYM's original battlesuit from Avengers Mansion. She embarked on a life of crime as the second Yellowjacket, joining the MASTERS OF EVIL before turning against that group. Her efforts to go straight earned her reserve member status in the Avengers, and a place with the GUARDIANS OF THE GALAXY. Yellowjacket II tragically died at the hands of IRON MAN, who at the time was under the mental control of IMMORTUS. **DW**

◎ **YOUNG AVENGERS** *see opposite page*

◎ **YOUNG X-MEN** *see opposite page*

YUKIO

FIRST APPEARANCE Wolverine Vol. 1 #1 (September 1982)

REAL NAME Yukio (full name unrevealed)

OCCUPATION Adventurer, former assassin **BASE** Mobile

HEIGHT 5 ft 9 in **WEIGHT** 130 lbs **EYES** Brown **HAIR** Black

SPECIAL POWERS/ABILITIES Highly skilled athlete, martial artist, and knife-thrower.

Yukio started out as a thief, running with GAMBIT, before becoming an assassin in the service of Japanese crimelord Lord Shingen of Clan Yashida. Her employer sent her after WOLVERINE; however, she eventually befriended him and his X-MEN teammates, particularly STORM. Wolverine grew to trust Yukio so much that he left his foster daughter Amiko in her care. Yukio and Amiko were attacked by OMEGA RED and LADY DEATHSTRIKE. During the fight, Yukio suffered crippling injuries from which she eventually recovered. **DW**

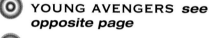

YOUNG AVENGERS

In a possible alternate future, a young robotics student named Nathaniel Richards is saved from death in the year 3016 by his future self. Nathaniel also learns that he is destined to grow up to become Kang the Conqueror. Horrified, the 16-year-old flees to modern-day Earth, hoping to circumvent his fate by securing help from the Avengers, Kang's greatest enemies.

Unfortunately, Nathaniel arrives soon after the SCARLET WITCH has disassembled the current team. He breaks into Stark Industries (*see* IRON MAN) and uploads the central processing unit of the recently destroyed android the Vision, finding a failsafe program that pinpoints the next generation of super-powered youths. Calling himself Iron Lad, Nathaniel quickly recruits them and trains them for a battle with Kang.

When CAPTAIN AMERICA and Iron Man learn of this new team, they try to convince the teenagers to disband before they get hurt, but Kang arrives and demands the return of Iron Lad so that destiny could fulfil its preordained course. Otherwise Kang would not exist! In the resulting battle, Kang is killed and Iron Lad must accept his destiny in order to prevent the destruction of the current timeline. **TD**

YOUNG AVENGERS
1 Wiccan
2 Stature
3 Hulkling
4 The Patriot
5 Kate Bishop

After leading the team against Mr. Hyde (left), Patriot admitted he had taken a mutant growth hormone to increase his physical powers.

FACTFILE
MEMBERS AND POWERS
IRON LAD (Nathaniel Richards)
Scientific genius with a suit of psychokinetic armor that responds to his thoughts.
WICCAN formerly Asgardian (Billy Kaplan)
Projects mystical energy.
KATE BISHOP
Olympic-level athlete and weapons-master.
STATURE (Cassie Lang)
Size-changing abilities.
HULKLING (Teddy Altman)
shapeshifter with healing factor.
PATRIOT (Eli Bradley)
Enhanced speed and agility.

BASE
Formerly Avengers Mansion, New York City

FIRST APPEARANCE
Young Avengers #1 (February 2005)

FACTFILE
MEMBERS AND POWERS
ANOLE Superhuman speed, reflexes, and coordination, plus regeneration, wallcrawling, and camouflage.
BLINDFOLD Telepath able to see past, future, and present.
CIPHER Undetectability and phasing.
DUST Living sandstorm.
GRAYMALKIN Superhuman strength, invulnerability, and night vision, which all increase in darkness.
INK Tattoos that grant various abilities.
MIRAGE (DANI MOONSTAR) None.
ROCKSLIDE Psionic creature who can telekinetically form a superstrong body from rock.
SUNSPOT Solar power control, superhuman strength, and flight.
WOLF CUB Wolfman form and enhanced senses.

BASE San Francisco

FIRST APPEARANCE
Young X-Men #1 (May 2008)

YOUNG X-MEN

In the aftermath of M-Day, CYCLOPS—the leader of the X-MEN—assembled a new team of mutants called the Young X-Men to bring down a new BROTHERHOOD OF EVIL MUTANTS. Ironically, this group was composed of former NEW MUTANTS Cannonball, Magma, Dani MOONSTAR, and SUNSPOT. Initially, the team members were Blindfold, Dust, Ink, Rockslide, and Wolf Cub—and secretly Cipher—but when they discovered that their Cyclops was actually X-Men foe Donald PIERCE, they united with their targets to defeat him. Before he was captured, however, Pierce managed to kill Wolf Cub.

Afterward, the real Cyclops made the team official and asked Sunspot and Moonstar to train the Young X-Men. Blindfold left the team, but Anole joined to replace her. The team eventually broke up, with many members joining the latest version of the NEW MUTANTS. **MF**

YOUNG X-MEN
1 Rockslide 2 Anole 3 Graymalkin 4 Cipher
5 Dust 6 Ink 7 Sunspot

ZABU

FIRST APPEARANCE X-Men #10 (March 1965)
REAL NAME Zabu **OCCUPATION** Companion to Ka-Zar
BASE The Savage Land, Antarctica **HEIGHT/WEIGHT** Unrevealed
EYES Green **HAIR** Orange
SPECIAL POWERS/ABILITIES Two long saber-like teeth; great
strength and agility; unusually intelligent for a saber-tooth tiger;
lifespan extended by gases in the Savage Land's "Place of Mists."

Zabu is the last known saber-tooth tiger on
Earth. The dominant predators during the Ice
Age, saber-tooths still survived in the Savage
Land, until nearly all of them were exterminated
by Savage Land natives. When Maa-Gor and his
Swamp Men slew Zabu's mate, the infuriated
tiger hunted them down. Zabu attacked Maa-
Gor just as he was about to kill Kevin Plunder,
the orphaned son of an explorer. In the ensuing
struggle, Kevin shot Maa-Gor, wounding him,
and thereby saving Zabu's life.

Ever since, Zabu and
Kevin have been loyal
companions, and
Kevin is known
today as the jungle
lord KA-ZAR, which
means "Son of the
Tiger." **PS**

ZARAN

FIRST APPEARANCE Master of Kung Fu #77 (June 1979)
REAL NAME Maximillian Zaran
OCCUPATION Mercenary **BASE** Mobile
HEIGHT 6 ft 1 in **WEIGHT** 235 lbs **EYES** Blue **HAIR** Red
SPECIAL POWERS/ABILITIES Skilled with a wide range of ancient
weapons, including nunchakus, shurikens, maces, bows and arrows,
staffs, and knives; he can also fire a gun.

A former British MI6 agent and now a
mercenary, Maximillian Zaran's career has been
chequered to say the least. After defecting from
the British secret service, Zaran
worked for Fah Lo Suee, Fu
Manchu's daughter, but she
cut his contract short. For a
time, his apprentice took
over his identity, but once
that was resolved Zaran
joined Batroc's Brigade.
During the Civil War (see
pp. 84–5), he was forced to
work for the Thunderbolts.
Recently, he registered with
the US government and
joined the Fifty State
Initiative (see pp. 118–9).
AD, MF

Z'NOX

FIRST APPEARANCE X-Men #65 (February 1970)
BASE Z'nox, Huz'deyr solar system, Andromeda galaxy
SPECIAL POWERS/ABILITIES Villainous race boasts highly
sophisticated technology and are able to move their homeworld
through space.

Although unable to
subvert the SKRULL
dominance of their
home galaxy
Andromeda, the
warlike Z'nox were a
highly sophisticated
and deadly race of
world conquerors.
When PROFESSOR X
learned that a Z'nox
invasion force was
heading towards

OUR VICTIMS LAUNCH YET *ANOTHER* PROJECTILE AT US!

Earth, he went into complete seclusion, leaving
the mutant shapeshifter the CHANGELING to stand
in for him. As the fleet approached, Xavier
combined his mind with those of the X-MEN
and the Earth's entire population to psionically
repel the attack. **AD**

⊙ **ZODIAC** *see opposite page*

ZALADANE

FIRST APPEARANCE Astonishing Tales Vol. 1 #1 (December 1970)
REAL NAME Zala Dane (allegedly)
OCCUPATION High priestess **BASE** The Savage Land
HEIGHT 5 ft 9 in **WEIGHT** 125 lbs **EYES** Blue **HAIR** Black
SPECIAL POWERS/ABILITIES Zaladane is a sorceress who
possesses assorted spell-based abilities.

The High Priestess of Garokk, Zaladane led
believers against the other tribes of the Savage
Land in a bid for power. Zaladane's sorcery
transformed Kirk Marston into the avatar of
Garrok on Earth, and she supported
him as his second in command. After
her bid to conquer the Savage Land
had been foiled, Zaladane's mutates
abducted Lorna Dane, the X-Man
known as POLARIS. Posing as
Lorna's long-lost sister, Zaladane
succeeded in transferring Polaris'
magnetic abilities to herself, albeit
temporarily. Thereafter, in a failed
bid to control all of the magnetic
forces on Earth, Zaladane ran
afoul of MAGNETO, who
overwhelmed her with his own
superior magnetic might, and left
her for dead. **TB**

ZARATHOS

FIRST APPEARANCE Marvel Spotlight Vol. 1 #5 (August 1972)
REAL NAME Zarathos, **OCCUPATION** The Spirit of Vengeance
BASE The netherworld dimension of Mephisto
HEIGHT 20 ft **WEIGHT** 225 lbs **EYES/HAIR** Not applicable
SPECIAL POWERS/ABILITIES Virtually immortal demon; uses
magic to enhance strength, height, weight. Can employ levitation
and project magical blasts of concussive force. Can project cold fire
that sears the souls of his enemies.

Zarathos is a demon who journeyed to Earth
before the Dawn of Man. He slumbered until a
sorcerer awoke him and offered to trade souls for
his aid. MEPHISTO, lord of the underworld, grew
jealous of a cult that grew around Zarathos and
enslaved him, sending him to possess humans in
the causes of sin, corruption, and vengeance. In
recent years, Zarathos became bound to stunt
motorcyclist Johnny Blaze and later to bike
messenger Danny Ketch, transforming both of
them into the demonic GHOST RIDER. **TD**

ZOLA, ARNIM

FIRST APPEARANCE Captain America Vol. 1 #208 (April 1977)
REAL NAME Arnim Zola **OCCUPATION** Criminal biochemist
BASE Weisshorn Mountain, Switzerland
HEIGHT 5 ft 10 in **WEIGHT** 200 lbs
EYES Brown **HAIR** None
SPECIAL POWERS/ABILITIES Brilliant geneticist; can mentally
project his intelligence into any of his creations.

During the late 1930s, Swiss geneticist Arnim
Zola discovered a tome of Deviant science and
learned how to create artificial life. He built
himself a new body, with a brain inside its chest,
a holographically-projected face, and an "ESP
box" for a head. Zola became a valued
member of Hitler's Third Reich, preserving
Hitler's consciousness after his death in the
form of the Hate-Monger. Zola's
creations have included Primus
and Doughboy, as
well as bio-
plastoids that can
impersonate any being. A
frequent foe of CAPTAIN
AMERICA, Zola is also responsible
for resurrecting the RED SKULL
into a copy of Captain America's
own body. **DW**

FACTFILE

MEMBERS AND POWERS

ARIES
Shoots fire from his horns.

AQUARIUS
Carries a gun that fires blasts of electricity.

CANCER
Superhuman strength, ability to create and control torrents of water.

CAPRICORN
Superhuman leaping and climbing abilities.

GEMINI
Can split into two bodies, can grow to huge size and strength, can project energy.

LEO
Superhuman strength and leaping ability.

LIBRA
Can fly, can become intangible.

PISCES
Can easily maneuver underwater.

SAGITTARIUS
Advanced archery skills.

SCORPIO
Wields the powerful Zodiac Key.

TAURUS
Superhuman strength.

VIRGO
Highly skilled in creating and using machines.

BASE Mobile

FIRST APPEARANCE

(in shadow) Defenders #49 (July 1977); (fully seen) Defenders #50 (August 1977)

ZODIAC

ZODIAC
1 Aquarius **2** Virgo **3** Gemini **4** Aries **5** Leo **6** Capricorn **7** Sagittarius **8** Libra **9** Taurus **10** Pisces **11** Cancer

Zodiac is a criminal organization, made up of intelligent androids. Each member of Zodiac is based on a zodiac sign. There was also another organization called Zodiac made up of 12 human criminals. The original human Zodiac was formed by Cornelius van Lunt and intended to rule humanity. Eventually they were all killed battling the android Zodiac. The second (android) Zodiac was formed when Jacob Fury (Scorpio from the original human Zodiac and brother of Nick Fury) gained possession of the powerful Zodiac Key. The Key unlocked Fury's potential for evil. Fury became the android Scorpio, and with 11 other androids, each representing a sign of the Zodiac, he took on the AVENGERS.

ZODIAC ATTACK

Several other Zodiacs have cropped up since then, some led by a single member of the Zodiac and others featuring all 12.

Recently, an all-new Zodiac surfaced, a single villain who killed the second Zodiac team and who planned to bring down Norman Osborn (*see* GREEN GOBLIN). **MT, MF**

Scorpio wields the Zodiac Key, which can fire energy bolts and teleport people and objects from one dimension to another. It was sent to Earth by the Brotherhood, a cult from another dimension that believes that the Key's existence depends on constant conflict between good and evil.

ZOMBIE

FIRST APPEARANCE Tales of the Zombie #1 (August 1973)

REAL NAME Simon William Garth

OCCUPATION Former businessman **BASE** New Orleans

HEIGHT 6 ft 2 in **WEIGHT** 220 lbs

EYES White **HAIR** Black

SPECIAL POWERS/ABILITIES Superhuman strength and regenerative ability.

A ruthless businessman named Simon Garth treated his employees with contempt. Eventually, his gardener, Gyps, became so upset that he killed Garth and resurrected him as a zombie. For two years the zombiefied Garth wandered the Earth, initially controlled by Gyps and later by one despicable individual after another. However the love of a good woman restored Garth to life for a short spell, enabling him to put his affairs in order. Although he then became a zombie once more, a benevolent voodoo priest intervened to help Garth end his undead existence. **AD**

ZZZAX

FIRST APPEARANCE Incredible Hulk #166 (August 1973)

REAL NAME Inapplicable **OCCUPATION** Purveyor of destruction

BASE Mobile **HEIGHT** Variable (max. 40 ft)

WEIGHT Negligible **EYES /HAIR** Inapplicable

SPECIAL POWERS/ABILITIES Unlimited electricity-manipulating powers including flight, super strength, and the ability to fire electrical bolts of concussive force.

Zzzax is a living electromagnetic field, formed by a bizarre accident that took place at a Consolidated Edison nuclear power plant. By absorbing the electromagnetic brainwave energies of its victims, Zzzax gained a limited degree of sentience and fashioned itself into a crude humanoid form. Zzzax can grow in size by draining energy from its surroundings, a tactic that it has employed when battling its most frequent foe, the HULK. For a while, General Ross's consciousness controlled the creature, but he soon abandoned that. Zzzax later escaped from the Raft super prison, but She-Hulk recaptured him once more. **DW, MF**

THE MULTIVERSE

Countless Universes of Heroes

The mainstream Marvel Universe is only one of countless possible universes in the multiverse. Most full universes are known by the name "Earth" attached to an identifying number. The regular Marvel Universe is Earth-616, although almost no one in that universe knows of it as anything other than "home." Many of the universes have their own versions of familiar characters, although they may be drastically different from each other. Most people live their lives in a single universe, never knowing anything of places beyond their own. A rare few, however, travel between the universes frequently. We live on Earth-1218.

1602

In an alternate world (Earth-460), the Purple Man uses his powers of persuasion to become US President and exiles Captain America into the past of Earth-311. This disrupts that universe's timeline so badly that modern heroes begin to appear at the turn of the 17th century; for instance, Sir Nicholas Fury works for Queen Elizabeth of England. Later, after the timeline has been fixed by the removal of Captain America, many of the heroes move to the New World, which is populated by dinosaurs along with the native peoples.

Alternate versions of regular heroes and villains band together to save the multiverse as the Exiles.

EARTH X

The future of Earth-9997 is a dark time. Black Bolt has released the Terrigen Mists into the atmosphere, causing many humans to become mutants. Controlling the US food supply, Norman Osborn (Green Goblin) makes himself US President and has Iron Man build robotic versions of the Avengers for him. The new Galactus (Franklin Richards) eventually saves the world. Later, Captain Mar-Vell persuades Thanos to use the Ultimate Nullifier on Death, then helps to make Mr. Fantastic—who has built a Paradise for the dead in the Negative Zone—into the new Eternity.

The transparent Machine Man served as the eyes for Earth X's Watcher.

EXILES

The Exiles are a Super Hero team assembled by the mysterious Timebroker to solve problems in the multiverse. The Timebroker is actually part of an insectoid alien race that is trying to repair the damage it did to the multiverse. The creatures live in the Panoptichron, a transdimensional space from which they can monitor several other realities at once. The leader of the Exiles uses a device called a Tallus to communicate with the Timebroker, helping to keep the team on track. Due to the dangerous nature of their jobs, the Exiles have a high turnover rate, but there are always replacements ready to take the place of the fallen.

ULTIMATES

On Earth-1610, the heroes who have been around the mainstream universe for decades have just developed, and sometimes have done so in unique ways. SPIDER-MAN, for instance, is just a teenager in high school, Nick Fury is African-American—although he still wears an eye patch—and the AVENGERS are known as the Ultimates. There are far fewer superpowered people in this world, and the number was recently reduced when MAGNETO went on a murderous rampage to avenge the deaths of QUICKSILVER and the SCARLET WITCH and flooded New York City with a tidal wave.

Until recently, the Ultimate universe seemed like a younger version of Earth-616, but it has now diverged in important and substantial ways.

SQUADRON SUPREME

One of the most enduring crossovers between universes happened when the Avengers traveled to Earth-712 and met the top hero team there, the Squadron Supreme. Years later, the Squadron's members decided to try taking over and running the world, but when this went bad they exiled themselves to Earth-616. They returned to find their homeworld overrun by ruthless corporations. They've also had encounters with people from the Ultimate universe (Earth-1610) and a darker version of their own team from Earth-31916.

WHAT IF....

The WATCHER often travels to different universes that are extremely close to Earth-616 but diverge at one critical point or another, such as "What if Uncle Ben had lived?" Sometimes he visits universes in which a regular hero appears in a different time, like Captain America as a fighter in the Revolutionary War. Other times, the issues the Watcher examines are more complex and posit a series of different paths taken during massive events like the Civil War (see pp. 84–5) or the Secret Invasion (see pp. 326–7).

ZOMBIES

A zombie version of the SENTRY entered Earth-2149 and, with the help of Magneto, began infecting superpowered people with a virus that turned them into the living dead. Magneto mistakenly thought the infection would only harm humans, leaving mutants alive. The zombies retain most of their powers, but their hunger for human flesh regularly overpowers them. After they run out of food, the superpowered zombies try traveling to new universes filled with fresh meat. They have managed to reach Earth-1610 and Earth-616 universes.

ACKNOWLEDGMENTS

TOM DEFALCO would like to thank Mark Gruenwald who believed that people would enjoying reading books like this and was the driving force behind the original Official Handbooks of the Marvel Universe. HOO-HA, my friend!

TOM BREVOORT would like to thank Stan, Jack, Steve and all the rest, for doing the hard part and coming up with all of these characters and concepts in the first place.

MICHAEL TEITELBAUM would like to thank Danny Fingeroth for the invaluable loan of the books and for his generosity in sharing his knowledge of the Marvel Universe, and Peter Sanderson for his help in identifying some of the characters; Alastair Dougall for bringing me on board and for his endless help and patience; Mike Hobson and John Romita, Sr. for the magazine (nod to Tom D. there as well!); Stan Lee, Steve Ditko, and Jack Kirby for starting all this; and my mom and dad, who—back when you could buy two comic books and a piece of gum for 25 cents—always gave me that quarter.

ANDREW DARLING would like to thank Keith Martin for those hyper-detailed responses to tricky questions, and the guys at Travelling Man in Manchester, who rescued me more than once. Big cheers go to Simon Beecroft for putting me forward for this gig, Alastair Dougall, who kept coming back for more, and Laura Gilbert, who couldn't quite get away. Finally, special thanks go to Ruth, who now knows a lot more about the Marvel Universe than she did, and Elijah—always a welcome distraction.

DANIEL WALLACE would like to dedicate my work on this book to the memory of my friend Dan Zoch, who introduced me to Marvel comics.

PETER SANDERSON would like to thank Jeff Christiansen, Tom Brevoort, Mike Fichera and Sean McQuaid for helping me resolve some continuity conundrums

DORLING KINDERSLEY would like to thank Thomas Murphy and Jeff Poulin at Marvel; Mark Perry at Avalon Comics and Will at 30th Century Comics; Lindsay Kent, Amy Junor, Elizabeth Noble, Laura Gilbert, Alan Cowsill, Laura Baxter, Lynne Moulding, and Cynthia O'Neill for editorial assistance; Guy Harvey for design assistance; Marian Anderson for the index.